Buddha Yoga

Cultivating the Yoga Path of the Buddhas,
Bodhisattvas and Guardian Spirits

WILLIAM BODRI

Copyright © 2019 William Bodri.

All rights reserved. No part of this book may be used or reproduced in any manner whatsoever the without written permission of the publisher, except in cases of brief quotations in articles and reviews. For information write:

Top Shape Publishing LLC
1135 Terminal Way Suite 209
Reno, NV 89502

ISBN: 0-9998330-3-0
ISBN-13: 978-0-9998330-3-2

DEDICATION

The *Sandhinirmocana Sutra* talks about four ways of cultivating cessation and contemplation practice.

The first two methods were turned into my books *The Little Book of Meditation, Color Me Confucius* and *Meditation Case Studies* that define the Hinayana, Vedanta and Stoic paths of cultivation.

The second two methods became *Culture, Country, City, Company, Person, Purpose, Passion, World,* the book *Move Forward: Powerful Strategies for Creating Better Outcomes in Life* (which contains my life philosophy) and this book. Together they define the Mahayana path. They define how Buddhas and Bodhisattvas set out to master phenomena and change fortunes, accomplish vows, and how you can practice their Yoga of cultivation and activity to at the minimum become a guardian spirit.

Nyasa Yoga, Visualization Power and *The Little Book of Hercules* define the Vajrayana and Yogic paths that include kundalini yoga, *kriya* yoga, Naropa's inner heat yoga, *nei-gong, nei-dan* and *anapana*. What physically, mentally and energetically happens to you along this path is found in *Meditation Case Studies*.

Detox Your Body Quickly and Completely together with *Look Younger, Live Longer* and *Nyasa Yoga* define the Taoist and scientific path of cultivation.

This book is dedicated to those people who want to become enlightened through any pathway, and if they don't succeed, still want to prepare for becoming a Bodhisattva benefactor or guardian spirit in the afterlife who can compassionately help the affairs of men.

CONTENTS

	Acknowledgments	i
1	From the Original Energy to Everything	1
2	Your Physical Body is the Structural Template for Your Higher Bodies	28
3	Life Purpose	51
4	Yoga Practice Methods	87
5	Optimal Practice Schedules	142
6	Foundational Study	161
7	An Excellent Temple or Spiritual Center	265
8	Making Donations to Support Spiritual Training	281
9	Minimizing Life Regrets	285
10	Arhat Yoga	300
11	Raising Money for Masters and Spiritual Training Centers	350
	Appendix: Sample Types of Emptiness Meditation	452

PURPOSE

It saddens me that so many people take up the practice of meditation and spiritual cultivation, but don't make any significant progress during their life. After they die and their subtle body comes out, they are introduced to the proper cultivation methods that bring results quickest, and then ask, "Why didn't anybody tell me this, but let me waste my time during life? Why didn't they tell me about the proper activities and practices that lead to better results than just regular religious observances or mild cultivation efforts?"

This book is meant to help such aspirants. It teaches the best methods to get spiritual practice results *now* and fully reveals the non-denominational stages of spiritual achievement, although the most important one is the deva body attainment because the correct spiritual teachings become openly available once you attain it. Since most people during life will still not succeed in attaining this initial fruit of the spiritual path, which is an independent spirit body, it prepares you for possible guardian spirit activities after death for those who desire a worthwhile life purpose or mission of helping humanity. This is the quickest way to earn the merit required for the deva body achievement.

Lastly, because so few spiritual teachers are knowledgeable about anything other than religion, and thus are limited in their abilities to help/advise ordinary people, this book also trains budding spiritual leaders to become more knowledgeable about crucial topics that can really help people's lives, and also helps them by revealing a number of ways to arrange and fund a spiritual center.

1
FROM THE ORIGINAL ENERGY TO EVERYTHING

Let's start with some basics.

Christianity said that everything in the universe started with "God the Father" who was pre-existing. He always is and always was.

Hinduism calls God "Parabrahman," "True Self" or "Supreme Self." If you trace all the energies and phenomena of the universe back to an ultimate origin, that primordial foundation of everything must be the True Self or self-nature since It is the Source from which all things arise. It is your self-nature. You arose out of It composed of It so you are It in essence and It is your True Self. The foundational nature of your own self must at its utmost be this primordial absolute essence that precedes Creation - Parabrahman.

Buddhism calls God the "original nature," "fundamental essence," self-nature or *dharmakaya*. Buddhism says that this primordial source is pure, changeless, blissful, and eternal. It is immaculate, unqualified, signless, omnipresent, and imperishable. Its purity is like the emptiness of space wherein you can see no divisions, attributes or characteristics. Because of Its purity this fundamental essence is absolutely devoid (empty) of anything other than Itself (emanations, attributes, characteristics, energies, phenomena) and is thus imperceptible. It is just one state, substance or essence that, having no parts or components or issuances or evolutes or attributes because of Its ultimate purity, is itself unknowable or unfathomable by thoughts and mental images.

Judaism says God is "Ein Sof" (infinite) prior to self-manifestation, prior to His production of any spiritual realm that has attributes and phenomena. The mystical *Zohar* explains, "Before He gave any shape to the world, before He produced any form, He was alone, without form and without resemblance to anything else." This view accords with the other religions. The original nature of everything is not a chaos but an immaculate void empty of energies, forms and phenomena.

Islam says that the primordial level of existence is "Allah," a primordial divine essence transcending (prior to) manifestation that exists as primordially pure Alonehood (*Abdiyat*) at a level of non-Creation.

Confucianism, following the principles of the *Yijing*, calls God the "Supreme Ultimate" that transcends the evolutionary birth of all other universal energies, phenomena and characteristics such as Yin and Yang.

In short, the original fundamental nature of the cosmos is not a being or person although It is often referred to in an anthropomorphic manner such as "He." It is one single, pure, unknowable essence that transcends all evolutes or creations. Mind and matter ultimately come from this foundational source or fundamental nature that we might want to call an ultimately pure singular essence or substratum.

Somehow the universe originates from God, the original nature that is our fundamental essence. How does this happen?

Christianity calls the universe "Creation" or the "Word" and due to Biblical contents Christians believe that "in the beginning God created the heavens and the earth" through a sequence of events. Some Christians say that Creation proceeded ex-nihilo, meaning out of nothingness. This is because the primordial Supreme Essence - the source essence of the universe - seems like a great void, emptiness, or nothingness since It is without attributes. It also seems like Emptiness since It is Unmanifest at the time of Creation due to the fact that It doesn't yet contain any evolutes from Itself.

When not literally following the Bible, the Jewish esoteric tradition says that before Creation there was only *Yesh* (nothingness) or Ein Sof, and that by Divine Will we had *Yesh me-Ayin*, the creation of emanated realms that were essentially the creation of something from nothing. Jewish theology is that "He turned His nothingness into something." All created things are complex while *Yesh* is simple, meaning a pure Oneness of substance that is the same, equal everywhere.

Buddhism says we don't know how Creation happened or occurred out of an original, primal, absolute nature that is impossible to transform into anything else because It is changeless, free from modification - there is only Itself there. Changeless in nature, It is singularly alone and perfectly pure which means there is no differentiation within its wholeness and thus no chance or way for It to transform into anything else. It says we are *ignorant* about that process of Creation because logic says Creation cannot occur since no change can transpire to an absolutely changeless essence, so Buddhism calls the first step of creation "Ignorance." Ignorance means we don't know how the first step of evolutionary phenomena occurred since something changeless in nature cannot change to produce an evolute.

Using the ideas of personification, Hinduism calls Creation the "play," "desire" or "will" of the absolute even though Parabrahman is not a person and therefore there can be no such thing as will, play or desire in the process of Creation. If creation occurs then it is just a natural process. Hinduism also recognizes that if Parabrahman (the source essence) had become the world then Parabrahman would have undergone some distortion or change, but of course this cannot happen since It is changeless. Thus it says that the Gods cannot conceive of a cause to produce the universe at the stage of Parabrahman, which is why Buddhism says we are "ignorant" about the process. Parabrahman is Itself a self-so existence and the causeless cause that is not in any way associated with whatever is an inseparable part of it, pervading it as an evolute.

To get around various quandaries involving this changeless purity issue, some schools of Hinduism postulate that there is a Nirguna Brahman (God without attributes) that is matched with a Saguna Brahman (God with attributes), and these two principles have no control over each other. They say that the process of emanation does not arise within Nirguna Brahman because It is changeless. Rather, Creation or emanation arises within Saguna Brahman, also known as Ishvara, and appears in the form of relationships between causes and effects where present evolutes serve as the cause for subsequent evolutes to evolve. Furthermore, all the causes, effects and evolutes are linked together in an infinite net of interdependence within Saguna Brahman where all levels of manifest reality and all phenomena are interpenetrated by one another with infinite cause and effect interrelationships.

Nirguna Brahman is therefore the causeless cause of whatever appears within It, but is not involved in the acts of evolution/Creation that characterize Saguna Brahman since It does not create or cause anything because no change ever occurs to It. It is the *support* because It is the fundamental, foundational, primordial essence. All things are derived from the primordial essence and are inseparable from It. However, all evolution only happens to the first evolute, also known as Saguna Brahman, Ishvara, Shakti, *Prakiti* or the embryonic essence *tathagatgarbha* of Buddhism that is the ground of all produced things, but a production itself rather than the original nature. It is the edge of conventional reality. In some religions this is called the Matrix Womb of Creation. In Christianity Shakti is the Word.

Gorakhnath of the Nath Yoga tradition describes the first emanation of the original nature (*Anama*, the nameless, self-existent One) as *nija-shakti*, and states that *nija-shakti* is completely indistinguishable from the original nature, but somehow becomes immanent within It. In other words, *nija-sakti* is the first manifest aspect (first evolute) of the original nature that can be called a transcendent aspect of creation or manifestation. *Nija-sakti* has the attributes of absolute purity, motionlessness, imperceptibility, and eternity (eternally present with the Nameless One, or foundational essence). For meditation purposes is described as like an undisturbed state of consciousness that is not different from the absolute nature and yet is unaware of anything.

Islam calls Creation an emanation or effusion from the absolute that occurs in a process of Divine Descent. According to this scheme the First, Original or Primordial level of existence is Allah, an incorporeal unmanifesting existence that is the original nature or source essence just as identified in every other religion or spiritual school. This is *Alam-i-HaHoot*, the Realm of He-ness (Is-ness). It is the primordial Divine Essence prior to manifestation and which exists as Alonehood (*Ahdiyat*). According to Sufism, *Ahdiyat* is primordially pure and incapable of being conceived; this essence exists and cannot be exemplified with anything. It is at the primordial level of non-Creation and somehow everything emanates from It despite its absolute purity or aloneness that therefore lacks causes.

From the First (Allah) or Real emanates the existence of a second. According to Islam this is an utterly incorporeal substance called *Alam-i-YaHoot* (the Realm of First Manifestation) that is an existence dependent on the first which *appears* different from its own essence (Allah) and yet is not a separate, independent entity. It is *Wahid-ul-wujud*, or Unitary Existence since it encompasses Everything – the Shakti of Hinduism. In Islam *Alam-i-HaHoot* is said to have no attributes (like *nija-shakti*) and yet the first manifestation of *Alam-i-YaHoot* is by definition an attribute. To explain it one must say that the attributes of God are neither other than God nor identical with Him. They are *appearances* and thus seem different or apart from Him but they cannot be other than Him since they are Him. God permeates everything since everything is God-substance.

Some spiritual schools postulate a purely mechanical or naturalistic process of creation, and say that somehow the universe just evolved or formed due a first spark or impulse from an absolutely pure substrate that set off an endless sequence of transformations. However, once again this begs the question that if the original nature (the absolutely pure foundational substrate) cannot change then how did it give birth to everything?

Vedanta gets around the issue by saying that since the absolute nature doesn't change, then all other existences are like a dream that don't truly exist, and thus you don't need to worry about them since they are illusions that are unreal. Only the original nature is Real since It is unchangeable, motionless, eternal and thus dependable, which are the qualities of Reality.

Furthermore, from the standpoint of the original nature that is Everything, they also don't exist since all that exists is Itself and only Itself.

The Greek Parmenides taught that reality was a single unchanging Being whereas Heraclitus wrote that all things flow, so one was talking about the unchanging absolute Reality that exists in a state of Unmanifestness, and the other about conventional reality that appears to us because of conscious experience. In Plotinus you will find similar views on the metaphysics of emanation "from the One."

Christianity says the universe or Creation is the "Kingdom of God" that is brought into being through a series of progressive creative acts.

Buddhism calls the emanations of Creation "karmic formations," or a set of energies and manifestations that develop into other consequential energies and manifestations through a complex interdependence of cause and effect relationships. They all develop through a process of "dependent origination." Buddhism says that everything that develops is conditional on the existence of everything else, and every single phenomena manifests through a complex web of infinite interdependence (cause and effect) tying everything together into one scintillating, ever-changing whole. Every member, piece, part, component, phenomenon, form, energy, etc. of that whole of manifestation is characterized by "impermanence" since every part is ceaselessly changing, which makes conventional reality like an ungraspable dream. Only the original nature never changes.

In Buddhism the original nature is also called the *dharmakaya* and sometimes Buddha-substrate. It also uses a term *Tathagatagarbha*, which means the womb or embryo of production that is equivalent to the Saguna Brahman or Shakti of Hinduism that gives birth to everything. This womb of production is also called the storehouse, container or alaya. The alaya (Shakti or realm of manifestation) is like an ever-changing, fluctuating medium; it is not the unchanging ultimate substance of Reality but its first-level projection. It contains all the forms and functions, laws and principles of the universe, which are its second-level projection. The world of life and death we know are later level evolutes.

Regardless of the fact that the universe consists of infinite energies or phenomena, Buddhism in the *Avatamsaka Sutra* clearly says that this is a case of "All in One, and One in All. The All melts into a single whole wherein there are no divisions in the totality of reality." In other words, all things taken together should be considered as one single body. The single body of all phenomena and energies is also just the original nature. The original nature and the realm of phenomena are one and the same. All genuine religions agree on this principle.

Hinduism calls the manifest universe "Shakti" to also denote a moving, seething mass of energy and manifest phenomena constantly in a state of flux and transformation. Shakti is often compared to a dancing woman since (a) the universe is always moving like a dance and (b) Shakti is like a mother's womb that gives birth to all things. Everything ultimately came from formless Parabrahman, which is alternatively called changeless Shiva, *Purusha* or Nirguna Brahman and other names. When the unmanifest formless original essence is called *Purusha* then Its manifest aspect is called *Prakiti*, which is Shakti or the *Logos* (Word).

Islam says that somehow everything emanates from the primordial level of non-Creation, Allah, despite Allah's absolute purity or aloneness, and it is through "complex interaction" that the various realms gives rise to one another and mundane reality.

Taoism says the universe arises from a primordial void and is like a giant vessel, vat or container of ceaseless "transformations." The *Daodejing* (*Tao Te Ching*) simplistically explains the process of creation by saying that "the One gave birth to a Second, next a Third manifestation arose and then 10,000 things."

Confucianism relies on the *Yijing* for its view of phenomena which says that the entire universe comes from *Taiji*, the Supreme Ultimate that is a formless, eternal, self-sufficient, perfect, primal absolute reality that transcends all the manifested, conditional phenomena of the universe which themselves are all characterized by ceaseless "change."

Hence Buddhism characterizes the realm of manifest Creation as *impermanent*, Taoism says it is always involved in *transformation*, Confucianism describes it as characterized by ceaseless *change*, Hinduism characterizes it as always *moving* (dancing), and Islam characterizes it as produced by *complex interactions*. Once again these are all similar ways of describing the same thing. The only Real, non-changing substance or essence of the universe – and which is thus perfectly pure, infinite without borders, self-existent and eternal – is the foundational, primordial self-so essence. All manifestations within It lack absolute existence or inherent existence.

Many spiritual schools or religions, like Judaism, say the universe originated ex nihilo, out of nothingness or Emptiness, but this is only because you cannot mentally conceive of a formless nothingness but they wished you to create a mental image of something empty, clear and peaceful as a practice for the spiritual path. For instance, a meditation instruction offered by Moshe Cordovero for Judaism is: "Whenever one forms a conceptual image of God, he should immediately backtrack, recoiling from the false notion, as any notion is shaped by man's spatial world. Rather, he should 'Run and Return' towards imagining Divinity, and then reject it." This type of instruction is meant to help one in meditation to cultivate an empty mind free of mental attachments.

In Judaism the pre-existing nothingness of the ex-nihilo creation process simply means the absolute purity of an essence without emanations, differentiations or attributes is like empty space. Infinite empty space without borders is akin to nothingness. If someone ends up pondering the ultimate source as a type of nothingness, they will abandon (clinging to) thoughts in that attempt and then they will be naturally meditating. Moses Maimonides of Judaism therefore concludes that the highest form of praise we can give God is silence, which means eschewing thoughts to be like this/Him. Buddhism, Hinduism, Taoism, Yoga and other religions also say mental silence is the Way.

Naturally everything that exists in manifestation must come from an original primordial something – a First Principle, an original essence or fundamental source nature rather than an inert absolute nothingness – but It must be so pure, transcendental or refined that It seems like a "formless nothingness" everywhere compared to all its evolutes that appear within It but are It in their absolute existence.

This is what "nothingness" really means in such dialogues – a pure essence or whatever so empty of phenomena that the purity of its nature can only be referred to as nothingness, empty like the void of space. This solitary essence shares no resemblance with any of its evolutes but is a primal substrate - an absolute existence or true reality - that is perfectly pure, changeless, stainless, immaculate and eternal. It is a self-so, self-evident existence that never changes by differentiating into something new, and yet somehow manifestations have arisen within It.

This is why a yogic text like the *Siddha-Siddhanta-paddhati* by Gorakhnath states that *Anama* – the Nameless origin (fundamental nature) that is self-existent, self-made, and self-manifest – gave birth to the first evolute of *nija-Shakti* that is eternal, pure, motionless, imperceptible *and an undisturbed state of consciousness*. The first evolute was described as a peaceful, pristine state of consciousness because this skillfully leads you to meditate according to this description – you should meditate with a formless, empty mind that is akin to undisturbed consciousness.

In fact, the only reason evolutes are described as consciousness, or the original nature is described as consciousness (ex. "Luminous Mind") in spiritual schools is to encourage you to meditate in such a way that you don't hold onto your thoughts, thus mirroring the nature of empty space that lets all things appear without the obstruction of resisting them or clinging to them. During meditation practice you should let thoughts appear in your mind, become aware of everything that arises, but you shouldn't cling/attach to anything. In this way you are practicing pristine awareness, luminous mind, non-attachment, or being like the original nature. The descriptions within spiritual schools are just expedient means to lead you to this type of meditation practice.

As another example, within Sufism the first evolute of *Alam-i-YaHoot* is an essence described as "like awareness." Although it is really an essence, sphere, energy level, or plane of manifestation it is said to be able to know of its own existence, so the descriptive schemes of Ibn Sina and al-Farabi call it the "first intellect." Once again, this is simply a form of skillful means to get you to meditate by creating an image of this in your mind. Only a sentient being can have consciousness, rather than an energy or plane of existence, so this is just a method of explanation that prompts you to practice meditations where you are just consciousness without thoughts. You would be practicing emptiness meditation if you were like this. The emphasis on consciousness has only this purpose since "emptiness meditation" is the major method of achievement on the spiritual path.

Everything within Shakti (the manifest universe) automatically develops from the one changeless ultimate Source, and manifests due to natural transformations of interacting causes and effects. The manifest realm of energy and phenomena proceeds mechanically due to scientific laws of dependence that rule transformations, and through these transformations life was eventually produced.

Life is a special type of manifestation that is often capable of consciousness. "Sentient life" means the ability to know and think via thoughts, called Knowledge. We are among the class of manifestations called "sentient living beings" who have evolved out of uncountable transformations and unlike insentient matter can think and reason. We can generate Knowledge. We can know the world. Through understanding and reason we have determined how to cultivate better lives and higher states of existence. We can determine wise courses of action and improve our behaviors in the world to achieve goals. We can penetrate countless realms of knowledge and through logic trace our beingness of existence back to the unmovable, unchanging pure original nature, which is what we ultimately are.

Confucius said we must trace all things back to their ultimate source, which is the original nature, the primordial essence. Buddhism says we must cultivate the mind to discover its ultimate essence, which is also this source nature. Islam says we must become one with Allah through an unveiling process that strips away the planes of existence. *Patanjali's Yoga Sutras* say, "The highest value a Yogi aspires for lies in re-absorption of primary constituents into their world-ground. Such a state supervenes upon total dissolution of the bodily and psycho-mental life, which is pure consciousness or feeling of void."

While the road of spirituality poses the ultimate attainment as *moksha*, liberation, salvation, emancipation, *nirvana*, release, Buddhahood, selflessness, egolessness, enlightenment or self-realization, you should consider the path of tracing yourself back to an ultimate essence as a pathway of cultivating higher bodies, each of a progressively higher transcendental substance. Each is composed of a higher or *more subtle form of energy* which Buddhism calls "winds." Each body vehicle is also more blissful than the previous from which it was generated.

The roads developed in religion to allow you to do this are called spiritual cultivation. They are roads that help you trace the human manifestation of the original nature back to the one absolute source, or God, and the human manifestation or evolute includes your body and its ability to form consciousness. You must trace them back to their ultimate root source by generating spiritual bodies (that have a concomitant or attendant stage of consciousness) of more refined substances/energies until you obtain the final one composed of the first effusional plane of the absolute nature ... or the highest evolute that is physically possible.

All the various teachings of religion are primarily expedient constructions with one grand purpose only: to enable you to accomplish this great task of realizing the source nature of the universe, which is your True Self. That's when you become a Buddha - a fully accomplished, fully perfected and completely enlightened being because of your transcendental body together with all the abilities and powers thus attainable.

Finding the One Source, which some call "God," is therefore the entire purpose of cultivation proper. By cultivating a body of the highest energy realm possible you can end up living an incredibly long period of time in that body and escape the ceaseless chain of transmigrations called reincarnation.

People decide in life to cultivate spiritual practice privately on their own or together in groups. Those groups can be a person's family, a community of followers within a tradition or under a teacher, or even a more formal organization with strict cultivation rules and schedules such as a monastery.

In most cases ordinary people can only devote a little bit of time during the day to the pursuit of spiritual cultivation. Some, however, can spare more time than others. Since progress is a function of the time you daily spend in practice together with the consistency of your practice over time, some people decide to become solitary sadhus, religious mendicants within a tradition, or decide to join a community of fellow strivers so they can practice more. This enables them to practice 5-6 hours per day, which is the average amount of time that top musicians and Olympic athletes devote to practice. When individuals decide to devote their whole life to this journey they often become monks and nuns, swamis, rabbis or priests of a particular tradition, whatever it may be.

This book is about how to do this in the most efficient way with the little time you have in life, and how to prepare yourself for success at this task in the afterlife if you don't finish the task while living. Consider that if you spend a great deal of time in spiritual cultivation but don't succeed during life, you don't want all that time to have gone to waste. This book will tell you how to prevent that possible waste by making sure that your actions accumulate into a positive result of worthwhile merit. If you don't succeed in spiritual cultivation you can still succeed in other ways.

What is the sequence of spiritual progress that all must pass through? It is described as a pathway that spiritualizes/purifies both your physical body and your consciousness. It also requires you to purify/improve your behavior. Therefore spiritual success necessitates a physical body attainment and mental attainment, namely the purification of your thoughts and actions since they are behavioral deeds controlled by your thoughts. The major technique for this is the practice of meditation and contemplation on proper thinking and behavior that you then adopt and make part of your life.

Most spiritual schools promote meditation in order to emphasize the practice of purifying/improving your thoughts and consciousness workings in general, but the *real* fruit of the spiritual path is actually a new body attainment – a new spiritual body in addition to the body you already possess. The new body is essentially a copy of the old but composed of a more transcendental level of energy, and consciousness is something that simply comes along with it since that body is still you and you are still a conscious sentient being. Your mind in that body is the same as the one you now have, but a higher body will give you extra capabilities. All sentient beings naturally have mental abilities commensurate with the structure of their body's nervous system, and thus any "purification of consciousness" that "lifts it higher" actually refers to "better" thinking where "better" means wiser, more compassionate, more virtuous, more effective and so on.

In practical terms, the desired outcome of the spiritual path is that you develop a sequence of spiritual bodies and start thinking and acting in better ways. What is considered better? When your thoughts and behaviors are impregnated with more virtue and higher values, you discard errant habits, and you adopt the mindset and start cultivating more behavior to help others.

There are five body attainments or steps on the spiritual path back to the original nature. You can consider them the stages of transcendence.

In Hinduism the five bodies are the physical body, subtle body, Causal (Mental) body, Supra-Causal body and Para-atman body. These are also called the *annamaya* (food), *pranamaya* (energy, Qi or Prana), *manomaya* (mental), *vijnanamaya* (wisdom or intellect), and *anandamaya* (bliss) *koshas* or sheaths.

In Buddhism these are the form body, deva body, Wisdom body, Dharma body and Buddha body (as mentioned in the *Diamond Sutra*). They are also referred to by the five skandhas: the form skandha, sensation skandha, conception skandha, volition skandha and consciousness skandha. The higher body attainments (past the physical body) also correspond to the four dhyana, four stages of Arhats, and the Bodhisattva bhumis where every two bhumi levels refer to one body level attainment.

In Vajrayana Buddhism you have the physical body, impure illusory (subtle or deva) body, purified illusory body, wisdom light or clear light body, and perfect *sambhogakaya* (Reward body or Enjoyment body).

In the Nath Yoga tradition there are the physical body or *stuhla deha*, purified subtle body or *suddha deha*, body of vibrations or *mantra deha*, wisdom light body or *jnana deha* and then the body of Immanence.

In Islam these are the gross body, subtle body, Mental body, Universal body and Shiva-atma or Paratma body. These correspond to the realm of the physical body (*Alam-i-Nasut*), realm of intelligence (*Alam-e-Malakut*) that corresponds to the subtle plane, realm of power (*Alam-i-Jabrut*) that corresponds to the Causal plane, the "second manifestation" or realm of Absolute Unity (*Alam-i-LaHoot*) that corresponds to the Supra-Causal plane (also known as the "Soul of Mohammed" or *Rooh-e-Qudsi*), and the realm of first manifestation (*Alam-i-YaHoot*) that is also known as the "Light of Mohammed" (*Noor-e-Mohammed*).

In Taoism the five bodies are said to be composed of Jing, Qi, Shen, Later Heavenly Qi and Primordial Heavenly Qi. Qi means Prana, "wind element" or energy. Each new body attainment corresponds to the rank of being a new type of Immortal, which are equivalent to the Buddhist Arhats.

In Christianity we have the five ranks of the body, soul, spirit, Kingdom of Heaven and God the Father.

In Confucianism the five bodies correspond to the stages of faith, beauty, grandness, sage and then divineness taught by Mencius.[1]

These are the names for the five bodies, or ranks of attainment on the spiritual trail, where each higher body is composed of a more rarified energy (transcendental material) than the body it was birthed from, and therefore

---

[1] See *Color Me Confucius* for a fuller description of these bodies and stages of attainment in Confucianism.

resides on a different plane of existence called a heavenly realm or Pure Land which the lower body cannot reach. A higher body attainment remains invisible to all lower bodies.

When as a human being you attain the subtle body this event is considered the "initial fruit" of the spiritual path, and the momentousness of this achievement is called enlightenment. This is enlightenment because you become a first stage Arhat, called a Srotapanna in Buddhism. This is what should be the target for the human potential movement, but its faithful haven't a clue.

The first dhyana of Buddhism is not attaining some trance state but attaining this extra body that abides in the subtle realm of the earth, which means an invisible realm all around us but populated by beings so subtle we cannot see them or measure their energy. This is the realm of "Heaven" where people live after death until reborn in a higher or lower body. When a master seems to be in a trance or samadhi, such as the first dhyana, it is simply because his higher bodies have gone elsewhere to perform certain tasks, thus he or she is preoccupied elsewhere.

When you attain the fifth body of Immanence or complete *sambhogakaya*, it is called Complete and Perfect Enlightenment, the stage of No More Learning, or "*nirvana* without remainder." This is the Great Golden Arhat stage of attainment.

The immediately preceding clear light body attainment stage, which equates to the Arhat's enlightenment of "*nirvana* with remainder" (*nirvana* with remaining dependency), is often called the state of universal oneness or union. This is the stage of enlightenment that most people normally think about, which is the stage of a full Arhat, although properly speaking the feat of first attaining the subtle body, or deva body, is enlightenment. As previously explained, this stage of a Srotapanna is one of the Arhat stages, and thus a stage of enlightenment.

The subtle body attainment, also known as the deva body, should be your target objective for your spiritual practice, for you must first attain this foundational body composed only of Qi in order to develop the others. Each new body is derived out of the energies of the lower body vehicle and each has special powers pertinent to the realm of energy to which it belongs (resides).[2] To attain the subtle body you must do inner energy work such as the practices taught within my book *Nyasa Yoga*.

The very first stage of spiritual attainment above the human body is this subtle body composed of Qi, the deva body, which can leave the physical body at will after its attainment. With this attainment you become a

---

[2] See *God Speaks* by Meher Baba.

heavenly being or deva while living, but now with two bodies at your disposal (your physical body and this subtle body which are both linked to one another). Because of possessing a deva body, which becomes the new center of your life of two bodies, you attain all the typical spiritual powers of a deva such as being able to develop mastery over the elements, quickly travel far distances (to be able to see and hear things there), enter the bodies of humans causing them to become subject to your will, helping people remember things forgotten (but stored within their brain neurons), and so forth.

These standard abilities of devas (spirits or lower heavenly beings) explain why saints who attain this stage can exhibit what we call miraculous abilities. They can "perform miracles" simply because they have another body that can do these things that are the perfectly ordinary capabilities of those bodies. In other words, miraculous abilities exist simply because a saint has attained one or more of the higher spiritual bodies attainable through cultivation and mastered the normal powers that are the common functional abilities of those bodies which, although ordinary abilities to beings at that level, seem miraculous to those with denser bodies who inhabit lower planes of existence and don't know what is going on. When a saint or sage (prophet, guru, master, swami, etc.) exhibits superpowers it is one of his higher bodies performing the feat, or possibly a higher-bodied friend or group of friends doing so. It is not that the powers come from God or that God performs the miracle. It is somebody performing the special feat with a body that can do those things as a natural ability. This is something people get confused about.

Superpower attainments correlate to how many bodies you cultivate (different planes of being you have access to) and whether you train to actively master the abilities normal to the plane of each body of higher composition. For example, as a human you have all the capabilities necessary for learning how to ski, surf, play the violin or roller skate but if you don't train then you can't exhibit these skills. Similarly, devas have subtle bodies made of Qi but can only master certain exceptional abilities in the Qi realm bound to our earth if they train and practice. The same principle applies to spiritual masters.

What are the standard capabilities of a deva, namely their siddhis? Yoga clearly tells us. *Anima*, the ability to reduce their subtle energy body to a small size. *Mahima*, the ability to expand their subtle energy body to a large size. *Garima*, the ability to make their subtle energy body heavy; *laghima*, the ability to make it lighter. *Prapti*, the ability to travel anywhere at will (since the subtle body can pass through matter). *Vastva*, or control over natural forces (when you train to be able to do so); *Isitva*, supremacy over nature (for similar reasons). *Prakamya*, the ability to attain whatever one desires.

Unfortunately, most people who enter a monastic life or become an ardent follower of a religious tradition will not attain the deva body during their lifetime. However, because they practiced spiritual cultivation all their life they will have created the chance to easily attain it after death since they will have purified their body's Qi to a major extent due to their spiritual cultivation practice, which will thus either prevent or delay another subsequent human reincarnation. Without this attainment while living, often they may feel that they have wasted their life on spiritual efforts even though they made great progress towards this attainment that will bear fruit after they pass away.

This book will help you maximize your chances of attaining the initial fruit of the path - the first milestone of the cultivation trail - which is the attainment of that independent subtle body (spirit body, astral body, illusory body or deva body) that can leave and return to your physical shell since it is now the true center of your life. *Nyasa Yoga* gives exact methods for how to speedily cultivate your internal energies to attain it in the quickest manner possible. It involves cultivating/purifying both your Yin Qi and Yang Qi, as well as cultivating emptiness meditation, a pure mind and good conduct. This book goes over methods and schedules that will even help you maintain compliance with the necessities of the cultivation effort. It is hard to sustain the momentum of a cultivation effort, and to sustain your commitment to practice it is best to set up a regular practice schedule that embodies just enough variety to keep you going.

Whether you are a Christian monastic or mendicant, Buddhist monk, Hindu sadhu or swami, Muslim Sufi, Jewish rabbi, yogi or Taoist, this book can help you attain the goal of the deva body achievement, which is the first fruit of the spiritual path for *all* genuine spiritual traditions. All genuine religions want you to attain this accomplishment. If you don't attain the subtle body attainment then you have no spiritual ranking despite any honors or status appointed to you in the world. The world may call you a Pope, Patriarch, Prophet or some other honorific title, but if you don't have the deva body attainment at the minimum then you have no special spiritual standing at all.

If you don't attain the deva body in this life time then this guidance will still prepare you for the higher spiritual body attainments that you can work on achieving *after* you die (before you reincarnate into a new life yet again). As the great Tibetan master Tsongkhapa said, if you don't succeed during this lifetime you can still succeed in the afterlife. Furthermore, it will help you prepare for a Bodhisattva's career as a *deva protector* or *guardian spirit* (or Orisha in the Yoruba religion) who performs various services for the world of humans, doing good and beneficial things helping them succeed, despite a full and busy life in Heaven. This is the first book telling you how to do this.

It sounds funny that you can start training yourself to become a Bodhisattva Protecting Spirit or Guardian Deity of your own choosing *if you so choose* to be that in your heavenly afterlife. However, when people die and the Qi-based subtle body imprisoned within their physical shell is liberated, making them devas or spirits who will then experience an earth-bound heavenly life, they can use their new stage of life to perform all sorts of helpful activities for humans.

You can therefore start to train now along a Bodhisattva path of cultivation so that you can render *big* service to others when you become a deva. Look at your current record of charitable contributions, or how you currently spend your free time, to get an idea of what you are really interested in. What issues have you been supporting in life or trying to protect? What is the light in the world that you wish others to see? Your life might be hampered now in so many ways that you cannot help as much as you'd like in certain areas, but the afterlife opens up countless possibilities to pursue your personal interests for shepherding functions as does the life of a master who achieves the first dhyana (deva body) and higher.

The helpful efforts of devas who intercede for humans are considered a form of Bodhisattva behavior, compassionate activity, or selfless service and this pathway of unselfish service can be taken as a road of cultivation – Karma Yoga. In fact, no one will help you attain higher bodies on the spiritual path unless you are an ethical, virtuous human who exhibits the tendency of wanting to help others. If you don't have this type of merit then no one will volunteer to spend the extensive time and effort required during the Twelve Years of a kundalini awakening to help you strengthen and then free a subtle body inherent within your human body's structure. If you are not a good person, no one will help you for this length of time as the transformation requires constant daily effort.

Naturally you will have to continue training after death to achieve any particular spiritual powers and abilities necessary to act as a helpful Bodhisattva or guardian for humans when you become a deva, but in terms of intellectual study there is fantastic information available right now that can help prepare you to become an expert in the very areas where you might want to become a helpful force and benefactor. You should start to study these materials now. Always study the best that there is, which is what I have tried to identify for you although the cited sources of what I consider "best" will certainly change over time.

You either become a Bodhisattva or not based upon your own decisions and efforts. There are other things to do in Heaven because children need teachers, people need barbers and doctors and everything else you need on the solid earthly place. It is just that life is more enjoyable in Heaven, but it is still filled with people involved with occupations. So if you think you might want to become a guardian spirit of some sort to help shepherd, protect and lend benefit to certain types of human affairs, it makes sense to start now to master the knowledge and skills required of your area of interest and to start participating in that very role you want to exercise. Craft your character, craft your training and craft your participation in related activities. Furthermore, you can also strive to make merit in that area by contributing to others in some related way.

As a monk or nun or other religious functionary who only studies spiritual texts, you are ill prepared to be involved with anything other than religious matters once you initially attain the deva body. What skills and knowledge of anything other than religion would you then have? People are all seeking a better life but how can you answer them? Therefore *it is wise to supplement your spiritual efforts to develop other skills and master other topics than just religion.* There are many mundane skills and topics you should consider mastering not just for when you attain the deva body, but so you can do other things in this life too. To solely study religion and spiritual topics while neglecting practical human affairs and mundane realms of expertise makes you rather useless. Try to develop other skills at the same time. For instance, Trappists learn to work while cultivating, and in the Arab world it was taught that Moslem rulers should also train in some practical craft skill (such as carpentry, weaving, medicine, etcetera) other than just rulership. You must learn other skills and how to think in other ways than that required of your predominant role in life now. Ways of thinking and skills are abilities you can take with you into a new life, as well as karmic merit.

Additionally, you should also consider the following. Say you spiritually cultivate very hard during this life but don't succeed in attaining the first spiritual stage of the deva body. Unlike ordinary people who don't meditate, your Qi will already have become somewhat purified and strengthened before your death so that it will be easier to make cultivation progress in Heaven. Because of your cumulative cultivation efforts during earthly life you will be far ahead of other people who pass away without having cultivated since you will have already laid the foundation for success in higher body attainments. The purity and integrity of your subtle body will have already been strengthened. The more pure your body attainment the longer that heavenly body vehicle will live.

This is why you should cultivate meditation during life as it will prolong your stay in Heaven even if you don't succeed in generating the deva body from spiritual practice. You will always be that much further ahead than everyone else who doesn't cultivate - as long as your spiritual practice includes meditation and *nei-gong, nei-dan, anapana,* Naropa's inner heat yoga and other forms of internal Qi energy work rather than just reverent religious devotion to a deity, participation in religious ceremonies or other functions and intellectual study.

Many devas compassionately choose the occupation of a Bodhisattva "protective spirit" or "guardian deity" who uses their powers to protect countries, religions, towns, rivers, families, individuals, organizations, occupations, missions, etcetera in the human world that they can see around them even though we cannot see them. Their main intercession is by affecting human consciousness. They commonly give people thoughts to do good deeds and as explained in *Meditation Case Studies* they train in how to do this. When "miracles" happen in life they are not "due to God" because a changeless original essence is not a being and cannot act. Miracles are due to the intercession of regular spiritual beings simply because they choose to help you. There is no Ultimate Power over all who orders anybody to do anything, just as you have your own free will to do whatever you like in the world.

In other words, miracles do happen because of higher spiritual beings trying to help humans, but not because of a changeless absolute foundational substratum ordering people around. As the Jewish sage Moses Maimonides said, "There is, in truth, no relation in any respect between God and any of God's creatures." In other words, God does not act, but God's creatures act according to their own wills and inclinations without anyone being in ultimate charge, and those actions never produce an effect on God. The original nature is a changeless essence that cannot change so the only help you receive from Heaven is from devas and spiritual masters who hear your pleas or see your situation and decide to intervene however they can.

To become a Protect god (guardian spirit) you not only have to master all the normal powers of a deva, which are the powers a spiritual master learns to use upon attaining the deva body, but one must become educated on matters relevant to what you want to do. For example, if you want to become a protector of agriculture and farming then you should learn about farming details such as soil, seeds, weather, planting, harvesting and so forth. If you want to help people with healing, you must not just learn how to help them with your Qi energy but actually study the topic of medicine and healing. If you want to become a "Mahakala" or wealth engendering spirit you need to know the roads and methods that normally lead to wealth. Since you would be guiding people by thoughts to help them make money you would need knowledge and skills in business management or investing to know how to influence people properly.

The *Avatamsaka (Flower Garland) Sutra* of Buddhism lists several different types of Protector Deities or guardian spirits, which as stated are devas or spirits that become a guardian, patron, benefactor, shepherd or protector of a particular place, nation, culture, lineage, occupation, craft, activity, or function. Most cultures have special names for the individuals who choose this type of selfless service for the benefit of others. You can train to become one of these patron protective spirits which are in every country and location. Among those mentioned in the *Avatamsaka Sutra* are the following:

- City protect gods and guardian spirits
- Nation-sustaining guardian spirits
- River-ruling guardian spirits
- Ocean-ruling guardian spirits
- Mountain-ruling guardian spirits
- Lake-ruling guardian spirits
- Forest-ruling (Trees and forest) guardian spirits
- Weather-ruling (Rain-making) guardian spirits
- Religion or Faith protect gods and guardian spirits
- Temple or Sanctuary (Bodhimandha) guardian spirits
- Wisdom guardian spirits
- Treasure guardian spirits
- Nature guardian spirits
- Happiness and Joy guardian spirits
- Medicine-ruling (Healing) guardian spirits
- Military guardian spirits
- Justice guardian spirits
- Wealth and Money protect gods and guardian spirits
- Travel guardian spirits
- Crop (Agriculture) guardian spirits
- Space element guardian spirits
- Wind element guardian spirits
- Fire element guardian spirits
- Water element guardian spirits
- Earth element guardian spirits
- Light abilities guardian spirits
- Music and Singing guardian spirits
- Skillful Transformation guardian spirits

Of course Buddhism and Asian culture in general recognize many more categories than this such as fertility protection deities, trade and craft patron deities, wealth (money) generation deities, relationship guardian deities, education (wisdom, intelligence and learning) guardian deities, afterlife protector gods and many more. The words guardian, protector, patron and so on are used interchangeably as are the terms deva, spirit or deity.

In Japan these spirits are called "*kami*." In Christianity these spiritual helpers are called "tutelaries" or tutelary spirits (deities) that are guardians, patrons or protectors. Christianity also has "patron saints" of locations (villages, towns, cities, landmarks, countries), occupations and trade crafts whom you can call on for various forms of protection, help and assistance including even illnesses and dangers. Those answering such calls are the human beings who cultivated the spiritual path, attained the deva body and then higher bodies, and then decided to devote themselves to these special sorts of benevolent help for human beings, namely you and me.

Christianity, Buddhism, Hinduism, Shintoism, Taoism and Islam all have patron saints and guardian deities who take care of nations, towns or cities as well as spirits handling other "offices" or functions. In ancient Rome, there was also the *genius loci* who was the protective spirit of a place. The *genius loci* was a tutelary deity who was responsible for the health, happiness and wellbeing of all the residents of that location, which is what a guardian spirit, protective deity, Bodhisattva or Buddha does. In Islam there is also the tradition of deceased Sufi masters working as the patron saints, protectors and heavenly advocates beneficially interceding for Muslim nations, cities, towns and villages. This description is also quite accurate.

In short, countless religions promote the *patron saints* of shrines, temples, churches, mosques and other holy places because they truly exist. There are also spiritual guardians of industries, hospitals, universities, legislatures, the arts and so on. Basically, spiritual beings who choose to help mankind will intercede in human affairs when they can although karma is sometimes stronger than any intercession they might render.

It is not idolatry or worship to beseech help from those who have attained higher spiritual bodies and want to help us, such as deceased Sufi or Christian saints. Bodhisattvas, Buddhas and guardian spirits want to help us. By virtue of possessing a body composed of the etheric substances of a higher plane they can shrink that body (*anima*), enter into people's brains and project ideas and their will, which is called the power of subjugation. This is how they typically help others. However, you shouldn't expect more success in any of your endeavors other than that suggested by the phrase, "God helps those who help themselves." An Arab phrase similarly runs, "Trust in God but tie your camel."

Once you pass away and become a deva yourself, which is the fate of all human beings who "die and go to Heaven," you will still be earth-bound unless you cultivate the higher spiritual bodies that access even greater transcendental realms called "Pure Lands." Access to Pure Lands becomes available when you attain the Causal body and higher. As a deva with a subtle energy body made of Qi you will happily live in the subtle etheric realm of the earth until you die in that heavenly life and are reborn again. During your heavenly (subtle realm) life, you can choose to intervene in human affairs to protect, prosper or benefit any human endeavors you want. Or, you can just live a happy life until you pass away without accumulating any merit that will make your subsequent life all the better.

Rather than wait for the afterlife or a subsequent incarnation, you can train to become a patron deity or guardian spirit *now*! If you are trying to succeed at spiritual cultivation in this life, it also makes sense to do some preparatory work in training yourself to become the type of Buddha, Bodhisattva, savior, helper, patron, benefactor or protector you would ultimately want to become later when freed of current life restrictions.

What are some of the other types of activities, functions or causes you might choose to protect as a guardian spirit? From examining the many charitable organizations that exist we find that some people devote their entire lives to humanitarian missions such as eliminating hunger, relieving disaster outcomes with aid, and improving public health (especially in impoverished nations). People often make contributions to charities involved with human rights, animal welfare, wildlife conservation, environmental protection/conservation, medical research, the wellbeing of children, international development, arts and culture (libraries, museums, performing arts), community and neighborhood development, educational support, social services, commercial research and religious activities.

To emphasize this principle of helping others through compassionate service of a particular avenue, Buddhism has special lessons on this topic which it calls the Mahayana (Great Vehicle) Path of compassionate activity. It makes a special point of identifying various Buddhas and Bodhisattvas who have developed special skillsets and are especially devoted to certain types of calling. They represent *you* if you attain the deva body and then choose a similar type of mission. You can call upon these Buddhas and Bodhisattvas for assistance in times of need, such as:

    Medicine King Bodhisattva Bhaisajyaguru
    Great Vow and Savior of Beings in Hell Bodhisattva Ksitigarbha
    Great Wisdom Bodhisattva Manjusri
    Power of Wisdom Bodhisattva Mahasthamaprapta
    Great Compassion Bodhisattva Avalokitesvara
    Great Benevolence and Joy Bodhisattva Maitreya
    Great Meditation and Spiritual Practice Bodhisattva Samantabhadra
    Supernatural Danger Protection Bodhisattva Sitatapatra
    Great Power and Esoteric Secrets Bodhisattva Vajrapani
    Great Success in Work and Achievement Bodhisattva Tara
    Wealth, Prosperity, Abundance and Fertility Bodhisattva Vasudhara
    Great Dharma Protector Bodhisattva Skanda

In Hinduism, for special help in life people are taught to call upon major deities such as Ganesh (good fortune, prosperity, wisdom and success), Saraswati (arts, music, intelligence and learning), Kubera (wealth), Lakshmi (good fortune, wealth and well-being), Durga (combating evil), Shiva (spiritual cultivation), Dhanvantari (healing), Kartikeya or Murugan (martial arts, warfare), and countless other deities, which are basically Buddhas and Bodhisattvas known by a different name. The Vasus assistants of Indra and Vishnu are also often called upon for success in certain types of cultivation exercises because they have mastered the elements – Agni (Fire), Vayu (Wind), Prthivi (Earth), Suray (Sun), Soma (Moon), Dyas (Space), and Varuna (Water). There are also Adityas and all sorts of other Hindu gods just as there were in ancient Greece and Rome. During the classical days in Greece and Rome the Buddhas and Bodhisattvas would also masquerade as deities so that human beings could call upon them for help and assistance. This is the occupation of the Buddhas and Bodhisattvas.

As explained in Buddhism, these deities, which are Buddhas, are actually human beings within our world who have succeeded at spiritual cultivation, attained the higher spiritual bodies, and decided to stick around helping us rather than go off to live in higher Pure Realms. They are people who succeeded in enlightenment, which means attainment of many higher transcendental bodies, and then with their long lives masquerade as ultimate deities when they are just humans with many bodies due to their cultivation. When you call for help they hear your pleas, and they try to render assistance where they can although they are hampered by the karma of situations. Training to become a guardian spirit, and acting that way in this life through charitable contributions or unselfish personal efforts to help others, prepares you for such an achievement. Such training is a type of Yoga. This type of individual is the one who succeeds on the spiritual path because they will be helped by higher beings on the road of attainment.

Thus Buddhism upholds the ideal of the Bodhisattva savior who devotes themself to the mission of liberating people and relieving them of suffering. A guardian spirit or protector deity who does this is also a "Bodhisattva," and the Buddhist sutras record many deities who vowed to protect places, teachings and even individuals who follow the cultivation path, thus becoming Bodhisattva protectors. Hinduism poses the ideal of the Avatar who incarnates in the world to do good and fight evil, who is also a Buddha or Bodhisattva protector. For instance in the *Bhagavad Gita* 4.7-8 the typical role of an Avatar is explained: "Whenever righteousness wanes and unrighteousness increases I send myself forth. For the protection of the good and for the destruction of evil, and for the establishment of righteousness, I come into being age after age." The ancient Greeks posed the idea of a hero whose wisdom, courage, actions and self-sacrifice saved the country in time of peril.

Christianity poses the ideal of the Christ-Savior who espouses charity, kindness and benevolence, and who comes to save the world by sacrificing himself for others. This is also the ideal of the Bodhisattva savior. Sikhism has the example of Guru Nanak, who taught selfless service on behalf of others and the need to fight injustice. Zoroastrianism espouses the ideal of choosing good over evil, while Confucianism espouses the ideal of perfecting yourself and then making a contribution to your family, state and country. As Confucius's student Master Zeng said, "The Master's Way lies in exerting all of one's effort and relating to the needs of others. That is all."

These are all examples of the Bodhisattva or Buddha way. It is a path of service to other beings to help relieve their suffering for after all, they are all our brothers and sisters despite different appearances since they too are the same original nature. We are all the same original nature.

Many people who succeed at spiritually cultivating multiple bodies choose to hang around the earthly sphere and perform various deeds to help the beings on all the realms lower than their highest body. They can now see and interpenetrate all those lower bodies, and thus render beneficial influence to them. As a form of skillful means that is part of a career of assistance, it is also common for all successful spiritual cultivators to masquerade as various gods and deities by responding to the prayers or mantras people use to request their divine aid. This has been going on for thousands of years throughout every country, culture and religion. They perform this masquerade chicanery because most people call upon non-existent beings for assistance, such as deities and gods, and therefore they answer those calls by impersonation.

This is something you will find out about after you die, or upon success in attaining the deva body, and is explained as "skillful means." The methodology of skillful means, where you deceive someone in order to save them, is explained in the *Lotus Sutra* and is based on the fact that people will not listen to the truth. Naturally the spiritual Bodhisattva men and women who take on these compassionate jobs also take on deva students and help them achieve the Tao (attain higher bodies) because of their devotion to helping others. No one will receive help from spiritual beings in attaining the Tao unless they are kind, virtuous, ethical people. It takes a full Twelve Years of such masters running their own Qi through your body to wash your Qi/Prana using their own in order for you to attain your own independent deva body, the process being called a kundalini awakening, and only the ethical, kind and virtuous can achieve such devoted help and attention. You really need merit to deserve such attention.

Mantras and prayers have therefore been created in many religions that ask for assistance from various gods, deities, local protector spirits, patron spirits and saints, Immortals, guardian spirits, gurus, sadgurus, masters, prophets, swamis, sages, Bodhisattvas and fully enlightened Buddhas who have attained the Immanence body and higher. These are all just human beings who either attained enlightenment while alive, or are reborn in Heaven as devas and then attained the Casual body, Supra-Casual body,

Immanence body and yet higher.

In Hinduism various mantras are available for requesting assistance from such beings for the pursuit of spiritual progress, health, wealth, business success, justice (victory in court), intelligence, skills in the arts, peace of mind, protection, the overcoming of enemies, relationships, and more. In Christianity there are patron saints who people pray to for various sorts of help as well. In Sufism people pray to the past saints (Sufi masters who passed away) for help too. In many religions a long list of past masters, rabbis, Sufis, saints, etcetera are sometimes recited in prayers because this attracts their notice and calls attention to your situation. You will find this behavior in nearly every religion because if the individual is enlightened it will provoke a response. However, your karma might be too thick for any real help to be rendered.

To the extent they can help, the needs of human beings crying out for aid are ministered to by the people who succeeded in spiritual cultivation and then specialize in certain types of aid, helping where they can to the extent they can. As explained, people who succeed on the path train to use their higher bodies in various ways that might render assistance, devoting themselves to certain efforts, but usually the most that they can do is give people thoughts, strength, energy or connections to others who might help them. A living spiritual master devotes himself to helping all his students in various ways, unbeknownst to them, but there is always only so much you can do, especially when someone has the fixed karma to suffer. Someone who has reached their time and is fated to die will die despite all their merit and all your prayers. Sometimes karma just has to work itself out.

The primary form of Bodhisattva help provided to people is by altering consciousness, i.e. giving people thoughts and ideas that can help them to solve problems themselves because you usually *do* have to do all the solving work yourself. For instance, the thought to call someone on the phone, a brilliant idea of inspiration, strength and courage that seems to appear out of nowhere when needed, and sometimes even lucky breaks are some of the things that can be given to people without their knowing the source. As another example, there is rarely such thing as "being psychic" such as knowing someone is going to call you by telephone because you have the superpower of foreknowing the future. It is usually just a deva who goes into your brain to give you that thought because he or she is practicing his powers and has advance knowledge of the phone call. Devas, Buddhas and Bodhisattvas are practicing little things like this all the time.

You should *never* expect miracles if you call upon higher powers for aid and assistance because you must follow the earthly road of consequences and do most of the work for handling problems yourself. Calling for aid and assistance will not stop a bullet whereas heeding that inner urge to avoid danger will prevent the trouble in the first place. Astrology teaches to remove yourself from the circumstances, or remove the circumstances, and you can change your fortune. This is why many masters go into retreat when bad fortune is due.

The point is that some things cannot be prevented or helped because the karma is too thick and cannot be changed (fixed), but people who do succeed in enlightenment can and do help people whenever they can to what extent they can. But what can you do when your primary technique is typically giving people thoughts or loaning them energy?

Even so, the act of offering assistance when devas and higher beings do not have to act at all (they have busy lives of their own after all) is why they are called compassionate Bodhisattvas and Buddhas or Guardian Deities.

The important point is this, which is called practicing Buddha Yoga, Bodhisattva Yoga or Guardian Spirit Yoga. You might call this a type of Karma Yoga as well. You can actually start training to become a Buddha or Bodhisattva by doing what they do, and by learning how to give to others good advice (thoughts) and wise judgment, inspiration or motivation, peace of mind or confidence, resources (wealth or connections) and other forms of aid. Learning how to make others healthy, such as raising their Qi by giving them Qi, is also something you can train to do. The three standard forms of charity include giving others wisdom, wealth/resources (and solving the problems of the poor) and fearlessness, which means courage and a sense of safety and security. You can train to offer in all these ways.

If you want to become a big Buddha then as part of Buddha Yoga you must train in virtue, wisdom, discipline, perseverance (grit), concentration and visualization. Furthermore, there are topics you can start to study now rather than waiting for the deva body attainment or afterlife, and skills you can begin to master. Life continues even after death, and you can start to accumulate an expertise now that you can use in the afterlife or in your next incarnation. The goal you should strive for is best articulated by Buddhism which says that you need to become fully accomplished, fully skillful, fully compassionate, fully wise, fully perfected. This requires training *now* in various ways – it requires you to work at self-improvement. This is why I am revealing the pathway of the guardian spirits, which is basically Bodhisattva or Buddha Yoga. Many who pass away tread this path.

Essentially the purpose of life is whatever you choose it to be. Life purpose or purposes for your life are a subjective thing - something you choose and define yourself. Life purposes are something you consciously create yourself. At the very ultimate source of consciousness everything is empty and phenomena are non-existent, but out of this emptiness, void, abyss, chaos, unmanifestness, non-differentiation, formlessness or purity the universe is somehow born. Similarly, out of this ultimate infinite freedom of potential you are free to create your own directions for your life. You can define life to be about whatever you want it to be by the choices and actions you make. Stay true to yourself and do that! What are you here to do? What value do you want to create for society? You define your own purpose and future. You define your own destiny by your efforts. You can shape your thoughts to be whatever you want to accomplish. Whatever you choose to accomplish you can work to accomplish. Whatever you select to build you can start to build. Whatever you want to master you can start to master. Talent can be learned, purposes can be served. Wherever you want to apply your efforts you can do so and achieve a result. You can even transform your personality if you determine to do so.

Your own inner directives can guide your purposes within life and your purposes for life. No one can guarantee a perfect result or even a completed result for whatever you wish to accomplish, but you can definitely get started and work towards completion to the extent of your abilities and resources. That is the choice you have with your time. It is simply a matter of deciding to commit to something and then undertaking that engagement.

If you think there is some ultimate meaning or some ultimate reason for life, then you are wrong. Life is something that simply appeared in the universe over time, like everything else. The purpose of life is just life – living protoplasm that exists just like uncountable other types of phenomena that exist. However the purpose of not life, but *your life*, is whatever you ultimately choose it to be. This is where meaning comes into the picture, so what will you choose?

Some types of life have no sentience, like viruses which live mechanically, and others such as ourselves do, which is a great miracle. Consciousness is the great miracle of the universe, the great treasure of all treasures, the wish-fulfilling gem that makes all things possible. Within life you are constrained by circumstances, including karmic limitations, but within those limitations you have comprehension so can solve problems and surmount challenges to make of life what you want to the best of your abilities. As stated, no one can guarantee you any success but spiritual forces can even help you to some extent if you call upon them for aid.

Just as you can send the electrons of an atom into a higher orbital shell if you inject the atom with energy, so you can elevate your life to a higher heights and break karmic bonds if you cultivate and receive spiritual assistance from the Buddhas and Bodhisattvas for your efforts. In *Move Forward: Powerful Strategies for Creating Better Outcomes in Life* and *Color Me Confucius* I even showed how individuals like Benjamin Franklin, Yuan Liao Fan, Frank Bettger and others did this in their own lives to break karmic destinies, stubborn habits and fashion entirely new fates and fortunes. You can overcome habits, insecurities and emotions that block you or hold you hostage such as fear, blame or guilt and thus free yourself from being stuck in patterns and mindsets that inhibit your life. In *Culture, County, City,*

Company, Product, Person, Passion, World I also showed how some people chose a deep life purpose of creating value for society and gathered together with others for related missions to create great positive change in the world. This is the Buddha and Bodhisattva way. This is Karma Yoga.

In the ultimate sense there is no such thing as an independent being, ego, I, personality or life in the universe. All things have developed from the one fundamental essence through a mechanistic set of transformations linked to everything else in existence. There are just phenomena, or you can say just one phenomenon – Shakti – and whether you refer to Shakti or individual phenomena you differentiate via your mind they are basically, fundamentally, inherently the primordial essence. We just happen to be one of the transformational results or evolutes that is called a "living being" rather than a non-living object or force, and because of having consciousness we can perceive, think, and know. Because of consciousness we can produce Knowledge. We can also craft our own destiny, and choose whether we will practice kindness and compassion in the world or not.

Everyone saying "I" is in deepest truth just referring to the one original nature since that is our Supreme Self – you are that one Self in All. In the ultimate sense, "I" means the original nature announcing itself via the thoughts/words of a sentient being. As the ultimate essence, It is the real unchanging Self from which we all are derived, so our foundational substratum is the only "I," the only true core, the only True Self. It is the only self-nature, or independent self. And since it is empty of restrictions but perfectly free that it can create endless possibilities, or lives are also ultimately free that we can direct them along any avenues of creation and accomplishment we choose.

So are we "living beings"? We are just phenomena linked to all other others in one large soup of energy and phenomena that is one whole. You need a mind to discriminate parts within it, but the smallest building blocks are separate, individual items that never become non-individual and thus never *really* compose any wholes. To say we are independent egos, souls, entities or living beings is really just a convenient way of speaking. It's just a relative way of carving out phenomena within a soup where nothing is actually a proper part of anything and no true composite objects exist.

As phenomena that are all inherently equal because of being the original nature, or being Shakti, I say you must put aside fear and define for yourself your own life purpose. Decide what you want to do in the universe and make use of everything to achieve it, for the universe is yourself and nothing bars you. There are always obstacles due to cause and effect relationships but you can try to become or do whatever you want.

Being the Self, choose your own destiny in the universe rather than just going along with karmic fate. Create that fate yourself by making it anew in each instant, changing each situation that comes to you for the better. Make of yourself what you want to make of yourself and do what you want to do in the world. If you fail, then so what? Life is in the doing, in the attempt. Since no fate or fortune can be guaranteed, it is in the trying that we must find happiness and fulfillment.

I want you to think about "minimizing your regret functions" so that at the end of life you have involved yourself with what you wanted to do and won't regret not having lived the way you wanted. Don't leave personal desires unfulfilled so that upon your deathbed you will look back regretting you didn't do what you wanted. You don't want to leave with unfinished business. When interviewed, people who are dying of terminal illnesses rarely say they regret having tried things in life that failed, but consistently regret not having delved into what they truly wanted to do. Don't be that way. Just be true to yourself and try to accomplish what you want! No one actually cares that you fail or succeed so stop worrying about other people's opinions. They are not carrying a scorecard about your life and their opinions don't matter, so be authentic, be an original, be true to yourself.

There will always be obstructions, challenges, limitations and karmic bonds hampering human beings in their efforts to accomplish things in life. This includes obstructions to the personal goal of finding joy, peace and fulfilling self-expression. With life there always come unavoidable pains and suffering. There are always problems, obstacles, challenges and setbacks. As a living being it is therefore your job to learn how to use cause and effect to wisely guide changes to produce results you want rather than just complain without lifting a finger and accepting things as they are. As the *Yijing* says, you have to learn how to "master the changes" to mold situations to produce a future you desire. Those purposes you cannot achieve in one life you can always set out to achieve in a subsequent life.

With this in mind, does it not make sense to start training to achieve the deva body now, before passing away, by taking up the road of spiritual cultivation? At the same time, doesn't it also make sense to prepare to become a guardian benefactor – which all devas, spirits or heavenly beings can do – since that is what enlightened individuals typically end up doing despite all of the other options available in the universe? There must be some very good reasons for that pretty consistent decision.

You should set for yourself a goal of becoming some type of Buddha, Bodhisattva or guardian spirit, which is Buddha Yoga. You should start cultivating meditation, inner energy work and start mastering the bodies of knowledge and skills that would be relevant to the type of helper, guardian, benefactor, Buddha or Bodhisattva you would want to become. You must start training to be a force of light in the world for when you finally get the chance. This training means intellectual study, participation in those activities you wish to master, cultivation work and self-improvement.

2
YOUR PHYSICAL BODY IS THE STRUCTURAL TEMPLATE FOR YOUR HIGHER BODIES

When someone is going to enter a monastic, mendicant or other committed religious life, the target is explained in terms such as pursuing *moksha*, liberation, spiritual salvation, enlightenment, self-realization, achieving union with God, dedicating oneself to God, becoming more spiritual and so on. While the goal is also usually described in terms of purifying or spiritualizing your consciousness, actually all of this can be substituted by an easier and more accurate explanation.

All paths of the spiritual life involve attaining a sequence of higher spiritual bodies, each one generated out of a previous body composed of denser substances. In other words, each new transcendental spiritual body is composed of progressively higher or more subtle etheric energies than its parent body that is denser, less pure, coarser, more material, more polluted or "lower" in composition. Higher bodies are always freed from within the condensed matrix or shell of agglomerated energies that compose a lower body, and thus are born from a process of transformation due to your cultivation (of its vital force) that liberates a higher energy from being tightly bound with grosser (more material) evolutes. Until you reach the highest body possible (considered the highest perfection or eternal self), each body is considered an inanimate container of something higher – a more transcendental soul or spirit. Thus man may "become like gods."

Each higher body is thus more "divine" or transcendental – a higher inner reality – and thus leaves behind a lower nature or karma attached to a lower realm. Therefore religions which state that the spiritual path involves freeing the soul, purifying the soul, leading us closer to God, returning us to God, leading us to unity with God, leading us to transcendence or becoming one in spirit with the source of all energy are correct. Since each new higher transcendental body and realm of being is more pleasant than the lower it surpasses, these spiritual attainments not just bring you closer to the Fountainhead but free you from bondage to lower realms of suffering, disharmony and evil. Thus a new body attainment means you purify your inherited karma; a new body represents a higher quality of life. With these higher spiritual bodies you can do many things to help the lower realms you then surpass. You can find a destiny with others who are performing extraordinary feats doing good and beneficial things for humanity, the world, our galaxy and the universe.

None of the major goals of religion can be achieved without attaining one or more of these transcendental bodies. To attain a higher spiritual body until you attain the highest possible, which puts reincarnation at bay for a very long time, is actually the goal of the spiritual path. This is how the spirit evolves towards transcendence.

Since this is the purpose and outcome of the spiritual path, and these higher bodies are the "reward" or "enjoyment" vehicle for your efforts, and since each new body is simply a *copy* of a previous lower body although composed of higher energies invisible to the lesser, one of your goals on the road of spiritual practice is to *perfect the health of your body* since it is the basic template for these higher bodies.

The first of these higher body attainments is a transcendent or more purified subtle body – less dense than our physical body – composed of Qi (Prana) that can leave the human body at will and travel the subtle realms. The subtle realm interpenetrates the denser earthly plane, and is what we normally refer to as Heaven. Upon the attainment of the subtle body, which is often called the first dhyana, astral body or deva body achievement, one becomes a spiritual master at the lowest ranks of spiritual attainment.

Let us be clear: every *genuine* spiritual master of every school, religion, sect and tradition has achieved at least this lowest body composed of Qi/Prana energy or they would not be a spiritual master. Great rabbis, priest, monks, swamis, gurus, patriarchs, archbishops, sadgurus, saints, masters, etc. all attain it from spiritual practice. With more spiritual cultivation work they can generate a yet higher body out of its matrix.

When you die you too will "rise again" in a subtle body double composed of Qi, which happens to everyone upon death, only your spirit body will have fewer powers and capabilities than a master's because you didn't create it through the power of yoga. It will exist because it was always there inside the matrix of your physical body. It exists even now as an energetic substrate or inner scaffolding that impregnates your current body, and is always ejected upon physical death. When you die it simply detaches from the physical body, which is like its shell or husk, but a spiritual master learns how to strengthen it, purify it and detach it while alive so that he can use this higher self to do good deeds. This body, and others if he works to attain them, are what gives him spiritual powers.

The subtle body attainment achieved through spiritual cultivation goes by a variety of names such as the will-born body or deva body (Buddhism), *yin shen* (Taoism), *sukshma deha* (Nath Yoga), purified Prana body (Tamil Siddhas), astral body (western alchemy), impure illusory body (Vajrayana) and countless other terms since it is a common phenomenon that every successful individual develops on the spiritual path. It is commonly recognized by nearly every *valid* spiritual tradition in existence because all true saints achieve it.

Since the first body attainment is the subtle body that is a pranic copy of the physical body, and since all other higher bodies are derived from each other with each new one based on the previous body it is birthed from, logic says that you should work hard to make your current physical body – which becomes the ground template for the first subtle body attainment – as healthy and as excellent as possible. This gives rise to concerns regarding your diet (food), exercise to develop and learn how to control your muscles, medicine to cure internal organs and illnesses, and whether or not you fix skeletal imbalances to align your posture and physical structure.

Hinduism says that each progressively higher spiritual body is not only more subtle, etheric, pure or transcendental than the lower one, but also lives longer than the lower. Nonetheless, despite the higher excellence for each new body the cycle of births and deaths (reincarnation) continues until you attain a Supra-Casual body, made of what Chinese call Later Heavenly Qi or Clear Light substance (that other schools like Taoism call Emptiness), that can live so long that we say nearly forever.

Buddhism says that finding one's original nature, which corresponds to the clear light, Dharma body or Supra-Causal body attainment of fourth dhyana enlightenment (*nirvana* with remainder), is one's last human lifetime. Ramalinga Swamigal explains that the *jnana deha* body of enlightenment becomes identified with universal life and is "oned with eternity." The *Thirumandiram*, which is a classic of yoga and tantra by Siddhar Thirumoolar, says (841) that through sexual cultivation (that moves your Qi) and many other cultivation techniques you can achieve the fruit of the path and then "you may live on earth a million, trillion years." Other teachings from yet more spiritual traditions also clearly state that the higher bodies live longer and longer periods of time, and are nearly immortal. In Taoism, these stages of achievement are actually called Immortals.

Since all these spirit bodies are copies of the present body you now have, one of your main concerns is to work on making your body as healthy and excellent as possible. This then enters into the fields of diet, medicine, exercise, bodywork and pranayama. When you preserve your body via healthy ways you preserve your Qi, which is necessary for success in spiritual cultivation.

Let us talk about this in terms of two directions, namely (1) health concerns for you as an individual and (2) health concerns if you were the head of a monastery, nunnery or large tradition and had hundreds or even thousands of monks or nuns (students) under your care whose health was your responsibility. These discussions can update some management practices that are hundreds to thousands of years old.

In the second case I would not just have to worry about the proper structure and operations of the monastery (see Nan Huai-chin's *Basic Buddhism*) but about the health and education of all the sadhus, swamis, monks and/or nuns under my charge. The medical issues for so many people would be enormous, and health care costs substantial as a proportion of my budget. Prevention is the only logical solution.

Unfortunately, money will always be an issue since few people donate to the care of the very people who will become enlightened and actually help them invisibly in life once they attain the subtle body. This is why I encourage donations to those spiritual institutions that train people for enlightenment. These are the people who will answer the public call of prayers and requests for help from God, all the time masquerading as deities, angels, Buddhas, saints and so on when intervening in human affairs to help. In any case, the road of health involves both prevention and treatment but let's focus on prevention and low-cost methods of treating medical conditions.

PHYSICAL DETOXIFICATION

The first issue of preventing illness is to regularly detox your physical body of accumulated poisons, which often end up causing disease, in order to set up a foundation for better health and prevent all sorts of illnesses in the future such as cancer. After an initial detoxification effort one can set up a schedule to detoxify your body on a regular basis. This is not only good for your health but good for your spiritual practice too. It's good for your life, and good for spiritual cultivation.

Spiritual cultivation is a process that involves opening up your Qi channels throughout your tissues, which are populated by various blockages and obstructions, so that the etheric duplicates within them can be cleared of restrictions and strengthened. These impediments to Qi flow exist on the level of the physical and subtle body, and they are related to poisons and tangled muscle fibers that have not been stretched or opened through and through. Therefore detoxification will help with spiritual cultivation, as will the stretching of your muscles since this will enable energy to flow more smoothly within your body.

Here are the main efforts you must do for spiritual cultivation – stretch all the muscles of your body, lead your Qi/Prana and at times *force* your Qi/Prana to pass through those muscles (and organs and other tissues), detox your body of harmful substances that it has accumulated over the years, eat well to build good cells, and restore the health of any damaged internal organs. Basically, get yourself into optimal health.

The earliest stages of spiritual cultivation always involve purging the body of poisons at a coarse level of detoxification. Your Qi/Prana is aroused because of spiritual practices, pushes through the body's tissues, and the poisons within those tissues are pushed to the surface of the skin to be expelled (which is why cultivators often experience rashes and skin eruptions) or are discharged through other channels of elimination. In India this is called kundalini yoga while other schools call this purification or purgation. You should consider purification both a creative and cleansing process.

Essentially then, *the earliest stages of cultivation are all a process of physical detoxification and purification.* Spiritual cultivation itself is often described as removing the unwanted, impure elements from the body via the process of burning, namely kundalini yoga or *nei-gong* that raises your Yang Qi. Since the onset of disease is a problem often caused by the buildup of toxic substances within the body, detoxification is necessary as a yearly preventive measure. Therefore for both health concerns and the spiritual path one of your first tasks for cultivation is to detoxify the body in order to take care of your body.

The idea of purifying or transforming the physical body necessitates that you work towards cleaning out what is essentially a cesspool. Every year you should also undergo some degree of herbal detoxification to rid your body of cellular wastes and organ toxins, especially toxins in the intestines, liver and kidneys. *Detox Cleanse Your Body Quickly and Completely* teaches you how to do this in the quickest and most cost effective manner possible using the fewest supplements as possible. Pranayama practice helps you open your Qi channels as well and push poisons out of your body.

Detoxing your body to remove poisons from your system will slowly improve all health conditions and also your spiritual cultivation. This is because herbal and other detoxification regimens will help purge your body of poisons that are impediments to health. Detoxifying your body will help you purify your Qi and Qi channels running through every tissue and atomic bond within your body. With less poisons in your body, your Qi won't have to do as much work to expel toxins from body tissues to create a smooth circulatory flow that eventually generates the subtle body.

Remember that the subtle body is composed completely of Qi energy, so during the process of spiritual cultivation you must move your Qi everywhere to purify and strengthen the inherent subtle body duplicate within the physical body. The Qi duplicate within all your tissues must be transformed. Even the European medieval alchemy-cultivation text, *Atalanta Fugiens*, explains this.

Human beings are animals, and if you have ever dealt with animals in the wild you will find that they have a strong smell and strong energy due to the untransformed raw Qi that flows within them. Humans are the same way in that uncultivated people tend to have Qi/Prana that flows less smoothly than others, and seem coarse and crude to others because of this. Because of cultivation the Qi/Prana flows within an individual will essentially open, purify and smoothen, and that crudeness or rawness will go away. Some people will begin to smell more pleasant as well. This is part of the meaning of Qi purification. While detoxification helps a body seem externally cleaner the practice of spiritual cultivation helps the Qi/Prana within it become purified, as does character training, moral development and any self-cultivation that aims to elevate the human being above base materialistic worldliness and its animal nature.

You should always accompany the process of spiritual cultivation with detoxification efforts because you might not succeed in cultivation, but you will still benefit from any detoxification efforts you make. Everyone who wants to start cultivating, or who just wants better health, should make an effort to clean their body of accumulated wastes and chemical poisons every year. When Qi starts stirring within you it will open up your body tissues, which is a process of purification, and the physical equivalent is the external practice of detoxification that you should add to your life too.

Detoxification is a complicated, multi-step process that can involve many different approaches. My books *Detox Cleanse Your Body Quickly and Completely* and *Look Young, Live Longer* teach ways to accomplish both coarse dredging and more refined levels of detoxification of your physical body. Pranayama practice helps to detoxify your Qi body as well. Here is a simple synopsis of the steps to take to detoxify your body.

First, stop adding to the problem by creating an even greater toxic load. The first step to improved health is to stop consuming poisons that destroy your health. Stop smoking and exposing yourself to harmful chemicals. Breathe cleaner air and drink cleaner water (use water filters in your home). Change your diet so that you are eating clean foods (non-GMO, organic if possible) and stay away from garbage junk food. With less poisons coming in, your body will have a chance to catch up on cleansing your system of those already accumulated inside if you help it out a little bit with the right herbs and supplements.

The second step is to start cleaning out any toxins that have already accumulated in your body tissues or block your channels of elimination, especially if you frequently experience constipation. Consider enemas or colonics for cleaning your intestines. Consider various detoxification herbs/supplements for your liver, kidneys and connective tissues. As stated, *Detox Cleanse Your Body Quickly and Completely* can especially help in this regard because it guides you through the supplements and protocols that work best for cleaning every part of your body.

Yoga has a number of detoxification protocols for the stomach and so forth, but cannot get rid of chemical toxins in the body except through the purging effects of pranayama and meditation. *Prevent and Reverse Atherosclerosis*, by Stanton Reed (a pen name of mine), is excellent for those with clogged arteries and cardiovascular issues because it provides natural remedies for cleansing arteries.

Third, "clean the pipes" within your body so that wastes can be more readily eliminated and excreted. This means improving the efficiency of your body's circulatory system and its channels of elimination. For instance, the supplement nattokinase dissolves long-standing blood clots in veins and arteries, Detoxamin (a rectal suppository) chelates arterial walls to remove any unwanted mineral scaffolding, and the protocols of Linus Pauling and the Nobel Prize winning Doctors Robert Furchgott, Louis Ignarro and Ferid Murad can help to clean arteries and veins of excess plaque and cholesterol that coat their walls. PMCaox or Life Assure can do this as well if you take the product for about one year. Once again, you can find such information in *Prevent and Reverse Atherosclerosis*.

Fourth, increase blood circulation and oxygen exposure to your tissues via deep tissue massage, castor oil packs, far infrared saunas, and chiropractic adjustments when needed. Start practicing yoga exercises or martial arts (stretching) and breathing exercises that help to open up Qi channels and circulatory routes via manual rather than chemical efforts.

CHIROPRACTIC ADJUSTMENTS & BODYWORK

Your subtle body, once generated, can live for hundreds of years while the Causal body can last even longer and the Supra-Causal body longer still. Since you can retain your body for an incredibly long time, you want it to remain in excellent top shape condition, which means you should practice good habits that create a healthy body.

One of those good habits is your posture and demeanor ... you don't want to live for hundreds of years with a twisted spine or lousy posture.

Who wants to live for a long time with back pain? These types of things don't automatically fix themselves upon death so you have to work on fixing them during life. Like etiquette, you must work at mastering it.

Think of it this way. Your body is the only vehicle you are assigned and if it breaks down you still have to live in it. Whatever its condition, that's the template that gets copied as your subtle body. The shape of your afterlife body is the body you have now until you are reborn into a new one. Therefore, do everything possible to work on its health, shape and functionality *now*. Chiropractic adjustments, from a top level practitioner, are therefore paramount. So are AMIT method adjustments (invented by Dr. Craig Buhler) to get all your muscles working.

To succeed in generating the subtle body you need to practice meditation, which in turn depends upon the health of your nervous system and spine. Since you will usually be assuming a lotus posture for meditation practice and sitting erect, your skeletal alignment is important. Your posture and skeletal alignment determines how you will hold yourself and move in the world (your posture, carriage and gait) as well as how your Qi flows within you.

Together with your breathing, heart rate and blood pressure, the correctness of your structural alignment also affects the creation of thoughts within your brain. If your spine has a good structural alignment this will help with your meditation efforts to cultivate an "empty mind," "mind of detachment," "purify consciousness," "cultivate a mind like the original nature" and so forth.

Since your spinal alignment is very important, the best advice is to get regular chiropractic adjustments so that your skeletal structure becomes perfectly aligned. This will help with health, meditation, mental functioning and peace of mind. When the bones in your back are aligned you will feel fantastic and move with greater ease because you corrected your structural biomechanics. Furthermore, you should perform lots of *anapana*, *qi-gong* or *nei-gong* work on moving the Qi around in your spine, and up and down the spine, to open up Qi channels heading into your brain (hundreds to thousands of revolutions of Qi per day), but always make sure that your skeleton is aligned and you practice good posture.

If you are the head of a monastery, you should arrange for all the monks and nuns to get regular chiropractic adjustments now and then. This will improve everyone's posture, fix any skeletal misalignments people many have developed, improve people's blood circulation, and help with their meditation efforts. Sometimes chiropractic adjustments can even reduce high blood pressure or other seemingly unrelated health issues.

Chiropractic adjustments make sure that the central nervous system is properly online. The net result of chiropractic adjustments is that people will feel better and can often permanently eliminate any back pain without needing medication. This is important for spiritual practice.

For postural help to fix problems and physical therapy work you might also pursue the Feldenkrais method, Aston patterning techniques, Egoscue and the NeuroCranial restructuring method of Dr. Dean Howell related to the Nasal Specific Technique developed by Dr. J.R. Stober of Portland. A wide variety of bodywork therapies are also available such as Rolfing, Hellerwork, Swedish massage, active-release technique (ART), advanced muscle integration therapy (AMIT) and the Graston technique. There are many others. You can find many ways to "fix" your body mentioned in *The 4-Hour Body* by Timothy Ferriss, which is excellent.

I am particularly impressed with Dr. Craig Buhler's revolutionary AMIT therapy which I highly recommend. This technique recognizes that muscular problems in one part of the body are often caused by problems elsewhere, whereas ordinary physicians will usually only treat the problem area and not the true cause so that the problem never gets cured. We all incur injuries through life and our bodies normally heal them for a total resolution, or our body *adapts* around the problem. For instance, if a muscle becomes overloaded with strain or stress, it either tears *or is inhibited by the body in order to protect it*. It will be deactivated (and thus "weakened") through a series of reflexes called proprioceptors and part of its load will be shifted elsewhere. To cure the first muscle you have to release the adaptation too, which ordinary doctors don't know to do.

Your body has a natural priority in inhibiting the functioning of tissues in order to protect more valuable tissues. It will first sacrifice muscles, then joints, lymphatics, viscera (organs), nerves, veins, and finally bones - in that order – before affecting arteries since if they tear you will die immediately. Your body will inhibit the movement of muscles or joints in order to protect more important components higher up on the list, and ultimately to prevent arteries from tearing because this would kill you. In terms of movements, when one muscle is injured your body will shift its load to other muscles, and this will occur in a cascading manner that will eventually affect many muscles in order to relieve the strain put on one. The nervous system plays a central role in determining these adaptations, so to return things to normal you must normalize specific circuits within your brain.

If a muscular injury isn't solved, our nervous system adapts into other tissues to take over some of the muscle's function. Your nervous system normally adapts by throwing stress into the muscle next to the muscle that can no longer handle load, and this adaptation is then locked into your neurology to produce altered movement patterns. Basically, your neurology stops using an injured muscle and shifts load to other muscles instead. The problem is that it often never switches back to using its original brain map, but starts preferring the alternative muscles forever.

Once "switched off," Buhler says that no amount of bodywork, yoga, or exercise will fully turn a muscle back on again. The symptoms of injury might seem to go away, and all muscles might seem to be working, but the adaptation means that the primary muscle stays weak to some degree even after recovery. Part of its load will stay shifted to other muscles, and those adapting tissues bearing extra stress will always be at a mechanical disadvantage due to the excess load. The adaptations will eventually weaken making them prone to be the next injuries. When those muscles become injured, then yet another group will play the role of adaptation in a cascading fashion. This is why when a muscle becomes tight ("won't fire under a load") you must treat *the reason it has become inhibited* – the core problem. To restore order you must also treat the adaptation, which are the muscles that have taken on extra stress in order to protect others that have weakened.

Through AMIT therapy muscle testing, muscles found to be weak or "shut off" because of prior stresses, accidents or bone misalignments are first identified and then restored to normal functioning by treating their mechanoreceptors. Connected to the brain map for the each muscle's usage are at least seven critical points that, once stimulated, will cause the brain to switch back to fully using that muscle instead of the other adaptations that previously assumed part of its load.

In other words, by stimulating seven reflex points connected to a muscle you can reactivate it back to full functioning and relieve the extra stress on adaptive tissues. A muscle will normalize because those seven points specific to the muscle, when stimulated, will restore its functional role to its former preeminence within your brain map of muscular loading priorities.

Stimulating these critical points – the weakened muscle's origin and insertion points, neurovascular point, neurolymphatic point, spindle cells, its acupuncture point, and two organ or gland reflex points, you cause the brain to "turn back on" the pattern for optimal muscle functioning so that it no longer locks onto adaptations. It takes ten minutes to reactivate a muscle, but AMIT therapy can honestly reactivate frozen or weakened muscle conditions and restore their functioning to normal almost instantly. Afterwards you will find yourself with more stability and strength, and a greater range of muscular motion. As a result, AMIT therapy can treat very stubborn chronic and acute musculoskeletal ailments. For instance, people with tight hamstrings are usually suffering because their quadriceps are shut down, and when AMIT therapy reactivates the quadriceps muscles then most hamstring issues instantly disappear.

If you want to have a very healthy body you should first adjust your spine to be straight through chiropractic adjustments. Next, "turn on" (reactivate) all the muscles in your body through the AMIT method because many of your muscles have been inactivated due to injuries over time, and you want to restore their full functioning. Chiropractic adjustments will also tend to hold once you do this. Only afterwards will passive muscle exercises such as yoga and Pilates, or active exercise such as dance (ballet), sports and the martial arts, be able to reach their full flower.

This is the sequence of adjustments to attain a more perfect body. If you are planning on living forever, fix your posture, turn on your muscle via the AMIT method (since no other therapy will turn them back on), and then exercise/stretch them to try to define each one and gain control over their movements. Also remember that diet and exercise, over time, will change the shape and composition of your body.

STRETCHING & EXERCISE

To liberate the soul from matter by generating the subtle (deva) body you must open up all the Qi channels within your current muscle tissues since your inherent deva body is the exact duplicate of your physical body. One method that quickens the process is stretching your muscles – thus dissolving any obstructions along the muscle Qi channel routes – while also doing meditation and other spiritual practices that force Qi/Prana through those muscles. This is what helps purify the deva body quickest. Many yoga practitioners and martial artists have attained the subtle body due to relevant Qi/Prana exercises like this, so these are good practices to undertake. They will improve the pattern or shape of your body too.

All stretching methods, to be most effective at helping you generate your deva body, should be combined with pranayama, visualization and mantra practice. As explained in *Nyasa Yoga*, the optimal procedure is to stretch every muscle of your body to definition while doing visualization and Mantrayana on each muscle group being stretched to send Qi/Prana through them, and also while they are relaxed. This will help you not only become healthier but prepare a strong foundational base for a quicker generation of the subtle body. In the best of all worlds you want to gain individual control over all your muscles because as a deva made of Qi you will practice controlling the energy movement in each one, so start learning that control now.

Therefore exercises such as yoga, Pilates, dance, acrobatics, Foundation training (Dr. Eric Goodman's technique of corrective bodywork exercises that stretch all the muscles in a chain), or the martial arts are great for training muscles. Therefore you should investigate some form of soft martial arts (*Tai Qi Quan, Akido, Yi Jin Jing, Baguazhang, Xing Yi Quan* and *Akido*), Zdorovye, yoga practices, dancing, or other stretching exercises that are suitable for you, and then start practicing regularly. Stretching is better than body building or strengthening muscles.

What you want is some form of stretching exercise that produces power, flexibility and control over individual muscles and their movements. The problem is that most of us have adopted improper movement patterns over time, and we have to break those old patterns with the right exercises. You want flexibility, posture, and strength changes to happen fast so I believe that Pilates, yoga, dance and Foundation training are some of your best bets. Foundation and Feldenkrais training, for instance, focus on establishing correct basic fundamental human movement patterns before you add any resistance to a flawed way of doing things. If you want to pursue swimming instead of these alternative routes you should learn the Total Immersion method, invented by Terry Laughlin.

When combined with breath and movement, stretching can help open up your tissues so that you look younger, feel better and live longer. You want your body to get into the best condition possible, preparing for the Qi channels (*nadis*) to open, and these stretching or exercise techniques will definitely help you accomplish this.

Kettlebells, although not a stretching method per se, are another great form of exercise that can help an overweight person become thin and a thin person gain muscles (weight). The Slavic physical system Zdorovye is also another martial arts-related possibility to investigate. Mini-trampolines (rebounders) and pogo sticks, as strange as it may sound, are also a great form of exercise as the tensional vibrations they produce in a body will exercise all its cells. Few exercises can do that.

The key to the quickest success for opening your muscle channels is to *stretch each of your muscles so that they can be seen with definition*, and try to move your Qi through them while stretching them. When you are practicing any form of stretching it thus helps to have color-coded pictures of the muscles being stretched in front of you during each stretch to help guide your visualization focus for *anapana, nei-gong* and *nei-dan* Qi practices, which are basically the same as kundalini yoga, *kriya* yoga, and Vajrayana cultivation techniques. The optimal thing to do is stretch every muscle of your body to definition while doing visualization and Mantrayana on each one.

The "best exercise in the world" is useless if you don't practice it, and so the best exercise for you is the one that helps you that you will bother to continue doing. Without adherence to an exercise schedule, you can talk about "optimal" all you want, but it is just mouthing air. You need to physically practice. I prefer people to try gentle stretching exercises like yoga and Pilates or Foundation training. I especially like yoga and Pilates because they were designed to enable you to isolate individual muscles during stretching. If you practice dancing exercises, this is also a way to help stretch, open and gain control over your muscles too.

Of particular note, Z-health training helps to open up your joints and Chinese *Yi Jin Jing* is great for tendon stretching. I always put exercises in an ordering scheme as follows - concentrate on the joints, tendons, muscles, and then movements. Thus you have circular Z-health movements for joints; *Yi Jin Jing* stretching for tendons; yoga, Pilates, Foundation training, or activated isolated stretching for muscles; dance, martial arts and athletics for muscle movement. Before all of this, however, you might spend some money on AMIT treatments in order to "turn on" all your inactivated muscles.

In a sense, one of our brain's primary functions is movement, for without movement you cannot survive and cannot even communicate. What is the sense of having higher thoughts of cause and effect if you cannot even move your lips to communicate with others? Therefore, learning how to make your body move in special ways, under the control of your mind, and learning how to control your inner energy and emotions, are purposes you should pursue through exercise and athletic instruction.

When it comes to martial arts, which also constitute a form of stretching that can be combined with inner Qi movements (*nei-dan, nei-gong, anapana*) to help open up your channels, consider "soft" martial arts that will not permanently hurt your joints rather than Karate and Judo, which are hard martial arts known to damage people's joints.

The results of scientific studies definitively prove that regular exercise reduces mortality and increases life expectancy, but it should be practiced in a gradual, prudent manner so you don't hurt yourself as you get older. The soft martial arts are wonderful in teaching you how to develop and use your Qi/Prana energy in tune with muscles and movement, but you have to use inner energy work, such as the methods in this book and *Nyasa Yoga*, to cultivate your Qi as well. For related advice see *Internal Martial Arts Nei-gong*.

In short, to become more fit and prepare a better foundational base for the successful generation of an independent subtle body that can leave your physical form at will you should regularly exercise posture and combine Qi movements with that practice, and should develop a better posture, especially one that will lend itself to meditation practice.

Buddhas and Bodhisattvas will always help you cultivate your Qi but they are not going to help you attain a subtle body that lives for hundreds of years if your body gets so out of shape that it causes you pain and discomfort every day. Who wants such a body forever? Therefore if you want to get out early then work at perfecting the form and functions of your physical body through diet and exercise and postural alignment.

KUMBHAKA RETENTION PRANAYAMA

Traditional Chinese Medicine says that "one hundred diseases start with Qi (wind)." Your health depends on your Qi and oxygen intake, which are improved by pranayama practice, so you should practice pranayama breath retention exercises on daily basis. In particular, you should practice *kumbhaka* (breath retention) pranayama exercises where you hold your breath for as long as possible before exhalation. If you want to achieve big progress through yoga you have to practice a lot of pranayama breath work and *nei-gong* practices to move your Qi so that you can learn to gain control of its inner movements. Adding visualization efforts helps your practice.

The *Geranda-Samhita* contains eight *kumbhaka* pranayama techniques, called "pots," that spiritual adherents are strongly advised to master to help their spiritual cultivation as preparation required for a spiritual body. If you combine these *kumbhaka* methods with the nine-bottled wind pranayama technique from Tibet (as featured in *Visualization Power*), they can help you transform your Qi channels very quickly, which is why most yogis who succeed recommend them. They are the basis of inner *tummo* heat yoga too.

Kumbhaka pranayama that involves holding your breath is one of the most important practices for making cultivation progress quickly. With pranayama you hold your breath for as long as possible, as gently as possible (using as few muscles as possible), in order that your body internally is forced to open up Qi channel obstructions. Then your Qi/Prana will begin to flow smoothly through your channels. Most people cannot hold their breath for very long, but if you combine pranayama exercises with the breath retention exercises taught for freediving you will usually be able to immediately double the amount of time you can hold your breath quite quickly.

The *Geranda-Samhita*, *Hatha Yoga Pradipika* and other yoga texts all contain *kumbhaka* pranayama exercises. In my opinion, four pranayama exercises are among the best. These include (1) *Bhastrika* "bellows breathing" pranayama, (2) *Visama Vritti* "uneven breath" *Anuloma* pranayama or *Surya Behdana*, (3) *Kapalabhati* "skull shining" pranayama, and (4) nine-bottled wind *kumbhaka* (nine round breathing). A good master will give better advice than this since I am not an expert on all the pranayama techniques available.

Learning control of your breathing eventually leads to control of your vital force or Qi. Thus pranayama is an entry vehicle for learning to gain control of your vital force, Qi or Prana. Superficial respiratory pranayama is akin to *qi-gong*, and when you can finally grab hold of the Qi/Prana of your body, circulating it here or there according to your will, the practice becomes *nei-gong* or kundalini yoga. Holding your Qi/Prana fixed at various points within the body, rather than in the lungs, is another type of related vital energy practice.

SEXUAL ACTIVITIES

Some cultivation paths allow for sexual activities, with a devoted partner, in order to help you rouse your internal energy to open up your Qi channels. Sex is then a matter of health and Qi channel practice. Sex is the quickest and easiest way to move your internal energy, which is why it can feature within the cultivation path under the right conditions. For those monks and nuns whom are allowed to have sex on the spiritual trail because they are under the auspices of an enlightened master, here is what you need to know.

Sex is an important part of life most people will not want to do without. In fact, many sworn-to-celibacy masters who generate the subtle body at a young age end up marrying a partner in Heaven (such as another human who has attained the deva body) so that they have a partner on the path, and practice sexual cultivation in the upper realms to help move their Qi/Prana in order to attain the yet higher bodies.

Because they help to maximize sexual pleasure and exercise muscles in the pelvic region (thus opening the Qi channels therein), women should learn kegel exercises and the yogic practice of *mula bhandha*. Men, including monks, should also practice *mula bhandha*. Laymen should train themselves for being able to do karezza, which is lovemaking without ejaculation, even if they never engage in sex. They must practice exercising the muscles in the pelvic region in order to open the channels in that localized area.

Even monks need to learn how to energetically move their Qi throughout the different parts of their body to open up all their Qi channels, and learning *mula bandha* helps them do so for the pelvis. A monk or nun should still practice to master *mula mandha* even though they refrain from sex.

All men need to conserve their semen (*Jing*) and Qi on the cultivation path; if you lose your Qi through the outlet of sexual ejaculation then that energy won't be available for opening up Qi channels. On the other hand, whenever sex is used in cultivation you should match sexual activities with the "immeasurable joy" practice of Buddhism and the methods of moving your Qi/Prana taught within this book and *Nyasa Yoga*.

In other words, you want to match the mental state of immeasurable joy with your sexual technique, sexual pleasure and sexual excitation as this will very quickly stimulate your internal Qi to move within you. The "immeasurable joy" meditation is used because people have too many embedded mental restrictions about sex to fully let go and enjoy themselves during intercourse, and "immeasurable joy" will tend to override their mental blockages.

During sexual congress you should adopt the joy and passion of happiness and bliss and use sex use it to move your Qi/Prana to open up different areas of your body. That is the essence of sexual cultivation. Either the energy aroused does this naturally on its own, or you cause it to penetrate other areas through different positions, tempos, mental guidance and so on.

When the Vajrayana school talks about using sexual "desire" on the spiritual path the translation is incorrect. The correct translation is to use sexual excitement, and sexual pleasure during sexual congress since these will move your Qi. You are after Qi movement through sexual passion. This is another way to open up your Qi channels for spiritual practice, and is used in Vajrayana, Taoism and the Kaula Yoga schools of India. The method of using emotions to *excite the Qi throughout your body*, such as immeasurable joy or sexual excitement, is taught within *Nyasa Yoga*. Many emotional cultivation methods such as bhakti reverence can move the Qi/Prana within you too.

CULTIVATING INTERNAL ENERGY & MEDITATION

Chinese Taoism has a saying: "By cultivating your essential nature only, without cultivating your Qi and channels, the *yin* spirit will not become a saint in 10,000 kalpas."

In other words, if you only practice meditation but don't engage in inner heat yoga, *anapana*, *nei-gong* or *nei-dan* practices to cultivate (stimulate and move) your internal Qi/Prana energy then you won't attain the first step of the path - a deva body composed of Qi, a subtle etheric body that can independently move within the world's earthly plane. You must perform inner energy work, moving your Qi everyday throughout your body, to generate the subtle body quickly. Static meditation practice that does not move your inner energy is not enough, but that is the mistake of many schools and traditions including the Zen school and Vedanta in particular.

Taoism also has another famous phrase: "If you only cultivate life and do not cultivate the fundamental essence, this is the first sickness of cultivating practice." In other words, if you only cultivate your Qi/Prana (life force) and body structure (Qi channels) through *nei-gong* exercises of internal energy work but don't practice meditation to cultivate an empty mind that mimics the empty, formless purity of the original nature, then your practice method is incorrect.

You cannot just focus on transforming your physical body and its vital energy. You must practice meditation work as well, especially witnessing meditation practice which leads to character improvement. Success in attaining the spiritual body requires (1) formless mind meditation and (2) inner energy work that moves your Qi/Prana everywhere inside you, which you should do hundreds of times per day for the quickest results.

The proper road of spiritual practice is a quick path that involves inner energy work on your Qi/Prana to transform your subtle body (called Deity

Yoga) and various forms of emptiness meditation wherein you don't cling to thoughts but simply watch your mind with awareness, or try to imitate states of true emptiness. If you join Deity Yoga (Nyasa Yoga type inner energy work) with the view of emptiness then success on the path is quickest. This means that to generate the subtle body you have to (a) practice empty mind, non-attachment meditation and (b) do lots of inner energy work to move the Qi/Prana around within your body.

Esoteric Buddhist master Ratnakarashanti said, "If one cultivates only the inner energetic body (subtle body), you cannot become fully enlightened merely through that because the fulfillment of (yogic) activities is not complete. Or, if you meditate on emptiness and don't focus on the deva-like subtle body (and its higher stages of purification), you will attain Buddhahood in many countless eons but not quickly. Through cultivating both, however, you will attain the highest perfect complete enlightenment very quickly because doing so is very appropriate and has special empowering blessings."

By practicing meditation diligently and continuously, we can say that your life force (your Qi or Prana) gets purified to an extent that it "attains divinity." Why? Because you can attain a deva body that way, and by continuing with more cultivation that Qi body can attain a Causal body of a yet higher transcendental substance, and that spiritual body can attain a Supra-Causal body, and next an Immanence body composed of Primordial Heavenly energy and so on. Thus we can say that cultivation "divinizes" or "spiritualizes" your body.

This is the idea of *theosis*, deification, beautification, ascension or glorification in Christianity. For a revolution in Christian teachings, it would be appropriate to pose spiritual work as becoming "like Christ through divinization," and thereby joining the community of saints to "become sons of the highest." The appropriate Christian spiritual path can be posed as becoming like what Jesus is Himself who "became man to deify us." This would be the appropriate spiritual pursuit of a Christian, for "You are gods" John 10:34 encased within a physical shell.

Clement of Alexandria wrote: "Yea, I say, the Word of God became a man so that you might learn from a man how to become a god." There are many quotes from Church Fathers along these lines that Christians should work to attain the deva body including words from Paul the Apostle, Clement of Alexandria, Justin Martyr, Gregory of Nyssa and many others. Such passages include, "We all, with unveiled face, beholding the glory of the Lord, are being transformed into the same image from one degree of glory to another," "He was made human so that he might make us gods," "he who obeys the Lord and follows the prophecy given through him ... becomes a god while still moving about in the flesh."

There are many passages from both the Old and New Testament that it is possible for man to become deified, to become a god by grace. Basil of Caesarea basically summed it up when he said, "becoming a god is the highest goal of all," which is the entire purpose of the spiritual path in order to escape the lower realms. The first step is to attain the deva body made of Qi/Prana, which is a god's body. Next there is the Mantra/Causal body made of Shen that is generated from within the deva body, then the Dharma spiritual body composed of Later Heavenly Qi/Prana from the Causal body, and finally the body of Immanence composed of Primordial Qi/Prana energy. Attaining the deva body *is* to become a god as is attaining the yet higher bodies.

It is a pity that Christians do not practice in the best possible way for this to happen when the path is openly taught in the eastern religions. It is mostly monks and nuns within the Christian tradition who succeed. However, many of the church hierarchy today in countries, especially the heads of the Eastern Orthodox Churches, have also attained the subtle body, Causal body, Supra-Causal body and Immanence body. Regular people, however, do not know this or even understand that there are standard levels of achievement.

Many more levels of body attainments are possible although we normally restrict the discussion to only five bodies in total, one earthly and four transcendental spiritual bodies termed "divine." Eventually we can attain a body of such transcendental substance that it is an extremely high evolute, and hence is termed "oned with eternity (the original nature)."

The higher the body, the closer it is to the original nature in terms of evolutionary planes of transcendence. As explained in *Nyasa Yoga*, we can say that through cultivation we divinize/spiritualize the body through spiritual practices, which is why we can have these higher attainments. Regardless, this entire pathway starts with the health of the body, for as Shakyamuni Buddha showed, you cannot achieve enlightenment if your body is unhealthy or you destroy your body on the cultivation path by engaging in overly fierce ascetic practices.

The gist of the spiritual path is that you must cultivate both your body and mind, your internal energy and conduct, in order to attain enlightenment. Without good conduct and virtuous ways, no one is going to help you achieve the deva body, which is why moral provisioning, ethics and virtue teachings are the first stage of the spiritual path. It is a stage of seeking. You must cultivate mental emptiness through the practice of meditation (see *Meditation Case Studies*, *The Little Book of Meditation*) and do internal energy work through practices like yoga *asanas*, pranayama, *anapana* Qi smoothing practices, visualization practice with Nyasa Yoga, *nei-gong*, *qi-gong*, inner heat yoga and so on. The Yoga schools explain that the physical body must be "burnt out by the fire of yoga" when all your kundalini or Yang Qi starts arising and clearing your Qi channels of obstructions.

Without a body you simply don't exist. There is no such thing as consciousness without a body vehicles containing a nervous system that creates consciousness. You need a healthy body as the template for attaining the higher body vehicles, the *sambhogakaya*, which is a set of spiritual bodies linked together (including a link to the physical body) that can each operate independently in separate realms. Basically, the initial fruit of the spiritual path is a subtle body composed of higher transcendental material (Qi or Prana) that can live in the heavenly realm, and when you cultivate the Causal body, Supra-Causal body and beyond you gain access to even higher transcendental realms, i.e. Pure Lands composed of higher etheric essences.

As the Tamil Siddhas and Taoists explain, the physical body is therefore a treasure and should not be squandered in vain. It is the great miracle of the universe. It is from the basis of a healthy physical body that you can attain a deva body, which is a guardian spirit's body, and from that initial subtle body you can attain the higher body accomplishments of the path to become a Bodhisattva or Buddha.

It is not that you "realize your mind" and then attain the *sambhogakaya*. It is that you attain a *sambhogakaya*, or set of linked transcendental bodies, and this is enlightenment or self-realization. This is the road of liberation from the lower realms. The *sambhogakaya* attainment means enlightenment, not "realizing the *dharmakaya* attainment is enlightenment and produces the *sambhogakaya* attainment." Most Buddhist literature deceives people on this principle, as a form of skillful means as taught in the *Lotus Sutra*, in order that they stick to meditation and emphasize it in their spiritual practice. Attaining dhyana means attaining the subtle body, which is a perfect copy of your physical body with the same memories and mental abilities. There is no empty mind in your new body, just a body with a concomitant, attendant consciousness for that body double which is composed of higher substances. You attain a new body but have the same consciousness as the old one.

Furthermore, you need a healthy body and proper spiritual exercises to generate the Qi necessary for the transformations required to attain the subtle body, so start working on making your body healthier, and start working on inner energy work. Even if you don't succeed in cultivation you should do this.

DIAGNOSIS, FOOD, DIET, SUPPLEMENTS, REMEDIES

The last topic of body cultivation has to do with preventing health problems through diagnosis and then intervention. Spiritual cultivation will cause your Qi/Prana to arise and bump into latent illnesses that will cause problems to erupt, as explained in *Tao and Longevity* (Nan and Chu). There are many ways to handle this.

Here are some hints for head monks and nuns who must manage the lives of aspirants. If I had to take care of many monks and nuns with limited funds, I would want to regularly analyze their state of health with as little cost as possible for prevention purposes. With diagnostic information I would then know how to intercede on their behalf with preventive measures or curative intervention. There are several ways to do this.

First, head monks/nuns should create family trees of each junior monk or nun where each relative on the tree is labeled by the diseases they have (diabetes, arthritis, heart problems, etc.) and causes of death if they passed away. This information on disease propensities, together with diagnostics, can help you spot potential problems that can be modified through preventative diets, appropriate vitamin-mineral-herbal supplements and other measures. Diets can especially be altered to nutritionally prevent or treat diseases based on this information. Prevention is the key, just as one should prevent accepting too many vaccinations because of the damage they can cause when in excess.

Let me provide some examples of nutritional prevention. If there is a history of prostate cancer in the family the individual should avoid milk, add flaxseed to their diet, and regularly take inexpensive herbs to also help prevent prostate problems. If heart disease runs in the family (the number one killer in the United States) a whole-food, plant-based diet has been repeatedly shown to prevent the disease or stop it in its tracks. Certain supplements taken proactively can often prevent cardiovascular disease. For instance, nattokinase can eliminate blood clots while *Prevent and Reverse Atherosclerosis* (Stanton Reed) reveals many orthomolecular cures for reversing cardiovascular disease. Nattokinase can also help reduce high blood pressure permanently as well while chiropractic adjustments and magnesium-calcium supplements can also help.

In other words, start by collecting the genetic health history of each person's family since this will have a bearing on their own illness tendencies, and the supplements most likely to work best at preventing illness. Do this for yourself as well. Once you understand the conditions and research the typical natural cures and diets for those propensities that run within a family, recommending those interventions for people *now*, especially when other diagnostics reveal problems in those directions, will often prevent the problems. If people take the herbal cures regularly for a disease that has not transpired but whose genetics lie within their family, there is a good chance the condition will not materialize. You can in many cases live — by taking the proper supplements and diet that are remedies — in a preventive mode in order to prevent certain disease likelihoods from occurring.

Next, you can finally perform some diagnostic tests to be used too. The most common form of diagnostic test is a bloodwork or blood chemistry. *Blood Chemistry and CBC Analysis* (Bear Mountain Publishing, Jacksonville: Oregon, 2002) by Dick Weatherby and Scott Ferguson can teach you how to nutritionally intervene for various health conditions based on blood markers being within or outside of their optimal ranges. You can also reference *Detox Cleanse Your Body Quickly and Completely* for short examples on how to do this. In time genetic testing companies such as 23andMe.com and others will be able to spotlight potential health problems and also recommend natural interventions as preventatives.

Since bloodwork exams for hundreds or thousands of people are too expensive, there are other non-invasive diagnostics which don't cost money but which can also identify potential health problems before they blow up into bigger problems. One such technique is Chinese pulse taking for diagnosis and herbal-based recommendations for health issues. However, this may require an expensive TCM practitioner whereas inexpensive *electronic forms of pulse taking*, which also indicate interventional remedies, may be superior.

There is also expensive western electronic diagnostic equipment, like the Asyra electrodermal screening machine, that can electronically diagnose potential health conditions and recommend remedies. The Chinese have developed similar types of electronic equipment which make Traditional Chinese Medicine diagnoses and recommend inexpensive Chinese patent medicines for intervention. You would have to do research to determine which is best for your situation.

Now for food. Keeping the body in good health is a duty, otherwise we shall not be able to keep our mind strong and clear. There are countless diets out there espoused for good health and/or spiritual progress. Those following spiritual pathways often choose the vegetarian or vegan route, but the key issues (assuming cost and availability are not issues) are whether they supply sufficient energy and nutrition. Nutrition includes whether the foods you eat provide you with the necessary vitamins and minerals in sufficient quantities. Many people, for instance, weaken on a vegan diet over the long-term because of nutritional deficiencies concerning iron, vitamin B-12, various amino acids and so forth.

The basic dietary rules of modern nutrition include cutting down on sugars and grains, especially as these foods cause people to gain weight quickly and become obese. In one phrase, "avoid sugar and foods that turn into sugar quickly, especially those that are white in color (wheat, bread, pasta, potatoes, rice, etcetera)."

The idea is to stay away from carbohydrates that quickly turn into sugar in the body, so the "best carbs" are low glycemic carbohydrates known as "slow carbs." Furthermore, one should *consume as many colored vegetables as possible* while avoiding the "whites" (wheat, bread, pasta, ...) to a high degree since they are typically the ones that spike your glucose levels. You should also consume good fats (cod liver oil, fish oil, olive oil, coconut oil, butter) rather than bad fats (corn oil, soybean oil, margarine, mayonnaise). Cis-fats are good, trans-fats are bad.

People should also eat a diet that is as much organic and non-GMO as possible. Furthermore, you should only eat foods to which you are not sensitive or allergic. You should also add probiotic foods (such as kimchi, sauerkraut, natto, tempeh, pickles, kombucha, kefir or *real* yoghurt) to your diet because you need healthy bacteria in your intestines and this how we have historically supplied them. Check out the Price-Pottenger Foundation (PPNF.org) for more information along these lines. The biggest and most important advice – which is pretty universal in diets – is to avoid sugar, especially soda and fruit juice, and foods that turn into sugar quickly such as refined carbohydrates.

Eating the right foods is the simplest way to supply yourself with the countless nutrients that will maintain your health or increase your energy for the spiritual path; a feeble body will have difficulty succeeding since it will lack sufficient Qi/Prana. If you want to boost whatever you are doing then you can do fresh fruit and vegetable juicing while also adding a super green or super red powder to the juice because its many nutrient-dense ingredients, in a powder form that makes them extremely easy to digest and absorb, takes away the problem of having to decide what individual foods or supplements to take.

These nutrient-dense food powders help insure against insufficient nutrients and minerals in your diet. You should rotate between different green/red brands as you finish any bottle so that you sequence through different formulas with different ingredients over time. Cod liver oil can be added as well. Juicing and super green/red powders will help to build, strengthen, and nurture your health, and are great for young children. They will fulfill the requirement of eating supplemental foods, herbs, grasses and minerals that Shakyamuni Buddha and the Taoists recommended as explained in *Look Younger, Live Longer*. Even if you cannot follow these suggestions, follow this basic rule: eat healthy and don't eat crap. Most of all, stay away from bad oils/fats, sugar and refined carbohydrates.

Along the lines of eating nutrient-dense foods that are good for you, there is a special importance to adding nucleotide-rich foods to your diet (which come from breast milk, sardines, Brewer's yeast, anchovies, mackerel, lentils, most beans, animal liver, oysters, chlorella algae and spirulina algae) since they are easily digestible and readily supply the ingredients necessary for repairing RNA and DNA. Since chlorella and spirulina are found in most green powders, you can get them in your diet through this particular avenue.

Now for supplements. Start eating right and take the fewest but best nutritional supplements that will help you with your health, energy and anti-aging efforts, and thus will help you on the spiritual path. *Look Younger, Live Longer* contains a list of the fewest but most powerful supplements to take for health and anti-aging purposes. It even provides teachings that can be co-jointly used with Nyasa Yoga to help quickly transform your physical body for spiritual practice.

The right diet and supplements can help turn back the biological clock, help you regain your health, help you live longer and of course prepare you for the spiritual trail. Pranayama exercises can help you accomplish this as well when done in conjunction with meditation practice. It is said in Buddhism that the mother of Vasubandhu and Asanga fed them all sorts of herbs to make them smart (such as the Lion's Mane mushroom that helps nerves grow in the brain), and in *Look Younger, Live Longer* I have provided a list of foods for the young that will make them healthy too.

You should use the right vitamin-mineral-herbal nutritional supplements to help correct any biochemical deficiencies you already have and to provide helpful nutrients that might prevent or reverse conditions like diabetes, heart disease and cancer. The right diet and supplements can help prevent genetic health problems that have a tendency to run in your family.

If your bloodwork suggests a list of potential supplements, how do you know which ones to use? Here is the method I use. You can note the common health failings that appear in your family tree and cross-reference the typical supplement remedies for those conditions against any supplement recommendations that bloodwork numbers would suggest. Creating a family tree of health conditions is therefore extremely useful. For instance, if diabetes runs in your family and you do not have it but your glucose levels are on the high side, daily supplementation with cinnamon, berberine and *gymnema sylvestre* can help you prevent it. If you have a condition unrelated to diabetes whose possible remedies also include berberine, guess which supplement you should definitely regularly intake?

As explained in *Move Forward*, you can use nutritional supplements to go against your own genetic predispositions (family genes) and avoid or even reverse genetic tendencies that run in your family. You can definitely defy your genes with the right lifestyle, diet and nutritional supplements. Look to LEF.org for indications as to which supplements might help a health condition or books like Jonathan Wright and Alan Gaby's *Nutritional Therapy in Medical Practice: Protocols and Supporting Information*.

3
LIFE PURPOSE

Ice, steam and ocean waves are nothing but water. No matter what the shape or form in which water appears it is always water just the same. Similarly, a thousand ornaments made out of gold are still nothing but gold. To think that ornaments of gold are anything else but gold due to their different shapes is just a grand illusion. From the perspective of gold, if it had consciousness it could look at all the ornaments and say, "It is all me, there is nothing there but me. There isn't any such thing as rings or necklaces … there is just me." On the level of gold, from its absolute standpoint ornaments exhibit no trace of independent This-ness that is non-gold.

We too are equally just derivatives, aspects, effusions, evolutes, transformations or manifestations of the original source nature, the Supreme Ultimate, primordial substance or original essence. We are just phenomena ultimately composed out of this fundamental essence like the ornaments of gold made from gold, but with one major difference from most other phenomena that have manifested in the universe. The major difference is that we can think and feel because we have consciousness and thus Knowledge.

But what is really happening when we think to produce Knowledge and develop some type of understanding? What happens is that Knowledge is just knowing itself. There is really just Knowledge being produced within a body vehicle and it is just referencing itself in a reflexive arc. It happens inside a phenomena we conventionally call a person, who is actually just the original nature in an effused form. So we might think we are special phenomena within the universe, but we are just phenomena that can spin Knowledge that understands itself, and we call this a living being.

It is not a person but Knowledge that is actually the true experiencer of everything. The I-thought of a doer or experiencer is just Knowledge and that is what "understands." There is no independent, inherent self-so self. There is just this Knowledge automatically being generated in a body vehicle and this body of Knowledge is doing everything, even thinking the thought "I am." That whole body unit, called a sentient being, is just another phenomenon in the universe with the special characteristic that it automatically generates Knowledge as part of its functioning. We call it an "independent sentient being," but it is certainly not independent and it is really the functioning of Knowledge that is doing everything rather than a "being."

Of course, Knowledge is what makes us a sentient being. Conventionally we call ourselves a living being, self, person, *atman*, *jiva*, and so on whereas we are just another phenomenon (albeit having consciousness) that is ultimately the original nature. Conventionally we are an effusion that is connected to everything else in existence, like a single particle moving within a grand soup that doesn't actually compose anything. We cannot see all the energetic connections of magnetism, electricity, gravity and other forces that permeate and compose us, but they are there. It is impossible to unravel the total causes and effects for our existence. We are like a drop of water in the ocean that in being a drop of the ocean is just the ocean itself. This is how we are connected to all beings and all things.

Think of it this way. We have a body with a brain and nervous system that generates Knowledge or knowing (thoughts). The master thought of all thoughts is an inherent thought of being a "I," which is also part of the body of Knowledge that our nervous system automatically generates. The concept of being an I, ego, self, person or being is also composed of a number of thoughts, and so that I-concept is also Knowledge. Without that self-thought ("I") there is no such thing as consciousness being possible for there has to be a self-referential center, or "I" who is an experiencer or doer. Consciousness needs a self or doer but that doer-unit, when you think about it, is just more Knowledge operating a program that produces consciousness rather than an independent person, being, entity or soul. Essentially, on a conventional level you are just your body along with its Knowledge processes for generating sensory perceptions and conceptions.

The I-thought is Knowledge and thinking as well as sensory perceptions are just Knowledge as well. You seem to know things because Knowledge can self-reference itself – it is referencing memories of labels and names and definitions stored in your brain that are Knowledge, including the thought of being an "I am" which arises automatically, mechanically within us because of our structure. Other living beings, such as viruses, don't have this capability.

You know yourself in Knowledge, that knowing is Knowledge and the knower is Knowledge. It is all just Knowledge referencing itself in a circle. Therefore in a grand sense the Knowledge we generate through thoughts and conceptions, despite its usefulness, is all just a relative illusion. It is all conditional on what we already know and nothing is absolute within that circle of Knowledge. There is no such thing as an independent living being, there is only Knowledge knowing itself in a limited vehicle that can generate Knowledge that makes knowing possible. When we know something it is actually Knowledge knowing Knowledge, so as the *Diamond Sutra* of Buddhism explains, where is there a person in all this? It is just an automatic process going on.

There is no *absolute* validity to anything we know and sense either, but all our sense perceptions and thoughts work for us to produce a world! Who can say what the universe is *really* like, however, because other beings/animals see, hear and taste things entirely different from us, and think quite differently as well. We are just automatic phenomena that can generate conditional Knowledge.

This is the nature of consciousness – it is a reflexive form of illusion, delusion or self-deception that actually works. It works according to cause and effect to produce understanding, but there is no one who understands, and yet understanding is there. Furthermore, in the ultimate sense there is only the cloudless original nature that lacks any traces of cause and effect due to its purity of one substance, and within It there is nothing except Itself. Everything that has appeared within It is a transitory, fluctuating illusion – an apparent existence that is momentary and ungraspable like a dream lacking inherent reality even though we think of things as stable forms and phenomena. The Knowledge knowing itself with us is all conditional, relative and not absolute like the changeless original essence. Yet it works for us.

Knowledge, thinking, consciousness or awareness are all made possible not because we are pre-existing immortal spirits, but simply because a biological machine, the human body, has evolved in the universe with the functional capability of producing knowing, memories, thoughts, emotions, and conceptions – which we in aggregate call consciousness, awareness or Knowledge – because of its structure. Plants and viruses and rocks do not have this capability but the human form does because of its neural structures, and thus is sentient. That's all we can really say.

Consciousness is thus the great *miracle* of our existence because most of the universe does not have it so cannot comprehend. Magnetism doesn't have Knowledge, argon gas doesn't, an electron doesn't, a cloud doesn't, the sun doesn't, space doesn't but we do. These other phenomena have no recognition of anything. They simply have qualities or properties and function in certain ways according to certain laws. Without consciousness we are the same as them; even with consciousness we are, in a sense, the same as them because we too are just phenomena that developed out of the original nature. All phenomena are equal but our difference is that we have knowing or Knowledge that makes us conscious or sentient, and we can cultivate transcendental bodies that free us from lower states. There is really just one equality that truly exists, namely that all phenomena are equally composed of one original essence that evolutionarily appears in various forms, so being It have no fear and choose the route of cultivation.

Since we have consciousness, the question is what to do with it. The cultivation path of transcendental self-perfection, ennobling ourselves to spiritual heights by mastering our thoughts and behavior so that we can improve situations that remove suffering and bring joy, is Buddha Yoga.

An amazing capability of higher consciousness is that we have discovered how, through spiritual cultivation practices, to generate a higher subtle body out of the energy of the denser human body. By making use of our life force and engendering transformations of our Qi to purify its nature, we can strengthen an internal Qi body double and cause it to emerge from the physical body shell at will to attain a subtle body. We can do the same thing with that subtle body and then generate an entirely new but different spiritual body composed of yet a higher transcendental substance or energy called Shen.

The subtle body, attested to by many religious saints, exists on a transcendental plane because it is made of Qi or Prana rather than matter. It exists at the level we normally call Heaven, which includes an etheric earthly plane all around us and other higher, transcendental Pure Lands of being. The higher bodies can travel Pure Lands that are not earth-bound whereas first stage masters, and people who die, can only experience the earth-bound heavenly plane of existence.

Qi/Prana is a different energy than magnetism, electricity, nuclear forces, radioactivity and so on. We cannot yet measure it, and so we certainly cannot find/see the higher bodies transcending it. We don't even know that there are entire civilizations of existence on higher planes throughout the universe – uncountable numbers of them. Of this, until you die and receive the teachings that all heavenly beings learn, you know nothing.

Here is a summary. Using the same process of generation with some minor differences, the subtle body can generate from within itself yet another body duplicate composed of a yet higher transcendental essence, energy or substance called Shen, and this forms the Causal body. The heavenly beings of earth, for their own spiritual practice, are working on precisely *this*.

From that Causal body one can continue with spiritual practices to generate a yet more transcendental and longer lasting body double called the Supra-Causal or Dharma body composed of yet higher energies (namely Clear Light energy or Later Heavenly Prana) that is still linked to all the prior lower bodies. At this stage you can even generate and project temporary spiritual bodies, made of the denser energies (the lower evolutes) you have ascended from, and use them to perform various functions in the world simultaneously.

This is the occupation of Buddhas and Bodhisattvas to give human beings help in life, and they do so by giving people thoughts and energy. If you have a high enough body you can even generate physical copies of yourself that others can see and touch. Many traditions have stories of masters doing this, but the capability is only possible with attainments much higher than the subtle body. If you only have a subtle body attainment then this is impossible. The really big superpowers only come from much higher body attainments than this first deva body accomplishment.

A man or woman can keep cultivating upwards to create more transcendental bodies countless times if they put in the effort, so it begs the question, why all the effort? What is the ultimate purpose to all this work and to those bodies and lives if you generate them? You must determine your own purpose if you are to live seemingly forever in the universe with these higher bodies. What will you do with them ... just be a consumer or enjoyer of good fortune? The lower bodies can all be used as appendages for the highest body, which becomes the true center of your life, so the question arises as to why you would bother maintaining them after you attain something higher.

From the highest viewpoint there is no such thing as a self-existing independent being, soul, personality or life in the universe. We are just manifestations, phenomena that can think that are infinitely connected to everything else in ways we cannot see. Everything in the universe is just a complex derivative of the original substance/essence with each separate phenomenon seeming independent but not independent at all. Why? Because every phenomenon is linked to everything else through a complex, infinite chain of interdependent origination. Nothing exists by itself so there are no independent phenomena; nothing is self-so with an inherent existence except the original, primordial, self-so fundamental essence.

All phenomena have their own unique properties, functions, aspects, attributes and capabilities different from all others. The truth of the matter is that sentient life is just one of these many possible manifestations. It exists, and if it didn't exist then other things would still exist without consciousness existing in the universe. If life didn't exist then so what? At one time it surely didn't exist. Now it does. In the future maybe it won't. Who can say? All we can say is that it is rare and precious to us since we have thinking, but certainly not precious to anything inanimate. In terms of the original nature's viewpoint, if it could have one (since it isn't consciousness nor a being with any organs of knowing), everything is the original nature only so there are no "things" that exist at all. To the original nature, whether there is or isn't life, so what?

Life is just something that has developed in the universe along with everything else that has developed, and therefore there is no ultimate purpose or significance to life other than the meaning you decide to give to it. The meaning of your life are the activities you do for they define what you are about. You are a conscious being with thoughts who can think about such things and devote your life to purposes according to your free will. So what will you do with your life that is ultimately born from the cosmos? What mission or purpose is worthy of your existence? What is it that you will subscribe to as your ideal? What is the light that you want others to see through your efforts?

Ask yourself, "Who am I and what do I stand for? What do I want to make my life about?" Not a single life is permanent, so what goals are worthy of you such that you should spend your limited precious life force, energy time and resources working towards their achievement? The tricky thing is finding a purpose, goal or mission that you can be passionate about because it is truly worthy, and then focus on this objective for an extended period of time. What will it be? What larger identity are you seeking?

Your ultimate *ground of being* is no different from the ultimate ground of being of the universe. It is the same with me. Our equality is ultimately the same. However, your life is a unique manifestation of that ground state different from mine, as are your goals and aspirations. Your beingness is under your control because you are sentient with thoughts and willpower. You have karma from past lives, but you created that karma so you can change it during this life as I teach in *Move Forward* and *Quick, Fast, Done*. You can control your actions and behaviors, regardless of what comes to you, so you are in charge of your destiny. You can change bad habits, cultivate new skills and virtues, even create a new personality. You can make use of your life in whatever ways you want and strive to achieve whatever you want.

The meaning of life is therefore whatever you select it to be, whatever you choose to be your own personal target, aim, purpose, mission, commitment or objective – however you use your energies and actions. You cannot ask why there is life, but you can ask what is there to live for and then live for that. This is why I asked you to think about becoming a Guardian Spirit, but you don't have to take the Bodhisattva path if you don't want. You can choose to become an automated vehicle of consumption to find your happiness, or take other paths too.

Even so, you should still strive to make your life worthwhile if you want to find contentment and the peace and happiness that most everyone longs for. As King Solomon of the Bible wrote, you certainly won't find it through material goods and experiences. I truly suggest that you give your life purpose some thought, and then start cultivating the ways of any Buddha or Bodhisattva you might want to become, for that really is a type of life purpose! It is possible to move in any direction of accomplishment you desire although it will require study, cultivation, and effort. Nonetheless, you should invest in your future best self.

The purpose of life is not just so that some lump of living protoplasm, because of "selfish genes," can pursue survival and then replicate some version of itself before it disappears. The purpose is whatever you take as your higher mission, aspiration or calling as you continue onwards through eternity, or until it all ends if you believe there is some termination point. Life is its own purpose, and therefore the ennobling of life is whatever we want to make of it that raises it higher. That ennobling should become the purpose of your existence. Take the high road, don't take the low road. Make your life count by living a bigger life.

Don't let your life become like a leaf tossed in the wind that blows this way and that because it follows circumstances instead of a direction. Choose for yourself a higher calling or mission within this effervescent scintillation called the universe, a purpose that will provide you with fulfillment and satisfaction. Become your best self. Fulfill your potential. Make life count. Winning isn't always possible so put that thought aside and instead just do your best in whatever you do. This will require study in wisdom and skillfulness.

After you think about this and decide upon some possible directions, the next step is learning the skills to help you tread those paths and finding, building or associating with the people and things that will help you achieve them. You don't have to do things by yourself but do need to associate with whatever can help you achieve the goals, missions or purposes you want to pursue. You have to find the designs that will help you achieve your desires, goals, purposes, missions or objectives, and associate with other people who can help you achieve them.

Whatever directions you ultimately choose, they are something you can work towards. You can chart a course of actions towards any accomplishment you want to achieve but must afterward dedicate your actions towards its fulfillment. What is the desired outcome that you want to produce?

Think about it this way. What will be the consistent dedication you choose for your existence? What are you going to try to bring about? What is the light you want to bring to the world?

When you watch a video of the galaxies in the universe, such as that produced by the Sloan Digital Sky Survey ("A Flight Through the Universe"), or the stars within our Milky Way galaxy alone (see stars.cromeexperiments.com), and then realize that life goes on forever within this vastness but you are insignificantly small in terms of the whole shebang, it pretty much comes down to the line of Rick Blaine in Casablanca, "It doesn't take much to see that the problems of three little people don't amount to a hill of beans in this crazy world." Your life is pretty much insignificant in terms of the vastness of the universe so how do you make it matter? Through self-purpose. Through purposes for your life.

This being the case, how can you make your life more meaningful by finding a self-purpose? Well, what skills and talents would you like to acquire that will help you do or achieve something worthwhile? If you had absolutely no obstacles or obstructions, what would you want to do in the universe? What function or role would you want to play? What type of Buddha or Bodhisattva, with ultimate powers, would you want to become?

There is *no* master "plan for you" in the universe other than the path you choose for yourself. You indeed have karma from past lives that is working itself out in this life but you can create your own path in life different from this karma due to skillful causes on your part. Self-cultivation for personal achievement must be part of that mix.

Karma indeed comes along as a consequence for how you behave and we all are bound to some circumstances (such as the need to go through puberty, the need to breath oxygen and eat food, our karma, etc.) but you essentially create your own fate in life. The great unfortunate thing is that most people do not proactively choose to do so but let the circumstances of life create a road for them, and thus they don't create and live the future they really want. Nonetheless, everyone always creates consequences by how they live and thus a future appears according to our actions. Wouldn't it make sense to put more consideration and planning into creating those karmic outcomes?

Karmic consequences, meaning the results of cause and effect, indeed happen to everyone because of what we build/do in this life together with our accumulations from past lives, but much of what happens to us is built unknowingly because of ignorance rather than because of careful choices and careful actions. This is why we need to develop greater wisdom or understanding of how things work and what normally happens if we hold to some road of behavior. This is why people read the works of wisdom writers such as Baltasar Gracian, Benjamin Franklin, the Stoics, Plutarch, and so forth.

Up and down you have been bobbing through countless lives without generating the higher spiritual bodies whose ultimate longevity provides some restful respite along with powers to accomplish great deeds in the world. Why? Because you did not direct your energies in the right way. You did not work on helping others so that the merit of this pathway became available to you; spiritual beings won't help others achieve the higher bodies if they don't have the basic tendency to help others. You have not been generating higher consequences but simply living for yourself and suffering what has come along due to your past actions. The Buddha or Bodhisattva path gives you access to the highest spiritual and material achievements, and a way to transcend the difficulties of life. Now it is finally available to you.

If you are wise and adopt the pathway of Buddha Yoga then you can become a more active participant in the universe who actually builds something wonderful because of your activities. You have the power to make life something of much greater significance, *even cosmic significance*, because you can choose to build anything you want just like the accomplished Buddhas and Bodhisattvas. It just starts with a decision. Through dedication to a higher noble direction/purpose you can create a future fortune of greatness.

This is what a hero does. This is who a hero is. Empowerment, or authority, is not something given to you by others so that you can tread the path of a hero. Empowerment is something you assume for yourself just as Napoleon crowned himself Emperor of France rather than have someone else place the crown on him. You are the ultimate authority of your own life and its trajectory. You give to yourself your own empowerment or permission to do whatever you want, and of course there will be consequences for whatever you do because cause and effect is the nature of the cosmos.

You must therefore select your own course in life and then move in that direction, so invest purpose into your actions. It is all in your hands to decide whatever purposes your life will be about. You can eventually become a master of anything if you stay with it long enough, but the road always starts with study, immersion in that activity, and the commitment to practice it.

Few people at a young age know enough to choose any ultimate pathways for their life. However they can choose things they would like to study or master, and directions they might want to try. Passion doesn't always come at the beginning of something, but only after you put in the hard work of individual effort to become excellent at it. Once you have passion or skills at something then you can choose to become a benefactor, protector or guardian of that activity.

There are obstacles for everything in life, but you are ultimately free to choose and then create whatever you want in the universe. You are the original nature, so why not? When you face obstacles and obstructions then wisdom, perseverance, timing and skillfulness are keys to surmounting them. Your life purpose is up to you, but consider that endless lives lie ahead. Therefore choose carefully what you want to do knowing that there is an endless horizon ahead of you.

What is then worthy of your efforts? Anything can be accomplished, but achievement takes skills and learning. It takes preparation. That being so, should your efforts be spent on a tiny goal that isn't worthwhile, or should you exert yourself towards a far longer-term, broader-minded objective? What should you try to create, and what should you try to protect? What is in line with your inner sense of transcendence? What aim or aspiration gives you energy and inspiration? What is it the world needs that you want to help supply?

You are free to accomplish whatever you set out to do in the universe because you will have the time. However, this does not mean you can block bad karma coming to you. You will have to learn how to deal with it. To accomplish anything you will have to learn how to deal with whatever you encounter as obstacles and obstructions. Two obstacles stand out clearest: circumstances and yourself.

Swami Sivananda of Rishikesh once said, "You are the architect of your own fate. You are the master of your own destiny. You can do and undo things. You sow an action and reap a tendency. You sow a tendency and reap a habit. You sow a habit and reap your character. You sow your character and reap your destiny. Therefore destiny is your own creation. You can undo it if you like because destiny is a bundle of habits. Purushartha is self-exertion. Purushartha can give you anything. Change your habits, change the mode of thinking and you can conquer destiny." As also explained in *Color Me Confucius*, the skill at getting things done is changing yourself and doing what needs to get done.

What Swami Sivananda said is that you can create a life of your own design through self-exertion. You can even change yourself - your personality, habits and behaviors - because you are the one in charge of yourself. The stories of Yuan Liao Fan, Benjamin Franklin and Frank Bettger within *Color Me Confucius* and *Move Forward* show there are ways you can change your personality and habits to break the hold that karma has on you. This is what allows you to create a new fate, fortune and destiny outside of karmic bounds. Benjamin Franklin, in particular, showed how a person's character could become noble though constant self-correction. You can also study the life of Dwight Eisenhower, George Washington and Abraham Lincoln to see how they also practiced self-control and worked on transforming their personalities to change their fortunes.

Ancient Hindu astrologers have often said that there would be no purpose to predicting fate or destiny unless there were also a means to change it. While teaching that karma from past lives is a fact, Hinduism says you can change it and your future fortune. But what new goals or new future are worthy of you with an endless future ahead? What auspicious circumstances would you like to build for others or yourself, and what skills would you like to have, now knowing that talents can be learned (see *The Talent Code* by Daniel Coyle) and you can indeed attain them? What objectives are worthy enough of you that they should become part of your total life purpose? In your own mind, what efforts are worthy of your beneficial sustenance and protection?

Religions offer us some guidance on these topics.

The highest ideal of Christianity is exemplified by Jesus who sacrificed himself for others. The teachings of Christianity are that Jesus sacrificed himself for people's benefit, and that we should love and serve one another according to his example. People who emulate his example therefore engage in incredible charitable activities for the world, which is a great outcome from his teachings. Jesus taught that we should be of service to one another by doing for others what we would appreciate others doing for us.

The highest ideal of Hinduism is that of the Avatar who descends from the divine to become human in order to rescue people from disasters, empower the good and fight against evil. The Avatar saves society by solving deep problems and restores balance by establishing righteousness once again when evil has become too strong.

The ideal of Sikhism set up by Guru Nanak can be seen in the vegetarian community meals freely provided to all, which are considered a task of service to mankind. The free meal, called *langar*, represents the equality of all people and the importance of charity to help one another. Sikhs are also known to fight against any sorts of social injustice.

The ideal of Confucianism espoused by Confucius is that we should fulfill our relationship obligations to our family and friends as well as to our community, country and leaders. However, in so doing we should not impose upon others what we would not wished imposed upon ourselves. As with Christianity, we should love other people and work for their betterment.

Confucius said that during our lives there is a mission we must all work to accomplish. It is a great mission that is the singular core of the human life purpose, which he called the "Great Learning." The three objectives of the great learning are that we are to cultivate, regardless of our status or circumstances in life, to find our "bright virtue," to benefit other people (which Confucius called loving the people or teaching the people), and to never stop until reaching the highest good.

Zen master Nan Huai Chin said that one's life purpose should be to "realize enlightenment, save people and save the world." The Confucian Chang Tsai said that the ideal purpose is to "Establish true mind for the universe, direction for humanity, re-establish the discontinued studies of the ancient sages, and establish great peace for 10,000 generations." The Yogi Tirumalai Krishnamacharya said, "Rid your body of its impurities, let your speech be true and sweet, feel friendship for the world, and with humility seek wealth and knowledge."

In the light of these standards, a true life purpose is not to just do better for oneself, which you should work to do, but to do better for humanity and the world as well. What will your choices then be to create the Great Betterment? What purpose or purposes do you want to serve?

The highest ideal of Buddhism is the Mahayana Bodhisattva or Buddha of cosmic vows whose compassionate activity entails undergoing sufferings and burdens without complaint to teach others the path of enlightenment, relieve their suffering and free them from misfortunate situations. The Bodhisattvas and Buddhas are enlightened individuals who have, since attaining their higher body achievements, devoted themselves to accomplishing great vows (purposes) that take care of people while also helping them to realize the divine as well. They internalize their aspirations and values so that they don't break their vows and are not shaken by any storm. They become benefactors, guardians or protectors over all sorts of worldly efforts. Their elevated position is something you can start working towards now by donating your money or efforts to charitable causes, or by studying to master some field of endeavor that you would want to help prosper and shepherd.

Greatness is not where we stand but the direction we are heading in life because of what we do with ourselves. Greatness and nobility arise in us because of what we do. The Bodhisattvas and Buddhas, because of the vows they have made and actions they thereby perform, are role models who might inspire you to do great deeds yourself and be greater than you otherwise might not be. They select their own compassionate missions and then work to fulfill their vowed commitments. Those become part of their life purpose.

Although many root causes of their personal suffering have been eliminated forever, if one is to exist nearly forever one must have a worthy target or purpose for one's existence other than just surrounding oneself with luxurious enjoyments and engaging in conspicuous consumption. Each Bodhisattva and Buddha has chosen special missions they want to execute for long periods of time, and while they try to help everywhere are especially committed to compassionate forms of wise and skillful action in certain fields of expertise to help others.

Basically, they are individuals who attain many transcendental bodies and then develop special skills and expertise in certain areas in order to help mankind. Naturally these skills don't just appear because you attain transcendental bodies. You have to gain those skills and capabilities from study and training, building your expertise in the directions of your choosing.

The world has loads of spiritual literature, but very little discusses the idea of a cosmic mission that can run across multiple lives and even eternity. Buddhism actually discusses this in several sutras including the *Diamond Sutra*, *Lotus Sutra* and *Avatamsaka Sutra* among others.

In the *Diamond Sutra* it is taught that you can sacrifice heaps of jewels worth more than galaxies or even countless lives throughout millennium but the merit you achieve by such deeds is still not as great as attaining enlightenment. In the *Lotus Sutra* it is taught that the Buddhas live endless lives as long as eons, and during that time accomplish vast, uncountable deeds for the helpful sake of all living beings.

In the *Avatamsaka Sutra*, Shakyamuni Buddha introduces many galaxies by name and even describes their inhabitants. The Sloan Digital Sky Survey offers an incredibly accurate 3D view of this universe ("A Flight Through the Universe") that Shakyamuni described, and today we know that there are countless inhabitable planets around stars. The stars of our galaxy can be seen in stars.chromeexperiments.com. In just our galaxy alone it is estimated that there are between 40 and 100 billion habitable planets that can support life. Viewing the vastness of the cosmos and knowing there are innumerable, uncountable world systems and beings within it, and knowing that there is life everywhere that is cyclically reincarnating again and again in endless fashion, the question arises as to the purpose of it all.

There is no ultimate purpose as imposed from an all powerful external agent. The only purpose of your life is what you select to do as your own mission or calling. In the *Avatamsaka Sutra* the measure of success is enlightenment (attaining the "infinite life" or longer-lived bodies) since it enables you to jump out of the infinite rounds of reincarnation in the lower realms. Success is also using these bodies in compassionate activity to help others.

Buddhism offers many role models of individuals who succeeded on the spiritual path and who took cosmic vows to help this whole conglomerate of world systems and beings. According to the Buddhist sutras, all the Bodhisattvas achieved enlightenment through the power of their vows because those vows propelled them forward to keep working hard at cultivation, self-improvement and offering (altruistic charitable activities and generosity on behalf of others). There is not one single Bodhisattva who was enlightened without first making great vows. The ideal of Buddhism, and of the cosmic Bodhisattvas and Buddhas, is for people to succeed at enlightenment and then devote themselves to various types of service that improve the welfare of living beings. The purpose of life is then a life of purpose, but a Buddha or Bodhisattva decides upon that purpose himself.

Thus there is the Medicine Buddha who has vowed to endlessly help sick and physically disabled people in all respects so that they are thereafter blessed with good health, both physically and mentally. You actually become a Medicine Bodhisattva yourself in regular life when you become a doctor, nurse, volunteer ambulance driver, or donate to hospitals and medical charities. When you learn CPR, acupuncture or herbal medicine with the intent to help others, even such humble beginnings start to give you the skills or contributions related to the larger direction of becoming a Medicine Buddha. They prepare you to become a Medicine guardian spirit after death.

Limited by time and resources, all people are constrained in what they can do to help others in the world. However, this is the nature of the world so one cannot complain. That being the case, all people must start from wherever they are right now, doing whatever they can, to help others in the various directions they choose. If you want to master any particular skills or become a guardian spirit of any type, it is necessary to form your own Bodhisattva or Buddha vows of what you want to accomplish in life, and the calling you want to devote yourself to achieving. Then you need to start training yourself in the directions that will give you the knowledge, skills, merit and contributions related to those directions.

Avalokitesvara, also known as Kuan Yin, has vowed to listen to the cries for help in the world and provide aid to all who are suffering in various difficulties. He has vowed to always stay in this world helping beings by listening to their cries for help and responding with rescuing aid. He has vowed to help people end all their troubles, sufferings and difficulties. He has vowed to destroy all the realms of suffering while practicing mental equanimity at all times and cutting off all mental fetters and knots. He took the immeasurable vow to save all sentient beings, and even guide them to different world systems if they want to be reborn in a different realm.

Ksitigarbha, the Earth Store Bodhisattva or "Hell Buddha," has vowed to help all living beings who are dying, in purgatory (hungry ghosts) or in the hells. Specifically, the great vow undertaken by Ksitigarbha Bodhisattva is to liberate all beings from hell before he himself becomes a fully perfected Buddha. The compassionate vow of Ksitigarbha is, "If I do not go to the hells to help the suffering beings there, who else will go? ... If the hells are not empty I will not become a Buddha. Only when all living beings have been saved will I attain complete enlightenment (Bodhi)."

The wisdom Buddha Manjushri has made eighteen great vows, Samantabhadra has made ten great vows, Amitabha Buddha (*Sutra of Infinite Life*) has made forty-eight great vows, Maitreya has made ten great vows and Shakyamuni Buddha made five hundred great vows that you can read in the Buddhist sutras. Reading these vows inspires people to perform similar charitable acts, make similar vows and increase their cultivation efforts in order to gain the skills and abilities to help others. You can actually take such vows yourself and start working toward their fulfilment, which is a type of Karma Yoga. When you do you are on the road of the Bodhisattvas and Buddhas whose first step is to become a guardian protector of some type.

These particular Buddhas and Bodhisattvas are just a few role models for the many directions in which you can devote yourself after you attain a nearly immortal spiritual body (actually, properly speaking you attain a *set of bodies* since each lower body will be linked to the next higher, which will live longer than the lower). What directions would be worthy of your efforts? What would you want to accomplish? In *Culture, Country, City, Company, Person, Purpose, Passion, World* I brought up the examples of individuals who devoted their lives to various missions, and the Bodhisattva vow tries to get you to think of such things.

The people who attain the subtle body (first dhyana attainment) can immediately start doing many things to invisibly help people without their knowing, and will live a long time in that body. It lasts far longer than the subtle body people normally attain after death, for theirs is weaker since most people do not cultivate. Those who attain both the subtle and Causal body (third dhyana attainment) can do even more good to help others. Those who attain the subtle body, Causal body and Supra-Causal body (fourth dhyana attainment) can do more still. Those who attain the subtle, Causal, Supra-Causal and Immanence bodies (complete and perfect enlightenment) can do the most.

You can achieve these bodies in this life if you cultivate correctly. Many people do although they are usually the swamis, sadgurus, gurus, masters, mazjoobs, chief rabbis, head monks, archbishops, cardinals, patriarchs, etc. at the highest commitment of spiritual practice or religious organization. It takes a devoted consistency of practice effort over a long period of time, and intensity of practice effort. A concert pianist, and Olympic sports athletes, typically practice 5-6 hours a day, and so do many of the people who finally attain the deva body attainment.

Therefore, what vows will be worthy of your efforts? What will make a difference in peoples' lives? What skills and activities should you start to study and master if you want to be able to give the right type of thoughts and invisible aid to others? What cosmic vows are worthy of your time, and what skills and excellences do you want to master?

As an illustration of the great vows made and carried out by the Buddhas and Bodhisattvas, we can examine in detail the twelve great vows of the Medicine Buddha as reported in the *Sutra of the Vows of the Medicine Buddha Healing*. Those twelve vows undertaken by the Medicine Buddha to relieve beings of their sufferings are as follows (paraphrased):

1. I vow that my body shall shine as beams of brilliant light on infinite and boundless worlds, showering on all beings, getting rid of their ignorance and worries with my teachings. I will help all beings to become like me with a perfect status and character, upright mind and soul, and finally attain enlightenment like the Buddha.
2. I vow that my body be like crystal, pure and flawless, majestic with merit and virtue, radiating rays of splendid light to every corner, brightening up and enlightening all beings with wisdom. With the blessings of compassion, I will help all beings strengthen their spiritual power and physical energy so that they can succeed in all their endeavors.
3. I vow that I shall grant by means of boundless wisdom, all beings with the inexhaustible things that they require so they are without the slightest want, and relieve them from all pains and guilt resulting from materialistic desires. Although clothing, food, accommodation and transport are essentials, they should be utilized wisely as well. Besides self-consumption, the remaining should be generously shared with the community so that all can live harmoniously together.

4. I vow to lead those who have gone astray back to the path of righteousness. Let them be corrected and returned to the Buddha way for enlightenment.
5. I vow that I shall enable all sentient beings to observe precepts for spiritual purity and moral conduct. Should there be any relapse or violation, they shall be guided for repentance. Provided they truly regret their wrong-doings, and vow for a change with constant prayers and strong faith in the Buddha, they will receive the rays of forgiveness, recover their lost morality and purity, and not fall into evil destinies.
6. I vow that all beings who are physically disabled or sick in any aspect, or who are ugly, dull, blind, deaf, mute, deformed, paralyzed, hunchbacked, or afflicted with skin disease, insanity, or various other sicknesses and sufferings, will through me be blessed with good health, both physically and mentally. I will help them all become endowed with upright features, keen intelligence, and perfect faculties. All who pay homage to Buddha faithfully will by me become free of sickness and suffering.
7. I vow to relieve all pain and poverty of the very sick and poor who are oppressed by many illnesses and who are without aid, without a place to turn, without a doctor, without medicine, without relatives, and without a family, who are poverty-stricken and filled with suffering to be cured of their sicknesses. The sick will be cured, the helpless helped, and the poor will be assisted by me.
8. I vow to help women who are undergoing sufferings and tortures and give rise to a deep loathing for having a woman's body because they are oppressed by the myriad sufferings of being female, and seek transformation into men in the next life. By hearing my name, paying homage and praying, their wishes will be granted and they will ultimately attain Buddhahood.
9. I vow to free all beings from errant paths, evil thoughts and their control. I shall lead them to have proper views by inculcating them with righteousness and honor so that they gradually cultivate the practices of Bodhisattvas and quickly realize unsurpassed enlightenment.
10. I vow to save prisoners who are bound, interrogated, whipped, fettered, imprisoned, sentenced to execution, or subjected to endless disasters, hardships, abuse, and humiliation so that they are torn by grief and distress and suffering in body and mind. Those who are sincere will be blessed by my supreme powers

and be freed from worry and sufferings.
11. I vow to save those who suffer from starvation and thirst and those who committed a crime or created all kinds of bad karma in order to obtain food. If they hear my name and faithfully cherish it they will obtain delicious food and drink and afterwards settle in ultimate peace and happiness.
12. I vow to save those who are poor and lacking clothes so that day and night they are troubled by mosquitoes and flies, and by cold and heat. If they come across my name, cherish it with sincerity and practice dharma to strengthen their merits, they will be able to achieve their wishes.

The Medicine Buddha constantly works toward accomplishing these tasks for all beings, working to help them using his thoughts, energies and by performing countless actions on their behalf.

Many guardian spirits, who help people who are sick and respond to mantras for medical assistance, are also announced in the Buddhist sutras. Here are a few from the *Avatamsaka Sutra* whose names provide us with some idea of their virtues, personalities, excellences, expertise or method of cultivation: Medicine-ruling Spirit Auspicious; Medicine-ruling Spirit Candana Forest; Medicine-ruling Spirit Pristine Radiance; Medicine-ruling Spirit Universal Renown; Medicine-ruling Spirit Shining Pores; Medicine-ruling Spirit Pervasive Healing and Purifying; Medicine-ruling Spirit Roaring Loudly; Medicine-ruling Spirit Banner of Light Eclipsing the Sun; Medicine-ruling Spirit Clear Vision of the Ten Directions; and Medicine-ruling Spirit Replenishing Energy and Brightening the Eyes.

In Indian and Chinese culture these Medicine Buddhas, Bodhisattvas and healing guardian spirits or deities sponsor all sorts of mantras that contact them for help in pain relief (back pain, rib pain, stomach pain, etc.) and assistance for healing medical conditions such as diabetes, ulcers, sprains, wounds, eye troubles (cataracts, eye pain, eye infections, swollen eyes, etc.), nail diseases, migraines, sunstroke, cancer, teeth problems and dental diseases, piles, jaundice, high blood pressure, skin disease, small pox, measles, fever, urinary diseases, pregnancy, menstrual pain, hernia, gland disorders, poison, scorpion stings, dog bites, wounds, leprosy, asthma, breastfeeding, bleeding, panic attacks, vomiting, and so forth.

Another Buddha whose vows are often read are those of Ksitigarbha, also known as the Earth-Store or Hell Buddha who as previously stated ministers to those who are sick, dying or have entered the hells and inferior states of being. In the *Original Vows of Ksitigarbha Bodhisattva Sutra*, Ksitigarbha Bodhisattva speaks to Shakyamuni Buddha and explains the vows he has been undertaking for countless lives.

"I teach and transform obstinate living beings like these in the evil age of the five degenerations, causing their minds to be regulated and tamed so that they abandon the false and return to the true. However, there are one or two out of every ten who still have evil habits. I too transform into hundreds of thousands of millions of emanations and employ many skillful means [for living beings]. Some beings are of keen capacity: they immediately believe and accept upon hearing [the Dharma]. Some are reaping the results of wholesome [deeds]: they achieve accomplishments through energetic encouragement. Some are ignorant and dull: they return [to the true] only after long being instructed. Some have karma that is heavy: they do not give rise to respect [for the Dharma].

"Living beings like these types are each different. I therefore transform into emanations to guide them across to liberation. The emanations are manifested in the forms of a man, a woman, a deva, a naga, a spirit, a ghost, or a mountain, a forest, a stream, a plain, a river, a pond, a spring, or a well to benefit people, so that they all may be guided across to liberation. The emanations are also manifested in the forms of Sakra, Brahma, a wheel-turning king, a householder, a king, a high minister, a government official, or a bhiksu, a bhiksuni, an upasaka, an upasika, or a sravaka, an arhat, a pratyekabuddha, a Bodhisattva, or others to teach and guide living beings across. It is not only in the form of a Buddha that I have manifested before them.

"You see how, kalpa after kalpa, diligently and arduously I guide difficult-to-teach, obstinate, wrongdoing, suffering beings such as these across to liberation. Those not yet regulated and tamed experience ripened effects according to their karma. If they fall into the lower realms and undergo great suffering, you should remember what I am earnestly entrusting to you now in the Trayastrimsa Heaven: Help all living beings in the saha world from now until Maitreya [Buddha] arises in the world—cause them to a attain liberation, to leave all suffering forever, and to meet [Maitreya] Buddha and be given prediction.

"At that time, emanation Ksitigarbha Bodhisattvas from the various worlds returned together to one form, and weeping from pity and great love, he said to the Buddha, 'throughout many long kalpas Buddhas have guided me, so that I am able to attain inconceivable spiritual power and be replete with great wisdom. My emanations fill worlds as numerous as the sand grains in hundreds of thousands of myriads of millions of Ganges Rivers. In each of these worlds, I transform into hundreds of thousands of myriads of millions of emanations. Each emanation guides hundreds of thousands of myriads of millions of people across, causing them to revere and take refuge in the Triple Gem, leave samsara forever, and reach the bliss of nirvana. As long as they do good deeds in Buddhadharma, even if such deeds are as little as a strand of hair, a drop of water, a grain of sand, a speck of dust, or a bit of a minute down hair, I will gradually guide them across to liberation, causing them to gain great benefits. O World-Honored One, please do not be concerned about future living beings who have unwholesome karma.'

"Thus he said three times to the Buddha, 'O World-Honored One, please do not be concerned about future living beings who have unwholesome karma.'

"At that time, the Buddha praised Ksitigarbha Bodhisattva, saying, 'Excellent, excellent! I will help in your aspirations. You will be able to fulfill the profound vows taken throughout many long kalpas, finish guiding [beings] far and wide [to the other shore], and immediately attain bodhi.'"[3]

This sutra excerpt basically explains that Ksitigarbha Bodhisattva has attained the Immanence body that then confers upon him the capability of emanating (upon need) countless astral subtle body projections that can enter into people's brains and give them thoughts. This capability of emanating body projections (called *nirmanakaya*) on a vast scale especially occurs at the Supra-Causal body attainment level (*nirvana* with remainder) and higher. Prior to that attainment level you have to use your own subtle or Causal body to appear before others or enter into them, but starting at the Supra-Causal level you can create many instantaneous projections or emanations to do such jobs and then dissipate them when finished. If human beings can see such a projection, it is called a *Yang shen*, which is Chinese Taoist terminology. Many people who report seeing their master in two places at once (bilocation) are actually seeing one of his *Yang shen* emanation bodies. Countless individuals have written of such stories.

At the Immanence body level your capabilities are even greater, and at body attainments superior to this your attainments are greater still. This is why Nagarjuna said:

> The seventh (stage of Bodhisattva development which corresponds to the Supra-Causal body) is the Far-going. ... he becomes a lord of the gods of Paranirmitavasavartin heaven. ...

---

[3] Jeanne Tsai translation from the Fo Guang Shan International Translation Center.

The eighth is the Immovable. ... He becomes a Brahma, lord of a thousand worlds, unsurpassed by Saints and Hermit Buddhas. ... The ninth stage is called Good Genius ... He becomes a Brahma, lord of a million worlds ... The tenth is called Raincloud of Dharma (Immanence body level attainment), because the rain of the excellent teaching falls, and the Bodhisattva is consecrated with light by all the Buddhas. He becomes a lord of the gods of the Pure Abodes, a supreme great lord of the sphere of infinite wisdom.[4]

Ksitigarbha Bodhisattva has basically stated his vow that he will use uncountable *nirmanakaya* emanations to continually help counter sentient beings' negative thoughts and guide them to better states of being. He will keep doing this forever in his long-lived bodies, and since the higher the bodies he attains the longer he lives, we are talking about a nearly infinite lifetime ... equivalent to waiting for all beings in the universe to become enlightened. With the prospect of living forever, what would you choose to do to occupy yourself? What tasks, goals, purposes or objectives would be worthy of your aspirations? You will have absolute freedom to support, protect and promote whatever you want because no one binds you. What would be your Bodhisattva vows, and how would start training now so as to be able to fulfill them?

Manjusri, Samantabhadra, Avalokitesvara and Maitreya have also vowed to use their abilities to transform into hundreds of thousands of forms (meaning that they will project *nirmanakaya* "emanation bodies" to enter into people to give them thoughts, emotions, courage, energy, strength, healing, comfort, dreams, motivation, inspiration, aspirations and so forth) in order to help people in all sorts of hidden ways. This is what you do when you achieve enlightenment.

When billionaires and kings die they are nobodies in Heaven because their money is gone and they didn't bring anything with them. They should have brought merit with them, but they take little to Heaven if they didn't do any good deeds. They no longer have a staff, company, money, possessions, retainers or anything major and are stuck with the fact that they did a lot of bad deeds and didn't use their money, resources or position to perform any great acts of altruism, philanthropy or charitable merit. Many did not bother to cultivate any special skills either. Basically they squandered their merit during life, and didn't create

---

[4] *The Christ and the Bodhisattva*, ed. by Donald S. Lopez Jr. & Steven C. Rockefeller, (SUNY Press, Albany: New York, 1987), p. 86.

any great good karma of service to others to bring good fortune with them into a new life. Politicians and kings find themselves no longer as people of power or influence, so no one listens to them or bows at their mere presence. What was it all for if they did not create an enduring legacy that continued to help others after they were gone … to have made some difference they lived at all? Most swelled, foamed for a moment, and then disappeared into oblivion. After years of hard training and struggle, it is common for Olympic medal winners to experience states of depression after their win. What was all the training for now that it is over? Think deeply on this well-known fact.

The only thing you take with you upon death is your personality, behavior and your accumulation of karma or merit. Good karma is accumulated by performing good deeds to help others, while bad karma is accumulated by doing evil, unethical or bad deeds. Good karma is what you want to be accumulating in life, and the size of the help you render can be considered the size of your karma.

It is strange that a poor sadhu that you might daily ignore - dirty, scantily clad, with unkempt hair and meager rations - might actually be enlightened as he sits there and uses his *nirmanakaya* emanations to perform helpful functions everywhere without your notice. That is the great one living resplendent in Heaven while you see a dirty body below, and he or she doesn't care that they don't seem rich on the earthly plane because their real life is in a higher body that resides in a more pleasant existence. The human body you see in the world is like an appendage tethered to their higher bodies which they continue using like a tool until the karma is ripe for it to disappear.

This is another reason you should always monetarily contribute to monks and nuns, swamis, sadhus, padres, priests, rabbis, and others who might actually be enlightened (they have at minimum a subtle body), or are qualified for enlightenment, for they hate asking for money yet need personal funds just like everyone else but have no way to earn it. Hampered by a lack of funds, how do you think they feel despite the fact that they know more than everyone else and are running around trying to help people and fix unfortunate affairs? If you solve some of their problems then they will have more free time to help more people and do greater deeds than if encumbered by too many earthly fetters.

If enlightened, in return they will not only start protecting you in unseen ways as a return for your kindness but those personal funds, rather than just funds contributed for a monastery, nunnery, temple, church or mosque, will free them from some basic concerns so that they can do more good deeds in this world without people knowing.

My point is, donate some personal funds to some spiritual monks and nuns or other religious functionaries for their own personal use when you can, especially when you see they are poor and need it. I suggest making this a habit twice a year, and whenever you encounter a worthy. As the sage Nisargadatta said, "There are people in the world who do more good than all the statesmen and philanthropists put together." He was talking precisely of these people.

The *Sutra in Forty Sections* of Buddhism says, "Feeding a hundred evil people is not as good as feeding one good person. Feeding a thousand good people is not as good as feeding one who upholds the precepts. Feeding ten thousand people who uphold the precepts is not as good as feeding one Srotapanna (someone who has attained the subtle body). Feeding one million Srotapanna is not as good as feeding one Sakadagami. Feeding ten million Sakadagami is not as good as feeding one Anagami (someone who has attained the subtle body *and* Causal body). Feeding one hundred million Anagami is not as good as feeding one Arhat (someone who has attained the subtle body, Causal body and Supra-Causal body). Feeding one billion Arhats is not as good as feeding one Pratyekabuddha. Feeding ten billion Pratyekabuddhas is not as good as feeding one Buddha of the past, present and future" (someone who has attained the subtle body, Causal body, Supra-Causal body and Immanence body)." Although figurative, the numbers indicate that the higher one's highest spiritual body, the more people one can help.

In the *Surangama Sutra* of Buddhism, Samantabhadra Bodhisattva said: "World Honoured One, I always use my mind to listen in order to distinguish the variety of views held by living beings. If in a place, separated from here by a number of worlds as countless as the sands in the Ganges, a living being practises Samantabhadra deeds, I mount at once a six tusked elephant and reproduce myself in a hundred and a thousand apparitions to come to his aid. Even if he is unable to see me because of his great karmic obstruction, I secretly lay my hand on his head to protect and comfort him so that he can succeed." In Buddhism Samantabhadra always rides a six-tusked elephant that is white in color to symbolize purified sexual desire. It represents a man's pelvis because the elephant head symbolizes his sex organs and its six tusks represent the six nerves exiting each side of the sacrum. So yes, Samantabhadra rides a six-tusked elephant everywhere because it represents his pelvis.

If you succeed in enlightenment you can generate countless *nirmanakaya* emanation bodies just like Samantabhadra and project them to do good things in the world, such as to give people thoughts and ideas. The higher your transcendental body the further you can project yourself in the universe and the more you can do.

When you succeed at enlightenment, which can happen in this life if you get the right master and work hard enough at cultivation, you too will also have this capability (as do many masters in the world), so you must start to think now upon what activities you would perform and vows you would undertake if you attained enlightenment. What are you involved in now, what do you find yourself doing? Those are some of your interests. With that in mind, you must start to think about what you might train to deal with and master.

While in the Buddhist sutras many Buddhas and Bodhisattvas announce their vows regarding the ways in which they will help people, the saints in other religions offer similar help to humans but don't announce it so overtly. Many Christian saints, Sufi saints, Jain saints, Taoist legends, Confucian sages, Hindu saints, Buddhist great monks, and enlightened rabbis are said to respond to prayers or perform protective functions for various occupations, festivals, institutions, locations and so on.

In Hinduism, many enlightened individuals have left us countless mantras they created, as a sort of telephone number, that people can recite to request different types of assistance from enlightened beings that masquerade as famous deities such as Ganesh, Kali, Saraswati, Shiva, Krishna, and so forth. Sometimes their help can change your karma, but do not expect miracles without helping yourself as much as possible. When people encounter difficult situations it often (but not always) means heavy karma that cannot be changed. Nevertheless, sometimes higher powers can bend things just enough so as to improve your situation from what it would be, but it is hard for you to know this.

In order that people call upon these saints for help, spiritual texts provide us their names and mantras or sutras they sponsor (respond to) when someone reads them. The Buddhist sutras even provide lists of the ways in which various Buddhas and Bodhisattvas will help people if individuals establish a connection with these masters.

For instance, Shakyamuni Buddha describes twenty-eight kinds of benefits in the *Original Vows of Ksitigarbha Bodhisattva Sutra* that can be received by people who pay homage to Ksitigarbha Bodhisattva. "Pay homage" simply means to think of the Buddha and pray/mantra for help and assistance in order to establish a connection. Their homage will establish a karmic connection with Ksitigarbha so as to earn his watchful concern and assistance of various types:

First, devas and nagas will protect them.
Second, their wholesome results will increase daily.
Third, they will accumulate superior causes for holiness.
Fourth, they will not retreat from bodhi.
Fifth, their food and clothing will be abundant.

Sixth, they will not be infected by diseases or pestilence.
Seventh, they will not be in disasters of flood or fire.
Eighth, they will not fall victim to robbery or theft.
Ninth, people who see them will admire and respect them.
Tenth, spirits and ghosts will aid and support them.
Eleventh, women [who wish to] will be reborn as men.
Twelfth, [if reborn as women] they will be daughters of kings and ministers.
Thirteenth, they will be good looking and with perfect features.
Fourteenth, they will frequently be reborn in the heavens.
Fifteenth, they may be emperors or kings.
Sixteenth, they will have the wisdom to know past lives.
Seventeenth, they will fulfill their wishes.
Eighteenth, their family members will be happy.
Nineteenth, untoward dire occurrences will be eliminated.
Twentieth, they will forever leave the karmic paths.
Twenty-first, they will pass through safely wherever they go.
Twenty-second, their dreams at night will be peaceful and happy.
Twenty-third, their deceased relatives will leave suffering behind.
Twenty-fourth, they will be reborn on the strength of their past merit.
Twenty-fifth, holy ones will praise them.
Twenty-sixth, they will be intelligent and have keen faculties.
Twenty-seventh, their hearts will be replete with kindness and compassion.
Twenty-eighth, they will ultimately become Buddhas.

According to the culture, many people also construct shrines for saints, deities, Buddhas and Bodhisattvas within or outside of their homes. This is not without merit because these small shrines usually become used by heavenly beings who choose to become guardian spirits under the tutelage of a fully enlightened Buddha. For instance, the same *Original Vows of Ksitigarbha Bodhisattva Sutra* records how people who pay homage to Ksitigarbha Bodhisattva will receive certain benefits:

First, their lands will be rich and fertile.
Second, their families and homes will ever be in peace.
Third, all their deceased relatives will be reborn in the heavens.
Fourth, the living will enjoy greater longevity.
Fifth, they will obtain what they seek with ease.
Sixth, they will not suffer disasters of flood or fire.
Seventh, events that cause depletion (bad becomings) will be eliminated.

Eighth, they will not have bad dreams (nightmares).
Ninth, they will be protected by guardian spirits in their daily comings and goings.
Tenth, they will come across many causes of holiness.

These benefits become possible because Bodhisattvas, guardian spirits, local deities and dharma protectors make them possible. Why would they bother to take on such tasks? You cannot have significance in life if it is all about you. You get your significance, joy, contentment and satisfaction through altruistic service, offering and even sacrifice for others. Once you start working for others all the Buddhas, Bodhisattvas, deity protectors and guardian spirits will start protecting you. This is the benefit of Karma Yoga.

Accordingly, many Asian cities and villages construct a suitable residence for the city's guardian protectors, or shrines to pay homage to them. These are the protective spirits of a place, sometimes called protect gods. In Indian culture these are the *Sapta Matrikas*, city protect gods or guardian deities in Chinese culture, *grama devata* village deities in Tamil Nadu (India), *kami* in Japanese Shintoism, *Landvaettir* in Norse mythology, and *Genius loci* in Roman religion. Other cultures use different names but they all refer to the same type of beings.

Whenever a master reaches a high enough stage and is ready to leave this world, he will sometimes publicly announce his Bodhisattva vows. Such was the case of Sufi master Sai Baba of Shirdi, who announced "Eleven Promises" to adherents after his departure. Although a Moslem, these constitute Buddha vows like those made by Ksitigarbha or the Medicine King Buddha:

Whoever puts his feet on Shirdi soil, his sufferings would come to an end.
The wretched and miserable would rise into plenty of joy and happiness, as soon as they climb the steps of my Mosque.
I shall be ever active and vigorous even after leaving this earthly body.
My tomb shall bless and speak the needs of my devotees.
I shall be active and vigorous even from my tomb.
My mortal remains would speak from my tomb.
I am ever living to help and guide all, who come to me, who surrender to me and who seek refuge in me.
If you look at me I look at you.
If you cast your burden on me, I shall surely bear it.

If you seek my advice and help, it shall be given to you at once.
There shall be no want in the house of my devotees.

Life goes on forever, and each Buddha or Bodhisattva has decided upon their own activities and life purpose within that foreverness. You are a Bodhisattva if you work for people's benefit even if you don't succeed in spiritual cultivation. Therefore you should decide what directions are of interest to you so that you can start working or developing skills along those avenues while living. With a deva body you gain a new life free of most worldly restrictions and constraints, and with that life you will be free to do whatever occupation or charitable activities you want. Therefore you should start training now, even if it seems just a little. That little bit is enough to start creating the karma you need for a grand fruition. When you speak of life purpose, studying the vows of various Buddhas and Bodhisattvas will demonstrate the possible types of activity that one can become involved in.

Since they have attained spiritual bodies that live nearly forever, which is the spiritual trail and standard accomplishment of anyone who cultivates towards enlightenment, the question of meaning comes down to selecting worthy missions and personal efforts other than just doing what life requires for survival. You must start thinking of vows, commitments and aspirations and start thinking about what to train for were you to engage in a cosmic mission. In other words, what type of Buddha would you want to be? What powers would you want to have? What services would you want to be rendering?

There is no ultimate Heaven or resting place in the universe since everything is impermanent. Considering that fact, and that we are in a realm of forever transformations, what missions are worthy of your life essence? What should you devote yourself to accomplishing if money, power, fame or fortune are not the issues at stake? What are the causes or issues that matter to you that you have an urge to do something about? Are you contributing any money or efforts to such causes now? Are you in any way acting as a guardian spirit already?

Wealth is a highly insufficient motivation for someone who will attain numerous spiritual bodies that will live incredibly long lives, have the capability to travel subtle planes and Pure Lands, and be able to give people helpful thoughts and energies. With many spiritual bodies you will actually finally be able to do something about solving some of the sufferings in the world. What is it that you would want to do? That is something you must think about. Once you decide what type of Buddha or Bodhisattva you'd like to become, why aren't you moving in that direction? Why aren't you training to do something about it?

There is great folly in the idea that successful careers will bring people life fulfillment. Your career should enable you to perform your higher calling, but they rarely do so. While a vocation may reward you with fame or incredible sums of money, many people may not feel any satisfaction at all in what they do to earn a living. Most people complain about their jobs and don't like what they do, but are stuck in a hole because of the necessity to make an income. They are dependent upon a wage and an employer, who they might not even like. As a result they usually end up living an empty script for their life and are just miserable. But, if you look for money and security that is all that you are likely to get. Chronic dissatisfaction is likely to be your outcome without a higher life purpose to hold you up.

Confucius even spoke a little about a proper career in his Appendix to the *Yijing*, writing, "Deeds leading the people of the world to settle peacefully is called career (cause and undertaking)." In other words, acting to help the world by benefiting mankind and society is a career. On the other hand, setting up a business or working for a monthly salary is not a career but a vocation. Thus, most of what people do for a living is a vocation, not a career. To be a merchant, for instance, is not a career but a vocation. It is a way to make a livelihood but not your ultimate mission in life. Work that you do simply for money constitutes a job, occupation or vocation, but isn't your true career. A Bodhisattva or Buddha vow is a career.

What most people really want to do, since they have a time frame that is only as long as this life, is make good money to support a great lifestyle. Within that lifestyle they make the mistake of equating acquisitions, entertainment or exotic experiences with happiness and contentment, and unfortunately this trio is usually only accessible because of money. If you then say that getting money is the most important thing in life then you will spend your life completely wasting your time. As Alan Watts once said in a speech, "You will be doing things you don't like in order to stay miserable doing things you don't like doing. It is incredibly stupid to spend your time doing things you don't like in order to continue spending your time doing things you don't like, and to teach your children to follow in the same footsteps. It's all a wretched *nirvana* – it never gets there."

Would you like to know what the definition of "folly" is? It is consuming the greater part of your life making a living rather than fulfilling the higher purposes in your heart that elevate and ennoble you and your life's efforts. Even if you feel it might be out of reach, you must take steps to elevate yourself to some exceptional purpose.

The Dalai Lama once said, "Man sacrifices his health in order to make money. Then he sacrifices money to recuperate his health. And then he is so anxious about the future that he does not enjoy the present; the result being that he does not live in the present or the future. He lives as if he is never going to die, and then dies having never lived."

People waste their entire lives doing unimportant things, and when their time is nearly up they regret what they didn't do and what they did do to get what they got, which they then admit was not worth the price. They struggle their whole lives for financial success and when they finally get it discover that it lacks meaning. People should believe that somehow, somewhere their efforts are helping the world in some way and devote themselves to that. How many can say, "I did something positive for the world today – I made a meaningful difference"?

Benjamin Franklin once wrote a related and highly instructive story about his early life as a boy, called "The Whistle," to teach the principle that people "pay too much" in life for careers and vocations that are not worthy of their time. It runs as follows:

> When I was a child, seven years old, my friends, on a holiday, filled my pockets with coppers. I went directly to a shop where they sold toys for children; and, being charmed with the sound of a whistle that I saw on the way in the hands of another boy, I voluntarily offered the storekeeper all my money for one.
>
> I then came home and went whistling all over the house, much pleased with my whistle, but disturbing all the family. My brothers and sisters and cousins, hearing about the bargain I had made, told me I had given four times as much for it as it was worth.
>
> This put me in mind of what good things I might have bought with the rest of the money; and they laughed at me so much for my folly that I cried with vexation.
>
> This, however, was afterward of use to me, the impression continuing in my mind; so that often, when I was tempted to buy some unnecessary thing, I said to myself, "Don't give too much for the whistle," and so I saved my money.
>
> As I grew up, came into the world, and observed the actions of men, I thought I met with many, very many, who gave too much for the whistle.
>
> When I saw anyone too ambitious of the favor of the great, wasting time in attendance on public dinners, sacrificing his repose, his liberty, his virtue, and perhaps his friends, to attain it, I have said to myself, "This man gives too much for his whistle."
>
> When I saw another fond of popularity, constantly employing himself in politics, neglecting his own affairs, and ruining them by that neglect, "He pays, indeed," said I, "too much for this

whistle."

If I knew a miser, who gave up every kind of comfortable living, all the pleasure of doing good to others, all the esteem of his fellow-citizens, and the joys of benevolent friendship, all for the sake of accumulating wealth, "Poor man," said I, "you do indeed pay too much for your whistle."

When I met a man of pleasure, sacrificing the improvement of his mind, or of his fortune, to mere bodily comfort, "Mistaken man," said I, "you are providing pain for yourself instead of pleasure; you give too much for your whistle."

If I saw one fond of fine clothes, fine furniture, or fine horses, all above his fortune, for which he contracted debts, and ended his career in prison, "Alas!" said I, "he has paid dear, very dear, for his whistle."

In short, I believed that a great part of the miseries of mankind were brought upon them by the false estimates they had made of the value of things, and by their giving too much for their whistles.

So it is that many people in the world are alive but not living due to the prison of occupations/vocations which do not suit them. They aren't happy because of what they must give up of themselves to continue in that unsatisfying line to make money. What initially seemed fun, interesting or romantic about some subject often disappeared after they made it their profession. Because of an unsuitable job or career it is as if they have cut off access to any inner joy, happiness, or vitality they once had. They might inwardly feel that they have a much higher calling, but they often feel miserable because they aren't involved with it.

People want to follow their dreams but they also wish to take care of their loved ones, so sometimes their financial responsibilities make following their inner dreams impossible. It is a wasted life when people know what they want to do but are working at something different they don't value. At the end of their lives such people are disappointed.

People might not be able to quickly identify what it is that they truly wish to do in the world, such as a career mission like the Buddhas and Bodhisattvas have vowed, but people can use them as role models for inspiration until they find their own vows. The best thing you can do until you find your own vows is actively contribute to many charitable causes until you eventually find your own calling.

For instance, a hadith from Islam recounts that Mohammed said we should carry on with life doing good deeds until we find what we want: "Carry on doing good deeds, for everyone will find it easy to do such deeds that will lead him towards that for which he has been created." If you cannot think of appropriate Buddha vows for yourself right now you can start thinking about it. At some point your deepest aspirations will finally hit you and then you will know what you want to do.

Spiritual cultivation, which leads to the attainment of the subtle deva body, will let you finally be able to do things, such as become a guardian spirit. This is the route that Buddhas and Bodhisattvas have chosen in trying to heal the ills of mankind. However, you must think about what you might do as a vow if you chose to become a Buddha or Bodhisattva and started working on specific activities to create a karmic impulse and stock of merit. What cannot be accomplished in this life because of circumstances can certainly be accomplished later if you have a strong enough desire and commitment. How will you show any interest other than through some preparation?

My advice is to be an original. Be authentic and true to yourself as much as possible. Don't be a lemming who just follows the crowd and does what others say is right or proper. Do the good acts you want to do. Think for yourself and follow your own code of ethics, for sometimes society is quite wrong. Work towards your own objectives. Don't die with a hole in your soul from denying what you want to accomplish with this life. Don't be afraid but manage the risks and strike out, even if just a little, for what you want to experience or accomplish.

Most people never touch upon what they really want to do in life, not even in their idle hours or as a hobby. Instead they imprison themselves in a life of unsatisfying work and waste away hours at frivolous past times like useless television or the internet. They don't lift a finger to travel in the most profitable directions they are interested in. They are born an original, but most people sadly die copies because they follow the crowd rather than their own authentic selves. Everyone needs a wake-up call or warning, and you are getting it right now.

The man or woman who remains in the wrong career when they have the *free choice and ability to change* lives the life of a lie. They live the unsatisfying life of the "company man" who must resolve himself to nerve-deadening standards of conformity. Your life cannot find completion if it settles for a routine that lacks fire.

Michael Masterson in *Automatic Wealth for Grads* said, "Somewhere inside you a fire is burning. It is your core desire—your desire—your deepest, truest idea about what you'd like to do and the person you'd like to become. If you can vent that fire, it will give you all the energy, imagination, and boldness you need to make your life full, rich, and satisfying. If you ignore that fire, it will consume everything that is potentially great and good about you. It will burn out your secret hopes, desires, and passions, one at a time, and leave you – as an older person reflecting back on your life – with a cold, charred core."⁵ Question: is your life structure as it is now consonant with your Dream?

Masterson would say that you should tap the passionate sweet spot of your life and get in sync with the real you to start doing what you really want in your heart and soul. Become more in touch with what you are all about. Seek out that path which makes you feel most deeply and vitally alive, along with which comes the inner voice that says, "This is the real me. Forget the higher income. This I want to do." Seek out work with a good purpose and higher calling. Work on something you value - spend your life on something important that will outlast it. Live for something bigger than yourself, something bigger than you are. Life is too short to be little, so create a larger aim of leaving a legacy. Play the long game knowing that there are multiple lives ahead.

You can be a great source of positivity for the world, and through endless lives as well. All of us have a greatness specific to us, our own greatness no one else has. Start bringing that greatness to the forefront. Find out where your greatness lies, decide upon your transformative ambitions, and if you aren't there yet then start taking the steps of study, skills development and self-improvement – self-cultivation – to get there. There are things where you want to be your very best, where you want to be impeccable. What are they? There are ways in which you want to have consummate conduct. What are they? There are ways in which you may want to make a difference. What are they? Start doing them even if your actions seem small and insignificant.

Look for more than just a job if you can get it. Look for a direct link between what you do and a higher meaning. Try to make your life more contributive to a greater cause and if you cannot, then use your free time to start preparing for what you would later do if you were able to become a guardian spirit. Start chipping away at creating a new future now. Start cultivating the character and ways of the Buddha, Bodhisattva, protect god or guardian spirit you want to become.

In an interview with John Chrichton the advertising legend David Ogilvy once advised people: "Be more ambitious. Don't bunt. Try to hit the ball out of the park every time. Compete with the immortals. Try to make whatever you do the greatest that anyone has ever done. You won't always succeed but reach for the stars. Don't bunt. Be more ambitious. Ambition is the key. Try to do remarkable things. Try to be great. It is the lack of ambition that cripples most people."

You should be this way with your life and your efforts, especially when you discover your inner calling! Success is disguised as work, so

---

⁵ Michael Masterson, *Automatic Wealth for Grads,* (John Wiley & Sons, New Jersey, 2006).

involve all your abilities and potentials in whatever you choose to do. Use your faculties to fullest force in all your efforts and live up to your full potential. This is the way of a Bodhisattva warrior who lives their best, doing their utmost to bring about whatever they desire. You are the original nature, so what is there to worry about? Manage the risks and then just do it.

You don't have to be the best in the world at anything, just the best you can be. You don't have to be #1 in the world. Just try to "be so good that others cannot ignore you." Walt Disney put it, "Do what you do so *well* that others cannot resist telling others about you." That in itself will help to propel you into the category of greatness.

Furthermore, in training to be your best what is as important as the skill you desire is the character traits that you develop simultaneously. Rather than just a skill, when training to be your best you should put time into developing attendant, accompanying character traits/virtues that are linked with that accomplishment. This is what is important, but training should always be about improving your habits, personality, and character for the better to become the best version of yourself.

Your historical biography is not equal to destiny, and your past is not equal to your future. With training and effort you can remake yourself into anything you want. Personalities and habits can be changed and talents can be learned. You can develop any skills you want to master, travel anywhere you want to go, and do whatever you want to do. Decision is the ultimate power of a human being that enables him to change the direction in which he is heading and move in a new direction he desires. Use decision to your advantage. I suggest you choose a path of study and then immerse yourself within it to become more proficient in the direction of your heart's calling. What does the phrase "benefit the world" look like to you? The famous poet Rumi once said,

> There is one thing in this world that you must never forget to do. If you forget everything else and not this, there's nothing to worry about; but if you remember everything else and forget this, then you will have done nothing in your life.
>
> It's as if a king has sent you to some country to do a task, and you perform a hundred other services, but not the one he sent you to do. So human beings come to this world to do particular work. That work is the purpose, and each is specific to the person. If you don't do it, it's as though a priceless Indian sword were used to slice rotten meat. It's a golden bowl being used to cook turnips, when one filing from the bowl could buy a hundred suitable pots. It's a knife of the finest tempering nailed into a wall to hang things on.

You say, "But look, I'm using the dagger. It's not lying idle." Do you hear how ludicrous that sounds? For a penny, an iron nail could be bought to serve the purpose. You say, "But I spend my energies on lofty enterprises. I study jurisprudence and philosophy and logic and astronomy and medicine and all the rest." But consider why you do those things. They are all branches of yourself.

Remember the deep root of your being, the presence of your lord. Give your life to the one who already owns your breath and your moments. If you don't, you will be exactly like the man who takes a precious dagger and hammers it into his kitchen wall for a peg to hold his dipper gourd. You'll be wasting valuable keenness and foolishly ignoring your dignity and your purpose.[6]

You have a reason to be here in life, but that reason is whatever *you* decide that reason to be. Your reason and purpose are your own. They don't come from anyone else. In the entire universe, you are unique and whatever you choose to do, whatever actions you choose to make, they are entirely your own choice. My advice is to use the Buddha and Bodhisattva vows as an inspirational motivation for discovering what issues really matter to you and then setting forth upon that path. Now is the moment to do so, because few ever make the effort. Life is too short not to be ambitious.

A life purpose is different than the purpose of life. Life is its own purpose, therefore how you use your life is your life purpose. My suggestion is this ... since life is its own purpose, bring meaning to your life by ennobling it. Decide on the light you want to bring to the world and then *be that light*. Decide on the happiness you want to bring to others, and then create that happiness and joy. Decide on the types of fulfillment you want to give or provide to others, and then start doing it, even if they are just small steps. This is how to develop a fulfilling life for yourself.

There is a popular myth that there is something God wants you to do in your life, but this is just wishful thinking. There is only what you personally want to accomplish, what you personally decide to do. Choose ennoblement. Choose your best self. Bring a greater purpose to the elements of your life and to your life as a whole. Work on your

---

[6] Robert Ullman and Judyth Reichenberg-Ullman, *Mystics, Masters, Saints, and Sages: Stories of Enlightenment*, (Conari Press, York Beach: ME, 2001), p. 28.

relationships because they keep people happy and healthy.

The Buddhist sutras provide memorable examples of Buddhas and Bodhisattvas who are role models of devotion to causes and missions which they have themselves personally chosen. You can do the same. For yourself, there is a whole new exciting journey ahead of you when you decide upon your own type of commitment and vows.

You have to read the cosmic vows of these tireless Buddhas and Bodhisattvas and then ask yourself, "For me, what tasks in life are worthy of my efforts? In my own heart, what tasks are worthy of a life of commitment? What is interesting to me? What type of Buddha or Bodhisattva do I want to become? As a Buddha, what goals would I want to achieve and what vows would I want to accomplish?"

These types of questions can help you find a life path greater than just a simple money-making occupation. It can help you decide where you will put your free time and efforts. We all have a deep human need to not only direct our own lives (to live independently on our own terms), but to learn and create new things, and to do better by ourselves and our world. But what will you choose to do along these lines?

People are motivated by all sorts of things in life – empowerment, transcendence, aliveness, accomplishment or the most material objectives such as money, power, status, fame, sex, social influence and so on. If something matters to you then you must start thinking about shaping your life so that its structure and activities, such as going to the gym or eating a better diet, start creating whatever you want to pursue. Try to pick the high road of ennoblement, betterment, self-improvement and consummate conduct rather than just the road of experiential consumption.

All things must pass away, but your actions will endure in a never-ending chain of consequences proceeding forward forever. For good or bad, this is the legacy you will leave behind in the world. The highest legacy is to leave behind a better world than what you first encountered. In other words, to make a contribution that will change lives and improve situations for the better.

You are unique amidst everyone who has come and gone in the world and are called upon to a personal purpose. What will it be? What type of Bodhisattva, benefactor or guardian will you choose to become? What missions do you want to empower and protect? What type of light giver do you want to become for the world? To become that, whatever it is, you must cultivate and study to achieve it.

So how do you discover your real purpose in life? I mean the real reason why you are here, the very reason you exist. I'm not talking about your job, your daily responsibilities, or even your long-term goals. I'm talking about any inner ache in your soul to make a difference.

You have to decide you want to ultimately accomplish in life. To accomplish something requires the acquisition of skills, study and application. It requires require grit and perseverance of effort. When you do feel a pull towards some purpose, activity or goal that you believe reflects your inner self, then pursue it fully and vigorously with great intent. Follow this road to become who you really are.

What personal vows are worthy of you? Here are some examples typical of aspirants following the Buddhist path:

> I vow to become enlightened (a Buddha)
> Save uncountable numbers of sentient beings
> Master the study and application of infinite dharmas, bringing best practices everywhere
> Cut off all mental afflictions for myself and others
> Master skillful means to accomplish my tasks, and transform all situations I encounter to something better
> Master the way of perfect virtue and purity of mind during all my activities
> Eliminate the causes of suffering while establishing happiness, joy, courage and inspiration for others in their place
> Practice good deeds, never practice evil deeds, prevent evil and harm from arising, remove (cut off) evil and harm that exists, and remove the obstacles that prevent goodness from arising but fertilize those good roots instead.
> Do all the good I can, in all the ways I can, in all the places I can, in all the times I can, to all the people and situations I can, as long as ever I can

As explained in *Color Me Confucius*, what people typically do is recite their personal vows at the end of the day after mentally reviewing their day's activities and reporting those activities to Heaven. In Asia they do this every evening after making an offering of a few grains of rice and small cup of water to feed hungry ghosts.

What I suggest is to review the day's activities at the end of the day, light a stick of incense and report what you did to Heaven, and then make a to-do list for tomorrow. The important point is to review your day's activities, noting where you went wrong, and determine not to repeat those errors. Then reaffirm your vows nightly to keep your commitment to self-improvement fresh. At the end of a week I would also review the entire week's activities, and also use some time to plan for the week ahead. This is all explained in *Quick, Fast, Done*.

4
YOGA PRACTICE METHODS

The objective of Yoga is to take a man or woman back to their original source - their root nature. This is supposed to result in eternal bliss and peace as a reward.

Yoga takes interest in explaining the process of emanation/Creation only so that you can understand (1) the reverse process that retraces all things back to their ultimate root origin, the formless source nature, which involves cultivating spiritual bodies composed of progressively more subtle substances and, (2) to give people a model for meditation practice which mimics the original nature that is empty of all things and yet lets all things (Shakti) develop within it without interference.

Thus, you need to train your consciousness to allow thoughts to arise within it but you shouldn't cling to them unless you are practicing concentration. If they are afflictions you need to learn how to cut them off, which is learning how to manage the mind, and you need to undertake a pathway of practice that purifies your mind so that afflictions don't arise in the first place.

One idea is that the emanation of phenomena can all be traced back through planes of existence, each more subtle than the next, to an original, fundamental, pure source essence. Similarly, thoughts can all be traced back to a pure empty state of consciousness/awareness where thoughts are as yet unborn/unmanifest.

After this understanding is established, Yoga then tells us that the yogic path involves (1) cultivating the physical body (made of Jing or semen) through *asanas*, breathing, inner energy work and meditation to purify your internal subtle body composed of Qi/Prana until it can leave the physical body at will, (2) cultivating your subtle deva body made of

Qi/Prana with similar purification techniques to attain the higher Causal body composed of a more transcendental, subtle material (Shen), (3) cultivating the more transcendental Causal body you have attained in order to generate the clear light Supra-Causal body composed of Later Heavenly energy, (4) cultivating the Supra-Causal body to attain the more transcendental Immanence body composed of Primordial Heavenly energy and so on. Each transcendental body substance gets progressively closer to the transcendental first emanate of the original source essence. The higher body attainments free you from birth and death in the lower realms forever.

Taoism poetically describes this process saying that Jing transforms into Qi, Qi transforms into Shen, Shen transforms into Emptiness (which is another term for the Clear Light, Supra-Causal body of Later Heavenly Qi that is also called the Dharma Body), and you have to break through that Emptiness body to get to the Tao. This means that the Immanence body attainment, or supreme stage, arises from within the Supra-Causal Dharma body.

Along this pathway one therefore always (5) mentally dissociates from any body attainment, refusing to identify with it as your final real Self so that you always work to move forwards. Your True Self is a final, primordial, self-so unchanging pure essence that isn't a being and therefore has no consciousness or knowing. It is always described as a oneness of peace/bliss that you are supposed to realize through meditation. But, the great prize is actually a body attainment.

This then is the real pathway of *moksha*, liberation, salvation, spiritualization, self-realization or enlightenment that results in peace, bliss, completeness, and freedom from suffering because each higher realm is better than the last, each new body is more comfortable and has more abilities than the last, and the attendant mental state of each higher body is a more progressive stage of peace, equanimity and bliss.

Therefore while cultivation is commonly described as a mental path it is actually also a body cultivation path because "higher consciousness" comes along with a new body attainment. It is not that a purer consciousness wins you a new body attainment. You have to do a lot of energy work to get a new body, not just meditation work, and better states of consciousness naturally come along with that new body attainment! The only reason that consciousness quiets in the human mind is because the Qi pathways in the brain open up due to better energy flows within it, so even at this level a "higher purity of consciousness" is achieved due to spiritual cultivation that works to physically transform your body. The degree of mental afflictions you experience in your mind as not just due to karma and your environment or actions but to the type of body you possess.

When you attain a higher body you will experience a better mental state as a result of possessing that better body. Life in a higher realm is better too. What you need to understand is that without a body there is no such thing as an individual consciousness. It appears within a body capable of sentience, and that sentient being can either develop its body and thought capabilities to their fullest or not.

The main reason cultivation is described as a mental path is because adherents, ignorant of body attainments, will think they are making spiritual progress if they are always improving their behavior due to watching their minds and striving to cultivate mental peace through meditation. If they focused on body attainments only (Qi cultivation) and constantly saw that they have not achieved the subtle body or made substantial headway along those lines then they would get discouraged from practice and simply stop. Therefore meditation practice is employed. People achieve mental realizations and think "I got it."

"Skillful means," as described in the *Lotus Sutra*, is therefore used on an ignorant population to manage its expectations. Spiritual practitioners are steered towards meditation and mental watching practice to purify their minds and behavior. This will improve their lives even though it doesn't lead to significant Qi cultivation by itself. Furthermore, they are steered away from most Qi energy practices since most people won't succeed with them anyway.

Cultivation is not solely about body cultivation, but is mind-body cultivation involving purification of your mind, behavioral perfection, and physical transformations to produce an independent subtle body. Most religions only explain spiritual work from the aspect of mind cultivation and behavior rather than body cultivation. They describe it in terms of mental peace/emptiness, clear thinking and virtuous behavior in accordance with reason, and allowing thoughts to always arise without clinging to them just as the original nature (or space) allows phenomena to arise within It without attachment. Thus the spiritual cultivation path is explained in terms of mastering consciousness, but the goal of inert mental blankness or "having no thoughts" is not the spiritual path. When you don't exist or are sleeping this is a state of having no thoughts, and how is that proper cultivation practice? Consciousness is the great prize of the universe, so the cultivation path is all about how to develop it, control it, master it and use it properly.

The primary reason for emphasizing your mind and behavior is because masters with higher bodies know that most people will not succeed in attaining the subtle body while alive due to the lack of ethical purity and the required practice consistency necessary for real cultivation progress. Sometimes their karma just isn't ready either. Hence they emphasize the mental aspects of practice that will still lead to positive results: clear mental awareness so that you can police your thoughts and behavior and subsequently better your life. Better behavior also means forgetting self-centeredness and performing unselfish acts of merit such as by becoming a benefactor or guardian of helpful activities in the world.

Nevertheless, the ultimate purpose of spiritual cultivation is to enable you to return to your most ultimate origin and attain mental bliss by cultivating more transcendental bodies because as *Patanjali's Yoga Sutras* say, "The highest value a Yogi aspires for lies in re-absorption of primary constituents into their world-ground. Such a state supervenes upon total dissolution of the bodily and psycho-mental life, which is pure consciousness or feeling of void."

How do you do this? How do you cultivate your body to such a high extent that you can even turn it into its constituent components? You have to be on a cultivation path where you work to attain higher and higher transcendental bodies; creating bodies of higher transcendental energies from denser bodies is the same thing as cultivating to attain the world-ground or fundamental nature.

Each spiritual body is of a higher (more transcendental or purer) type of energy that is actually already inherent in your coarse physical body, which can be considered a condensation of all sorts of higher levels of energy that science does not yet even know exist. Along this pathway of cultivation you can even learn how to dissolve your physical body into Qi and then reassemble it again because your higher bodies still exist in a form that maintains its original structure.

An example from Swami Rama within *Living With the Himalayan Masters* will illustrate one of the many different ways that accomplish this. One time Swami Rama was visiting his grandmaster who provided the following demonstration.

> My grandmaster said, "I am going to give you wisdom. I am going to demonstrate for you." He said he could leave his body and enter someone else's body and then come back to his own body again. He said he could change his body at will. The thought flashed in my mind, "He wants to cast off his body and wants me to immerse it or bury it," but suddenly he said, "It's not that." He was replying to my thoughts. He instructed me to go inside the cave and again check if there was any outlet or hidden door, but I had already lived in that small cave for more than a month, and I thought there was no point in checking the cave again. I did as he ordered, and as I had seen before, it was a small rock cave with only one entrance having a wooden portico outside. I came out and sat under the portico with the lama next to me. He told us to

come nearer to him and hold a wooden plate which was like a round tea tray. When we held the tray, he said, "Do you see me?"

We said, "Yes."

In my ignorance I said, "Please don't try to hypnotize me. I won't look at your eyes."

He said, "I am not hypnotizing you."

His body started becoming hazy and that haziness was a human form like a cloud. That hazy cloud human form started moving toward us. Soon in a few second's time, the cloud disappeared. We found that the plate which we were holding started becoming heavier. After a few minutes, the wooden plate again became light as it was before. For ten minutes the lama and I remained standing holding that plate and finally sat down waiting in great suspense and awe for something to happen. After ten or fifteen minutes, the voice of my grandmaster told me to get up and to hold that wooden plate again. When we held the plate, it started becoming heavier and again the cloudy form reappeared in front of us. From the cloudy form, he came back to his visible body. This amazing and unbelievable experience was a confirmation. He demonstrated this *kriya* once again in a similar manner. Perhaps that day will never come when I can speak about this to the world. I would like to do so, because I feel that the world should know that such sages exist and that the researchers should start researching such secret signs. Miracles like this show that a human being has such abilities and in the third chapter of the Yoga Sutras, Patanjali, the codifier of yoga science, explains all the *siddhis*. I do not profess or claim that such *siddhis* are essential for self-enlightenment, but I want to say that human potentials are immense, and as the physical scientists are exploring the external world, the genuine yogis should not stop exploring the inner abilities and potentials.[7]

When the mind and body reach the highest level of transcendence, this is the highest spiritual attainment because that is almost the original nature. A total dissolution of becoming the singular essence that is the original nature (base state of existence) means there is no mind or body anymore, or even existence except being the original nature, and that is not the purpose of self-cultivation. That is extinction, annihilation or non-existence. You shouldn't become annihilated on the spiritual path

---

[7] Swami Rama, *Living with the Himalayan Masters*, (Himalayan International Institute of Yoga Science and Philosophy of the U.S.A., Honesdale: PA, 1986), pp. 424-426.

... the ideal is simply to cultivate as high a spiritual body as possible that is as close as possible to the base energy of the universe since that would be the composition of the highest body and the commensurate mental state is blissful or peaceful.

Many schools and sages explain this. The Vedanta sage Nisargadatta said, "The primary purpose of meditation is to become conscious of, and familiar with, our inner life. The ultimate purpose is to reach the source of life and consciousness." The source of life and consciousness is the original nature.

Nisargadatta explained that the whole world exists in awareness or consciousness, which projects worlds in our minds because we have thoughts in our brains, and once consciousness turns off then everything vanishes (just as in sleep). Nisargadatta likes to say, "When consciousness turns back to its source then it vanishes. ... The crown jewel of spiritual studies is that one should stabilize in the One without qualities." This explanation is worded to encourage the practice of meditation once again.

Similarly, he said "what is beyond both thought and no-thought, supporting both, is the supreme state, a state of utter stillness and silence. Whoever goes there, disappears. It is unreachable by words, or mind. You may call it God, or Parabrahman, or Supreme Reality, but these are names given by the mind. It is the nameless, contentless, effortless and spontaneous state, beyond being and not being. ... By itself the light [of consciousness] can only be compared to a solid, dense, rocklike, homogenous and changeless mass of pure awareness, free from the mental patterns of name and shape. ... [Attributes] appear and disappear in my light, but cannot describe me. The universe is all names and forms, based on qualities and their differences, while I am beyond. ... I know there is a world, which includes this body and this mind, but I do not consider them to be more "mine" than other minds and bodies. They are there, in time and space, but I am timeless and spaceless. ... This state is entirely one and indivisible, a single solid block of reality. The only way of knowing it is to be it. The mind cannot reach it. To perceive it does not need the senses; to know it does not need the mind. ... It is not perceptible, because it makes perception possible. It is beyond being and not being. It is neither the mirror nor the image in the mirror. It is what is—the timeless reality, unbelievably hard and solid. ..."

Of course the sage Nisargadatta had attained the Immanence body that is a higher copy of the physical body but composed of much higher transcendental energies. That body has thoughts within its consciousness stream just as the human body does. Otherwise, without thought you wouldn't exist at all as a knower of anything. He was simply explaining his understanding of matters in a way that encouraged meditation practice.

When particular words in a religious text strike you, that recognition on your part is like a flare or beacon that can cut through the billions of human thoughts being produced in the world to notify higher-bodied beings about your study, and then they can arrive to help you via a *nirmanakaya* emanation. Mantras, holy texts, and even religious sculptures and paintings are monitored by Buddhas in this way, who have vowed to help people who recite such texts or look at "sponsored" religious figures and paintings.

Nisargadatta also explained that the consciousness workings in our brain are like an infinite web that instantly and simultaneously reflects all memories, names and labels so that thoughts can manifest the whole of the material, biological, mental, and spiritual world that presents itself to us. In other words, it references all our memories and thought processes so that it can make sense of what it encounters and form a world of mental recognition for us.

Nothing exists for each of us outside of our consciousness. Without consciousness there is no "I" nor world because without thoughts there is no way to know anything. Consciousness is just a bunch of thoughts in the head that spin a picture of a world for us that works, even if that picture is imperfect or incomplete, and the primary thought is an I-thought center without which there can be no sense of I and others.

Nisargadatta also said that the substance of the mind itself is fundamentally, originally, and eternally pure and clear. Other than pointing to the formless original essence that is the true nature of everything and thus need not be mentioned, he is basically suggesting that you think of the mind as like a pool of clear awareness that is naturally empty of thoughts but allows them be generated as needed. In other words, the natural state of consciousness is peaceful and clear, but empty mind has an infinite capacity to form thoughts that reflect phenomena.

This is an explanation that also encourages meditation practice as the spiritual path while bypassing body cultivation altogether. The focus in Vedanta, as in Zen, is on what we would call pure consciousness, empty mind, pristine awareness, mental purity or mind cultivation while missing the second part of the equation, which is the necessity for cultivating the Qi/Prana of your body so that your inner subtle body can be purified and strengthened. Inner energy cultivation requires many different types of exercises to stir your inner vitality, and this is the energy yoga of the path. If you don't engage in this type of Yoga, you won't "become enlightened" or "attain the Tao" in millions of years. The Zen school and Vedanta do a great disservice by not clearly telling this to individuals.

"Tracing things back to their ultimate origin," as taught in Yoga, Vedanta and Buddhism, is also something Confucius instructed us to do. Confucius espoused a path of mental introspection for tracing consequences back to original causes so that individuals could learn the principles of better behavior for handling situations. Tracing things back includes tracing thoughts back to unmanifest consciousness, meaning (like Nisargadatta) empty consciousness that is a state unmanifest of thoughts but aware and ready to give birth to them. Confucian mental witnessing is one such trace-back practice.

Confucianism says we must discover our inherent "bright virtue," which is Nisargadatta's pristine clear awareness of the mind that is absent of thoughts – unmanifest/pure consciousness that is the treasure of sentient beings. Discovering that the natural state of the mind is empty brings peace.

Yoga contains a very large set of practices to help us trace both our consciousness and bodies back to their one source. Thoughts can be traced back to clear consciousness, but consciousness itself, and the physical body, must ultimately be traced back to the original nature. Along these lines, Jesus said that we should become one with the Father, the original nature. Advaitism and Hinduism say that we must become Brahman, which is also a name for the original nature. Jainism says we must regain our pristine glory. Islam says that we must remove the veils that screen us from Allah.

Now Confucianism tells us to find our bright virtue, which we can take as meaning either our original nature or pristine awareness. Tibetan Buddhism teaches us to search for the root of consciousness (the root of being conscious) - the light beyond the mind, the clear nature of the mind beyond thoughts. Christianity calls this the uncreated light of the mind. Other schools call it the natural illumination of the mind, base illumination or luminous mind. All these terms are various ways to refer to clear awareness as a type of pure, empty consciousness.

The pathway to spiritual achievement is two-fold: one of the paths involves meditation for calming and purifying (emptying) your mind so that you touch upon empty consciousness at times, and the other path involves inner energy work (kundalini yoga, *anapana*, Nyasa yoga, Naropa's Prana/Qi yogas or *nei-dgong* for transforming your physical body to generate the subtle body and beyond. You need both of these to succeed.

The meditation path includes many techniques. There are many ways to "purify consciousness" such as by witnessing your thoughts or concentrating on a topic to quiet your mind by banishing distractions. You cannot block your thoughts or emotions from arising, and in fact need them to survive. The question is whether you should listen to whatever arises in your mind, and so you need to practice a detached witnessing of your thoughts to learn that they don't need to control you. In time they will quiet and you can reach a state of presence, or mental purity that we colloquially call emptiness or empty mind. But thoughts are still there as long as you have existence, so "emptiness is misunderstood."

In order not to waste your time in buying hundreds of meditation books, I think these are among the best on meditation techniques:

Color Me Confucius (Bodri)
Twenty-five Doors to Meditation: A Handbook for Entering Samadhi
    (Bodri and Lee)
Meditation and Its Practices: A Definitive Guide to Techniques and
    Traditions of Meditation in Yoga and Vedanta (Adiswarananda)
Meditation Techniques of the Buddhist and Taoist Masters (Odier)
The Little Book of Meditation (Bodri)
Meditation Case Studies (Bodri)
Vijnana Bhairava

If you want to succeed quickly on cultivating your Qi that once purified becomes the deva body that can leave your physical shell at will, there are only a few excellent books on internal energy work (*nei-dan* or *nei-gong*) and transforming your body that you need to study. The best books on tantric internal energy exercises to cultivate your body are as follows:

Nyasa Yoga: Kundalini, Prana, Chakra and Nadi Cultivation Techniques
    (Bodri)
Yajnavalkya (trans. A.G. Mohan and Ganesh Mohan)
Tibetan Yoga and Secret Doctrines (Walter Evans-Wentz)
A Systematic Course in the Ancient Tantric Techniques of Yoga and Kriya
    (Satyananda Saraswati)
The Six Yogas of Naropa (Glenn Mullin)
Readings on The Six Yogas of Naropa (Glenn Mullin)
Dharana Darshan: Yogic, Tantric and Upanishadic Practices of
    Concentration and Visualization (Niranjanananda Saraswati)
Kriya Secrets Revealed (J.C. Stevens)
Visualization Power (Bodri)
Look Younger, Live Longer (Bodri)
Detox Cleanse Your Body Quickly and Completely (Bodri)

The best books to explain the *gong-fu* of the path, which are the common changes that occur in your physical and subtle bodies (and consciousness) as you start to purify them due to meditation and yogic exercises, are the following:

Tao and Longevity (Nan and Chu)
Meditation Case Studies (Bodri)
The Little Book of Hercules (Bodri)
Meditation and Its Practices: A Definitive Guide to Techniques and Traditions of Meditation in Yoga and Vedanta (Adiswarananda)
A Systematic Course in the Ancient Tantric Techniques of Yoga and Kriya (Satyananda Saraswati)

I consider these some of the best books for the cultivation trail. Unfortunately many of them are my own, which is not because I want book sales. It is a highly unsatisfactory state of affairs where I had to write them to fill in the gaps where information was unavailable to the public. Some other books that I highly recommend:

The Yoga of Siddha Tirumular (T.N. Ganapathy, K.R. Arumugam, Geetha Anand)
The Yoga of Siddha Boganathar (T.N. Ganapathy)
Master Key to Self-Realization (Shri Siddharameshwar Maharaj)
God Speaks (Meher Baba)
Discourses (Meher Baba)
Hatha Yoga Pradipika
Be As You Are: The Teachings of Sri Ramana Maharshi (David Godman)

As to changing your mindset, attitudes and behaviors – "purifying" consciousness and your actions – I wish I had a longer list of books but these will get you started:

Color Me Confucius (William Bodri)
How to Win Friends and Influence People (Dale Carnegie)
Liao Fan's Four Lessons (Yuan Liao Fan)
The Autobiography of Benjamin Franklin (Benjamin Franklin)
How I Raised Myself from Failure to Success in Selling (Frank Bettger)
The American Reader (Bodri)

Here is the gist of it. If you want to start practicing cultivation to generate the subtle body, you are sure to get lost without an enlightened master. You will spend tons of money and waste years not knowing what to do, which involves lots of meditation work and inner energy cultivation. Without a master, who will work on your inner subtle body with their students?

My best advice is to find the head of a tradition or great monastery of many monks (and nuns) since they are usually enlightened, although there are also a number of rabbis, priests, Sufis and so on have attained the deva body and have students willing to work on transforming your body's Qi and channels. If an enlightened master is in charge of a large group of monks and nuns, however, then it is easy to throw you into the roster schedule of individuals whose Qi has to be worked on; he or she and his enlightened associates are working on many at the same time in a continuous fashion, so by associating with them you will get out earliest and without problems. The responsibility of working on the Qi of all these individuals forces a great master into regularly scheduled Qi work on their bodies, like a factory production process, that a solitary adept will usually not do in an efficient fashion. Also, if he belongs to a large tradition you will know whom to turn to if he dies.

You also must do two things: (1) start meditating and, (2) start working on transforming your body and its Qi by doing inner energy work every day. By reading these books and skipping useless ones you will quickly find the right practices. It is all a matter of Qi Yoga in the end where you try to first ignite and then grab your body's vital energy and move it everywhere, swishing it this way and that way inside you many times per day. At other times you let go of your Qi and thoughts and rest in inner meditation, witnessing the contents of your mind without attachment. That is the quickest way to open your Qi channels.

Spiritual practice is all a matter of Yoga in the end. It is all a matter of Yoga to transform your Qi and channels. In other words, it is all about doing *nei-gong/nei-dan/anapana* work hundreds to thousands of times per day in various ways, and also meditating where you let go of thoughts but aim to cultivate a clear mind that knows its own thoughts without getting entangled in them and losing the state of presence.

Furthermore, if you are not a virtuous, ethical person then no spiritual master is going to help you initiate the kundalini purification process despite all this work. They certainly won't make the 24-hour per day commitment to work on your body for twelve years (see *Nyasa Yoga*) to wash your Qi/Prana to help you generate the deva body. This is why being a good person and ethical training is an essential part of the path.

For our benefit, Shakyamuni Buddha surveyed all the different cultivation methods within the India of his time and compiled them into ten large categories he called mindfulness practice or mindfulness training. These include:

- Mindfulness of the Buddha
- Mindfulness of the Dharma
- Mindfulness of the Sangha
- Mindfulness of Practicing Discipline
- Mindfulness of Practicing Generosity
- Mindfulness of Cultivating to Attain to Heaven
- Mindfulness of Cultivating Your Breath, Vital Energy or Qi/Prana
- Mindfulness of Mental Peace
- Mindfulness of Cultivating Your Body
- Mindfulness of Death

Here is a short explanation of some of these techniques which you can also choose as practice vehicles.

(1) Mindfulness of the Buddha practice is like bhakti yoga in that it involves concentrating on a sacred or divine figure such as Jesus, Padmasambhava, Krishna, Shiva, Vishnu, Surya, Kartikeya, Ganesha, Devi, Shakti, Isis, Buddha, Guru Nanak, an Imam or some other great deity or spiritual teacher, and then identifying with or holding those thoughts on a moment-by-moment basis. As a result, that being if enlightened will connect with your body and use their own Qi to help transform yours to help purify and strengthen your subtle body. In actuality, an enlightened individual who assumes responsibility for masquerading as that individual in your vicinity will be responding to your practice if it is ardently sufficient.

When you feel your energy stir inside your body during cultivation practices it is usually due to interventions like this, or due to the self-generated emotions of sincere veneration for a great religious figure, such as Amitofo Buddha. Emotions can move your Qi so many methods have been developed in various religions to arouse your emotions to stimulate the movement of your Qi or Prana, and deep religious veneration (another form of Buddha mindfulness) is one of those techniques. Singing devotional songs gives rise to Yang Qi also.

"Mindfulness of the Buddha" is not a method restricted to Buddhism, but simply uses the word "Buddha" to denote an enlightened individual of spiritual stature who has succeeded on the cultivation trail – someone who has attained an Immanence body or higher. When you think of them they will know it and connect with your Qi. When you recite their mantra or prayers they will usually connect with your Qi also.

In Buddha mindfulness practice an enlightened/ascended spiritual being is to become the object of one-pointed concentration so that you establish a Qi-connection with that person, or a masquerading representative, who will then generate a *nirmanakaya* projection body to go within you and start transforming your Qi and channels via its own energies that will then move yours. This is why some traditions tell you to visualize "becoming one" with a spiritual great or with your own spiritual guru. Or, just by envisioning and feeling you become one with them you create a type of Qi purification effort by yourself.

Let me provide a useful example of cultivation practice related to Buddha mindfulness in some ways. Actually it is more akin to the Buddhist cultivation practice of the four immeasurables, but the method is instructive nonetheless.

One of my friends, Frank, was once a young electronics engineer and Vice President for a large defense contractor. At one time he helped invent integrated circuits necessary for the U.S. Navy to be able to place sonar buoys across the world's oceans, record the passage of all submarines passing by, and then beam the information to shore for processing. While in a meeting with a large navy staff of senior officers and the chief admiral of the navy, despite his very young age he was able to override the chief admiral's authority in the meeting – an incredible feat never done before – by projecting his own authority Qi outwards during the meeting. Going against the admiral's announcement at the table, he told the admiral and all present that his company would be the lead contractor on this project instead of a subsidiary contractor. The admiral had just stated that the main contract would go to someone else, and had never once in his lifetime had his orders rejected. The room was stunned, but Frank had his way.

I asked Frank how he was able to do this in a room full of admirals, captains, and other powerful naval commanders who regularly had their orders obeyed without question, and who were clearly above him in age and pay grade. He said he trained for it. He explained that he used a special exercise technique to cultivate a character trait he especially wanted, namely authority. Analogously, you can also cultivate the particular character traits of a Buddha you want to become like by also copying Frank's technique.

Frank explained that he used to sit in his room and visualize himself as an authority all would listen to, and would project his Qi energy outwards impregnated with a feeling of authority until he could successfully imagine it filling his entire room and he sensed that extension. When he had mastered projecting that feeling of authority filling a room, he then repeated the same practice in a larger room, and next an empty concert hall, and finally an empty sports stadium! He created a character trait he wanted to cultivate, concentrated on feeling it both inside him and projecting it outwards around him, and finally was able to successfully project immense authority into the outside world.

Another friend, hearing this story and understanding the basic principle, now practices projecting the ability to bring prosperity and helpful business deals to other people. By continuously doing this, over time he will slowly change his habit energy, personality, and fortune in a vastly positive way. Who knows what good karma it will bring? The point of this story is that this is how you can develop the virtues or character traits of the Buddha or Bodhisattva you wish to become. Therefore, you can use this method as a form of Buddha mindfulness.

This is also similar to the four immeasurables practice of Buddhism, only in this case you are cultivating unique virtues, qualities or character traits you want to possess/master that are not the standard four immeasurables. You can definitely change your personality over time by adopting new character traits that you also emphasize by using these immeasurable-type meditations and other related techniques. This method is a way of developing those qualities within yourself, such as by every day meditating that you have a particular personality trait and feeling the Qi of that trait within you. Of course, you have to bring that behavior into the real world as well.

The practice entails projecting your Qi outwards permeated with a large feeling of this virtue or character trait you want to develop, just as Frank practiced cultivating "authority." Through the force of permeation over a long period of time, by sitting in a strong envelope of the Qi of this personality trait and by then acting in this way during real life situations you will slowly change your personality and character. Even an idle moment of time, such as when standing in some line or watching television, can be used to advantage with such practices.

If you do this consistently, it will imprint your Qi (aura) and even your body cells with the new trait you practice imagining being and having, especially if you start acting that way and put that trait into effect wherever possible. This will change your fortune and destiny including your personality in subsequent incarnations. This technique explains why people who receive organ transplants from others will often start to exhibit some of the personality traits of the organ donor. This is because the donor's organ cells had become impregnated with the Qi of their personality, and thus their organs carried a bit of their personality traits into the new organ recipient.

In Paul Pearsall's *The Heart's Code* there is the case of a 52-year old male heart transplant recipient who started to like rock music, instead of the classical music he preferred, after receiving the heart of a 17-year old boy killed in a car accident. Similarly, a female 35-year old heart transplant recipient, who received the heart of a 24-year old call girl and topless dancer, experienced an incredible increase in her libido after surgery and took on some of the call girl's prior sexual proclivities. So in whatever way you live this will be imprinted within your Qi. If you imprint your Qi with a new character trait developed during meditation, then you can slowly reprogram yourself to build a new character.

The more you act or become a certain way in terms of character traits, personality and emotions, the more this will become imprinted on your Qi. This is what changes your fortune and personality since they are not set in stone. If you try to change, transform, purify or override your "basic programming" through immeasurable meditations – such as of infinite joy, courage, confidence, authority, leadership, cheerfulness, love, kindness, mirth, humbleness, vigor, generosity, adaptability, optimism, serenity, patience, carefulness, goodwill and so on – you can certainly do so.

You can use this method to inculcate a virtue that you lack, or try to overcome some of your character defects. This is a way, in addition to mental watching, that helps you change your behavior. On the spiritual trail you should try to cultivate so that you become full of virtues while eliminating bad behaviors. Only firm resolve, by daily using a method such as this, can help someone eliminate their personality flaws and enhance their desired virtues. Benjamin Franklin did this as did Yuan Liao Fan, and their stories and methods are found in *Color Me Confucius*.

When you see Buddhist monks with a naturally joyous temperament, many times it is because they consistently practiced the infinite joy practice of Buddhism (one of the four immeasurables) in a previous life and thereby created for themselves that personality trait in this life, or practiced it in this life. Similarly, women who are especially attractive in this life usually cultivated certain behaviors and emotions in a previous life that bore the fruit of being beautiful in this one.

If you wish to become more beautiful/attractive *now* and in the next life there are certain things you can do. First, you can donate to charities like Operation Smile or Smile Train (that fix cleft palates) to set up karmic causes for beauty. Second, you can also cultivate the emotions of happiness and joy that you express in your face since this is extremely attractive to men regardless of anyone's physical appearances. Negative attitudes, on the other hand, can ruin your complexion by making lines and creases appear on your face. If you practice the infinite joy meditation while smiling and feeling happy, and project it outwards, this *will* make you more beautiful to others.

Patti Stranger, the "Millionaire Matchmaker," wrote that highly eligible, rich men were looking for happy vibrant women without an attitude who smile and have joy in life, so by cultivating those characteristics in this life through this "immeasurable happiness meditation" you will not only improve current circumstance but set up the karmic causes for more beauty in the next.

Deity yoga is similar to Buddha mindfulness practice. In deity yoga you are also supposed to practice imagining that you become a perfect being with special qualities and energy in order to also cultivate your Qi, which is a similar practice. Here a Buddha is replaced by a deity, and of course if the deity is enlightened that means they are a Buddha. The deity you use for your practice is called a *yidam*.

Various groups of enlightened masters specialize in responding to any Qi practice for a particular deity *yidam*. During deity yoga meditation practice, you are to identify your own form, attributes and mind with those of the deity for the purpose of transformation. Sound familiar? This is Buddha mindfulness. Examples of *yidams* include the meditation deities Chakrasamvara, Kalachakra, Hevajra, Yamantaka, Vajrayogini, Hevajra, Guhyasamaja, Marici, Vajrasattva, Tara, Avalokitesvara, and Kalachakra, all of whom have sadhanas for this type of practice.

In deity yoga, which is a form of Buddha mindfulness as well as Qi cultivation, there is a generation stage and completion stage of practice. During the generation stage of practice, a practitioner establishes a strong familiarity with the *yidam*, deity or Buddha by means of visualization and a high level of concentration. During the completion stage of practice, a practitioner focuses on methods to "actualize the transformation of their mindstream and body into the meditation Deity by meditation and yogic techniques of energy-control." Thus you can see how this type of practice ends up basically being Qi, Prana or kundalini cultivation that starts with Buddha mindfulness efforts.

In terms of Buddha mindfulness you are supposed to visualize, concentrate on and then "link" with the Qi of the individual you are focusing on in order that they recognize this fact, generate a *nirmanakaya* to enter into you in response in order to help transform your inner Qi body, or help you change your thoughts and behavior. When an ordinary electromagnetic field enters the body it causes charges to move and currents to flow, whereas if a spiritual being enters your body and moves his or her Qi, it causes your Qi/Prana to move and purify.

This is the basic method that masters use to help students "purify," transform or spiritualize their Qi so that they can generate the independent subtle body and higher. This is the secret basis behind nearly every spiritual path of cultivation. It is hard to stir or activate your Qi just on your own without engaging in a lot of *tapas*, or cultivation work. Therefore other beings have to enter into your body and use their own Qi/Prana to help you.

If you are trying to become like someone you admire, such as in the sports or business fields, you can employ the similar NLP method of modeling their behavior in order to try to duplicate their excellence. This entails copying their physiology (breathing and posture), beliefs, strategies, behavioral patterns, and how they do things. Actors do this all the time, and you can also change your Qi/aura in this manner if you consistently try to cultivate what you feel inside your body as the emotion or characteristic you want to develop.

Writers who like the style of famous authors can learn to write that way if they continuously read their books and write out entire sections of their literature over and over again until they've copied their style to some extent. Singers also commonly do this as well. With Buddha mindfulness you simply link with a Buddha's behavior and Qi in hopes that this will turn into a significant form of Qi purification/cultivation.

(2) Mindfulness of the Dharma (Teachings) is like jnana yoga and involves studying cultivation teachings deeply enough to follow cultivation ways in almost everything you do. Success in dharma mindfulness uses the road of understanding spiritual teachings and always applies them everywhere to help you learn mental detachment and cultivate a proper mind and behavior. *Color Me Confucius* teaches the proper way to do this.

When you study spiritual teachings and combine your understanding with how to run your life, this is dharma practice or dharma mindfulness. It is to be aware of the dharma at every moment in time, which requires that you must constantly watch your thoughts. Hence it involves a form of constant witnessing meditation practice.

An example of dharma mindfulness is where you always recognize the inherent selflessness of phenomena (because everything is connected), the emptiness of the ego since you are simply Knowledge knowing Knowledge, and the illusive nature of reality (because your own thoughts spin the world you see) so as to always be letting go of holding onto your thoughts and conceptions. Then you are mentally cultivating emptiness naturally.

You also won't take things so seriously when you understand this view perfectly. Thus the ability to laugh at yourself and not take yourself too seriously, the ability to take the ups and downs of life and say "So what?" falls into this category of practice.

By always remembering dharma teachings, you will develop a free and fluid mind that can detach from thoughts, but focus and concentrate when necessary. When you are clear about the contents of your mind but don't cling to them, this is real life meditation practice. Mastery of this method will lead to clarity, which is what various schools call awareness cultivation or the development of a pristine mind.

(3) Mindfulness of the Sangha practice involves relying upon an

accomplished living master or saint, or groups of accomplished monks in a living tradition, for your own spiritual progress. To succeed in attaining the subtle body you definitely need to find an enlightened teacher, and many traditions will serve. It is a big secret that many chief rabbis, Eastern Orthodox Christian monks, Sufis, swamis, sadgurus and so on are enlightened. Even some martial artists attain enlightenment who latch onto good masters to practice meditation, and inner energy work. The misdirection of the Zen school makes everyone think it only has to do with the mind whereas cultivation progress stages have to do with body attainments.

The Zen school literature has promoted so many wrong notions that many people have been led astray and squander years in fruitless Zen practice without cultivating their inner energy, which they'll then have to do after they pass away. All the Zen stories lead you to mistakenly believe that enlightenment is some type of mental realization, whereas it really means that you attain the subtle body. Everyone who has spiritual bodies knows who else has attained those stages and who has not. Thus no one has to be "tested" on their enlightenment as you find in Zen stories because all the masters know who has attained the requisite spiritual bodies. Practitioners don't have to "realize their original nature." They simply attain the subtle body and presto they are enlightened and have entered the stream of higher body attainments.

The point is that you need to find a tradition containing many enlightened monks/masters, or an enlightened master who will help you transform your Qi and channels with inner energy work and sponsor you through the Twelve Years of kundalini transformations. They don't have to be eastern yogis, swamis, gurus or masters. Many western individuals, such as Padre Pio, Seraphim of Sarov, and Hazrat Babajan attained the Tao. Once enlightened masters collect deva students around them who will work with them to help you transform your Qi and Qi channels within your body. The masters of every school and tradition do this, without exception, but regular people don't know this until the afterlife when everyone sees what is really going on and then takes up the proper religious/spiritual practices.

For this effort, in my personal opinion it is better to associate with a large spiritual tradition of known successes rather than a layman spiritual master. Furthermore, it is best to be located near a large temple or spiritual center with many monks or sadhus, and it is especially useful to be in a country with a tradition of countless masters such as India, Bhutan or Tibet. Ramana Maharshi's ashram, located near the holy hill of Mount Arunachala that hosts the Annamalaiyar Temple, is a perfect example. Maharshi would say that the mountain was holy, but through misdirection he was actually referring to the many devas and masters of the Annamalaiyar Temple who help practitioners. As to the mountain itself it is nothing special at all. If you are located or spend time near such a temple with lots of devas undergoing practice, they will help your practice efforts, which is the secret of places like Arunachala and famous monasteries or other cultivation centers.

Many of the patriarchs of the Eastern Orthodox Christian churches have attained the higher bodies, as have some of the Chief Rabbis of countries, Chief Muftis and the heads of the Buddhist councils for most countries too. They just won't tell you, and it is standard practice to deny it. In mindfulness of the sangha practice you rely on these living enlightened teachers and their associated body of accomplished monks/nuns for instructions, guidance and Qi/Prana cultivation help (rather than Shiva, Buddha, Jesus, Guru Nanak, Padmasambhava etcetera) to attain the subtle body.

One version of sangha mindfulness, similar to Buddha mindfulness, is to intensely visualize a living or deceased spiritual master who had gained enlightenment and identify with them in your mind, which makes them know of your effort and often prompts them to send Qi (generate a *nirmanakaya* that possesses you) to help transform your own Qi/Prana. This is Buddha mindfulness practice, but because the master is an unknown rather than a recognized bigwig it is considered sangha mindfulness practice even though he or she are actually enlightened.

(4) Mindfulness of Discipline and Virtue practice, which is emphasized by Confucianism, Greek Stoicism, Christianity and Vinaya Buddhism, involves a constant witnessing of your mind so that you can immediately cut off mental faults and errant behavior when you see them occurring. Thus you will cultivate a detached, cleaner mental state of purity by always watching/policing and correcting your mind. You basically watch your thoughts all the time and when you notice errant behavior you stop it. You immediately cut it off. When you notice errant thoughts you immediately cut them off or transform them into something else. *Color Me Confucius* lists many of the major ways to do so.

Furthermore, you try to enrich every action with good thoughts and emotions (*samskaras*) whenever appropriate so as to slowly beautify your character. For example, if you eat food you should try to do so with a sense of gratitude that expresses deep emotional thanks for how difficult it is to produce it. Positive emotions added to your actions as a type of consistent, deep impregnation – instead of a fleeting transitory thought – help to make actions more benevolent. This will change your karma, although in some situations you want to train to act automatically without any extra thoughts or emotions at all. Martial arts are an easily understood example of this.

The mind has two types of functions you should try to master through cultivation – deliberate thoughts you create through intention, and automatic or unintentional thoughts. You have to learn how to control both of these although the most difficult to conquer are the habitual or unintentional thought processes that automatically arise when you encounter phenomena. In *Color Me Confucius* I show how to master the automatic afflictions that usually arise in an untamed mind.

This spiritual road can also be called Mindfulness of Morality practice, which can purify a person's Qi just by itself. The meditation practice of cessation and observation (witnessing) is a form of morality mindfulness, and the Confucian practice of self-correction (so as to avoid behavioral mistakes) and Buddhist Vinaya self-policing also fall within this practice technique. This road is described in *Move Forward: Powerful Strategies for Creating Better Outcomes in Life* as well as *Color Me Confucius* and *Meditation Case Studies*.

(5) Mindfulness of Giving or Generosity practice is like the path of Karma Yoga and Action Yoga. It entails forgetting yourself and your own needs while cultivating benevolence, good deeds, and acts of charity and beneficence for others. It involves giving up self-centeredness to cultivate kindness, compassion, and unselfish giving.

Mindfulness of giving/charity also involves cultivating a detached state of mind that always lets go of thoughts. You can attain mental peace by not holding onto thoughts but by giving them away, and through this route you can cultivate mental emptiness. Christianity especially emphasizes this pathway.

Weeding a garden will enable flowers to grow without encumbrance, and this removal of weeds (symbolizing errors in behavior) is equivalent to mindfulness of discipline and virtue practice. If you add fertilizer to the garden, which is akin to mindfulness of giving practice (and efforts such as the authority cultivation method previously described) this will also produce an uncountable number of blossoms.

In other words, mindfulness of giving also means to actively *go out of your way* to perform acts of charity and good deeds wherever you are. John Wesley accordingly said,

> "Do all the good you can,
> By all the means you can,
> In all the ways you can,
> In all the places you can,
> At all the times you can,
> To all the people you can,
> As long as ever you can."

This nicely encapsulate the principles of mindfulness of giving practice. When you make contributions to various philanthropic charities, or lend your time and energy to some good cause, or simply help a neighbor or friend in need, this is mindfulness of giving practice. When you help any worthwhile effort, this is mindfulness of giving practice too. All these types of giving will create for you great good karma in the future.

What do you think you do when you become a Bodhisattva or Buddha? With the ability to generate *nirmanakaya* projection bodies you therefore emanate countless bodies to help those in need by giving them thoughts, energy as in healing, or emotional support such as fearlessness, confidence, feelings of secuoirty/safety and strength. Or, you can give people mental peace too. These are all mindfulness of giving/offering practice, also known as Karma Yoga. Such giving is the major occupation of a Buddha or Bodhisattva. By practicing to do this now you build up the merit to become a Buddha and practice the results of having become a Buddha. Whenever you practice generosity to others you are indeed a Buddha.

According to Buddhism the three types of offering include giving others Teachings (Dharma), Wealth/Resources, and Fearlessness. Fearlessness means giving people confidence, courage, motivation and emotional support. You should start to practice all these forms of charity.

(6) Mindfulness of Heaven (also known as Mindfulness of Deities) practice, as exemplified best in Hinduism and Christianity, is another road where you devote yourself to good conduct, virtuous ways and personal purification so that you will ascend to Heaven upon death, and then be able to make spiritual progress from there.

In mindfulness of Heaven practice you basically work on perfecting your behavior and doing lots of good deeds so that you are definitely reborn in Heaven rather than a lower realm. You devote yourself to purifying and uplifting your mind and behavior. Christianity teaches this road of cultivation, and if you become an enlightened priest, monk/nun, bishop, archbishop, patriarch or pope it is sad that this is practically the only road for leading people upwards other than *theosis* (divinization).

Once an individual becomes an inhabitant of Heaven, which means you die and become a deva along with everyone else who dies, he or she can then use their more fortuitous circumstances to make upward progress in their spiritual cultivation. Hence, this road of practice means to become a good person and do good deeds so that you are reborn in

Heaven, and there you can cultivate the real dharma for further progress.

Since for most of human history the average lifespan was only forty years, to attain the Tao (the deva body) before death would require you to use the proper practices and to start spiritual cultivation at a young age. Since most people start late and since most people (99+%) will never attain the Tao during their life, their target should be a heavenly rebirth after dying due to good behavior where they will have access to better teachings and a chance to make this progress due to better circumstances.

Therefore most masters do not talk about kundalini yoga, *nei-gong*, *anapana*, Vajrayana, etc. teachings (which cause troubles to arise) and instead focus on just teaching people meditation, which by itself achieves inferior results but positive results nonetheless. Another reason not to introduce such teachings is to prevent people from attracting the involvement of devas that is sure to happen when you engage in the road of energy work, as the Twelve Year kundalini transformation period is simply hellish, which is why few describe anything about it.

(7) Mindfulness of Breath, Vital Energy, Qi or Prana practice, such as *anapana*, *qi-gong*, *nei-gong*, *nei-dan*, kundalini yoga, inner heat yoga, *kriya* yoga and pranayama exercises, involves breath control and breathing exercises to help open up your Qi channels, usually by force. It also means using your will to move your Qi/Prana throughout your body, guiding it everywhere to open up sectional areas.

Most individuals do not know that breathing practice also means moving the Qi/Prana within your body by using your will. Nearly all the esoteric techniques for transforming your body have breathing practices as their foundation since they are the basis of inner energy work; you can use your respiration to move your Qi (*qi-gong*) and then eventually train in using your will (thoughts) to move it where you want (*nei-gong*).

The *kumbhaka* pranayama breathing practices, where you hold/retain your breath, are especially recommended for opening up your Qi channels and getting this process started, but you must also practice all sorts of *anapana* practice as well where you try to move your Qi/Prana within you.

With *anapana* you try to feel the Qi in every part/segment of your body when you breath in and out, and then you try to move it to open "blocked" areas. This too is cultivating your Qi and channels, as explained in *Nyasa Yoga*. In *anapana*, "hot" and "cool" breath means Yang Qi and Yin Qi respectively. *Internal Martial Arts Nei-gong* provides some minor *anapana* exercises for smoothing your Qi/Prana when your body feels uncomfortable.

Any type of exercise where you attempt to become aware of the Qi or energy of your body, and then try to move it in various ways and control it, falls into this category of practice, so it includes *kriya* yoga, kundalini yoga, raja yoga and so forth. Qi/Prana practice is breathing practice, breathwork or vital energy work and inner energy work is breathing practice. In other words, breathwork should be Qi/Prana practice although you should start with respiratory breathing and the feelings it generates within your body. In cultivation one proceeds from *qi-gong*, which is breathwork involved with respiration, to *nei-gong*, which is internal energy work that involves moving your Qi or Prana.

This type of Yoga is actually the basic transformational yoga of the spiritual path in each and every religion! Chanting, prayer recitation, mantra practice and so on, because they move your breath and thus your Qi in a rhythmical fashion, are basically breathing practices, namely the road of mindfulness of breathing/Qi. The entire process of generating a subtle body involves cultivating (purifying or transforming) your Qi so that the inner deva body can finally leave your physical shell whenever you want, but you have to pass from external breathing practices to internal energy work to attain this achievement.

During the Twelve Years of kundalini transformation countless spiritual masters and their students are constantly passing in and out of your body and moving their Qi everywhere in order to purify your own. This requires them to gain control of the Qi movements within their bodies, which devas train at doing all the time, so you can and should start practicing this now as the *nei-gong* Yoga of the path. It is the basic Yoga of spiritual practice. This is the basic Yoga of the path. The spiritual path isn't just about empty mind meditation because the transformations necessary to your body involve Qi/Prana work. Empty mind practice helps those energy current movements to become initialized, but the Yoga work is Qi movement in the end.

(8) Mindfulness of Mental Peacefulness practice, which basically involves meditation practice that rests the mind, namely the aforementioned "empty mind" practice, is the basis of many spiritual schools. As explained in *Meditation Case Studies*, which provides several dozen emptiness or peacefulness practices based on the *Vijnana Bhairava* (see this book's Appendix), you mentally imitate the peaceful nature of *nirvana* enlightenment (the original nature) by letting go of the thoughts that arise in your consciousness. Then they will eventually die down and you will develop a degree of mental peace.

If you imagine that your mind is empty like space, or try to imagine your state of consciousness before you were even in existence, this type of no-thought meditation also falls into this practice category. It attempts to cultivate a type of empty consciousness and teach that peace is the mind's natural state. Imagining that you are simply space that lets everything arise and depart within it is also a mindfulness of peace practice. It simply means to practice meditations that cultivate a quiet, empty, peaceful state of mind.

What is missing in Vedanta, Buddhism, and other cultivation schools that talk about the non-dual stainless purity, motionlessness, and peacefulness of the original nature is that they neglect to directly link this to meditation practice. They miss this one step so you are supposed to figure this out. Your mind is to naturally be like this (called emptiness) but not inert in the sense that it blocks thoughts from being generated, which is ignorance. In other words, you don't cultivate having no thoughts, but *no clinging* to thoughts since this results in a reduction of wandering thoughts that we normally call "no-thought."

You should mentally let everything arise, just as does the original nature since It gave birth to Shakti that is always moving, but you shouldn't attach to mental going-ons. If negative afflictions arise you use skillfulness to cut them off or change them into something else. The natural state of the mind is clear and unmanifest, empty of thoughts, but it takes effort to realize its natural state of quiet peacefulness. When people mentally experience that state it's called "seeing the Tao" and some take the experience as realization but it is *not* enlightenment.

Mindfulness of mental peace practice does not mean to obstruct or suppress thoughts, but to let them go (don't cling to them) and not be bothered by them.

(9) Mindfulness of the Body practice involves cultivating the body in various ways such as through Yoga, the martial arts, dance, and other exercise modalities that eventually include our old friends, namely various *nei-gong* inner energy practices in order to transform your Qi and Qi channels.

Since the spiritual path is basically Yoga, this route includes all the body-based techniques of exercising your muscles and moving your Qi to open up your channels, ignite your kundalini and generate the subtle body. It involves body excellence and mastery of movement.

Here is the important issue. Since the subtle body is a perfect copy of your physical body, if you want your subtle body to be in great shape then you better work on perfecting the health and form of your physical body through manipulation, exercise and diet. You must also learn how to control the movements of your body, and its internal energy, using your mind.

If you are not in great shape that result won't happen overnight. Transforming your physical body begins with a better diet and an exercise program. Three books that might help get you started are *Internal Martial Arts Nei-gong*, *How to Detox Cleanse Your Body Quickly and Completely* and *Look Younger, Live Longer*.

(10) Mindfulness of Death practice is the final set of cultivation techniques from Shakyamuni Buddha's ten large categories, although by now you might correctly surmise there might be even more practice categories that he didn't mention. Mindfulness of death involves prompting you to let go of all thoughts and situations since they are impermanent, thus destined to leave (die), but also reminds you to take things seriously since you could die at any moment.

Mindfulness of death involves remembering that death takes away everything, you could die at any moment, and therefore you shouldn't tightly cling to things, especially the thoughts within your mind. This turns it into a type of meditation practice. Mindfulness of death leads to abandonment of mental clinging since you realize that you cannot take anything with you upon death. Furthermore, remembrance of death should motivate you to make life count, to do your best and strive to achieve or experience whatever you want to do and experience in life before you die. Your life should be bigger than it is, and mindfulness of death should help you abandon any fear that prevents you from being authentic to yourself and stepping out to do whatever is your true heart's desire. Live life like you're gonna die because one day you're gonna. That is mindfulness Sof death practice. Make life count!

Many death-based exercises fall into this category of practice. For instance, the Tibetan bardo practices are a related form of this road of practice used by those who are passing away.

Ramana Maharshi practiced a death meditation exercise where he imagined that his life was slowly withdrawing from his limbs, his senses were no longer functioning, and death was approaching. As he imagined that the flow of his thinking was beginning to stop and consciousness was disappearing, he would let go and remain in what simply was. This is a type of emptiness meditation that falls into this category.

Imagining a state of annihilation or extinction where you do not exist anymore (Zen: "What were you before your parents were born?"), thus producing a state of peace due to the release, is also a mindfulness of peacefulness or death cultivation practice.

Perhaps the most important type of mindfulness of death practice is recognizing that death is inevitable and then (1) making a will for your family so that things go smoothly upon your demise (buying sufficient life insurance as well), and (2) making a list of goals you want to achieve in life (so that it counts) or a bucket list of things you want to experience before dying and then working on them. Someone who wants to become a Buddha also (3) creates a set of vows, aspirations, missions or commitments that they would assume as a Buddha or Bodhisattva and which they start working on while alive.

THE SURANGAMA SUTRA

In the *Surangama Sutra*, Shakyamuni Buddha also revealed ten roads of practice that help individuals cultivate their bodies and Qi/Prana in order to help their spiritual cultivation. He stated:

"Some practitioners with unflagging resolution cultivate longevity through eating special foods and perfecting the diet of what they eat. When they have perfected this method of cultivation, they are known as earth-bound immortals.

"Some of these practitioners with unflagging resolution to cultivate longevity ingest special grasses and medicinal herbs to preserve their bodies and live a long life. When they have perfected this method of cultivation, they are known as flying immortals.

"Some of these practitioners with unflagging resolution ingest special minerals and stones to preserve their bodies and live long lives. When they have perfected this method of alchemy, they are known as roaming immortals.

"Some of these practitioners with unflagging resolution to cultivate longevity cultivate themselves by mastering their breathing and Qi. When they have perfected their Qi and Jing, they are known as space immortals.

"Some of these practitioners with unflagging resolution to cultivate longevity cultivate their saliva [the "sweet dew" salivary hormones produced at advanced meditation levels] and perfect the way of internal lubrication. When they have perfected this method, they are known as heavenly immortals.

"Some of these practitioners with unflagging resolution to cultivate longevity make themselves strong by absorbing the energy essences of the sun and moon. When they have perfected the inhalation of this purity, they are known as penetrating immortals.

"Some of these practitioners with unflagging resolution to cultivate longevity use mantras and special *nei-gong* (internal alchemy Qi exercises) cultivation techniques to preserve their bodies. When they have perfected this means of cultivation, they are known as immortals of the lesser way.

"Some of these practitioners with unflagging resolution to cultivate longevity master mental concentration and perfect the way of meditation to preserve their bodies. When they have perfected their method of mental concentration, they are known as illumination immortals.

"Some of these practitioners with unflagging resolution to cultivate longevity cultivate through sexual union to help preserve their bodies and live a long life. When they have perfected this method of cultivation to achieve harmonization, they are known as Jing immortals.

"Some of these practitioners with unflagging resolution to cultivate longevity cultivate the understanding of heavenly and earthly transformations which they apply to their bodies. When they have perfected their spiritual cultivation, they are known as immortals of the highest order."

These ten methods are extensively explained in *Look Younger, Live Longer* along with other anti-aging methods. Let's take an in-depth look at these ten basic methods Shakyamuni mentioned so that you can understand how to add them into your path of cultivation practice.

(1) Special Foods and Perfecting the Diet

The first method of supplemental practice, said Shakyamuni, is that you should follow a diet of special foods that will help you on the cultivation path. Basically you want to be eating nutrient-dense foods rather than junk foods.

There are foods you should avoid and foods you should eat that will supply the nutrition that is most beneficial for health and cultivation purposes. In particular, men need to avoid foods that stimulate sexual desire (garlic, ginger, onions, leeks, etc.) because if a man loses his semen and Qi through ejaculation then it won't be available to open up the Qi channels within his body.

From today's modern nutritional science we would also advise avoiding sugar-laden foods or foods that turn into glucose easily (such as the grains, rice, wheat and potatoes), foods that produce allergic reactions or sensitivities, GMO foods, bad fats rather than good fats, and junk foods which hurt your body rather than supply nutrients.

A cultivation diet would not necessarily be vegetarian but should indeed be biased toward organic fruits and vegetables that have many different colors (since the many colors indicate many different phytonutrients). The easiest way to ensure this would be to ingest superfood green or red powders either with freshly squeezed juices or liquids like rice milk, almond milk, etc.

Nucleotide-rich foods will also readily supply the food components necessary for RNA and DNA repair. Flooding the diet with nucleotide foods that make such repair easier would be a wise course of action.

Please see *Look Younger, Live Longer* for more details. One update ... the best supplement for natural vitamin D is probably Blue Ice Fermented Cod Liver Oil (GreenPasture.org), which should be used for long-term darkness retreats.

The general rule to "eat healthy" is compounded by the fact there are many competing notions on what type of diet is best (raw food, vegan, vegetarian, no sugar, no wheat, no GMOs, etc.) that it is difficult to separate wisdom from radicalism. Along these lines I prefer the balanced food guidelines espoused by the Price Pottenger Foundation: eat whole, fresh, unprocessed (non-GMO) natural foods; eat only foods that will spoil; eat naturally raised or wild proteins (fish, chicken, beef, etc.); eat whole (full-fat), naturally produced milk products, preferably raw milk and fermented products such as whole yoghurt, kefir, whole cheese and fresh raw sour cream; use only traditional fats and oils (butter, animal fats, extra virgin olive oil, expeller pressed sesame and flax oil, coconut oil, palm kernel oil and palm oil); take cod liver oil regularly to supply your body with vitamin A and D; eat fresh fruits and vegetables, preferably organic; eat whole grains and nuts (that have been prepared by soaking, sprouting or sour leavening to begin to neutralize phytic acid and other anti-nutrients); include enzyme-rich lacto-fermented vegetables, fruits, beverages and condiments in your diet on a regular basis; prepare homemade meat stocks from the bones of naturally raised animals; use herb teas; use spring water or filtered water for cooking (and bathing); use unrefined sea salt; use a variety of organic herbs and spices for cooking; use unrefined and natural sweeteners (in only mall amounts); cook in glass, stainless steel, or good quality enamelware.

(2) Special Grasses and Medicinal Herbs

Shakyamuni Buddha's second method of supplemental practices was to eat special herbs, plants and botanical substances for their biochemical health, longevity and cultivation benefits, as well as for their ability to stimulate your Yang Qi into arising. This includes many types of herbs, such as adaptogens, that help make you healthier by balancing your internal body chemistry. You can find a list in *Look Younger, Live Younger*. Modern nutritional science, Indian Rasayana practices, Indian Ayurveda and Traditional Chinese Medicine have also identified many herbs that can be helpful to the body for cultivation purposes.

(3) Special Minerals and Stones

The third supplemental practice which Shakyamuni Buddha mentioned was ingesting special metals and minerals. Here one can supplement the diet with some form of easily absorbable minerals such as Shilajit (which contains at least 85 minerals in ionic form as well as fulvic acid and humic acid), kelp tablets, colloidal mineral liquids and mineral concentrates. Some companies that at present produce superior mineral products include Purest Colloids, Trace Minerals Research, Marine Minerals, and Goldstake Minerals.

While pregnant, a mother-to-be should consumer bone broth soups so that their baby will have healthy joints, and Shilajit or other easily absorbable mineral products like kelp powder or green powders. By supplying a fetus with trace minerals and vitamins during gestation you maximize the chances for a perfect body to be formed without birth defects. However, a woman who wants to get pregnant should start any type of vitamin and mineral supplementation well before pregnancy.

(4) Mastering Your Breath and Qi (Prana or Vital Energy)

Shakyamuni Buddha said that the fourth type of supplemental practice for cultivation are breathing exercises. This includes breath retention techniques, inner Qi movement exercises, and Qi balancing techniques. These techniques should usually be practiced together with visualization efforts.

There are many types of breathing practices you can use in spiritual cultivation, most of which cultivate your Qi and Qi channels. The most important type are *kumbhaka* pranayama practices of breath retention since they use force to help you open up your Qi channels quickly, and don't require energy supplied by an etheric master. Using breath retention techniques is like using a match to ignite fire, in this case the potential energy in your body (known as kundalini or Yang Qi energy).

The second type of breathing exercises are Qi balancing techniques, such as taught in Taoism, and the alternate nostril breathing techniques of Yoga. You can find more on these techniques in the books *Nyasa Yoga* and *Internal Martial Arts Nei-gong*.

If you feel uncomfortable inside your body, you can use visualization practice together with your mind and will to move your Qi into those areas to smooth out the uncomfortable feelings. This is Qi balancing, namely *anapana* practice. The Six Healing Sounds of Taoism (see *Look Younger, Live Longer*) fall into this category, but most people do not practice them correctly because they do not move the Qi of their organs during practice. You must know how to move your Qi/Prana internally.

The *Geranda-Samhita* also contains eight *kumbhaka* pranayama techniques, called pots, which spiritual adherents are strongly advised to master to help along these lines. If you combine these *kumbhaka* methods with the nine-bottled wind pranayama technique from Tibet (as featured in *Visualization Power*), it can help you transform your Qi channels so that you attain a subtle body more quickly. A trick to being able to hold your breath much longer is to watch Youtube videos on freediving breathing exercises, and to use those techniques right before breath retention. This usually doubles the amount of time you can hold your breath. A good master who had many students would have them time their best retention periods each year, and give an award for the best performers as a sort of contest.

The famous *Hatha Yoga Pradipika* of Indian Yoga also contains many pranayama techniques stating, "Pranayama should be practiced daily so that impurities are driven out of the body and purification occurs. ... By proper practice of pranayama all your diseases will be eradicated. ... According to some teachers, pranayama alone removes internal impurities and therefore they hold pranayama in esteem and not any other cultivation techniques." This basically means that breath retention techniques will help you open up your Qi channels. Yoga is really the pursuit of being ale to control your muscles and Prana/Qi within your *nadis* (Qi channels).

Basically, pranayama will not just help to make your breathing more efficient, but will help you activate the vital energy life force (Qi/Prana) within your body, which is what is important, and therefore help to open up the energy pathways in all your tissues. This will help you activate your kundalini and thus generate a subtle body more quickly.

But pranayama isn't the only type of practice to employ. *Anapana*, and other *nei-gong* internal Qi movement techniques where you swish your Qi hundreds to thousands of times per day in selected areas of your body, moving it this way and that, constitute the basic Yoga practice of opening up Qi channels and strengthening your inner subtle body so that it can leave and return to your physical body as you wish. Sometimes you should move all the Qi in the entire right side of your body, and then the left, and then the top half followed by the bottom, or in your left arm or right arm or trunk or legs or head and so on. Devas practice Qi movement techniques like this all the time. If you want to develop the deva body then so should you.

You can concentrate on visualizing a flame or body of light in your body to ignite internal Qi movements, or strive to move your Qi this way and that, and sometimes you should just rest in emptiness while your Qi moves all on its own. There are many types of cultivation exercises for activating your Qi so that it can start the practice of subtle body purification.

(5) Cultivate Your Fluids and Saliva

The fifth method of supplemental practice is to cultivate your body's water element (fluids) such as saliva. This refers to cultivating your hormones by generating and swallowing a special sweet salivary hormone that is released during advanced stages of meditation practice. The *Hatha Yoga Pradipika* poetically refers to it saying, "The Yogi who drinks the pure stream of nectar from the head will become free of disease, attain longevity, and their body will soften and become as beautiful as a lotus stem."

You can also find mention of the meditation phenomenon of sweet saliva in Nan Huai-chin's *Tao and Longevity*, the medieval *Atalanta Fugiens*, and Swami Satyananda Saraswati's *A Systematic Course in the Ancient Tantric Techniques of Yoga and Kriya*.

Stimulating, collecting and swallowing your saliva, as commonly taught in Taoism, is another technique along these lines. However, the real meaning of this method is to cultivate the hormones of your body, which are a messaging system responsible for all sorts of chemical reactions that keep you physically functioning. By doing visualization and Qi movement exercises over your glands you will help to keep your glandular system healthy. To do so, you basically perform visualization practice on the glands within your body to send Qi to those areas, while spinning the Qi around them and within them. This will help to keep them healthy.

It is dangerous to try to manage your body's hormone levels through hormone supplements like testosterone or estrogen, but a number of adaptogen herbs can help you attain hormonal balance. Bodybuilders use steroids to change their bodies, and these are to be avoided as well except, of course, for medical purposes.

(6) Absorb the Essences of the Sun and Moon

The sixth method of supplemental practice Shakyamuni Buddha mentioned was to absorb the energies of the sun and moon, which means imagining that you absorb the pure Yin and Yang energies from celestial bodies, or the environment, in order to supplement your own Yin and Yang Qi energies. You basically try to absorb into your body the energy from the sun, moon, earth, stars, or planets.

This is typically just imagination, but an imagination effort that cultivates your Yin Qi or Yang Qi. Why is this an imagination? Because you are absorbing these energies all the time since they surround you and bathe your body constantly. How can thinking about absorbing them bathe you more or draw their energies into you? This is just another imagination-based practice to help you move your Qi/Prana.

To do this type of practice you can envision the light energies from the sun, moon or planets embracing your entire person (usually pouring in through the top of your head), reaching inside you as far as the bottom of your abdomen and pelvis (visually imagine energy filling your whole body), and giving you the feeling of being completely illuminated within and without. After you imagine that your body becomes filled with energy, you must imagine that your whole body become luminous and shines brightly with these energies whether they be Yang Qi (sun), Yin Qi (moon), Fire Qi (Mars), etcetera.

Other practices for absorbing energy from the sun, moon, stars or other planets involve actually, truly feeling those energies such as sunlight or moonlight. With these methods you must physically gaze at the sun, moon or stars (such as the Big Dipper or Polestar) in order to feel their energy and try to absorb their essences. To succeed with this method requires special conditions of time (such as the full moon for lunar energies) and place (high locations with clear skies), but some individuals work at it despite the difficulties.

Once again, this is a type of Qi cultivation practice, so it is important to use your mind and will to move the Qi within your body everywhere while (imagining) that you absorb these energies. Just trying to mentally absorb them, without inner Qi movement efforts, will do nothing for you. After all, your body is exposed to these lights and energies all the time without moving your Qi at all.

If you use any technique of trying to absorb Yang Qi you should also balance it with a practice of absorbing Yin Qi, such as the energy of the moon. *Nyasa Yoga* explains techniques for cultivating your Yin Qi. Tantras from India say, "Every male aspirant has to realize the latent Female Principle within himself, and only by becoming female is he entitled to worship the Supreme Being *(vaamaa bhuutvaa yajet paraam)*." The meaning is to cultivate one's Yin Qi, such as by imagining that you absorb the energy of the moon, imagining that you turn into a woman as a sexual fantasy or Qi cultivation technique, and so on which are all methods explained by tantric and Vajrayana masters.

The best results for absorbing lunar Yin energy are achieved around the full moon of each month when the lunar light is brightest. At that time you can best imagine you are absorbing/pulling the cool Yin Qi energy into your body through the top of your head and then also absorb lunar moonlight though the eyes, pulling it into the brain and sending it to the back of your head. An alternative is to pull the lunar energy into your heart-chest area or whole body, which is best.

When yogis in India sit under the hot sun while surrounded by cow dung fires, unbeknownst to you they are cultivating their Yin Qi at the same time otherwise they would not be able to stand the heat. When yogis in Tibet go out into the cold snow and try to raise their kundalini energy to melt it and keep warm, which Yoga schools call radiating inner fire, they are cultivating their Yang Qi at the same time, otherwise they would not be able to stand the cold. These are not absorption methods, but simply indicate Yin and Yang Qi types of cultivation.

There are both Sunlight and Moonlight Buddhas, which are enlightened people who help with all these techniques, and probably mantras for all these practices that call on them for help and assistance. Shingon Buddhism from Japan, incidentally, also has a cultivation method based on the planet Venus.

The basic idea of this technique is to augment your own Qi from the Qi of a greater celestial source, whether truly or just imagination, and to use that extra energy to help strengthen all the Qi atomic bonds within your body. This will create an extremely healthy body. There are two schools that especially have these absorption techniques – Chinese Taoism and Indian Yoga.

(7) Mantra and Special Cultivation Techniques

The seventh special cultivation method is to recite mantras. There are mantra practices that will help you to quiet your mind because reciting sounds while listening to them will definitely quiet your thoughts. There are also mantras that call on spiritual beings to help you activate and purify your Qi energies, which transforms your Qi.

The most effective mantra practices are Mantrayana and Nyasa exercises that help transform your body. Most people have never heard of Nyasa practices that combine mantra recitations with visualization efforts on body sections while you also try to visualize, feel and move the energy (Qi) within those regions. You try to move your energy in order to transform/purify the Qi channels in some vicinity. In Taoist practice you try to grab the Qi of a body region and move it hundreds to thousands of times in revolutions of various shapes thus performing all sorts of different types of Qi movements within your body.

An individual practicing Nyasa selects a part of their body, focuses on it with concentration while visualizing that it is either shining with light or changes color. They also recite a mantra (sometimes as if from within that location thus vibrating it) in order to move Qi to that area and open up the Qi channels in that immediate vicinity. When so doing you must try to physically *feel* that area being focused upon and the energy sensations within it.

Remember, you are trying to do Qi/Prana cultivation, not mantra recitation. You must continue working on each body part until one by one you have done this for all the sections of your body, and then you do your entire body as a single unity. Sometimes you also try to generate special emotions during the practice such as courage, excitement, liveliness and so on since they will help you generate Yang Qi during the practice.

All these techniques work to open up the Qi channels of your body, your *nadis*. By using visualization as the energizing, vitalizing, activation or innervation mechanism to move your Qi, you try to progressively increase the size of the body region affected until you can feel your Qi stimulated everywhere. You want to eventually cultivate the Qi of your entire body as a single unit, but to get to that point you have to start on smaller, more manageable sections as done in weightlifting. This type of work takes years.

You always try to stimulate, energize, stir up or move your Qi using this method, but you do so for smaller/fractional body sections until you can do the entire body completely as one whole. Once you reach a state of harmonious fullness of Qi because it feels balanced, you should let go of attaching (clinging) to those sensations and mentally rest in a blissful state so that your Qi channels will naturally open without any effort. The Qi that has just been activated/stimulated into moving will be what subsequently opens your channels.

As another example, when people are told to visualize that their body is a roaring pillar of fire (or on fire, etcetera) they should try to whip up all the energy within their body like a roaring or flickering fire, simultaneously give rise to a state of joy, and then keep that sensation of warm moving energy alive for as long as possible while visualizing that you are a fire. The ideal result is to have your Yang Qi warm energy start energetically moving everywhere like the blazing flames of a fire. In Tibetan Buddhism the monks and nuns practice generating heat as well through their own varieties of kundalini cultivation.

You can also imagine that a blazing fire is burning away your flesh and bones and eventually reveals a transparent, crystal clear perfect body beneath the final ashes, which is done in Jainism. While doing so, you should recite any special mantras connected with that technique because that will tell Buddhas and Bodhisattvas to send *nirmanakaya* and/or students to help you with your practice.

(8) Meditation

The eighth method of practice is simply the practice of meditation. You must meditate nearly every day in order to obtain the benefits of opening up your Qi channels to help create your deva body. Moslems, for instance, pray five times per day which is why many Sufis attain enlightenment due to spiritual practice of such frequency. Olympic athletes typically practice 5-6 hours per day, as do professional musicians. Only members within spiritual traditions usually have the time to devote themselves to such extensive efforts.

As previously stated, the best how-to meditation guides with a variety of techniques are within:

Color Me Confucius (Bodri)
Twenty-five Doors to Meditation: A Handbook for Entering Samadhi (Bodri and Lee)
Meditation and Its Practices: A Definitive Guide to Techniques and Traditions of Meditation in Yoga and Vedanta (Adiswarananda)
The Little Book of Meditation (Bodri)
Meditation Case Studies (Bodri)
Vijnana Bhairava

(9) Sexual Intercourse with Discipline

The ninth method of practice is sexual intercourse to help with cultivation practice, which is known as *karmamudra* in Vajrayana Buddhism. The Qi, Prana, life force or vital energy within your body can be stimulated or activated through sex to help open up your Qi channels and transform your physical and subtle bodies. This is one of the fastest ways to do so, and is practiced, along with kundalini yoga, by heavenly beings. The practical basis is to use the internal energies aroused by sex to flood all the sections of your body with energy, and you utilize sex to do so since it is already a basic biological function that normally gives rise to joy and internal energy movements. The *asanas* of lovemaking, in conjunction with the accompanying joy, bliss and passion, are to be used to produce a passionate flow of energy in the bodies of the partners.

The idea of using sexual intercourse as a cultivation practice is that a man and woman should have sex (without the man ejaculating to experience semen loss, although female orgasm is allowed) while experiencing sexual excitement so as to move their Qi and thereby open up their Qi channels due to its internal movements. Even sexual thoughts, which normally excite men and women, will cause someone's internal Qi to move. Physical sexual cultivation is far superior to imaginary sexual fantasies (*jnanamudra*), although fraught with appropriate dangers such as sickness, pregnancy, an abusive tendency to use others, and so forth. Despite Tibetan Buddhism teaching about *jnanamudra* you should not do it at all.

Different positions and tempos during love-making naturally cause your inner Qi energy to move. Good sex causes your Qi to arise and different sexual positions allow you to move that energy to different parts of your body. Your emotions are important in this process as different emotions cause different Qi flows to arise, so it isn't just the physical excitation/activity that matters.

For instance, practicing the four immeasurables of Buddhism (infinite joy, compassion, loving-kindness and equanimity) will cause your Yang Qi to arise within your body and will make an imprint on your long-term personality and behavior. Organ transplant stories prove that the character traits of the donor are sometimes transferred to the recipient due to being permeated with the Qi of the donor. Those emotional likes and dislikes sometimes get transferred to the recipient. That being the case, this means you can permeate your own Qi with emotions or traits you desire, and thus you can transform your personality and behavior in this life, and sculpt yourself for a better future life, by engaging in this type of cultivation practice.

To do so you are not supposed to just think about selected traits you wish to have but must *actually become them*. It is like an actor who has to play a certain movie role that imitates an individual, and who then starts walking, talking and thinking like the person they are to play so that their character traits become second-nature. Such activity will give rise to a certain type of Qi within your body, and your cells and subtle body will be imprinted with such traits as a permanent feature. In a similar vein, during sexual intercourse the passion, bliss and joy of sex should largely envelop you along with the emotion of love, and you can then use sexual intercourse as an activity for Qi cultivation.

This route of using sex to transform Qi channels is used in some spiritual traditions (Chinese Taoism, Vajrayana Buddhism and the Maithuna practices of Hindu kaula tantra yoga) to help transform the physical body. However, the effectiveness of the efforts decline tremendously if a man ejaculates because he will lose both his Jing and Qi in the process. Those are the essences one must retain in order to transform your Qi and open up your Qi channels. The pressure men feel from not having sex is pressure of the Qi channels being opened, so when men lose this energy they lose their chances for great cultivation progress. Hence, Yoga schools always emphasize that men should not lose or waste their semen.

(10) Matching with Earthly & Heavenly Conditions

The last method of practice mentioned by Shakyamuni Buddha was to match oneself with heavenly and earthly transformations because they involve Qi energies, and by matching with stronger Qi forces you can use them to open up your Qi channels.

Heavenly and earthly transformations refers to the influences of the four seasons as well as any local geographical *feng-shui* energies. It also refers to various astronomical phenomena since those energies definitely affect the Qi flowing within your subtle body. Furthermore, it refers to personal astrological influences too.

For this, astrological squares, oppositions and quincunxes represent forces fighting one another in a negative fashion while trines and conjunctions represent forces adding to one another in a beneficial, coherent fashion. Sextiles are not necessarily positive but typically represent a heavy mixing of planetary energies that produce a strong interaction. In any case, this method applied to astronomical or astrological phenomena is to swim with the tide, not against the current, and to use the strong energies of the tide to help transform the energies within your body.

Planetary and environmental influences can affect the Yin and Yang energies of your body, and therefore can help you open up your Qi channels or hurt you depending upon whether they are harmful or helpful and whether you accord with them or try to go against them. The idea of cultivation is to go along with nature and *use any natural beneficial energies to help open your Qi channels and transform your inner subtle body composed of Qi.* You should piggyback on free energy to your benefit.

The idea of matching yourself with earthly and cosmic conditions is therefore to use these energies (or any other you can identify) to help transform your Qi for the development of the inner subtle body, and thus you want to be swimming with the flow of these energies in a helpful fashion rather than fighting against them. Also, if you know you have an astrologically auspicious time to make progress cultivating your Qi by using some special type of practice technique then use it.

Chinese culture identifies earthly and heavenly forces using "ten heavenly stems" and "twelve earthly branches" while other cultures use planets or refer to the "five elements" (earth, wind, fire, water, space) to categorize them. There are also the different forces available during the different seasons. You want to use these powerful energies whenever possible to greatly supplement your Qi so that it helps open up your Qi channels. You must adjust your practices appropriately.

Success in spiritual cultivation is not about the number of books you read. *It is all a path of Yoga practices in the end, especially internal energy work practices!* Because of this, you need to set up a daily practice schedule of inner Qi work, along with meditation work, and stick to it through thick and thin. Consistency of complying with a practice schedule that involves you in a large variety of cultivation techniques *simultaneously* is what will bring the quickest results. Repeat: If you want quick practice results you should "simultaneously practice a large number of different cultivation techniques, each based on different principles for moving your Qi/Prana, on a consistent, regular basis."

Every day you need to recite mantras, practice meditation and pranayama, move your Qi by practicing inner energy exercises, maintain sexual discipline so you don't lose your internal energy, and try to become a better person. The inner energy work is most important because it takes years to build up the foundation of Qi channel cleansings before your real kundalini (Yang Qi) can awaken, but when it finally does then the deva body is assured in twelve years' time. To succeed at cultivating the subtle body, however, you must spend countless hours in meditation and doing energy work ahead of time, and you have to become a better person. The result comes from long meditation sessions after your Qi is somewhat purified, and from cumulative practice hours. The more work you do, especially when based upon different practice techniques, the better.

Spiritual cultivation is basically a process of devoted Yoga practice (such as these exercises) that essentially involves cultivating your mind and Qi. We can say this is mind-body practice, but all the talk about emptiness, consciousness, original nature and so on all comes down to doing special forms of Yoga in order to first generate the subtle body, or deva body that is the first dhyana attainment, while not clinging to your Qi and thoughts.

Once you can pop out of your physical body with a subtle body composed of Qi then the rest of any spiritual teachings can be easily obtained. Therefore you don't really need extensive religious teachings. You just have to be an ethical, virtuous, moral person or no one will help you attain the deva body. A Sufi, for instance, just needs to do the cultivation work that will ignite his kundalini and then after he pops out twelve years later he can get any teachings that aren't available in Islam. He will then be introduced to the *real teachings* that correct any mistaken notions he adopted because of Islam. The same goes for Christians, Jews, Buddhist, Hindus, Jains, Sikhs and so forth. Everyone discovers that their religion has false beliefs and errors ... big ones!

This is the same for anyone, so spiritual study is, in a sense, overrated other than teachings on ethics, morality, character training, values and virtuous behavior in accordance with wisdom. Remember that the virtue-driven life purifies your Qi as well. What is important is meditation, internal energy work and behavior – moral training. It's all about proper behavior. Virtuous behavior is important because as you will find when going through the difficult Twelve Year kundalini transformation period, many who already achieved the Tao have powers but are abusive assholes with little restraint.

Power corrupts everyone, including people who attain spiritual bodies. They sometimes become arrogant, self-centered, self-assured and abusive in behavior (which is normal for the elites in most societies) when they should become more interested in self-improvement and self-correction. A Buddha is someone who is devoted to helping others, and is always cultivating virtue and helpfulness rather than power, fame, status and so on. Just because someone is a monk or nun doesn't mean they are pure or proper.

If you don't transform/open up your Qi channels you won't transform your physical body to be able to generate the deva (subtle) body of Qi, which is the same as attaining any of the samadhi or dhyana mentioned in spiritual texts (when someone is in samadhi or trance it just means they are using their higher bodies to travel the spiritual realms, which is why they are non-responsive). You won't sufficiently purify the physical body that is the template for higher body vehicles of a more transcendental composition.

Enlightenment is actually a body attainment, and the concomitant "enlightened" mental attainment comes with that body attainment as the natural accompaniment. However, various spiritual texts are worded so that people think it's the other way around and work primarily on meditation to "purify consciousness." As a result of this "skillful means that deceives," most people who cannot succeed in this lifetime will still work at meditation and by watching their minds improve their behavior, which is needed for the path.

There are an incredible variety of spiritual practices you might use in your own cultivation. While professional musicians and athletes typically train several hours per day for six days a week, no one wants to spend that amount of time meditating each day. Compliance to a regular practice schedule, and boredom are issues. To simplify the decision process of what to practice, I always tell people what I wrote in *Move Forward*, which is that there are four or five basic methods (foundational cultivation exercises) that they should turn into a daily practice schedule if they possibly can. Those methods will get you 90% of the results. You have just been introduced to those basic techniques, although the book *Nyasa Yoga* contains even more information.

Each of these basic methods works to transform the body *based on entirely different principles*. You never know which cultivation principle or practice will work best for you, since everyone is different, so by using several methods together (each based on different principles of Qi purification) you will maximize your chances for success in attaining the subtle body quickly. Therefore, try to combine several methods together for the quickest results in igniting your kundalini, transforming your Qi and opening up your Qi channels. At the minimum you should be practicing meditation, mantra, pranayama and *nei-gong* (inner energy work) practices every day.

In Buddhism these are the "intensified yoga practices" that prepare you for the kundalini awakening, which then results in the Twelve Years period of advanced Qi transformations/purification, supervised by many masters with higher bodies, that finally produce the deva body of the first dhyana. If you engage in ardent cultivation work, your efforts are called "preparatory practices" before you attain the deva body.

COMBINE YOUR PRACTICES

We have already gone over many cultivation methods but here is a reminder of the most important.

The first of these methods is mantra practice, *japa* or prayer recitation, which doesn't require you to set up a special time period for practice. However, you should practice it in such a way that it becomes Mantrayana, or Mantra Yoga. You do this by trying to move the Qi in your body at the same time you recite the sounds, such as by feeling or moving it in different sections of your body according to the sounds.

Another derivative is to identify with a divine form, imaginatively feeling their energy within your body, while reciting a mantra or prayer to them, which is then Buddha mindfulness along with Qi cultivation. You can also just recite mantras to quiet your mind.

You can practice reciting mantras at any time and anywhere, but should try to practice a certain minimum number per day or for a certain time period per day. It is actually best to set up a regular practice schedule to recite at the same time each day and then the enlightened beings overseeing those mantras will more easily fit you into their schedule. Never forget to focus on your Qi during mantra practice instead of just mindlessly mouthing sounds over and over again, unless you just want to quiet your mind.

People always say reciting mantras calms your mind, but mantras also actually call on a particular Buddha family for assistance in flooding your body with Qi (enlightened beings move the Qi within your body by projecting *nirmanakaya* into you, and moving the Qi of that *nirmanakaya* to affect your own) to help purify it via transformation. If you think of your teacher while reciting then he/she will do so if enlightened.

You should pick several main mantras you consistently recite, although you should test new ones every now and then. Usually people feel warmth or energy moving inside them due to a mantra's usage, and that's the sign of a good mantra where the spiritual beings "behind it" are doing an active job. Of course their proficiency can change after a while, so periodically test new mantras too.

Many masters responsible for helping people who recite mantras don't really do a good job, which is why you should test mantras to see if they move your Qi. For quickest results, mantra practice should always be turned into Mantrayana practice, as explained within *Nyasa Yoga*, because this is the quickest way to use sound, visualization and the power of divinization to transform your inner subtle body of Qi using your own efforts rather than somebody else's energies. If you take this road you will get a good result even if spiritual beings do not help because your progress will come from your own athletic efforts in using your will to move your Qi around inside you and thereby purify your subtle body.

The second practice I recommend for everyone is some type of daily emptiness or witnessing meditation practice. If you want to succeed in attaining the subtle body, you *must* practice meditation. Specifically you must always be watching your mind in order to (a) calm your thoughts to reach a higher degree of inner mental quiet, (b) learn detachment from your thoughts, and (c) upgrade your behavior because of self-policing your thoughts and behavior.

Vipassana or mental witnessing practice is the practice people typically think of when they hear the word "meditation." You basically sit down and start watching your thoughts without adding any extra energy to the process, and in time they will die down. You stay mindful of the witnessing, so it is also called mindfulness, watching or observation. Sometimes the word "contemplation" is used, but it more properly means thinking about things in order to understand them or become wiser about them.

You must set up a schedule that forces you to do meditation every day if you want to succeed in spiritual cultivation. Several books have already been mentioned that teach this and other forms of practice.

To help transform your physical body, you should also do some form of *kumbhaka* (breath retention) pranayama breathing practices. Holding your breath forces Qi channels to open internally within your body. Every time you do *kumbhaka* pranayama practices you should record the amount of time you can hold your breath and you should keep a record of your progress in chart form. In that way you can challenge yourself to surpass previous retention records, and also visually see how you are progressing. Don't strain yourself so much that you hurt yourself, which can happen for pranayama retention exercises that require exertion. Visualizations that you are purifying your physical body can be added to breath retention exercises, and they should be ultimately followed by thought-free (emptiness) meditation work.

Next, you must also do some form of stretching exercise. This is absolutely essential because you want to stretch every muscle fiber to remove knots so that you smoothen the flow of energy within your body as much as possible. The body you have is the body shape you will get as a deva, only it will be composed of Qi energy. Therefore, work at exercise to improve its form and appearance if you want a better body.

To this end people normally practice yoga, Pilates, Foundation training, weightlifting, dance and the martial arts. I like to combine muscle exercises with Mantrayana and focused visualization on each of the muscles being worked on during a workout session. You can, of course, also easily do this with Yoga and Pilates or martial arts.

The point is to stretch every muscle so it can be seen with definition while doing visualization and Mantrayana practice on each one. You should do this work without stretching your muscles too. This will help you not only become healthier but prepare a base for the successful generation of the subtle body in the shortest time. When you are practicing, it helps to look at color-coded pictures of the muscles being stretched to help guide any visualization practices. *Visualization Power* teaches you how to do this.

During the stretching of your muscles you should try to move your Qi through them. Rotate your Qi, swish it, move it here and there, but try to energize it. As previously explained, the soft martial arts stretch muscles with movements but you should take these skills to the next level by matching their movements with Qi and breathwork. By adding visualization, energy work and Mantrayana onto a muscle as it is being moved/stretched you can open up all its Qi channels fastest and create the subtle body in less time than average.

You should practice pranayama, mantra and internal energy work *together* with stretching exercises to quickly transform your Qi and channels. This is what makes Yoga the effective spiritual practice vehicle it is intended to be. Pranayama, by itself alone, will force your Qi/Prana through your muscles.

All exercise routines should always include women learning kegel exercises and *mula bhandha* in order to open up Qi channels in the pelvic region. Men should practice *mula bandha* as well, even if monks.

For the fastest results in opening your Qi channels you must practice *nei-gong* and *nei-dan* exercises, which are internal energy movement routines of kundalini yoga involved with moving your Qi internally. Inner *nei-gong*, *nei-dan* or *anapana* exercises are practiced in order to move your Qi within your body parts, and thus purify your Qi/Prana and your body. Yogis practice hundreds to thousands of repetitious inner energy movements per day when undergoing certain training regimens such as *kriya* yoga and kundalini yoga. You can *move* your Qi/Prana along your muscles, or try to *excite* the Qi/Prana in every cell of a body section, or *feel* the Qi in entire sections, move it around like water or wind leading it everywhere, suffuse an area with the feeling of saturation and so on.

There are all sorts of methods you can try in order to bath all your cells with Qi, in a sense washing them over and over again.

Warning: the first few times you do this your body muscles may lock up the very next day where it feels impossible to move, but this is normal and quickly passes. It proves that Qi exists, otherwise you wouldn't get this response. *Meditation Cases Studies* goes over all sorts of physical results from this process. It also proves that you are working somewhat correctly. The techniques within *Nyasa Yoga* fall into these Qi movement practices.

You need to cultivate every individual part of your body – through mantra practices, breath retention pranayama exercises, stretching and so on to activate-stir-energize and then move your Prana/Qi to open up the *nadis* or Qi channels within all sections of your body. You can focus on large body sections (such as head, chest and lower body) or specific body appendages/parts (such as arms, legs, trunk, head, etc.). There are lots of ways to do this, and countless practices available.

The more you move your Qi along body parts as pathways, flooding your body sections with Qi as done in Nyasa yoga, kundalini yoga, *kriya* yoga or *nei-gong* the quicker you will open up your Qi channels and transform your physical nature. This is what prepares your body for the Twelve Year kundalini awakening. Remember that you must flood entire body sections, limbs and organs with Qi (using visualization, mantras or imagined energy movements powered by your thoughts and will) to activate your Qi and open up the pathways instead of visualizing single lines or points. There are countless techniques for doing this, and the books mentioned on tantric yoga reveal many methods.

Usually these techniques are kept secret because once you start doing them the devas will come to help, and they have absolutely no discipline in their behavior. They will f*ck you over in order to prove their stage of powers to their teacher. The devas are always eager for enjoyment, so they love to play with your thoughts and emotions to do so. Your health or other conditions are not their concern, so if you begin such work you need a master to protect you whom you can go to for help. The devas will practice giving you thoughts, emotions, visions, and making you do things under their control. They'll play all sorts of tricks on you for their training games such as making you believe certain people are enlightened. There is nothing you can do to prevent this living hell.

If you undergo the twelve-year kundalini transformation process to attain the subtle body, the suffering is even worse. The first one hundred days are usually terrible with lots of visions, hearing of voices, violent internal Qi movements, the arising of sexual desire, etcetera. You will usually be assigned a deva who is to go through the same process as you to attain his Causal body at the same time they are working on your subtle body, and who will therefore be your companion. If you are unlucky you will get one who is below average, and if lucky someone who is above average. Typically the Causal-bodied devas are talking through him, and he and others lower with just subtle bodies will be practicing using you, and Supra-Causal devas will be practicing using multiple bodies to handle everybody. At the early stages they will all pretend they are demons or ghosts to stimulate your Yin Qi from the fright. This system is wrong if you must go through this suffering to attain *moksha* or liberation, but this is it. The masters working on your body won't do so twenty-four hours per day for twelve years unless they are also having fun teaching their students, whom they treat as the primaries, so you are basically screwed if you go through the process and your teacher is incompetent at controlling them. Usually it's just monks or nuns who can make it through this process because the monastery system supports and protects them as they go through it.

For twelve years you can never trust anything devas say because they are always practicing mental control techniques and don't want you to know what is going on. They will often try to make your Yin Qi rise, which is why they put you through all sorts of worries, anxieties and frights such as disguising themselves as evil demons, devils and ghosts to provoke a Yin Qi response within you. At later stages you will seem to be mumbling or talking to yourself as they practice talking through you. They will make negative reactions arise within you all the time, so you really need to be a strong person to go through this. It is even tradition for them to warp your thoughts over time so that you hate your master and criticize other teachers by the end of the Twelve Year period, or think other people are enlightened who aren't.

Whatever you do, never start using pornography during this Twelve Year period because they will use all you have seen/watched against you to raise your sexual desire and basically destroy your vitality and body by stroking the impulse for sexual excess, such as masturbation. They themselves cannot rise above their own animal nature and they will end up destroying you as they use you for sexual cultivation teachings. The "Fifty Mara States" chapter of the *Surangama Sutra* even warns about this, so never get involved with pornography or imaginary sexual partners (*jnanamudra* teachings) as taught in Tibetan Buddhism, for all the visions of naked women and imaginary sexual partners that masters such as St. Anthony, Padre Pio, John Vianney, Swami Muktananda, Yeshe Tsogyel, etc. go through are fake. They are illusions put into your head during this process so that your Yang Qi arises, but when masters do this to teach their students they also become abusive of you. If you engage in that type of practice by constantly looking at pornography and visualizing a consort, devas will grab hold of you for their own practice efforts and make your life a living hell. In nature it is the alpha animals who have sex while the beta animals watch, so abandon the desire to watch pornography to eliminate lots of problems. Fifty percent of divorces even state that pornography was an issue.

Everything you have ever done in life – an accumulation of impressions – is stored in your brain neurons as memory, and Heaven (subtle-bodied devas, Causal-bodied devas, Supra-Causal-bodies devas, etcetera) makes a habit of reading what everyone has done in life by reviewing their memories, including what you cannot remember. This is why living masters know what you did in life, or know your thoughts. You can never hide anything from Heaven no matter how hard you try. Therefore, even if you are not a cultivator you should never engage in evil, bad, unwholesome deeds in life. All will be known because the spiritual beings around us ("in Heaven") are watching. They just laugh at people, which is why they have a tendency for abusing you during the Twelve Year kundalini period.

During the twelve-year period of kundalini changes your past deeds will all be brought up again and again especially those involving wrongs, guilt, shame, fright, inappropriateness, character flaws, past mistakes and so on. The memories will come up as well as feelings of guilt, shame and regret at the same time when devas use them for practice. The twelve-year period is so uncomfortable that masters never discuss it, and it's best to hitch yourself to a tradition early, that involves lots of *living* enlightened masters, if you want to go through it. Now you know why masters typically only teach self-awareness, yoga and meditation practice.

You must Protect and Prosper yourself during this time because devas will not protect you from anything but land you in trouble, just as the *Surangama Sutra* warns. If they gain control they will cause you to damage your health, body, wealth, relationships and nearly everything, and then laugh and leave. This is why spiritual masters have created the fictitious story that kundalini energy is too powerful for most people, would burn out their body, or create insanity. Rubbish and nonsense! It is devas that are the problem due to their lack of self-control, and their teachers who allow too much leeway because of the fun. If one of them causes you to do something stupid, or they do something new, it will probably be repeated 10,000 times with you as the sufferer, so you need a master nearby to protect you from such behavior. Such excesses are explained in the "Fifty Demon Mara States" section within the *Surangama Sutra*, included within *Meditation Case Studies*.

The problem becomes complicated as devas practice giving you thoughts, especially thoughts that cause your Yin Qi to arise (such as fear, guilt, shame, sadness, embarrassment, anxiety, despair, powerlessness, depression, sadness, discouragement, worry, etcetera) or thoughts that cause your Yang Qi to arise (such as pride, anger, reverence, joy, happiness, love, hope, sexual desire, etc.) as part of their training and in order to help purify your Qi/Prana. As Meher Baba explained, they will try to affect your thoughts and your emotions, which are harder to affect. Lacking restraint and self-control, they are like a hoard of animals or locusts without any concern of your circumstances, including your health, safety and job or relationships.

Both your Yin Qi and Yang Qi have to be transformed on the spiritual path in order that you attain a subtle body, and spiritual masters will work on cultivating your Yin Qi directly by stimulating their own Qi inside you while giving you Yin thoughts, and work on transforming your Yang Qi directly while giving you Yang-type thoughts. Or, they may work on your Yang Qi while giving you some Yin thoughts, or work on your Yin Qi while giving you some thoughts that raise your Yang Qi. They will mix thoughts and types of Qi but never let you know what is going on. You need a living master to protect you through this process, which is why usually only monks, nuns and sadhus or swamis, protected by their tradition, can stand it. Some go into retreat for years to pass through it. If your master is too old he may die while you go through it, so make sure you are involved in a tradition with lots of enlightened masters whom you know so that you have many helpers.

Masters will sometimes use one of their spiritual bodies to violently vibrate your Yang Qi while using another body to give you thoughts of worry or anxiety so that you generate some Yin Qi, and blend the two in various proportions to help you purify your subtle body. They themselves practice using multiple *nirmanakaya* to control your Qi and thoughts and emotions on different levels, disguising it as if coming from different individuals. This is the training to become a Buddha and use your multiple bodies. However, the methods used for training, by using you, are in my opinion unethical because they abusively go too far. People get hurt and many try to kill themselves. Devas justify all sorts of abuse because they have the power, you cannot do anything, and it's fun. The best way I can describe their behavior is by using the words abusive, arrogant, stupid, excessive and hubris.

Once you start doing kundalini cultivation types of inner energy work, masters will rush in with their students to teach, and will create all sorts of problems because their students take priority over you and they "have no skin in the game" (personal consequences or factors at risk) if they cause you harm, or cause you to do harmful things. They will just walk away. Who will protect you?

If you do something stupid because you succumb to their pressures then you will get hurt and they will just walk away laughing, so edit any of the strange impulses you feel compelled to do during the road of spiritual cultivation (such as yell during a church service, take drugs to see what it is like, write a strange letter, give *all* your money to the poor, hire a prostitute, etcetera). If you ever do something stupid or errant because of these influences, especially when you know it is wrong, they will endlessly try to cause you to repeat the same errant behavior during contests to see whose powers are stronger than your will, so don't ever do a single thing wrong, errant, stupid or of vice when under these influences. They will try to make you repeat unfortunate behaviors endless times. Damage, in most cases will be irreversible.

Most masters, knowing that you will not succeed on the spiritual path, therefore want you to stay away from the kundalini (Qi) cultivation techniques, which are the only things that get you the Tao (subtle body). They want you to stay away because you will have to deal with devas playing with your thoughts and energy and you won't be able to handle it. The honest truth is that you can move your Qi on your own, but your Qi usually moves *significantly* only because someone enters into you and uses their body of energy (moves his or her own Qi) to move your Qi.

Devas (what the West calls "angels" or "spirits") are around you every moment. They include people who have passed away such as your parents or ancestors and individuals born in Heaven. They know everything people think and do, so are used to looking down on (disrespecting) human beings when they see all the stupid, wrong and evil things being done everyday and all the crazy justifications people use for their behavior. The behavior of devas is not like we see in movies where angels are angelic. They are regular people who can see everything we do and eventually adopt the habit of looking down on and laughing at human stupidity in order to deal with seeing all the crap, crime and evil they see. Because of laughing at us all the time, and knowing that we don't know better at many of the cons going on, many develop an abusive condescending attitude of disrespect towards humans. They will attack you in hoards again and again under their own teacher's tutelage in order to practice reading your memories and giving you thoughts.

Devas under a master's training will practice giving human beings thoughts and emotions, or blocking them, or giving visions or dreams, or getting you to do things. Surprisingly they will ~~screw~~ f*ck you over for their own training purposes, without restraint, because they think that everything they do to you, including harm, is permissible since they can always walk away without personal consequences. There is nothing you can do or say to stop it unless you have a powerful group of enlightened masters as your protectors, so don't ever do anything foolish or you'll suffer the consequences. This topic is briefly explained in *Meditation Case Studies* and I wish to emphasize it again and again like Shakyamuni Buddha did in the *Surangama Sutra*.

This bothersome trouble is why no one ever discusses what goes on during the Twelve Year period of kundalini transformation during which hundreds of masters and their students will run their Qi throughout your body continuously 24 hours per day to purify its atoms, and put you through mental hell at the same time. Jesus went through it, Shakyamuni Buddha went through it, Naropa went through it, Abraham went through it, Yeshe Tsogyel went through it, Padre Pio went through it, Saint John Vianney went through it, Swami Muktananda went through it, everyone goes through it to attain the deva body – everyone without exception! No master will ever tell you what he or she went through because they don't want anyone to think they are schizophrenic or be scared away from the spiritual path, so they refer to it simply as a period of trial and tribulation. Shakyamuni Buddha revealed a little by giving a lecture on "Fifty Demon Mara States of Delusion" that appears within the *Surangama Sutra*. I translated this lesson in *Meditation Case Studies* while also providing many case studies of deva-caused illusions and mental problems such as voices in the head. *Meditation Case Studies* is non-denominational and because of its valuable contents should be given to ardent practitioners of every religion.

Once again, a kundalini awakening is not dangerous due to "awakened energies." What is dangerous is devas making you do things that harm your life. They will put you through wave after wave of mental anguish to test their powers during this period of time and to determine their skill level. This is why few masters tell you how to do internal energy practices but teach mantra, meditation or yoga instead. Otherwise you might become a candidate for abuse by devas who will then want to practice on you. Therefore it is best to do this only if you have an enlightened master who can subject them to some level of restraint. Note: most swamis, gurus, and masters are *not* enlightened.

As stated, Shakyamuni Buddha described what typically goes on during the Twelve Year period in the *Surangama Sutra* section of Demon Mara States, translated in *Meditation Case Studies*. As an example of the abuse you pass through, when Abraham of the Bible was going to sacrifice his son on an altar this event clearly indicates that he was going through the introductory phase of this Twelve Year period and was caught in a miar of deva manipulation and delusion. He was in a state of delusion controlled by devas and masters, for why else would you listen to someone and attempt such a crazy thing thinking it is the command of God?

Many such cases are described in *Meditation Case Studies* to help you stay away from harm. The case of Jesus being tempted by Satan and Shakyamuni Buddha being tested by Mara are just watered down descriptions of this Twelve Year process. Those stories just hint at what went on during a multi-year process, but by no means explain it clearly. You must protect yourself during this period from doing something wrong or harmful to yourself because the devas will try to force you to do so, and get you in trouble and walk away. Always protect yourself during this period.

When the control exerted over you feels coarse, akin to the "coarse thought" of the first dhyana, it is a deva making the effort. When the control is a little smoother, it is a product of third dhyana thought, namely a Causal body attainee who is exerting influence. When the control or thoughts that exert control over you are very smooth or fine, this is classed as the thought type of the fourth dhyana (or higher) and refers to a Supra-Causal or Immanence attainee demonstrating how to do it to his or her students. Those individuals have absolute control over others by using their *nirmanakaya*.

That was a long discussion of the dangers of the kundalini awakening period, but it had to be transmitted even if repetitive because Shakyamuni Buddha's warnings were not enough.

Moving on, next we have visualization, inner focus or concentration exercises to help develop mental stability and a "one-pointed mind." Many concentration methods teach you to practice keeping your mind on a topic for an extended period of time, and this helps to banish other wandering thoughts that might distract you. *Visualization Power*, *Sport Visualization for the Elite Athlete*, Tibetan sadhanas and Hindu deity sadhanas (of Kali, Heruka, Lakshmi, etc.) can help you practice this technique although they are also training vehicles for your emotions and Qi movement. The Vajrayogini sadhana, white skeleton visualization method, and concentrating on marma points and acupuncture meridians on your body are all good forms of visualization practice.

Some people are qualified for sexual cultivation (*karmamudra*) on the spiritual path, which means sexual activity with a partner to move your internal energy in tune with sexual activity. To be more efficient at this technique women should practice kegel exercises, and both genders should practice *mula bhandha* in order to open up Qi channels in the pelvic region. No one is qualified for this technique unless they also practice meditation and inner energy work, such as through using pranayama, *anapana*, kundalini yoga and the white skeleton visualization method. In the white skeleton visualization you visualize that your body and bones are burned by fire, turned into ashes, the ashes turn into dust and then drift off into emptiness until nothing is left. In some versions you move the Qi/Prana of your body around all your bone sand body tissues to generate the feeling of fire within.

With yogic determination, men should learn to be successful at karezza (coitus reservatus), which is lovemaking without ejaculation so that your energy is still available for opening up your Qi channels. Despite the attention to non-ejaculation, they should still fully experience the joy, excitement, physical bliss, passion and happiness of sex along with internal energy movements throughout the body that happen during intercourse.

Please see internet pictures related to "mapping emotions on the body" which show where we most feel emotions like love, happiness, anger, etcetera inside our bodies. According to these diagrams, love and happiness can be felt throughout our *entire* body, which is why sex - since it gives rise to such feelings/emotions - can be used as a powerful method to move your Qi/Prana and open up your Qi channels everywhere. In other words, it is a way to transform your body. Sex can indeed be used in cultivation to help open up your Qi channels if you "stay with the fire at the beginning and avoid the smoke at the end."

Male assists female and female assists male in this practice; both are trying to help the other move their Qi and feel physical bliss and sexual excitement during acts of sexual passion. Men must learn energy control and yogic control for this technique. During sex the couple are to saturate their body with the wondrous (blissful) feelings of Qi movement connected with sex, and are to absorb themselves in the bliss of sexual excitement and happiness that moves their Qi. The mantra "Ohm Ah Hung Lah Rah Tah Soh" is often used by those practicing sexual cultivation to open their Qi channels through that technique.

Buddhism says that Shakyamuni, before he left his palace to become a monk, was married and surrounded by dancing girls but was celibate and never slept with them. Before leaving the palace he is said to have used his superpowers to give his wife a child by pointing his finger at her. Of course this symbolized his penis, which means that he engaged in sexual intercourse. He gave his wife a son through sexual congress and ejaculation that caused pregnancy, not through superpowers, but you cannot say this out of respect. He was a normal guy.

Vajrayana Buddhism, Chinese Taoism and Indian Kaula Yoga paths allow/teach sexual practices so that people can use sex to internally move their Qi to help transform their Qi and channels, but to be qualified you need to do a tremendous amount of prerequisite work with the white skeleton visualization technique, *kumbhaka* pranayama and many *nei-gong* and kundalini yoga practices to start purifying your Qi. Without that foundation your efforts will be useless.

Lastly there are two practices that go hand-in-hand with any other techniques you may use. The first is study of cultivation dharma, as you are doing now, and the second is working on transforming your behavior using the methods within *Move Forward*, *Color Me Confucius* and

Culture, Country, City, Company, Person, Purpose, Passion, World. For instance, a wonderful method to emulate is the practice of King Kulashkekhara, a famous saintly king of ancient India who would carefully watch his own behavior during the day and then submit a report of what he did at the end of each working day to his deity. This was similar to Benjamin Franklin's and Yuan Liao Fan's method of character development. I suggest King Kulashkekhara's technique for every household.

Those who make character observation a daily practice, starting from a young age, will be able to better transform themselves into noble human beings. A ledger of merits and demerits, and using methods similar to the four immeasurables (ex. authority Qi projection), are ways to ennoble your character and life though constant witnessing, self-assessment, contemplation and self-exertion. In particular, if you work on perfecting your behavior in conjunction with practicing generosity you can become a person of consummate conduct, and thus qualified for help in attaining the deva body.

In short, your short set of daily cultivation practices, each which works to transform your Qi and/or consciousness according to different principles, best includes:

- Mantrayana or simple Mantra/Prayer recitation
- "Emptiness" and Witnessing Meditation
- *Kumbhaka* Pranayama
- Stretching exercises with attendant inner energy work (Yoga, Pilates, Martial Arts, etc.)
- Kundalini Yoga (Nyasa Yoga, Naropa's inner heat yoga, *kriya* yoga, *anapana, nei-dan* or *nei-gong* inner energy work to move your Qi)
- Visualization – Concentration exercises
- Liao Fan's Method for self-policing your behavior

In the field of investing, Benjamin Graham said he started selecting stocks by concentrating on thirteen important financial factors he had worked very hard to identify. After many years of experience he reduced his selection process down to seven or eight factors, and at the end of his career he had reduced it down to just two factors of significance that determined whether a stock was a good or bad buy.

In baseball Bill James reduced all the various player statistics primarily down to OBP, the percentage of time a player got on base (On Base Percentage) because concentrating on this one figure alone produced game wins. Through his simplification of principles down to the very basics he absolutely revolutionized baseball, and teams who followed his statistical guidance started producing winning streaks.

As another instance, in the field of horse race betting, Beyer's Speed Figure was developed to compare thoroughbred horses. Thoroughbreds run in all sorts of races of different lengths and different conditions so it is hard to compare their speeds, but past information from all the races of varying distances has been reduced down to a single speed figure.

The point from these examples is that there are thousands of things to study or practice in the field of spiritual cultivation but it primarily comes down to a simple three: inner energy work, meditation, and good behavior. Practice wise you have to do a lot of inner energy work to ignite the kundalini transformative process, but most schools emphasize meditation instead and ignore the inner energy work for transforming your body so that the subtle body can independently form. This deflection of interest is a giant mistake, and haunts schools such as Zen, Vedanta, Christianity, and so forth. People waste years of effort because they are not told to make efforts to cultivate their Qi/Prana.

Zen and Advaita Vedanta are particularly misleading in this regard, and most Zen/Advaita practitioners waste their lives meditating without ever doing the inner energy work that will bring them the first dhyana enlightenment, namely the subtle body attainment. In the heavenly realms the devas are all concentrating on energy work since they can make their bodies larger, smaller, lighter, heavier, etc. at will. Because they can move their energy in various ways they are always practicing energy work, and are the ones who will move the energy inside you and ignite your kundalini energies.

Remember that spiritual cultivation is a matter of generating bodies of higher transcendental substances that are, as a linked collection, called the *sambhogakaya* in Buddhism. The way Hatha Yoga explains this is that you have to resolve the constituents of the body back to their original essence, which actually means to spin out of the physical body a subtle body, to spin a Causal body composed of higher transcendental substance out of the subtle body, a Supra-Causal body of higher nature out of the Causal, an Immanence body out of the Supra-Causal, and so on. You "spin" a new body out of a lower one, like the Hindu legend of the gods stirring soma, because you have to revolve your Qi/Prana throughout your body over and over and over again for years to create an independent new body of higher transcendental substance.

The process is not limited to five bodies, but teachings will not go beyond these first five for a variety of reasons. Each body substance gets closer to the constituent primal energies of the universe since each is more refined or transcendental. Therefore you are resolving the constituents of the body back closer to their primordial energies every time you generate a new higher body vehicle. You can only see bodies at your level of existence and none of those at a higher energy level. With each new body your mind becomes clearer, and you attain extra body/energy capabilities pertinent to a body composed of the energy of a higher plane.

The *Mahabharata* of India says *pavitranam pavitram yo mangalanam ca mangalam* – "The closer we go to Him, the purer we become. And the farther we go from Him, the more we become vulnerable to impurities." You can interpret this in terms of body substances for there are entire realms where the beings are composed of transcendental substances far higher than our own, and therefore their body compositions are "closer to the original nature." The dense earthly plane is lowest of all, hence extremely impure.

Islam also reveals the five bodies of attainment, and talks about five planes of emanation that veil Allah, and which must be removed for us to see His face.

Confucianism says to trace all things back to their Source, the Supreme Ultimate. Confucianism also says we are to master the changes of phenomena, which Taoism also emphasizes. In particular, Taoism says we must investigate the transformations of nature and learn to manage them. We must understand how people normally behave and use our understanding (wisdom) to help guide them.

In Taoism, a main principle is that man can by observation and study learn the principles and energies that rule nature and then use them to transform his body, uplift his life, and even guide humanity to higher states of peace and prosperity. Those body transformations include not just better health but even such things as generating a subtle body.

As with Taoism, the school of Shaktism has both the goal of liberation and the goal of gaining ascendancy over the forces of nature. Therefore various masters of the Shakti path would investigate nature by carrying on experiments to gain a detailed knowledge of the workings of the cosmos. To them, personal salvation is too small a goal as they desire mastery over phenomena too. This is similar to the Taoist view.

The Kaula school of Hinduism has also adopted this viewpoint because it affirms a positive approach to spiritual cultivation, embracing all virtuous avenues as a means for spiritual evolution. In the Kaula school you don't need to be a sadhu or ascetic to succeed in spiritual cultivation. Laymen and laywomen can do so too. Sex, music, love, business dealings, art, social life, athletic pursuits, even food, are all possible helpmates for cultivation, spiritual evolution and the uplifting of mankind.

The Kaula school maintains that whatever is pleasant and positive can be integrated into the spiritual path, which does not have to be entirely ascetic or restrictive like Hinayana Buddhism. In the Kaula school the physical body is not an obstacle to be tortured through ascetic practices. It is considered a condensation of the energies of totality, and therefore a contracted form of the universe. In other words, it is a condensation of higher etheric forces that are therefore concealed within it, and this is what makes the spiritual path possible. The spiritual path, by letting you attain higher transcendental bodies through the hard work of personal effort, releases the higher energies from their mixture with the lower. This is basically the cultivation process in total.

The Aghori path of India reminds us, "Your body is not even a speck of a speck of dust when compared to the universe. When you have not yet understood the energies working within your body born out of human intercourse, then how can you possibly know anything about the workings of the universe born out of divine pulsation, and the energies that govern it? …

"Aghor is beyond Tantra. Right now you do not understand even the energies working within your body. These energies, on an infinite level, hold all of universe in all the ten directions and govern its function. He, who after understanding these energies on an infinite level attains command over them, is an Aghori or Aghoreshvar. But what would you know of this when you do not even understand the energies that reside within you and hold your entire existence together. Then to attain oneness with that ultimate reality, the source of these energies and the mother of all creation, Goddess Jagdamba, who resides beyond even these energies, is simply out of the question and several births away from you."[8] This is reminiscent of the demonstration given to Swami Rama.

In other words, even on the Aghori path, which most Hindus shun out of fear or disgust, you eventually master the various energies of the cosmos by also generating the transcendental bodies that progressively move you closer to the original nature, which in this school is called the Goddess Jagdamba.

In Mahayana Buddhism universal salvation for everyone is the goal. The vows of Buddhas and Bodhisattvas are emphasized because engaging in compassionate activity to help people is the entire goal of the cultivation path. Altruistic activity to help others is the practice of the path, the purpose of the path, and the result of the path. Such service exhibits success on the path. The Mahayana focuses on compassionate activity that makes helpful efforts for others. You try to

---

[8] Manoj Thakkar, Jayesh Rajpal & Nupur Agrawalp, *Aghori: A Biographical Novel* (Trident Book, India, 2017), p. 254.

succeed in cultivation in order to save others.

The Hinayana path focuses on strict disciplinary rules for managing your mind and behavior. The goal is to create merit to succeed in the path for yourself.

In Vajrayana Buddhism you are specifically taught how to tap into your Qi energies to ignite the kundalini within your body and quickly transform your Qi to attain the subtle body and higher. It focuses on Qi cultivation using inner energy work while the Mahayana focuses on meditation and altruistic behavior.

The idea in spiritual cultivation is not just to ignite spiritual energies within yourself, but guide them in a beneficial fashion to go through all your bones, joints, organs, body sections and tissues to help strengthen your inner Qi body so that it can eventually attain independence and leave your physical shell at will. This is how you attain the first of many higher bodies, namely the deva body. Once you generate that body, then you have to repeat the process with that new body to gain yet higher body attainments composed of even higher transcendental energies.

Spiritual practitioners devote their entire lives to this pursuit under the guidance of teachings to "clarify their mind" and "discover the source of consciousness, or "realize their original nature," but what it actually entails is body and energy Yoga. At the same time practitioners are working at meditation, their master and many others are using their own Qi to move the student's Qi in order to get the Qi transformation process started and keep it going.

Once attained, the question arises as to your life purpose with a nearly immortal body that gives you powers over lesser creatures who don't have your body attainments. Therefore the spiritual path also comes down to vows or commitments, ethics, morals, values, virtue and proper behavior. While the spiritual path is essentially the practice of Yoga, the end result should essentially be consummate conduct.

With successful spiritual cultivation you will attain a set of spiritual bodies that will live a very long time, so what do you want to do with those lives? Each body can do different things in different realms simultaneously, acting quite independently of each other. Think of the vows of the Buddhas and Bodhisattvas ... what is it you would want to accomplish?

In an infinite eternal universe with endless lives of reincarnation one after another, or one single life that lasts a very long time, this then becomes the crux of the issue. How will you spend your energies? What purposes or causes are worthy of you? What would be your vows or areas of interest? What do you want to do or achieve?

Why not start acting that way now and start accumulating the skills and merit to make it happen? Such is Buddha Yoga.

5
OPTIMAL PRACTICE SCHEDULES

What is the best training or practice schedule for spiritual cultivation? What should you be doing on a daily or seasonal basis throughout the year to get the best results since the weather, especially mugginess or humidity, can hamper the internal movements of your Qi/Prana?

In spiritual cultivation we want to obtain the maximum results for the most minimal efforts. We want the highest results in minimal time. We want to maximize the Qi/Prana results we can possibly get for the minimum amount of practice effort, especially since no one has the time (or interest) to practice. Therefore there is an optimal and non-optimal way to do things.

Since we want to find the optimal way that gets the best results with the smallest effort in the quickest time we should turn to the field of sports training for some insights. Sports training teaches how to train for maximum results in the safest, quickest and most advantageous ways.

Training should take into account fundamental principles just as when Benjamin Graham found he could reduce investing down to just two stock characteristics, and Billy Beane found that he could reduce hundreds of baseball considerations primarily down to OBP (on bas percentage), a sabermetric statistic invented by Bill James, to win baseball games. As previously explained, Andy Beyer, who was a horse racing columnist for the *Washington Daily News*, did a similar service for horse racing by coming up with a formula called the "Beyer Speed Figure" that basically incorporated all past racing information for a horse into a single speed estimate. All these men reduced hundreds of complicated factors down into just a few relevant principles for their decision making.

Why repeat this information? You have to understand that you should look at cultivation practice scientifically. Take all the information you've ever read and simplify it into *just a few basic principles of practice*, and rely primarily on those principles to guide yourself rather than many meaningless concerns or superstition. "What is this practice doing for my Qi, how can I improve that result, and how can I get a quicker and deeper result?" Remember, simplify everything down to a few fundamental principles to guide yourself and your practice. If you look at the matter in terms of fundamental principles instead of thousands of principles, and stay focused on applying those principles, then you can make progress.

What is our target in spiritual practice? Purification of your mental processes, a general quieting of your mind from the reduction of wandering thoughts, and transformation of the physical body (its Qi and channels) enough to prepare for the kundalini awakening that then initiates a Twelve Year period of Qi transformation before your subtle body can emerge. All the intensified yoga preparatory practices have the purpose of getting you ready to go through this Twelve Year period. They all involve cultivating your Qi/Prana and also involve various types of emptiness meditation.

What is the main preparatory pathway? Once again - inner energy work on the Qi throughout your body, and meditation (empty mind) practice. Don't forget making vows and engaging in better behavior.

What is the challenge to practice? Basically, no one wants to practice. Most of us practice infrequently, and we tend to practice incorrectly or just use one method when many would be better. Most importantly, meditation and Qi/Prana energy practice have a very low compliance rate. No one has a lot of time to practice and few people practice with consistency (or even correctly) because most of us just don't want to practice. Moslems are lucky in that they are forced to practice (pray) five times per day, which is why many succeed, and many Christian monks follow a monastery's schedule that causes them to regularly practice on a daily basis as well, but most of us rarely practice and don't want to practice.

Why? Because it is tedious, boring, monotonous, tiresome, routine, repetitive, uneventful, uninteresting. Therefore, continued compliance with a practice schedule is an issue. We need to either be forced into practice, or create variety that beckons us to become more interested in regular practice so that we voluntarily comply with a regular practice schedule.

Few people want to sit in meditation every day and try to empty their mind or watch their thoughts. It's boring, and they don't want to spare the time or make such an effort. To say it "produces bliss" is in most cases a lie as well because most people are uncomfortable sitting there. No one wants to do endless, repetitive energy work either especially if it seems that the practitioner isn't getting any results and the effort will require years. Hence people seek a master to supervise them and keep them on track, who should tell them what is going on and what they should do, but most masters won't tell you what it is all really about, which is generating the subtle body as the foundation of higher spiritual attainments.

The only people who can thus easily commit to a long-term schedule tend to be monks and nuns or other religious professionals who are supported (so they need not worry about an income) and *scheduled to practice on a daily basis* (typically under supervision) because they have to follow the rhythms of their monastery, nunnery or tradition. As explained, Islam is an exception because every Moslem prays (can practice cultivation) five times daily due to a schedule that *all* Moslems must follow.

Most people stop practicing because of boredom, monotony and the seeming lack of progress from just meditating. To motivate yourself to practice, you therefore need to inject some variety into your practice schedule. Along these lines, it therefore helps if you set up a number of multi-day special sadhanas (practices) to be performed one after the other, and start telling yourself "I must finish this special practice" when you are in the midst of one. This will help you to continue practicing until you are due to start a new sadhana. One after the other, the novelty will help pull you along to the progress you desire.

Sticking to cultivation practice over a long period of time is a fundamental problem, so how can we structure our practice effort in such a way that we maximize our staying power, and keep up the motivation to stick with meditation/cultivation training?

One method ensuring a higher compliance rate with practice is to join together with others to cultivate in a group that has a regular practice schedule. When Christians go to Church on Sunday this is the one hour per week that they will be "practicing," but are they really accomplishing anything significant in terms of Qi/Prana purification and mental quieting when they attend such infrequent, brief services? One hour per week can hardly be considered adequate spiritual practice if you have the objective of significantly changing your Qi and Qi channels. As explained, Moslems have it better because they adhere to the tradition of praying five times a day.

Another excellent method is when a master privately instructs a student to practice a particular method for a certain period of time, and then supervises their progress. Masters can train students through a progressive series of preparatory Qi work to prepare their bodies for a kundalini awakening in this way. This is done for monks, swamis, gurus, etc. in a variety of spiritual traditions and is akin to the process of a coach training professional athletes. This is a superior method for great spiritual masters to adopt, namely telling students, "I want you to do this particular practice so many times/hours per day for this amount of time. Then come back to me. Use this mantra when doing it."

A third way is for individuals to practice on their own quite regularly due to self-motivation. They must keep to a strict cultivation schedule via willpower just as athletes do when self-training. One great way to do this is to link specific forms of practice to the different days of the week, which adds variety to the overall routine. Variety breaks up monotony and will help you to continue practicing.

For instance, in weight-training people usually vary their workout according to the day of the week. Since inner Qi work to move your Qi everywhere (*anapana, nei-gong* or *kriya* yoga etcetera) is also time consuming because you must try to move/circulate/revolve and even wiggle your Qi/Prana hundreds to thousands of times per practice session, one way to do a really good job is to concentrate on smaller limited sections of the body on different days of the week as in weight-training. Then you will be sure to do the entire body one or more times per week instead of just partially doing it, with a very bad job, and then crapping out.

While one should always do full-body Qi/Prana cultivation at the end of such practices to link all your Qi together into one whole, and also end all Qi-based movement methods with emptiness meditation that lets go of thoughts and body sensations while resting in the comfortable body feelings generated, this type of routine is focused but incorporates variety. As a result of a limited focus on different body segments each day, you will have a higher chance of actually intensely concentrating on each different body section and transforming its Qi with whatever *anapana, nei-gong,* kundalini yoga, *kriya* yoga or Nyasa yoga practice you use. That's because this takes less time than doing the whole body, and hence you'll be more likely to complete the work. For some people, "Today I work on the lower section of my body," or "Today I work on my arms," "Today I work on my lower trunk," etc. is far more motivating and subject to continued effort than doing the same thing every day, getting tired at it and then stopping Qi-based work because of monotony and boredom.

At the end of such practice, always do full-body Qi practice, and then cap it off with emptiness meditation during which time you don't cling to the Qi movements or sensations within your body, but let them reach a state of harmony and balance on their own. Remember that devas can make their bodies of Qi larger, smaller, lighter or heavier. They are always practicing to attain control over every part of their energetic body. Therefore while practicing Qi control over parts of your body, don't forget to try to feel the Qi of your entire body during part of your practice session, which I am calling full-body Qi. *Nyasa Yoga* introduces a variety of single body unit Qi practices but you can surely make up your own.

Weight-training experts typically concentrate on exercising different muscle groups either once per week, twice per week, or three times per week. This gives their muscles a chance to sufficiently rest and recover between sessions. Now because *nei-gong anapana, kriya* yoga, kundalini yoga, Nyasa Yoga, etc. work on moving your Qi energy in a region and you need to repeat countless repetitions of Qi movement per day (as in martial arts training), most people will not finish a session that works on their entire body. They will get tired and then drop the entire practice. Therefore you can split up inner energy work into work on different sections of your body on different days of the week. But always end a session by trying to cultivate the Qi/Prana of your entire body as a single unit, as that is what devas train to do, and then engage in empty mind meditation practice at the end.

Remember the 80/20 rule that you want maximum gain for minimum effort - you want the lowest training frequencies that get the job done and you want to use 20% of the efforts or exercises that produce 80% of the results.

For your consideration, here are a few of the standard weight-training schedules that you can review to obtain ideas on how to segment the Qi/Prana cultivation work required on various parts of your body. Of course this is not directly applicable to cultivation work but is simply meant to give you some ideas of how you can break up the task of cultivating parts of your body on different days of the week:

The 3 Day Full Body Split:

Monday: Full Body Workout
Tuesday: off
Wednesday: Full Body Workout
Thursday: off
Friday: Full Body Workout
Saturday: off
Sunday: off

The 4 Day Upper/Lower Split:

Monday: Upper Body Workout
Tuesday: Lower Body Workout
Wednesday: off
Thursday: Upper Body Workout
Friday: Lower Body Workout
Saturday: off
Sunday: off

The 3 Day Upper/Lower Split:

Week 1
Monday: Upper Body Workout
Tuesday: off
Wednesday: Lower Body Workout
Thursday: off
Friday: Upper Body Workout
Saturday: off
Sunday: off

Week 2
Monday: Lower Body Workout
Tuesday: off
Wednesday: Upper Body Workout
Thursday: off
Friday: Lower Body Workout
Saturday: off
Sunday: off

The Rotating Push/Pull/Legs Split:

Week 1
Monday: Chest, Shoulders & Triceps
Tuesday: Back & Biceps
Wednesday: off
Thursday: Legs & Abs
Friday: off
Saturday: Chest, Shoulders & Triceps
Sunday: Back & Biceps
Week 2
Monday: off
Tuesday: Legs & Abs
Wednesday: off
Thursday: Chest, Shoulders & Triceps
Friday: Back & Biceps
Saturday: off
Sunday: Legs & Abs

The Push/Pull Split:

Week 1

Monday: Chest, Shoulders & Triceps + Quads & Calves
Tuesday: off
Wednesday: Back & Biceps + Hamstrings & Abs
Thursday: off
Friday: Chest, Shoulders & Triceps + Quads & Calves
Saturday: off
Sunday: off

Week 2
Monday: Back & Biceps + Hamstrings & Abs
Tuesday: off
Wednesday: Chest, Shoulders & Triceps + Quads & Calves
Thursday: off
Friday: Back & Biceps + Hamstrings & Abs
Saturday: off
Sunday: off

When doing Qi/Prana work within your body the point is that you can work on your body in sections. You can work on the right side of your body and then the left. You can work on the upper half and then the lower. You can work on just your arms, or just your hands in one day. You might work on just your pelvis, or spin, or head, or toes. You can work on seven different sections according to the nerves of your spine. There are all sorts of ways to partition practice schedules where you try to gain control of the Qi/Prana within your body and move it in a way that it washes through all the tissues within body regions. During the twelve years of a kundalini awakening, masters and their students will be doing this for you continuously, so during the stage of preparation, or intensified preparatory practices you should also be doing this type of work.

It is hard to keep up the motivation for this type of tiresome energy work, and for straight meditation too. Therefore, each type of cultivation method can benefit from a different type of motivational, inspirational impetus to help you continue doing the practice.

For mantra practice, the way to achieve this is by setting a minimum number of mantra recitations to do per day which you can count via prayer beads, a rosary or mechanical/electronic clicker. You can recite mantras anytime but if you make an effort to recite mantras *at the same time every day* this will help the enlightened beings overseeing that mantra to work you into their schedule more easily for Qi assistance. Any time you recite mantras long enough you will eventually attract the attention of enlightened masters who have undertaken a vow to respond to *that* mantra, and who will send you an etheric *nirmanakaya* copy of their body to enter inside you and help transform your Qi. This is why masters tell you to always "mantra

Buddha's name" or recite a specific mantra of some type that someone will respond to.

For pranayama, it should be performed on a daily basis several times per day. However, some people like to rest 1-2 days per week to give their body a chance to adapt to the stress. To increase adherence to maintaining *kumbhaka* pranayama breath retention practice – which no one likes to do – you must always challenge yourself by recording your average breath retention time, or best time for each practice session, and plot this on a graph. Every time you practice anew you should look at the graph and try to increase your breath retention holding period to surpass your previous best record. That's a form of motivation too.

For meditation practice, you need to commit to a daily practice effort and you can help maintain compliance by meditating at the same time every day, or by marking "practice done" on a calendar with an X, check mark or other mechanism. Some people like to increase the time they meditate more on weekends and less during the week.

These are all just various ideas as the best schedule is one you arrive at because you can follow it.

THE 24 SEASON CALENDAR

Chinese have a seasonal calendar, based on the dates of solstices and equinoxes, which segments the year into twenty-four two-week periods. Each period of two weeks corresponds to specific earth energies that regularly arise at that time of year to dominate the local environment. Each two-week period has its own specific characteristics including a typical weather pattern and periodic natural events that usually occur at that time in nature such as plant germinations, animal migrations and so on.

These periods are important because different types of cultivation work can benefit or be hampered by the local earth energies and the weather. For instance, the Indian monsoon season made it impossible to travel from one location to another, so Shakyamuni Buddha set up that period as a time during which monks should undergo a meditation retreat. This has become the annual three-month Vassa retreat practiced by Theravada Buddhists, which is based on the lunar calendar, and during which time monks typically devote themselves to intensive meditation practice in one location.

The principle is that a person should adjust their cultivation schedule at certain times of the year based on heavenly (astronomical or astrological) phenomena, earthly phenomena such as the weather, and also based on local circumstances. Adjustments should take into account the predominant energies of special periods and the weather within your location. Universal or local *feng-shui* energies are bigger than you, and can either help you or thwart your cultivation efforts. Try to use them in your practice. The big problem is fighting against humidity, which tends to hamper any efforts to move the Qi within you. This is why cultivators prefer arid, dry locations.

The idea of *feng-shui* is that the wind and water elements battle in nature and also within your body. Since the wind element represents your Qi and your body is composed of 70% water, finding harmonious conditions for cultivation always involves avoiding severe dampness and humidity. Under those adverse conditions your Qi/Prana has to struggle to move within your body to open up Qi channels (*nadis*), which is another reason Buddha designated the rainy season as a time to push especially hard for meditation progress. Sexual desire tends to arise at such times too.

Timing and locale are both important for progress in spiritual cultivation. Some times and locations are better for cultivation efforts than others. For instance, due to the weather your cultivation progress may be hampered at certain times of the year, but some locations are always blanketed with Qi that can help push open a practitioner's Qi channels, and some simply have more enlightened masters in the vicinity. Having more masters who reside in the vicinity is the most important factor for spiritual progress, which is why India is a particularly good place to cultivate.

In general, it makes sense to have a different cultivation emphasis during the four seasons of the year, which can be marked off in segments as short as one week or two weeks. One of the ways to do this is by using astronomical phenomena. One can also time their practice using personal astrological indications as well.

MOON

In astrology the moon represents the mind, females or femininity, Yin Qi, emotions, memory, receptivity, moodiness, sensitivity, mother, breasts, body fluids, uterus, water, beauty and Monday.

Since the moon has both waxing and waning periods that influence your internal energy in different ways, these two lunar periods can be used for specific cultivation sadhanas. In fact, since the moon affects the mind and emotions, specific sadhanas for special Qi cultivation techniques can be scheduled for practice according to the various phases of the moon. Typically they involve Yin Qi sadhanas (*Nyasa Yoga* has collected several of them), which means various ways to cultivate your Yin Qi.

Most of the lunar calendars across various traditions are based on the celestial motions and positions of the moon which stays about 2 ½ days in each astrological sign. Both Chinese and Indian almanacs, for instance, consider the various phases of the moon or its position in signs, lunar mansions and nakshatras as "celestially auspicious (favorable) occasions" for certain activities. This includes certain types of cultivation.

There are several astronomical events that are perfect for special types of cultivation effort because at those times the lunar energies that might stimulate your Qi are strongest or weakest. Those events include the new moon, full moon and to a lesser extent eclipses. These are special times to cultivate various aspects of Yin Qi as specified by an enlightened master. A perfect example is that some people try to feel the lunar energy inside them around the full moon, which is a great period for cultivating your Yin Qi.

SUN

In astrology the sun stands for your soul, males or masculinity, leadership, and Yang Qi. It also represents the heart, back, spine, vitality, body heat, courage, enthusiasm, generosity, optimism, entertainment, ovens, stadiums and Sunday. Therefore some people practice specific cultivation sadhanas focused on the heart, courage, generosity, etc. based on the sun's position, or whether the day of the week is Sunday. There is also both an Indian and Chinese sadhana for absorbing the energies of the sun through the eyes. In Chinese Taoism and Hindu Yoga there are various methods to absorb the energies of other planets and constellations including the Moon, Venus, Big Dipper or Pleiades.

The sun changes astrological signs every thirty days, and astrological principles tell us it throws off different energies during those twelve periods of the year. Some of those periods may be particularly useful for cultivation practices of a particular type. If you want to make use of the energies of the sun to augment your cultivation progress, the only big question is whether to use the Vedic calendar of Jyotish (Indian astrology) or the western sun signs astrological calendar to determine when the sun changes sign. Since these two calendar systems differ, the overlap of the two is only true way to know when the sun is *really* in Leo, Cancer, Capricorn, etcetera. The overlap is a very short window.

The next question is what type of practice to transform your Qi and channels would be best augmented at that time since the natural energies of the sun during that period can affect your astrological fortune, your mental state and internal subtle body/energy of Qi. In other words, what cultivation technique is best to practice during a particular time of the year in order to benefit from the special energy given off by the sun at that time?

When the sun first enters a sign there is a burst of new energies that can be taken advantage of for cultivation purposes. The middle of a period is when the energies are considered strongest, which would be around the 15th day into a new sun sign. However, in astrology the energies of a transit or progression are most strongly experienced three or four degrees prior to becoming exact, at which time the aspect has spent most of its power. This leads to a different conclusion as to when energies are truly strongest, i.e. when they will affect you (help you or hurt you) the most. In any case, extra spiritual effort undertaken at these times can help you break the monotony of regular practice if you exert yourself for that brief 3-5 day stint.

For instance, in the field of money management the first three days of a new month (and last two days of a previous month) are when we consistently see new money entering stock markets (since people receive paychecks or reinvest month-end funds), which tends to push the markets upwards. If the sun provides new types of positive energies when it changes sign, and *if* they can be helpful for cultivation, doesn't it make sense to try to make use of them for cultivation purposes too? You might want to try to capture energies when they are increasing the most, rather than at a static high, if that is when you can most feel them or benefit from them.

The sun moves approximately one degree per day in the sky for approximately 30 degrees per month. Indians typically break a solar month into three sections of 10 degrees each to encompass the entire 30 degree range of the sun's travel with the central 10 degree sector supposedly exhibiting the strongest powers of the period's energies. Chinese culture also states that the central section of any time period represents the strongest energies of that designated period. Since it takes the sun approximately 30 days to travel a sign, we can also use those ten-day sections as special periods to also vary our cultivation schedule/practice. Doing so will help break up the monotony of regular practice.

Since a regular calendar month also contains natural sections of days and weeks, we can use the ordinary calendar month - which is constructed without any relationship to astrological phenomena - to mark off periods of particular cultivation emphasis.

MERCURY

Mercury represents the mind, thinking, nervous system, breathing, movement, memory, messages, communications, reason, contracts, publishing and Wednesday. Mercury can stay in each sign for approximately 14 to 30 days depending upon its motion.

You can use the signs of Mercury as a marker for reading and study, pranayama, water-related visualization practices, or reciting a new mantra on top of your standard mantras. By periodically practicing new mantras you can establish a connection with new Buddha family every two to four weeks, and test out different practices during that period.

VENUS

The transit of Venus in an astrological sign lasts between 23 days and two months. That time period can also be used for different types of cultivation sadhana that might make use of any energy influences from Venus, however large or small, that might help you transform your Qi/Prana and channels. Just the fact that you decide to devote yourself to practicing a particular cultivation technique for the limited time that Venus is in a sign will add impetus, urgency and motivation to your efforts, thus helping with adherence to cultivation work – "I'll keep doing this for as long as Venus is in this sign."

The basic idea behind all these suggestions is that you might try practicing especially hard (at a certain type of cultivation effort) as long as an astrological or astronomical event lasts. You might use its presence as a motivation to work hard at cultivation for a certain period, namely as long as the event lasts. A commitment to practice does not seem as artificial when linked to the movements of a celestial phenomenon, thus this approach will boost practice effort.

When two planets make aspects in the heavens - such as a conjunction, trine, opposition, square, etc. - one might use that event to engage in cultivation practices that symbolize the energies of the event as well. When there are astrological aspects to your own astrological natal chart, this might give indications for certain types of practice to perform too.

PLANETS

According to astrological teachings, the energies from planets can be categorized as strong or weak, exalted, beneficial, detrimental, and so on. When they are closest to the earth their energies will have more influence affecting the Qi energies that comprise your subtle body, so will be more strongly felt. These can be harnessed or tapped into for cultivation purposes.

For instance, during a particular Mars transit or astronomical phenomenon you might devote yourself to a special type of Agni practice, fire visualization effort, or kundalini cultivation exercises to make use of every bit of positive influence. Hinduism offers many types of Agni mantra for fire element cultivation. If many people perform the same sadhana at the same time, especially if they form a group, Buddhas will know that and make arrangements to put a special emphasis on helping all those people doing the same sadhana together. Their work becomes more efficient, easier to handle and you get a better result when a group of people do it together.

Thus, planets entering new signs or other astrological phenomena also represent an opportunity (or one could say "excuse") to vary your cultivation practice. Variety helps you maintain your motivation to continue practicing. Just as people get tired of eating the same food every day, they look forward to variety to break up the monotony of their daily cultivation work. What then helps is timing particular types of cultivation effort according to specific type of astronomical or astrological phenomena.

The monotony of the regular work year is broken up by holidays and special celebrations, which in India leads to different types of cultivation effort, and a similar thing should be done for your cultivation efforts so that you don't stop cultivating because of boredom. Chinese culture, for instance, breaks the year into five seasons and one can engage in a different type of practice per season.

DAYS OF THE WEEK

Another of the best ways to institute variety in your practice schedule, and become more well-rounded in your cultivation results, is to practice a different type of cultivation effort for each day of the week. As each day of the week is named for a different planet, one can use this symbolism to designate different cultivation practices for each day to keep your cultivation varied and interesting. Let's see how to put this into action. The planetary correspondences to the days of the week are as follows:

Monday – Moon
Tuesday – Mars
Wednesday – Mercury
Thursday – Jupiter
Friday – Venus
Saturday – Saturn
Sunday – Sun

Since Sunday is matched with the sun, which represents Yang Qi or masculine energies, in addition to your normal cultivation schedule you might practice specific Yang Qi activities, do Agni fire visualization practices, recite Vairocana Buddha's mantra, imagine that you are sunshine, perform Buddha mindfulness of a heroic, courageous enlightened deity, and so forth on Sundays. These are all sun, fire or Yang type cultivation practices. Imagining that you are just light (sunshine) is another Sun practice. Many others are possible.

Since Monday is matched with the moon, which represents Yin Qi, feminine energies, youth, water, thoughts and emotions, … you might on

Mondays cultivate your Yin Qi by reciting lunar mantras, worshiping a feminine deity through Buddha mindfulness, performing water visualization sadhanas, and so on.

Since Tuesday corresponds to Mars, which stands for the fire element, energy, courage, bravery, confidence, aggression, wrath (anger), and war, you might consider the following practices on a Tuesday: Agni fire visualization practices, Vajrapani practices, Mahavira's Jain fire-visualization practice, Kartikeya mantras, imagining that your body burns into dust and becomes emptiness, etcetera. The Tibetan *tummo* practice of imagining your body as a fully blown up hollow balloon with a little glowing object inside that is giving off heat and light is also a fire visualization practice commonly used to generate kundalini energy (Yang Qi). A common and very powerful pranayama practice is to inflate your entire body with breath, as in blowing up a balloon, and holding that state while doing visualizations and/or Qi/Prana swishing inside it to open up tissues.

Various types of fire visualization practices include visualizing that (1) your body burns with a fire that entirely burns away all impurities inside it, (2) you become a pillar of surging flames that exists as happy joy, (3) you become the internal body of the shining sun – bodiless without any torso – always generously offering light and warmth to the entire universe, (4) your body becomes immaterial sunlight that universally shines everywhere with transparent clarity and (5) your bones start burning away all your flesh and your body becomes a mass of roaring flames that you feel vibrating until what is finally left after the burning away is a transparent crystalline body that replaces your old. These are just sample practices; many others are possible.

Since Wednesday is matched with Mercury, which stands for the water element and thoughts, you might consider the following practices on Wednesdays: (1) imagining that you are an infinite ocean of consciousness without a body, (2) imagining that you have no body at all but are instead an immeasurably large emotion of bliss that is so great that it fills the entire universe, (3) performing *nei-gong* work by spinning the Qi around your seven glands, afterwards using your will to connect them together with Qi, (4) swishing your Qi hundreds of times everywhere in your body to wash your muscles, tissues, bones and organs, and so on.

Since Thursday is matched with Jupiter, which stands for the wind element, devotion (prayer), religion, … you might consider that this might be a good day to spend extra time on *kumbhaka* pranayama practice (or do something special like measure your breath retention time if you don't normally do so on a daily basis), chanting, mantra recitation, religious study or worship, and swishing your Qi/Prana around your body like wind. Swishing your Qi around inside you is *anapana* practice or *nei-gong*. The wind element stands for energy, so imagining that your entire body is just energy and stirring it around is another way of cultivating the wind element.

Since Friday is matched with Venus, which stands for the space element and love, it might be a day to practice the Buddhist exercise of imagining you are universal loving kindness, practice empty space meditation or empty body practice.

Since Saturday represents the planet Saturn, which stands for the earth element, solidity, bones, patience or hardship, you might consider putting extra effort at this time into doing (1) the white skeleton visualization practice, (2) imagining that all your bones or your entire body shines with a brilliant bright white light, (3) yoga or other exercise routines that stretch your muscles, and so on. These exercises all cultivate the solid physical body since Saturn symbolizes bones and solidity.

As you can see, there are all sorts of practices you can use or develop on your own based on the symbolism of the day of the week. For best results you would do your Qi/Prana practice first and when finished you would end your practice session with some type of emptiness meditation, such as the several dozen emptiness meditation methods revealed in the appendix.

NUMBERS OF BODY SECTIONS

Another type of practice related to the week that introduces variety into your practice schedule is to number each day of the week from one to seven. Then one can perform inner energy work, *anapana, nei-dan, nei-gong* and other forms of Qi practice on the body in one, two, three, four, five, etc. sections to match with the numerical significator of the day, thus keeping up the variety for meditation practices. The partitioning of the body into one, two, three, four and more segments, and appropriate Qi practices, is explained in *Nyasa Yoga*. "One section" is full-body practice.

For instance, on day one you could practice Mahavira's whole body fire visualization, Hakuin's duck egg meditation that involves feeling the Qi within your entire body as a unit, Vajrapani visualization that activates the Qi of your entire body, the Buddhist white skeleton visualization, or just trying to feel/move/mobilize/link all the Qi of your body as one unit. All these methods treat the body *as one single unit* and try to affect the Qi of it as one whole. The number of that day is "one," as you would expect.

For day "two" you would practice any technique that cultivates the body's Qi/Prana in two sections, such as the Ram-Vam method within the *Mahavairocana Sutra* and *Yajnavalkya* (Neem Karoli Baba recites Ram-Nam instead that often sounds like Rahlam), Taoist practices that cause you to run your Qi up and down your spine or up your spine and then down the front of your body (or center of it) hundreds of times per day, and so on.

For day "three" you could practice reciting "Ohm Ah Hun," "Hreem

Shreem Kleem" or other three syllable mantras following the rules of Mantrayana where you also try to simultaneously feel the Qi/Prana in three separate sections of your body, each connected to a different mantra sound-syllable. The most common three sectional partitioning includes the head together with the arms; chest and arms; and waist to legs. Don't worry about overlapping the cultivation sections for different sounds.

For day "four" you might teach the four part (four chakra) internal *nei-gong* method taught by Chinese Grandmaster Lu Zijian and also found in *Tsongkhapa's Six Yogas of Naropa* (Glenn Mullin translation). You can also practice reciting four syllable mantras such as Kartikeya's "Om Ah Sou Aim." The practice of cultivating the body in four sections is a staple of many traditions, and is found in the *Atalanta Fugiens* from Medieval Europe.

For day "five" (which might be a Friday) you might cultivate the Qi of the body in five sections as is done with the "Ohm Ah Vah Lah Hung" Vairocana mantra, or other five syllable mantras. The five sections would be the head together with the arms, heart region of the chest, mid section of the body, lower belly, waist and legs ... or some equivalent that feels more comfortable to you in terms of getting results.

For day "six" you might practice the six Taoist healing sounds on six organ sections of your body, making sure that this is used as a method to move your Qi rather than simply reciting sounds.

For day "seven" you might focus on doing *anapana, nei-gong, nei-dan* etc. work on the seven chakras. In *Nyasa Yoga* you will find the only correct description in print of the seven chakras within the body with their actual location and meaning. They are just sections of the body and spine that you concentrate on during inner energy work, and not spinning vortices or some other crazy nonsense.

5 ELEMENTS

Another type of relevant practice is to practice a sadhana for each of the five elements according to the weekday. One example would be to generally follow the supposed pattern of the birth of the universe starting with empty space and progressing to the wind element, fire element, water element, earth element, and turning that sequence into Qi cultivation exercises as follows:

1. SPACE – Imagine that you are empty space in all directions simultaneously without any thought-constructs, experiencing emptiness all around you. Concentrate on yourself in the form of a vast firmament, unlimited in any direction whatsoever. Imagine being the spatial vacuity in all directions around you and rest your mind in

that state. Stay aware but let your thoughts dissolve (don't attach to them) as you become the empty space everywhere without a body or mind. Cast aside the body and ignore the fluctuations of your mind as you become the empty space you see. If anything arises as your thoughts, let them arise within you without attachment because you are just infinite empty, bodiless space that cannot hold to them but lets everything arise within it. Rest your mind in that visage of infinite empty space without holding onto any thoughts that arise. Such is the nature of the original nature that is the purest of the pure, yet gives birth to all things without any attachments or clinging, letting each phenomenon follow its own course. Now you are emptiness that just witnesses without attachment.

2. WIND – Start moving your Qi all over your body everywhere, whipping it up like a torrent of wind, stirring it everywhere using your mind and will (with attendant emotions such as joy or excitement if appropriate). After you stimulate it everywhere, harmonize the feeling of Qi within you as one calm, peaceful whole and rest in that more comfortable feeling that then encompasses your entire body. Alternatively, slowly recite a mantra in tune with your breath and observe the void of emptiness that occurs at the end of the protracted pronunciation. Doing this each time you recite a mantra such as Om-Ah-Hung, Hreem-Shreem-Kleem, Om-Ah-Sou-Aim, etcetera, you will eventually attain an experience that is mentally quiet, free of wandering thoughts. Stay in that emptiness when you reach it without giving rise to more recitations.

3. FIRE – Imagine that a bright energy enters into the top of your head from the universe, or is being projected into you from the universe, a spiritual deity or your own spiritual master. It enters in through the top of your head and settles into your heart and belly where it becomes a pillar of flames. Fill your belly and body with this fiery energy and imagine that your entire body, including your limbs, becomes ignited into a blazing fire that slowly burns everything away. *Feel* that energy moving and its warmth as it burns away your flesh, bones and every part of your body. After feeling the moving Qi inside you everywhere for some time, burning away everything of dross matter, visualize that the only thing left of you is a crystal pure, transparent, immaterial body form of pure energy.

4. WATER – Contemplate that your body and the entire universe simultaneously become filled with a giant ocean of surging great bliss. After being fully saturated and permeated by this bliss, which flows

inside your body and mind, let go of all human thinking and let the mind rest in this blissful feeling without thought. Let it gradually subside into calmness while your body feels comfortable, yet do not cling to it. Let your awareness still function in this state so that you know any thoughts that arise within your mind and their meaning, but do not encourage their arrival or discourage their departure. Simply remain in a state of clear, pure, pristine awareness while your Qi energy flows like water everywhere within you. Imagine you are an ocean of this energy.

5. EARTH – Try to feel the substance of your entire body as a single unit. Try to feel its heaviness or material substance by trying to simultaneously feel all the energy of you body as one unit. Try to feel your muscles everywhere simultaneously. Penetrate all the various parts of your body by consciousness, feeling all the parts of your body as a unified wholeness of soft energy. Next, once accomplished then contemplate that the skin of your body becomes like an outer wall and that there is nothing inside it but empty space. You might also imagine that there is nothing inside your body's components because they are empty inside - contemplate that the constituents of your body such as your organs, bones, and flesh become pervaded with mere vacuity (emptiness). Imagine that your body progressively becomes like an empty sack but that your mind becomes limitless, infinite in all spatial directions and that you then have no body at all. You are just the empty space that cannot attach to anything. Rest your mind in empty space just like this. Imagine you are bodiless without a container or vessel of any sort and rest your mind in the empty space you become. In that empty space continue watching/knowing the thoughts that rise in your mind but do not follow them. Simply know them with awareness.

6. DISSOLUTION – Imagine that the whole universe is successively dissolved from a gross state into a subtle state, from a subtle state into space, and then from space into a formless transcendental state that lacks any attributes or distinctions. Rest your mind in that final formlessness. In the same manner, allow your mind to be dissolved away into unmanifest consciousness and then the emptiness of great quiet, peace and bliss that is a nothingness.

7. LIGHT – Imagine that you are a single point of light within an ocean of infinite light. Try to feel that you become that entire ocean of light, which has no form. You are light, only light, without a body or form.

Let that point of light that you are merge in the infinite ocean of light and then rest in that state of bodiless infinite light and bliss.

These are just samples of how you might take the five elements and turn them into cultivation methods, and how you might use a different one for each of the seven days of the week. It is not by any means fixed in stone or all-inclusive because you can change the sequence or develop many other methods from these basic ideas. For instance, during an earth element emphasis you might practice the white skeleton visualization technique where you visualize the bones within your body shining with a bright white light, and upon completion your body turns into dust and then empty space. The point is to equate each day of the week with one of the five elements and then perform a different type of related practice on each day. Consciousness and perception are considered elements in some cultivation schools, but in the example provided are replaced by light and dissolution.

On any appropriate day you also might mentally excite and then violently swish/shake your Qi hundreds of times everywhere as if it were moving like wind, like fire, or like water. Cultivation Yoga is basically moving the Qi in your body in a repetitious fashion hundreds to thousands of times for each organ, limb, segment, section, etc. until you cultivate your entire body and get it ready for the kundalini awakening. In *qi-gong, nei-gong, nei-dan, anapana,* Vajrayana, tantric, *kriya* or kundalini Yoga practice you do this every day by spinning or revolving your Qi countless repetitions all over your body. For the earth element, you could practice a different type of inner energy work that concentrates on the solid elements of the body.

The basic point is to do many different types of energy work on your body because cultivation is all a matter of Yoga in the end. If you just think it is about sitting meditation practice you will get nowhere. You will never develop a foundation for the subtle body. This is the big mistake you make from reading Zen texts and Advaita Vedanta. You must meditate *and do inner energy work* to prepare for the Twelve Year kundalini transformation period that gives rise to a deva body and makes you a spiritual master.

Another point is that people stop cultivating because they become bored and then they don't want to maintain a practice schedule. They want variety in their cultivation schedule, and want to develop new skills instead of just sitting there with an empty mind meditating, or watching their thoughts, or repetitiously moving their Qi/Prana. By turning the days of the week, or months, or astronomical phenomena into special practices that last only for only a short while, you can keep yourself motivated to perform a wider variety of Qi cultivation techniques and other cultivation methods to help you purify and strengthen your inner subtle body. This will definitely speed your progress on the path. Your spiritual study should be varied too and encompass practical matters that help humans, which we will discuss next.

6
FOUNDATIONAL STUDY

Let's say you become enlightened. This means that through spiritual cultivation practice you were finally able to develop various spiritual bodies, each made of a more refined substance than the previous one, that are still linked together and able to independently travel different planes of existence to perform independent activities. To others they seem like independent lives but they are more like extra appendages to the highest body, which becomes your central life vehicle. By attaining the first body, the subtle energy or deva body (called the illusory body in Tibetan Buddhism), you are officially "enlightened" although people usually equate the Supra-Causal body (equivalent to the fourth dhyana, Clear Light Body or Dharma Body) with what they would consider the standard definition of Buddha enlightenment. Nevertheless, the subtle body is a stage of Arhat attainment (Srotapanna), so it is a stage of enlightenment – the first dhyana.

Attaining these higher bodies is the true spiritual path for the saints and sages of *all* religions, only it is kept secret and thus most people don't know about it. They think that the spiritual path is attending religious ceremonies, practicing rituals or cultivating quiet mental states that somehow give you insight into the original nature of the universe because by meditating you might experience varying degrees of mental silence and bliss. This wrong view keeps people busy with cultivating meditation practice.

The idea (in Zen) that someone must test you to see if you are enlightened is bogus – you either have the extra bodies or not, so all masters already know you are enlightened, and so do you. Enlightenment is not a mental realization but a body achievement and a more blissful consciousness comes with it. The Zen school is extremely misleading in this way, and has people wasting years because while they practice meditation they are not performing inner energy work in order to generate the deva body that is the first significant fruit of the path.

Zen school stories, in particular, are extremely misleading to adherents. Zen doesn't even tell people that the first dhyana achievement means the subtle body attainment, but if you read various Buddhist texts, such as the *Surangama Sutra*, the information is there clearly. It's in Hinduism too as well as in Taoism, the Nath Yoga path and Sufism. Most every spiritual school leads people into believing that enlightenment is some form of thought realization or empty mind attainment, which causes people to meditate, when *it is really a body attainment* and your "clarity of consciousness" for each body attainment is a concomitant, naturally associated with, attendant accompaniment that comes along with that new body.

If you want to attain enlightenment via the Zen school you must cultivate inner energy work on your Qi/Prana using methods such as kundalini, tantric, and *kriya* yoga or Chinese *nei-gong* and *nei-dan* and Buddhist *anapana* practice. This is the fastest road to success other than just the "stillness" meditation of Zen dhyana. Don't be mislead by all the Zen stories that seem to suggest that enlightenment is some type of mental realization, or samadhi of no-thought. "To know yourself as Brahman, the original nature, is self-realization." There, now you know everything along those lines, but for real enlightenment you still have to practice energy work. Knowing that the mind's natural state is empty of thought is seeing the Tao, realizing the self, but it isn't enlightenment.

Zen is from Buddhism, and Buddhism champions *anapana* practice, which is inner Qi movement yoga like *nei-gong*. It also teaches the white skeleton meditation, which should involve moving your inner energy in addition to just stable visualization and concentration practice. You have to engage in inner energy work like this, which India calls kundalini yoga, to reach the first dhyana of Buddhism and generate the "will-born" body that we also call the deva body or subtle body.

Don't be misled either by Hinduism and the Yoga schools that say that the mind or ego reaching a state of dissolution is liberation. This is just meant to cause you to meditate more. All the Yoga schools are dependent upon kundalini yoga, which is the *nei-gong* practice of cultivating your Qi/Prana and circulating it everywhere in your body so that you can attain the first of many spiritual bodies. Telling you to abandon the ego is just a form of meditation practice to cultivate mental emptiness or formlessness.

Spiritual paths typically hide the path of body attainments, which is called cultivating the *sambhogakaya*, Reward body or Enjoyment body, under descriptions of skandhas, *koshas*, samadhi-dhyana attainments, *bhumis*, Zen koans, levels of consciousness, bliss states, and so forth. It's all a charade to keep people misinformed so that they keep practicing meditation, otherwise they would get discouraged and give up practice.

Once again, enlightenment is really a body attainment, and with that more etheric body you will have an attendant, concomitant consciousness that is more clear than the consciousness level pertaining to the previous, denser body. Nevertheless it is just a regular form of consciousness at that level all the same, and because it resides on a higher energy plane you can come to know the thoughts of sentient beings on lower planes. In attaining a higher spiritual body you are just duplicating your physical body and mind at a more transcendental level of physical composition, that's all.

If you just cultivate meditation you will never gain the higher bodies, and if you just cultivate inner energy work you won't get them either. You must cultivate both – emptiness meditation *and* inner Qi yoga. Cultivation is mind-body Yoga, but people are usually particularly deficient in their inner energy cultivation!

Starting with the subtle body attainment, you can then use your extra body or bodies to know people's thoughts and their memories by entering into their brains and "reading the neurons." This is a skill that every deva is taught. This is one of the things accomplished masters teach their students during the Twelve Year kundalini transformation process; they take students into your brain (the ten-foot square room in *Vimalakirti's Sutra*) to watch how thoughts and emotions are formed, and practice giving you thoughts and controlling your actions, which is hell for the practitioner.

When new thoughts are formed in the brain the process of neurons lighting up from the chemical processes and energy interactions is described in the Buddhist sutras as vajra banners flapping in the wind, jeweled nets, arrays of light, raining flowers, multi-colored clouds, wondrous shining ornaments, and so forth. In particular, the *Avatamsaka Sutra* is replete with such descriptions. These are esoteric secrets that only the initiated know.

Once achieved, you can use your spiritual bodies to (project them to faraway places and) know things at a distance, and with the higher bodies you can sometimes know the template for the future. You can go into people to read their thoughts and memories, give people thoughts, and give them energies to help them during sickness or help transform their bodies for the spiritual path. You can practice skills that can sometimes affect the elements, such as becoming able to generate rain in response to requests such as seen in Hopi Indian ceremonies. Many small and great superpowers become available, from using the higher bodies, if you train to achieve them.

You will live a long time in your higher bodies and will want to make an helpful impact on the world, whose problems you can now see since no one can hide anything from you. In Chinese culture it is said that the Kitchen God sees everything in your household that happens and reports everything you do to Heaven. Well, this is true in the sense that all the devas can see what you are doing and thinking, and there is nothing you can ever hide.

Whether it is lying, stealing, cheating, murder, gossip, adultery, drug use, etc. every deva can find out if they want. Heaven knows all the things you do secretly so you cannot hide anything. A living master trains to be able to accept all he sees and knows.

Don't think you can hide anything from the devas around you. They know everything you do and why you do it. "Heaven knows," which is why it is said that people are judged upon their deaths. This is true. Everything you have done or experienced during life is stored in your neurons, and will be known and used to fashion your future karma.

Upon enlightenment you will probably want high-level people with power, influence or wealth to come and consult you for advice because you will want to make an impact on the world, but there are two major problems.

First, you are a nobody. You are probably considered a lowly monk, nun, swami, rabbi, priest, sadhu, etc. that most people normally ignore in life because people typically ignore everyone of that status/occupation. You might be a high-level religious functionary, but still a monk, nun, rabbi, etcetera just the same who would be normally ignored because of your occupation.

Second, even though you now have these powers you only studied spiritual topics during your life that are useless for intervening in the real world. You basically studied "useless materials" whereas what people actually want are solutions to practical problems. At best you studied morality teachings, but very few practical affairs unless you worked for a living. You can go into people's minds and try to give them thoughts, but why are yours any better than theirs? Sometimes they are, sometimes they aren't.

Buddhism therefore says you need to study five topics if you aspire to become a perfect Buddha: (1) spiritual cultivation and the cultivation path, (2) causation (logic, philosophy, psychology, religion and the human social science such as history, economics), (3) sound (literature, music, linguistics, the active literacies), (4) medicine and healing, and (5) practical techniques (the skills associated with modern science and technology). Confucius encouraged people to master Six Arts: ritual, music, archery, charioteering, calligraphy, arithmetic as well as knowledge of poetry and history. These were important for the life of his day. Once again, monks and nuns usually know little to nothing about any such things at all so have trouble helping people. This is a deficit that needs to be remedied.

The problem is that monks and nuns rarely study additional things other than meditation topics or religion because they think this is the spiritual path and they neglect thoughts of the future, namely what they would do if they really succeeded in enlightenment. When they can finally generate the subtle body they find themselves useless at being able to help people because they just don't know enough about anything other than religion. In olden days politicians, monks and nuns were the most intelligent strata of society, which was usually largely composed of illiterate farmers, and now everyone else is more talented, skillful, and intelligent than these groups of people. You need to study materials other than holy texts to become more useful to society and help them with your deva body! During life cultivators therefore need to start developing some special skills, knowledge, and excellences that can help the world.

Ordinary people who cultivate during life and then die, whereupon they obtain a subtle energy deva body for the remainder of their heavenly life until they again reincarnate, finally have some access to limited spiritual powers and want to help human beings, but they too did not study special skills or fields of knowledge/expertise and cannot help people much at all either. They simply don't have ample knowledge and skills.

Since you can only give people energy or thoughts, but aren't a master of their specialties themselves, the best you can do is look within their brains and help them to decide what to do using their own small world of ideas stored in their memories. You can only give them thoughts, and of course, sometimes an independent outsider's view of someone's situation is helpful and superior to their own. Without special knowledge, skills or expertise the default option is learning how to shrink your subtle body into a small size, enter into people's brains, and give them thoughts to do good things or stop doing bad things.

Even with these powers, the problem in wanting to help others is a lack of skills, knowledge and mastery of their own specialties even though you learn how to be a quick study in understanding a brain's total contents for a topic. You can understand what people think, and master a synopsis of important facts and principles quickly using higher bodies, but you still cannot master their skills in yourself. For that, such as learning how to play the violin, ride a skateboard, surf or fly a plane, you need to practice. You cannot just download how-to information in your head, like Keanu Reeves in *The Matrix*, and then be an instant master of it. Therefore you need to study to increase your wisdom to master many lines of intelligence and start practicing new skills and paths through immersion.

The path of cultivation includes study and practice, but in today's world the study aspect has to be enlarged to encompass *other areas* than just spiritual practices/religion in order that you can become very helpful to people in the real areas of life in which they commonly ask Heaven for assistance. After all, when people pray to God for help it is usually an enlightened Buddha and his or her students who respond to the call. "Dharma" doesn't just pertain to spiritual study but study of all sorts of bodies of knowledge that can be helpful to other human beings. A saying runs:

Study and practice. It is hard to become human, but having become human
One should vigorously practice the Dharma.
Do not waste time; this is like entering the mountain of treasure
And returning empty-handed and with regret.[9]

While most people take this to mean that you should primarily study cultivation topics, it also means mastering special skills that you would need if you were to magically become some type of sage, Immortal, Buddha, Bodhisattva or Guardian Deity. If you could magically choose to become some type of saint, sage, immortal or deity whose responsibilities were to be of a certain nature, what would they be? What would you select as the functions you would oversee for mankind? What would be worthy of your efforts? What is worthy of an obsession that would make a difference in people's lives? What light would you want to project into the world?

Okay, now that you know that, what skills and knowledge do you have to study and master to move in that direction? What should you be associating with?

You have already seen my list of books on meditation, tantric yoga, and cultivation gong-fu. If there are special cultivation topics or skills to be learned then many other specialized books are available. But what about study in order to master the topics that most people ask about in life other than spiritual cultivation, namely medicine-health issues, money-wealth-business-career-success issues, relationship issues, children and education issues, national rulership-governance-policy-prosperity issues, and arts-cultural-educational issues? There are Bodhisattvas and guardian spirits that specialize in dealing with, protecting and supporting all of these areas.

If you want to become a Bodhisattva, Protect God, guardian spirit or Buddha it doesn't just automatically happen that you have skills and knowledge in everything after you obtain multiple bodies one by one. Do you really know what a Buddha or Bodhisattva is? They are just people like you and me who cultivated, succeeded in attaining the extra spiritual bodies, and then practiced to learn more skills and techniques with these bodies as well as new topics *so that they could help people* with their influences, and then did so.

As soon as you get the subtle body you are considered enlightened, an Arhat, *arihant* or *jivanmukta*. You are a junior-stage Arhat but an Arhat nonetheless. If you then start helping people rather than go on to live comfortably in Heaven or the Pure Lands without assisting them you are

---

[9] *The Way to Buddhahood*, Master Yin-Shun, trans. by Wing H. Yeung, (Wisdom Publications, Boston, 1998), p. 38.

considered a Bodhisattva. If you continue cultivating bodies you can become a fully enlightened Buddha upon the attainment of the fourth dhyana (Supra-Causal body) or Immanence body.

If you are an asshole you will still be an asshole with those attainments. If you only know religious texts you will still only know religious texts with those attainments even though you can check people's minds and learn any fact or principle you want to know quite quickly. If you are greedy, power hungry, want fame or sex or power, or get angry easily you will still have those character flaws with those attainments. Nothing changes, you just get an extra body or more. As a person you're not any better.

Do people with personality flaws become enlightened? Yes. Do people change just because they become enlightened by gaining the extra bodies? No. You have to work at self-cultivation to change your personality, behavior and habit energies or tendencies, which is why I emphasized *Color Me Confucius*. You must work on changing your own personality and behavior even after you attain the deva body, otherwise you'll end up hurting people with your powers. Unfortunately, many people stop doing so after attaining the higher bodies. They think their job is done and become arrogant.

A Buddha is simply a person who cultivates extra spiritual bodies and then uses them to try to help others, but if you don't have sufficient knowledge and skills you will be limited in how you can help. If you want to become knowledgeable about a topic, you must study it and practice it. You have to lay down a foundation of knowledge. To attain skills you have to practice until you reach a level of mastery. You must practice to gain proficiency and then expertise.

From my own studies, here are some of the best current sources that will familiarize you with certain topics that are of interest to most people seeking help. By no means is it all inclusive or conclusive. In studying a topic, you want to accumulate a foundational base of the best information, ideas and methods out there, the very best models and templates from which to build a higher and more complete understanding. These lists are far from complete, of course, but can help you get started.

MEDICINE & HEALING

If you want to become a healing Bodhisattva, guardian spirit (health/medical specialist benefactor) or have aspirations to become a big Medicine Buddha such as symbolized by Bhaisajyaguru, Dhanvantari, Asclepius, Enrile, Sekhmet or Baosheng Dadi, then in addition to one's spiritual cultivation there are several topics one should study.

You should learn how to become optimally healthy yourself by reading or attending courses on the appropriate topics of health and then applying those lessons to your own life. The major topics one should study, in addition to learning common medical knowledge and remedies, are the practices of the alternative health field and nutritional information related to cures and diets.

What do people most seek in the area of health? In addition to ways to heal themselves and eliminate health issues to find relief, most people seek high levels of health and energy, methods of longevity or methods that reverse aging, methods that maintain brain health, knowledge on how to eat better and maintain a proper diet, methods for losing weight, and methods for stopping addictions and recovery.

Remember that if you were to become a great monk or nun or other spiritual leader, people would come to you with all sorts of health issues because regular medicine has failed them. Therefore you should know which doctors are best in your area for certain common conditions (especially cancer, heart disease, Alzheimer's disease and diabetes), and become especially knowledgeable in the alternative or complementary health fields that the establishment often rejects since when regular medicine fails people will be looking for alternatives that work.

Consider that people who pray to God, or mantra to Buddhas or deities for medical assistance, need help. They will either have no access to medical care at all, will already be under professional medical care (that may or may not work) and need more assistance, or are already seeking alternative medical care because conventional care has failed them. You need to be able to direct people to the best conventional and alternative doctors and/or procedures and remedies. You should become knowledgeable in these areas. To this end you should study the fields of:

- Diet and Nutrition
- Vitamin-mineral and nutritional supplements
- Herbal medicine (Traditional Chinese herbal medicine, Indian Ayurveda, South American and western herbs) – the key is learning the functions of herbs and how to use them, in particular what herbs to combine in what measure, how to prepare them, and how to adapt a formula over time since no formula maintains top effectiveness for decades
- Detoxification and cleansing
- Environmental remedies to create a healthy home such as air filters (ex. Pure Air Doctor equipment), EMF radiation protection (ex. anti-radiation Silverell clothing), water filters, etc.
- Bodywork modalities such as massage, lymph drainage, strain-counterstrain, chiropractic therapy and other muscle manipulation

therapies like Egoscue, cranial sacral work, IMT, Rolfing, AMIT method, etc.
- Homeopathy
- Acupuncture, Acupressure and Marma Points
- Nutripuncture - a new modality similar to homeopathy but using microdoses of minerals
- Energy modalities (Reiki)
- Alternative medicine diagnosis methods – Chinese pulse taking, tongue diagnosis, iris diagnosis, VEGA and Asyra electrodermal screening machines, kinesiology muscle testing, reading bloodwork, etc.

I want you to think deeply about the fact that most monks and nuns have virtually no skills and special knowledge except those involving religious texts and ceremonies, but like every human being must learn how to deal with their own body vehicle, which ultimately becomes the product of the path. The ignorance of most spiritual training is overwhelming because it ignores mundane things that help mankind and which, as a Buddha or Bodhisattva or guardian spirit, you would want to master to provide that assistance. This type of study should proceed in parallel with spiritual training so that religious functionaries become well-rounded and *more useful than ordinary human beings* rather than just religious functionaries.

Most people on the path neglect their bodies (which is why Zen Master Bodhidharma taught the monks of China how to do tendon exercises, which eventually became Shaolin gong-fu) even though it becomes the template for the deva body that will live longer than an average human life span. You have to keep your human body healthy so you must exercise on the spiritual path. Stretching is particularly important as it can help Qi/Prana flow within you. The deva body becomes the template, in turn, for the Causal body because it is created out of its matrix of deeper energies too. And so on it goes ...

Furthermore, most religious heads and spiritual representatives usually have people come to them asking all sorts of questions about health, yet they don't even know the best doctors for referrals in their community, or the contents of the best alternative medicine newsletters that can supply ready solutions. This should be remedied.

When you read the vows of the Medicine Buddha you will find promises (commitments) to help people who are sick and poor but lack medicine and aid. You will find promises to help the physically disabled, prisoners, people starving or dying of thirst, and individuals so poor they lack clothes. Many charities offer aid along these lines such as Doctors Without Borders, Jaipur Foot, Amnesty International, or CARE. Are you contributing? If you want to become a Medicine Buddha or medical protector deva/deity, what can you do, even if the steps are but small, in that direction now?

A big Buddha not only tries to render assistance in individual cases like this but puts his mind on big scale national health issues, like a statesman who is seeking solutions, in order to work on prevention and cure. Prevention is always better than pursuing cures, which may or may not work. He focuses on solving the causes of deficiency in a nation such as by making sure it builds sufficient sanitation infrastructure to prevent disease, emphasizes national hygiene, establishes clean and healthy food sources, and removes pollution from the environment. He wants to make sure that the nation adopts sanitary health habits (makes them into customs), and works to make sure that medicine, trained health professionals and medical facilities are readily available and reasonably priced, etcetera. If you support such movements or purposes you are establishing the causes to become a great Medicine Buddha or Bodhisattva.

My priority for improving a nation's prosperity is to attack the big causes of death and destruction first and then move to lesser issues. This means working to prevent/end warfare, end plaques, end famines and hunger, establish good health conditions and then create jobs, income and education. Preventing death comes before working on economic prosperity, so hygiene, health and hunger are priority issues.

As to health issues in a normally functioning society, basically you want to learn how to fix people's health problems or direct them to people who can, and help them feel more alive, awake, energetic and better in their own skin. The body wants to be healthy but there are usually habit barriers that stand in the way such as a bad diet, so becoming healthy often entails learning how to do things properly that you have been doing wrong for a long time, such as improving your diet. You want to learn and disseminate information on the proper ways to do things in the area of health. Diet is one of the most important areas.

The "establishment" medical system in every country is readily available to people so it is the alternative, or complementary field that the general public needs information on and access to. As a monk, nun, swami, rabbi, priest or other religious functionary you usually cannot become a doctor, so to help people you should really develop familiarity/expertise in the health alternatives field, which is very easy to do just by reading the right books and health newsletters.

The video interviews of Dr. Joe Mercola (Mercola.com) can get you started on learning the best of the alternative medical options and their practitioners. The Price-Pottenger Foundation is also a valuable resource, as is the Life Extension Foundation for their health reports on medical conditions and supplements which might help. Over time other sources will arise too. You should learn the hard facts about GMOs, amalgam fillings, cholesterol, vaccines, fluoride, ozone and EMFs.

For environmental medicine equipment solutions for cleaning up your home see *Look Younger, Live Longer* and check out the teachings of Dr. Dietrich Klinghardt via his Youtube videos, the wonderful materials of David Getoff (Naturopath4you.com), and TooMuchEMF.com. This pertains to water filters, air filters (Pure Air Doctor is a great brand), ozone equipment, house lighting, cell phone protection, and so on.

Since people will often tell you about miracle supplements that helped cure their disease, before accepting such conclusions you should run the story past possible logic filters such as the following: the disease ran its natural course, the disease is of a cyclical nature with ups and downs where the cure coincided with a cyclical down, the placebo effect may have been responsible, the individual credited the wrong thing, their original diagnosis may have been wrong, the patient confused a temporary improvement with a cure, and their psychological needs distorted what they perceived.

The Medicine Buddha has vowed, "If people are sick I will save them, if deformed I will fix them, if they are not pretty I will help them become more beautiful, if they are embarrassed I will protect them, if hungry I will feed them, if they don't have any clothes or housing or shelter then I will supply them, if they want education I will arrange for them to be taught, if they want children I'll help them conceive, if they want to change genders then I'll help them do so for their next life, if their sense organs are defective then I will help restore them." You can contribute to charitable causes that focus on these conditions too, or learn the skills of correction for some of these problems yourself.

Just directing people to an excellent doctor, chiropractor or bodyworker is being a Medicine Buddha since it helps people solve their health problems. You don't have to be a health/medical expert, but by directing individuals to others who can solve their problem you will accumulate great merit and generate a field of blessings. Train to do that.

What are some good cultivation practices that are specifically related to becoming a Medicine Buddha? There are yoga and Pilates exercises, pranayama breathing exercises, the white skeleton technique visualization technique, kundalini yoga, inner energy work according to anatomy and so forth. Whatever methods involve the body, its energy, healing and health ...

One other powerful thing you can do is take the vows of the Medicine Buddha. You should read his vows, update them for today's world, and then recite the new vows you subscribe to on a frequent basis. Furthermore, you should write down for each vow a list of people or organizations you admire who best exemplify making the effort to fulfill those vows since their example might help to inspire you. Next, frame this and put it on the wall where you can see this all the time.

Lastly, there is the field of study and for health information as stated I often rely on the selections of the Price-Pottenger Foundation.

WEALTH

If you want to become a big Wealth Buddha like Kubera, Lakshmi, Mahakala, Vasudhara, Tsai Shen Yeh or the Fuk Luk Sah, Daikoku, Aje, Jamablaya, or a wealth/money guardian spirit, in addition to spiritual cultivation there are several topics one should study. One should learn the best knowledge that this world system can offer in the fields of wealth creation through entrepreneurship, business development and management or investing. All people want more money so this is something to study if you want to be able to advise them. The final goal is not wealth per se but enough money so that people can attain financial freedom and live an independent life of their own choosing.

Here are just a few of the areas you can study to become of enormous value to others in advising since they are the concerns of most entrepreneurs and businessmen:

- Marketing and Innovation
- Sales
- Business Growth
- Management
- Becoming Rich
- Investing
- Career Selection

Here is the briefest summary of some major principles for these topics. It is by no means conclusive but simply meant to get you started at becoming more knowledgeable in minimum time with minimum reading.

Peter Drucker said, "Because the purpose of business is to create a customer, the business enterprise has two – and only two – basic functions: marketing and innovation. Marketing and innovation produce results; all the rest are costs." Therefore you should familiarize yourself with the best methods for each of these two pillars, especially marketing.

Innovation: For innovation, which includes creating new products or services, you should start by familiarizing yourself with the materials of Doug Hall (*Driving Eureka!*) including an especially hard-to find CBC news feature about the innovation techniques of his Eureka Ranch. Also study TRIZ (a method for generating inventions), the Maker Faire, *A Technique for*

Producing Ideas (James Webb Young). The goal is to learn how to turn innovation into a reliable science that produces meaningfully unique products. Such inventions can be marketed through the techniques of my book, *How to Create a Million Dollar Unique Selling Proposition*, whose structural insights can also help you create unique products. Doug Hall is the individual whose ideas you should particularly study.

Alex Osborn, the "O" within the advertising agency BBDO, also invented a number of brainstorming strategies for coming up with creative ideas and innovations. When trying to come up with new ideas or approaches you might employ his SCAMPER checklist from *Applied Imagination: Principles and Procedures of Creative Problem Solving* – Substitute, Combine, Adapt, Modify-Magnify-Minify, Put to Other Uses, Eliminate, Reverse-Rearrange. Osborn, the inventor of classical brainstorming, used this checklist to try to turn an existing idea into a new one:

- Substitute? Put to other uses? New ways to use as is? Other uses if modified?
- Adapt? What else is like this? What other idea does this suggest? What does this tell you? Is the past comparable? What could I copy? Whom could I emulate?
- Modify? New twist? Give it a new angle? Alter the meaning, color, motion, sound, odor, taste, texture, form, shape? Other changes?
- Magnify? What to add? More time? Greater frequency? Stronger? Higher? Larger? Longer? Thicker? Heavier? Extra value? Plus ingredient? Can it be duplicated, multiplied or exaggerated?
- Minify? What to subtract? Can anything be taken away? Made smaller? Condensed? Miniature? Lower? Shorter? Narrower? Lighter? Omit? Streamline? Split up? Understate? Less frequent?
- Substitute? Who else instead? What else instead? Where else instead? When else instead? Different ingredients? Other material? Other processes? Other power? Other place? Other approach? Other tone of voice? Other time? Someone else?
- Rearrange? Interchange/swap components? Alter the pattern, sequence or layout? Transpose cause and effect? Change place? Change schedule? Earlier? Later?
- Reverse? How about opposites? Turn it backward, upside down, inside out? Reverse roles? Change shoes? Turn tables? Turn other cheek? Transpose positive and negative?
- Combine? How about a blend, an alloy, an assortment, an ensemble? Combine units, purposes, appeals or ideas?

Marketing. Good marketing is the crucial characteristic for business success. However, sales and marketing are the weakest links in the majority of small businesses, which is why small businesses remain small, but they are the only thing that results in profits because nothing happens unless you sell something. To make a business grow, you have to generate sales through marketing and sales efforts.

Companies succeed because they sell, and sales depend upon good marketing which is often more important than "how good you are." While good marketing can cover many sins, it cannot fix a bad product and cover over its flaws. Marketing guides your advertising, and along these lines customers should be treated with respect, for as the famed advertising guru David Ogilvy said, "The consumer is not a moron. She is your wife."

Marketing is part behavioral psychology and part mathematics. If you don't optimize your marketing efforts then you will lose in two ways. First off, you won't get the sale but instead your competitors will capture it, and will put that profit into their bank account. Next, your competitors will turn around and use that money in their own marketing campaigns to get your other customers. Furthermore, when you permanently lose an existing customer you lose their lifetime value in profits, whatever revenue they would have also generated through upsell opportunities in the future, the sales you would have gotten from their referrals, and as dissatisfied customers they will discourage others from using you.

The referral customer is the most profitable, loyal, reliable, cost efficient, and easy to negotiate with type of customer you can get so you don't want to lose them because of bad products or services. It will cost you six times as much to get a new customer to replace the one you lose, which is why reducing customer turnover by 5% can increase profits by 25%. Companies therefore need a customer retention program rather than simply expecting customer loyalty. Even temples, ashrams and spiritual centers need to keep this in mind.

For learning marketing you might start by studying the many works of Dan Kennedy, Jay Conrad Levinson's *Guerilla Marketing*, *Money-Making Secrets of Marketing Genius Jay Abraham and Other Marketing Wizards: A No-Nonsense Guide to Great Wealth and Personal Fortune*, the books and interviews of David Ogilvy (*Ogilvy on Advertising*, *Confessions of an Advertising Man*), all the marketing strategy and positioning works of Ries and Trout, and information on how to create a unique selling proposition (USP) since this is the very first step to an excellent product and good marketing.

To learn about the USP you can read *Jump Start Your Brain* (Doug Hall) and *How to Create a Million Dollar Unique Selling Proposition* (Bodri). The very first step of marketing, and I mean the very first step, is getting the USP right, which is why I wrote a book on how to create one to help businesses. If you can get this right then you can help most businesses make more money. Marketing methods change dramatically every few years so focus on basic, foundational strategies and principles like the USP.

For learning about advertising and applying that knowledge to products and businesses, a great course of study would include Claude Hopkins (*Scientific Advertising, My Life in Advertising*), Rosser Reeves (*Reality in Advertising*), *The 100 Greatest Advertisements* (Julian Watkins), Robert Cialdini (*Influence: The Psychology of Persuasion*), Al Ries (*The 22 Immutable Laws of Marketing, The 22 Immutable Laws of Branding, Positioning* and more), David Ogilvy (*Ogilvy on Advertising*), Eugene Schwartz (*Breakthrough Advertising*), Victor Schwab (*How to Write a Good Advertisement*), and the books of Joseph Sugarman. The absolute best book on copywriting (recommended to me by many professional copywriters) but a totally unknown title is Anthony Flore's *Quick Start Copywriting System*.

In a sense copywriting, wordsmithing, and most of the active literacy skills can be considered a form of Mantrayana to be applied on the "body of greater society" in order to influence it to move in a certain direction just as mantra sounds are used to influence/move the Qi within your own body. Words have the power to affect people through their influence, just as art does through its visual imagery. Such skills can be used for good or bad, so it takes the highest ethics to use them properly.

Press Releases: Paul Krupin once created a single sentence formula for press release success: "Tell me a story, give me a local news angle, and then touch my heart (make me laugh or cry), make my stomach churn (with horror or fear), hit me in my pocketbook, or grab my gonads."

Blair Warren once wrote the following lesson on persuasion: "People will do anything for those who encourage their dreams, justify their failures, allay their fears, confirm their suspicions and help them throw rocks at their enemies."

Sales: If you are not selling then you are not making money in business. Most people think of selling as a despicable, deplorable activity but without sales companies will have no profits. Without profits there is no local employment or tax revenues for the government. Without government revenue social services for the public cannot be provided, including the administration of justice and police protection. So sales are king. Furthermore, everyone is selling. Models are selling their beauty and athletes their performance skills, which are their ability to entertain and amaze. Even doctors and lawyers are selling a service to make a profit to live, so everyone is selling something or they are not in business. Sales can and should be a noble activity done with integrity and the aim to help others by satisfying their needs.

Even great monks and nuns should study the sales process and sales psychology in order to learn how to match with people and influence them for the better with integrity. Devas use possession to get people to do what they want so the purpose of reading sales and persuasion books is to master an alternative, which is to use powerful findings from the fields of persuasion, influence and NLP in moral applications. In a sense mastering the field of persuasion involved with sales or presentations is a subset of Mantrayana mastery.

Understanding the psychological principles and mental aspects of selling opens up a whole world of understanding. For instance, the basic cycle of persuasion is to first establish rapport (see *The Power of Business Rapport* by Michael Brooks), and then attempt to persuade. Matching your body language with another person (see the teachings of Kevin Hogan), so as to reach nonverbal communication, is one of the many NLP methods you can study for gaining rapport with other individuals, such as by matching your breathing and posture with theirs. Learning body language is a useful skill for all interactions; communication with others is 7% verbal, 38% vocal and 55% body expression, so how you hold yourself and your appearance are important. Persuasion techniques also include inducing reciprocity by giving a gift, or showing respect via a compliment and making others feel special. Robert Cialdini wrote the definitive book in this area, *Influence*, which everyone should read.

In Bodhisattva Yoga, you always practice good grooming to look your best, keep a healthy and fit body, cultivate an excellent posture, try to articulate well, practice good manners and etiquette, and cultivate social confidence. Along these lines, I think Cary Grant is an excellent male role model. There are many books and courses on these topics (such as *Dress for Success* by John T. Molloy and Alan Flusser's *Dressing the Man*). Strange enough, sales training, which teaches you how to dress, hold yourself, establish rapport, get along with people and service them, actually helps you prepare to become a Bodhisattva.

Understanding that people are motivated by different things can also help you make sales. People have metaprograms or internal patterns by which they process the world to help determine, direct and guide their behavior. In any field of persuasion you need to understand these metaprograms and appeal to them and people's desires, addressing the question, "What's in it for them?"

For instance, in making decisions some people prefer convenience to cost. Some people make decisions by deferring to thinking and judgment while others defer to their emotions. Some people seek pleasure in life while others are motivated by avoiding pain. Some are motivated by possibility while others focus on necessity. Some are extroverts while others are introverts, and some prefer the big picture while others want specific details. There are many types of metaprograms that run peoples' lives and their decision making. Inside their brains, people commonly evaluate alternatives differently than others.

Let's delve into peoples' motivations just a little to help understand this better. All people have different priorities in life and *want to obtain* different things such as health, time, money, popularity, comfort, leisure, a better appearance, security in old age, praise from others, social advancement, more enjoyment, or self-confidence. People *want to be* various alternatives such as good parents, up-to-date, gregarious, efficient, sociable and hospitable, creative, proud, "first" in things, recognized as authorities, or influential over others. Some people *want to* express their personalities, acquire or collect things, win others' affections, resist being dominated by others, satisfy their curiosity, emulate the admirable, improve themselves generally or appreciate beauty. People may also *want to* save time, worry, doubts, embarrassment, money, work, discomfort or risks. We all have different motivations and things we are after. We also do things in different ways and for different purposes. As further examples, status-oriented people tend to do things to impress others; experience-oriented people do things because they are fun, exciting, challenging or adventurous; and principle-oriented people do things when actions meet their values and subscribe to their code of ethical beliefs.

Robert Cialdini revealed the eight universal laws of persuasion in *Influence*, which help you penetrate through all these metaprograms, and you are urged to study this book and *The Science of Influence* (Kevin Hogan) if you want more. Hogan is an excellent teacher of persuasion and influence techniques. However, many other psychological principles can be learnt with further study such as Alpha strategies that make your offers to others more attractive, Omega strategies that reduce the resistance you experience with a counterparty, and Delta strategies that involve asking people to go into the future and imagine how they will feel if they comply with your advice. Powerful phrases for changing minds fast and for winning compliance include "because," "Imagine (while taking someone to imagine the future)," as well as "don't feel obligated."

Improving yourself for greater sales effectiveness, when done in the form of service, can be a powerful form of self-cultivation. Along these lines see *How I Raised Myself From Failure to Success in Selling* by Frank Bettger and other materials in the line of consultative selling. For sales training you can study many masters such as Brian Tracy, Tom Hopkins, Chet Holmes and too many others to list.

Another skill is getting used to cold calling, which is trying to sell to perfect strangers. One individual whose course might be of interest is Ari Galper ("Unlock the Game"). Ari has valuable lessons on mastering a relaxed vocal tone and has people practice saying, "It's not a problem" in a natural, comfortable way to relieve sales pressure. By also studying the psychology of cold calling people can move towards the Buddhist idea of fearlessness because they will learn to develop confidence by getting over their fear of rejection.

Related to this, one of the greatest things you can ever do to improve your sales career is tape record and critique one phone call a day that you make. Jay Abraham teaches us to find the very best phone salesman, record what he does, break it down, analyze it, improve it and make it your own in order to increase your sales. You can improve it by adding NLP to the content as well as "magic" words or phrases. You should model the best and then optimize it. As Frank Bettger demonstrated in his book *How I Raised Myself From Failure to Success in Selling*, you have to work at always improving your sales skills. If you add one skill or technique to your arsenal a day, that's 5 a week, 20 a month, and 250 a year then your skills will improve dramatically.

One of the big secrets of sales training is sales scripting, pioneered by Donald Moines. The power of words also comes through in *Magic Words That Bring You Riches* (Ted Nicholas), *First Hundred Million* (E. Haldeman-Julius) and *Tested Sentences That Sell* (Elmer Wheeler). As an example, the phrase consistently found to work best in generating sales at retail stores when shoppers come in to browse is, "What brings you into the store today?" This could be adapted to temples and other holy places to prompt individuals to divulge what help they are seeking when they visit, namely, "What brings you to the temple today?" Once you have an answer then you can direct them to the appropriate resources.

Another phrase to use with people is to tell them, "Share with me ..." Also, if you add the words "Donating = Loving" to any fundraising letter at the appropriate place you are likely to increase donations. If in door-to-door requests you say, "Would you be willing to help by giving a donation? Even a penny will help" it will tend to double your donations instead of just saying, "Would you be willing to help by giving a donation?" Words matter.

You need to know that after selling over 100 million books for a nickel a piece, Haldeman-Julius found that people were primarily interested in four major life subjects: sex, love and romance; self-improvement; free thought, skepticism and controversy; and entertainment. These are the things people are typically seeking in life. A fact confirming his observations is that the information products easiest to sell deal with sex and sexuality; money and finances; inspirational, motivational, personal or religious belief themes; health and wellness; sports, hobbies and entertainment; technology (such as computers or software); and employment.

Business Growth: Here are some very basic principles to understand about business development. Famed investor Peter Lynch said there are five ways to increase the earnings of a company: (1) reduce costs, (2) raise prices, (3) expand into new markets (new products), (4) sell more in old markets, and

(5) to close operations, factories, products, etc. that lose money.

Three other ways to grow your business: (1) every year introduce new products or penetrate a new market/country to create a new alliance, (2) make at least one acquisition per year to acquire assets and distribution networks, (3) make growing your existing product or business a regularly scheduled objective every week (and establish annual reviews that force you to innovate). The best meeting schedules to do this that will keep your company aligned and on track are found in *Mastering the Rockefeller Habits* (Verne Harnish). The excellent companion volume is *Scaling Up*.

A key point to remember is that businesses usually have an inside focus and outside focus. For instance, in founding Sears, Roebuck and Company Richard Sears would concentrate on the company's marketing while his partner Julius Rosenwald would work on managing the company's internal operations. If a company's external marketing isn't working well then its sales will lag. If it isn't doing well in terms of internals it may also go bankrupt due to budgeting and cost control issues, productivity problems and other operational issues. One of the biggest problems is controlling cash flow. You can be showing a paper profit but go bankrupt because customers aren't paying you on time, and you therefore run out of cash.

In advising people on improving their business profitability you must remember the simple teaching of Jay Abraham who said there are only four principal ways to build your business: (1) get more customers (increase the number of your customers), (2) get them to spend more money with you per transaction by increasing the average purchase size (increase the average dollar amount per sale), (3) get them to come back more often (increase the repurchase rate by increasing how frequently they buy from you), (4) get them to stay with you longer rather than buy from someone else (extend their buying lifetime by increasing customer loyalty so they stay a customer for longer). He also taught that you need to determine the lifetime value of a customer and spend on advertising less than this value, in effect buying a customer for less than their lifetime value in profits to you.

Another way of looking at it is as follows. To increase the profits of a business you have several options: you can increase the number of customers (grow your customer base), increase the amount of business customers do with you (increase the average purchase size, transaction value, repurchase frequency and loyalty), decrease your expenses, and increase your productivity (do something better by optimizing it, speed up production, and so on).

If you are the leader of the firm, yet another way of growing your business is to make your mission big enough that the dreams of all your employees, vendors and customers are themselves fulfilled by working with you. This will attract them to you and win their support, which will help you to grow. When a company has a core ideology or mission that gives guidance and inspiration to people inside that company then it will attract people with a similar mindset, which helps it to succeed. This is yet another reason why companies should define a fundamental reason for existence that guides the firm beyond just the pursuit of making money.

In terms of choices for the corporate executive, he has only five capital allocation choices: invest in existing operations, acquire other businesses, issue dividends to stockholders, pay down debt, or repurchase stock to drive up the price. He also has three means of generating capital: via internal cash flow, debt issuance, and equity issuance. These choices are discussed in *The Outsiders* (William Thorndike).

There are hundreds of great business books available, but I especially recommend reading the biographies of men who greatly succeeded in business. You might accordingly study such men as John D. Rockefeller, Andrew Carnegie, Charles Schwab, J.P. Morgan, Cornelius Vanderbilt, Sam Walton, Walt Disney, Alfred Sloan, Henry Ford, Michael Dell, John Welch, William Hewlett and David Packard, Thomas Watson, William Procter, Leon Bean, Fred Smith, and so forth. You don't want to become impressed with their wealth. You want to learn how they thought, notice the skills they mastered and how they managed people. I especially recommend *The Unpublished David Ogilvy* for management lessons, and also books by Mark McCormack and Harvey Mackay.

Management: Darren Hardy's *The Compound Effect* and *The Slight Edge* (Jeff Olsen) touch upon the power of small, incremental changes along with momentum to build great results. Success is most often achieved not by great leaps, but by incremental improvements. Therefore you must commit yourself to this approach of constant incremental improvements in life. Specifically, by repeating small disciplines with excellence and taking small, ever-increasing steps you will progress yourself forwards.

Bill Bonner put it this way: "Success is usually the product of compound effort over time. It takes time to develop contacts. It takes time to develop trust – both of your own team and outside clients/customers/associates. It takes time and experience to develop the hunches and instincts that are useful in real life. It takes time too to understand other people and learn how to work with them. It also takes time to build a foundation of human financial capital that allows you to take advantage of the insights and opportunities that experience bring you.

"Time does not work in a linear, mathematical way. As with compound interest, time pays off geometrically. As contacts, experience, wisdom innovations and intuition are added one to another, your opportunities multiply. A $100,000 deal that you might have done when you were 25 grows into a $1 million deal 5 years later. And instead of doing two deals a year, you might do 10 per year.

"This is also why it is important to put in lots of time. The leading figures in their industries put in thousands of hours – usually far more than their competitors. They may appear to be 'gifted.' Their achievements may seem effortless. But they are almost always the product of time.

"Not only that, but the time spent at the end is much more powerful than the time at the beginning. You can see this by looking at charts of compound interest. Starting from a low base, the first series of compound interest produce little difference. But at the end, the results are spectacular.

"Start with a penny. Double it every day. At the end of a week you are still only adding 32 cents per day. By the end of the third week, however, you're adding more than $10,000 per day. So you see, the last increments of time are much more important than the first. ...

"Compound interest works because each addition is then put in service to earn another increment of gain. Compound effort works the same way Every insight, innovation and useful contact helps bring on another, bigger and better one. ... The longer and harder you work at something, generally, the more success you have."[10]

One of the most powerful principles to learn for management is the 80/20 principle, where 20% of your efforts/activities produce 80% of your desired results. This principle appears everywhere such as in sales where 20% (or some such small figure) of a company's products typically produce 80% of sales revenues, and are therefore the most important ones to concentrate upon. Richard Koch has written many books on this principle. One of its greatest applications is to hold one-hour-per-week workshops that focus on 20% of company problems or challenges that will produce 80% of the improvements desired.

The key to effective improvement for any business is to get a handful of people in a room for one hour each week and talk about what to do to drive marketing, sales or fix particular problems. Big breakthroughs can come from the sharing of ideas at just one hour per week, which can be used at temples and spiritual centers. The idea is to work on developing solutions to challenges. The way to manage people is to get them to do weekly meetings that strategically work "on the business," not "in it."

Chet Holmes ("The PEQ Workshop" series of video tapes that are excellent, and *The Ultimate Sales Machine*) is one of the best experts at company meetings. At one time he managed nine divisions of a company for Charlie Munger (partner of Warren Buffett), doubled the sales volume of each, most within 12 to 15 months, and again doubled sales for several years consecutively. An incredible track record from incredible management

---

[10] Bill Bonner and Will Bonner, *Family Fortunes: How to Build Family Wealth and Hold on to It for 100 Years*, (John Wiley & Sons, New Jersey, 2012), pp. 146-148.

skills.

Holmes's super valuable method for running a one-hour workshop to address challenges or solve problems is as follows: (1) Appoint a workshop leader and then get everyone in a room and put a topic to be solved up on the board – the purpose of the workshop (ex. how to improve airline safety, how to reduce customer returns, how to increase sales for a new product), (2) Ask everyone in the group to *write down* 3 solutions on paper without calling them out, giving them two minutes to do so, (3) Write down everyone's ideas on a flipchart while eliminating duplicate ideas, asking questions to clarify the ideas, and refrain from any criticism that an idea is "dumb" or "stupid," (4) Get everyone to look at the list on the board and give the group 30 seconds to write down what participants believe are the top ideas/solutions with a priority of 1-2-3, (5) Organize a vote where you ask everyone in turn for their top three choices with ratings and mark slashes for 1-2-3 against each idea, (6) Determine the winning solution(s) by tallying up the slashes. Cut off everything past the top five or six benefits, solutions, etc. and particularly focus on the top three. Also, keep a full record of everything suggested.

Next, each person should then think of a new assignment or task where they can integrate the top three ideas into next week's working schedule and get everyone to implement it that week. Ask for the implementation ideas for the top three solutions and write them on the board, rank them as done previously, and select the top three assignments for the group to implement. Finally, write a memo summarizing the top three problems, proposed solutions and implementation strategies and tell the group to implement them. You should file this in a 3-ring binder that becomes the record of such meetings for a year. The big boss can review this for every department, and thereby manage the company effectively this way. New employees can read it to get up to speed in very little time.

At next week's meeting you need to review the actions taken and their results. You must determine what worked and how it can be improved because some "solutions" don't work at all initially and need to be constantly rejiggered until they produce the results you want. This proactive way of managing is "working on a business" rather than "in the business." This is the proper way to manage.

Overall you must repeat this process every week with new topics, or the very same topics until you get a good solution. A big boss doesn't have to personally come up with all the solutions to the problems of his company himself (see Martin Edelstein's book *"I" Power*). He simply needs to surround himself with talent better than himself, which is the approach that many business people use, such as Hugh Hefner who developed Playboy.

Jay Conrad Levinson, author of *Guerilla Marketing*, said that Hefner was not talented in writing, but he surrounded himself with the best writers and editors. He had no talent in photography, so he brought in the best photographers or purchased their photos from the outside. He knew people who were great art directors and artists and used them to supplement his lack of skills in art. By surrounding himself with talent where he was lacking, he built the Playboy empire. I know of a multi-million dollar supplement manufacturer which also grew because the owner made it a strategic principle to surround himself with talent better than himself. He had a vision and simply surrounded himself with the very best lawyers, accountants, marketers and so forth to build his giant firm. *Rich Dad, Poor Dad* author Robert Kiyosaki advised doing the same thing.

What executives, such as CEOs and top managers, should do is simply assign problems or concerns to departments to solve. Those departments should hold group problem solving sessions conducted in the manner described. He or she can then manage the departments by keeping up-to-date with the recorded results that are kept in a 3-ring binder, and intervening with department heads as appropriate.

When trying to implement an idea you can go through the very same procedure. In a workshop you might ask a team how they are going to implement an idea. Everyone should write down their ideal structure (bullet style) and then the workshop leader asks each in turn their solutions, which are written on the board. The leader must work through the ideas, guiding the group as it goes, and establish a "perfect" structure using everyone's ideas. That done, they must then put out a memo describing the results of the meeting that lists the new procedure/solution to be followed. Into the 3-ring binder it must also go.

Most importantly you must examine, observe and police the new procedure in action. The leader or manager should also personally perform the task or procedure. Skip this step if you want to fail! By trying it yourself you'll know when and how it is working or not, and why. Furthermore, if you don't watch its execution, even if you told people to do it the results will usually be subpar if you just delegate without inspection. "People respect what you inspect," so you must think of yourself as a military general who performs inspections, takes random observations and makes sure things are implemented in order to protect lives.

At the following week's meeting, you should go over the procedure and refine it based on the results, asking each person what they precisely did and how it worked. New ideas or procedures rarely take hold immediately, so you may have to repeat this process for 6-8 weeks with the goal being incremental but continuous improvement. Eventually a synthesis will occur where the new procedure/solution finally becomes how people think and operate. Then all you must do is continue to refine it regularly.

This is a great way to manage a firm, and can fix many problems without having to resort to policies. Actually, this method is priceless and worth the price of this book alone, but few realize this until they start using it.

A similar approach to fixing problems, which avoids creating lots of conflicting policies, is to contact the source of a reported problem to get an understanding of the situation (with evidence); contact the person responsible for solving the problem and ask them if they know about it and how much they know; and then ask them to "copy" you their solution (resist the urge to suggest a solution or create a new policy) which ensures that the problem gets solved, the solution makes sense, and it makes sense in the context of the whole business and its operations. This type of disciplined approach for fixing problems helps to prevent the creation of a large bureaucracy and countless internal rules and regulations that stifle creativity and business function.

Business Miscellaneous: James Altucher once said, "You're not going to get rich buying stocks. Put the money into reading, writing, learning, starting your own business. Investing in yourself is by far the best investment you can make." Andrew Carnegies gave essentially the same advice, which is to invest in yourself to become successful. Robert Kiyosaki (*Rich Dad, Poor Dad*) also said that personal development and self-improvement, and the money spent on it, is always a wise investment.

Robert Allen introduced the notion that everyone should try to develop multiple streams of income (*Multiple Streams of Income: How to Generate a Lifetime of Unlimited Wealth*) in order to become wealthy. Every year someone becomes a star writing about new ways to make money and accumulate wealth, and how to help yourself financially. Typically the solution involves real estate or leverage of some sort (options, futures, margin stock trading). Avoid the trading field as you have a high likelihood of losing money, perhaps 98%. If you ever approach the investment field for excitement, rather than purely for profits, you are doomed to failure. If you invest in something you don't understand, you will fail with certainty.

One of the best investments is to start your own business, but what type? Locational astrology can often give you insights as to the type of business you can be successful with in your location, the timing of maximum success, and location(s) where you can best succeed. Use it.

The *E-Myth* (Michael Gerber) is a must read for entrepreneurs that helps them understand they are to grow and market a business that can be easily duplicated rather than create a job for themselves. After reaching a certain stage, the owner should spend their time focusing on marketing and strategy rather than being tied up solving minor day-to-day problems. In addition to strategy and marketing, a leader should spend time on selecting managers who can perform well and be the future of the firm.

For referral marketing systems see Jay Abraham's *93 Extraordinary Referral Systems* and a similar internet collection by Perry Marshall. For networking there is *Endless Referrals* (Bob Burg), and *Dig Your Well Before You're Thirsty* by Harvey Mackay (all his books are excellent as are those of overlooked American sports agent Mark McCormack). For time management and productivity tips see *Quick, Fast, Done* (Bill Bodri) and *Getting Things Done* (David Allen). Some of the principles for radical productivity include touching papers just once, making to-do lists, planning your day by scheduling the time required for tasks, and prioritizing so that you always do the most important (most productive) tasks first.

Dan Kennedy has a tape series on accumulating wealth that is really excellent, and one of the golden nuggets inside is his rule to hire people whose parents owned their own business. These typically are the *best employees* since they saw their parents *doing everything*, so they did not grow up emulating a pattern where they only performed just their own tiny little job function. This rule is also worth its weight in gold. Similarly, Wayne Green suggested that in in applying for a job you might say something like, "Look, you have a whole bunch of things you need to get done and no one (or not enough people) to do them. I'll do them and if I don't know how I'll learn." Surprising, Michael Senoff on his HardtoFindSeminars.com site posted an interview with a Silicon Valley "Mr. X" business success who suggested that hiring ex-policemen, ex-FBI, and ex-intelligence operation professionals was problematical because they had "limited views of positive business ethics." Don't expect high ethics from prosecuting attorneys in the legal field either.

As a general rule, when in doubt about a potential employee then don't hire but keep looking. "Hire slowly but fire fast" is a general rule ... if an individual doesn't work out then that bad apple can spoil an entire organization so fire misfits quickly, especially internal politicians. David Ogilvy also said, "Sack incurable politicians." Also, put your best people on your best opportunities, not your biggest problems.

The general rule is that you cannot grow revenues faster than you grow good managers. A company's real assets are its people. Actually, people are not your most important asset, but rather the "right" people are your most important asset, and this often has to do with character. This is why Dan Kennedy was predisposed to hiring people who saw that their parents did everything without complaining.

"Casting" as a form of hiring is important because people don't change that much. It is hard to instill within people what is not already present in their character, so in hiring decisions it is often best to select people who already have the character traits you need for the position, or who fit in with the company's core ideology, and to use what is already in them rather than try to train them to have something that isn't there. You select them by their inclinations and personalities, which is casting, and then add training. For example, one airline company executive said that in hiring stewardesses they recorded the room of faces and only hired those who were always smiling and listening to the speaker as he/she talked, thus selecting people according to a personality trait they wanted. Managers should select employees based on talent and personality, set expectations of the right outcomes, motivate them, and develop them by helping them find the right fit.

When you must fire someone, one of the best firing speeches I ever encountered, whose source I cannot recall, was the following: "Listen, this isn't working out for you. Everybody is great at certain things and this is not what you are good at, and as a result you're holding yourself back. You'll never get ahead in this job and I'll never put you ahead in this job. The best thing I can do for you right now is to let you go so that you can find something where you will do great." The internet offers many good verbal scripts for letting people go.

In *David Ogilvy, An Autobiography*, Ogilvy alternatively suggested: "1. Give him the bad news at the very beginning of the interview. It is cruel to lead up to it. 2. Don't tell your victim he is incompetent or repulsive. It is awful to be sacked; to have your self-esteem obliterated can ruin a man for life. 3. As soon as you have delivered the bad news, talk to the poor devil as if he were your brother. Tell him what you would do in his shoes. 4. End the interview by taking him to lunch the following day. This makes him feel that dismissal does not imply personal rejection." Food for thought – there are lots of alternative ways to do this. Do some internet or other types of research for the method that suits you and the situation best.

Becoming Rich: Famed investor Ken Fisher explained that there are ten major roads to riches: starting a successful business of your own; becoming CEO or an extremely high paid executive of an existing firm that will reward you well; hitching yourself to the coattails of a superstar visionary who is going places and riding along his wave of success; becoming a celebrity yourself and turning fame into wealth; marrying into money; using the law to take money from other people (suing them); capitalizing on or leveraging other people's money to make your own money; inventing an endless future revenue stream such as book or invention royalties; making money from real estate using the power of leverage; saving money, avoiding debt and investing well.

To understand how to get rich, you should read the biographies of some of the richest people in the world to see how they became wealthy. A large part of that wealth is due to their astrological fortune, namely their fate from past life karma. People to study should include Crassus (*Lives of the Noble Greeks and Romans*), Warren Buffett (*The Snowball*), J. Paul Getty (*How to Be Rich*), Andrew Carnegie *(The Autobiography of Andrew Carnegie and the Gospel of Wealth)*, Jacob Fuger *(The Richest Man Who Ever Lived: The Life and*

Times of Jacob Fugger), and John Rockefeller *(Titan: The Life of John D. Rockefeller)*.

In analyzing the *Forbes* billionaire list you'll find that most of world's richest people came from the fields of business and finance; oil, chemicals, energy and manufacturing; retail and consumer goods; real estate and construction; tech. Some of the business fortunes were made based on the model of a tiny profit duplicated on innumerable transactions, others focused on making big profits on a moderate number of transactions, others focused on making money through the power of leverage, others created virtual monopolies for steady income, and others bought tremendous resource assets on the cheap that deliver a continuous stream of revenues for revenues.

There are all sorts of business models inherent in the billions made by billionaires, and you need to understand some of these basic wealth models. A major point is that those who become rich were typically entrepreneurs who owned their own business. Singers, actors and athletes can become rich, and sometimes you can become rich through a high salary, but entrepreneurship offers the most common pathway to wealth. Along these lines *The E-Myth* by Michael Gerber should be read.

Many billionaires followed the same pattern that Warren Buffett used, which was to find good businesses, for sensible prices, producing attractive returns (strong profits), which could then be reinvested in more businesses of the same kind. Buffett never invests in anything he does not understand. He has always sought durable competitive strengths from what are essentially quasi-monopolies (businesses whose earnings are protected by a "moat"), businesses with able and high-grade management, and businesses that manage capital and cash flow against clear metrics that show good returns on the net tangible assets required to operate the business.

Jim Collins wrote *Good to Great* and *Built to Last*, both fantastic books which emphasize that the best companies in the world focus on managing just a very few metrics and stick to their core game to remain profitable.

One should also recognize that business people can easily become "errant men of business" such as when cigarette manufacturers deny that smoking causes lung cancer, investment bankers sell their worst holdings to their clients and then actively bet against those customers, oil companies conduct fracking operations that permanently destroy the ground water resources of the nation, pharmaceutical firms manufacture drugs that kill but hide those results so that they can continue to sell products to make money, and so forth. How to avoid becoming an errant man of business is covered in *Color Me Confucius* and *Culture, Country, City, Company, Person, Purpose, Passion, World*. In one sense, the right job and career, and avoiding the path of errant men of business, is part of the eightfold path of Buddhism – right view, right resolve, right speech, right conduct, right livelihood, right effort, right mindfulness, and right meditative practice.

Andrew Carnegie said: "No man can become rich without himself enriching others." This should become one's guiding principle … becoming rich should be the result of rendering service to humanity, fulfilling a need and even helping your partners become rich rather than concentrating on just yourself. Andrew Carnegie's book *The Autobiography of Andrew Carnegie and the Gospel of Wealth* would be a mainstay for anyone wishing to learn about the road to wealth. Carnegie would be the first to point out that business success comes from hard work – working your ass off. However, when you grow and create a business and then see people getting jobs out of your efforts, create families, and send children to school because of what you do it is a wonderful feeling that you have moved the world forward.

In addition, more millionaires have read the book he "commissioned," *Think and Grow Rich* (Napoleon Hill), than almost any other business book in history. It should definitely be read along with *How to Win Friends and Influence People* (Dale Carnegie), *The 7 Habits of Highly Effective People* (Stephen Covey), *Rich Dad Poor Dad* (Robert Kiyosaki), *Influence: The Psychology of Persuasion* (Robert Cialdini), and *The Autobiography of Benjamin Franklin*.

For individuals, especially those in their twenties who aren't businessmen but wish to become rich, there are the financial lessons to be mastered in *I Will Teach You to Be Rich* (Ramit Sethi), *The Total Money Makeover* (Dave Ramsey), *Super Investing* (Bill Bodri) and *Rich Dad Poor Dad* (Robert Kiyosaki). Kiyosaki taught the invaluable lesson that the rich know the difference between an asset and liability; an asset is anything that generates money while a liability is anything that regularly takes money from your pockets for upkeep (boat, car, golf clubs, plane, home). In *Super Investing* I cover the investment principles and rules that have consistently worked over a 100-year time frame, as well as basic investment rules that rarely make it into print. A structure is revealed to enable you to create a family legacy of wealth that will last for several generations. In *Breakthrough Strategies of Wall Street Traders* I revealed interesting trading strategies and investment philosophies that will benefit you.

To understand the millionaire mind you can start by reading *The Millionaire Next Door* and *The Millionaire Mind* by Thomas Stanley, *Rich Dad Poor Dad* (Robert Kiyosaki) and *Secrets of the Millionaire Mind* (T. Harv Eker).

Investing: As *The Richest Man in Babylon* (George Clason) says, money comes to those who save it, money stays with those who avoid debt, money multiples for those who invest it, money stays with those who entrust it to wiser investors, money is lost in get-rich-quick schemes and when you invest in things you don't understand. Debt is particularly a problem, for most people go bankrupt because of too much debt, especially medical debts. Business and personal bankruptcy often arrives from too much debt, so avoid it as much as possible. Inadequate cash flow becomes the issue.

Wealth from investing is a function of time where abundance originates due to the slow growth of wealth via wise investments. Abundance happens because of well-designed intention followed by well-designed actions taken over and over again until their positive results accumulate. In the field of investing this means selecting the right investing methodology and religiously applying it over time despite the ups and downs of the market. See *Super Investing* and *Breakthrough Strategies of Wall Street Traders* to learn how to do this.

For those who wish to learn the field of investing there are the momentum methods of William O'Neil, and profitable trading methods within *Breakthrough Strategies of Wall Street Traders* (Bill Bodri), *Inside the House of Money* (Steven Drobny), *The Alpha Masters* (Maneet Ahuja), *The Hedge Fund Edge* (Mark Boucher) and the excellent series of *Market Wizards* books by Jack Schwager. I do not recommend people enter into the trading field at all because 98% will lose money, especially with commodities, options and futures trading. They should focus on investing rather than trading or speculation. Furthermore, people need to learn the lesson that just because prices are speculatively elevated it doesn't mean that somehow they actually belong there. They should have a value relative to the cash flow they will throw off to the investor and deliver into his wallet, otherwise they are probably in a bubble.

As I revealed in *Super Investing: 5 Proven methods for Beating the Markets and Retiring Rich*, there are only two primary ways to make money in investing that have worked for a hundred years in the past and probably will continue to do so into the future - value investing and momentum investing. Wesley Gray, interviewed in *Breakthrough Strategies of Wall Street Traders*, told me he evaluated thousands of investment systems and came to the exact same conclusion. Once again, only two methods work over the long term: value investing and momentum investing.

Furthermore, you can practice creating a well-diversified portfolio, or concentrating your investment funds in just a few investments that you feel will be winners. Prudence suggests diversification whereas some wealthy people suggest that concentration is the only real way to get rich, but of course this is only if you are lucky enough to pick winners. Jimmy Rogers states that if you approach investments with the idea that you can only have twenty investments in your life you'd be very careful at picking them and would create a better chance to pick winners with that mindset.

Value investing can be learned through *The Intelligent Investor* (Ben Graham), *Getting Started in Value Investing* (Charles Mizrahi), *Value Investing* (Bruce Greenwald), and by studying the methods of Walter Schloss and Warren Buffett. AQR Capital Management once analyzed Warren Buffett's investments to discover the secret of his success. An AQR working paper called "Buffett's Alpha" reported, "In essence, we find that the secret to Buffett's success is his preference for cheap, safe, high-quality stocks combined with his consistent use of leverage to magnify returns while surviving the inevitable large absolute and relative drawdowns this entails. Indeed, we find that stocks with the characteristics favored by Buffett have done well in general, that Buffett applies about 1.6-to-1 leverage financed partly using insurance float with a low financing rate, and that leveraging safe stocks can largely explain Buffett's performance." Another invaluable paper is *The Superinvestors of Graham-and-Doddsville*, by Warren Buffett himself, which is a reprint from the Columbia University Business School.

The reality of what Buffett actually does is buy high quality firms that are cheap. I have a slightly different take on Buffett in *Super Investing* that is very similar. You have to buy very good businesses for an undervalued price, like buying a dollar for thirty cents, and compound the cash they throw off by investing in similar quasi-monopolies that also throw off cash you can compound. *Super Investing* contains all my investing and macro-economic insights from years of research on Wall Street and hundreds of investment book readings. It was written for parents to teach children, and for aspiring super investors, with the idea of providing a methodology whereby you could create a family legacy of mega-wealth.

The single most reliable measure of stock market valuation ever developed, which can be used to forecast future stock returns, is the ratio of equity market capitalization (non-financial equities) to corporate gross value-added (of non-financial companies included estimated foreign revenues). This figure is computed by investment manager John Hussman of Hussman Strategic Advisors whose forward return estimates are invaluable. Value investor Warren Buffett divides the total market capitalization of the U.S. stock market by the gross national product, or GNP, to determine whether stock prices are cheap or too expensive.

Incidentally, in 2009 Warren Buffett was being interviewed by CNBC reporter Becky Quick and was asked which single economic indicator he would want available for determining the state of the economy if he were stranded on a desert island and had access to only one number. He actually mentioned two - "freight car loadings" and "truck traffic" data. There is also an ocean going equivalent for the health of the world economy, which is the Baltic Dry shipping rate index. This is also known as the Baltic Dry Index or BDI. The velocity of money is yet another powerful indicator largely ignored by mainstream analysts. For true statistics on the economy (inflation, unemployment rate, GDP growth, etc.) you should turn to ShadowStats.com, produced by John Williams, and the independently produced Chapwood Index of inflation.

Momentum investing can be learned through *Quantitative Momentum* (Wesley Gray) and *Dual Momentum Investing* (Gary Antonacci). Successful momentum investors and their stories are also featured in *Breakthrough Strategies of Wall Street Traders and Momentum Masters* (Mark Minervini and Bob Weissman).

For asset allocation and where and when to invest over the long term, one can study *DIY Financial Advisor* (Wesley Gray), *The Ivy Portfolio* (Mebane Faber) and *Super Investing* (Bill Bodri). A knowledge of contrarian investing, where you purchase assets on the cheap because they are out of favor, is important to the long-term investor as is knowledge of crowd psychology. Asset allocation along the lines of contrarian thinking, where you buy undervalued out-of-favor assets, should follow the long-term Kondratieff cycles, demographics trends, and innovation waves discussed in *Culture, Country, City, Company, Person, Purpose, Passion, World*. If you use a MACD indicator on monthly or quarterly prices you can often come up with overbought and undersold indications for long-term investing.

To avoid losing one's head in speculative asset bubbles when everyone gets into a buying frenzy that ultimately collapses, one must study Elliott Wave theory, Gustave Le Bon's *The Crowd*, *Reminiscences of a Stock Operator* (Edwin Lefevre), and *Extraordinary Popular Delusions and the Madness of Crowds* (Charles Mackay). Charles Mackay warned, "We find that whole communities suddenly fix their minds upon one object, and go mad in its pursuit; that millions of people become simultaneously impressed with one delusion, and run after it, till their attention is caught by some new folly more captivating than the first." Several individuals, such as Didier Sornette, have found that financial bubbles and crashes exhibit unique mathematic behaviors known as increasing log-periodic oscillations around the rising trend, which lead to a projected critical point for the beginning of a market crash that can be used for forecasting purposes.

If you want to study the financial markets, you need to study the economy. If you study the economy, this leads to trying to understand the global economy along with trade deficits and budget deficits. Who talks about this most coherently? The hard money, hard asset (non-fiat currency) advocates. Some people call them gold bugs out of derision. They often talk about the lessons of monetary history (ex. Michael Maloney in the "Hidden Secrets of Money" video), which repeats over and over again. Thus you can learn the financial lessons of history from gold proponents since they study sound money the most.

Various books such as *Probable Outcomes* (Easterling), *Unexpected Returns* (Easterling), *This Time is Different* (Reinhart and Rogoff), *Bull's Eye Investing* (Mauldin), *Endgame* (Mauldin), *Riding the Millenial Storm* (Vittachi), *Tomorrow's Gold* (Faber), *The Fourth Mega-Market* (Acampora), *The Great Boom Ahead* (Dent), *The Great Crash Ahead* (Dent), *The Fourth Turning* (Strauss), *Boom, Bust and Echo* (Foot and Stoffman), *Stock Cycles* (Alexander), *The Kondratiev Cycle* (Alexander), *Leading Sectors and World Powers* (Modelski and Thompson),

Long Cycles in World Politics (Modelski), *Resource Wars* (Klare), *Why Countries Fail* (Acemoglu and Robinson), *Currency War*s (Rickards), *The Great Super Cycle* (Skarica), *Conquer the Crash* (Prechter), *The Real Crash* (Schiff), *How Rich Countries Got Rich and Why Poor Countries Stay Poor* (Reinert), *Breakout Nations* (Sharma), *Investment Biker* (Rogers), etc. all have interesting offerings on this subject of macro-trend investing.

To understand this I would start with my two books, *Super Investing* and *Culture, Country, City, Company, Person, Purpose, Passion, World*. They deal with long-term economics, national supremacy cycles, innovation cycles, the principles for how countries become rich and how people become wealthy by tapping into macro-trends. They offer views and information that are not taught in any traditional curriculum.

One intriguing miscellaneous: buying real estate is all about location, location, location. However, the best forecasting method that I've ever encountered for real estate property prices in countries is the *inverse dependency ratio*. The age dependency ratio is the sum of the young population (under age 15) and elderly population (age 65 and over) relative to the working-age population (ages 15 to 64). Available for countries, this population statistic can forecast the future demand for real estate, and thus property price trends, for decades going into the future.

Career Selection: Careerwise you have a few options. You can either (1) work for yourself by owning your own business, (2) work for someone else, including institutions (such as a hospital or university), or (3) work for the government.

Employees must recognize that the individuals who have the highest chances of getting raises, bonuses and big paychecks are those who know how to bring in money and do so. These people usually occupy positions in sales, creating products and managing profits. They bring in the revenues so they get paid the most. For the biggest possible income, you need to develop a career in these areas, especially sales.

It is a funny thing that many people struggle their whole lives for financial success and when they get it discover it lacks meaning. Then they suffer from chronic dissatisfaction. Many don't feel that their efforts are enriching the world in some way, and feel that their most inner Dream is unconnected with their life. For job security, the typical fields are careers in accounting and computer related services, but you are secure only if you add value to an organization that is profitable since bankruptcy saves no jobs. Furthermore, if you are only looking for money and security that is all you are likely to get, not career satisfaction.

When people are trying to determine a career or occupation, typically they are shuttled to books such as *Strengths Finder* (Tom Rath), *What Color is Your Parachute?* (Richard Bolles), and *The Pathfinder* (Nicholas Lore).

However, I encourage books like *Automatic Wealth for Grads* (Michael Masterson), *So Good They Can't Ignore You* (Call Newport), *The Talent Code* (Daniel Coyle), *Talent is Overrated* (Geoff Colvin) and *The E-Myth* (Michael Gerber). Small businesses and entrepreneurs, rather than big businesses and corporations, are what create the most jobs in a country.

Many religions teach us to avoid careers that involve harmful activities (such as alcohol since it leads to destructions caused by intoxication, weapons that lead to violence and killing, exploiting people and so on) that you can find symbolized in Shakyamuni Buddha's teachings about Right Livelihood. The basic idea is that with the right knowledge of "dharma" you will be motivated to right conduct in life and avoid careers that contribute to harm, cause harm or produce bad karma for yourself and others. Hinduism and Indian philosophy flat out state that pursuing *artha*, or wealth, profit and success in life, is perfectly proper. So is pursing *kama*, or enjoyments and pleasure as part of life. The only caveat is that they should be pursued in the right way; you should only pursue what is proper, namely what is ethical, virtuous and righteous. Therefore, while you choose a career in part due to income, you should also consider whether that job or career embodies a good purpose. If not, keep looking. Most people find their careers unsatisfying until they find what they consider their dharma.

For career selection I highly recommend the services of astrologers for some advice, especially Vedic astrologers and locational western astrologers (see JulianLee.com) who will redraw your natal chart by moving it to your current living location or where you intend to live. Locational astrology is a neglected field but absolutely the right way to make predictions, and they are so extremely accurate they are often astounding compared to traditional western astrology predictions. This is what you should turn to since most people cannot obtain a genuine *Nadi grantha* palm leaf reading from India, or *Tieh Pan Shen Shu* reading from Hong Kong. See *White Fat Cow* for details.

Don't play with your life but hire the most experienced locational astrologer you can find before you make a fateful decision worth hundreds of thousands to millions of dollars, as well as your future comfort and happiness. When you move you tend to reconstruct yourself in a new location according to your new locational rising sign and the new location of planets in houses. Your personality and traits will start to change with a new birth chart, which will produce new phenomena for you in your life.

By focusing on the sign, ruler and occupant of the tenth house of career and the second house of money, one can come up with some excellent career suggestions. By determining favorable long-term progressions and transits to the house rulers (such as Venus/Jupiter trine, sextile or conjunct the tenth house career ruler) you can also determine the big positive trends for decades, and can then move to locations where you can harvest these favorable trends. However, no chart is perfect for all areas of life.

When you move to a new location that is good for one area of your life it may be bad for another, such as relationships with your spouse (the seventh house). If the fourth house of home is afflicted in a new location you are considering then you will never feel comfortable or happy in that location even if you are making lots of money and your career is fine. As one master astrologer told me, "No life is perfect. They all have ups and downs and everyone who enjoys great good fortune in one area of life experiences misfortune in another."

CITY AND NATIONAL PROSPERITY

The principles of uplifting and spreading civilization, culture, cultivation, good conduct, cooperation and charity – these are the topics to master when you want to become a Buddha and especially when you want to become a protector deity or Orisha for a city, state or country. My book *Culture, Country, City, Company, Person, Purpose, Passion, World* was actually written as a training vehicle for such aspirations.

All cities and countries have protect gods, which are Buddhas, Bodhisattvas and guardian spirits that work to protect the welfare and prosperity of those locations. For instance, a number of city protect gods appear in the *Avatamsaka Sutra*, namely City-ruling Spirit Jeweled Peak Illumination; City-ruling Spirit Wondrously Adorning Palaces; City-ruling Spirit Pure Jewels of Joy; City-ruling Spirit Pure and Free from Worry; City-ruling Spirit Flower Lamps and Blazing Eyes; City-ruling Spirit Clear Manifestation of Blazing Banners; City-ruling Spirit Flourishing Blessings Brightness; City-ruling Spirit Pure Radiance; City-ruling Spirit Fragrant Cowl Adornment; and City-ruling Spirit Wondrous Jeweled Light.

Some of the protector deities for temples and spiritual places (a bodhimanda) also mentioned include Bodhimanda Spirit Banner of Pure Adornment; Bodhimanda Spirit Sumeru Jeweled Brilliance; Bodhimanda Spirit Thunderclap and Banner-like Characteristics; Bodhimanda Spirit Raining Down Flowers Wondrous Eyes; Bodhimanda Spirit Flower Garlands Bright Cowl; Bodhimanda Spirit Raining Down Jeweled Ornaments; Bodhimanda Spirit Heroic Fragrance and Vision; Bodhimanda Spirit Vajra-Colored Cloud; Bodhimanda Spirit Lotus Flower Brilliance; and Bodhimanda Spirit Dazzling Wondrous Light.

Over time, empires and countries develop their own character and civilization. Civilization is a set of ideas, knowledge, values, institutions and achievements of a society at a certain time. Culture is fundamentally a set of beliefs that are shared by a large group of people. It is a pool of information stored in a population that gets transmitted to people through a social learning process, and therefore is a primary influence in forming people's character. Culture is definitely one of the primary determinants of character formation. If you want to become guardian spirit or protector god for a city, region or country, which is a national guardian, in addition to one's spiritual cultivation there are several topics one should understand that deal with the long-term issues of civilization, prosperity, and culture of the people you want to protect. Prosperity is not just a matter of avoiding war, improving health and advancing economics but of the character and behavior of a people.

When you read history you must understand that the elite class of society, which includes the king, his ministers and the richest or most powerful strata of men and women in a country, were always concerned with how to make their country rich, how to put that wealth into their own pockets, and how to maintain power, particularly how to manage the public to avoid being toppled. They were interested in obtaining power, influence or control over every national axis such as the military, political, economic, social, religious and intellectual spheres. One can even study ancient Sparta to learn how the elites put an emphasis on using power to keep the Hoplite underclass in subjugation. This same concern reappears constantly throughout history, especially in the bloody track record of Marxism and Communism.

Only if you understand this, and understand what John Taylor Gatto and many others have taught,[11] which is that the elites in today's world have followed the historical pattern of subsidizing movements that dumb the public down and take freedom away from individuals, can you understand why certain memes are transmitted to the public by the Deep State, the media and press, philanthropic foundations, and think tank institutions. The purpose is to engineer the masses to be submissive, and the propaganda methods of Edward Bernays and other scientific methods are used to do so.

The Century of the Self British film documentary by filmmaker Adam Curtis reveals just a tiny bit of how people in power tried to use the ideas of Walter Lippmann and methods of Bernays to guide herd instincts and control the opinions of the masses in this current age of democracy.[12] They supported programs to control/direct the inner psychological life of the masses because of the need to create consumers in a mass production economy.

One can start to understand the mass psychology of crowds from *The Crowd: A Study of the Popular Mind* (Gustave Le Bon), *Extraordinary Popular*

---

[11] "The Ultimate History Lesson: A Weekend with John Taylor Gatto," accessed August 29, 2018, https://www.youtube.com/watch?v=YQiW_1848t8.

[12] *The Century of the Self*, Adam Curtis, accessed August 29, 2018, https://www.youtube.com/watch?v=eJ3RzGoQC4s.

Delusions and the Madness of Crowds (Charles MacKay), *Manias, Panics and Crashes* (Charles Kindleberger), *Elliott Wave Principle* (Robert Prechter), *Socionomics* (Robert Prechter) and *Contrarian Investment Strategies* (David Dreman). Many manias, especially asset bubbles, require both a compelling story and ample credit to support them just as mass movements require a motivating issue and financial support too. To learn how to produce social change within inflexible communities you can read Saul Alinksy's *Rules for Radicals*.

A famous Alex Jones interview with Aaron Russo also revealed how the Rockefellers funded "women's liberation" not because it was a good thing, but because they were interested in achieving two primary objectives. The first objective was that American elites wanted to increase the tax base by having women work. The second objective was to break up the strength of the family and get children in school at an earlier age, which would happen if mothers were not at home because they were working. The purpose was so that children could then be indoctrinated on how to think and would start considering the state as their family.[13] I provide this interview in *Husbands and Wives Were Connected in the Past*.

Another interview, of Soviet defector Yuri Bezmenov conducted by historian G. Edward Griffin, clearly reveals that nations will use long-term playbooks of "invisible" strategies to try to destabilize and then gain supremacy over other nations.[14] This is actually true and not some conspiracy theory. When retired 4-star U.S. Army General Wesley Clark, previously Supreme Allied Commander of NATO, announced the U.S. plans that Iraq, Syria, Somalia, Libya, Sudan, Iran and Yemen were "to be taken out" over a series of years, he revealed the same type of planning even in the United States. Long-term, large scale economic development plans that will fund companies for years, especially favored government contractors (like Bechtel and Halliburton), also fall into this category.

Hence, if you want to understand how countries are destabilized or led down different paths you can study the interview of Russian defector Yuri Bezmenov (interviewed by G. Edward Griffin), the interview of Aaron Russo by Alex Jones, the workings of foundations cooperating with intelligence agencies (see *The Deliberate Dumbing Down of America* by Charlotte Iserbyt), the methods used by George Soros for destabilizing the Soviet regimes, the efforts of NGOs, the propaganda methods of Edward Bernays (*Propaganda*) and advertising methods of Albert Lasker (*The Lasker Story: As He Told It*), etcetera. To understand such interventions in South

---

[13] "Alex Jones Interviews Aaron Russo," accessed August 29, 2018, https://www.youtube.com/watch?v=N3NA17CCboA.
[14] "Deception Was My Job" or "Soviet Subversion of the Free World Press," accessed August 29, 2018, https://www.youtube.com/watch?v=jFfrWKHB1Gc.

America I refer you to *Confessions of an Economic Hit Man* and *The Life and Times of America's Banana King*.

Lasker must be read with Bernays since Lasker used similar techniques inside the United States to shape public opinion. Aftewards, you will then be able to understand why many rich industrialists of the past eras would fund political and intellectual movements that promoted capitalism since this was the source of their fortunes (whereas socialism and communism would raise their labor costs), and why governments fund subversive organizations to fracture the cohesiveness of other nations. This is touched upon in *Color Me Confucius* since Confucius warned against this.

What one must come to understand is that there are definitely long-term plans put in play by various parties – in the military, economic, financial, educational, health, social, etc. fields – in order to change the culture of nations for various purposes, most of which are nefarious in the sense that they equate into a loss of freedom for the public and more control by elite parties with their own agendas. *Seeds of Destruction* explains this type of engineering in the field of agriculture. Historian Eustace Mullins explained how he found a voluminous trail of historical documents to back up this conclusion for many other fields.

Interestingly enough, Dr. Dave Janda explained that President Ronald Reagan had a policy that every high level official entering his administration be taught a certain principle before assuming office, which is that the Left-Right, Democrat-Republican, Liberal-Conservative dichotomy was just a fictitious smokescreen for the real battle actually being waged all the time, which was always an up-down axis of more freedom or more control over the populace (oppression). The fight between Republicans or Democrats didn't matter because the real fight was always more control or less control over the population.

For an inkling of real politics and geopolitical strategy you should read *The Fourth World War* (Count de Marenches and David Andelman), *The Evil Empire* (Count de Marenches and Christine Ochrent), and the geopolitical strategies of Kuan Tzu (*The Means to Win* by William Bodri). Other tacticians, geo-strategists, mega-historians or related people of interest to study include Sun Tzu (*The Art of War*), Zhuge Liang, Han Fei, Clausewitz (*On War*), Thucydides, Kautilya (*Arthashastra*), Ibn Khaldun (*Muqaddimah*), Machiavelli (*The Prince*), Cardinal Richelieu, Talleyrand, Metternich, Otto von Bismarck, Camillo Benso of Cavour, and Frederick the Great. To understand strategies one will be forever helped by reading the Chinese geopolitical classic *Romance of the Three Kingdoms*, and watching the "more than excellent" 2010 "Three Kingdoms" television version available (with English subtitles) on Youtube in 94 episodes. This will train you greatly and affect you deeply. After watching these videos you will understand strategy.

Those with strategic military and geopolitical aspirations need to familiarize themselves with the theories of Alfred Thayer Mahan on sea power, Mackinder's Heartland theory, the history of the British-Russian struggle for domination of central Asia called "The Great Game," petroleum politics, the history of large entities controlling resources sold/used on a continuous basis (grains, tea, silk, cotton, oil, medicine, minerals, timber, etc.), and new geostrategic ideas such as *The Pentagon's New Map* (Thomas Barnett). After digesting such information one can start to fathom the many geopolitical implications of China's "New Silk Road" initiative that is greater in scope than the Marshall Plan instituted after World War II, eliminates any dependence on the U.S. dollar, will power China's economic growth for decades to come while reducing dependence on the U.S. as a final customer market, and all the while escapes the reach of U.S. military intervention.

To understand this geopolitical initiative, you must understand that America's "winning" of WWII produced a peace dividend that allowed nations to lengthen their supply chains and manufacture products in other countries, at lower prices, for their own eventual consumption. All that America demanded in return was that other nations use its dollar in trade and follow its lead in return for its international policing to enforce peace.

The Bretton Woods system, created upon this foundation, was essentially a maritime empire of an Anglo-American alliance that controlled global sea lanes for an open trade model where the American consumer was the main attractor. Presently, China and Russia are trying to create their own competitive land model by building roads, railroads and bridges so that Eurasia and Europe can trade with each other at high speed on land instead of using the oceans, thus bypassing American or British sea power and interference.

China and Russia want to circumvent the Anglo-American control of sea lanes and shorten cargo time by 80% by using high speed rail through the New Silk Road initiative. This will also power their economies for coming decades. Russia's regional aim is an economic connectivity agenda for Greater Eurasia. Therefore it wants to connect China's northern provinces with Eurasia via the Trans-Siberian and Chinese Eastern Railway to help it develop its agriculture, minerals, lumber, oil and gas resources. Contrast this with America, which has no long-term trade plan at all.

At the same time, the per capita income in China ($15K) is slowly converging with that of America and the G7 nations (about $60K) as China builds a middle class of consumers. This middle class, in China alone, will eventually be ten times larger than the American consumer base that previously helped to build world trade, and the EU middle class will be twice the size of America's. Once the land bridges are built between Asia and Europe, and the Asian consumer has a higher per capita income, this will probably cut out America from the prosperity equation, especially if the

Chinese currency wins a greater share of the trading currency function.

This is one of the reasons why many of the American wars and military interventions (Ukraine, Afghanistan, Syria, etc.) are located in the border states between Asia and Europe, although there are other reasons as well. Most wars are about commerce, trade routes, asset resources, infrastructure and money flows. The big question is who will control the New Silk Road and what will happen to the Anglo-American alliance since China will use the fast transportation routes to enrich itself as a top priority. China will not abandon its prosperity goals just to be friendly with other nations. China, for instance, is divesting itself of its U.S. Treasury bonds by using them to pay for infrastructure projects along the New Silk Road (and projects elsewhere), and is trying to free itself from any U.S. dollar dependence, as is Russia. The U.S., as per geopolitical concerns, must make moves to counter this and strive to keep other nations from abandoning the dollar.

Previously China purchased boatloads of U.S. Treasuries as America imported low cost Chinese goods and paid in dollars. In a sense, China was therefore exporting both product and labor deflation to America, lowering the prices of both domestically. The United States ignorantly exported its manufacturing base and fundamental productivity to China, which gutted America's middle class, but the U.S. somewhat protected itself by creating a false prosperity through asset booms (ex. housing and stock market bubbles) and by flooding itself with cheap Chinese products.

Now China is building a land empire with the New Silk Road initiative and financing its own growth and the rise of the Chinese consumer, so it is now exporting inflation. It is now competing with America for resources and trying to rebalance itself away from dependency on the United States. It has become a serious competitor on the global stage by becoming a technology juggernaut whereas the U.S. has spent decades and $7 trillion on useless wars in the Mideast that gained it nothing except enemies and ill-will. China, on the other hand, has gone up the value chain in developing its economy and is now pursuing sophisticated technologies and high-quality manufacturing. Seeking independence from U.S. influence, America now sees the Chinese competitor as an enemy to its own prosperity.

The key geopolitical points are that China is now dumping U.S. Treasury bonds, building up its industry, and becoming an efficient competitor to the Anglo-American sea lanes. It is developing the South China Sea, which is also a trade superhighway. It is also graduating more engineers (and high IQ individuals) to build its nation as is India, whereas the U.S. is graduating more lawyers and replacing industrial engineers with financial engineers who try to create wealth by reshaping the forms by which you can buy debt. Both India and China are educationally focusing on math and the sciences to spur innovation and future economic growth. Both are building the finest new infrastructure while America watches its infrastructure crumble.

Russia is importing skilled labor (while America welcomes unskilled immigrants into its population base) and creating relationships to help develop its own natural resources, agricultural output, and build its manufacturing base. While Russia used to be an agricultural importer, it is now an exporter. Russia is also aiming to turn itself into a civilizational bridge that fuses many cultures, so is aiming at producing a new paradigm on a cultural and ideological level rather than just focus on geopolitical and geoeconomical grand strategy. As a strategy Russia uses its conventional and nuclear arsenal as a deterrent against provocations, as well as its large natural gas shipments to Europe. China is also establishing strong economic relationships with Africa, which the U.S. previously ignored, in order to secure sources of raw materials for its future. Perhaps it will try to gain control over these countries with debt, imitating the "Economic Hit Men" practices of the West, but only time will tell.

China and Russia are also buying up gold (rather than U.S. Treasuries, which they are dumping) as insurance in case American debt goes bankrupt or the U.S. currency experiences hyperinflation because of excessive debt, excessive money printing and a loss of confidence in the dollar due to the consequences of all these geopolitical processes. If their U.S. Treasury bond holdings crash in value due to the global recognition of too much U.S. debt that cannot be repaid (such as the fact that U.S. borrowing costs now exceed U.S. tax income, so taxes will never be sufficient to pay back the debt in arrears *and the U.S. will have to issue even more debt to pay these costs that will never produce a benefit in terms of investment, growth, or productivity*), or because global banking systems enter failure and require a reset, China and Russia plan to make up their losses through the subsequent emergency rise in gold prices that would be expected. Then they will also be able to buy international assets on the cheap if there is a U.S. or global debt default. By purchasing precious metals that will maintain their value during a crisis they will be "the last men standing" after any financial calamity, and will have the funds necessary to buy up assets at bargain prices. In short, if sovereign bonds drop in value then gold investments will make up the losses, and will enable the two countries to buy assets on the cheap after all the dust settles on ruinous positions that leave all other parties bankrupt.

Because the U.S. is in a position of world hegemon due to the U.S. dollar being the world's reserve currency and main vehicle for global trade, China and Russia plan to bypass its usage and knock the U.S. out of preeminence by eventually replacing the dollar with a gold-backed trade system. As a larger proportion of world trade is conducted outside of the U.S. dollar, the consequence will be fewer U.S. Treasury bonds held in foreign banking systems, and thus a lesser ability for the U.S. to finance its debt. America will suffer from increasing inflation, higher interest rates, and won't be able to borrow whatever it wants whenever it wants. This will hamper America's ability to simply print up dollars to buy international assets on the cheap, fund its deficits, and finance its military forays into other countries. To counter America's military might, both China and Russia have also turned to solutions that focus more on defense rather than offense so that no one dares attack them. In particular, Russia now leads with low-cost, high tech weaponry that is superior to America's, but the United States cannot openly admit the superiority of Russian weapons.

To become a big time national protect god (or statesman) you need to understand such current issues including the various policies of empire building, the motivational rationales used to justify it, and interpretations of history that involve geopolitical motivations for war or economic development. For instance, you should understand that the present U.S. geopolitical strategy is first and foremost about maintenance of the Petrodollar through all means possible including military might, without which the U.S. dollar cannot remain the world's reserve currency for long (see *Bankism* by Bodri). The Petrodollar and the dollar as the world's reserve currency are together the #1 concern of U.S. grand strategy and geopolitical strategy. This is explained in *Super Investing* and *Bankism*.

You must also understand the words of Nickolas Spykman, who was one of the intellectual founders of the realist school in America foreign policy, geopolitics and geostrategy. In *America's Strategy in World Politics* Spykman once wrote, "There are not many instances in history which show great and powerful states creating alliances and organizations to limit their own strength. States are always engaged in curbing the force of some other state. The truth of the matter is that states are interested only in a balance which is in their favor. Not an equilibrium, but a generous margin is their objective. There is no real security in being just as strong as a potential enemy; there is security only in being a little stronger. There is no possibility of action if one's strength is fully checked; there is a chance for a positive foreign policy only if there is a margin of force which can be freely used. Whatever the theory and rationalization, the practical objective is the constant improvement of the state's own relative power position. The balance desired is the one which neutralizes other states, leaving the home state free to be the deciding force and the deciding voice."

With this in mind, one can start to unravel some of the objectives of American grand strategy and geopolitics. For instance, for the World Bank and IMF the U.S. made sure that its large share gave it veto power over any loan or policy. Without veto power over judgments, the U.S. has also never accepted membership in any type of world court, and insists on veto power at the United Nations. The U.S. also considers international finance an arm of its Federal Reserve, State Department and Pentagon. These are all instances of geopolitical moves where the desire is for your own country to control foreign territory, revenue flows and assets, shape international policy and other states' foreign policy.

In no particular order, aside from maintaining the Petrodollar and the dollar's usage in world trade and as a reserve currency, the other major geopolitical concerns of American grand strategy are to maintain the revenues and profits of the military-industrial complex; maintain the prosperity of America's banking complex; enrich the nation economically; attain worldwide control of continuous mega-revenue streams (food, agriculture, fertilizer, minerals, timber, pharmaceuticals, petroleum, water) via patents, laws and strategic ownership mechanisms; obtain ownership and control of the assets, resources and raw materials of other nations or deny other nations access to those resources for their development; secure free entry into foreign markets in order to trade/exchange goods; control or influence the banking systems, financial institutions and capital markets of other countries to the greatest extent possible; put other nations into debt servitude in order to control/suppress them; control/capture the monopolistic profits of the illegal drug trade (and other illegal activities) so they can be used for secret off-budget projects; impede the domination of landmasses or regions by other powers; destabilize the Mideast to both control oil revenues and create security for Israel; prevent collusion between lesser states so that they cannot come together in a unified coalition that presents a powerful counter-force to U.S. interests; and destabilize other countries in order to raise their costs and create troubles which will neutralize or eliminate them as top global competitors, or simply block their development in order to remain a hegemon over them. This includes blocking the growth of any competitor nation's development in high tech if it threatens U.S. technological, economic or military superiority. The idea is to set up things in such a way that America prospers and can project its power on a global scale where it can enforce its own will upon, or simply influence, the most powerful states and international events for its own favor.

These are the actual unstated pillars of U.S. grand strategy, or geopolitical strategy. As you can see, many objectives involve the idea of pushing oneself up by pushing others down rather than facing others on a level playing field of equal, clean competition. No such thing exists in geopolitics, for it is all about national power and advantage and the money flows or trade routes that a winner captures.

Military conquest, treaty, subsidization, suppressing social change, legal bindings, debt obligations, economic penetration, blackmail or bribery, assassination and regime change are all methods used by national players jockeying for supremacy. There is no such thing as fairness in grand strategy for it is a struggle over power, money and supremacy. As Reinert pointed out in *Why Rich Countries Got Rich and Why Poor Countries Stay Poor*, it is common in grand strategy for leading nations to consistently mislead weaker nations into following the worst possible strategies in order to keep them in a weaker, subservient position so they may be exploited. Britain tried to do this to America during its after-independence formative years. No country wants to allow competitors to arise that might hurt its own power base or prosperity.

As I pointed out in my book *Bankism*, misleading others includes promoting the idea that each nation should have a private central bank (owned and controlled by non-government entities) that issues money at an interest cost to the government whereas many nations that grew rich did so by rejecting this policy. See *The Public Banking Solution* by Ellen Brown for a history of the successes behind this solution.

You cannot make an economy more prosperous by printing money, which only increases a nation's debt load. If printing money could make a nation rich then everyone would be doing it successfully, but of course this doesn't happen. Furthermore, you must recognize that the people who make/issue the money make the rules in a nation. This mirrors Mayer Amschel Rothschild's purported statement, "Let us control the money of a nation, and we care not who makes its laws." Bankers in an economy, who are authorized to create money out of thin air, only have power because they can make money and use it for their own ends, which enables them to control many matters. Who said they are qualified for positions of power and authority, and have the wisdom to make the right decisions for public welfare when they are precisely interested in only their own prosperity?

Unfortunately, the United States has recently sabotaged itself by adopting grand strategies that have weakened its own economics, such as by outsourcing its industry to other nations and thus destroying its own internal manufacturing base. It gave a free tax ride to multi-national corporations who outsourced its productive abilities. It liquidated its middle class while maintaining a false prosperity charade that it kept on-going via cheaper imports, easy debt and asset bubbles. As a primary strategy this policy lead to trade deficits, transferred technology to competitors, destroyed domestic employment and is basically a colossal failure.

The United States had previously held a great multi-decade advantage in development because of its educational system, strong focus on research and innovation, and immigration policies that enticed the best talent to come to America. It also offered an attractive lifestyle of privacy and freedom that said "no" to oppressive government control and coercion. Furthermore, because the world destroyed itself in World War II, thus damaging its major competitors, it was catapulted into a top economic spot that it could maintain for decades, but now other nations have caught up with their educational systems, industrial bases, and capital markets.

The United States has also lost additional legitimate income by turning to debt and asset bubbles as stimulus rather than focusing on selling more products and services to other nations. By emphasizing consumption for its growth model, America has also ended up purchasing more goods from countries that invested in their own capital stock and infrastructure while neglecting its own development. By supporting policies that lead to ever-increasing housing prices, it has produced a faux prosperity of over-inflated property values where young workers now even cannot afford homes but must live with their parents. If America does not produce stable jobs for the younger generations that pay enough for them to buy a home and raise a family then the nation is in serious trouble, so it must work to recreate an economy that benefits the working American.

Basically, a consumption-driven economy based on debt, and a financial system designed to coerce ever higher levels of debt to fuel consumption, cannot succeed without population growth and sufficient prosperity. Without population growth consumption declines, debt declines and asset prices decline. Without prosperity people cannot pay any interest on debt. Increasing national debt which reaches an extreme always ends in a debt default of ultimate collapse that takes an economy down with it.

In the case of rising property prices, the long-term appreciation rate is less than 3.5% per year, and when prices grow much faster than this over the long-run then people are eventually priced out of being able to own their homes. Young families therefore cannot form, and small businesses cannot pay rents even though they are the backbone of the economy. This result is the opposite of national prosperity.

As explained within *Bankism*, as a new grand strategy the U.S. must reindustrialize in a grand national program. It must forge an internal grand strategy for everything from macroeconomic stability to environmental health to ways to unleash the economic power of America's 3,000 counties, for prosperity starts at the city and county level and aggregates upwards. Unleashing prosperity will entail promoting small business growth, championing innovation and inventions, emphasizing technical education, promoting self-responsibility/reliance as a national characteristic, and eschewing debt enslavement for the population. It must start giving preference to community decisions instead of federal control, and emphasize small businesses rather than corporations since entrepreneurs create the most jobs. It must free small businesses from excessive taxes and regulations. This includes overhauling the tort system since it inhibits innovation, risk-taking, new businesses and growth. America must also stop the practice of private sector revolving doors to government agencies that protect corporate monopolies, as in the pharmaceutical and agricultural fields, and no longer give a free tax ride to multinational corporations. The campaign finance system must be overhauled such as by forbidding non-living entities from making campaign contributions.

While the rest of the world is succumbing to a tyrannical and oppressive

100% surveillance mentality that suppresses free speech and criticism, it must turn its back on this tendency for control that Ronald Reagan warned about and instead focus on freedom, democracy, rights, transparency, privacy, jury nullification and rule of law. America should try to make itself the place where talent wants to come again because the U.S. is absolutely free of the oppressions sprouting up everywhere else (see *Culture, Country, City, Company, Person, Purpose, Passion, World* for a discussion of placemaking). Just as it practices *realpolitik* in the field of foreign affairs, it must now pursue a *realeconomik* that benefits society rather than elites. It must pivot for a new productive purpose that benefits the populace rather than the new nobility of parasitic financial and corporate elites who have made deals with entrenched government/political operatives.

One of China's most successful epochs was the Tang dynasty, which did things so well that many other Asian nations emulated its methods. The U.S. must follow the same design of once again becoming a model all want to emulate. In the United States money has become like a horse that has gone wild and torn itself free from spiritual and cultural values. Somehow the U.S. must tie money back to values creation in the spiritual and cultural fields, and once again emphasize factors beyond the boundaries of pure materialism. Over the past few decades it has chipped away at any values and value creation processes other than those of money-making. Now it needs to start protecting the public's spiritual life that holds to higher values not in the money world, but which are projected into the physical world. As in the example of Tang Dynasty China, America needs to start projecting an inspiring spiritual radiation, but one that is not divorced from science.

Asia is rising and has only begun going up the S-curve of development by concentrating primarily on commercial culture. Now that Asian educational systems are on par with those in the West, and Asia has an equal availability of capital and technology, its development trend will not stop whereas America (the outgoing hegemon) is stuck in a denial mindset that insists it will be forever preeminent. How can that be, since the American consumer is already no longer the center of the global economy? America is assuming future greatness based on the mythology of previous greatness born from eras in which it had grown rich through hard work, sacrifice and thrift.

The U.S. is trying to hold onto its premier position with failed, outdated policies. American grand strategies for foreign policy and security policy must in the future be based on sound principles of power management instead of passions, ideology and unbridled favoritism. The U.S. will no longer be able to afford to be the policeman of the world, intervene in other countries at will, and maintain hundreds of military bases without an economic return, especially as the dollar is continually abandoned for trade payments by other nations and reduced in importance as a reserve currency.

As part of its foreign policy grand strategy, the United States must stop inventing and exaggerating threats to America's homeland security that cause massive defense spending, intense busywork that has nothing to do with the real safety and security of America, and draconian losses of domestic rights and invasions of privacy. It must abandon far-flung military missions designed to enforce America's hegemony. The U.S. is only producing an immense generational fiscal crisis and international ill will from useless, profitless incursions that accomplish nothing.

In the future, other countries will no longer be willing to finance America's continued gain so it has to start competing once again. Its competitiveness must start at the local level with small businesses that grow into large businesses because of policies that foster an excellent business environment. It should turn to Catherine Austin Fitts's plan, based on analyzing the cash flows of thousands of American counties that engage in "participatory budgeting," for unleashing local prosperity that can aggregate into national prosperity and national renewal. The leitmotif or primary pillars of a new grand strategy should be that power and capital must decentralize to the local level in order for the prosperity forces to become unleashed, there must be election reform, and we must unleash the potential at the local level by allowing it more leeway in economic decisions free of Washington's control. This is how the country was originally built.

The leitmotif must change to promote competition instead of monopoly, and capitalism instead of fascism and authoritarian government control. It must cleanse corrupted ideals by systemically decentralizing power and eliminating the neo-feudal dominance of an entrenched political and financial elite. A national strategy that benefits the country (all the citizenry) should offer a level playing field to all innovators and capital, and then lets free opportunity attract the voluntary opt-in of the most productive players on the planet. It must abandon the idea that wealth is created by the debt-leveraged inflation of real estate and financial asset prices, and must prevent debt levels from growing to economic levels that burden taxpayers and shrink the economy.

In short, the focus must now turn to manufacturing, industrialization and the production and export of real goods. The notion must be taught within society that one now earns steady income and gets rich over time through innovations that produce tangible capital formation, not by increasing stock prices or real estate prices. Throughout history the banks that have gone bankrupt and imperil economic systems are always involved in trading and speculation, so this needs to be curbed.

As a grand strategy, the U.S. must now embark on a national redesign of government regulation and function that fertilizers its productive capacity (turning it towards the production of real goods rather than paper goods and services), protects its resources (such as the water table), unleashes human and financial capital (at the county and small business level), empowers community governments, encourages risk-taking (such as by reforming tort and bankruptcy laws), insures social mobility, and promotes a national cohesiveness of shared purpose and forward development rather than divisiveness. It must encourage the development of new forms of private capital formation to fund businesses rather than remain dependent on banking loans to finance capital formation. It should let community banks and credit unions have more leeway in community development decisions rather than more federal control over their processes. This alone would reengineer government investment to improve small businesses.

As part of grand strategy, America's bankers must also learn a new trick of leading regional development in order to produce a new source of demand for consumer and industrial goods, similar to what America did in the postwar decades. It must also put a new emphasis on export creation. Through tax incentives and less regulation it must attract the most productive talent and capital on the planet that will then, given a secure playing field of opportunity free of parasitic predatory elites, build the country. The focus should be centered on, "How can we grow small business and employment?" America must also stop trying to be the policeman of the world. China's growth, for instance, came from investing in China while America invested in its military. China's infrastructure is new and high quality while America's is crumbling from neglect.

As a national protector you must further understand how governments use secret tactics to maintain themselves such as false flag attacks (covert actions carried out to look like another party did them), fake news (disinformation propaganda for political advantage), economic hit men and assassination jackals, coercive engineered migration (overwhelming another country's capacity to cope with migrants in order to pressure political interests), color revolutions, proxy armies and humanitarian interventions (funding the army of an opposing power when you cannot fight directly with another country). A protect god understands the strategies used by rulers and power blocs. They are fully aware of the secret methods going on behind the scenes. Only if you understand that these methods exist can you even be considered as qualified for a high leadership position.

For ancient theories on how to rule people or nations you should furthermore read various Chinese classics and Roman history. Of special usefulness are books like *The 33 Strategies of War* (Robert Greene), the strategies of Edward Bernays, *Confessions of an Economic Hit Man* (John Perkins), *The Three Strategies of Huang Shih Gong*, the Chinese classics *36 Strategies* and *The Sixteen Strategies of Zhuge Liang*, *The Integral Management of Tao* (Stephen Chang), *Thunder in the Sky: On the Acquisition and Exercise of Power* (Thomas Cleary), *The Book of Leadership & Strategy* (Thomas Cleary), *Rule the World – The Way I Did* (Chanakya), *The Six Secret Teachings on the Way of*

Strategy (Ralph Sawyer), and so on. The Chinese probably offer the best classical literature on rulership and strategy, and you can find many illustrated AsiaPac comic books containing such lessons. I highly recommend all the AsiaPac comic series, especially for children. The British to their great credit have successfully applied Lao Tzu's Taoist strategies in their governance of other nations and their techniques should be studied, particularly the methods of the East India Company that was able to control an incredible number of people with so few.

To be a protect god, one must understand the Yin and Yang of strategy and timing (where opportune timing allows you to accomplish more with less effort) in order to be able to understand the processes of natural transformation destined to occur for specific processes. When strategy is applied to the great masses of people, the highest ideals of ethics and morality must be applied in conjunction with application of skillful means as taught within *The Lotus Sutra* of Buddhism. A key issue is how to affect the minds of men on a vast scale, which you can understand by studying the methods of advertising, marketing and public relations. For this you should study the works of David Ogilvy, Robert Cialdini, Claude Hopkins, Rosser Reeves, Ries and Trout and others. As you can see, the same names and topics keep popping up over and over again. There are basic lessons you need to learn to really understand the world.

In *The Masks of God* Joseph Campbell wrote, "The rise and fall of civilizations in the long, broad course of history can be seen to have been largely a function of the integrity and cogency of the supporting cannons of myth, for not authority but aspiration is the motivator, builder and transformer of civilization. A mythological canon is an organization of symbols, ineffable in import, by which the energies of aspiration are evoked and gathered toward a focus." In recent times, Germany used this approach of promoting mythic symbols to guide the masses during the Third Reich.

In *Propaganda* Edward Bernays wrote, "The conscious and intelligent manipulation of the organized habits and opinions of the masses is an important element in democratic society. Those who manipulate this unseen mechanism of society constitute an invisible government which is the true ruling power of our country.

"We are governed, our minds are molded, our tastes formed, our ideas suggested, largely by men we have never heard of. This is a logical result of the way in which our democratic society is organized. Vast numbers of human beings must cooperate in this manner if they are to live together as a smoothly functioning society. …

"It remains a fact that in almost every act of our daily lives, whether in the sphere of politics or business, in our social conduct or our ethical thinking, we are dominated by the relatively small number of persons, … who understand the mental processes and social patterns of the masses. It is they who pull the wires which control the public mind, who harness old social forces and contrive new ways to bind and guide the world."[15]

In today's world, various groups compete using sophisticated techniques in attempts to engineer public perceptions through memes and media propaganda. You simply need to be aware of this; ordinary people remain ignorant. The whole purpose is designed to create legislation for social engineering that benefits their own ends. In order to promote self-serving policies they secretly attain control of the press and other powerful bodies with public influence in order to "manage the narrative," which means to manage the consensus that their agendas and actions are okay. However, the highest method of influencing a population is by promoting the example of men of superior moral qualities and consummate conduct rather than through fake news and propaganda promoted by all sorts of media outlets. A Bodhisattva should want to inspire a moral transformation of the people by examples of excellence and social contribution. Gandhi was this sort of individual as was Dr. Ron Paul.

Confucius said that he broadened himself with culture and restrained himself with proper standards of behavior ("rites"). One should desire that the social structure of every country is internally harmonious rather than whipped up into divisiveness by special interest groups both inside and outside of it. A Bodhisattva should understand that such divisive efforts are always going on. Standards of behavior that assist in taming society and emphasize group cooperation and shared ideals help to produce harmony between its disparate elements. They help maintain society and social order. Thus it is important to establish proper codes of conduct within a country.

In India, for instance, the proper "Dharma" includes loyalty to laws and morality, service and sacrifice to deities, obedience to the state, love of one's family and purity of social life. One's obligations to society and mankind are spelled out in a framework of cooperation rather than divisiveness. China has a Confucian work ethic that produces hard workers, and the Protestant work ethic is prevalent in many prosperous European nations. Islamic states tend to have populations loyal to their religion rather than government. Such types of ethos (guiding ideals) color the character of a nation and can amplify or diminish its prosperity. A Bodhisattva tries to help create positive ones for a nation.

Even after attaining the deva body whereupon you can see what humans are really thinking and doing everywhere, even behind closed doors, the *Surangama Sutra* states that you should not abandon or destroy the normal ways of religion etc. that help to order and pacify society even though you will now find that many religious tenets you previously believed, and which

---

[15] Edward Bernays, *Propaganda,* (Ig Publishing, Brooklyn: NY, 2005), pp. 37-38.

the masses hold dear, are truly bogus. In other words, even though you attain the deva body and then discover that many religious teachings are falsities and lies, you should not disparage or try to destroy anything helpful if it helps to pacify society. You should try to support and uplift religious practices via transformation, and try to free society of any strange ossifications it undergoes because of religion. This is a standard principle.

Even when we hold beliefs based on totally false information, they have an impact on our lives. Most of the beliefs we personally hold dear in life are not based on any reality at all but have simply been absorbed from our environment since we were young. They are based on information we have absorbed from society, our parents, and from a whole variety of sources that have imprinted themselves upon us. The degree to which we accept beliefs, even if untrue, changes us and alters how we act which is why religion, even if false, can often elevate societal behavior.

One of religion's positive functions is to instill within society pacifying beliefs along with the norms of ethical, virtuous behavior. Beliefs act on us even if untrue and we usually end up living in a manner consistent with them. Therefore the falsities one discovers, even if true, can still be used to help guide mankind. What one must determine is whether the ethics, virtues, values and culture promoted within society are high enough.

When you find out that other ordinary individuals who have the *sambhogakaya* body are masquerading as Buddhas, deities, gods and so forth in order to help people, there is no reason to teach this in greater society if it will cause harm rather than good. Most people cannot accept this truth anyway. Only the few people with enough wisdom and merit who will go through the Twelve Year kundalini awakening process to produce the deva body, which will involve daily contact with these individuals, will truly end up understanding this valuable information. Or you, since you're reading this book, and of course everyone who dies and then discovers the truth.

What Confucius called "rites," which comprises social customs and conventions generally accepted as the formal standards of proper conduct in society, provide a starting point for the cultivation of individual morality. They are important in every society, and usually come from religion. Standards of behavior serve a different function than the law, but just because social conventions allow/promote certain activities this does not mean they are correct or moral. It just means that they are traditional behaviors and when wrong it is our duty to correct them. Foot binding in China, the suicidal self-immolation of widows in India, slavery in Brazil and America, child brides, the cutting off a young girl's clitoris in Islam, and girls being forbidden to go to school to get an education are all examples of errant "traditional" ways that were eliminated or need to be eliminated.

People normally try to restrain their actions so that they are in accordance with the socially accepted rules of propriety and etiquette, which are the "rites" of Confucius. To train oneself to conform to propriety is humanity, which is raising ourselves high above worldliness and our animal nature. This is the basis of spiritual cultivation because if you do not do this then you will not receive any help on achieving the deva body. You won't become a virtuous, ethical or good human being if you don't work on raising yourself higher than your animal instincts and desires.

What is the way so that man can, on a daily basis, master himself and return to propriety? For this we have the teachings in *Color Me Confucius* with the role models of Benjamin Franklin, Yuan Liao Fan, Wang Yangming and others. In *The American Reader* I showed how American Presidents Washington, Lincoln, Roosevelt and Eisenhower also worked hard on personal development to change their typical habit tendencies, actions and behaviors. People's personalities are not set in plaster but can change through the efforts of self-development.

To practice propriety depends on yourself. Through propriety we preserve human decency and a respect for others despite divisive messages in society and strange themes promoted by political powers for their own ends. Confucius said that emphasizing proper behavior helps regulate and pacify society and is far more effective than employing laws and punishments.

What is the standard of ethics you should want to see in a city or country? Of course you want a people to be honest, trustworthy, fair and able to cooperate with one another, so these need not be mentioned. You should really want people to always be striving after high ideals in as many fields as possible, especially as people's ethics tend to be situation specific. You want them to never lapse in their pursuit of self-improvement. You want people to become perseverant in character development, learning and self-improvement for this is the road of self-cultivation upwards.

Fortune determines name and wealth, so Confucius felt that a man should not pursue fame and recognition, but only worry that he is not "polishing" himself through the efforts of self-improvement. Furthermore, he felt that a man should devote himself to civic contributions for the people just as was stressed in ancient Greece and Rome.

National prosperity usually occurs when society is cooperatively working together to make things better, and when the country as a whole is being guided by a *grand strategy* for economic development. The components of a grand strategy should include educating the people up to a certain level of knowledge and technology and keeping at the forefront of technological changes. A country must also develop sufficient infrastructure, including financing methods for business startups and expansions, and an immigration (and tax/economic) policy that attracts the smartest and most productive people since they will help to build the nation and move it forward. Regulations must encourage capital formation and investment whereby the investors keep most of their profits, which works as an incentive. Furthermore, the rule of law must be enforced fairly everywhere so that investors are protected from theft, otherwise why would they risk building a business in the country? Capital goes where it can earn the greatest returns, which has implications for labor costs and taxation. They should be as low as possible in order to keep pace with competitors who offer better deals. These are all common sense principles but many countries forget them.

There is a big difference between short-term and long-term strategies and policies meant to build nations. A statesman (Bodhisattva or Buddha) wants to craft strategies of development that are not just good in the short-term but also in the intermediate and long-term.

Economics: On the topic of economics and national wealth, the most important topic on the scale of grand strategy is knowledge of economic history and causation (see Martin Armstrong's writings) and understanding what a country or city must do to become prosperous, which is summarized in *Culture, Country, City, Company, Person, Purpose, Passion, World*. Grand strategy is the framework that guides not only foreign policy but prosperity policy for the nation. Its objective is what I call "The Great Betterment" of the country in all its axes and dimensions. For a good perspective you must understand such forces as Kondratieff innovation waves, demographics, and generational waves.

If one overly simplifies matters by thinking of the basic needs of society, a prosperous city should build ample schools and training facilities for the young, for adults it should create ample job opportunities via a great business environment, and it needs to create ample hospitals or medical care facilities for the elderly. Since a large proportion of individuals in poor countries have jobs related to farming and agriculture, it is important that a nation does not destroy this strata through low-priced food imports. On the micro-level, prosperity comes down to jobs, occupations and business opportunities for adults so that they can support themselves with an independent livelihood.

For modernizing a backwards nation you can study the successful examples of Peter the Great, the Japanese Meiji era, and other modernization successes such as Japan's transformation to become a manufacturing powerhouse in the 1980s by applying Deming's teachings on quality control. By consistently applying very simple ideas on quality control in its manufacturing sector, Japan went from being a poor country to one of the richest in the world. Adhering to one simple idea did this! The lesson is that by consistently, religiously, continually applying the correct idea over and over again in society, and hammering away at it for years, you can transform the entire fortunes of a nation, but you have to promote the right ideas and principles. Hans Rosling teaches this too. You must attack fundamental things at the root. Usually successful modernization efforts involve movements towards greater cost efficiency, higher productivity, abandoning traditional restrictions and free market economics.

An old Chinese saying runs, "After the granaries are full, people will be aware of proper behavior and ethics; and after the country becomes prosperous, education will be thriving." Therefore, before you can talk about the need for a higher degree of virtue and ethical behavior within a nation you must confront the problem of economics; without income many people will turn to crime because they have no other choice. In other words, ethics are usually situation specific. People won't normally lie, cheat or steal except in adverse circumstances, such as when facing starvation. Then even honest people will do what they must to survive. Solving economic problems therefore solves many social and ethical issues.

During prosperity the burdens of poverty borne by the people are relieved, and then you can see a blossoming in ethics and education. When hardships are removed, people normally return to the path of virtue and ethics. When hardships abound, sermons on ethical behavior will be ignored due to the necessities of life.

To understand money flows within an economy you should imagine the economy's money supply as contained within a balloon where the balloon becomes larger (inflates) as more money is printed, goods are sold to outsiders (exports) who pay cash that enters the balloon, or outsiders pour money into a domestic economy (the size of the balloon) to make investments. The balloon decreases in size when money flows outwards to buy foreign goods, or there is a collapse in asset prices that wipes out internal wealth.

Next, consider that all the money within an economy is involved in sectors such as businesses, real estate, stocks, bonds, precious metals, currency and commodities. When you squeeze one part of the balloon, which symbolizes putting a damper on investments in one sector (such as by increasing taxes on real estate to make it less attractive), you will cause the money to flow to other sectors just as the air in the balloon will be squeezed to other regions and inflate them while the grabbed section is pinched. Money always flows to where it can attain the highest returns, but returns are usually proportionate to the risks taken.

If you conduct another Einstein-type thought experiment making yourself Emperor of your country who owns absolutely everything, then it becomes easier to understand what policies to institute to bring about greater peace, prosperity and social stability in a nation. You imagine that you own everything, all the money and assets are yours, but various parties within the country can by their actions go to extremes that can cause you to reduce your total wealth or threaten prosperity and harmony.

By conducting such a thought experiment you will remove many complications to policy analysis. Through mental analysis you can determine which entities are becoming too powerful and threaten aggregate wealth and internal peace because they are destabilizing the nation or putting too much power in unscrupulous hands. Thinking thus, through this type of mental experiment you can create solutions in your mind for pressing problems.

Furthermore, as a Protect God or Guardian Deity of an economy you should understand the standard rule that if you advertise, subsidize, reward or promote a behavior you will get more of it whereas if you tax, denounce, ridicule, penalize or prohibit a behavior you will get less of it. This is how to guide the public into behaviors you prefer and away from behaviors that produce negative consequences.

Also, by mentally exaggerating situations to become extremely large or small, and determining the likely outcomes and consequences from such amplifications, you will understand the probable results of proposed policies - their direct and indirect side effects. This is another way to analyze proposals.

As a miscellaneous, one principle of economics that history has clearly proven is that wage and price controls do not work. When governments meddle in the economy this way, prices become distorted and so do investment incentives. Price controls are also a common precursor to hyperinflation, which usually erupts after massive money printing and when some line is crossed where a society stops trusting its government. If a government simply prints money for convenience, that is precisely how the Roman Empire was ruined. That is how the Weimar Republic was ruined also. There comes a point when the money printing becomes dangerous in terms of inflation and loss of public confidence in the government. You cannot just print money to create wealth.

Before you promote any type of policy, always search history for prior precedents to see the likely outcome. History teaches the lessons of what happened in the past and what didn't work, such as gun control laws usually being followed by repressive governments that committed aggressions against the public. Also, when governments forbid innovation to protect labor interests they usually caused the collapse of those industries because competitors elsewhere typically adopted those innovations.

Education: Educational policy has changed over the centuries, and throughout history has been tied into themes of filial piety, good conduct and religion. The general purpose of education should involve helping children change their personality and behavior (transform their bad behaviors and errant habits into good ones) rather than just develop their intelligence, provide them with skills, and give them knowledge. Education should also introduce them to ways to find the peace and purity inherent in their minds. It should also serve to help them create their own bedrock of principles so that they internally develop their own moral compass for life.

Education is an ongoing process that is not synonymous with credentialing and does not end when schooling ends since it entails constant learning and self-improvement. For instance, in *The Education of Henry Adams* the author wrote that his traditional education failed to help him come to terms with rapid changes in science and technology over the course of his lifetime, and so he had to resort to self-education past schooling. Benjamin Franklin's example also emphasizes the need to become a constant, life-long self-learner interested in self-improvement and open to whatever is new, which is said to be one of the common most traits of wealthy individuals. When you listen to the autobiographical interviews of great men on WebofStories.com you will find that most of them were self-taught to some degree.

What would be a powerful addition to education today is if someone linked the stages of cognitive development to specific childhood lessons that challenged the budding neural pathways at that same age, thus helping to develop the neural pathways to their fullest at their most opportune time. Furthermore, there would be a great benefit in teaching the same types of lessons each year at the same seasonal time due to astrological reasons, which would help lessons take hold and make a deeper impact on children. Unfortunately, no one does this.

There are three traditional core purposes for education that a nation must consider when developing a curriculum. Those purposes are:

1. To produce "good, virtuous people" who have ethical, moral standards (an inner sense of right and wrong), good characters, who can get along with others in harmonious, cooperative relationships, who are self-disciplined and responsible, who act out of principle, and who have a deep sense of their inner life that cherishes values other than pure materialism. This is the "spiritual purpose" of education, which is to teach children the difference between right and wrong, instill within them a sense of goodness, and help them develop positive human qualities and virtuous character traits. This directive of education produces "good people," ethical living and "kind neighbors."
2. To produce "good citizens" who truly love and care about the fate of their country, society and family and who are willing to strive for the public good and improve society through their personal civic contributions. This is the "public purpose" of education, which in addition to teaching patriotism, social commitment and participation in community life also includes

teaching children how to live peacefully together with others in cooperative, united communities tolerant of the fact that other members may cherish different ideas, values and ways of living.
3. To train people to be able to earn an honest living, to be able to live in the world in an independent, self-reliant, self-directed way that is not a burden on society. This is the "private purpose" of education, or economic purpose, which is to help individuals find some particular talents or skills with which they can work to make a living. It is the "independent livelihood" purpose of education, which is to train children through education to make their own independent way in the world standing on their own two feet.

There are countless educators and approaches you can read about (see *The Taihu School* or Sudbury school for instance) but for today's world I think people should especially familiarize themselves with John Taylor Gatto and his fourteen themes of the elite education curriculum. After much research Gatto felt that the elite prep schools teach fourteen important educational themes not taught in ordinary school curriculums:

1. A theory of human nature (as embodied in history, philosophy, theology, literature and law).
2. Skill in the active literacies (writing, public speaking, persuasion skills).
3. Insight into the major institutional forms of the country (the government structure, courts, corporations, military, education).
4. Repeated exercises in the forms of etiquette, good manners and politeness based on the truth that politeness and civility are the foundation of all future relationships, all future alliances, and access to places that you might want to go.
5. The ability to do independent work.
6. Energetic physical sports are not a luxury, or a way to "blow off steam," but the only way to confer grace on the human presence, which can later on translate into power and money. Also, sports helps you not only learn to control the movements of body muscles but help you practice handling pain and dealing with emergencies.
7. A complete theory of access to any place and any person.
8. Responsibility is an utterly essential part of the curriculum; one should always grab responsibility when it is offered and always deliver more than what is asked for.
9. Arrival at a personal code of standards (in production, behavior and morality or ethics).

10. To have a familiarity with, and to be at ease with, the fine arts; learning cultural capital.
11. The power of accurate observation and recording. For example, you can learn to sharpen your perception by learning how to draw accurately.
12. The ability to deal with challenges of all sorts.
13. A habit of caution in reasoning to conclusions.
14. The constant development and testing of prior judgments: you make judgments, you discriminate value, and then you follow up by "keeping an eye" on your predictions to see how far skewed, or how consistent, your predictions are.

While these fourteen themes are what Gatto found that the elite prep schools teach, George Wythe University has a representative list of skills that it feels makes an "educated person" at the university level:

1. The ability to understand human nature and lead accordingly.
2. The ability to identify needed personal traits and turn them into habits.
3. The ability to establish, maintain, and improve lasting relationships.
4. The ability to keep one's life in proper balance.
5. The ability to discern truth and error regardless of the source or the delivery.
6. The ability to discern true from right.
7. The ability and discipline to do right.
8. The ability and discipline to constantly improve.

For self-study, KhanAcademy.org and TheGreatCourses.com offer internet courses on a variety of subjects that can expand your worldview and broaden your knowledge horizons. TheGreatCourses.com, favored by billionaire Bill Gates and others like myself, has a good course on developing learning skills ("How to be a Superstar Student"). *How to Become a Straight-A Student* (Call Newport) and similar works are used by many students to help *learn how to learn* by "studying smarter rather than harder."

It is unfortunate that schools do not teach the very topics that would really be of help to students such as how to manage their personal finances, self-defense, negotiation skills, etiquette and social skills, cooking, time management and productivity skills, entrepreneurship, health and nutrition, survival and first aid, mind mapping, memory skills and speed reading.

Health: Throughout most of human history the average lifespan was only around forty years, and was low primarily due to infant mortality and issues related to lack of proper sanitation and hygiene. The three measures that reduce to a minimum infectious diseases in society are pure water, good drainage and proper isolation of the sick. Major scourges of mankind have been waterborne diseases, as well as plagues, parasites and ordinary infections. Wars, malnutrition/starvation and the general unavailability of medicine have also contributed to shorter lifespans.

To see how health measures have improved over the decades you can watch the TED talks (and other videos) of Hans Rosling which reveal the links between economic development, agriculture, poverty and health. Rosling used animations to transform development statistics into moving bubbles and flowing curves that make global development trends clear, and offered a level of abstraction that statesman and Bodhisattvas (who are destined to live a long life) can learn from. The point is that the state of a nation's health can become dramatically better over the course of just twenty years if the government adopts the right policies.

What types of leaders can create the right policies? Because the world is fast changing and requires our adaptation, our leaders need to adopt visions that choose the future or they will choose the past. The leader's vision is key. As historian Rufus Fears taught, we must prepare our future leaders to possess four critical qualities: (1) a bedrock of principles and fundamental truths they will hold to, (2) a moral compass, or sense of right and wrong, (3) a vision of what the people can become/produce, and (4) the ability to build a consensus to achieve that vision. Development is an on-going process and our leaders need to manage that process to create a more prosperous future.

There is an old saying that a prosperous country is where "The wind comforts the land, The soft rain brings its blessings in season, The people are hard working, The land is at peace." This beautiful couplet incorporates the idea that there are four elements of a country akin to the four elements of a human body that reach inner balance and harmony through spiritual cultivation. In other words, a country should be managed so that its components (wind element = customs and culture, water element = rain and prosperity, fire element = work, earth element = land and stability) can attain a state of harmonious balance, and the nation enjoys peace and prosperity as a result. A Bodhisattva strives to bring about the golden mean of prosperity that avoids extremes and balances all the sectors of society.

HISTORICAL DEVELOPMENT CYCLES

If you develop a deva body that lasts for hundreds of years (the Causal body and Supra-Causal bodies last even longer and survive when your deva body dies) you will want to understand how man progresses through great cycles of time and larger world historical processes. You'll want some guide path for understanding this long process since your longevity will be as long. I've created a small guide to this in *Culture, Country, City, Company, Person, Purpose, Passion, World*. Carroll Quigley's *The Evolution of Civilizations* might also be of interest.

As with people, you should understand that countries, cities and even civilizations are born, grow to maturity, reach their highest height, and then decline. If you live many hundreds of years, which is what normally happens with the deva body attainment, you will want to be able to reference the general pattern of the rise and fall of civilizations, countries, cities, cultures and so on because you will want to be able to guide people to more fruitful outcomes within these patterns. You will want to learn how to intervene in a long-term process in order to maximize human progress and happiness while encouraging the development of civilization and culture. You will want to the know the pattern of generational waves and other forms of societal and economic progress that normally appear within these long-term processes. Let's review some of the roadmaps to these matters.

Arthur Schlesinger (*Cycles in American Politics*) says that sometimes societies simply transition back and forth between a "We" phase and "I" phase; a national mood shifts back and forth between an emphasis on public purpose and private interests. He postulated a consistent cycle of liberalism and conservatism ("I" and "We") in America that might also extend to other countries. Williams and Drew (*Pendulum: How Past Generations Shape Our Present and Predict Our Future*) came up we a similar theory of "We" versus "I" generations, and found that it matched the famous generational waves of Howe and Strauss revealed in *The Fourth Turning* and follow-up books. This duality fits in with the Socionomics view of Robert Prechter who said that society swings between a positive and negative pole of social mood: optimistic vs. pessimistic, adventurous vs. protectionist, benevolent vs. malevolent, confident vs. fearful, daring vs. defensive, liberal vs. restrictive, ebullient vs. depressed, hopeful vs. full of despair, and so forth.

Of course others have created cyclical views of history as well. Alexander Tytler set forth a theory of the cycles that every democracy passes through, as did Polybius in ancient Greece. Crane Brinton in *The Anatomy of Revolution* set forth a theory of the typical behavioral pattern found within the English, American, French and Russian revolutions.

Prabhat Rainjan Sarkar set forth a vision of the evolution of macrohistory (the Law of Social Change) where specific types of classes assume the leadership helm of a nation in turn, sometimes through revolutions or a natural rotational development. Vilfredo Pareto and

Gaetano Mosca developed theories on historical change due to the circulation of elites within societies who eventually commit too much crime/vice and plunder too much wealth from the "lower" classes so that they are then deposed.

The dynastic cycle theory of China postulates that each Chinese dynasty rises to a political, cultural and economic peak and then declines because of moral corruption, loses the "Mandate of Heaven," and falls, only to be replaced by a new dynasty that initiates a brand new cycle of the same pattern. Sima Qian, the Grand Historian of China, felt that each Chinese dynasty began with a sage king of great wisdom and virtue (ex. Yu of the Xia dynasty or Chen Tang of the Yin dynasty) and ended with an evil, degenerate monarch. According to the Chinese view, people are typically happy when the dynasty is rising and turn violent or degenerate when it is in decline.

Other models suggest that excessive population growth is the underlying cause of state breakdowns in agrarian countries. This is because a growing population leads to a gradual fall in agricultural income per head (per capital production) due to diminishing returns, and any surplus normally available for the state shrinks when this happens. Eventually the productive surplus of food over bare subsistence is insufficient to provide for the state's needs, which is basically the ruling class that taxes farmers for its own existence. Unchecked population growth thus leads to fiscal insolvency.

Generational Theories: The Romans derived the concept of the saeculum, representing about ninety years, which stood for the first moment that something happened (like the founding of a city) until the time that all who lived at that first moment had died. The Romans felt that every people or civilization were only allotted a certain number of generations.

Ibn Khaldun in his Islamic masterpiece, *Muqaddimah*, also proposed that dynasties had natural lifespans like people and lasted no more than three to four generations of forty years each (which was about the lifespan of an individual in ancient times). He said each generation had an *asabiya*, or unifying sense of social solidarity, group consciousness, shared identity, or social cohesion that formed the community. He saw history as being due to the rise and fall of this *asabiya* of solidarity whereas the Chinese historian Sima Qian saw it due to the rise and fall of virtue. The views are similar if we consider *asabiya* as a form of virtue, or shared virtues as *asabiya*.

Ibn Khaldun's theory of history and the ending of a dynasty after successive generations is very instructive: "It reaches its end in a single family within four successive generations ... The builder of the family's glory knows what it costs him to do the work, and he keeps the qualities that created his glory and made it last. The son who comes after him had personal contact with his father and thus learned those things from him.

However, he is inferior to him in this respect, inasmuch as a person who learns things through study is inferior to a person who knows things from practical applications. The third generation must be content with imitation, and, in particular, reliance upon tradition. This member is inferior to him of the second generation, inasmuch as a person who relies upon tradition is inferior to a person who exercises independent judgment. The fourth generation, then, is inferior to the preceding ones in every respect ... He imagines that the edifice was not built through application and effort. He thinks that it as something due his people from the very beginning by virtue of the mere fact of their descent, and not something that resulted from group effort and individual qualities."[16]

In general, a first generation's *asabiya* is strong and brave, a second generation still has some of the original group's virtues but moves from privation to luxury, and the third generation has totally forgotten the period of toughness due to luxury, leisure, sensual pleasure and ease. This is what happens to successive generations of people over time, especially within rich families. The collective memory of a group is destroyed as older generations pass away and are replaced by younger generations disconnected from the struggles of the past and the values they necessitated. Akin to the worldwide observation that wealth rarely lasts more than three generations, the children of elites usually come into money and power without having developed equivalent talents and thus become decadent over time as they are no longer talented individuals who struggled to get where they are. Thus, by the third generation of an empire or dynasty it is usually characterized by a total dependence on or habituation to ever-increasing luxury rather than characterized by the original strengths of the founding generation.

Basically, within three or four generations, due to a gradual but progressive "softening of the fiber," the people within a nation undergo moral degradation and loss of collective solidarity too. They progressively lose their *asabiya* or capacity for collective, cooperative action. Then they become susceptible to conquest by a group with a stronger *asabiya* and motivating sense of legitimacy. This is why nations should not institute educational policies that soften the fiber of children by creating dependency and an aversion to risk taking, which can result in "snowflakes" and "strawberries" (which bruise from the slightest pressure). Nations as a policy must internally encourage independence, hardiness, responsibility and self-reliance.

As a short summary, Ibn Khaldun said that new dynasties achieve social cohesion and then grow tremendously, later become sedentary and wedded to luxury, and then become subservient to desire and decadence at the end

---

[16] Sohail Inayatullah, *Understanding Sarkar*, (Brill, Leiden, 2002), p. 210.

of their lives. That's when they lose their ability to defend themselves and their resources, and their ability to extend their influence over other groups wanes.

Sir John Glubb Pasha, military author and historian, also worked out a general history describing the internal cultural patterns of empires from the earliest pioneers to a final stage of conspicuous consumers who typically become a burden on a state. He wrote that empires go through a general life cycle of specific stages - which lasts a total of about 250 years or about ten generations on average - as they start to expand, mature, decline and collapse.

This meshes nicely with Peter Turchin's findings that state breakdowns occur at somewhat irregular intervals roughly two to three centuries apart. Pasha also supported the idea of a final decline characterized by deterioration and decadence, which was also supported by both Chinese and Arab observations (Sima Qian and Ibn Khaldun). The final demise appears as an age of decadence characterized by common features including undisciplined and overextended military spending, large government deficits, political dissensions and unrest, conspicuous displays of wealth, massive disparities between the rich and poor (massive income inequality), higher food prices, a common desire to live off a bloated state, the rise of frivolity, an immature obsession with sex and fine food, and debasement of a nation's currency. Supply and demand imbalances also tend to undo the social order over time.

Historian Carroll Quickly wrote, "The process by which civilization, as an abstract entity distinct from the societies in which it is embodied, dies or is reborn is a very significant one. There are at least five steps in the process. Civilizations die as (1) decreasing political security and the ending of law and order make property precarious and make personal violence an increasingly significant element in life; accordingly (2) long-distance trade decreases; as a result (3) town life becomes precarious and there is a general exodus from the towns as people try to find a place in which they can be attached in some stable social and economic relationship to the food-producing earth; obviously (4) there is a decline and even a disappearance of the middle classes (the property-owning, commercial, literate, city-dwelling group); and (5) illiteracy rises rapidly. Civilization reappears through the same five steps, each in reverse: (1) law and order are reestablished; (2) commerce increases; (3) cities appear and grow; (4) a middle class, between soil tillers and fighting men, reappears; and (5) literacy reappears as a technique of record keeping and distant communication for the middle class."[17]

---

[17] Carroll Quigley, *The Evolution of Civilizations,* (Liberty Fund, Indianapolis, 1961), p. 266.

It is also important to understand the generational cycles revealed by William Strauss and Neil Howe from researching generational biographies back to 1584 (see *The Fourth Turning, Generations: The History of America's Future, 1584 to 2069* and *Generational Dynamics: Forecasting America's Destiny*). To Strauss and Howe a generation usually lasts 21-22 years, although people sometimes round this down to 20 years so that three generations amounts to an even 60 years.

You should think of a "generation" as the predominant worldview of society as a whole for a period of time. A generation is a group of people who experience the same events and develop a similar mindset and way of looking at things. Rather than think in terms of years, you should think of a generation as the predominant worldview of a strata of society including how people within that age group look at things, make decisions, and what they value.

Any country can dramatically transform itself quite quickly, historically speaking, if it concentrates its planning on generational-based periods of time. A good principle is to measure change in proportions of sixty years, such as twenty, thirty or forty-year segments. Thirty years, which is (1) half of the sexagenary cycle, (2) approximately half of a Kondratieff economic wave as well as (3) the length of Saturn's orbital period, is one useful period of importance or planning purposes.

Twenty years is useful as the length of a generation. When we look at the work of Hans Rosling or the economic complexity work at Harvard (atlas.cid.harvard.edu) developed by Ricardo Hausmann, we can find that a country can become dramatically different in just twenty years of effort.

Forty years is a pattern encompassing two generations, and there are over 160 instances of 40-year generational patterns mentioned in the Old Testament. The exact phrase "forty years" appears fifty-four times in the Bible, and every time it refers to an epoch or window of transformation. Howe and Strauss said that society becomes entirely different every forty years by passing through successive 20-year cycles of what they call Idealist, Reactive, Civic and then Adaptive behavioral patterns.

A competing time period of consideration for planning matters is the Chinese 60-year sexagenary cycle, which is essentially the 60-year Saturn-Jupiter cycle. The Chinese sage Shao Yung is said to have offered an interpretive scheme of history using this cycle in a book on cosmology (*Huangji Jingshi*), but it is unavailable in English. He is famous for writing the *Plum Flower Numerology* (*Mei Hua Yi*) classic that has become the basis of many fate prediction systems.

The *Yijing* teaches that we have to learn how to guide the changes that happen during all these cyclical periods. I stress this in *Color Me Confucius* because the key to mastering phenomena is to master the changes possible for phenomena, which includes human affairs. All rulers are interested in how to manage large groups of men to states of peaceful prosperity, and the Bodhisattva should make this an ardent topic of study. Different strategies must be employed for different situations, locations, individuals and time periods. For instance, the laissez-faire principles of Taoism are typically useful in chaotic situations because they lead to chaos settling, whereas in stable conditions the Confucian principles of administration are used to preserve a golden mean of good conditions. Confucianism is equivalent to centralized control and central planning whereas Taoism is equivalent to laissez-faire policies, evolution and adaptive change.

That which is rigid, formal and inflexible such as centralized planning cannot adapt to rapid change and eventually vanishes, which is the essence of evolutionary dynamics. Centralized planning sees all the aspects of adaptive change – such as dissent, experimentation, decentralization and self-organization – as dangers to its hierarchical structure that especially benefits elites. In times of danger that require quick changes, you must defer to the adaptive philosophies of Taoism that let people work out their own solutions to problems in order that groups of people may survive.

National Supremacy Cycles: The famous Chinese strategic classic, *The Romance of the Three Kingdoms,* starts off with, "Empires wax and wane, states cleave asunder and coalesce." Another translation - "After a long split, a union will occur; after a long union, a split will occur." Basically, everything dies in the long run; impermanence rules the fate of empires and nations. Supremacy cycle scholars Modelski and Thomson accordingly said after much study, "Successive powers emerge as the leading nations of their time in roughly 150 year cycles." If a nation becomes preeminent, the question is not just why but for how long?

What are the requirements for a nation to become a preeminent hegemon, a supreme leader among other countries? History shows that the nation has to become independent of direct foreign influences (it should not be under anyone's control), attain agricultural self-sufficiency, and resolve its internal conflicts that could impede social and economic union. It must also be isolated from the center of active world events, exhibit an propensity of free trade and capitalist tendencies, and must start to acquire land and a widening sphere of influence without being blocked by the current world leader or other nations in its pre-supremacy stages.

Kondratieff wave analysis suggests that this happens in roughly 180-year periods involving three phases of power transfer, each roughly a 60-year Kondratieff cycle. In the first phase of power transfer (the first Kondratieff wave out of three within the larger pattern) the old supreme leader weakens, a new leader emerges and a depression is typically experienced by the new leader as it learns the ropes. In the second wave the new leader solidifies his position through trade and wealth accumulation, and his political influence and power increase. An economic depression eventually occurs that is lighter than the first one because bureaucracies and social safety nets have been built. In the third and last wave, less capital is available for new industries and innovations due to social welfare costs, there is stagnation of growth along with high inflation and socialist movements.

Governments may start to make large socialist promises, but as Margaret Thatcher said, "The problem with socialism is that, eventually, you run out of other people's money." People are always inevitably oppressed under socialism because the government takes an ever-increasing portion of their income, crushing them in the process rather than letting them spend their income in the way they personally deem best. Under socialism, no matter how hard you work or how much you succeed you won't improve your lot because the government will take most of the fruits of your labor. The burdensome costs of socialism eventually kill a nation.

Within each Kondratieff wave there is usually a five-stage pattern of development where each stage lasts roughly a decade or more. In the first decade, characterized by recovery, there is a tendency towards a conservative national mood, modest speculation, and protectionist foreign trade. In the second decade, characterized by wealth accumulation and sometimes war, the nation pushes to maximize its wealth via free trade. In the third decade, characterized by both prosperity and war, the nation tends to be progressive and reform-minded while practicing free trade. In the fourth decade, characterized by transition and stagnation, the nation tends to be internationalist but protectionist. In the fifth decade, characterized by a depression that ends the wave, the nation tends to become conservative, practice extreme protectionism, and suffer deflation as great debts are wiped out.

Mike Maloney even described seven monetary stages to an empire or country as it progresses through typical phases of development. Typically, (1) a country starts out using good money that is either gold or silver, (2) the nation develops economically and socially, and begins to take on more economic burdens through countless public works and social promises, (3) as its economic affluence grows so does the nation's political aspirations and it starts to fund a massive military, (4) eventually it starts wars because of a dangerous, combative foreign policy that causes its military expenditures to explode, (5) to fund the wars it steals the wealth of its people by debasing the coinage and printing money endlessly, (6) the populace senses the loss in purchasing power of the debased currency and loses faith in it, (7) a mass movement out of the currency into precious metals takes place. Everything seemed to be going so well until the country's currency suddenly collapses in an unexpected phase shift that sweeps everything away.

One can keep a pulse on the state of an economy through analysis using methods that technicalize fundamental information such as in Ned Davis's *Being Right or Making Money*, the work of Nelson Freeburg, Neftci probabilistic recession models (that should use *deciles* for data inputs to improve results), the special indicators within *High Yield Investments, Hard Assets and Asset Protection Strategies* (Bill Bodri) and so on.

All along the way throughout these phases – for the rise and fall of empires, countries, civilizations and cultures – things are as written in *A Tale of Two Cities*, "It was the best of times, it was the worst of times." There is always both good and bad throughout every phase of these cycles. Crisis is a time of opportunity for those who act quickly and have the resources to take risks and make advantageous moves. While most people suffer during a crisis, those who prepared for the danger or simply have good fortune can make their fortune. Crisis teaches the lesson that you should take opportunity when it arrives, and that opportune timing can be more beneficial than force because it enables you to accomplish more with less.

City Prosperity: The idea of supremacy cycles and the eventual fatality of preeminence can even be extended to the rise and fall of cities, which can certainly lose their glory. A quick survey of the largest cities in the world (*Four Thousand Years of Urban Growth*) shows that the largest is always eventually replaced by a newcomer. No one holds the standing of preeminence forever.

Cities can become great when they serve as a transportation hub for international trade and commerce, when they have good administration fair to all participants (including minorities) because of the rule of law, where there is tolerance of dissent so that intellectuals are not persecuted, and where there is good infrastructure. Among other reasons, cities fall because of war and invasion, because they aren't economically diversified, because they were on the edge of a large empire that fell, and because they overstretched themselves in projects they didn't understand, especially when they involved taking on too much debt. See *Culture, Country, City, Company, Person, Purpose, Passion, World* for the rise and fall pattern of great cities.

Political economist William Playfair said, "Wealth and power have never been long permanent in any place … they travel over the face of the earth, something like a caravan of merchants. On their arrival, everything is found green and fresh; while they remain all is bustle and abundance, and, when gone, all is left trampled down, barren, and bare."

Virgil once wrote, "The Roman state, just like all states, is doomed to die." In other words, God simply has not granted the boon of perpetuity to any empire, nation, city, tribe, race, religion or civilization. They all rise and fall, and you should strive to understand some of the more common reasons as to why and the typical patterns of failure.

I have high hopes for the new field of cliodynamics, invented by Peter Turchin, that tries to analyze these dynamic macrohistorical processes in an analytical fashion. His book *Ascendancy Cycles* reveals long historical periods of cooperation, peace and prosperity followed periods of inequality, political instability and misery. There are many competing models of ascendancy and decline, and all postulate competing structures of developmental phases.

For instance, Raymond Wheeler's climate cycles (*Climate: The Key to Understanding the Business Cycle* by Zahorchak) for describing government styles is another way of looking at long-term trends and cycles of civilization. After compiling twenty centuries of historical records on temperature, rainfall and other measures, Wheeler found, "A difference in mean annual temperature of no greater than 1.5 F, when prevailing consistently for no longer than half a decade, is sufficient, anywhere on earth, to start changes in the human behavior pattern in one direction or the other." Many historians will confirm that climate change leading to agricultural failure has frequently initiated mass movements of people. Wheeler also found, "Old civilizations collapse and new civilizations are born on the tide of climatic change. The turning points occur when cold-dry times reach their maximum severity."

Sun-spot cycles, which affect the weather, are a related force that can affect agriculture and thus economics. Alexander Tchijevsky studied man's emotions or excitability throughout 2,422 years of history as exhibited through wars, riots, revolutions, expeditions and migrations, and found they were linked to sunspot activity as well. Martin Armstrong has studied many such historical cycles.

AGRICULTURE & FARMING

In the *Avatamsaka Sutra* there are several crop-spirit Bodhisattvas mentioned: Crop-ruling Spirit Tender and Delectable; Crop-ruling Spirit Pure Light of Seasonal Blooms; Crop-ruling Spirit Robust Strength; Crop-ruling Spirit Increasing Essence and Energy; Crop-ruling Spirit Universally Producing Roots and Fruits; Crop-ruling Spirit Wondrously Adorned Circular Cowl; Crop-ruling Spirit Moistening Pure Flowers; Crop-ruling Spirit Accomplishing Wonderful Fragrance; Crop-ruling Spirit Delighting the Beholder; and Crop-ruling Spirit Immaculate Pure Light.

If you want to become an agricultural (crop or farming) protect god or guardian spirit, or have aspirations to become an Agricultural Buddha or Bodhisattva, in addition to one's spiritual cultivation there are several topics you should study. Over the past millennia we have moved from hunter gatherers to farmers and through advances in seeds, planting and harvesting equipment, fertilizer, pesticides and so forth we have solved many problems contributing to world hunger. You want to study the best agricultural practices that are not yet popular but *extraordinary* in the field of agriculture, since this is what people are not yet instituting.

For instance, while most farms make only $3-5K per acre, some unique farms following organic principles make $120-150K per acre. For ashrams, monasteries or convents/nunneries running farms, this is a ten-fold increase in income from making a few simple changes. A monastery, ashram or temple with a farm should check into this to maximize their income. Along these lines, the best three farms to study are: the Singing Frogs Farm (Paul and Elizabeth Kaiser), Four Seasons Farm (Eliot Coleman) and the Market Gardener (Jean-Martin Fortier).

The methods of Joel Salatin's Polyface Farm, available on video from Acres USA, are also extremely worthwhile to study. A very famous interview called the Fruit Guy Interview, by Michael Senoff, will also teach you how to earn one million dollars in cash profits per summer if you simply follow the methods to the letter.[18] This is another way to help finance a religious institution.

Every country has different types of crops and agricultural systems because of soil and climate conditions, but some agricultural principles are common everywhere. You need to know about what are best practices concerning soil health, seeds, planting (times and conditions), crop rotation, weed management, irrigation, weather (rainfall), fertilizer, pest control, and harvesting. Acres USA provides many books on these farming topics. TED talks also provide information on innovative, revolutionary farming techniques.

For instance, soil health and fertility can be improved through products like volcanic ash, the soil enrichment methods of William Albrecht, and radionics indications such as provided by Arden Anderson. For some people the insights/methods of Rudolph Steiner and Viktor Shauberger will prove of interest. Along the lines of radionics, devices such as the Quantum Tube broadcaster (if they work) might offer subtle energy solutions to farming problems, such as pests and fertility issues. Decreased irrigation costs and nutrient uptake can be improved through inexpensive water treatment methods such as Crystal Blue Water Structuring Units. Various mantras for crop growth are available in Hinduism and other religions.

As to rainfall, many people know that there are ceremonies where you can ask the local guardian spirits and protecting devas to produce rain, such as a Pueblo or Hopi Indian Rain Dance. You can learn how to do rain

---

[18] Michael Senoff, "Fruit Guy Interview," accessed August 29, 2018 http://www.hardtofindseminars.com/Fruit_Guy_Interview.htm

engineering yourself too. The absolute best information on weather engineering are the works of Trevor Constable such as *Loom of the Future: The Weather Engineering Work of Trevor James Constable*, "Etheric Weathering Engineering on the High Seas" (video), and his other videos. These materials show how to use very simple-to-construct esoteric devices for weather engineering whereas the government uses microwave energy and very large scale atmospheric heating devices such as HAARP. I have constructed Constable's rainmaking tubes myself after he taught me how to do so and surprisingly found them to work. They can create rain by pushing against atmospheric Qi until it bunches up into an agglomerated mass and then discharges as rain when the mass of Qi becomes too large.

To find the best day to try and cause rainfall, historical rainfall data for a region can be collected and put in neural network modeling software, such as that offered by TimingSolution.com, to create predictive models based on astronomical phenomena. The highest probability rainfall dates, in conjunction with real-time humidity and cloud conditions, would then be the best times for trying to artificially produce rain through Constable's methods.

Rain is so critical to agricultural prosperity, and thus national prosperity, that even Buddhism has a mantra for the naga spirits (in eastern religions any deva who helps to make rainfall using etheric Qi energies they learn and practice is called a naga) in charge of rainmaking: *Namah samanta-buddhanam meghasaniye soha.*

Desertification, which has destroyed many civilizations in the past, is a related problem that now threatens us globally, but there is hope of reversing the problem in some situations using "holistic management and planned grazing." A TED talk by Allan Savory, "How to Fight Desertification and Reverse Climate Change" (his grazing practices are followed at the Polyface Farm), showcases these techniques. The use of Acacia trees to re-green lands bordering deserts, and various other methods can also be used.

In case of a nuclear war, as a national priority we would have to turn to hydroponics and aquaponics until the soil was once again safe. These are also topics to study and perhaps master.

I have high hopes for three technologies used together to improve crop yields. First, the use of CRISPR alter crop genetics. University of California researchers found a strain of corn in the Sierra Mixe region of Mexico able to support nitrogen bacteria, and if those genes are passed to other plants that develop similar attributes they will all need less fertilizer. Second, the University of Illinois found out how to "hack photosynthesis" by increasing the efficiency of the Rubsico protein used in the detoxification line of photosynthesis so that plants grow faster and bigger. These two technologies might be combined together to produce superior yielding plants. CRISPR can also be used to create other wonderful crop features as well. Finally, the development of organic sprays containing minerals, amino acids and plant extracts, such as the seaweed-based product "Sonic Bloom," might be sprayed on plants via drones to help increase crop yields tremendously. These three innovations alone can dramatically increase crop yields and end hunger.

Some other interesting agricultural titles: *How to Grow World Record Tomatoes* (Charles Wilber), *Four Season Harvest* (Eliot Coleman), *The Winter Harvest Handbook* (Eliot Coleman), *The Rodale Book of Composting* (Grace Gershuny), *The Vegetable Gardener's Bible* (Edward Smith), *Gaia's Garden* (Toby Hemenway), *Mini Farming* (Brett Markham), and *Vertical Gardening* (Derek Fell). Forest gardens should also be studied. For agricultural books I always turn to the publishing firm *Acres USA* since it is a specialist on production-scale organic and sustainable farming.

ASTROLOGY & HOW TO CHANGE YOUR FORTUNE

Any denizen of higher spiritual realms has a strong grasp of the reality of various cosmic energies, such as the distinctive energies of the planets, constellations, nakshatras, lunar mansions and five elements of the seasons. For instance, the waxing and waning of the moon affects your Qi flow, just as the movement of planets and their proximity to the earth affects you as well. These are energies a Bodhisattva and Buddha must understand, so some study of these factors, however little, is in order.

Astrology and *feng-shui* deal with understanding these energies and are traditional paths used to attract people into the practice of spiritual cultivation because they deal with predicting people's fates and destinies. Masters of Hindu Jyotish (astrology) tell us that there is no use in knowing someone's future unless you can change it, so remedial measures for handling problems and changing people's fortune have been invented by various spiritual cultures. The "8M Method" in *Quick, Fast, Done* (and *White Fat Cow*) is the only book in the world that integrates worldly success principles with such supersensible principles, for changing your fortune.

There is fate, there is karma. It does exist and at times can be predicted. However, you created it so you can change it but most people just go along with it because they cannot detach from the habits, impulses and inclinations that impel them along the fate line they previously created, and which is to come due, as their karmic recompense. People talk of free will, but if they don't cultivate wisdom, clear awareness and transcend the pull of their emotions then they will always let past karma control them.

To create a new fortune you need a clearly visualized goal or plan. You need to cultivate the meditation practice of inner watching to correct your faults that impel you down old pathways and errant behavior when you notice it. You also need disciplined action to go against fate as revealed in the 8M Method. You have the ability to choose your responses to life, and using wisdom and persistence you must proactively create your own behavior, character traits and any new fortune that you want. This requires work, just as it requires work to learn a new talent or skill.

Vasistha's Yoga says, "What is called fate or divine will is nothing other than the action or self-effort of the past. The present is infinitely more potent than the past. They indeed are fools who are satisfied with the fruits of their past effort (which they regard as divine will) and do not engage themselves in self-effort now.

"If you see that the present self-effort is sometimes thwarted by fate (or divine will), you should understand that the present self-effort is weak. A weak and dull-witted man sees the hand of providence when he is confronted by a strong and powerful adversary and succumbs to him.

"Sometimes it happens that without effort someone makes a great gain: for example, the state elephant chooses (in accordance with an ancient practice) a mendicant as the ruler of a country whose king suddenly died without leaving an heir; this is certainly neither an accident nor some kind of divine act, but the fruit of the mendicant's self-effort in the past birth.

"... The wise man should of course know what is capable of attainment by self-effort and what is not. It is, however, ignorance to attribute all this to an outside agency and to say that 'God sends me to heaven or to hell' or that 'an outside agency makes me do this or that' – such an ignorant person should be shunned."[19]

In *Liao Fan's Four Lessons*, Zen master Yungu said, "Ordinary people are forever involved with wandering thoughts, so naturally their lives are bound to Qi, the forces of Yin and Yang, and fate. You cannot deny that fate exists, but only ordinary people are bound to it. Destiny cannot bind those who practice great kindness or great wickedness. For those who cultivate great kindness, the virtues they accumulate from kind acts is so great they can alter their original destiny for the better. The merits accrued can actually change their destiny from suffering to happiness, poverty to prosperity, and short lives to longevity. However, when a person's evil deeds are great and powerful, they will cancel out the fortune and prosperity predetermined in their original fate, and their life will be transformed from good to bad."

Then again, some things are so karmically fixed or fated that there is nothing you can do. As Ramana Maharshi explained, "The fate of the soul is determined in accordance with its *prarabdha-karma*. What is not meant to happen will not happen, however much you wish it. What is meant to

---

[19] Swami Venkatesananda, *Vasistha's Yoga*, (SUNY Press, Albany: New York, 1993), pp. 26-27.

happen will happen, no matter what you do to prevent it. This is certain. Therefore the best path is to remain silent."[20]

The point is that we all have some *fixed* karma, but you can change most of your fate, fortune and destiny for better or worse, especially if you practice very good deeds or very evil deeds in this life. Don't ever assume your karma is fixed or you'll stop trying to move ahead and make things better. When things don't happen the way you want there is the temptation to think it is destiny, but that's just a poor way of thinking for dealing with failure that produces solace for your condition and excuses you from more effort. As Swami Sivananda of Rishikesh once said, "You are the architect of your own fate. You are the master of your own destiny. You can do and undo things." I painstakingly laid out the how-to details for improving your life and accomplishing goals called the "8M Method," in *Quick, Fast, Done* based on what I originally developed in *White Fat Cow*.

In the West we say that people are influenced by their genes, but genes are not your destiny. Genetic influences can be overcome. The influences playing an impact upon the formation of your character and life go beyond genes and include your parents, family, friends, schooling, community, society, culture, religion, race, nation, environment, seasonal influences, planetary influences, past life influences, and personal experiences. As *Move Forward* explains, there are ways of training yourself and conducting yourself in life so that negative influences from all these quarters can be overcome. A person who sets out to do this is an exemplary individual, a man of consummate conduct, a superior man, a transcendental one. Therefore, Buddhas and Bodhisattvas are always working on self-improvement along these lines. They work on the forces of karma that produce the quality of one's life – their personality, behavior, cultivation, and good deeds.

To know the fate of an individual, unless you already have the superpowers available to the Causal body or higher, you need to know astrology. The various forms of astrology include western astrology and Indian astrology or Jyotish whose five principal styles are *Parashari, Jaimini, Nadi*, Tantric, and *Tajika*. The major style is *Parashari* while *Nadi* readings, if they can be found can reveal amazing details of your life.

There is also Chinese astrology whose principal styles are *Ba Tzu* or the Four Pillars of Destiny, *Zi Wei Dou Shu* or Purple Star Astrology, *Qi Men Dun Jia, Da Liu Ren*, 9-Star Ki, *Tie Ban Shen Shu* also known as Iron Plate Spiritual Numerology. There are also several other schools of astrological techniques but these are the main ones.

Chinese believe that success in life is based on five areas of influence, which are: (1) *Ming* or fate, which is decided at birth and can be known but

---

[20] Ramana Maharshi, *The Spiritual Teachings of Ramana Maharshi*, (Shambhala, Boston, 1988), p. 1972.

not changed, (2) *Yun* or luck, which fluctuates with time but is predictable, (3) *feng-shui* or environmental influences, which can be manipulated so that we reach a higher level of what our luck allows, (4) *Dao De* or virtue and character, which brings us good karma and good will from others, thus lifting the fortune, (5) *Du Shu* or education and footwork, which stands for the work we must do to actualize our luck.

Most who study astrology in the West start out with western astrology and then turn to Jyotish (Indian astrology) because it has much better predictive abilities. Western astrologers often tell me the story of how they turned to learning and using Jyotish because it allowed them to make better predictions than the methods of western astrology alone. Chinese astrology also has powerful predictive abilities, but most Chinese methods are difficult to learn because there are few texts available in English. Chinese usually only study Chinese astrology while Indians typically restrict themselves to various forms of Jyotish.

Regardless of the form of astrology one chooses to study, one should become familiar with most of the ordinary astrological significators such as the meaning of planets, signs, houses, house lords, transits, progressions, dasa bhuktis, yogas, and so on. Transits and progressions can manifest as (1) thoughts, (2) sensations in your body, (3) what you see, hear or notice through your senses (perceptions) around you, (4) actions you take, (5) or events and occurrences that happen to you. The main questions people usually ask astrologers concern matters of career and wealth, relationships and health issues. As a tendency, men tend to focus on issues of wealth and career while women tend to focus on relationship issues.

One highly overlooked but extremely powerful form of western astrology people should consult is locational astrology, which changes the natal chart by recasting it for your present living location. This is the right way to do astrology to obtain the most accurate predictions and the one I recommend, but there are very few experts for the technique. Because Chinese and Indian astrology were developed at a time when people rarely moved from their birth location, they did not incorporate its powerful insights into their methodology. Astrocartography attempts to make a stab at the insights of locational astrology, but explains just 3% of the findings available with locational astrology.

As stated, the purpose of astrology is to help you understand the influence of cosmic energies on your life, and *know your fortune so that you can change your fortune*. It takes more than positive thinking to do so. For this you can consult the remedial measures of Indian Jyotish and Chinese *feng-shui*, as well as the western methods of character development, goal setting, and the importance of grit, unremitting perseverance, coping skills and concentration combined with mantra, meditation and merit as explained in *Quick, Fast, Done* (Bodri) and *Move Forward* (Bodri). Some people study the

Yijing to learn how to change their fortune, meaning how to guide their actions to change situations, but the *Yijing* is rarely used that way.

The big principles to remember are that a good astrologer is invaluable, and astrology can alert you to potential opportunity. It may not give you exact predictions, but it can give you a range of potentials from the high-end to low-end for certain transits and progressions. There is no bad thing in your charts that *has* to happen, just as there is no good thing that *has* to happen either. However, there are periods when the potential for certain events is high. You should use astrology to identify those periods of potential, and push forward when it is beneficial while withdrawing from efforts when detriments lie ahead. As Shakespeare wrote in Julius Caesar, "There is a tide in the affairs of men. Which, taken at the flood, leads on to fortune; Omitted, all the voyage of their life is bound in shallows and in miseries. On such a full sea are we are now afloat, And we must take the current when it serves, Or lose our ventures."

So sometimes astrology can alert you to events that will most probably happen in your life, but you must always give yourself a chance to change a predicted fortune, especially if you know about it. In particular, avoid the toxic conditions that are a preamble or prerequisite for a bad fortune to manifest. By removing yourself from those conditions, such as by becoming a monk and refusing marriage, sometimes a bad fortune can be prevented. By doing less, meditating or going into retreat during a problematical period you produce less opportunity for your actions to produce unfortunate results. During bad transits do less acting or act in a more limited way so that bad fortune has less of a sphere to manifest. The more actions you take during a bad transit the more that trouble seems to expand.

Remember that you alter the manifestation possibilities of transits, progressions and yogas as you alter/transform the contents of your mind and body, which you accomplish through personal cultivation. Astrology usually only indicates the potential for events to happen, and you must use those times and circumstances to help make things go the way you want. It is important to emphasize that you must *work* to get the results you want in life even under favorable astrological aspects and progressions – they are not guaranteed by your astrology or by requesting Buddhas and Bodhisattvas for help.

There is a wonderful ancient story that perfectly illustrates this principle. At one time there were two farming brothers who were very poor, so the elder brother decided to pray day and night to the God of Wealth, asking to become rich. While he prayed, he let his younger brother do all the hard work in plowing and planting the fields. After the older brother had spent a considerable time in making supplications, the God of Wealth magically assumed the form of his younger brother and went to visit the elder, who became angry at seeing that his younger was not working the fields. When he asked the younger brother why he wasn't working, the disguised God replied, "Brother, day and night you pray in the temple, hoping to obtain considerable wealth. I also want to do the same as you. Through pledges and vows and abstention, I too wish to gain considerable wealth."

The elder brother responded, "If you don't plow the field and plant the seeds, then how will we ever gain the wealth and abundance we desire?"

The younger replied, "Oh, is that how it works? Do you mean that we have to plant and work the fields to get rich?"

The elder brother was stunned at this reply, whereupon the God of Wealth threw off his disguise and resumed his celestial form saying, "Now is the time I can finally help you because your mind is finally open, and you can accept the truth. So listen carefully to what I have to say. Only if you practice generosity and giving can you become wealthy. Your previous karmic causality has made you poor because you did not practice generosity, offering and all forms of charity. That is why you are poor. So even though you ardently beg me day and night for wealth and riches, how can you obtain them without this karmic past?

"Take for example a fruit tree. If it is wintertime, you cannot obtain any fruit, no matter whether you served a thousand or a million gods to get it. The same principle applies to money. Because you previously did not develop any karmic causality, but yet you still beg me for wealth and riches, you cannot get it either. But when the fruit is ripe in season, you will naturally obtain it without even asking. Everything is obtained because of prior formations; to obtain something you must perform the appropriate actions and set the right formations into motion. What can imploring the gods do about it?"

As stated, astrology can indicate your potentials, but if you do nothing to actuate them then you won't get any results. There are a lot of potentials most people have, but if they don't have the necessary merits then they won't achieve them either. You have to work to produce the results you seek, for it is the law of the universe that nothing comes free. However, by using astrology and knowing of transits and progressions you can know when you might plant seeds to get the best results.

One of the recommendations that I often give young people is to find a great astrologer for predictions, as they are worth their weight in gold but difficult to find. In particular, before moving to a new location you should check with a relocation (locational) astrologer who might be able to tell you how you will like the new area and how your job/career or marriage in that location will fare. This is because a relocated natal chart becomes the primary chart over your birth chart after you move.

A move to a new city may cost thousands of dollars. It will also be worth hundreds of thousands of dollars in terms of the salary you get or house you buy, so spend the money on an excellent relocation astrologer before you make such an important decision. They can tell you ahead of time whether you will like your job in that new location, and whether you will like the area as well. Typically it is by moving sufficiently far eastwards or westwards will change your chart and fortune whereas moving northwards or southwards will not change your fortune significantly.

Everyone has astrology authors they like, and with so many reading and learning options available it is hard to say who is best. I cannot give you a short list of the best books to study, but personally like the works of James Braha (*Ancient Hindu Astrology for the Modern Western Astrologer*), Rick Houck, B.V. Raman, Myrna Loftus and Sakoian & Acker, as well as many others.

MARRIAGE & RELATIONSHIPS

Many people will come to a great monk or nun for help in finding a spouse, or for marriage counseling. Some want to find a spouse, some a soul mate, and some are considering divorce, which is at the 50% rate or higher. I have put some of my thoughts about this in *Husbands and Wives Were Connected in the Past*.

Seeking a Spouse: There are many mantras that people can use to attract a husband or wife, called *Vashikaran* in Hinduism, and when recited used the enlightened Buddhas and devas will indeed try to help you find a spouse for a loving relationship. Your past karma, and your willingness to change yourself in this life, will determine the nature of the relationship you experience, such as whether you will marry a "soul mate" or just someone you have karma with. You must be a certain way, which includes being intent on improving yourself and working on your relationship, in order to connect with a "soul mate."

Astrologically speaking, you should use progressions and transits to find useful times and appropriate mantras in conjunction with locational astrology to try to find a spouse when you really decide to get married. Even if such efforts work, remember that there is no such thing as a perfect spouse, and as the Chinese say, "70% is good enough." One of the keys to a good marriage is avoiding deal breaker conditions in the first place, such as a potential spouse who is toxic because of their habits and personality. Furthermore, moving to a new area (if it is sufficiently far away either eastwards or westwards) will usually change your astrological houses and the planets within them, and thus the nature/happiness of your marriage relationship will change too because of the move.

Once married (or while dating), you should remember the rule in life to maximize the wellbeing of any relationship for as long as it lasts, however long or short that will be. The rule: Make it as good as you can for its life span. How good your marriage is will be a function of your past life merits (your past life relationship with that person) and *the efforts you put into the relationship in this life*, so do the best you can to make it the best you can for as long as it lasts. Remember that marriage requires work! The rule in cultivation is to turn every situation you encounter into something better, so you should try to do this within your marriage relationship. As stated, locational astrology can show a new location where a marriage can blossom, heal troubles, and reveal locations where a marriage will simply disintegrate because of the environment through no fault of your own. Try to use it.

In terms of marriage specifically, I always advise people to remember a phrase found above the Imperial shrine in Hangzhou, China:

> Husbands and wives were connected in the past,
> Whether their connections were good or bad those connections never fail to meet again.
> Sons and daughters are basically past debts.
> Some come to collect from you and some come to pay you back but they only come on account of debt.

If you marry someone it is usually because of a previous relationship, strong or weak and for good or bad, from a past life. You natal chart will reveal the characteristics of your spouse.

The idea of finding a mate and marriage ties into the topics of sex, fertility, love and romance. People marry for many reasons and all are equally valid as long as you take responsibility for your decision to marry. In other words, if you marry primarily for money and security you cannot complain that you don't feel passion in the marriage, but must accept their lack because you married for something else.

Should you enter into a marriage that you know is doomed to fail, or try to pay off what you feel is a karmic debt in another way such as when there is an unexpected baby? The decision is up to you, but if you marry for a reason other than love than you should be willing to bear the normal consequences of that particular form of marriage.

Before marrying I suggest you determine the degree of compatibility with your spouse by running through the questions in works such as Susan Piver's *The Hard Questions: 100 Essential Questions to Ask Before You Say "I Do."* Divorce expert Dr. John Gottman says that women having butterflies before a marriage is almost always a sign that deep inside they know there will be trouble which typically turn out to be true, and that they shouldn't get married to *that person* in the first place.

It is said that there are six things that women are highly attract towards in men:

- Money, Riches or Means (great wealth and possessions imply he can "support" you)
- Power and Influence (power implies "safety" – he can "protect" you)
- Fame or Status
- Good looks
- Exclusivity (royalty, already married, hard to get, affiliations)
- Personality (humor, creativity, romance, mystique, intelligence).

People jokingly tell men that if you don't have any of the top five attractive factors on this list then all you are left with to capture a woman's heart is your personality. They also tell men that if from the start you don't rate 70% or better on a woman's attractiveness/approval scale then nothing you do will ever put you into the category of dating material. For each woman you must rank at least 70+% on her approval rating from the start and cannot climb into that level later.

As a bit of fun, women sometimes say there are eight types of men. The first four types are Lover types including the (1) Bad boy (dangerous and thrilling), (2) Adventurer (fun and exciting), (3) Seducer (sensual and sexy), and (4) Artist-musician-poet (moves her emotions and is an enigmatic complex). These four types appeal to women who desire fun, excitement, passion or challenge. They might appeal to women who want/need their emotions stirred, for good or bad, and therefore seek someone who "makes them feel alive."

This explains the best selling within romance novels which women buy to stir their emotions: opposites attract, a love triangle, an abductor and hostage situation, forbidden love, protector/bodyguard and damsel in distress situation, adversaries, deserted island or stranded together theme, arranged marriage, amnesia story, Pygmalion mentor and protégé story, Cinderella rags to riches tem, beauty and the beast theme, fish out of water theme, different classes, bad boy/good girl or popular girl/nerd story, ugly duckling transformation story, best friends become lovers, and partners struggle jointly to beat a common enemy.

The second set of male Provider types includes the (5) Mr. Successful who provides a great lifestyle and stability, (6) the Daddy type who controls her and tells her what to do, (7) the Regular guy (down to earth, loyal, stable), and (8) the Ass kisser who always agrees with her or gives her whatever she wants. Women are attracted to certain types of men, and these well-known categories are fun to talk about.

Fair is fair, so we can turn to some well-known stereotypes for women looking to marry. The eight categories postulated by Vin di Carlo are quite fun in this regard, but you should remember that there are many other equally interesting categories developed by others, all of which can lead to lively discussions.

To Vin the (1) Hopeful Romantic girl is old fashioned and wants an honest, deep emotional connection with a man. She is waiting for the perfect man to fit the role she determines in her life, and holds back until then. The (2) Connoisseur is extremely selective and finicky about men and doesn't fall for conventional male tricks and techniques. If she is attracted to you then she gets attached very quickly. You have to be socially savvy and work very hard to date her. The (3) Cinderella woman is classy and quickly gets intimate. She loves to fall in love, craves romance and passion, always has a man and gets her heart broken often. The (4) Modern Woman is friendly and cool, not exclusive, and wants fun and comfort. She is open about being intimate with men, is not afraid of her sexuality, but will not sleep around until she finds the right partner. She wants one guy but will date around to find him. She makes a great girlfriend and wife. The (5) Playette has many guy friends, is flirtatious but doesn't sleep with them because she enjoys attention and respect and knows they will diminish is she sleeps with anyone or starts dating them. She is sexy and sweet but keeps her emotions a secret. To pursue her you must not pressure her or smother her. The (6) Private Dancer is a giver with lots of passion inside. She is selective about men, easier to sleep with than the Playette, but normally pursues power and money. She is very picky and only gets involved with guys who contribute to her life. She has to think they are above her own social status level. The (7) Social Butterfly dates a lot and sleeps with many of those men, but only those whom she is friends with. She is hard to catch. You have to be aggressive to pursue her without being needy. Finally, (8) the Seductress is liberated, the most sexual of all the types of women, actively pursues her goals, and demanding. She is a master manipulator in life. You have to be strong and confident without being needy to gain her.

Men, not surprisingly, want to pick up women because they are looking for sex with attractive partners who may or may not turn into mates. But good looks aren't the most important thing for a stable, long-lasting marriage since few women are super models, and neither are most men. Although everyone prefers an attractive mate, as they get older both partners become wiser and realize that compatibility is the issue. A fulfilling life depends on the quality of your relationships, not your appearance.

Chinese culture is very pragmatic about the selection of a wife, saying, "the ugly wife is a treasure at home." The Chinese man tends to think of the wife in a more functional rather than sexual or sentimental way so while he wants a Playboy model, like everyone, he realistically expects that his wife will not be as physically attractive as a Playboy model. He wants a wife who will take care of the family, take care of the parents, cook the food, and help him raise their children together as a team. You can read *The Chinese*

Secrets for Success: Five Inspiring Confucian Values by YuKong Zhao to see how this culture wants to raise a family.

The problem with women who want to work in a career is that they cannot fulfill this mother and wife role as well as in the past, and they sometimes start losing their femininity due to stresses in the world of modern business. Sometimes their lives *is* a choice between having a good career or a good marriage and family.

Why do men and women marry? For many reasons, and sometimes not because they have found Mr. or Mrs. Right but simply because of family pressure or they want to have a baby while time is running out. All these reasons are valid, and all have consequences.

Some other books of interest: *The 5 Love Languages: The Secret to Love that Lasts* (Gary Chapman), *Men are From Mars, Women are From Venus* (John Gray), *Love & Respect* (Emerson Eggerichs), *The Relationship Cure* (John Gottman) and *His Needs, Her Needs* (Willard Harley).

Divorce: The divorce rate is approximately 40-60%, depending upon the country and culture, and may climb even higher going into the future. Since the couples of today do not need each other for survival; since television paints an unrealistic picture of perfect/wealthy marriages that most people cannot achieve; since most people are now impatient and want quick results in marriage and everything else; since couples both want to work rather than concentrate on the family; since children are not needed as cheap labor for a family farm; since society no longer pushes a couple to stay together when there are marital difficulties; and since women are usually no longer dependent upon a man's income for her future, the reasons to stay together during marriage difficulties are weakening over time.

One must remember that you must give up your ego to the marriage bond in order for it to thrive, which means that when you compromise you are not giving up your ego to your partner *but to the marriage*. Remembering this fact helps to preserve marriages through difficulties.

There are also mantras available to help prevent divorce, but sometimes separation is best so that you do not continue to create bad karma by staying together within a bad relationship. Many people will even use the excuse that "they want to cultivate" as a reason for divorce when they really just want a divorce, and this reason is just a way out that the spouse cannot argue with. When marriages become old and one partner wants out, they often seek a "no fault" excuse that they can use to justify the separation.

Furthermore, researchers state that approximately 25% of couples will have an affair during their marriage, and genetic testing reveals that from 5-15% of children in marriages are illegitimate with the higher percentages correlating with lower economic strata. About 50% of divorcees also cite internet pornography as a contributing issue, so it will probably become a marriage issue if one of the partner delves into pornography too frequently. With couples watching "perfect" couples and families on television, which also tends to display wealthy lifestyles out of reach, there are many situations that are contributing to weaker families and higher divorce rates.

Divorce specialists say that women have affairs due to a variety of reasons such as shifting hormones, bedroom boredom, greater confidence, because the mommy stage is over, or because they are feeling neglected. However, one expert summarized the reasons by saying it is usually due to a lack of passion and that women are looking for situations that can "make me feel alive." This explains the attractive potential of the first four types of "lover" men and gives you pointers as to successful conduct in the dating field. All women have different buttons that push their emotions, but one of the keys is to make her feel alive, and for each person that's different.

Aside from the causes of abuse (substance, gambling, drug, alcohol, physical or mental, etc.), and the fact that the economic situation of women is considerably better than ages ago so that she does not need the monetary support of the husband for her survival, many divorces are due to the fact that marital partners cannot match in five particular areas. For a marriage to succeed the partners must have (1) sexual compatibility in the bedroom, (2) communications compatibility where they respect and regularly talk with one another with honesty, (3) interest compatibility so they like doing some enjoyable things together and have some activities of mutual interest, (4) they must have something they want to *build together* - a common dream or vision that is the purpose of the marriage such as the desire to build a family, travel together, succeed in politics or build wealth, and (5) they should not overly disagree over money matters.

For instance, research shows many marriages are low-risk when husband and wife view themselves as a team, which is reason #4. Some are prone to divorce because the couples are personality incompatible, which are reasons #2 and #3. For instance, a wife might typically press to solve problems and want to discuss them, but the husband might commonly dismiss her concerns, which is a frictional difference that might lead to divorce.

Researcher Dr. John Gottman has developed models that are close to 94% accurate in predicting which couples will be divorced within three years time, and which explain what drives the process of incompatibility. He believes that strong marriages have at least a five-to-one ratio of positive to negative interactions. When that ratio starts to drop (because the couple is not saying nice things to one another) the marriage becomes at risk for divorce.

Gottman also said that in a healthy marriage the martial partners usually bid for each other's attention throughout the day, seeking recognition of the other through signs of acknowledgement. They should turn towards each other in response to those bids since this is a very crucial factor in maintaining the relationship's success.

Another characteristics of successful marriages is that the partners are kind to each other. Yet another powerful factor predicting divorce is how couples react to arguments with the best course of action being to talk about a conflict, fight or argument after it has happened. Gottman found that couples should talk immediately and openly about what just occurred, figure out what went wrong to resolve it, and discuss the topic while trying to understand each other's feelings.

Gottman also identified that there are four major negative behaviors that typically predict divorce, and so should be avoided:

(1) criticizing the partner where you turn a partner's behavior into a statement about their character,
(2) speaking in contempt (anger and disgust) of the other partner during conversations where one party sees the partner as beneath them while they are superior,
(3) defensiveness, where you play the victim in tough situations with your partner,
(4) stonewalling or emotional withdrawal from interaction (blocking off a conversation to avoid conflict) with your partner.

In summary, Gottman's general prescriptions for avoiding marital conflicts are to turn toward your partner when they want interest from you, say positive things in a 5:1 ratio or higher, celebrate the hard times you have been through together, and examine whatever they want you to notice. You can easily find many of his books on marriage and harmonious relationships.

Pregnancy: Most couples want children, but some do not. Fertility is an issue that has plagued mankind for millennia, and there are countless mantras that beseech higher powers for children. There are also the concerns of not wanting children until it is the right time.

Most women have been taught to know their fertility cycle and when they are most likely to become pregnant according to the cycle of menstruation. Natural birth control can also be practiced by using the Billings Method, also known as the Ovulation Method or Mucus Method. It was developed by Drs. John and Evelyn Billings of Melbourne, Australia because the Rhythm Method is not reliable. The birth control failure rate is 1.2% whereas according to John Billings, "The combined biological failure rate and user rate of the ovulation method in Tonga was 0.69 percent." The technique, which you can read about in *The Ovulation Method*, is as follows.

"The Billings Method is a one-step reading of a woman's cervical mucus, performed by the woman herself in a moment and without internal examination. Every day, she gently wipes her labia with clean, dry, white toilet paper. She looks at the paper to see if there is any mucus on it. If there is, she is likely to be fertile. If the mucus is wet and slippery, and can be easily stretched, then she is very fertile. If the paper stays dry, she is likely to be infertile that day. On the day of the most wet, slippery, clear mucus, she is most fertile of all. This day is called the peak day, and is the very day she ovulates. She will also feel wettest on this day. She remains fertile for three days after the peak.

"It does not matter how old the woman is, nor does it matter how long her menstrual cycles are. Unlike the Rhythm Method, there is no need for regular menstrual cycles. There is no need to fit into a normal, clockwork 28-day model. If a woman has short menstrual cycles, she will ovulate early. If they are long, she will ovulate late. The mucus is there at ovulation, regardless. If she misses a period, there will simply have been no ovulation, and therefore no fertile, wet mucus that cycle. A woman does not even have to know to read and write to use the Billings Method effectively. Trials in the South Pacific nation of Tonga between 1970 and 1972 showed high levels of acceptance and success with the Billings Method.

"Abnormal temperature, such as a low fever, will interfere with the temperature method of birth control. It will not obstruct accurate readings with the Billings method, however. Abnormal vaginal discharges, also, do not prevent a woman from recognizing her state of fertility. Given the knowledge, any woman can use the Billings Method for her entire reproductive lifetime without financial cost. And, obviously, unlike medical methods of birth control, there are no harmful side effects with the Billings Method."[21]

Such information can be combined with the findings of Czech psychiatrist Dr. Eugen Jonas reported within *Astrological Birth Control* (Sheila Ostrander and Lynn Schroeder) if his method is correct. Dr. Jonas wished to help the many women who desired pregnancy and had been trying in vain for a long time. Based on studying thousands of pregnancies, he supposedly found that the times of the greatest fertility for women are based on the relationship of the Sun and the Moon at the time of the woman's birth - the same phase of the moon as that in which the woman was born. For instance, if a woman was born with the Sun and Moon at a 60-degree angle, as occurs five days after the New Moon, she would become highly fertile when the Sun and Moon were at a 60-degree angle each month and for a period on either side of this peak period regardless of her menstrual cycle.

To avoid pregnancy, in addition to avoiding sex during ovulation Jonas

---

[21] Andrew Saul, *Doctor Yourself*, (Basic Health Publications, North Bergen: New Jersey, 2003), pp. 96-97.

suggests that a couple should also abstain on (and for several days prior to) the day that the Sun and Moon repeat the exact angle they made with each other at the moment of the woman's birth. A woman born at the exact moment of the full moon would abstain during, and for several days prior to, the full moon since that is when she would be most fertile. Since sperm can survive for as long as three days it is recommended that one abstains for three days before the repeated phase angle if no pregnancy is desired. When combined with abstention during ovulation, this modified rhythm method is, according to Czech researchers, 98% effective as a birth control method.

This method is questionable. I have doubts about this methodology, but believe it must be reported because someone will research it if I pass it along, as I just have. Even so, at worst it simply provides some extra days to enter into the bedroom other than those based on hormones if you want a baby. As long as you are not using it as a guide to prevent pregnancy we could say that no harm is being done other than possibly ignorance.

If one desires pregnancy, it is important for the man to maximize his fertility. Zinc supplements (50-100 mg daily along with copper) will increase sperm counts and megadoses of vitamin C for a few weeks (6,000 mg per day) will also increase sperm production. This will produce more sperm, stronger sperm and better swimming sperm.

A woman should detox prior to wanting to get pregnant (see *Detox Cleanse Your Body Quickly and Completely*) and then start taking fertility herbs when she is ready. It is also essential that prenatal vitamins start to be taken *several weeks before conception* in order to boost a woman's vitamin levels to prepare for the first few weeks of pregnancy, which is when the most fundamental decisions about the shape of a baby's body will be made. Sufficient vitamins will help to prevent birth defects. Repeat: if you want to get pregnant you should start taking multivitamins *well before* the pregnancy.

Once pregnant, everyone desires a healthy baby without miscarriage. Dr. John Lee provided indications as to when natural progesterone would likely help to prevent miscarriage, especially for women who had repeated miscarriages or were getting older and worried about pregnancy due to their advanced age. The main secrets to having a healthy baby are the right diet and taking vitamin supplements, and starting well before pregnancy.

Most everyone knows that pregnant women should avoid alcohol, drugs and cigarettes, but what they don't know is that vitamin C helps hold a pregnancy from the start and is essential for helping the baby form strong connective tissue that it will have for the rest of its life. Dr. Frederick Klenner MD gave very large doses of vitamin C to over 300 women and found no complications in any of the pregnancies or deliveries, but did notice that the vitamin C babies were the healthiest and happiest. Specifically, Klenner gave 4,000 mg during the first three months of pregnancy, 6,000 mg per day during the second trimester, and 8,000-10,000 per day during the third trimester. Since we are all deficient in vitamin C, and since it is used to make strong connective tissues, I like the "vitamin C babies" approach.

Since the B-vitamins also help prevent birth defects, and since most babies are vitamin D deficient even when their mothers take prenatal vitamins, every woman who wants a healthy baby should be taking megavitamins during pregnancy as recommended by their doctor, Cod liver oil, and mineral supplements such as Shilajit. Eating the right foods and supplements can also have long-lasting beneficial effects.

In *Deep Nutrition*, Catherine Shanahan MD and Luke Shanahan found that if you want your children to be extremely healthy, intelligent, able to excel at sports and *so physically beautiful that they are striking* then the expectant mother should be eating a surplus of complex nutrition that avoids sugar and vegetable oils during pregnancy. She has to eat nutrient-dense foods and take ample supplements to avoid nutrient depletion in order to produce a baby with the best skeletal development, which translates into better facial features and appearance. This is why I recommend vitamins, green and red vegetable powders, bone broth soups, Cod liver oil, olive oil, and mineral supplements such as Shilajit during pregnancy.

The most attractive children in a family are typically the oldest or, in families of three or more, one of the first two children because of better maternal nutrition during gestation or better womb circulation for the second child. The avoidance of nutrient depletion, which can be countered by the right foods (such as bone broths) and supplements, tends to produce the most favorable looks. An aspiring mom who is pregnant needs to avoid frozen, canned, vitamin-poor foods and a generally unhealthy diet for the best looking and healthiest baby. Naturally she should avoid alcohol, drugs, cigarette smoking and other vices as well since these are poisons that hurt the body.

If the mom is malnourished because she doesn't eat nutrient-rich foods then it will affect the skeletal structure and features of the baby. The demands of producing a baby draw down maternal stores of all sorts of nutrients, so for the best looking babies a mom has to eat very well and take supplements.

Children: Remember what the sign above the Chinese Imperial shrine said? "Sons and daughters are basically past debts. Some come to collect from you and some come to pay you back, but they only come on account of debt."

In *Light on Relationships: The Synastry of Indian Astrology* (Hart deFoew and Robert Svoboda) the authors wrote, "A child who comes to you with a horoscope of destitution does so because your own destitution karmas have also ripened and are waiting for you to consume them. The child is as much an instrument of your karmic fulfillment as you are of its.

"Similarly, a child who comes to you destined to enjoy prosperity has come to you because you, too, are destined to enjoy some prosperity. If you do right by that child, your mutual prosperity may develop yet further. If you mistreat it, you will be garroting the goose that is ready to lay your own golden eggs. Students of the law of karma marvel at the elegant sort of neutrality that involves both parties, often unconsciously, in creating their own situations."[22]

SELF-MASTERY & CHARACTER DEVELOPMENT

The pursuit of self-actualization or self-perfection is the "Great Learning" road of self-cultivation taught by Confucius (see *Color Me Confucius*). It entails the pursuit of skills, character development, and the impregnation of ethics and virtue in all your behavior. Among other terms, you might consider this the pursuit of purity, higher being, self-perfection, spirituality, consummate conduct, right living or ennoblement.

Interestingly enough, it is usually the successful people in life who are most interested in becoming better people, including improving their skills and behavior along the lines of the Great Learning. They also tend to contribute to the world more than others.

Let's focus on the aspect of improving our personal virtue and ethics, which is raising ourselves above our animal nature.

Confucianism categorizes people into different groups according to their varying degrees of moral cultivation, which is the cultivation of ethics, proper behavior or virtue. A morally exemplary person is called a "superior person" ("gentleman" or "man of consummate conduct"); those who are gentlemen but also help others to cultivate themselves are "men of humanity"; and those who can extend benevolence to all people and bring succor to the multitude are "sages."

Moral self-cultivation is a continuous process that we should all commit to throughout our lives, and is an essential part of the Great Learning. While not born perfect you can be come more perfect, talented or skillful through a practical path of training. You can become the best version of yourself. You can become more than what you were born with. You can become the light you want others to see. Talents and skills can be learned while personality flaws and bad habits can be changed for the better.

We can all learn how to manage our weaknesses and develop our

---

[22] Hart deFoew and Robert Svoboda, *Light on Relationships: The Synastry of Indian Astrology*, (Samuel Weiser, York Beach: Maine, 2000), p. 171.

strengths. We can all adopt new values. We can all learn how to become superior people of consummate conduct, and from this as a basis cultivate to become a sage. If you don't decide to tread the road of ethics then no one will help you complete the transformations for attaining the subtle body. You'll just have to cultivate in the afterlife.

Everything revolves around ethics, but what are ethics? There is a saying in China that the ears are deaf to virtue or right and wrong until the stomach is full. Only when people are no longer hungry can you speak to them about virtue and ethics and impact the audience. Furthermore, a Chinese saying runs, "After the granaries are full the people will be aware of proper behavioral standards and ethics; and after the country becomes prosperous, education will be thriving." This is something that a Wealth, City or Country guardian spirit needs to keep in mind. Only if you first bring prosperity to a region or family of individuals can ethics then prosper for it is hard for people to stay ethical when they are poor and hungry.

Nevertheless, what are some ethical principles you can use for guidance in life? What are the foundational basics of ethics?

- Doug Casey: "Do not aggress in any way against another person or their property."
- Chamfort (*Products of the Perfected Civilization*): "Enjoy and give pleasure, without doing harm to yourself or to anyone else – that I think, is the whole of morality."
- Kant: "Act in accordance with the maxim that your actions should [be so justified that they] become a universal law." In other words, don't do anything if you think it isn't proper enough to become a universal law.
- John Wesley: "Do all the good you can, in all the ways you can, in every place you can, at all the times you can, with all the zeal you can, to all the people you can, as long as ever you can."
- Buddhism: "Do all the good you can, cut off any evil when you encounter it, don't block any unborn good from being born, but never let any unborn evil arise."
- Confucius: "Don't do to others what you would not have them do to you."
- Jesus: "Do unto others as you would have others do unto you" and "Love thy neighbor as thyself."
- Old Testament: The Ten Commandments
- Yoga: the Yamas and Niyamas

The golden rule of dealing with others is not imposing on them what you do not want imposed on yourself. For instance, history shows that elites typically become oppressive and harm others without any power once they get into power themselves, for power corrupts. Elites tend to impose on the weaker whatever they want or desire, and tend to justify it with all sorts of nonsense. Treat people as you want to be treated is the rule.

The formal principle which should guide you in relationships with others is to first conduct a type of thought experiment of how you would feel in place of the person(s) who will be affected by your actions. If you would be unwilling to be treated in the same way you imagine, then you should not do what you are considering. At least consider, "If situations were reversed, how would you like to be treated? How would you want the situation handled?" In considering an action you should also ask, "Does this raise me above my animal nature?"

How to Win Friends and Influence People (Dale Carnegie) is one of the few books that everyone should read. It talks about the soft skills involved in leading people, how to appeal to noble motives, how to become genuinely interested in others and create enthusiasm, and in general how to handle interpersonal relationships. Carnegie pointed out that in interpersonal relations you must know how to draw the best out of people. What do men want? Lincoln said all men crave to be appreciated, Dewey said the deepest human urge is to be important, and Freud said that apart from sex the chief desire of men is to be great.

Most people go to spiritual teachers (such as monks, nuns, rabbis, priests, masters, swamis, etc.) with problems and want help. Many of those requests center on personal behavioral problems rather than requests to help them out of a specific situation such as a lawsuit or illness. How can you help people get what they want?

Without the specifics of a situation, we can only talk about how to help people change their behavior – their typical mindset way of thinking, habit energies, tendencies and consistent behavioral patterns. We all need ways to prevent ourselves from pursuing past habitual patterns that are bad for us. How to change habits is explained in *The Power of Habit: Why We Do What We Do in Life and Business* (Charles Duhigg) and *Color Me Confucius*, which reveals various techniques such as Stoic philosophy, ACT and mindfulness practices. In all these methods we should remember the adage,

> Watch your thoughts for they become your actions.
> Watch your actions because they become your habits.
> Watch your habits because they become your character.
> Watch your character because it becomes your destiny.

Changing our habits and character flaws, and policing our behavior, is the pathway to consummate conduct. Sometimes we need to eliminate flaws from our personality/behavior, which is akin to weeding a garden, and sometimes we need to add fertilizer to the garden to make things grow, which is working to develop new character traits that we want such as through immeasurables meditations. You can and should, through the right techniques, cultivate the qualities of the Buddha you want to be.

Pick a Buddha whose values, virtues, and vows impress you, or inspire you to be the same way if you could. Think about whatever interests or virtues infect you with the desire to be greater than you are now, and then vow to become a Buddha of that type even if you know of no one who has taken that road. You absolutely, positively can get rid of the imperfection layers you've built up over the years and get in sync with the real you, the core of who you really are, by vowing to and then taking steps to cultivate the way of the Buddha you want to be. This is the path of Buddha Yoga.

Plato says that when young we need to learn to take pleasure in virtuous actions even if we don't fully understand why. We must form habits that teach us to like them. Aristotle even pointed out that virtue, which is the control of the appetites by reason, is actually a kind of habit. He felt that if you learn what is good for you and then develop good habits to practice it and ultimately learn to like it, this is the key to success and happiness.

The famous actor Cary Grant, adored by millions including countless men who wished to imitate him, once explained, "Everyone wants to be Cary Grant. Even I want to become Cary Grant. ... I pretended to be somebody I wanted to be until I became that person, or he became me."

By taking steps to become the way you want to be, and by practicing immeasurable meditations along those lines, you can become more like that very person. You can develop the character traits of any individual you respect or want to become like, including a god, Buddha or deity you admire. You can become a Buddha with a cosmic mission if you want, but you have to envision a clear idea of what you want to become and then take active steps in the positive direction you desire. Start doing what is close to your heart even if you can only apply a little effort in that direction. In time the seeds will bear fruit, and if not in this life then in the next. Don't be afraid to reveal yourself, but take some positive steps, however small or insignificant, in the Buddha direction you desire.

This approach belongs to the field of character development, self-improvement, moral development, or virtue training. Athletes, in their sports training, also use this approach. Character training and personal development is either something that others guide you through or something you undertake yourself via a regular committed course of self-improvement.

Since we cannot talk about what others may train you for, we must talk about your own options for self-guidance, which is how past leaders typically became great. Surprisingly even past American presidents took this route. In other words, they worked on and trained themselves. You absolutely can become someone quite different from how you are now in terms of how you think, what you believe, what you feel, how to appear to others and how you behave if you train yourself to become different. You certainly will be different thirty years from no. The question is whether you let those changes happen to you or guide them yourself.

For this task you need good teachers or should read about men who changed themselves and their methods. Confucius, Liao Fan, Benjamin Franklin, and many others are all on the table as are the biographies of other great men who persevered in order to accomplish great goals, and who worked hard at transforming their flaws of behavior. I was amazed when I found out that Presidents Washington, Lincoln, Eisenhower and Teddy Roosevelt all developed the practice of self-cultivation to change their faults and behaviors, and molded themselves into the type of men they wanted to become. Hence, they didn't just become President of the United States through luck or skill, but because they worked on changing their personalities.

Your personality is not set in stone. As stated, thirty years from now you will be an entirely different person. You can either train yourself to develop in a direction you want or you can be like most people and let circumstances shape you. A Buddha, Bodhisattva or guardian spirit chooses the road of cultivate themselves and developing their personality and behavior in the directions they choose.

As individuals we become quite different from one another not just because of genes but due to habituation. Habituation means soaking up and getting used to the influences of our culture, environment and education, and taking these influences as normal. When young it is therefore important to be exposed to morality tales and be given examples of moral heroes so that we have a chance to see great behavioral models. Heroes are effective totems of motivation because they tattoo themselves on our psyche as role models. They serve as role models that can imprint positive aspirations upon us and thereby elevate us and lead us forward.

To this end there are McGuffey Readers (over 120 million sold, attesting to their popularity), the stories of Horatio Alger, Chinese moral stories, Indian spiritual tales, and many other success stories or hero tales involving ethics and morals that help form character. Every country and spiritual tradition has them.

Goals: A major, major character trait to develop in life is grit and perseverance in the face of difficulties, the will to never give up. Sometimes this is called "stick-with-it-ness," maintaining concentration, or samadhi, which means the concentration/commitment to stick with a problem until it is solved, such as the devoted effort required to win a war. To change their fortune or circumstances, people must learn how to conquer hurdles and challenges to persevere over difficulties to achieve success. There is always a way open to achieve for the determined soul with grit. Even if you are not brilliant, if you simply persist at working toward a goal you will tend to get rewards.

William James also said, "To change one's life: 1. Start immediately. 2. Do it flamboyantly. 3. No exceptions." Individuals often use the GAMA formula for doing just that. The first step of GAMA is defining your Goal – what you want. The second step is determining and then doing Actions that take you there. The third step is Measuring whether you are on/off course, remembering that what gets measured gets managed (gets attention) and measurement ends argument. Lastly, always Adjust (change) your course of action according to the results you are getting.

When I once asked persuasion and influence expert Kevin Hogan the best means to create a program for personal change he said to set up a sequence of daily steps such as in Tony Robbins's 30-day *Personal Power* series. Basically, "Success is achieved by repeating small disciplines and taking small, ever-increasing steps." Break up your objectives into segments, and work on them individually.

We spend dozens of years in school, but school doesn't teach us how to make our dreams, goals and ambitions come true. How strange this is if school is to prepare us for life! Only by first setting and then working to achieve our goals do we get in charge of our destiny. Worthy goals and ideals give our lives meaning and purpose and make them bigger, but no one teaches us to take the time to crystallize them or how to achieve them.

Napoleon Hill's method of goal setting is to fix in your mind exactly what you want, determine what you will give in return to get it, and establish a definite date by which you will achieve it. Next you must create a definite plan for achieving it and then *begin at once*. You also must write out a clear and concise statement of these decisions and describe the plan of action. Finally you must read the plan aloud, twice a day, morning and night, and imagine yourself in possession of that accomplishment.

Brian Tracy similarly said that goal setting involves deciding exactly what you want, writing it down, setting a deadline, making a list of everything you are going to have to do to achieve your goal, organizing this into a plan, taking action on your plan immediately, and resolving to do something every single day that moves you forward. Goals are value-neutral, he taught, meaning you are likely to achieve them whether they are good or bad, so why not create wonderful, life-enriching goals? Is this not what Buddha Yoga, or training to be a guardian spirit is about? Without goals, Tracy taught that you will "follow the followers," but if you work on your goals you will be in charge of your destiny. You will follow your own values and interests in life.

Goals must be written down because your mind needs crystallized details in order to shape your actions. For instance, you cannot hit a target you cannot see, so you must clearly formulate goals in your mind and *write them down on paper*. Furthermore, your goals should ultimately wrap around a meaningful purpose for your life – a compelling life mission – because you are only successful in life to the extent you can achieve your own happiness, so you should pursue the goals you seek for happiness and contentment.

You must be specific, measurable and realistic when creating your goals. Don't set goals too high or low, don't make them vague or conflicting. Part of seeking goals, after writing down in exact detail the outcome you want, is to regularly practice visualizing that you achieve that outcome while working towards them (see *Visualization Power* and *Sport Visualization for the Elite Athlete*). Furthermore, when writing down goals you should do so in the positive because the subconscious cannot distinguish between the positive and negative.

How do you determine the action steps to take to achieve what you want? To determine those steps, think everything through backwards to see how to achieve the final goal, or model yourself on someone who has already achieved what you want and use the methods/steps they used.

As you progress towards a goal's fulfillment, you should also continually monitor and even measure your progress in order to provide feedback and should review your progress daily. This is why I tell people to keep a cultivation practice schedule and also record their progress at pranayama efforts. Also, in seeking goals you should also reward yourself at milestones as you work towards the final achievement.

In the business field, goal setting is now known as OKRs, or Objectives and Key Results. Objectives are goals we seek to achieve; key results are how those top-priority goals will be attained with specific, measurable actions within a set time frame. For more information see *Measure What Matters* (John Doerr), and remember that we respect what we inspect, meaning that we respect what we measure. Measuring progress keeps goal targeting in active mode.

Self-improvement: One of the most beneficial self-help, self-reliance, self-improvement mindsets that builds character is the attitude of thinking like an immigrant: "Nothing is owed me, I need to find my niche and go after it working harder than everyone else. I need to think like an artisan and do an extra job of quality so that I stand out from others."

This is the attitude that built America, and the opposite of a snowflake or strawberry culture that shields children from conflicts or anything uncomfortable, thus setting them up for a lifetime of pain since they cannot adapt to the real world and handle its inevitable problems. The real world teaches us that we must adapt to a quickly changing reality to survive and thrive, and children need to learn this lesson, as well as the lesson that life involves pain and setbacks. A nation's success depends on the younger generations, but are we teaching them the right lessons? Are they expecting free handouts or reality?

Furthermore, an important attitude is to develop the learning mindset, and to become a lifelong reader. It is said that what separates the rich apart from the poor are books; the rich read them to learn skills and get ideas while the poor do not. The rich, therefore, are on a constant road of self-improvement when they become lifelong readers/learners. They always try to learn and master new skills, such as negotiation (see *Never Split the Difference: Negotiating as if Your Life Depended on It*). Some random but highly useful books on various skills you might want to learn: *Pitch Anything* (Oren Klaff), *Fanatical Prospecting* (Jeb Blount), *Influence* (Robert Cialdini), *The Science of Influence* (Kevin Hogan), *Never Split the Difference* (Chris Voss and Tahl Raz), and more.

Long-term success, if not from luck or fate, comes from investing in yourself and then doing something to make your own success. Study but then practice, immersing yourself in what you want to become or achieve rather than just reading about it. Get in and do it so that you *become real*. Appreciation of a skill or topic must turn into mastery through concentrated practice, and this is achieved through immersion. Once you have skills and talent then you can build the success you envision.

Training. If you want to train people in spiritual cultivation, you need to know the most efficient methods of training to achieve the best results in the shortest period of time. Most traditions are bad at this but simply follow the methods used for millennia without knowing whether they are truly best or not. There is a lot of inefficiency in the process. As stated, the cardinal principles are to *simultaneously* use a lot of different methods based on different principle is for moving your Qi and calming your mind. There are inner Qi exercises and emptiness meditation practices based on the teachings of non-duality. You must practice both, not just the road of meditation.

You cannot just engage in three versions of emptiness meditation practice, for instance, and think you are using "different techniques based on different methods for cultivating your Qi." You must try to open up your Qi channels through pranayama. You must try to move your Qi through *nei-gong* and *anapana*. You must try to move your Qi through Mantrayana. You must engage in yoga practice or other forms of stretching and exercise while using visualization, Mantrayana and feelings to guide your Qi through your muscles.

You must basically try to simultaneously use, during the same day, many different types of cultivation techniques that will move your Qi based on different principles, and after you activate all the Qi within your body you try to smooth it out into a harmonious, comfortable feeling of bliss and stay in a quiet state of witnessing. First Qi practice, then emptiness meditation so that it can settle. *Anapana* practice, where you try to smooth out your Qi wherever it feels obstructed, can help you reach a state of body harmony.

To understand how to train people, you should familiarize yourself with the deep practice and deliberate practice methods that Olympic athletes use as discussed by Daniel Coyle (*The Talent Code, The Little Book of Talent*), Geoff Colvin (*Talent is Overrated*) and Anders Ericsson (*Peak: Secrets from the New Science of Expertise*). You need to learn how to break a skill you want to learn into chunks that can be mastered and then re-connected back together again into a whole. You need to know about behavioral psychology of rewarding behavior and that intermittent reinforcement (unpredictable random rewards in response to desired behavior) is the most powerful motivator on the planet.

In many fields a cornucopia of information has been reduced down to just one or two principles, instead of dozens, that you must concentrate on for success. The same goes for spiritual cultivation. For instance, with pranayama the principle is to hold your breath as deeply within your lungs as possible, using as few muscles/energy as possible, for as long as possible. For mantra practice, its effectiveness is based upon who is answering the call at the other end of the mantra as some Buddhas are better at working on your Qi than others. Some Buddhas put more energy into answering calls for help and are less distracted by other efforts. Mantra practice can be improved by adding light (visualization), emotions (fervor) and muscle movements to the sound (mantra) work, which then becomes Mantrayana practice. In terms of transforming your body, Mantrayana practice is thousands of times more effective than just reciting a mantra. Yoga, Pilates, stretching and so on can be improved by combining exercise efforts with Mantrayana.

Once you understand training principles you can make your practice succeed more quickly. The following cannot be over-emphasized: the key is to use many different types of cultivation practice simultaneously in a practice schedule you keep in order to move your Qi – meditation, Mantrayana, yoga, pranayama, visualization and self-improvement, etcetera.

William James said, "The greatest discovery of my generation is that a human being can alter his life by altering his attitudes." NLP and EFT (the emotional freedom technique) teach this also. Therefore you should learn how to become a master of your mood at all times, and as a life skill in general. A sunny disposition is worth more than fortune because sometimes you cannot change your fortune but you can still learn to be happy. To get out of a state of misery and move into a happier state, it helps to smile and act as if you are in a happier frame of mind. In time you can train yourself to be this way just as you can cultivate peace of mind through meditation practice.

Along with NLP, EFT, ACT and cognitive behavioral therapy, the most powerful methods for changing your attitudes, habits and behavior are the ones I put in *Meditation Case Studies, Color Me Confucius, Move Forward* and *Quick, Fast, Done*. It is by a system of daily mindfulness, measurement, and self-appraisal that you achieve desired virtues, which is the law of constant self-improvement that leads to a better life promise and behavioral perfection. Engaging in self-improvement is the real road of cultivation. To become a guardian spirit you are engaging in self-development.

THINKING BETTER – CRITICAL THINKING

As human beings, we are lucky to be among the animals that have higher consciousness and can think deeply, and we must train our thinking if we want to elevate and ennoble ourselves or improve our living standards. Thinking logically, and developing the intellect and sciences, is how society has progressed forwards.

Ayn Rand said, "Man's mind is his basic tool of survival. Life is given to him, survival is not. His body is given to him, its sustenance is not. His mind is given to him, its content is not. To remain alive he must act and before he can act he must know the nature and purpose of his action. He cannot obtain his food without knowledge of food and of the way to obtain it. He cannot dig a ditch—or build a cyclotron—without a knowledge of his aim and the means to achieve it. To remain alive, he must think."

According to Rand, human beings must choose their values in life. Whether a person's actions lead to fulfillment and whether a person will act to promote his well-being is totally up to him. This is not hard-wired into his physiology. Hence the need for a culture impress upon society the need for constant self-improvement.

History shows that man made progress over the eras when he emphasized clear thinking, logic, reasoning, investigation and rationality over guidance by emotions or superstition. This (rationality) is what you must emphasize on the road of cultivation. In ancient times people were taught grammar in addition to reasoning and logic, which were emphasized in a number of traditions such as Vedanta, Buddhist Abhidharma, Jewish Talmud study, Sharira study, and so forth. The purpose was teach logic and intellectual consistency. Today we teach science instead.

In ancient times when most people were illiterate, did not go to school and were uneducated, monks and nuns and other spiritual officials became some of the most educated in society through study of religious texts. Today they are not the most educated, skillful, talented or wise. One of the purposes of their religious studies was so that they could help guide others to moral ways, but also to help guide societies upwards to progress. Thus there was an emphasis on teaching religious functionaries how to think properly and to become leaders. If they don't touch upon some of the fields of study within *Buddha Yoga* today, however, how can they say they are qualified to guide others?

In the *Odyssey*, Homer accentuated the excellence of the mind and intelligence, shrewdness, cleverness, wit and wisdom for winning. Wise thinking was emphasized, so how do you teach people proper thinking skills? One factor is to stress shrewdness, logic and reason over a strict regime of political correctness. A disciplined study of logic, science and the ability to reason clearly are desired abilities we want to develop. Logic and reasoning – the keys to thinking and analyzing ideas – are the key methods by which science, law and political discourse were developed in the world.

Along these lines is to learn the principle behind the famous Latin principle "*cui bono?*" (to whom is it a benefit, who benefits from this?) used to identify crime suspects. When you are trying to figure out who might be behind some engineered event the first thought should be of the order of *cui bono*? ... who profits, who benefits, for whom is this good? Cicero once used it in a legal case he was arguing, saying, "The famous Lucius Cassius, whom the Roman people used to regard as a very honest and wise judge, was in the habit of asking, time and again, to whose benefit it be?"

The Chinese warlord Cao Cao consistently uses this wisdom principle to his own benefit in the strategy classic, *The Romance of the Three Kingdoms*. The principle is so powerful that is can be used to immediately decipher the culprit behind false flag attacks secretly used by nations in order to destabilize others. "Trace the money" is another similar principle that can unravel clues as to who is ultimately responsible for some act.

When there is a change of state in some expected result, another principle is to ask, "What did we do differently before this happened? What conditions were different this time before it happened?" This type of questioning, stressed by Kepner and Tregoe in *The Rational Manager*, has helped me immensely in life. When something unexpected happens, you must always ask, why is this situation different? What part of the situation or process changed right before this happened? Osborn's questions for creativity are also very helpful.

Another example of proper thinking, and of the power of observation, is the deductive work of private detective Sherlock Holmes who used logic and observation to solve crimes. His famous phrase of deduction was, "When you have eliminated the impossible, whatever remains, however improbable, must be the truth." If of interest you can read *A Few Lessons from Sherlock Holmes* (Peter Bevelin).

John Paul Getty (*How to Be Rich*) once said that many blunders in life result from a failure to distinguish between fact and opinion (hearsay), and

Sherlock Holmes was a master at getting to the facts and abandoning emotions since they interfere with the intellect. Like the Jains, he emphasized avoiding preconceptions, superstitions and other factors that get in the way of seeing clearly, which is cultivating right perception. This is actually spiritual cultivation since it entails cultivating the capabilities of our consciousness, learning how to use consciousness correctly. Holmes taught us to check our beliefs against the facts, and to be ready to discard your ideas if they did not conform to the facts. While you should strive to believe what is likely to be true, not to believe what you wish to be true, you should always be willing to alter your ideas upon new evidence. This is wisdom.

Most people don't know that the marvelous deductive processes of Sherlock Holmes were inspired by the marvelous diagnosis abilities of a surgeon, Dr. Joseph Bell, and incredible deductive abilities of Zadig described within *On the Method of Zadig* (Thomas Huxley). The method of Zadig is to make conclusions based on an understanding of cause and effect, namely what we may conclude from an effect to the pre-existence of a cause able to produce that effect. An understanding of causation, which entails the mental science of logic, is what we must teach to children and ourselves. In Buddhism "causation" not only includes logic, philosophy, religion, psychology and physical science but also history and economics. "Causation" means studying the laws of nature that rule phenomena, and the reliable tendencies in human behavior and human affairs.

Why should we emphasize *cui bono*, "what changed this time?", and the methods of Sherlock Holmes? John Taylor Gatto stressed that proper deductive reasoning (the ability to reason clearly) is one of the Elite Private School Curriculum themes found most often in the elite prep schools that produce national leaders. Gatto said that the elite prep schools are different from ordinary public schools because they teach children to discern truth from error regardless of the source or the delivery of information. They teach the ability to ask hard questions that challenge prevailing assumptions, and how to use the rules of logic and inference without jumping to conclusions. Thus they develop the proper use of the mind – cultivation!

In his study of these schools, Gatto found that the elite prep schools consistently teach children that they should always test prior judgments. They are taught to make judgments but also told to keep an eye on their predictions to see how they are doing, and to re-evaluate when things aren't going as they thought they might. They are taught to examine history and form principles therefrom that will help them create models of expectations. Ordinary schools do not teach students that cause and effect sequences typically produce second- and third-order effects or feedback loops, but the elite schools do. They teach the ability to understand interrelationships and see the connections among many different disciplines, ideas and cultures.

Basically, at the most elite prep schools the children are taught to think inductively, deductively and dialectically. They are taught how to confront information in the form in which it is delivered to people all over the world, distinguish the important from the trivial, quickly assimilate needed data from masses of irrelevant information, and then conceptualize and reorganize the information into new patterns. In *Weapons of Mass Instruction*, Gatto recently recounted nine qualities essential for adapting to the world of work that touch upon thinking habits:

1. The ability to ask hard questions of data, whether from textbooks, authorities, or other "expert" sources. In other words, do we teach dialectics?
2. The ability to define problems independently, to avoid slavish dependence on official definitions.
3. The ability to scan masses of irrelevant information and to quickly extract from the sludge whatever is useful.
4. The ability to conceptualize.
5. The ability to reorganize information into new patterns which enable a different perspective than the customary.
6. The possession of a mind fluent in moving among different modes of thought: deductive, inductive, heuristic, intuitive, et al.
7. Facility in collaboration with a partner, or in teams.
8. Skill in discussion of issues, problems or techniques.
9. Skill in rhetoric. Convincing others your course is correct.[23]

Another lesson Gatto discovered was the objective to sharpen children's abilities of observation and perception by teaching them how to draw correctly. Drawing teaches you the art of accurate observation, which was emphasized in the movie *Kim* (with Errol Flynn), based on Rudyard Kipling's work about an English orphan in India who was taught to accurately observe everything in order to become a spy for the British "Great Game." In the movie the orphan Kim is taught by the shopkeeper Lagan how to make careful, accurate observations of whatever he sees and to remember coded messages with perfection. Within the movie appears the principle that it is important to teach children super memory skills, which no one teaches at school despite their incredible importance and usefulness. Our educational systems are negligent in teaching the most useful skills for success in life.

The idea of accurate observation and then careful deduction is definitely related to accurate thinking. As stated, the tales of Sherlock Holmes, who is

---

[23] John Taylor Gatto, *Weapons of Mass Instruction: A Schoolteacher's Journey Through the Dark World of Compulsory Schooling*, (New Society Publishers, Canada, 2009), p. 72.

famous for his rational mind and logical powers of deduction, reveal mental powers dependent upon recognizing or determining sequences of cause and effect. The shrewd Judge Dee of Chinese detective novel fame, falls into the same category.

The Romans used to emphasize *lux vitae ratio* – logic is the guide of life, which emphasizes similar lessons along these lines. Buddhism teaches us to learn about linked chains of cause and effect, such as the links of dependent origination. For many religions, we are to tie this type of understanding into the belief that the evolution of our plane of gross matter comes from higher planes of rarified existence as a type of condensation. Basically, to rise above superstition and enter into the realm of science, you have to learn cause and effect.

Chinese spiritual culture also has an art of *xiang shu*, which is observing the environment (objects, situations, appearances) carefully to deduce events of the future. *Feng-shui*, palmistry, and other esoteric skills are all based on the art of observation combined with a large body of tested knowledge (for tendencies) that helps one make predictions. The emphasis on decoding the future is because of the view that remedial measures can be derived for improving situations due to their ability to alter the Yin and Yang of changing phenomena.

How might one familiarize themselves with proper ways of thinking that correct, or at least bring light to common thinking errors? You have to use reason and intelligence to arrive at wisdom. A few books come to mind that can help you develop greater thinking skills such as *Thinking, Fast and Slow* (Daniel Kahneman), *Fooled by Randomness* (Nassim Taleb), *The Tipping Point* (Malcolm Gladwell), *The True Believer* (Eric Hoffer), *Influence* (Robert Cialdini), *Freakonomics* and *Think Like a Freak* (Stevin Levitt and Stephen Dubner), *Predictably Irrational* (Dan Ariely), *Decisive* (Chip Heath and Dan Heath), *How to Lie With Statistics* (Darrell Huff), *Mistakes Were Made But Not By Me* (Carol Tavris and Elliot Aronson), *The Signal and the Noise* (Nate Silver), and *The Rational Manager* (Charles Kepner and Benjamin Tregoe). Many more will be written in the coming years that shed light on how we make common thinking mistakes, and how we should change our manner to start thinking correctly.

PERCEPTUAL TRAINING

The Buddhist sutras teach that people who attain the Causal, Supra-Causal, Immanence body or higher can visit Pure Lands where inhabitants teach/communicate in different ways other than by sound, which necessitates an ear. They can, for instance, teach by fragrances (Qi) in Perfume worlds, by offering light, by using their *nirmanakaya*, or by movement instead of speaking. If you learn sign language, for instance, this type of special movement gives you the ability to teach and communicate without using sound.

There are a variety of methods used to train the senses, and you can pursue them if you want to for fun. They are not important for cultivation purposes, but you will widen your world if you engage in multiple forms of perceptual learning. For instance, training can produce improvements in the ability to distinguish two points touching the skin. Vision can be trained with various devices to improve athletic reflexes. Hearing skills can be improved through training too.

The most important thing is to heal our body of any impairments in our sense organs because our physical body is the template for all the higher body attainments. The functioning of our senses organs can be improved and even restored through various nutritional supplements. In particular, hearing for the elderly, or the loss of taste, can be restored by ingesting Lion's Mane or zinc, respectively. You can use the Bates method for improving your eyesight naturally – it works! For pointers also note the following vitamin/herbal helpmates to improve sense perception:

- For hearing (sound) – Lion's Mane, alpha lipoic acid and aldosterone
- For taste (tongue) - zinc
- For smell (nose) - zinc
- For sight (eyes) – lutein and zeaxanthin, astaxanthin, vitamin A and beta carotene, eyebright, bilberry
- For touch (skin) - vitamin C, zinc, proline, alpha lipoic acid

To attain enough merit for the subtle body attainment it makes sense to donate to charities that help people restore defective sense organs, such as charities that supply vision services, seeing eye dogs or provide cataract operations. Donating to charitable organizations that help the deaf, help the blind, restore limbs using artificial appendages, and so forth is a means of developing the merit to attain the subtle body and also to become a Medicine Buddha.

Actually, when you make such contributions you *are* a Medicine Buddha because you are enabling the work to be done, and so in a sense you are doing it! Always think to cultivate the way of the Buddha you want to be. You should try to cultivate the character of the Buddha you want to become, and the ways of the Buddha you want to be. By determining what that ideal is, and then working towards it, you are achieving personal authenticity - becoming your most authentic self and presenting it to the world.

MARTIAL ARTS

If you want to become a martial arts guardian deity or Bodhisattva, or have aspirations to become a big martial Buddha like Kartikeya (Murugan), Xuan Wu, Wei-To (Entry Guardian) Buddha, Bishamonten, Ares, Minerva, Ogun, and so on then there are several skills one should master *in addition to* martial arts and one's own spiritual cultivation exercises.

First, naturally you must learn the martial arts. The goal is to master the physical self and one's physical energy. Seek a sensei or master teacher to help you establish the right practices, path and priorities and then practice diligently to incrementally progress to new levels of competence.

Also, use the training methods that Olympic athletes use to make progress most quickly as revealed by Daniel Coyle. To get to the highest levels of proficiency, you must combine mastery of physical movements with expertise in moving your Qi, which martial arts usually approaches through breathing but which you can approach through the Qi exercises within this book and *Nyasa Yoga*.

Second, there are other physical exercise modalities that will help with your pursuit to master martial arts skills. These include flexibility training regimes as found in Z-Health, Scott Sonnon exercises, Yoga or Pilates, Foundation exercises, and so on. As always, also go for chiropractic adjustments to fix your skeletal alignment and use AMIT therapy to "turn on" all your muscles. First fix your body's structure, and then start training on how to use it optimally.

Third, there are countless martial arts schools and courses for learning how to strike harder or faster and how to get stronger but there is some information missing from all these specialized topics. The practical information missing from all these approaches includes visualization work, breathing methods, internal energy work, and the fact that talent can be taught in stages. The works of interest that help fill in these gaps include:

- *Visualization Power* (William Bodri)
- *Sport Visualization for the Elite Athlete* (William Bodri)
- *Internal Martial Arts Nei-Gong* (Bill Bodri and John Newtson)
- *Nyasa Yoga* (William Bodri)
- *The Talent Code: Greatness Isn't Born. It's Grown. Here's How* (Daniel Coyle)
- *The Little Book of Talent* (Daniel Coyle)
- *Talent is Overrated: What Really Separates World-Class Performers from Everybody Else* (Geoff Colvin)
- *The 4-Hour Body* (Timothy Ferriss)

- *Body By Science* (John Little)
- *The Anatomy of Martial Arts* (Link, Chou and Kasturia)
- *The Inner Game of Tennis: The Classic Guide to the Mental Side of Peak Performance* (W. Timothy Gallwey)

Martial artists usually end up studying ancient strategy texts on warfare like Sun Tzu's *The Art of War* and a wide variety of other Japanese or Chinese military texts. These deal with victory in battle. Eventually military readers encounter Clausewitz, Jomini, Corbett, and other military strategists. For warfare they must also study the various teachings of John Boyd, who revolutionized modern warfare strategy with his emphasis on speedy reactions.

Even so, as Sun Tzu says, "To win one hundred victories in one hundred battles is not the acme of skill. To subdue the enemy without fighting is the acme of skill. Hence to fight and conquer in all your battles is not supreme excellence; supreme excellence consists in breaking the enemy's resistance without fighting." To win without fighting is supreme.

Above Sun Tzu in skill, strategy and wisdom is Kuan Tzu, who focused on winning without fighting. His methods have been used by the Prussians, Japanese and Rothschilds to gain supremacy in world hegemony. To study Kuan Tzu see *The Means to Win* (William Bodri).

SUMMARY

The principle behind this chapter is very simple. If you succeed at cultivation you can use your multiple bodies to become a Bodhisattva or Buddha who helps people in many different areas of life. However, while you will be able to enter into their minds and learn complicated topics quickly, you will still have to study and practice to learn particular skills in order to become their master. Just understanding how to play the violin doesn't mean you can play it. You need practice to master a skill, but talent can be learned.

Why not start studying now? If you don't succeed at cultivation while alive, you can still use the skills you develop now while working to become a Bodhisattva guardian spirit for some vow, commitment, purpose, offering or mission important to you. Instead of waiting for the afterlife, why not save time and start working to become a great guardian benefactor, Bodhisattva or Buddha now? Where there is a will there is a way. By acting in that function you will become that way.

Life goes on forever, so start now while you have the mind to do so and these teachings. You have incredible merit to have all these teachings in your hands at this moment. If you do succeed in getting out (attaining the subtle body), then when you succeed you can immediately start to work in areas you deem important to your calling. I don't want you to waste time or lack direction. I don't want anyone to say, "No one told me or I would have done things differently." Even if your steps are small you should take them. Consider a new and greater vision for your life that includes this path.

Most people who succeed at spiritual cultivation are religious professionals who study only religious texts, and when they attain the subtle body and higher are therefore quite useless in being able to offer help or advice in anything other than religious related things. They don't know how to do anything in fields other than spirituality since that is usually the only thing they studied.

What a waste! How unfortunate. They should always have engaged in several parallel fields of practical study so that they had skills in helping people in other areas of life, and therefore maximized their usefulness to humanity. That's what the spiritual path is all about, but most religious professionals neglect this common sense! This is also why I wrote this book, which is to help people prepare for helping others in all sorts of fields and areas of expertise other than just the road of spirituality and Yoga. By imitating the Buddha, Bodhisattva, Protect God or Deity you want to become you can become that way.

The whole point of cultivation is to become useful for the world, not to retire from it. To become useful you have to develop practical worldly skills and excellences that help other people, which is what Buddhas and Bodhisattvas do, and become actively engaged with people and events. Unfortunately, most everyone on the spiritual path is not doing this. They simply study spiritual texts, engage in the requisite yoga, and when they finally pop out with a subtle body they have to start learning how to help people. Pity that their teachers didn't encourage them to also pursue parallel courses of training. Pity that they waste so much time.

To help you get a hold on some areas that Buddhas need to know about I listed what I felt were some key basic principles and some of the best current sources, which of course will change over time. It's embarrassing that I often had to cite my own books, but I had to write them in order to fill in the gaps in the information arena since nothing was available. In a way, they can be viewed as revealing the Pragmatist, Hinayana, Mahayana and Vajrayana roads of cultivation practice. Example:

Hinayana: *Color Me Confucius; Meditation Case Studies; What is Enlightenment?; The Little Book of Meditation; Easy Meditation Lessons; Twenty-five Doors to Meditation; Socrates and the Enlightenment Path; Spiritual Paths and Their Meditation Techniques; How to Measure and Deepen Your Spiritual Realization; The Various Stages of the Spiritual Experience*

Mahayana: *Culture, Country, City, Company, Person, Purpose, Passion, World; Buddha Yoga; Color Me Confucius; The Means to Win (The Kuan Tzu); The Taihu School; White Fat Cow; Move Forward; Husbands and Wives Were Connected in the Past; The American Reader*

Vajrayana: *Nyasa Yoga; Visualization Power; Meditation Case Studies; Internal Martial Arts Nei-Gong; Sport Visualization for the Elite Athlete; The Little Book of Hercules; The Atalanta Fugiens Explained*

Practical: *Quick, Fast, Done; Move Forward; Super Investing; Bankism; Breakthrough Strategies of Wall Street Traders; High Yield Investments, Hard Assets and Asset Protection Strategies; The Means to Win (The Kuan Tzu); The American Reader; The Taihu School; Detox Cleanse Your Body Quickly and Completely; Look Younger, Live Longer; Prevent and Reverse Atherosclerosis; Super Cancer Fighters; How to Help Support the Body's Healing After Intense Radioactive or Radiation Exposure; Visualization Power; Sport Visualization for the Elite Athlete; How to Create a Million Dollar Unique Selling Proposition; The Claude Hopkins Rare Ad Collection; Husbands and Wives Were Connected in the Past.*

7
AN EXCELLENT TEMPLE OR SPIRITUAL CENTER

In *Why Do We Need a Temple?* Chaitanya Charan Das states that there are six functions or social services a temple should provide other than its function as a place of worship and religious services.

A temple or spiritual center should serve as a center for (1) tranquility and meditation practice, (2) healing or medication, (3) spiritual and practical education, (4) physical and mental purification, (5) love, and (6) community engagement. Some temples or centers offer all of these services, some offer a few, and some specialize in one or more.

Whether we are talking about a church, temple, synagogue, mosque, monastery, nunnery, wat, gurdwara, meeting house, ashram and so forth they are all aimed at serving the public and fulfill these roles to a greater or lesser extent. They all serve a particular function designed to help the people. For instance, many offer a location for religious services and/or showing reverence to a deity, which is a state of mind that in itself is one of the ways to cultivate spiritual practice. Surrendering to a deity is a type of giving up of your mind that silences thoughts. Bhakti practice also involves the emotions of reverence and devotion.

Let us examine how a great monk or nun, swami, sadguru, master, guru and so on should set up the functions of an ashram, temple or other spiritual center.

MEDITATION

Naturally a temple should become a center where people can find peace and tranquility upon visiting, and where they are also taught how to practice tranquility. Thus, it should be a quiet place where you can go to learn how to meditate, and where you can also practice meditation in an undisturbed fashion.

Even Christian churches and spiritual centers should be teaching meditation (which some sects call "centering prayer"), for one of the basic principles within Christianity is that you can approach God through inner silence since He is beyond rational thinking. As the Bible says,

> Be still and know that I am God (Ps 46:10)
> Be still before the Lord and wait patiently for Him (Ps 37:7)
> My soul finds rest in God alone (Ps 62:1)
> But I stilled and quieted my soul; like a weaned child with its mother [no longer clinging], like a weaned child is my soul within me. (Ps 131:2)
> For God alone my soul waits in silence; from Him comes my salvation. (Ps 62:1)
> To You silence is praise. (Ps 65:2)

If Christians take basic meditation practice and combine this with inner energy work, then Christians everywhere will see a new blossoming of their tradition unlike anything seen in history. Most of the eastern spiritual practices are already inherent within the Christian tradition in some form, which is why the Christian monastic system has been successful in producing enlightened adepts just as in the East. Unfortunately, people don't know this truth because the ways and results of spiritual practice are hidden. However, methods for the Christian public to make spiritual progress can be improved substantially from understanding basic cultivation principles.

For instance, the Sacrament of Baptism can be turned into a daily practice of visualizing and feeling cool energy entering into the top of the head that then washes your entire body everywhere. Then this practice that imitates Baptism, which is essentially *anapana* and *nei-gong* practice, becomes a type of inner energy work.

The principle that our body returns to ashes upon death, which is often recited by the Church (especially on Ash Wednesday), can also be turned into a daily spiritual exercise where you imagine that your body becomes a fire that burns away everything, reducing it to dust, and then empty space filled with light. Or, it burns away to reveal a transparent, crystal pure divinized body that can join the communion of saints. Other alternatives are naturally possible.

These two exercises of visualizing fire and water, done on a daily basis, can match the inner Yin Qi and Yang Qi kundalini energy exercises done in the East. The *Canticle of Brother Sun and Sister Moon* by Saint Francis of Assisi was written to hint to spiritual practitioners that they had to cultivate all the elements of their body, including their Yin Qi and Yang Qi, by using various cultivation methods other than just quieting prayer.

Since Christian prayer recitation, such as reciting the rosary or Hesychast prayer, is similar to eastern mantra practice that produces a calming and emptying of thoughts, this too can be taught to people in a way that is more clearly identified as emptiness meditation too.

Thus Christianity has the basics of Qi cultivation, good works/behavior and emptiness meditation ready for the masses if anyone bothers to teach them. The point is that even Christianity has meditation teachings and should be actively teaching meditation in its various forms too.

Sadly, while it is easy to meditate in churches you will find that few temples are constructed in such a way that there are facilities where people can come and meditate undisturbed on a regular basis. However, this is understandable as teaching meditation should not be the only function of a spiritual center. In fact, few temples that primarily are places of worship offer this service.

Nevertheless, a temple should serve as a quiet refuge from the stresses of life where people can momentarily devote themselves to higher sacred affairs, thus uplifting their spirits. They should offer a location where people can practice reverence and quiet contemplation, including imageless meditation. They should be a place where people can find some momentary peace from the stresses of life.

Even so, while distilled water may be pure, no fish can live in it. Despite the peace of the original nature and the fact that a temple should be a place where you can experience silence, it should also be active like the transforming universe. Thus, a good temple should also have a regular active life, but truly serve as a place where people can calm their minds and learn methods to do so on their own when away from its premises. It should serve as a refuge of calm in the storm of life. At times it should be bustling with activity, but it should also serve as a quiet place by its architecture, functions and design. It should provide an opportunity for people to calm their minds.

HEALING

Since ancient times temples and religious places have often been centers for healing. Since people today commonly know about the possibilities of western medicine, and since modern medical options are usually readily available in the locales where temples are normally found, a temple should serve the public by making available *alternative* medical healing information that is not normally available to the public, or which is even suppressed.

In other words, a temple should inform people as to what natural treatments, protocols, remedies, doctors, etc. are available as establishment alternatives, especially when conventional medicine fails. It need not make available information on conventional medicine since it is easily accessible. It serves the public by making available what people don't normally know or have available.

I think all great monks and nuns should subscribe to alternative health newsletters to keep abreast of the health field so they can advise people who come to them for aid. One of the requirements for being a Bodhisattva is to learn medicine and healing. To just be able to enter people's bodies and give them Qi/Prana energy for healing, or thoughts on what to do, is not enough of a skill in order to help. To me they should know about the best local and national doctors for the treatment of conditions, such as cancer, diabetes and heart disease, and the best alternative medicine practices as well since this information rarely reaches the public but often produces the "miraculous cures" people seek. LEF.org and Mercola.com, for instance, commonly offers such information.

In particular, a temple or spiritual center doing it right would provide not only referrals to conventional doctors considered the best for certain procedures or specialties (in that local area, state-wide, nation-wide or worldwide), but should be able to direct people to alternative medicine professionals. A temple is perfect for being a clearing house for information not normally transmitted by the traditional establishment (since people can normally find *that*), yet which works.

This includes information, courses or even retreats involving meditation, detoxification (how to rid your body of impurities), bodywork, and alternative health scenarios that save people when traditional medicine fails. I have written *Super Cancer Fighters*, *Look Younger Live Longer*, *Prevent and Reverse Atherosclerosis (Reed)*, and *Detox Cleanse Your Body Quickly and Completely* to help with this approach. Two books that should be readily at hand so that a spiritual leader can render service, or so that people can advise themselves, include Dick Weatherby and Scott Ferguson's *Blood Chemistry and CBC Analysis* along with Jonathan Wright and Alan Gaby's *Nutritional Therapy in Medical Practice: Protocols and Supporting Information*.

Many other fine publications could be added to this duo. They only give an indication of the ideal possible, which is to make a temple more useful to the public by having it disseminate helpful information and/or services. How wonderful it is when a great monk or nun, swami, master, sadguru, rabbi, etcetera becomes skilled in offering such advice, such as knowing alternative medicine approaches for health problems or where to send you for help.

In ancient times, "sleep temples" were built that also served as hospitals of sorts for the sick and wounded. An individual seeking healing of some type would come to this type of temple – which could be found in ancient

Egypt, Greece (Asclepeions) and the Middle East in general – and then undergo detoxification, meditation and chanting to ask for aid. Their dreams at the location, which were often influenced by Buddhas, Bodhisattvas and devas, would then be analyzed for clues as to remedies.

In Greece, sick individuals visiting a temple of Asclepius would go to sleep in the temple ("temple sleep") expecting that they would be visited by Asclepius himself or one of his healing children in a dream. During their dream they would be told what they needed to do in order to cure their ailment, and upon waking would report their dream to a priest who would then interpret it and prescribe a cure. In today's world, the equivalent might be a temple offering detoxification retreats, yoga retreats, Bates training to improve your eyesight naturally, and castor oil pack treatments which are extremely helpful.

In other types of temples across the world, Buddhas and devas perform different functions for human beings who come asking for help.

Devas, Buddhas, Bodhisattvas and so forth regularly visit temples to help the faithful with their Qi cultivation and with healing. The first three *sambhogakaya* bodies are composed of Jing, Qi, and Shen respectively. Medicine and healing for these three bodies – for our physical body made from Jing, internal energy or Qi/Prana that comprises the subtle body, and Shen energy that comprises our Casual body – can be made available at a temple. That should be one of its major purposes or functions.

Think of it this way. If you wanted to become a Medicine Buddha you should start learning traditional medicine, natural healing or alternative medicine now. Since "learning medicine" is for becoming a doctor and that isn't your profession, you should learn alternative medicine and natural remedies instead since absorbing those knowledge fields doesn't require a degree.

To help the public and to establish the basis for being able to help people with their health, we should find swamis, monks and nuns studying alternative medical treatments such as herbs, vitamins, Ayurveda, TCM, bodywork, etc. and offering help or referrals at a temple. Incidentally, you can find many old movies showing that temples, churches, and other spiritual centers were places offering healing during war.

EDUCATION

A temple can provide invaluable community service by serving as an educational center not just for specific types of moral, religious, spiritual cultivation and transcendence training but for learning specific types of skill. Naturally these would be the most valuable skills needed by people related to spiritual cultivation, but which are not normally taught at home or in the schools.

Wisdom Buddhas such as Saraswati, Ganesh, Manjursi and so on are masters of many types of skills and intellectual bodies of knowledge. Why can a temple or spiritual center not offer training in some of the skills and learning they are said to master but which are not taught in schools?

Children: For example, one of the purposes of education is the "spiritual" or "moral" purpose, which is to teach children ethics, morality, character and the difference between right and wrong through spiritual teachings. The goal of education is not just to give knowledge and teach good judgment but to provide examples of moral heroes, character strengths and to help children change their personality flaws and bad behaviors. For instance, how often are children taught to smile in order to defuse a situation, or to say a kind word? Temples can and should offer such relevant teachings as should churches, synagogues, etcetera.

Furthermore, most children lack extremely valuable life skills that are not taught in schools or at home. Since cultivation trains the mind, it is a natural fit for a monastery, temple, ashram, etc. to be a place where children are taught valuable *mental skills* they can use for life that are not taught elsewhere. Accordingly, a temple might offer lessons in:

- Super memory skills (see *Unlimited Memory* by Kevin Horsley, *Moonwalking With Einstein* by Joshua Foer, and *The Memory Book* by Harry Lorayne) and mind-mapping skills. Memory skills are ultra-important for life, and yet we fail to teach children all of the super memory tricks worked out over the ages that they might use. Even the how-to of how to study (see *How to be A Superstar Student*) isn't taught in school but is ultra-important and can be taught at a spiritual center as a course for children.

- Visual thinking skills, visualization skills and especially sports visualization (see *Visualization Power* and *Sport Visualization for the Elite Athlete*). Visualization skills, which are the training basis of many higher spiritual attainments, are a critical skill used by great inventors, artists, doctors and healers but no one teaches them. If such a course for children was offered by monks, nun, swamis, etc. at a monastery or other spiritual center (since they become masters of these skills themselves in certain traditions), this would be something I'd enroll my own children in learning. They provide a foundation of concentration skills useful for life as well as for the spiritual practices within most traditions.

- Mental math, which is the ability to do calculations in your head, can also be taught (see *Secrets of Mental Math* by Arthur Benjamin and Michael Shermer). This is another extremely valuable skill.

- NLP neuro-linguistic programming skills for understanding other people and helping children learn how to change their mental state, emotions and behavior at will. The big skill to teach children is how to change their emotions, viewpoints and intentions at will.

- The mental skills emphasized by John Taylor Gatto.

We are sentient beings in a cosmos overwhelming populated by insentient phenomena, and we happen to be rational animals who can think and reason. The spiritual path involves learning how to use our minds to fullest flower, developing its highest capabilities and yet we don't teach such consciousness skills anywhere. The spiritual path means mastering all the various functions of consciousness to their fullest. Temples can teach some ignored by our educational systems.

As pointed out in *Color Me Confucius*, the mind is capable of many deliberate functions that it can master, and we also must learn how to master the afflictive thoughts and emotions that automatically arise and impel us such as habit energies and tendencies. Such skills are not only useful for life but prepare kids for spiritual cultivation later in life should they choose to pursue it, and in the present time give them ultra-valuable skills for success.

Hence there are two types of mental functions to master – (1) deliberate or intentional, and (2) the automatic that we normally cannot control. Incidentally, in the body there are automatic functions such as the breathing rate or heart rate that we can learn to control through biofeedback training.

At temples, churches, synagogues, gurdwaras and other spiritual centers children should be taught moral stories and lessons on good character, ethics, virtue, values, and spiritual integrity. The ideas of karma (*Lao Tzu's Treatise on the Response of the Tao*, *Liao Fan's Four Lessons*), filial piety and character (*Lives of the Noble Greeks and Romans*) should be introduced to them along with spiritual texts. In particular, they should learn various methods for self-improvement, such as in *Color Me Confucius*.

The Stanford marshmallow studies on delayed gratification show that children who learn self-control have much better life outcomes, so self-control leads to a better life promise. Self-control is another word for discipline, which is a characteristic often attributed to Marines due to their training. The Greek Stoics also emphasized self-control and mental fortitude as a means of overcoming destructive emotions. Another character strength or personality characteristic that children should learn is the necessity to become a reader and lifelong learner.

Temples and spiritual centers should inform parents that in addition to a moral foundation they need to teach these particular lessons and more in order to prepare children for successful lives.

In India this overall effort is called instilling *samskaras* and in Chinese and European-American culture it's called instilling values. The western method for doing so most often centers around teaching the Bible or Biblical lessons in some way. Samples of useful titles that portray the eastern views include *How to Inculcate Good Sanskars in Children* (Vasant Balaji Athavale) and *The Chinese Secrets for Success: Five Inspiring Confucian Values* (YuKong Zhao).

Teenagers: Because of their age, teenagers not only need guidance to help them deal with their internal energies and sexual impulses, but as teenagers they also need to be presented with challenges that will build their skills and character, particularly physical challenges so that they develop their bodies and learn their physical limitations. In particular, they need to learn risk-taking as well as grit and disciplined perseverance in the face of difficulties and adversity, for these are critical skills for success in life. This is related to motivation and positive thinking, but the pragmatic aspect of this is akin to Stoicism.

Challenges also means that they should be presented with a smorgasbord of interesting physical skills they might attempt to master – skateboarding, baseball, fishing, building things, dance, martial arts, sports, etcetera. Challenges also include mental skills and mind powers (super memory, visualization, etc.), emotional skills (NLP for controlling their emotions), performance skills (acting, music or public speaking) as well as the physical skills just mentioned (martial arts, sports, dance, yoga, etc.).

As to physical challenges, teenagers need to learn how to control their bodies and their internal energy, and how to deal with pain. Since yoga and martial arts are excellent in these respects they might be taught at temples. The two principles, which are important for spiritual cultivation, are to learn (a) internal energy control and (b) external muscular control.

A gigantic skill that teenagers also need to learn is how to transform their mind-sets and emotions. Teens need to learn the technologies for how to change the way they feel, how to master their emotions, how to change their habits, and how to perfect their intentions to set beneficial goals and accomplish them (see *Move Forward* and *Quick, Fast, Done* and *Color Me Confucius*). They have to learn this *now* before they enter the working period of their lives and get sidetracked from self-development efforts.

The field of NLP teaches these skills, and the need for self-improvement, self-perfection, self-mastery and self-control can be taught at temples. This *is* the spiritual path. It is about becoming master of yourself and a better human being. Consider: if you do attain various spiritual bodies you will attain great powers over others, so you must be a moral, ethical person before masters will help you attain them and must improve yourself so that you don't misuse them to abuse others.

As they grow older, teenagers will be presented with all sorts of temptations (vices) that can end up costing large, draining sums of money and which can also even destroy their lives: drugs, alcohol, gambling, spending, smoking, substance abuse, etcetera. They must learn disciplined methods of self-control, and how to change their emotions at will to avoid impulses and urges along these lines (for one mistake can be fatal), which is a basic skill of inner development. Since these are matters of self-cultivation, discipline and self-control, the basics of some of these powerful techniques can be taught at temples since they are not taught at schools or in the home. In this way the temple serves the community as part of the vital ethical fabric of the nation.

If parents are interested in other things they should teach their children, but which are not necessarily temple material, they should listen to the lectures of John Taylor Gatto, especially those concerning the lessons of the elite private schools that are not purely fact memorization classrooms. I have included several of these lessons in my book, *Husbands and Wives Were Connected in the Past*. Gatto teaches, and I agree, that the easiest way to teach your children to become geniuses is to frontload them with huge amounts of diverse experiences, including what we would consider dangerous ones, but supervising them through the process (this includes sports).

This is closer to how children were taught in colonial America where everyone wanted an independent livelihood; children were exposed to *real life* which *is dangerous*. They weren't raised to be snowflakes or strawberries (which bruise easily) but to take risks and responsibility for their actions. There is a great human need for individuals to feel that they are in control of their own lives, and can do better by themselves and the world. We have to teach children the skills and support the character training that will enable them to accomplish this.

I very much like Gatto's observations. A sample: "Americans never went through the twelve-year wringer our kids currently go through [called schooling], and they turned out all right. George Washington, Benjamin Franklin, Thomas Jefferson, Abraham Lincoln? Someone taught them, to be sure, but they were not products of a school *system*, and not one of them was ever 'graduated' from a secondary school. Throughout most of American history, kids generally didn't go to high school, yet the unschooled rose to be admirals, like Farragut; inventors, like Edison; captains of industry, like Carnegie and Rockefeller; writers, like Melville and Twain and Conrad; and even scholars, like Margaret Mead. In fact, until pretty recently people who reached the age of thirteen weren't looked upon as children at all."[24]

Adults: Temples should be a place where adults can learn methods for changing their character, faults, and habits. This effort is the true, genuine meaning of self-cultivation rather than simply sitting in meditation, for once you attain a higher spiritual body life is still about your behavior. Related are lessons on how to change your life, fortune, fate or destiny. I have detailed this in *White Fat Cow, Move Forward*, and *Quick, Fast, Done*. In particular, the "8M" method for bringing about change or accomplishment teaches you how to do this.

Temples should also teach goal setting or achievement skills since adults need these methods for their lives too, but no one teaches this information in schools even though it will vastly improve human lives. To put it another way, by teaching people how to change their character, their habit energies, their faults, their fortune and behavior, they teach them how to change their lives and their destiny. This is also the product of goal setting.

Another important lesson to be taught is the law of karma so that people can factor it into making life choices, especially difficult moral or ethical choices when the right thing to do means less money, fame, power, status or more trouble and obstructions. For this I like to recommend Eva Wong's *Lao Tzu's Treatise on the Response of the Tao*, which was written by the twelfth century sage Li Ying-chang to explain action and karma from the Taoist point of view. India has similar teachings as does Buddhism. It is hard to do the right thing when it means a loss, but the right thing to do is the right thing to do. We must all do what is right simply because it is right. In particular, *Color Me Confucius* and *Culture, Country, City, Company, Person, Purpose, Passion, World* teaches how to prevent yourself from becoming an "errant man of business" who does the wrong things for profit.

In addition to meditation, two major roads of cultivation are concentration exercises and visualization practice. Concentration skills are especially important for training your mind to stay on track by abolishing disturbances. A temple should therefore always offer courses for college students, inventors, engineers, healers as well as aspiring yogis to help them train their minds in the skills of focus and concentration, such as through visualization practices. This is why I wrote *Visualization Power* and *Sport Visualization for the Elite Athlete* (and other books to offer other bodies of knowledge). It is especially useful to offer such skill-building courses to both children and adults. To put it another way, a temple or spiritual center should teach various *mind skills* that can be used for spiritual practice, or which can simply help your life become better.

---

[24] John Taylor Gatto, *Weapons of Mass Instruction: A Schoolteacher's Journey Through the Dark World of Compulsory Schooling*, (New Society Publishers, Canada, 2009), p. xv.

Naturally a temple might teach yoga, Pilates, sacred dance, martial arts and other physical skills that are related to the spiritual path although you should expect to find them at exercise centers, such as a YMCA, yoga center or martial arts dojo.

Great Men and Great Houses of Men: A great monk, who attains many spiritual bodies, should study various bodies of knowledge and become so knowledgeable about the big trends and events in the world, nation and society at large, as well as the future, that they can readily advise high-level individuals considering weighty state matters. I have talked about grand strategy issues, in a way never done before, to help you get up to speed. They should be able to readily talk with politicians, heads of state and CEOs because they have an excellent understanding of current affairs, know valuable information and can render good advice. This is what great monks and nuns who are enlightened have done throughout history, so use them *if* they are qualified. However, some who attain enlightenment are simply incompetent for anything other than spiritual affairs.

A truly great monk or sage can be an advisor, counselor, chief minister, chancellor or elder statesman if consulted on national policy and many have done so in the past. The history of the world shows that sages have served in such capacity to tremendous national benefit for certain nations. This is why Confucius remarked, "A gentleman stands in awe of three things: the will of Heaven, great men, and the words of the sages."

PURIFICATION

A temple should be a place where people can come to rest and purify their minds, which is mental purification. Since temples are often the location of meditation retreats they can serve as a center for purification of the physical body and inner subtle body. In fact, when the Qi/Prana (kundalini energy) in your body is awakened through spiritual practice and passes through your Qi channels this produces a purification of both bodies. Some people call this an empowerment or blessing, or even baptism, but the process is essentially purifying your Qi/Prana.

How can you help this process? By doing more cultivation practice of many simultaneous practices undertaken at the same time. Secondly, if your efforts are accompanied by the use of detoxification herbs and supplements to clean your organs and tissues then you will have less poisons within your body that need to be pushed out through the process of cultivation.

Fasting, as a method of "purification," is simply not enough if you want to clean your body, although there are great weight-loss benefits to intermittent fasting. Furthermore, if you want to do fasting, juice fasting is far better than water fasting because it supplies nutrients you can use to heal your body during the fast. In any case, since regular medicine does not stress the importance of detoxification to help purify your body, the cultivation path should do so.

Many diseases, and ill health in general, are due to the accumulation of chemical toxins and poisons within the body, which will become an increasingly larger problem as time goes by in the world. A temple or spiritual center can and should offer an accompanying detoxification protocol of natural substances (see *Look Younger, Live Longer* or *How to Detox Cleanse Your Body Quickly and Completely*) every time there is a meditation retreat. Or, they can simply offer detoxification retreats that also involve meditation practice in addition to herbal remedies of purgation. Or, a spiritual center should just make the best detoxification products available to people who come to visit, or simply inform them about them. The point is to make available to the public what isn't done elsewhere but will help their lives greatly.

Additionally, sometimes people reach a point in their life when they want to make a clean break with an old habit or old way of life, and need some way to announce their determination to turn over a new leaf. Temples should therefore also serve as a place where people can perform a small ritual or make a private vow signifying to Heaven their commitment to feed a new life, such as when a Mafioso or Triad member vows to never kill or hurt someone again. This, too, is a method of detoxification or purification.

A temple should offer teachings on how people can watch their thoughts and behavior, change habits and break afflictions. This too while doing good deeds is a type of unremitting purification of the body, mind and behavior. In short, a temple should serve as a refuge where people can cleanse or purify their mind, body and behavior, and should offer teachings or opportunities for the many ways to do so.

LOVE

Jesus and Confucius both said that we should love other people, which we should demonstrate through compassion, kindness and working on their behalf. Then we become the avatars of God on earth.

Aside from teaching meditation practice and offering a place where people can meditate, temples and spiritual centers should offer opportunities for people to show their love for others and higher powers. They should be a place where people can engage in devotion/devotional practices because bhakti, love and reverence for a deity or higher power are also methods of cultivation. A temple should serve as a place where you can give your heart to a higher power. It should be a place where you can also pause and reflect upon ways to compassionately help others in difficulty.

In the Tibetan Buddhist tradition, there is a practice of meditating on infinite loving kindness or infinite compassion. This is a derivative of the Hinayana practice of meditating on the four immeasurables (becoming infinite love, kindness, compassion or equanimity), and can be taught at most spiritual centers. This is also a method of training in love.

Individuals who practice this method slowly change their personality and mindset, and set up the karmic conditions to become more of that way in a subsequent life. Therefore I highly encourage this type of meditation practice, and bringing it into the regular world as a personality trait. For instance, Buddhist sutras state that one of the karmic causes for beauty is to smile and be joyful to all you meet, while avoiding negative attitudes. This type of personality trait is also one of the reasons men become attracted to women. By practicing this type of meditation on a daily basis, and projecting your Qi in this fashion, you not only become happier and more attractive in this life but set up the causes and conditions to be born with even prettier features in a subsequent incarnation.

The Christian ideal of good works, and sacrificing oneself for others can be taught as well. Of all the religions, I think that Christianity is the best one for teaching about love, which is shown through your behavior. Loving one another is one of the central messages of Christianity, and one of the reasons that Christians, as a group, are the largest contributors to charity in the world. In John 13:34 Jesus said, "A new command I give you: love one another. As I have loved you, so you must love one another."

Here is some food for thought on lessons that a temple, church, synagogue, mosque or other spiritual center might teach about love:

- Do not take revenge on others or continue to hate them, but love your neighbors as you love yourself. (Leviticus 19:18)
- Above everything, love one another earnestly, because love covers over many sins. (1 Peter 4:8)
- My children, our love should not be just words and talk; it must be true love, which shows itself in action. (1 John 3:18)
- No one has ever seen God, but if we love one another, God lives in union with us, and his love is made perfect in us. We are sure that we live in union with God and that he lives in union with us, because he has given us his Spirit. (1 John 4:12-13)
- Do all your work in love. (1 Corinthians 16:14)
- Be always humble, gentle, and patient. Show your love by being tolerant with one another. Do your best to preserve the unity which the Spirit gives by means of the peace that binds you together. (Ephesians 4:2-3)

- To conclude: you must all have the same attitude and the same feelings; love one another, and be kind and humble with one another. Do not pay back evil with evil or cursing with cursing; instead, pay back with a blessing, because a blessing is what God promised to give you when he called you. (1 Peter 3:8-9)

Rabbi Hillel once said, "That which is hateful to you, do not do to another. This is the whole Torah. The rest is commentary." Confucius said not to do to others what you wouldn't want done for yourself. Jesus said to love one another and do for others what you would appreciate them doing for you. Putting these ideas together, in terms of positive action and restraint, and you have the basis of love in expression rather than simply passive compassion.

The idea of doing good works, or love in action, is millions of times more important than sitting in meditation. The question to ask should not focus on the supposed sanctity or purity of an action as defined by some artificial rules, but whether an action helps or hurts another person. When you act to help others, this is the manifestation of love in action. A temple or spiritual center should be a place that promotes this.

COMMUNITY ENGAGEMENT

The proof of being enlightened is practical activity in the world to help others, so just as a master with many bodies tirelessly works for the welfare of hundreds to thousands of people, a temple should serve as a center for social activities and shared rituals that service the surrounding community. It should promote social cohesion so that people feel connected to the larger community. Thus a temple or spiritual center overseen by a wise leader should sometimes serve as a central place for arts performances or volunteering efforts where people's activities can help to make a better community by working for the happiness of others, especially the poor and unfortunate. Besides promising inner peace and harmony it should grow the social bonds of the community.

I once saw the Youtube video *Let's Do It!* explain how the country of Estonia was entirely cleaned of trash in five hours due to the grass roots volunteer work of community engagement organized by a few devoted individuals. California sponsors a yearly Coastal Cleanup Day on a similar theme. A temple can let its spaces be used as an organizational hub for such charitable efforts. It can serve as a central hub of voluntary activities for a community, thus demonstrating to the community that the purpose of spiritual practices and enlightenment is not to just save yourself but to help others. It should let people work as Orishas or Bodhisattva saviors for others.

Since 80% of the success of a Christian church is said to be due to the spiritual head, and 20% of its success is usually attributed to its degree of community involvement, this means churches are at risk of failure when the charismatic head leaves or passes away. This is another reason that community engagement, independent of the leader, should serve as one of the functions of a religious center. It will help to bind it together.

As Confucius once said, you first save yourself, then your family, then your community, state, and finally the world. With this as an inspiration and guide, in today's world it is very easy for a temple to run web-based charity sites like Kiva.org that can affect the world in giving ways such as micro-finance or micro-health efforts that truly make a beneficial impact. *Culture, Country, City, Company, Person, Purpose, Passion, World* details many such projects that have helped communities and the world.

The entire idea of cultivation is to save yourself, other people and the world, but this isn't possible if you just sit in meditation practice. You have to develop knowledge, skills and resources and actively engage with others. The Bodhisattva ideal is to practice active engagement with people and the world to help them better live and succeed on earth. It takes time to instill this mindset into a community so a religious center must continually stress the ideals of cooperation and altruism to help others. Guru Nanak, who founded Sikhism, did a tremendous job along these lines when he initiated the practice of the free community meal to help the poor within the community, and promoted the principle of fighting social injustice.

The multi-functional service nature of a temple mirrors the functions of an enlightened master who will be using his various bodies to help people within his community, especially his students. The higher their attainments, the more a master can proceed to a national level of helpfulness. Temples offer a way for them to interact in a caring dimension with the community.

Networks of mosques, churches, synagogues, gurdwaras and temples should serve as part of the foundation of a nation's culture. They can serve as centers for worship, education, inspiration, healing and spiritual cultivation. I have seen Buddhist temples with pathways lined by rows of statues of previous spiritual greats, and I think such walkways should more frequently appear around temples. However, I think they should be lined with statues of individuals who both cultivated themselves and made great contributions to the nation. Those are the real Bodhisattvas even if they did not become enlightened. A small list of such notables is found in *Culture, Country, City, Company, Person, Purpose, Passion, World*. In *The American Reader* I hope to reveal yet others.

By training to become a Buddha, Bodhisattva, protect god or guardian spirit you will in time become able to use your subtle body to render assistance to individuals, families, communities, states or nations. You can choose to help people with their health issues, give them useful thoughts, help to connect them with others, and so on.

REVELATION

Temples and spiritual centers should also disseminate the very best information "from Heaven" or "from man" that is helpful for the public, even if it goes against established norms. For instance, the medical establishment may frown upon natural remedies, but a temple should make available the names of alternative medical practitioners good at natural remedies, as well as names of the best traditional practitioners for certain conditions (such as cancer, diabetes, Alzheimers, heart disease).

If a catastrophe or emergency situation is due to hit a town, a great monk, nun, swami, etcetera who knows the future should prepare people with warnings. If a government has so mucked up the financial markets that a collapse or economic catastrophe is coming a temple or spiritual center should disseminate information to adherents to financially protect themselves. If a great monk or nun knows that the country will be invaded by another and become enmeshed in war, they should warn people as well. These are examples of information from man and from Heaven, namely foreknowledge of future events. Many masters in the past have provided such warnings.

Of course, if spiritual masters who truly know the future (rather than the countless fraudsters that abound) have not already established a reputation for such information because they never volunteered accurate "predictions" in the past, who will believe them at such a crucial time? No one will believe you when it really matters unless you establish a track record and reputation for accuracy ahead of time, and therefore become a voice to be listened to.

Basically, a spiritual center should disseminate information to the public that will help the public. This is the function of Buddhas and Bodhisattvas.

For sure, sometimes a great monk or nun *knows the future*, so they should disseminate any helpful information along these lines if it will help protect people or help them make better decisions. Knowing the goings-on in the supersensible realms, some of this information should be made available to people as revelation. Great monks and nuns do this all the time when they tell people their personal futures in private.

The point is that great monks and nuns and other religious professionals, with supersensible knowledge available because of their enlightenment, should warn the public of heavenly secrets that will help people manage their lives. They don't often do this, but this should become more common because the purpose of the extra body attainments is to help people rather than keep everything wrapped in superstition and mystery.

8
MAKING DONATIONS TO SUPPORT SPIRITUAL CENTERS

Let's say that when I become a Buddha I want the power to be able to give people clean water to solve sanitation and hygiene issues, and be able to quench people's thirst. It makes sense to start building up a stock of merit regarding water now, in effect becoming friends with water. For instance, I can learn how to swim and boat. I can learn to make rain where it is needed - like the Buddha deities Indra, Mari (Marriamman), Chaac, Tailoc, Lono and many others since every country has rainmaking and Bodhisattvas - via Trevor Constable's methods. I can support local efforts to keep rivers and lakes clean. I can practice water conservation. I can advise people on the best water purifiers for their homes. I can also start giving to water charities right now in order to start making a difference. Why wait?

"Now" is the key consideration. Most of all, *right now* I can be a Buddha or Bodhisattva with the ability to provide clean water to those who are thirsty by giving to charities that make clean water available to people all over the world, such as Water.org, Charity:Water, WaterAid, Water is Life, or HaitiWater.org. If that is one of the functions I want to be able to perform when I finally do become enlightened I can start to exercise it *now*, and later when I have more power and resources I will be able to do more. The lesson is to become involved now. Just get started by getting started.

There are a lot of water charities that serve communities lacking clean water. In contributing to water charities that serve a water mission I already become a Water Buddha, Bodhisattva or guardian spirit, someone who has the power to give water to others who need it. In involving myself with them, I am cultivating the ways of the Buddha I want to be, the skills I want to have of the type of Buddha I want to become. This is how Buddhas and Bodhisattvas developed the skills and powers they have. They simply started doing what they believed in to the best of their abilities rather than wait for a perfect situation.

The point is that you can learn certain skills, engage in certain activities, and even donate to certain charities that are all about the mission you want to support. You will not just build merit in that direction, but make the world a better place. By acting as the very type of Buddha or Bodhisattva you wish to become, by delivering upon the very skills you would like to have, you are practicing Buddha Yoga. By practicing the "result of the path" as the "method of the path" you become that vehicle and can claim those skills and merit.

CharityNavigator.org and CharityWatch.org can help you find the effective charities that fulfill any philanthropic missions that you might be interested in. By contributing to them you build up a stock of merit in those directions.

Another type of donation is to make gifts to religious/spiritual institutions such as monasteries, nunneries, churches, temples, synagogues, mosques, meeting houses, gurdwaras, shrines, and other places of spiritual study, practice and worship. Benjamin Franklin, for instance, was not a member of any organized church and rarely attended church services, but donated to the building fund of every church constructed in Philadelphia. Christianity was predominant, but he made one of the largest donations for the first synagogue in Philadelphia too.

Franklin urged his fellow citizens to donate "so that even if the Mufti of Constantinople were to send a missionary to preach Mohammedanism to us, he would find a pulpit at his service." In his autobiography he painted a picture of the practitioners of organized religion in a poor light, showing them as more focused on following their particular customs, tenets and practices than on really working on instilling the ideals of virtue and humility in their lives. However, he felt that churches and spiritual meeting centers might improve the general moral character of people and provide a sanctuary of peace for the public, thus helping humanity. Therefore he funded many regardless of their tradition.

I particularly like to give to temples, ashrams, monasteries, nunneries or other institutions that are training monks and nuns, mendicants, swamis, sadhus and so forth because these are the individuals who will attain enlightenment. Then they will be using their higher bodies to perform all sorts of service for humanity. Other than helping the public, to support individuals who are cultivating so that they can attain the subtle body (without them knowing that is the target) is the most important thing that a spiritual center can do.

Along these lines, don't ever think that western religious monasteries and nunneries are not producing enlightened adepts. Many are the westerner spiritual adherents who are enlightened even if they might be living in a small nunnery or monastery of just a few individuals. People overly focus on the Buddhist, Hindu, Taoist, Yoga and Jain traditions thinking that only these paths lead to the spiritual body attainments (enlightenment or liberation from the lower realms). How wrong they are. Other schools created mendicant traditions to produce the same outcome, which is why saints with superpowers (due to their extra bodies) appear in all sorts of traditions.

Think about it for a second. Once people die everyone arises in a subtle (deva) body, so the deceased of all traditions would find out what is really going on in terms of "masters" being produced elsewhere with multiple bodies and powers. Why would they then *not act* to create a similar pathway of accomplishment in their own religious traditions? The western schools produce just as many adepts, only they aren't paraded around as living saints, gurus, masters and so on.

Unfortunately, most temples, ashrams, monasteries, nunneries and other spiritual centers don't know how to raise money, and it's a never ending problem to seek funding for their continuance. They don't know what to do, or are shy or embarrassed to ask for financial support. They usually don't even know how to write a good fund raising request letter.

As we all are, they are a little bit afraid and reticent to ask for aid in maintaining their efforts. Our job is to relieve them of this burden and the embarrassment of having to ask for funds. Donating to temple and church buildings is nice, but if you want to produce a Buddha and accumulate the merit you yourself need for enlightenment then donating to training centers is one of the ways to go. It is especially important to help people who are training for the Tao, or who have the Tao, but who are in poor countries because while the income in poor countries is low they still have international costs if they want to travel or buy the right books or supplies that will help their lives and missions.

Funding individuals by personal cash gifts is sometimes where you can do the most good because some young monks and nuns, sadhus, swamis, students, etc. of quality may achieve enlightenment, and you will have helped them in this quest if you make a private gift to them of cash. They usually have no other source of income other than your contributions.

Twice a year, in the Spring and Fall, I suggest that you consider funding worthy monks and nuns, swamis, sadhus, monastics and mendicants etc. who have little to no money of their own but need it. They won't ask for it or tell you they need it, so you have to use your brain and seek them out to contribute.

If a training center has a great monk or nun or other such head religious functionary you might ask them, "who has talent?" so that you might donate some money to help those individuals. This will help a lot, *more than you can possibly imagine,* because everyone needs their own disposable income for little things, and without a source of income their cultivation is hampered. Think about making personal gifts where you feel it is appropriate. In some life you might become a monk or nun yourself to attain enlightenment, and you have to think how you would feel if you needed money, had no way to get it, and then someone helped you out of the blue.

Consider it this way. Everyone wants and needs money but is afraid or embarrassed to ask for help. Monks and nuns, especially, have no source of income but they need cash too. Travel costs money, books cost money, courses cost money, computers cost money, software costs money, supplies cost money, bodywork costs money, health concerns cost money, training costs money … these are all things that a tradition will not supply a monk, nun, or other initiate working on generating their subtle body. Therefore please consider making a donation to known and unknown worthies.

However, you don't want to be funding just another dumb person without skills who won't help society if they succeed, but should seek people with alert minds and compassionate habits who want to learn and master many skills so that they can help others when they finally do succeed. The greater their wisdom, because you funded their skills acquisition or study by giving them some monetary leeway and freedom *that you yourself would appreciate,* the more they will be able to help the world. Think of a contribution as funding a scholarship to make the world a better place. The public doesn't know it, but the enlightened are the individuals who answer our prayers for help and assistance using their higher bodies when they can.

If you helped one individual succeed you did a great deed for the world since they will be helping countless others with their spiritual bodies. If you just funded an ordinary church, mosque, temple or synagogue, who can say what the money went towards achieving?

Does the institution or people you want to support promote the right views arrived at through wisdom and analysis rather than just emotions or superstition? Do they exhibit a perfection in the intention and motive to compassionately help others with friendliness and kindness without pursuing self-benefit (which is desirelessness)? Are they always exhibiting unremitting, strenuous, vigorous effort along these lines? These three perfections of intention, view and effort are useful yardsticks for consideration.

9
MINIMIZING LIFE REGRETS

It is said that the number of breaths we take, and even the number of minutes of our life are fated. Furthermore, the only thing that can change these numbers is doing lots of merit and engaging in spiritual cultivation. Merit and spiritual cultivation are said to increase your life span whereas doing bad deeds and practicing evil ways is said to make your fortune far worse than what it is fated to be. One such result is cutting your life short. With this in mind, life should definitely involve two things among the many: spiritual cultivation and good conduct.

Aristotle said that happiness is the highest good that we all aim for in life. Scientists through research have found that several activities make us happiest in life – exercise, meditation, doing something we're good at where we abandon the wandering mind and reach a state of flow/concentration, experiential purchases (rather than material purchases), and performing altruistic acts of kindness. Note that kindness (good conduct) and meditation (spiritual practice) appear in this list.

From conversations with dying patients, the Australian nurse Bonnie Ware once made a list of the top five regrets of the terminally ill about to pass away. Looking back at their lives and knowing they were going to die, they tended to be extremely honest. Since the same themes commonly came up time and again, should we not rectify those areas in our own lives *now* so as avoid those same regrets, repeated by so many, when we are to pass away?

Here were the top regrets people most often mentioned ...

The first regret many lamented is that they did not have the courage to live truthfully. They were never authentic, true to themselves, and now it was too late. All their life they were living lies whether it had to do with their career, marriage, or pleasing others rather than themselves. The dying often said to her, "I wish I'd had the courage to live a life true to myself and not the life others expected of me." Another way of wording this was, "I regret that I never pursued my own true dreams and aspirations," or "I wish I'd lived a life true to my dreams instead of doing what others expected of me. I wasted my life that way."

In other words, on their deathbed many people still had unfulfilled dreams they wish they had pursued. Sometimes they phrased this as, "I wish that I had lived for myself more," but the common theme is that people felt unsatisfied as if there was a hole in their soul for not having ventured to do what they really, and perhaps secretly, wanted to do in life, whatever it was.

Right now I want you to imagine reaching the end of your life and looking back at all the time you spent on useless things that did not matter when there were things you really wanted to pursue that you totally left untouched. This is why I tell you sincerely to start training yourself now, as the Bodhisattvas do, so that one day you can later become a force for great good in a direction where you want to make a difference. You *can* become a Bodhisattva benefactor or guardian spirit of some special cause dear to yourself. As soon as you succeed in spiritual cultivation you can take on such responsibilities, but I'm reminding you that you can actively prepare for such a path of positivity now and even start treading it. You must start to cultivate and train in the areas of interest you have now.

You must carefully pick your career and occupation in life, otherwise you will be unhappy and unfulfilled upon your deathbed. People need a job, career, occupation or profession that produces income but life also needs to be meaningful. We are all restricted in life by concerns of money and other obligations, but in your free time (or with some free funds) you can certainly work towards a higher calling such as becoming a guardian benefactor of some type – the type you want to become.

What is the purpose of living if you don't like who you are, and you aren't doing what you feel you should be doing? All the money in the world won't help you if you don't like what you see in the mirror because of what you have become or are not doing. You won't like yourself if you have put aside what you know is truly important to your life. You have to start living a life of truthfulness and honesty to yourself and point yourself in the direction of something truly meaningful. You have the ability to both mold your character and your life in any way you want, so don't wait until the end of your life to make yourself happy and start doing what you want to do.

A second common regret of the dying was, "I wish I hadn't worked so hard." People lament the fact that they shackled themselves to the treadmill of their job and did not have the courage, which may have taken as little as one single step, to do more outside of work. They worked so much at the expense of their family and friendships that at the end of life they wished they had worked far less. What was it all for? What did they accomplish? What are they going to take with them into the afterlife? No one has ever had "He wrote a great business plan" carved on their tombstone.

Linds Redding, a New Zealand-based art director, who had worked at BBDO and Saatchi & Saatchi, wrote the essay, "A Short Lesson in Perspective" after he was diagnosed with lung cancer, which eventually killed him. Instructive for its insights on his life as a creative and on working so hard in general, Redding wrote as follows:

> Perhaps I am not alone in this assessment. Many people have their own idea of a person's life, without knowing what really goes on, on the inside. Some even envy the lives of their friends and colleagues, without realizing, their lives are much better. Now that I am out of that life, I am able to have a different perspective of my old life.
>
> And here's the thing.
>
> It turns out I didn't actually like my old life nearly as much as I thought I did. I know this now because I occasionally catch up with my old colleagues and work-mates. They fall over each other to enthusiastically show me the latest project they're working on. Ask my opinion. Proudly show off their technical prowess (which is not inconsiderable). I find myself glazing over but politely listen as they brag about who's had the least sleep and the most takeaway food. "I haven't seen my wife since January, I can't feel my legs any more and I think I have scurvy but another three weeks and we'll be done. It's got to be done by then. The client's going on holiday. What do I think?"
>
> What do I think?
>
> I think you're all fucking mad. Deranged. So disengaged from reality it's not even funny. It's a fucking TV ad. Nobody gives a shit.
>
> This has come as quite a shock I can tell you. I think, I've come to the conclusion that the whole thing was a bit of a con. A scam. An elaborate hoax. …
>
> Countless late nights and weekends, holidays, birthdays, school recitals and anniversary dinners were willingly sacrificed at the altar of some intangible but infinitely worthy higher cause. It would all be worth it in the long run …
>
> This was the con. Convincing myself that there was nowhere I'd rather be was just a coping mechanism. I can see that now. It wasn't really important. Or of any consequence at all really. How could it

be. We were just shifting product. Our product, and the clients. Just meeting the quota. Feeding the beast as I called it on my more cynical days.

So was it worth it?

Well of course not. It turns out it was just advertising. There was no higher calling. No ultimate prize. Just a lot of faded, yellowing newsprint, and old video cassettes in an obsolete format I can't even play any more even if I was interested. Oh yes, and a lot of framed certificates and little gold statuettes. A shit-load of empty Prozac boxes, wine bottles, a lot of grey hair and a tumor of indeterminate dimensions.

It sounds like I'm feeling sorry for myself again. I'm not. It was fun for quite a lot of the time. I was pretty good at it. I met a lot of funny, talented and clever people, got to become an overnight expert in everything from shower-heads to sheep-dip, got to scratch my creative itch on a daily basis, and earned enough money to raise the family which I love, and even see them occasionally.

But what I didn't do, with the benefit of perspective, is anything of any lasting importance. ... Economically I probably helped shift some merchandise. Enhanced a few companies bottom lines. Helped make one or two wealthy men a bit wealthier than they already were.

As a life, it all seemed like such a good idea at the time. ...

Pity.[25]

If a life lived entirely for work was so great, why do people on their deathbed lament, "I worked too much and never made time for my family. I wish I had spent more time with my spouse and children. I wish I had traveled more." Did that person then truly live a good life? Did their life amount to something of importance to others or did it amount to just a soul numbing walk through existence in order to gain a salary? Was it a meaningful life of significance, or just something hollow and empty?

The individuals who run about in life trying to maximize their wealth, sacrificing all sorts of other important concerns in the process, are also paying too much for that whistle. A better objective would be to minimize your maximum regrets such as dying alone, losing your humanity, and failing to sustain your family and attain enough wealth to avoid a bad ending. Pursuing the most wealth you can possibly achieve actually increases your chances of a bad ending in life, whereas a better path is to go

---

[25] Linds Redding, "A Short Lesson in Perspective," Accessed July 19, 2018, http://www.lindsredding.com/2012/03/11/a-overdue-lesson-in-perspective/.

after enough wealth that life is good and you avoid a bad ending. Furthermore, you cannot take that wealth with you and money only has value insofar as you use it. What are you using it for that has meaning?

So what might people have done differently during their prime years to make their lives a little more enjoyable? They might have given to charity to make others' lives better. They might have used it to take steps in the direction of skills their heart wanted to develop. They might have pursued goals, dreams and objectives that really mattered to them personally, and/or experiences that would have helped them to grow.

When we examine the most common items on bucket lists, which are lists people make of things they want to do before they die, we can find some common themes of what people are looking to experience in life other than just their job or occupation. The themes include adventurous experiences, experiences that are sublime that lead to wonder, experiences that are giving, and even skills development. For instance, here are some of the activities most commonly found on bucket lists:

> Buy a House, Start a Company, Fall in Love, Own a Dog, Donate Blood, Get in Shape and Achieve Your Ideal Weight, Get Six Pack Abs, Get a Professional Massage or Chiropractic Adjustment, Be Listed on a Patent, Learn Another Language, Learn Sign Language, Learn to Play an Instrument, Learn to Ride a Motorcycle, Ride a Segway, Connect With Past Teachers, Write a Story/Book, Try a Profession in a Different Field, Drive a Sports Car, Get a Tattoo, Go Skinny Dipping, Go Up the Empire State Building, See a Broadway Musical, Hike the Pacific Crest Trail, Drive Across the Country (Take a Great American Road Trip), Visit Yellowstone National Park, Ride a Hot Air Balloon, Eat a Texas Barbecue, Send a Message in a Bottle, See Your Favorite Band, Go to a Music Festival, Run a Marathon, Sleep Under the Stars, Go Horseback Riding, Go Whale Watching, Go White Water Rafting, Learn to Surf, Learn Scuba Diving, Kayak a Tranquil Lake or Rushing River, Go Skydiving, Go Dog Sledding, Experience Bungee Jumping, Go Ziplining or Parasailing, Experience Zero Gravity, Go Glamping (Glamour Camping), Swim with Dolphins, Ride a Camel, Ride an Elephant, Ride a Horse, Take an Alaskan Cruise, Travel the World on a Cruise, Set Foot in Every Continent, Bed Down in an Igloo, See Machu Picchu, Take an African Safari to See Magnificent Predators, Visit Stonehenge, View Paris from the Eiffel Tower, Sample Gelato in Rome, Feel the Heat in a Finnish Sauna, Visit the Taj Mahal in India, Gamble in Las Vegas, See the Northern Lights, Dive the Great Barrier Reef, Participate in Burning Man, Visit Romantic Venice and Ride a Venetian Gondola, Snorkel at the Great Barrier Reef, See Japanese

Cherry Blossoms in Spring, Spend New Year's Eve in New York, See New England in the Fall, See the Egyptian Pyramids of Giza, Visit the Grand Canyon, See the Northern Lights, Walk the Siq to Petra in Jordan, Walk Along the Great Wall of China, Visit a Volcano, Climb a Daring Mountain, Traipse through the Amazon, Visit Oktoberfest in Germany, Visit Carnival in Brazil, Celebrate Thailand's Festival of Lights, Experience the Colors of Divali in India, Visit Wine Spraying at La Rioja Spain, Experience Spain's Lat Tomatina Tomato Throwing Festival, Relive the Wild West at a Rodeo, and more.

In general, during life people want to experience, link with or identify with something grand and magnificent beyond themselves. They want to feel they are part of a larger meaningful whole. When people perceive that something is vast and wondrous they are often stopped in their cognitive tracks, and seek to remain in that sublime experience of outer grandeur and internal silence. Something vast in beauty cannot be accommodated by a person's mental processes. Because of the sheer enormity of wonder people's thinking shuts down and they experience mental peace. People go through life seeking this type of experience – a desire to experience something beyond themselves, a desire to reach the infinite. Bucket lists contain many activities that people hope will lead to such an experience.

Another dying wish was about maintaining friendships; "I wish I had stayed in touch with my friends" was a regret nurse Ware often heard. Most people have regrets about relational fractures and wish things had gone differently. Since not maintaining strong friendships was one of the most frequent regrets that the dying have, ask yourself right now what you are doing to maintain your friendships. If you are somehow lacking, pick up the phone and give someone a call. Send someone a card, flowers or another type of gift to show appreciation. Strengthen that bond of friendship through restoration and renewal. Many lament with deep regret, now that they are dying, "I should have been the bigger person and resolved my conflicts."

Basically, many of the dying lament that they should have made more time for their friends. They regret having lost touch with a friend, family member or a partner from the past. Since you know this now, why not do something about it so that you don't find yourself in this very same situation?

Nurse Ware said that many people also lamented, "I wish that I had let myself be happier." They wish they had smiled more, laughed more, danced more, created more. Many people become doctors, lawyers, engineers or officials and earn plenty of money, but this is no guarantee they will be happy and contented in life or cultivate their own well-being.

You have to stop *waiting to be happy* in life and create your happiness by adding it to your life right now. By shifting your viewpoint or perspective of situations (the way you think) you can choose to be happier. Happiness is always a choice, and looking back on their lives people commonly wish they had known this principle a lot earlier. They could have let themselves laugh more, love more, and have surrounded themselves with more positive people in order to change their "life influencers" for the better.

You can and must choose to make yourself happy, or let yourself be happy in life. Happiness is a choice. Many people, however, simply refuse to let themselves be happy or make themselves happy with what they have until it is too late. On their deathbed, many lament that they refused to move in a new direction that would have made them happier, such as change a career. Such decisions are all up to you. No one stops you.

One of the keys to happiness is not just to have appreciation for what you already have, but to be content with what you have and to see how far you have progressed rather than how far ahead you must still go. You have to learn contentment, but not be so satisfied as to kill any inner motivation to make things better. Happiness lies in changing thought patterns, so one must make a commitment to get out of old patterns and move to better situations and states of being.

Happiness is to be happy with the present, and is also earned by creating a new future in which you will be happier because it is absent of misery. You can also feel happiness by doing compassionate things for others. Making self-care part of our routine, which includes giving yourself a break and recharging, is a form of respite that gives happiness too. Most people actually find happiness in the soul of service, which is to actively make life better for others.

The Biblical King Solomon in *Ecclesiastes* (2:1-11) commented, "I said to myself, 'Come now, I will test you with pleasure to find out what is good.' But that also proved to be meaningless. I tried cheering myself with wine, and embracing folly – my mind still guiding me with wisdom. I wanted to see what was good for people to do under the heavens during the few days of their lives. I undertook great projects: I built houses for myself and planted vineyards. I made gardens and parks and planted all kinds of fruit trees in them. I made reservoirs to water groves of flourishing trees. I bought male and female slaves and had other slaves who were born in my house. I also owned more herds and flocks than anyone in Jerusalem before me. I amassed silver and gold for myself, and the treasure of kings and provinces. I acquired male and female singers, and a harem as well – the delight of a man's heart. I became greater by far than anyone in Jerusalem before me. In all this my wisdom stayed with me. I denied myself nothing my eyes desired; I refused my heart no pleasure. My heart took delight in all my labor, and this was the reward for all my toil. Yet when I surveyed all that my hands had done and what I had toiled to achieve, everything was meaningless, a chasing after the wind; nothing was gained under the sun."

A similar sentiment is found in *The Consolation of Philosophy*, by Boethius of the sixth century. Born into an aristocratic Roman family, groomed for power, living a life of privilege and receiving the finest education, Boethius married well and was made a Roman consul in his twenties. He wanted to make translations of Aristotle that would keep alive the classical tradition through the Middle Ages, and desired to harmonize Plato and Aristotle, but never got his chance. Appointed chief of staff of Emperor Theodoric's court, he was unjustly accused of treason, thrown into prison and wrote *The Consolation of Philosophy* on death's row. Boethius lamented that fortune comes and goes as it pleases and one should never rely on it. Happiness, he concluded, was not high position, wealth, honors, public esteem andreputation, fame and the advantages of high birth because (like King Solomon) he had enjoyed all these things and found them lacking. He felt that only by attaining God, the perfect good, could one find happiness.

The *Lieh Tzu* from Chinese culture provides further food for thought, "Some people think they can find satisfaction in good food, fine clothes, lively music, and sexual pleasure. However, when they have all these things, they are not satisfied. They realize happiness is not simply having their material needs met. Thus, society has set up a system of rewards that go beyond material goods. These include titles, social recognition, status, and political power, all wrapped up in a package called self-fulfillment. Attracted by these prizes and goaded on by social pressure, people spend their short lives tiring body and mind to chase after these goals. Perhaps this gives them the feeling that they have achieved something in their lives, but in reality they have sacrificed a lot in life. They can no longer see, hear, act, feel, or think from their hearts. Everything they do is dictated by whether it can get them social gains. In the end, they've spent their lives following other people's demands and never lived a life of their own. How different is this from the life of a slave or a prisoner?

"The ancients understood that life is only a temporary sojourn in this world, and death is a temporary leave. In our short time here, we should listen to our own voices and follow our own hearts. Why not be free and live your own life? Why follow other people's rules and live to please others? When something enjoyable comes your way, you should enjoy it fully. Don't be imprisoned by name or title, for social conventions can lead you away from the natural order of things. It doesn't matter whether you will be remembered in generations ahead, because you will not be there to see it."[26]

---

[26] *Teachings of the Tao*, trans. by Eva Wong (Shambhala, Boston, 1997), pp. 49-50.

Along the lines of being more happy, you will often hear the elderly looking back on life, judging matters, and then also saying that they wish they had spent less time worrying. Worrying cannot change things so they regret that they worried so much about everything.

Don't ever believe that worrying will help anything. It won't, so learn how to stop it. Move your mind into some other occupation instead. Start moving ahead instead of worrying by taking steps forward, for most worries never materialize anyway, and if you cannot do anything about something then resign yourself to that fate. Plan and dream, but take some positive steps, however small, that show you really want to create or experience something new and then work to create something better in your life. Don't just worry or complain about affairs. Do what you want to do, and especially what you can do in the direction of what you ultimately want to do. Prepare. You might not be able to be an ultimate hero, champion or become world famous in this life but you can certainly train yourself for powers and beneficence at a later time.

Nurse Ware said the dying often looked back and regretted not having expressed their feelings more saying, "I wish I'd had the courage to express my feelings." Typically people hold back or even repress their feelings in life. Sometimes they keep quiet and refrain from speaking to keep peace with others (such as to manage a situation) but later they feel that they should have spoken their mind instead of holding back and then experiencing resentment. This includes not speaking up or standing against bullies, often keeping silent just to fit in with the crowd.

However, sometimes they just didn't take the risk to express themselves more fully – "I wish I'd had the courage to express my true self." They weren't authentic to their own beliefs, especially when it came to stopping evil (because good people don't want to "get dirty" in establishing justice). They regret that they failed to hug their parents more often and tell them they loved them and appreciated all that they had done. They regret not having said "I love you" more frequently, especially in telling this to their spouse.

When asked about his single biggest life regret, the poet Sir John Betjeman answered "not enough sex." Sexual dissatisfaction was also commonly cited as a major regret by the dying, followed by frequent unfilled wishes to travel the world or change professions.

The book, *Eternal Sex* by Sam Biser, contains an insightful interview with medical herbalist Dr. Richard Schulze, who like Nurse Ware for a time treated only incurable patients who had but months to live due to some fatal condition. Since his patients were dying they were very honest about expressing themselves, and honest about revealing some of their greatest regrets in life.

In one of the book's chapters Dr. Schulze explained what he learned about one of people's biggest regrets - sex, which can be used on the cultivation trail when one's vitality and emotions are stirred up and channeled in the proper fashion.

> SCHULZE: When I was younger, I had time to spend with my Grandfather. I remember hearing a lot of very wise things from him.
>
> So, one of the things I decided I wanted to do with many of my patients before they died was to spend some quality time with them – the week before, the day before, the day of.
>
> They had been great patients, but we all die and they would invite me to parties, or want me to be with them when they died, so I went to many of my patients the day or the week that they died. I know that they're very wise and in most countries they are considered the elders who we listen to. Unfortunately, in our country we dope them, and valium them, and put them in nursing homes.
>
> And so, I would always ask them, "Do you have a message for my younger people? What would you want to tell them?"
>
> Almost every one of them had regrets. It's really sad to see people live to be seventy, eighty, ninety years old, and then sit on their deathbed and say, "I wish I would have done it differently."
>
> And so, I would always ask them, "Well, what are those regrets?" I kept a tally for a long time, and after about four or five years, I tallied it up, and the first regret always was: "I wish I had more sex."
>
> BISER: I never would have expected that.
>
> SCHULZE: That's the number one, the number one regret. ... They said, "More sex." I didn't expect that kind of honesty, you know.
>
> People also said, "I shouldn't have worried about what neighbors or others thought, because none of that mattered. I shouldn't have let my sex life wither away."
>
> The things they thought mattered – the embarrassment of expressing yourself to your partner, what you want, or how you want it, seemed like a big wall when you were younger, "Oh God, I couldn't say that to my wife or girlfriend."
>
> And then when you are dying, you look back and say, "It was the stupidest thing I did NOT to talk about it." What could be more normal or natural than to express sexual needs or desires to your mate or boyfriend or girlfriend? Unfortunately, by the time these people came to that great awareness, their sexual organs were dried and shriveled up, and their life was over.
>
> Older people said, "Why did we create such a barrier of

embarrassment and fear when we were younger?" They shared this with me, because they wanted younger people to know that they are going to regret it.

Older women would say, "I wish I hadn't been so frigid, I wish I hadn't been a prude," or, "I didn't want to say I wanted it, because I was waiting for him to do it, and he never did."

Women said, "I bought that red sexy dress, but I never had the guts to wear it, and now I have the guts to wear it, but I'm ninety-seven years old."

Men, a lot of times would look back at the past and say, "I wanted to ask a woman for a date, but I was too embarrassed," and they always regretted that.

One of the comments heard very often was, "I thought it was important when young to keep a sterile attitude about sex, and to not let my kids or neighbors know I did it with my wife."

Who gives a damn about what neighbors think when you are ninety-seven years old? These old and dying patients admitted they had been embarrassed to hold hands in public, or to kiss their mate in public, or even do it in a car, or any of the things that people are afraid to do. Many old people said, "I wish I would have done it in my car."

Women said "no" to a guy, thinking he would ask again, and he never did. All the fear was for nothing. What is going to happen if you hold hands or kiss? What is going to happen? There is tremendous fear that people have equated with sexual expression, and the fear goes away when it's too late.

BISER: *Fear goes away when your life is over, and the worst thing about it is, you don't have a second chance.*

SCHULZE: That was the saddest part of sitting with these older people. You can still travel when you are older. You can still be with your grand-kids. But, when you are 93, you can't go back in time and ask Becky Johnson out.

They would get a blank look on their faces and say, "I don't remember what I was afraid of." They couldn't figure out what the fear was all about.

I think what happens during our life is that we spend a good part of our life repressing our sexual feelings, and then when we are about to die, we think, "Gosh, that was a real mistake," – because death is, you know, a great awakening.

The second regret dying people had was always, "I wish I had travelled more"; and the third one was, "I wish I'd spent less time at work, and more time at home, or on vacations, or with my family."

But, sex always came up number one and it came up with the

women and it came up with the men. I found it to be sad.

We don't talk about sex, we don't share information with our partners, we don't discuss it with our partners, we don't tell our partners what we like, where it feels good, where to touch. And then we rarely talk about it to the outside world, and we don't talk to our children about it, and so we're all just silent.

It's the big silence. Sex is the big silent secret, and then when we're about five minutes away from our last heartbeat, we go, "I wish I wouldn't have done that."

And people will say, "Why was I so afraid? Why are we all so afraid?"

BISER: *And they'll say this on their deathbed?*

SCHULZE: Oh, absolutely. It's a very sobering experience to know you're going to be dead in about 24 hours. You don't have to worry anymore about offending anybody. You don't have to worry anymore about embarrassing yourself.

You really don't have to worry about much of anything, except where you're going to be next. I find that people get great when they get near death, and all we have to do is get them to be great when they're in the middle of life. We need to take that information, we need to learn ...

BISER: ... *to take that honesty and move it backwards into the middle of life.*

SCHULZE: Absolutely. I've had many patients get divorced because someone in the relationship had sex with one other person.

If that's all your love is worth with someone, in that you'll throw away twenty or thirty years of marriage because the person you love had intercourse with someone else, I personally think that's ridiculous.

And I think that it ends up being regretted. I've had people cry on their deathbeds because they left someone who had one moment of passion with someone else.

I had a man sobbing for hours, almost the whole day before he died. He was sobbing over the relationship he broke up with his wife, because he found out she was having an affair, and he deeply loved her and lived without her for the next twenty years. That's crazy. It's crazy.

I mean, come on, we're human, we do things like that. It's just horribly unfortunate that people really ruin their lives, they ruin their families.[27]

---

[27] Sam Biser, *Eternal Sex*, (University of Natural Healing, Charlottesville: Virginia, 1995), pp. 224-228.

The most powerful energies you can use for spiritual cultivation are sexual energies, which are your vital energies unleashed. Sex moves your Qi/Prana, which is why it is used in some spiritual paths. However, sexual activity can be misused, especially if you pursue sexual partners just for selfish reasons rather than for an honest relationship. This is why the first rule of discipline in Mahayana Buddhism is no sexual misconduct whereas with Hinayana Buddhism, which does not allow sexual relations for monks and nuns, the primary rule is no killing or harming others.

When they are in a healthy sexual relationship individuals can use sexual energies to help open up their the Qi channels in all their body sections. As Yeshe Tsogyel instructed, you must train to control the energy flows (Qi/Prana) within your body and then must enjoy sexual excitement and pleasure without losing your semen (for men) during sexual intercourse. Otherwise you stray from the path of Tantra, which is one of the quickest ways to transform your body because of all the Qi energy you stimulate inside you and can guide around to open up body areas. While men should refrain from losing semen as much as possible, women may experience orgasm without any detriment.

To monks and nuns without enlightened teachers, sexual relations are forbidden. This discussion, taken for what it is worth, is food for thought for non-monks and non-nuns able to cultivate with their partner and use the energies of sex for opening up their Qi channels. Qi channels, of course, doesn't mean just acupuncture lines but the atomic bonds between all the atoms of the body. When you feel energy moving inside you due to sex, you can often guide it everywhere just as you can via kundalini yoga exercises, *anapana*, *nei-dan* and *nei-gong*. Thus it can become a cultivation technique if you also practice certain other cultivation exercises as a foundational prerequisite and alongside it.

All being said and done, pretend you are eighty years old sitting in your chair reviewing your life. Do this exercise now and think back on all the things you did and wish you had done differently, your regrets.

Now imagine that a genie appears and grants a wish that you can live your life again in a second chance. What would you do differently?

You still have time ahead of you in this life. Maybe you are young enough that you don't need a genie, but just courage to change your course direction and trajectory. But let's go back to the genie. You can now live the life you wanted and be the light you wanted others to see the first time around. What will that light be?

I have listed some of the various types of Buddhas, Bodhisattvas, protect gods and guardian spirits so you can see various types of activities and the vows some have chosen for their lives. You can devote yourself to similar commitments … if you want. They can be something like you have read or entirely different since I only provided a few examples.

Whatever you see in life that inspires you can become a personal vow or commitment to spread elsewhere if you decide to take on that responsibility. The subtle body enables you to do many different things if you so desire. What is it you want to do or experience? What is your highest calling, the activities of a life well-lived? What is worthy of you spending your time, energy and life force? What goals will make yours a Bigger Life where you change people's lives in a joyous way that improves matters?

Death puts you in the same realm (the realm of subtle energy we call Heaven, although earth-bound) where you can start performing these deeds, but why not start acting in this manner now? By donating to charities, for instance, you not only accumulate the merit you need for enlightenment but help change the world along interests and passions you have chosen. What type of merit is most important to you? Furthermore, why not cut down on the time required to learn skills in the areas where you want to bring light (and change) to the world by beginning a course of study and training *now* to become a Bodhisattva benefactor or guardian spirit. Training is the Yoga path of the Bodhisattvas and Buddhas. Exercising vows is also Bodhisattva Yoga, Buddha Yoga or Karma Yoga.

Life is too short for you to keep it so little, and since you have sufficient freedom in life you should "make good art." Moments add up to a lifetime so put some higher purpose and meaning into your many life moments … at least some of them. Be the light you want others to see. Help create the positive change you want to see take hold in the world. Build the future you want others to experience. See your efforts from a more elevated viewpoint … work on building a cathedral rather than just a brick wall.

Make your life count, make it matter. Don't bunt but shoot for the stars. Start working towards becoming a great Buddha, Bodhisattva, spiritual benefactor, guardian spirit, a supporter or protector of various causes. Start cultivating the character, skills, knowledge, actions and methods of the Buddha or Bodhisattva you want to become.

Protect what is important to you, and start fertilizing the green sprouts of future greatness. Create some personal goals and objectives that will help the world and then go beyond those goals to an even larger aim. You are the one who has to decide what is important to you. Training for and then executing your own vows is Buddha Yoga.

How do you stay on track with what you decide? As explained in *Quick, Fast, Done*, around January 1st of every year I make a list of yearly goals – things I want to do and accomplish for the year. I keep this in a journal for the year, whose middle section is used to write out and keep track of monthly goals. I strike them off when accomplished, and on the last page I list my life goals, which I redo every year, along with Bodhisattva vows and bucket list type items. This last page can include Buddha and Bodhisattva vows that you want to make for the world as well as the galaxy in which we live.

I suggest that twice a year, in the Spring and Fall, you create a little ceremony where you write down these goals on a piece of paper and throw them into a fire as an offering to the universe of what you want to do for it, letting the Buddhas and Bodhisattvas know of your goals and vows. It might include what you also want to experience, or learn too, and other objectives with a worldly and/or universal significance.

I would also throw into the fire a list of bad habits I would want to work on changing that year, or virtues I would want to cultivate as explained in *Color Me Confucius*. The Spring and Autumn periods, reflective of times when energies in the world are rising (Spring) or being reaped (Fall), are also why I suggest making offerings to spiritual training centers or enlightened masters at those two annual times.

In the Spring the fire might be in the shape of a square pit, symbolizing the body's root chakra in the pelvis from which energies ascend, while in the Autumn (near Harvest Festival time) it might be in the shape of a spiral galaxy – the Milky Way.

The square fire pit in the Spring would symbolize all the chaotic, unchanneled energies that we carelessly expend throughout the year that might be turned towards higher accomplishments like goals and vows if we simply set our mind on achieving them, which the ceremony helps us remember to do rather than waste our energies carelessly. The spiral, galaxy-shaped fire ceremony in the Fall when most of the work for the year has been done (and thus most of your goals usually accomplished), would reaffirm your goals for the year and give you the chance to report to the galaxy what you hope to do for it in the long run. Since the end of the year would be right around the corner at this time, the Fall fire ceremony would help motivate you to actually finish any items still unfinished on your list.

When January 1st arrives, you should create a new list for the new year once again. Thus you have three touch points or reminders during the course of a year – New Year's day, the Spring fire ceremony and the Autumn fire ceremony – to help you accomplish what you most want in life as goals, vows, and efforts at self-improvement. Don't become a fatalist and don't succumb to inertia in life. Use this method to set goals for the year and for your life, and use these twice yearly reminders to push yourself to achieve them. They are goals you want for *your* life, and are not for any other person. So be true to yourself and use this as a way to push yourself into doing *what really maters to you in life* so that at its end you can look back without regrets and say "I did it" or "At least I tried."

Notice to All: Because of its importance I hereby make this chapter, "Arhat Yoga," and any sections thereof, copyright free to anyone to reprint without permission as long as they credit the author as William Bodri and attribute its source to this book, *Buddha Yoga*.

10
ARHAT YOGA

THE ORIGINAL NATURE[28]

The primordial substance, essence or energy of the universe which gave birth to everything is its original fundamental substrate, and is known by many names such as the Ultimate, Uncreated, Supreme Reality, "Highest, Clearest, Purest," the Supreme Beatitude, Source, true nature, absolute essence, original nature, absolute nature, self-nature, primordial essence, absolute purity, Suchness, or True Self.

In religious terms It is sometimes called Parabrahman, Brahman, Nirguna Brahman, Shiva, *Purusha*, God, Ein Sof, Supreme Ultimate, *dharmakaya*, Buddha-substrate, *nirvana*, *Anama*, Allah and many other names.

Being the original essence/energy that is the most fundamental and primal essence, logic necessitates that It must be uncreated, self-so, pre-existing or beginningless because It doesn't come from anything else. It has no coming into being. It is the primal, fundamental, foundational essence before myriad other things were created, and Itself was pre-existing from beginninglessness rather than created.

---

[28] See *Traditional Theory of Evolution and Its Application in Yoga* (Gharote, Devnath, Jha), *Maya in Physics* (N.C. Panda), *Avadhuta Gita of Dattatreya* (Swami Chetananda), *Astavakkra Samhita* (Swami Nityaswarupananda), *Dasbodh* (Shri Samartha Ramdas).

Since Its existence does not come from any prior cause or conditions It is therefore self-so, uncreated, present before the creation of the universe of myriad things started. It is their primal substance or essence, infinite and all-pervading. How could it be limited and bounded? Only phenomena are limited and bounded.

This primordial essence or energy or substance must, by logical inference, be a solitary singleness of one essence that is unmanifest into anything. It only exists as pure Itself. It must be a oneness, a single solitary whole Aloneness rather than two or more things. Since It is the only primal existent, Its immaculateness necessitates that It cannot have anything else besides It. It is the One Without Another, the Solitary One, the Pure One, the Immaculate without divisions.

This original essence must also be infinite because having borders would mean It transforms into something else at its boundaries, and then there would be two things instead of a single fundamental substance. Therefore It is partless, an unbroken infinite whole of single purity that does not undergo modifications such as by having attributes (which would constitute impurities within It). It is without changes, motionless, attributeless, unsullied or unclouded by phenomena so that It is continuous and everywhere the same. Being homogenous and changeless It has no precedent stage nor consequent stage, no increase nor decrease, no coming into being or transformation into anything else. It is always just Itself and only Itself – motionless, immutable, pure, infinite, eternal. It is everlasting due to Its changelessness, and thus the sole unchanging Reality.

For understanding's sake It is sometimes described as formlessness, void or Emptiness without attributes (qualities). Thus It is often referred to as non-dual or being like undivided endless empty space which is also pure, changeless, motionless, unshakable, and without attributes or differentiation. Any changeable entity, on the other hand, has a beginning and an end as well as attributes that can be described.

What is a change? It is the appearance of another characteristic of a substance while the previous characteristic has disappeared. This is called change, mutation or transformation. Any changeable entity has a beginning and end, and must decay whereas the primordial essence has no divisions, differentiations, or attributes to It. Without borders, It must be infinite in its eternal form. Changeless, It is without motion and immaculately pure and whole, a perfect oneness. When people think of It they often compare It to an emptiness like space, or the empty clarity of clear consciousness.

THE PRIMAL CONSTITUENT

All things, at their most fundamental level, are composed of this primordial essence. Therefore their composition, in the most absolute inherent aspect, is only this highest fundamental substance-essence-nature. Ultimately there is only this original essence and nothing else. It is the omnipresent, dependable, real part of you that can never be eliminated – your truest Self or self-nature.

You are this Self. Everyone is this same Self or primordial substrate, the foundational self substance. The real "I" in you is this unchangeable self-nature. You are nothing different from this original essence. You are the one Self in All. You are It, It is you, you are one of Its aspects, being It you are also the rest of the universe that is also you. You and It are no different from one another as is the case with all other things. Therefore, you are ultimately beyond birth and death. You were never born and will never die.

Just as gold can be made into various ornaments, those golden ornaments are in their primal essence only gold. From gold's standpoint, they are all just Itself, namely gold. Similarly, from the standpoint of the original nature there is nothing else in existence, no phenomena at all. There is just the original nature - just Itself. All subsequent evolutes (energies, forms and phenomena) are just Itself no matter what their shapes or forms. They are only It.

The original nature is therefore the Source, True Self or self-nature of all things. It is their fundamental substrate, their fundamental substance, their fundamental energy, their absolute self-nature, their innermost Self. All things, at their ultimate compositional breakdown, have It as their absolute essence or substrate (substance). A saying runs, "Although He existed in many forms He was single. He was there in all the elements and was all the elements." Thus the primordial essence is often called the source nature, fundamental nature or primordial substratum. It is the Self that is the Self of All. Ultimately there is only one entity, this fundamental Self. The universe is this pure existence itself.

EVOLUTES

Being eternal in nature this self-nature is changeless, being changeless It can never transform into anything else, and therefore It can never give birth to anything.

By a process therefore unknown, which Buddhism terms "Ignorance," this solitary essence somehow gave rise to evolutes that gave rise to further transformations and even more evolutes. Through complex interactions of cause and effect, the evolutes produced innumerable subsequent energies, forms and phenomena.

During the process of gold being formed into jewelry the substance of gold never changes at all, only its outward appearance or form. There is nothing separating one piece of gold jewelry from another as long as you are just looking at the gold. Analogy – all the various forms of the world are still nothing but the all-pervading original substrate appearing in various forms. A state of diversity somehow arises in oneness, but this is an illusion because it is all the foundational substrate nonetheless.

No one can conceive of a cause at the stage of creation but the evolutes in aggregate are called the Manifestation, Creation, Triple Realm, karmic formations, Shakti, *Prakiti*, the Word, Holy Spirit, all things, universe, attributes, forms, the Primal Illusion, Indra's web, Maya, Mara, samsara, and many other names. They are generated by the process we call creation, generation, production, emanation, manifestation, mutation, change or transformation and in essence they are the original nature.

Evolutes are constantly in a state of flux, movement, transformation, change, no-rest and vibration whereas the original nature doesn't change, and is motionless because of its changeless immutability. On the other hand, the realm of evolutes is characterized by impermanence, and so the realm of Creation is like a great illusion such as the reflection of the moon in water that lacks a permanent solidity that can be grasped.

When the wind flows in the sky it does not distort the sky in any way. You can in no way say that by the arising of wind space is broken. There is no distortion in the sky if darkness or light pervade it either. So when evolutes arise within the original nature there is no change or distortion within It. Nothing can produce an effect on It. However, new appearances do somehow arise just as wind somehow appears in a motionless sky.

These evolutes, energies, forms and phenomena (subtle elements) comprise what we can call various planes/levels of existence, also known as realms of being, that are populated by innumerable diverse phenomena. Many spiritual schools maintain that the world has evolved as a gradual condensation, crystallization or emanation from higher non-physical energies and essences, with the ultimate foundation being the changeless original nature.

Religions, and especially spiritual cultivation schools, typically talk about five planes of existence in additional to the primordial original essence. However, there are many more despite the abbreviated dialogue.

The causeless cause – the original essence – is in no way associated with whatever It inseparably pervades as part of It; inseparable means It pervades all evolutes that are, in their essential nature, It. It is the "I" or self-nature of all things so they cannot escape It, and being the only existent It is All, everything is It. Evolutes, appearances or manifestations are Its non-transcendental functions, attributes or aspects. They are what we call conventional existence, an ephemeral existence of constant change.

The two principles of the original nature and evolutes (Shakti) have no control over each other. The original nature is not involved in evolution since being perfectly pure and motionless/changeless It does not cause anything and thus is not the cause of any evolute. It does not perform any actions whatsoever. Nevertheless It exists always, everywhere and in everything as existential support. No change whatsoever ever occurs to It just as there is never any distortion in the sky when darkness or light pervades it. All changes only happen in the field of Creation, emanation, effusion, or manifestation. Evolution only happens to Shakti. From Shakti all is evolved. In *Purusha* nothing happens. Shakti is constantly in a state of flux and transformation.

From the standpoint of evolutes, as explained, we must say that the generation of each and every phenomenon proceeds and is governed by universal natural laws of cause and effect. All production, emanation, transformation, mutation, evolution, generation or creation of phenomena can be understood as a relationship between cause and effect. The cause and effect laws of transformation/generation may be as yet unknown, but all things arise and transform through definite laws of cause and effect, stimulus and response. An entity or entities as evolutes serve as the cause for subsequent entities to appear. As sentient beings with minds we have the ability to decipher some of these laws and make use of them to our own benefit. This is a necessity in order to live, so should we not also use this ability to make situations as good as possible? Such mastery requires learning and skillfulness.

The primordial essence is the causeless cause that is no way associated with whatever appears within It. It is inseparable from everything, pervading everything, but the two principles of Parent and Daughter, Host and Guest, Mother and Son, primordial original substance and Shakti have no control over each other. *Purusha*, the original essence, is not involved in evolution since it does not create anything. It does not cause anything and so is not the cause of any evolute because changes never occur to It. All changes only happen in Shakti, the field of emanations. Evolution or involution only happen to Shakti/*Prakiti*, from which all is evolved.

ALL PHENOMENA ARE IMPERMANENT

All the constituent forms of Shakti that make up the universe are always in motion. Thus their natures are impermanent, transitory or temporary which means that they lack an inherent identity. They all arise and pass away, and therefore lack a concrete identity, a solid inherent nature, due to ceaseless transformation. They all exist due to an infinite interdependence of causes and effects within the body of Shakti, so their existence is conditional upon everything else.

This is why all the phenomena within Shakti are termed "unreal." They are components of a shimmering, dancing "Grand Illusion" that cannot be grasped and held firm, and thus are like a mirage. Phenomena lack "true reality" because they do not remain the same whereas the original nature remains changeless, motionless, reliable, eternally present.

This lack of an enduring identity for phenomena has important consequences for the possibility of liberation from conditions that produce suffering in life, and lower states of being. Because phenomena, states of being, conditions or circumstances are impermanent we can change them. Because we have consciousness we can learn how to master their transformations to create better, higher states of being. This is our opportunity and birth right, and is only limited by our wisdom and skill.

All together the myriad individual phenomena of the universe comprise one single body whose most fundamental essence is the infinite original nature. All phenomena within this whole, or you can say the whole (All or Shakti) itself, are constantly changing or mutating because of infinite interdependence causing ceaseless transformations everywhere. Despite their separate individualities the whole universe comprised of Everything should be considered an effervescent, scintillating unity of one body. Although in continuous, interminable flux Shakti must be considered one single whole.

As an individual you are part of the single unified body of Shakti, the Word, and thus you form a unity with all the myriad things of the universe. They are therefore your greater body. Because of this linkage, you are responsible for what arises to some extent. You are the True-I, True Self or self-nature, and have the ability to fashion conditions and the future in any way you want. Once again, what do you ultimately want to achieve as a consequence for your greater body?

The unity of Heaven and man is one all pervading unity, so how will you devote your actions within this unity? What will you create? Where should your efforts be applied? There will always be consequences for what you think, say and do and for the impressions you give to others (that influences them) simply because of your existence and appearance. Why not choose a path where the consequences beautify your relationships and the world?

INFINITE INTERDEPENDENT CO-ARISING

Creation of a phenomenon is called its appearance, manifestation, rising up, or birth. Its continuance is called continued existence, sustained existence, or maintenance. Its dissolution is called its death, disposition, settlement or disappearance. In Hinduism these three phases of existence are symbolized by Brahma, Vishnu and Shiva.

There are laws that control the three phases of generation, maintenance, and dissolution for each phenomena. These are the laws of cause and effect (such as physics, chemistry, etcetera) that rule the transformations, mutations, evolution or changes for all phenomena. All things arise and disappear due to cause and effect, and when we cannot fathom the reasons for an event it is simply because we are ignorant as to the ultimate causes, but causes are there.

Furthermore, the existence of each singular phenomenon depends upon all other phenomena in the entire universal whole because all phenomena are interlinked in a giant infinite web of interdependent, intertwining causes and conditions that excludes nothing. All phenomena are infinitely interconnected, each having an existence that all others participate in, which is called "Indra's web."

No phenomenon has an existence of its own – an inherent existence – but always comes into existence in dependence upon all other things. The presence of all other things connected together creates a phenomenon, and so they share in its beingness.

Thus one can say that "each phenomena contains the entire universe" since the entire universe is involved/participates in the creation and maintenance (existence) of every single thing as well as its transformation into something else. If one single object in the universe changes, then the universe as a whole simultaneously changes. Doesn't it change if a single mote within it changes? Does that change not cause others too?

Simply put, the existence of each and every single thing is due to an infinite network of cause and effect, an infinite co-dependence. All things are therefore said to arise, appear or manifest because of all others. Everything is dependently arisen because of being depend on everything else, and each and every thing is therefore devoid of inherent existence.

This dependent arising is alternatively called simultaneous arising, infinite interdependence, interdependent generation, dependent origination, Indra's web, linked interdependence, simultaneous co-arising and many other names. An infinite chain of cause and effect is responsible for the appearance of any single phenomenon, although for practical use we limit causality chains to a smaller set of conditions.

What this means is that one entity or evolute cannot serve as the sole cause for a subsequent entity to appear. Actually, there is no such thing as a single cause or evolute being solely responsible for the appearance of any other manifesting phenomenon. The entire universal cosmos, through infinite interdependence, gets into the act. Everything is responsible for everything, which is infinite codependent arising.

Since the net total causes, conditions and circumstances that cause the generation or dissolution of anything are actually infinite, this means that things are not distinctly apart from one another. It is hard to say where one thing ends and another beings because of being linked in the grand unity of everything that produces all events. This multiplicity, however, is actually singleness. Furthermore, to handle affairs we simplify this immensity into simple, localized cause and effect relationships. To change situations and circumstances to your liking you will have to master these interrelationships.

Nonetheless, the appearance of any single phenomenon is determined from infinite prior causation with the whole cosmos getting into the act, and in Buddhism dependent arising is described as "this arises from that because of prior causes and conditions." The appearance of anything is completely dependent upon causes and conditions, namely the mutual interpenetration of all phenomena in infinite realms upon realms, mutually containing and interacting with one another. The fact that phenomena affect one another is called mutual perfuming or mutual interpenetration. This is the *Hua Yen* or Flower Ornament view of Buddhism, and in Confucianism is described as, "Man affects the Heavens and the Heavens affect (interact with) man."

Because of infinite interdependence and simultaneous arising, causes and effects are neither absolutely different nor identical with one another. Because everything is interlinked infinitely we cannot clearly say where one thing ends and another begins. Nonetheless, on the apparent plane they certainly seem different from one another but at their core they share the same essential identity because they are the changeless source nature.

All things arise in the One original nature, the One foundational substrate penetrates/comprises All, so from Its aspect nothing appears at all – It remains solely Itself. *Nirvana* and samsara are therefore inseparable and interdependent; there is no difference between them. The All melts into a single whole, the Unity is Shiva and Shakti, God and Creation, *Purusha* and *Prakiti*, empty space and emanations. Shiva and Shakti, God and the Word are the same. *Purusha*, the Holy Spirit (Shakti) and thus phenomena are one.

Christianity says, "In the beginning was the Word (Shakti), and the Word was with God, and the Word was God. The same was in the beginning with God. Through him all things were made; without him nothing was made that has been made" (John 1:1-3). In other words, the Word and God the original nature are the same thing. However, all created things proceed from the Word, Shakti, which has its beginning in God. Christianity does not say that the Word is beginningless but that the beginning of Creation initially starts with the Word. How the Word appeared it does not say. This accords with the teachings of all the other spiritual schools.

In the absolute reality there is only the single oneness of the primordial substratum. Whatever you perceive because of having consciousness (illumination or comprehension) is actually That alone despite apparent multiplicity. Within Alonehood arises apparent diversity, but the apparent multiplicity is nothing but an illusion hiding the single nature by screening it. Although the fundamental substance exists in many forms It is single.

Because we have a mind, we can discern these truths. Insentient phenomena lack mental illumination so cannot. We can discern the apparent multiplicity of phenomena and also discover the rules of cause and effect that rule them. We can use them to change situations for the better, guiding the changes of phenomena as we want. Doing so requires wisdom and skillfulness, training and application, which are factors you must cultivate in life. This is the Buddha and Bodhisattva way, which is to develop our understanding of matters, made possible by our possession of consciousness with its abilities of comprehension) and use that understanding together with our actions to create better states of the future.

Though the artful production of phenomena guided by our Knowledge and mastery of cause and effect, we can create personal, global and universal results that are good for everyone. The results of our efforts will manifest in the future when the appropriate conditions allow; efforts always have effects although those effects might not be exactly what we want so we must learn to be skillful in our efforts.

What we presently experience in our lives are the results of the aggregation of the past deeds of man and nature within this unity, including our own deeds. Each of us has our own individual effect on the world along with a personal fate that has developed due to our past actions and the shared karma of family, community, nation, and world.

All worlds/realms, including the residences of the heavens, are produced by phenomenal changes and the acts of living beings together with their interactions with phenomena. The reason why people share common circumstances and environments in these realms is due to similar seeds of karma. Just as individual lives are the fruit of personal causes, so does the world's appearance rest upon the quality of common karma such as the aggregate purity of consciousness of its inhabitants. This means we have a common responsibility to improve things, especially as it is all our physical body of manifestation.

CONSCIOUSNESS & KNOWLEDGE

Of the many phenomena that have appeared within this endless web of interdependence, one is called life. Life evolved because the right causes and conditions eventually came together. Some forms of life have sentience and some forms of sentient life, such as ours, are capable of higher consciousness because of their physical structure.

Consciousness is what goes on within our minds. Consciousness means knowing and perceiving, or having the ability to generate Knowledge via thoughts and perceptions that are stored in memories used to name, label and differentiate mental phenomena. Consciousness means the ability to cognize, which is to be able to mentally discriminate and give meaning (names and labels) to phenomena that arise within the mind. Discrimination means the knowing of differences, which means making comparisons or differentiating things. It means the ability to generate Knowledge.

In order for a discrimination of beingness (a recognition of conscious existence) to manifest within a living being there must be a discrimination of self versus others. For a sentient being to be able to cognize its beingness (self-existence) it must be able to discriminate some other state as juxtaposed to itself, otherwise it cannot fathom that it is an existent I and that there are others which are "not-I." In other words, the consciousness of a life-entity must develop a sense of an individual I which entails an I-thought, self-notion, subject-notion or ego-concept in order for it to have self-awareness of self-existence ("I exist" or "I am") and thoughts that others are "not-self."

Basically, if there is no "I-witness" there is no self-awareness or awareness of others. The knowledge of self also necessitates the existence of memory that can be used to compare and classify mental phenomena. Higher knowledge absolutely necessitates the existence of memories, which are used to make sense out of conceptual processes by giving phenomena names and labels that lead to a recognition (or building) of a world. Otherwise there is only chaos within the field of experience.

The ego, self-concept or I-thought is a special kind of meta-thought at the center of all other thoughts. This I-thought gives you the sense that "you" are thinking "your" thoughts when in fact nothing of the kind is happening. During the process of thinking it is essentially the thought process itself that is doing the thinking, not a permanent "I" that is an independent, inherent sentient being. The thinking process itself is automatically doing all the thinking and understanding without any self, *jiva* or *atman* being involved.

To be "a sentient being with consciousness" means that Knowledge within a physical body can be generated and reference itself in a self-reflexive arc. Knowledge (thought) itself – and not an actual being, soul, entity or life – is the ultimate experiencer of everything. It produces thoughts, interprets them, and produces an illusion of understanding.

Again, there is no real *atman*, self or living entity that is the ultimate doer or experiencer of any thought or action. It is the Knowledge created within a certain body that is doing all the thinking, knowing and understanding, and the process is happening automatically. The I-thought of being a personal soul self is therefore just a delusion or illusion.

In other words, thinking just happens but there is no one there thinking while it happens. During thinking, Knowledge is experiencing thoughts, that's all. Knowledge is doing all the thinking and understanding. Who understands this? No one – not a person or being – but understanding is still there.

Various kinds of thoughts arise in response to different kinds of stimuli, but they all arise automatically, mechanically. Everything happening within the mind, and in the universe, is mechanical or automatic due to laws of cause and effect that rule all. Everything arises, is sustained, and dies away due to cause and effect including the contents of your consciousness. Thoughts are expressed in a particular moment because the laws which govern consciousness cause them to arise, and they are replaced by other thoughts due to those same laws. What arises within your mind does so because of the mechanical functioning of Knowledge, that is all. You may not know the laws of cause and effect that rule the generation of thoughts within a consciousness, but they exist. Since we have consciousness the key is to learn how to gain control of our thoughts to bring about better states of being.

The universe operates in generating phenomena like a vast, perfectly oiled machine operating according to all sorts of causality laws. Only the unmanifesting original nature without characteristics, which is pure like empty space, transcends all this and is without rules of transformation.

Even though all sentient beings say "I" in reference to their small phenomenal self, saying "I" is actually the True Self of every being and all phenomena announcing Itself. Isn't that the case? At the deepest level, all men who say "I" are actually referring to the same self-nature, which makes us all brothers. Are we not brothers if we share the same parent? Do we not then have a responsibility to help one another rather than harm others since everyone is essentially related?

The most fundamental essence, our self-nature, is not the little self of the individual who says "I am." It is the infinite, beginningless primordial essence that is the self-so, uncreated, always existent Self. The great power of consciousness ultimately came from this Self of ours, and religions often teach meditation so that we mentally imitate the fundamental serenity of our foundational nature. The idea that our original nature is pure and undivided, without attributes, is the ideal objective of the mind produced by meditation practice, for it is taught that the natural state of the mind is empty like the original nature – equanimous, blissful, peaceful.

Now if you suddenly found yourself without the possibility of thoughts, how would the world appear to you? Would you see a world of separate objects? Could you recognize anything at all? You wouldn't be able to cognize any objects or recognize anything; there would be no world of existence. Without thoughts, there would be no perception of anything.

What you see as objects, or the world, are only appearances within your mind. At any moment of time, you are only experiencing your own mind, you are only experiencing the thoughts of your consciousness. You never experience the world, you only experience your own mind.

Your mind is your world of reality, and that reality is created based upon your memories, perceptions, thoughts and nervous system that generates that world within your consciousness. Other beings, such as animals and insects, see and experience the world differently than you. Your own five senses certainly don't give a full picture of the world, including all the forces that create for you a destiny of a moment. What you see is only a limited conditional reality pertinent to you, and sometimes inaccurate.

While a world of phenomena does exist outside of you, it is an existence whose appearance is only seen/experienced because there is a mind to know it. Your mind has formed various sensory images of it and has thoughts about it to interpret them and give them meaning. Every mind will see the world differently because of being colored by different thoughts (and because of different sensory apparatus), so the world and universe we see are *conditional* constructions, *dependent* constructions and have no absolute meaning other than what we ascribe to them.

Every being experiences life conditionally, which means dependent upon its prior memories, sensory apparatus, and thoughts generated at the moment. However, beings of the same type will share enough commonalities in their perceptual sensory apparatus, thinking processes and conventional names and labels to think somewhat similarly. In Buddhism it is said they share "similar seeds of consciousness."

Knowledge is generated by knowing and involves perceptions, conceptions (thinking, thoughts or intellectual operations), the master self-thought of "I," and the memory of names and labels. Memory is essentially a set of names and labels built up over time from experience and applied to new appearances within the mind to derive recognition. Thus it lets us distinguish, differentiate, identify, recognize or make sense of phenomena within consciousness. This is also called understanding, without which nothing could be recognized or known. Without that, chaos would be our field of perception.

Every thought generated within the mind has an internal meaning colored by all the other contents of the mind. The sense organs have their raw perceptual data turned into mental entities/images, and then these mental events are further synthesized or appended to by memories, thinking and the intellect to produce ideas, emotions, judgments and volitional acts. The intellect is constantly bombarded by a stream of sensory reports and automatically adds words, names and labels to make sense out of them. All these operations are simultaneously perfuming consciousness and its operations so as to generate new thoughts in turn, like an endless stream.

The sensory inputs and thoughts which actively perfume consciousness, and the consciousness which is perfumed, live and perish together while affecting the generation of new states of consciousness (thoughts) due to the blend; this is the principle of perfuming. By the perfuming stimulation of the brain (consciousness) the seeds/memories that lie within neurons are engendered to sprout in response due to the combinational aroma, flavor, blend, or light of the total mixture of inputs. Hence the term "perfuming" or "smoking," as what is produced takes on the aroma/flavor of what came previously.

As soon as the spinning of thoughts and seeds of memory are engendered to produce new thoughts, the consciousness which is perfumed acts in turn as a cause to perfume and mature other seeds of consciousness to generate new thoughts (states of consciousness). These three elements - thoughts that are born, the inputs which perfume/electrify them, and the seeds which are either stimulated (provoked into stirring) by this perfuming - revolve in a cycle, simultaneously acting as cause and effect. The consciousness produced is like a bundle of reeds stacked together where each reed is supported by the aggregate of all others. In this way, the causes and effects of consciousness can in some sense be considered co-dependent or mutually-reflexive.

The intellect is the "organ of thinking" that must make sense of all this, and its abilities of discrimination can be compared to a great army general who is interpreting all the information he's receiving from his sense lieutenants and local officers who are constantly issuing him reports. If we get rid of these sense reports then we have no more outside world, and then the only thing left for consciousness to work with is memory and the intellect itself, which is basically Knowledge functioning to produce thoughts that are more Knowledge. Knowledge is always just producing itself; there is no independent being, entity, soul or *atman* producing Knowledge. Knowledge is doing that all by itself.

To get any peace or quiet at all in the midst of this incessant activity, the army general has to separate himself from the ceaseless flow of these reports. The meditative act of "sense withdrawal" mentioned in Yoga, or "turning within," "turning away from the senses," or "cultivating one-pointed concentration to ignore distractions," "cultivating empty mind" or "abandoning thought" is thus a means for developing mental peace and quiet.

This is the practice of meditation. It involves imitating the original nature. It involves no longer internally clinging to the contents of consciousness – while continuing to let everything mentally arise – in order to gain the peace of mental calm, equanimity, serenity and stability. It involves helping you realize the natural peaceful state of your mind. It leads you to realize that any modification of the mind cannot be your natural state of being.

Buddhism, in particular, talks greatly about the workings of our mental processes because as Arhats all spiritual masters can shrink their etheric bodies, go into peoples' brains, and watch as thoughts form due to the electro-chemical processes going on. This is done by the Arhats (spiritual masters) of all religions, but Buddhism does the most to describe some of the operations of consciousness.

It is common training among the spiritual masters of all religions to read the memories of people stored in their brain neurons, which is why it is said that no secrets are kept from Heaven. It is also common for spiritual adepts with higher bodies to train on how to change people's thoughts and emotions, which is one of the primary ways by which spiritual masters and their deva students try to help individuals, though they are limited by the restrictions of karma that determine what a person is due to experience.

In the Buddhist Sutras the brain is symbolized by Vimalakirti's ten-foot square room where miniaturized Buddhas (practicing the *amina* superpower of shrinkage) arrive to teach an uncountable number of deva students. In the *Avatamsaka (Flower Ornament) Sutra*, the memory cells and neural pathways as they fire are symbolized by bright banners, wondrous adornments, flags, wisdom flames, arrays of lights, jeweled lights, shining pores, magical displays, pleasant thunder, flowers, wisdom fragrances, supreme clouds, banner lights, or precious sounds and other analogies.

Our experience as sentient life where all these things operate is all possible because of the great treasure of consciousness. In the universe, rare is the phenomena of life. With life, rare is the existence of higher consciousness able to form thoughts that enable beings to learn how to master phenomena, bring about better states of existence for themselves and others, and discern a spiritual path that enables them to develop ways to generate higher bodies where they can rejoin beings living on higher planes.

THE FIVE BODIES

Religions, and especially spiritual cultivation schools, typically talk about five planes of existence or being in additional to the primordial original essence. However, there are many more despite the limited dialogue. Because we have higher consciousness and the fact that the path is naturally open, human beings have the ability to cultivate bodies comprised of the energies/substances of these higher transcendental planes.

Each higher energy realm "closer" to the original essence, in terms of the layers/levels/sequence of causal evolution, is composed of more basic, subtle, fundamental, primordial, higher, or more transcendental energies than a subsequent evolute, which is considered denser or less pure. A denser evolute has all the higher energies inherently within it. As with all things, the energies of all these planes interpenetrate, and together comprise a single universal whole – Shakti, the Word.

Of the five planes or realms there is the (1) material plane, (2) subtle plane, (3) Causal plane, (4) Supra-Causal plane, and (5) Immanence plane that can be experienced by a human being who may possess a human body, subtle body, Supra-Causal body, and Immanence Body. These bodies are known by different in names in different spiritual schools.

As stated, all the phenomena of these planes exist because of a complex interaction of cause and effect spanning across all realms, energies and phenomena, in effect the result of a great mixing of infinite, co-dependent arising. One can particularly consider the phenomena of our material plane a condensation of higher energies since once investigated each phenomenon can be found to be composed of more transcendental energies. By the process of spiritual cultivation you can even generate a body composed of the energies from each of the higher realms by releasing them from within a body composed of materials from a lower plane. The most fundamental basis of all these energies and phenomena is the one primordial original substrate.

The physical body of the material plane is known as the food body, gross body, coarse human body, impure physical nature or body of flesh and blood. It is also referred to as the form skandha in Buddhism and *annamaya* ("foodstuff") *kosha* in Hinduism.

The subtle body is also known as the deva body, *yin-shen*, will-born body, astral body, impure illusory body, *suddha deha*, etheric body or body composed of Qi or Prana. It is also referred to as the sensation skandha in Buddhism and *pranamaya* ("energy") *kosha* in Hinduism.

The Causal body is also known as the Mental body, Mantra body, body of vibrations, *pranava deha*, Grace body or purified illusory body. It is composed of a higher energy known as Shen that is more transcendental than Qi. It is free of all lower gross matter and impurities. It is also referred to as the conception skandha in Buddhism and *manomaya* ("mind-stuff") *kosha* in Hinduism.

The Supra-Causal body is also known as the Dharma body, Clear Light body, Wisdom body, Buddha body, and is composed of what Taoism calls Later Heavenly Qi (energy, Prana or wind). It is also referred to as the volition skandha in Buddhism and *vigyanmaya* ("wisdom") *kosha* in Hinduism. This is the attainment that people normally think of when they hear the word "enlightenment," and it is considered *nirvana* with remainder.

The Immanence body is also known as the Complete and Perfect Enlightenment body, or Great Golden Arhat body composed of Primordial Heavenly energy. It is also referred to as the consciousness skandha in Buddhism, the stage of No More Learning, the *anandamaya* ("bliss") *kosha* in Hinduism, and the stage of *nirvana* without remainder.

GENERATION OF BODIES

The Yoga school says that the purpose of the spiritual path is to resolve the physical material body back into its most primal constituent components, which means cultivating higher transcendental bodies that are "closer" to the original nature in terms of their composition, namely the layers of emanation until the composition of your ultimate body is as high as you can go. The practice of Yoga has the purpose of taking man back to his Source (source-nature).

The Confucian school also says to trace all things back to their source, which can only be done by generating these higher transcendental bodies.

Hinduism says to cultivate a state of bliss, which is only attained by possessing a higher transcendental body as your major body vehicle since its existence is considered blissful compared to the earthly world. Hinduism also says that "the *atman* must return to Brahman," meaning that you must achieve a higher body attainment as close to the original nature (Brahman) in composition as possible. The ultimate purpose in Hinduism is to reach the source of life and consciousness, which is the foundational essence.

Buddhism says you must prove that all things come from the original nature by cultivating to achieve it, but you can only prove that all things arise from the primordial fundamental nature by cultivating transcendental bodies composed of higher and higher essences, each new one composed of a level of energy that is more primordial/transcendental than the previous. Each higher body leaves behind coarser elements from the old and is "closer" to the original essence.

Thus according to Taoism, out of a physical body you can generate a body of Qi, out of a body of Qi (the subtle body) you can form/generate a Causal body composed of Shen, out of a Shen body you can generate a Supra-Causal body composed of Later Heavenly energy, out of a body of Later Heavenly energy you can generate an Immanence body composed of Primordial Heavenly energy and so on.

Islam explains this by saying that spiritual development means passing through various planes or levels of divine manifestation, and at each level we transmute by shedding a skin. This spiritual path is called "the return," and has the same meaning as developing a new body of higher elements out of a body of coarser elements that belong to a lower plane. In Islam the planes of existence are said to be like screens that separate us from the highest purity of Allah. Islam says the purpose of spiritual cultivation is to engage in an "unveiling" or "tearing off of veils" to see God's face and experience unity with Allah, the original nature or Parabrahman.

Christianity teaches us to strive to seek communion with the saints (who have achieved heavenly bodies) and become one with God the Father Supreme through a similar process of divinization, deification, beautification, ascension or *theosis* that involves cultivating through your own efforts an incorruptible, refined, transfigured body of glory and power. It simply fails to disclose that there are many possible rather than just one.

Thus the various religions and spiritual paths word the cultivation of transcendental bodies, which is "attaining the Tao," achieving liberation, emancipation of the soul or realization (of higher bodies) in different ways.

The spiritual cultivation path for attaining the higher bodies entails transformations within your physical body to purify impure elements. The result is that you first purify the Qi/Prana of your physical body and generate from within it a body of transcendental elements that can leave your physical body at will – the subtle (deva) body attainment composed of Qi, or Prana. Spiritual cultivation is essentially a pathway of Yoga to cultivate your pre-existing Qi/Prana so that you can produce this independent spiritual body as the initial fruit of the spiritual path. When individuals die an internal body of Qi/Prana leaves their physical shell, but it is much weaker and more impure than this one that is purified through the kundalini transformation processes of Yoga.

On this cultivation pathway to generate the independent subtle body you must use your will to mobilize your Qi/Prana so that it circulates and spreads in every part of your body, making it go to your four limbs, internal organs, all bones of your skeleton, your tissues - everywhere. This is called cultivating your Qi/Prana, rotating your Qi/Prana, or revolving the "vital breath" of your body so that this Qi, Prana, wind element or energy penetrates everywhere.

You accomplish this via various spiritual exercises that stimulate your Qi/Prana and by moving your Qi/Prana with your will. If you cultivate the Qi/Prana of your body (your vita energy) sufficiently and in the right way, then out of your body's Jing and Qi you can eventually generate an independent spiritual body formed of your Qi/Prana that can then leave and return to your physical shell as you want. This subtle body attainment, known as the deva body, is the first stage/fruit of the genuine spiritual path.

This generation process occurs when the physical body is "burnt out" through the continual application of the "fire of yoga," and eventually produces the "divinized body," "purified body" or "perfect body" that is the subtle body. Once again, this accomplishment is just the first stage of the spiritual path. This subtle body, composed of "pure elements," is called the "house of kundalini" because moving the Qi/Prana within your body to cultivate its emergence is sometimes called kundalini yoga or *kriya* yoga, and these activities correspond to purifying your Qi/Prana. The subtle body (deva body) composed of Qi/Prana has free movement in the world although unseen by men.

The next stage of transformation is that the subtle body can through a similar process generate from within itself a more transcendental Causal body, Mental body, Shen body, or purified illusory body that is entirely free from all gross matter and impurities, including those still remaining in the subtle body composed of Qi. It is a transfigured body higher in composition than the subtle body, so it resides on a yet higher plane, and has more dominion over all the siddhas, or superpowers than the subtle body.

The next transformation is that the Causal body, with more cultivation, can generate from within itself a Supra-Causal body, also known as a Wisdom light body, Dharma body, Buddha body or bliss body. With this attainment, called *nirvana* with remainder, you can identify with universal life on the lower planes. In attaining this body you become a Para-mukta, meaning you attain Sivahood or what is typically though of as the enlightenment or liberation that leaves the coarser physical planes behind forever.

Going further through cultivation, this body can generate a body of Immanence said to be close to God Supreme, meaning that it is the most transcendental body compositional attainment you can reach, and thus is equivalent to Complete and Perfect Enlightenment or the perfect *nirvana* attainment. It is a Great Golden Arhat's body. Higher bodies are possible still so it is only a way posing a final termination target for your cultivation efforts.

This process of spiritual emancipation, liberation, *moksha*, self-realization or enlightenment starts by understanding that the ultimate evolutionary source of energy and matter, and thus life and its attendant consciousness, is the original nature or *dharmakaya*.

One proves this by purifying your body back to its most purified elementary forces, thus creating higher and higher transcendental bodies in the process. Each new body stays attached to the lower body from which it was generated, and each resides on a different plane. Each is capable of different powers and skills that you can master which can affect the plane(s) below its own plane of composition.

A set of these bodies linked together, or simply the highest body attainment you reach just by itself, is called the *sambhogakaya*.

THE STAGES OF ATTAINMENT[29]

An individual who cultivates the subtle body (deva body) is called an Srotapanna. This is the first stage Arhat enlightenment attainment. It is also called attaining the first dhyana in Buddhism or *vitarka* (coarse mental

---

[29] See *Nyasa Yoga, Move Forward, Color Me Confucius, God Speaks* (Meher Baba) and the story of Ramalinga Swamigal's cultivation (Vallalar).

grasping) samadhi in Hinduism. Its attainment is a birth by transformation.

With the subtle body the adept attains the eight yogic powers because the subtle body composed of Qi/Prana can change shape and form to become bigger, smaller, lighter, heavier and so on. This is why a subtle body can shrink itself to enter into a physical body, and learn to read the memories stored in someone's brain. Using this new body he can perform minor miracles (tricks) in the physical world such as converting a dry tree into a green one, stop railway trains or cars, fill a dry well with water and so forth.

The individual who cultivates the subtle body to a higher stage of purity is a Sadragamin, or second stage Arhat. This is alternatively called attaining the second dhyana or *vicara* (refined mental grasping) samadhi. Devas start out with a subtle body whereas humans start out with a physical body and must first cultivate an independent subtle body, which normally is ejected from their physical shell upon death. Thus this higher stage of subtle body purification, where the Qi/Prana of your subtle (deva) body is refined to a higher level of purity, is simply specified for the benefit of devas who already possess a subtle body. The first and second dhyana of Buddhism refer to subtle body attainments of different degrees of purity for bodies composed of Qi/Prana.

The individual who cultivates the Causal body is an Anagamin, or third stage Arhat. This is the third dhyana attainment of Buddhism or *ananda* (bliss) samadhi of Hinduism. Using this new body composed of Shen (a type of energy higher than Qi/Prana) he becomes capable of performing grand miracles such as giving sight to the blind, resorting limbs to the maimed and sometimes even raising the dead to life, but only of lower creatures rather than human beings. He can experience yet more of the different planes and worlds of the transcendental spheres.

The individual who cultivates the Supra-Causal body is a full Arhat, or "Buddha," which is called attaining the fourth dhyana, *"nirvana* with remainder" achievement or *asmita* (existence) samadhi in Hinduism. With this body he becomes capable of raising the dead and even creating new life. He can generate many *nirmanakaya* emanation bodies to do simultaneous activities, and even project one into a womb to be reborn in the world of men. A reborn *nirmanakaya* is an individual who usually attains the Tao (achieves the subtle body) at a very young age.

The individual who cultivates the Immanence body is a Great Golden Arhat, or Complete and Perfectly Enlightened Buddha. This is the Buddhist stage of No More Learning, or *"nirvana* without remainder."

These four higher bodies are all considered stages of "enlightenment," realization, spiritual attainment, spiritual salvation, divinization, *theosis*, ascension, deification or liberation. Devotees of all religions and spiritual streams can equally cultivate to attain them. They are the natural result of spiritual practice and not the monopoly of any person, sect, spiritual school, tradition, practice or religion. However, Buddhism, Hinduism, Jainism, Taoism, Sufism, Confucianism, Yoga and other traditions have different names for these common stages of achievement.

An individual on the spiritual path might cultivate prayers, mantra recitation, pranayama, concentration practice, stretching *asanas*, meditation, bhakti, *anapana*, *nei-gong*, kundalini yoga, visualization, sexual cultivation, mental introspection, a proper diet, good deeds and other cultivation techniques to attain the higher bodies, but if their cultivation of mind, body and behavior are insufficient they will not attain the first subtle body and rise to the spiritual realms during life.

Lacking sufficient cultivation, however, they will still achieve from their efforts a higher measure of good health, longevity and an improved fortune in this life and the next. For instance, cultivation efforts that affect your Qi/Prana can cure a man of disease, and in the absence of disease one will see health improvements and the prolongation of one's life, namely greater health and longevity. Furthermore, once they die such individuals will have an easier time of cultivating the higher bodies as a deva.

One who practices policing their mind and actions through mental watching/witnessing will also cultivate their character and good fortune due to the avoidance of error. A vigor for doing good deeds will also bear positive karmic fruit in terms of your Qi purification too. These attainments are therefore earned by human beings who cultivate to halfway between the spiritual and physical realms because of their efforts.

THE THREE REQUIREMENTS

The way to these transcendental spiritual attainments is essentially a Path of Yoga. In the final analysis, for success in religious practice and spiritual practice it is all Yoga in the end. The spiritual path is entirely a pathway of Yoga. There are three major requirements for success.

First, you must cultivate meditation practice.

Second, through various exercises and emotions you must actively cultivate the Qi/Prana (vital energy or wind element) of your physical body. This is sometimes called Qi purification, kundalini cultivation, *kriya* yoga or *nei-gong*. If you do not actively cultivate your Qi/Prana then the subtle body attainment will not likely be reached during this life.

Third, you must cultivate spiritual virtues, values and qualities, which is the road of self-improvement. You must engage in compassionate behavior that eschews self-centeredness and focus on helping others. Taoism symbolically says "you need to perform 3,000 great good deeds in order to earn the merit for self-realization," meaning that only those who work on purifying their behavior and unselfishly work on benefitting others can achieve the Tao. The spiritual path is not divorced from active compassionate effort to help others reduce their sufferings and find joy.

If you do not cultivate good behavior and virtuous ways, then no spiritual beings with higher transcendental bodies will help you achieve the higher spiritual bodies. Their help is necessary in stimulating, purifying and transforming the Qi/Prana of your present body so that you can generate an advanced subtle body from within your physical body. They must use their own energies inside you to move your Qi to help the process. Who will do that for you if you are not a virtuous individual?

If you do not cultivate your body's Qi/Prana, namely your vital energy or life force, then you will not be able to generate and free an independent spiritual body, made of Qi/Prana, from the matrix of your physical body shell. You must engage in many spiritual practices to cultivate/purify the Qi/Prana of your physical nature so that your internal subtle body made of Qi can finally be released while living. External spiritual help, in addition to your personal *tapas* or work at spiritual cultivation, is needed for this success.

If you are a man you must cultivate sexual restraint/discipline so as not to lose your Jing (semen) on this pathway. If you are a man and let the "elixir" leak then because of its dissipation your Qi/Prana will be lost upon ejaculation, and then that energy will not be available to open up Qi channels within your body to fully strengthen the spirit body duplicate of your physical body – your subtle body. "Without water in the boiler there is no steam in the pipes. Without gas in the tank there is no power in the car."

If you do not cultivate meditation practice then you will always cling to your thought tendencies, habit patterns and lower-level mindsets. You will not be able to fully rise above your animal nature and your monkey mind to improve your character if you don't learn how to free yourself of prior tendencies, which meditation helps you do. Furthermore, mentally clinging to thoughts as a habit will prevent the vital energy of your body from beginning to move, transform and purify. Also, without a mind of openness, you will not be able to accept all the good and bad that you will see with your spiritual bodies. Lastly, you must cultivate an empty mind centered on the pure self so that you can remain impassive to emotions and pleasure, and retain control over your body and behavior during the Twelve Years of the kundalini awakening when devas come and daily give you problems like a pack of barbaric animals.

If you do not cultivate witnessing meditation practice where you always watch your thoughts to improve your behavior then you will never cultivate virtue, propriety and the consummate conduct (in accordance with reason and wisdom) required of the spiritual path. You will never naturally refine your Qi/Prana to a higher level of excellence.

If you do not cultivate concentration skills so that you can develop mental stability, you will always flit from thought to thought without ever being able to discard mental distractions and afflictions, settle mentally, and find mental peace. You will not be able to get free of attachment to concepts, abandon language and find a state of blissful presence without much thought. A wandering mind is usually a distracted, unhappy mind whereas a mind that can concentrate finds bliss or can accomplish great things.

Without concentration skills you will not be able to remain focused for a long time so as to be able to solve problems that arise in life, or do great deeds. Concentration and commitment to a course of action (which is also a form of concentration or "staying-with-itness") are key life skills necessary for success and achievement for many types of ventures. Perseverance, determination, willpower, commitment, focus and grit are all matters of concentration, the ability to stay with something and "stick with it."

If you do not learn to cultivate an open (empty) mind that can accept everything then you will not be able to bear what you see with your subtle body when you become a deva, including all the hidden bad thoughts and actions of other sentient beings. It will then be difficult to practice kindness and compassion, which are primary prerequisites for success on the path.

Basically, "emptiness" meditation practice is necessary for cultivating your Qi/Prana, changing your behavior and attaining the subtle body.

CULTIVATING MEDITATION[30]

Most spiritual schools promote the spiritual path as seeing/realizing the original nature, which is empty of attributes like a void and therefore sometimes called "Emptiness," to encourage meditation practice. They say many things to promote the practice of meditation such as "the original nature is consciousness without consciousness," "the Self is pure Knowledge," "Brahman is the only witness," "the Pure Beingness is the same as awareness" and so forth.

They often make analogies about the original nature being like pure consciousness, luminous mind, empty mind, the ultimate "Witness" and so forth in order to encourage meditation practice. They want people to become aware of awareness itself, which is available because we have a conscious mind, and teach that we need to detach from mentally clinging to thoughts so that they internally die down and we can experience a higher state of mental peace that is akin to the natural state of the mind before thoughts are born. They also want people to look at their minds and learn how to control their thoughts and afflictions.

They commonly make the analogy that a relatively empty mind, pure consciousness or clear awareness is similar to the unmoving original nature, which is like continuous empty space without attributes, and that thoughts are similar to the Shakti or energy or Word that arises within It. They often say that the fundamental state of the mind is emptiness, the natural state of the mind is empty, or the fundamental nature of the mind is unborn or unmanifest and so on to encourage emptiness meditation.

Advaita Vedanta says that in the motionless original nature (Parabrahman) somehow there arose movement in the form of a manifestation of energy (wind), which occurred in the original essence that never undergoes any modifications. The real nature of that energy is therefore the unborn substrate like the void of space, from which all other phenomena are also somehow born.

In the same way, it is said that thoughts somehow arise out of the emptiness of clear awareness. They arise within pristine clear awareness through a process we don't fully understand, but they indeed arise and produce a conventional world of things for us in our minds. They mentally produce for us a conditionally derived world within our consciousness that

---

[30] See *Meditation Case Studies*, *Visualization Power*, and *The Little Book of Meditation*.

we take as reality. The picture of reality they create is quite limited. Also, the thoughts generated by the mind never stay and therefore exist in the nature of a dream. The same goes for the phenomena they create/recognize.

Most spiritual schools promote meditation practice since most practitioners will not succeed at generating the subtle body, but meditation practice will still help the faithful improve their lives in many ways such as by improving their mental clarity, health, longevity, behavior and fortune. Furthermore, spiritual masters normally want most people to refrain from energy work that will attract the participation of devas who will often cause troubles due to a lack of self-restraint, so they encourage meditation practice that will get all these other benefits instead.

Meditation will improve many areas of your life. For many reasons it is the foremost spiritual practice.

Meditation practice always leads to a purification of your Qi/Prana to some degree. Your Qi/Prana will automatically start to move when you let go of your mind/thoughts, and it will then start to undergo a process of purification due to those movements. By meditating you will therefore start to purify/transform your Qi/Prana and one of the natural results of more purified Qi is that you will experience greater longevity in Heaven before any heavenly death and rebirth. Virtuous conduct and positive emotions also purify your Qi/Prana and start purifying it of a coarse animalistic nature, but are not as directly powerful as meditation.

Meditation also trains people to focus their awareness on their mind's inner doings so that individuals can more easily police their thoughts, words and deeds (behavior) and become better human beings, which will improve their fates and fortunes. Meditation is the basis of introspection, self-policing, witnessing or self-regulation that trains your focus, attention and awareness so that you can bring thoughts and actions under greater volitional control, thereby improving your life and fortune.

In order to encourage the practice of meditation the original nature is often described as empty of attributes, formless, imperceptible, unknowable or unfathomable by thought, and even an undisturbed state of consciousness. The analogy with an empty, clear or pristine mind of awareness is deliberate. The description of an empty original nature is used to promote the practice of "meditation without attributes." It also prompts cultivation of a mind of dispassion that can, in imitation of the original nature, freely give up craving to become calm, peaceful, and blissful. Tirumalai Krishnamacharya said, "Knowing all objects to be impermanent, let not their contact blind you. Resolve again and again to be aware of the self that is permanent." Many such instructions from masters are available such as "Rest your mind in your essential nature."

Thayumanavar also instructed, "Ever-permanent, without any blemish, without any ignorance, without support, ever-full, undecayingly pure, far as well as near, like the Light beyond the three luminaries (Sun, Moon and Fire), the One Charm that includes all, overflowing with Bliss, undiscernible to mind or speech, standing as the Colossus of Consciousness—on that vastness of the beginning of Infinite Bliss, let us meditate."

Spiritual schools also commonly say that to recognize God (the original nature) is the ultimate aim in life. They say that the crown jewel of spiritual studies is that one should stabilize in the One Without Qualities that is similar to empty space without borders – your original nature from which everything is born, the ultimate mother of manifestation. This gives rise to forms of meditation practice that are images of emptiness in some way, and thus are called "emptiness" or "empty mind" meditations.

These are all didactic devices with an ulterior motive. No one can possess consciousness without a body because the structure of the brain is required to produce thoughts. Thoughts are needed for there to be Knowledge, awareness or consciousness, and all we can ever know or experience are our thoughts. No concept can accurately image something pure, infinite or empty of attributes. We can only mentally know images rather than a true ultimate purity. We therefore can never directly know the beingness of the original nature unless we ourselves are a state of non-existence, annihilation or total mental dissolution. Thus the idea is for people to try to cultivate emptiness in order to let go of their thoughts and Qi, but not to attain a state of mindlessness absent of thoughts.

Images of emptiness formed by the mind are not real emptiness. Therefore, "Nothing can be said about the condition of the absolute nature using thoughts." Nevertheless, teachings on the original nature give rise to the meditation practice of natural empty mind whereby you imitate the original nature by letting thoughts arise without mental clinging. It is colloquially said one can "become one with the Father" or "find Union with the Supreme" so as to also encourage meditation practice like this.

While consciousness is often described as a duality of pristine clear awareness and moving conceptions/perceptions where the background of empty mind is considered to be pure awareness/consciousness absent of thoughts, a state lacking in thoughts is actually non-existence or a nonexperience state such as sleep or coma where there are no thoughts at all. Actually, even in deep dreamless sleep or within a coma there is mental activity, but it is not very discernible. Some schools will say there are states of no mental content whatsoever, but is that really so, and of what benefit would that be for existence other than rest? Only if you are physically or mentally annihilated, extinguished or exterminated are there no thoughts at all.

The reason that meditation practice is promoted is because it leads to the purification of your Qi, the purification or transformation of your Qi leads to the attainment of the subtle body, the subtle body is the first heavenly spiritual attainment, and its attainment serves as the foundation for higher body attainments that are essentially the true spiritual path of transcendence that leads to consummate union with your spiritual Self.

The nature of our consciousness is that thoughts are born and perish again from moment to moment, ever streaming through the mind like a violent torrent of water that flows onward without rest. The sequence of thoughts that arise in the mind flows onward without interruption, never giving rise to mental peace. However, meditation practice can give pause to the ceaseless flow of thoughts and somewhat silence the torrent of consciousness so that you can taste the natural pristine nature of your mind. It is a way for you to slow down thoughts and find internal peace, called mental bliss. When that happens your Qi/Prana will start to transform.

Basically, consciousness encounters inputs from the visual, auditory and other senses, and because of these impulses is then continually stirred to perpetually maintain its onward flux. Consciousness is continually perfumed by impressions that continually form the seeds for new thoughts to be born. Every thought eventually perishes but before doing so serves as a cause that gives rise to new thoughts that are then born. Thus a thought never remains continuously single nor can stay even when you concentrate on holding one with stability.

Concentration, or being able to stay with a mental subject/activity for a long time, such as holding a thought with stability, is the basis of most higher accomplishments. Its importance has given rise to various forms of spiritual concentration practice such as visualization exercises to hold pictures in the mind for long periods of time as a form of mental training. By practicing concentration you learn to ignore or banish distractions within the mind that would normally interrupt your focus and attention. Furthermore, a focused mind tends to be a happy state of consciousness whereas a wandering mind tends to be a distracted, unhappy mind. All these points prompt the practice of meditation with attributes.

Contrast the ever-moving, ever-changeful, ever-vibrating Shakti that produces all phenomena within the changeless original nature that is all-pervading and omnipresent like space. Note the analogy with energy and empty space, and the analogy between empty clear awareness (said to be the natural state of your mind) and the thoughts arising within consciousness. Such analogies are often highlighted in order to motivate the practice of meditation – meditation without attributes, and meditation with attributes.

It is also often explained that in the motionless original nature (Parabrahman) that is continuous without attributes, somehow there arose movement in the form of a manifestation of energy (wind), which cannot occur in the original nature/essence that never undergoes any modification, and yet did thus producing phenomena. Analogously, the natural state of our mind is the pristine peace of the original nature that is free from emotion, excitement, desire, and other perturbations. It is this naturally pure, clean state of our mind that we need to learn how to cultivate.

It is also sometimes said that the natural state of your mind is like a clear light able to illuminate phenomena when they appear. Therefore the base of consciousness is sometimes called "uncreated light" by some religions. Even with these expedient explanations meditation is acknowledged to lead to a resting of thoughts that reveals the "natural state of your mind" that resembles the original nature absent of forms. This natural state of mind absent of thoughts is often called pure consciousness, luminous mind, or pristine awareness. To realize that the natural state of consciousness is empty is called "seeing the Tao," or "realizing the mind's true nature."

Thus we have three forms of mental training often used in spiritual schools: concentration practice to develop stability of the mind; witnessing practice where you watch your thoughts so that you can correct your attitudes and behaviors; and emptiness meditation which brings mental peace by imitating the original nature.

Naturally there are other forms of meditation practice and mind training as well, such as contemplation practice that exercises your mental powers of logic, analysis and discrimination for various purposes such as to analyze your mental processes, afflictions and their roots. Learning how to use your mind in different ways so that all its capabilities bloom is a celebration of the gift of consciousness that is part of the spiritual trail.

SELF-IMPROVEMENT TOWARDS VIRTUE[31]

The first stage of the spiritual path is a stage of virtue provisioning where you try to eliminate impure thoughts, habits and inclinations, abandon evil deeds and in their place cultivate more ethical, virtuous ways. It is a stage of seeking, study and self-improvement. You commence upon a path of cultivating virtue and higher values to transcend your animal nature, and by all people cultivating moral harmony within themselves society achieves civil harmony rather than chaos. You work on purifying your thoughts, words and deeds and practice mindfulness of your inner and outward behavior so that they can be purified and ennobled.

The goal is to cultivate a strong moral, ethical and virtuous basis of inner mental and outer physical behavior, along with a contagious beingness and joy for life. Another goal is to develop the habit of performing good deeds in mind, body and speech, such as selfless charitable work for others.

This foundational phase is also a stage of study where you first start to study spiritual cultivation teachings, and increase your stores of spiritual wisdom by studying spiritual texts so that you understand the cultivation path. This will help you live a morally virtuous life.

Christianity and Judaism use the Ten Commandments for ethical guidance, Buddhism speaks of the Ten Wholesome Actions, Moslems look to the Koran and Sharia for ethical guidance, Confucianism has the Five Virtues and Five Relationships, and Hindu ethics are to be found in the Vedas and Upanishads while Yoga distinctly points to Yama and Niyama. All schools and religions champion certain virtues, values and codes of conduct and have various scriptures on ethics as their foundational teachings.

Basically, ethics involves concepts of right and wrong behavior, meaning that there are things you do and things you don't do, things to refrain from and things to strive for in terms of your relationships with yourself, others, insentient phenomena, society, the environment, and the universe.

The primary rules of ethical restraint involve being respectful of others and therefore not doing to (imposing upon) others what you would not want them to do to you; not aggressing against another's person, property, health or liberty. Basically you refrain from doing harm to others or yourself. The primary ethical principles include more than just this short list and can be

---

[31] See *Color Me Confucius*, especially Chapters 6, 8, 9, 10 and 11, *Liao Fan's Four Lessons*, and *The Autobiography of Benjamin Franklin*.

found in most basic religious teachings.

For instance, in Hinduism the *Mahabharata* says, "This is the sum of duty. Do naught to others which if done to thee would cause thee pain." In Islam a Hadith runs, "No one of you is a believer until he desires for his brother that which he desires for himself." In Judaism the *Talmud* says, "What is hateful to you, do not to your fellow men. That is the entire law; all the rest is commentary." In Buddhism the *Udanavarga* states, "Hurt not others with that which pains yourself." In Christianity the *Gospel of Matthew* says, "So in everything, do to others what you would have them do to you, for this sums up the law and the Prophets." In Zoroastrianism it is said, "That nature only is good when it shall not do unto another whatever is not good for its own self."

The list of disciplinary rules also includes restraints of self-control such as injunctions not to steal, lie, kill, commit violence (non-injury), engage in cruelty, engage in sexual excess, overindulge in sensual pleasures and so on.

The active principles include treating others as you would want to be treated yourself, offering charity and kindness in compassionate concern for others' welfare, doing what you know is right rather than wrong, and more. Cultivating ethics is the act of cultivating joy for life along with higher values and virtues that ennoble your character and raise you above your animal nature, which purifies your Qi, conduct and fortune. Different individuals and religions have proposed diverse lists of "virtues" that are ideals of consummate conduct and self-perfection. They raise you above your animal nature by requiring you to gain control over your passions and desires so that they don't rule you. They entail elevating your thoughts, words and behavior, which is also called ennobling, purifying or spiritualizing them, and this also nourishes your vital force (Qi/Prana).

Wisdom demands that ethics be applied according to common sense and circumstances, and not according to unbreakable laws taken literally from religious texts that are never updated and ossify society, as has happened in Confucianism, Islam and Judaism. Jesus became a role model of proper behavior when he spoke of rescuing a mule on the Sabbath even though religious law said it should be a day without work. As another instance, while normally you would not lie you would not tell a murderer the location of his prey. The well-being of others is central to ethical decision-making rather than whether or not you break some written rule or code of conduct.

Rules and codes of conduct can be imposed on societies by governments, traditions, customs or religions, which will perfume the people in a certain way over time, but in reality ethics must be deeply internally cognized so that you do what is right despite outside influences and urgings. Wisdom and compassion are to be your goals and guides to true ethical behavior. One of the best principles for an ethical life is to simply refrain from harming others; don't do to others what you wouldn't want done to yourself.

To cultivate the road of self-improvement required of the spiritual path, which means purifying your behavior and the thoughts that give rise to it, you must always be watching your mind and policing your actions. You must try to eliminate automatic bad habits and form new good habits in their place. You want to eliminate internal mental and emotional afflictions that interfere with the determination of, and execution of, wise and skillful behavior. You want your attention to always be monitoring your behavior to bring it under voluntary control and in line with higher ways.

This is why you need to learn meditative introspection, witnessing or watching practice, and try to bring that habit with you into regular daily life.

One way of transforming errant behavioral habits that lack virtue, wisdom or skillfulness is through the method of inner watching, introspection, or mental witnessing wherein you continuously watch and police your thoughts and behavior through heightened awareness. You learn to do this through the practice of meditation. When bad thoughts or actions are noticed/witnessed you try to immediately cut them off and/or replace them with something better. When the right thoughts arrive to do good then instead of remaining complacent you should also rouse yourself with vigor to do those good deeds.

Another way of creating new good habits is through the immeasurable meditations, such as found within Buddhism, that involve perfuming or impregnating your mind, body, Qi/Prana and behavior with boundless positive impulses/emotions bound to take root and bear fruit in this life and the next. Cultivating a sunny disposition can be done in this way.

There are many others methods that help you change your character tendencies or habit energies, cut off bad thoughts and deeds, create good thoughts and deeds, and purify your mind.

You are trying to act with wisdom and skillfulness, which means that you should try to surmise the likely outcome of events if you act in a certain way, and then you should act in the best way possible after evaluating all your alternatives. You want to adopt best practices wherever possible, work to improve situations for the better by cutting off errant ways while supporting what is good, and act in a way that is not just expedient for the moment but best for the short-term, intermediate-term and long-term whenever possible.

All mental states that produce thoughts, words and deeds are accompanied by distractions, disturbances and afflictions. Cultivation practice and wisdom can help you dissolve mental afflictions at their root so that they no longer arise, or help you cut them off or transform them when they do appear. You must cultivate away afflictions to create mental purity and achieve inner peace despite the vicissitudes of life, and cultivate the Qi/Prana of your body to attain the subtle body and higher.

Eliminating mental afflictions that commonly arise within your mind is part of the spiritual path. Remember, on the pathway of spiritual transformation there must be physical health, ethical health, mental health, and intellectual health as your foundations.

GENERAL PRINCIPLES OF QI/PRANA PRACTICE[32]

In spiritual cultivation you proceed from study to practice, and from practice to study. You should mix the two just as flour and water are mixed together to make bread. You attain the goal from perfection in study and practice together because study alone will not strengthen and then set the inner subtle body free, which normally happens only upon death. In other words, study alone will not get you to the first dhyana attainment, which is a deva body, because it is only achieved through cultivation practice.

For the generation of an independent subtle body during life you need meditation work and energy work on your Qi/Prana. Furthermore, if you are not a virtuous person, spiritual beings will not help you in this process either. Therefore, it is impossible to succeed unless you are also a virtuous human being who is also devoted to improving himself by perfecting his behavior.

The principles of effective practice differ for each type of spiritual cultivation technique. They always take into account the welfare of your mind and body – you are never to hurt your mind or body through practice! You are always to preserve and improve your health and well-being otherwise it will be difficult to proceed and succeed. Remember, the deva

---

[32] See *Nyasa Yoga, The Yoga of Siddha Tirumular, Yoga Yajnavalkya*, etcetera.

body is a duplicate of your physical body, so don't harm it or disfigure it in any way.

The main objectives of spiritual practices are normally to calm your mind and stimulate the Qi/Prana of your body into moving so that this purifies your Qi/Prana and gradually strengthens your inner subtle body of Qi/Prana to the extent that it can finally leave your physical shell while you are alive. Then it becomes your main body of being although still attached to your physical body, which you learn how to control using that body. This is sometimes called "attaining control over the life process within your self" because Qi/Prana is the body's vital energy or life force.

You should practice as many different types of spiritual exercise as possible, each of which works according to different principles for transforming your Qi/Prana. Through *simultaneous* practice of many *different types* of practice at the same time, each which affects your Qi/Prana via *different principles*, you will maximize your chances for real Qi/Prana transformations that will purify its nature and produce the independent subtle body quickest. Since you don't know which techniques will work best for transforming your Qi/Prana, the use of multiple techniques simultaneously, each of which works on affecting your Qi/Prana according to different principles, is highly recommended.

For instance, one might during a single day practice meditation, Mantrayana recitation, pranayama, yoga stretching with visualization on your muscles, and inner *nei-gong* work (*anapana*) to move your Qi. This is an example of practicing multiple techniques simultaneously (on the same day or practice schedule) rather than just one per day or per practice session, each of which transforms (purifies) your Qi/Prana via different principles. The harder you work – the more types of methods you practice and the longer and more consistently you practice – the higher your chances for success, and the quicker your success if success is to come. Success is the result of consistent effort applied across time. The longer and deeper you practice the more profound will be your results.

Some of the major principles of practice for different spiritual exercises are as follows:

Mantra Recitation: Reciting mantras (or prayers) quiets your mind. It also transforms your Qi/Prana, which is typically accompanied by sensations of heat or warmth, because spiritual beings will respond to each particular one due to their individual vows to protect/help those who recite them. Different mantras, prayers, and spiritual songs (as well as books, passages, and spiritual texts) are "answered" or attended to by different enlightened masters who assume responsibility for them by transforming the Qi/Prana of practitioner who use them, so a good one is one that you feel moves the Qi/Prana within your body. To make this practice even more effective, combine the recitation with visualization, the effort of generating emotions which move your Qi/Prana, and try to stimulate/vibrate the Qi in different areas of your body according to the sounds. Then mantra or prayer recitation becomes Mantrayana.

Mantrayana: Certain mantra sounds work best at naturally vibrating (stimulating) the Qi/Prana in certain sections of your body through resonance, such as the sounds within "Om Ah Hung" affecting the Qi/Prana in your head and arms; chest region; and abdomen and legs, respectively. "Aim Hreem Shreem" (where "Aim" is pronounced "I'm") can be used to move your Qi/Prana in the same body sections respectively. Or, you can try to feel each syllable in your body *as an entire whole* with each recitation. Or, for instance, when reciting "Ah" you might feel the energy start in your head and move towards your feet as you hold the syllable, or start from your feet and move upwards, or start within your stomach area and move outwards, and so on for each syllable respectively. You can recite one, two, three, four or five syllable mantras to cultivate the Qi/Prana of that many different sections of your body respectively. You can recite mantras on certain *bindus*, *marma* points or acupuncture points too. If you recite mantras while trying to feel, move, excite or stimulate the Qi/Prana in different areas of the body, which can be helped by also simultaneously using emotional excitement or other enervation techniques, and if you also put your mind/will on those areas to move your Qi/Prana in conjunction with reciting and feeling those sound syllables within you, you will quickly stimulate your Qi into building a stronger subtle body. Adding visualization efforts to the body section at the same time - such as by using your imagination to mentally flood an area with bright light or change its color, etcetera - will also help to move its Qi/Prana. The best mantras have sounds that actually move/vibrate your Yin Qi or Yang Qi because those energies resonate in particular sections of your body just as "Om" seems to vibrate in the head and "Ah" resonates in the chest. "Ram" (Rang, Rahlam, Rah) and "Vam" (Vah, Vang, Lam, Lang, Nam) are also very useful. Some mantras are constructed to call for Qi/Prana help from higher spiritual beings, some work on moving your Yang Qi/Prana through direct resonance, some work on moving your Yin Qi/Prana, and some work on moving both your Yang Qi/Prana and Yin Qi/Prana. Therefore, mantras can "raise your kundalini," move/stimulate both your Yin Qi and Yang Qi, and particularly vibrate the Qi/Prana in certain sections of your body.

Meditation: A variety of meditation practices might be tried. Please see *Nyasa Yoga, Meditation Case Studies, Easy Meditation Lessons, The Little Book of Meditation, Color Me Confucius, Twenty-five Doors to Meditation, Meditation Techniques of the Buddhist and Taoist Masters* as well as the *Vijnana Bhairava* and Adiswarananda's *Meditation and Its Practices*. Many religions promote different types of meditation practice that can be tried.

Yoga Asanas/Martial Arts: Correct posture is an indispensable requirement for the successful practice of pranayama and sitting meditation. Any comfortable posture held for spiritual practice is an *asana*. That pose is best which continues to be comfortable for the greatest length of time while allowing you to cultivate your mind, emotions and body (Qi/Prana) correctly. Stretching your muscles by holding an *asana* posture will also make it easier for your Qi/Prana to move within them. You can either practice moving your Qi/Prana when your body is held motionless in *asana, bandha* and *mudra* positions (explained in Yoga texts) that stretch muscles, or when the body is moving (as in dance, martial arts, athletics). This is called "combining your breath" with your practice, although "breath" means your internal energy or Qi/Prana. Thus you should always practice combining your vital energy (Qi or Prana) with your physical practice in order to more quickly cultivate the subtle body. If you also combine visualization efforts on the particular muscles being stretched, and mantra practice on those same muscles in order to stimulate the Qi/Prana within them, and add emotional content during your practice time so as to stimulate your overall Qi/Prana into moving, you will greatly enhance your efforts. To transform a body into the healthiest state possible, diet and medical remedies and physical manipulation are important. For optimizing your body structure, first undergo chiropractic treatments to align your bones, next undergo AMIT therapy to activate all your muscles, and then engage in either passive exercises (Yoga, Pilates, etc.) or active exercises (dance, martial arts, etc.) in conjunction with inner Qi/Prana exercises and mental work.

Pranayama: Pranayama breathing exercises can stabilize your mind and have a therapeutic effect on your body. The first important step to breathing exercises is to master the *asana* of a stable posture and then afterwards pranayama. Pranayama is ultimately the control of the Prana/Qi of your body that is attained in stages. Pranayama expertise begins with the regulation of your respiratory breath(ing) and then proceeds to gradually gaining control over the life-currents or inner vital force of the body, namely your Qi/Prana. In other words, pranayama aims to help you start gaining control of the life-currents of Qi/Prana within your body through control of your breathing and breath. Later you can simply grab/move this Qi/Prana by your will, which then becomes *anapana* practice, *nei-dan* exercises, kundalini yoga, *kriya* yoga or *nei-gong* work. When Pranayama is attended by the mental recitation of any mantra, it is one hundred times more powerful than when unattended by any mantra recitation. If you simultaneously visualize Qi/Prana currents moving or held stationary within your body during pranayama practice and try to feel these energies, this will also increase its power. Pranayama attainments depend upon the intensity of the efforts of the practitioner. It is recommended to practice them two to four times per day when you are not tired, worried and have an empty stomach.

Kumbhaka Pranayama: The *Yoga-sutras of Patanjali* states, "Regulation of breath or the control of Prana is the stoppage of inhalation and exhalation, which follows after securing that steadiness of posture or seat." This is *kumbhaka* pranayama. Yoga texts have many exercises for *kumbhaka* breath retention, which can be learnt therefrom. If a breath retention technique is not practiced according to rhythmical ratios of exhalation, inhalation and retention, but for the purpose of holding the breath as long as possible, follow these principles: hold your breath as deep within your body as possible, for as long as possible, using as little force and as few muscles as possible, and then forcibly expel it as quickly as possible. Or, use whatever classical instructions are provided within the instructional text you are using. Combine with freediving exercises in order to learn how to learn how to hold your breath longer, and periodically measure the length of your retention period so that you can track your progress and try to improve upon best efforts.

Anapana/Kundalini Yoga: Kundalini Yoga, *kriya* yoga and *anapana* practice involve moving the Qi/Prana of your body in various ways via your will (thoughts), which is also basically *nei-gong* or *nei-dan* work. You train to push your Qi/Prana by using your mind such as by rotating/moving it hundreds to thousands of times per session in certain ways. You might focus on a body region to bring Qi/Prana into that area, or use your will to move it in various ways all over your body and especially in particular areas. The entire purpose is Qi/Prana stimulation to open up the Qi channels (*nadis*) in all your tissues, and to circulate your Qi/Prana over the molecules and molecular bonds of your atoms again and again and again. Masters will do this to your body continuously during the Twelve Year kundalini transformation process if you have the merit. Another method concerns fixing of the Qi/Prana in the various locations of the body and taking/moving it slowly, step by step, and stage by stage, to other sections of your body. For instance, the Yogi Boganathar suggests leading your Qi/Prana from the big toes to the ankle, knee, thigh, genitals, navel, heart, neck, uvula, nose, space between the eyebrows, forehead and crown of the head; *Yoga Yajnavalkya* has a different sequence. You can also hold your Qi/Prana at these vital points. A common introductory practice only is to also work on moving your Qi/Prana up and down your spine into your brain hundreds of times per day or to circulate it in loops and circular orbits and to hold it in various places. Also, specific activities of Qi/Prana practice in various parts of your body will bring different results/delights to a practitioner in accordance with their ability to move their Qi/Prana to these spots and rest in them. However, just as in martial arts you should practice moving your Qi/Prana hundreds to thousands of times per day for the quickest results of spiritual practice.

Visualization Practice: Practice holding images steady in your mind for as long as possible to build your powers of concentration. Also, practice holding images of Qi/Prana movement – such as flames, fires, lights, the sun, etcetera - in your abdomen, heart, brain, and other areas of your body as is done in Jainism (flames in the abdomen), Orthodox Christianity (flames in the heart), Buddhism, Taoism, Yoga Vajrayana, etcetera. If appropriate, add stimulating emotions to such mental images in order to help move your Qi/Prana. One yogic practice is to also visualize your Qi/Prana at certain points within your body and then take/move/lead it step by step, and stage by stage, to other locations.[33] This can help remove various disorders in different body areas. Also, you should practice visualizing light and/or colors at certain points within your body, and sometimes in special shapes. Another practice is to inhale to fill your entire body with breath, hold that state for awhile while feeling your Qi everywhere within you and visualizing that all your flesh is red in color, and then visualizing your bones shining bright white and giving off light as you exhale and afterwards, thus holding a state of empty exhalation while maintaining the visualization of your bones giving off shining light.

Sexual Cultivation: As practiced in several cultivation schools, use the emotional excitation and happiness-joy-bliss from the passion of sexual activity, which stirs your Qi/Prana, together with physical sexual technique to move the Qi/Prana in various regions within your body. Sex can be a powerful force for moving your internal Qi/Prana, as can sexual excitement. It is one of the fastest ways to transform the Qi/Prana of your body, but its pursuit leads to all sorts of violations, infractions, problems, misconduct and abuse so it is not allowed in most cultivations schools. Celibacy then requires extra efforts in restraint, pranayama and inner *tummo* heat cultivation instead using a variety of techniques. This need is also symbolized when Shiva opened his eye to burn Kamadeva, god of lust, and

---

[33] See *Yoga Yajnavalkya*, trans. by A. G. Mohan (Svastha Yoga Pte Ltd.,2013).

turned his body into ashes. Similarly, in the *Surangama Sutra* Ucchusmma was given the name "Fire Head" because he cultivated by contemplating/envisioning that his body became a mass of raging fire, after which he could cultivate the Qi throughout his body. However, the story of the supreme ascetic Rishyashringa bears relevancy that the rains must fall to end drought, and so a courtesan was required to match his ardent cultivation. For non-celibate cultivators, men should try to prevent ejaculation during sex so as not to lose their Qi/Prana (and have to cease activity) whereas women are free to orgasm.

Bhakti Yoga: As practiced in Christianity (by focusing on Jesus or the Virgin Mary) and in Hinduism (focusing on Krishna, Kali and other deities), the purpose is to self-generate ardent devotion to such a deep extent that your emotions end up moving your Qi/Prana all over your body. The ardent emotional states are also a form of "immeasurable emotion" practice taught within Buddhism. Bhakti devotional practice is meant to stimulate certain emotions and your Qi/Prana into moving. Simple reverence, as practiced in religious ceremonies and rituals, is also a form of meditation practice for quieting and purifying the mind that also affects your Qi/Prana.

Diet: Eat the right foods, minerals, herbs, and supplements to bring about a state of optimal health, including detoxification as necessary. Some foods, such as spicy cuisine, will make your Yang Qi arise while others will cause a cooling reaction within your body, thus affecting your Yin Qi. At times one can ingest certain foods to adjust the Qi/Prana of their body rather than just eat for health and perfect growth. For instance, during winter one can drink warming teas such as Pu'er, and during Summer cooling teas such as Jasmine tea to help adjust the body.

Yin Qi Cultivation: Sickness, fear, fright, anxiety, sadness, helplessness, depression, guilt, disgust, chills, thoughts of suicide, imagining that you absorb lunar energy from the moon (cool moonlight), water visualizations, attending funerals or cremations, visualizing/imagining that you undergo age regression, fantasizing sexually that you transform into a girl (femininity practices), etcetera are all situations and methods used to cultivate the Yin Qi/Prana of your body by giving rise to Yin thoughts that stimulate your Yin Qi into moving. It is most common to cultivate your Yin Qi by reciting the mantras/prayers (or performing the sadhanas) of female Buddhas, the Hell Buddha Ksitigarbha, performing cooling water visualizations that "wash" your body's Qi (Yin Qi is cool, not warm), or performing lunar energy absorption sadhanas. When sadhus in India sit under the hot sun surrounded by burning coals or burning cow dung, they are using special methods to cultivate their cooling Yin Qi. The female Mahavidyas of India

– Kali, Tara, Tripura Sundari, Bhuvaneshvari, Bhairavi, Chinnamasta, Dhumavati, Bagalamukhi, Matangi and Kamala – as well as the nine manifestations of the goddess Durgha represent different types of Yin Qi cultivation. Tara, Kuan Yin, and Zhunti are female Buddhas with appropriate mantras and practices as well. In ancient days the cults of goddesses such as Isis, Demeter, Diana etc. provided Yin Qi cultivation methods too. Many countries even have Yin holidays – such as Halloween, Mexico's Day of the Dead (*Dia de los Muertos*) or China's Tomb Sweeping Day – which are used by Buddhas to help transform the Qi of a large group of people on a vast scale. When people suffer nightmares or "see ghosts" this is sometimes due to spiritual beings trying to frighten them to influence their Yin Qi into arising, and when Zen masters develop irrational fears of death this is due to the influence of Buddhas and devas as well to make their Yin Qi arise. When you are sick it is easier to cultivate your Yin Qi since your Yang Qi is depleted at that time. For an adept going through the Twelve Year kundalini process who has reached the stage of Shariputra's goddess flower lesson within Vimalakirti's ten-foot square room – like Ramakrishna, Arjuna or Hercules in women's clothing - *Shikhandi and Other Tales They Don't Tell You* (Devadutt Pattanaik) is relevant.

Yang Qi Cultivation: Anger, pride, courage, triumph, confidence, euphoria, sexual excitement, exhilaration, enthusiasm, joy, cheerfulness, awe, optimism, love, strength, mirth, aliveness, masculinity practices, standard meditation practice, sunshine visualizations, attending weddings, active exercise, fighting, etcetera are all situations used to cultivate the Yang Qi/Prana of your body. Some foods cause a heating/warming reaction within your body which is also Yang cultivation. When Tibetan monks sit in the icy cold and melt the snow around them, they are using special methods to cultivate/activate their warming Yang Qi. Fire visualizations and kundalini Yoga exercises are typical Yang Qi cultivation methods.

Five Elements Qi Cultivation: While it is said that there are two basic types of Qi/Prana – Yin and Yang – one can also think of the body as being composed of the Qi/energy of five elements, or of many other components. Thus, methods have been developed to help you cultivate the Earth element Qi of your body such as through exercise of your muscles and diet which affects the composition of your physical nature, or the white skeleton visualization on your bones. The Water element of your body can be cultivated by emotional exercises (immeasurables absorption and projection) and visualization or *nei-gong* practice on your glands. The Fire or Warmth element of your body can be cultivated by kundalini practices and internal fire visualizations, and there are various ways to cultivate fire samadhi. The Wind element of your body can be cultivated by various pranayama, Mantrayana, meditation, kundalini, *kriya* yoga, *anapana*, *qi-gong*, *nei-dan* and *nei-gong* exercises that move/mobilize your inner Qi/Prana. The Space element can be cultivated by emptiness meditation practice and by imagining that your body becomes bodiless light. Wisdom can be cultivated by study and development of your mental powers.

Immeasurable Emotions Cultivation: The four Buddhist visualization and emotional immeasurable practices of infinite joy, kindness, compassion and equanimity are meant to help you cultivate your Yang Qi/Prana. They symbolize the four dhyana/higher bodies, and by dwelling in them (regularly cultivating them fully) you will slowly change your personality over time to develop those personality characteristics. You will also impregnate your cells and internal organs with those emotional energies, as proven by the fact that organ transplant recipients start taking on some of the personality traits of their donors after a transplant. You can also practice to cultivate emotions such as immeasurable/tremendous courage, valor, vigor, generosity, authority, certainty, positive energy, stamina, mirth, and almost anything else to help you change your personality and fortune. By engendering such large emotions, and holding those emotional states in mind and body like meat soaking in a sauce, through the force of permeation over a long period of time you will slowly affect the Qi/Prana of your body, your thoughts and finally your behavior. It helps if you watch your behavior and then act in those ways when opportunities arise. It takes vigor or effort to put the full-body emotional feelings into effect in your real life until those characteristics become a habitual part of yourself. The results will appear in this life and as character traits in subsequent incarnations. To make greatest use of this technique, during practice sessions or during daily idle moments (such as waiting in line somewhere) imagine suffusing, permeating or saturating yourself with the Qi/Prana/aura of the character trait you wish to cultivate, imagine also projecting it into your outer environment, and simultaneously try to *feel the Qi of that characteristic within you and everywhere*. When opportunities arise then retrieve that feeling and act that way. Consistently visualizing that you are a wrathful deity, like Yamantaka for instance, is another type of immeasurable practice designed to raise your Yang Qi/Prana, but it will also affect your pride and aggressive tendencies if you are not careful of the *yidam* you select and how you practice. When choosing a deity for Buddha mindfulness practice, such as Jesus or Krishna, you must be selective as to the types of emotions and thoughts you practice generating and holding onto at that time in order to move your Qi/Prana, as you are actually cultivating those same characteristics. For instance, many Hesychasts recite the Jesus Prayer "Lord Jesus Christ, son of God, have mercy on me a sinner." Note the difference between this and the feeling from alternatives such as "I give myself to you, Jesus Christ the Lord" or "I trust in you Lord Jesus Christ my Savior."

There are many other forms of Qi/Prana work that can be practiced in conjunction with meditation to help you transform your Qi/Prana and quickly purify and strengthen your inherent inner subtle body. Religious practice strengthens it as well but not so much as the path of Yoga herein explained. The key to the deva body attainment is firm resolution to consistent deep practice and a consistent practice schedule, perhaps keyed to the days of the week (as explained) or some astronomical phenomena for a specific sadhana period of time in order to establish some variety that will help you maintain continuance. The target objective is not just transformation of your physical body, but the control of your Qi/Prana by your mind/will. Successful practice also requires that you understand the principles underlying the effectiveness of the practice, as explained.

PHENOMENA ARISING DUE TO PRACTICE[34]

With spiritual progress it is common to see visions, hear unusual sounds or voices, smell beautiful odors, or feel sensations of energy moving within your body. Most of the visions and sounds are illusions projected into your brain by devas and spiritual masters. The inner sensations of energy movement, or feelings of hot and cold, etc. are due to Qi/Prana transformations within your physical body and subtle body, some of which are caused by spiritual beings moving their own Qi/Prana inside you to help you get the transformations going, and others caused by yourself.

Some people may seem to become psychic, but their psychic talents are typically also due to devas as well who happen to be working on your body to help transform your Qi/Prana.

After a true kundalini awakening initiates, the first 100 days will entail continuous and powerful Qi/Prana movements throughout your body 24 hours a day. You will likely hear many inner sounds/voices and see many illusions or visions. The process will continue for twelve years, and involve the assistance of countless masters and their deva students who visit your body to help transform your Qi/Prana for the generation of the deva (subtle) body attainment.

Unfortunately, the spiritual masters (usually the great ones within your

---

[34] See *Meditation Case Studies*, Chapter 4 & 6 and *The Little Book of Hercules*.

tradition, and their deceased predecessors who attained spiritual bodies) will also use you during this time to teach how to alter the thoughts and emotions of human beings, and being undisciplined this will be a period of intense suffering for you, which is why no masters describe it since they don't want to dissuade people from the path.

ARHATS, BODHISATTVAS AND BUDDHAS[35]

Arhats: The Arhat is one who attains one or more spiritual bodies, but primarily works on his own salvation and on satisfying his own personal interests and pursuits in the universe. Having attained the initial fruit of a subtle (deva) body or even more bodies, he primarily resides in his highest body and therefore is not especially enticed by physical sensual attractions/delights and worldly profits anymore since the material realm is the lowest realm that is no longer his primary sphere of residence. He identifies his highest body as his self, and his lower bodies are like appendages. He or she does whatever they want without any special commitment to other human beings. They develop skills and talents according to their personal interests, whereas the Bodhisattvas and Buddhas do so in order to make their capabilities in special skills accumulate into a powerful force that can succeed in accomplishing goodness on a vast scale.

Bodhisattvas: The Bodhisattva, having attained one or more higher bodies, is one who then spends a great deal of time trying to help others in various ways that better the human condition. He or she works on accomplishing personal vows, offerings or missions they have voluntarily chosen, and this is the road of Bodhisattva Yoga. While free to leave projects at any time because their participation is voluntary, the Bodhisattvas don't abandon people but involve themselves with all sorts of compassionate activity (some of which constitutes just "hit and run" efforts) to help them and the world. In personal training, they try to master various skills and dharmas, taking upon themselves the road of Perfection-kaya to master chosen paths with excellence. They work to master various dharmas, excellences or skills such as various powers, bodies of knowledge, and skills or functions. They try to learn how to proceed wisely in all activities (to do so with skillfulness and effectiveness for the result they want), which is Wisdom-kaya. They try to become masters of preventing problems, solve problems at the root so they no longer exist, and devote themselves to creating flourishing states of happiness, welfare, prosperity and abundance that remove suffering. Thus they try to become masters of the Greek concepts of *arête* (excellence or

---

[35] See *Culture, Country, City, Company, Product, Person, Passion, World.*

virtue), *phronesis* (practical and moral wisdom) and *eudaimonia* (human flourishing and prosperity). They master helpful intercession and influence by deed or presence in some form, which include active *nirmanakaya* projections, which is Compassion-kaya. They work to always better perfect their views, efforts and intentions. The Bodhisattvas focus on self-correction and active learning of what they must cultivate in themselves to move forward, trying always to rise above their basic animal nature. They try to transform their errant habits and transcend fixed traditions or prejudicial thoughts geared to narrow divisions of caste, race, religion, nationality, sexual orientation, gender, creed (or any other such distinguishing characteristic) so that they can help all beings without prejudice. They start to practice skillfulness (expedient means) in thought, word, deed and appearance – mastering their presence and functioning – trying to detach from fixed concepts of morality as well as rigid religious rules of purity and codes of conduct in order to contribute to the well-being and spirit of others. They see all errant situations as diseases that they aim to cure, and because diseases are not the same they recognize that remedies must vary according to the situation, and vow to master them all. They try to transcend all their current patterns of feeling and thinking to employ new and better ones, not being wed to any except what is best for the situation at hand as well as good for the intermediate-term and long-term too. They understand that as a manifestation of the original essence they are basically a cosmic function that can choose its own activities, and work to master their skillfulness and intercession in the directions where they choose to intercede as saviors who improve lives and liberate beings from suffering.

Buddhas: A Buddha is one who, having attained the higher bodies and presented now with the gift of a long life ahead, takes upon himself permanent vows to accomplish long-term missions. They perform devotion (bhakti) to those aspirations, principles and missions they wish to follow. Buddhas become willing to permanently take upon themselves the burdens of the world. They take the suffering of other beings upon themselves, swallowing poison like Shiva as well as insult, pain and criticism like Jesus and Maitreya, in order to relieve the bad conditions that affect others. Like a peacock which eats poisonous insects but in turn produces glorious feathers, they will assume troubles on purpose to produce beautiful results in return. Thus they will take upon themselves the burdens of the world and select roads fraught with difficulty and suffering in order to permanently improve situations for the better, such as by creating systems that automatically solve problems without their involvement. They know that any sufferings they assume will end in the long run, or be as dreams once they attain a higher body and work the lower body as an appendage, so they know that the bag of troubles they hoist upon their shoulders as a burden is light because it is ultimately empty. Thus through their various bodies they cultivate a fearlessness/courage of commitment and act without delay. Committed, they don't frighten of troublesome responsibilities but will suffer to accomplish the tasks they have chosen. Like a strong tree that grows roots and branches everywhere, they will take upon themselves a permanent presence in order to spread their influence, and strive to establish peace, prosperity, harmony and direction for all humanity. They try to model themselves on the ceaseless vitality of cosmic processes so that they can continue to maintain their commitment despite intermittent waves of weariness and fatigue during the ups and downs of events and circumstances. They have the potential to become like a cosmic function and so strive to become an unstoppable field of blessings that is like a force of nature. They exhibit the desire to help all men, and based upon their wisdom manifest activities in response to the needs of men. They inspire people to take up the diligent cultivation that leads to spiritual liberation which involves self-improvement, cooperation with others, charity, spiritual cultivation, and the promotion of culture and civilization. They teach individuals and societies how to behave and what they must cultivate, help in establishing those conditions, support all sorts of projects to improve basic human conditions and the cosmos, try to realize all aspects of God, and try to make every situation better than how they found it. They try to improve culture and civilization to improve people's quality of life and lifestyle so as to create the best possible life or living state for others. Although settled in the original nature, they never settle in one phenomenal state too long but make sure conditions always evolve forward and move ahead so that everyone progresses.

Every higher spiritual body lives longer than the average human lifespan, so upon achieving the higher body attainments you must choose appropriate tasks, goals, offerings, vows or commitments to give your longer life greater purpose and meaning, which will be a reflection of your Compassion-kaya, Wisdom-kaya, and Perfection-kaya.

While it is idealistic to assume that you can master all dharmas equally, in practice people will always be better at some things more than others. Therefore it is best to work at *specializing in some specific fields* rather than try to become a jack of all trades who is master of none. I have provided study guides in this book to help you get started at mastering some areas of expertise that might interest you, but they are by no means inclusive and better ones will appear over time. In the human world, large conglomerates that try to do everything are eventually broken up because they lose their profitability due to size and eventually fail at being really good at anything specific. Specialization produces skills and talent can be learned, but it takes committed effort.

HEART SUTRA UNDERSTANDING[36]

One needs to understand that your physical, subtle, Causal, Supra-Causal, Immanence body, and higher, are all essentially the pure original nature, and the pure original nature is no different from these bodies.

In Buddhism it is said that the form, sensation conception, volition and consciousness skandhas are the original nature, and the original nature is these skandhas. They are no different from one another. You are these bodies because without a body you do not exist, but you are also essentially the original nature so It is you.

Thus in one sense you cannot be termed as energy, nor any type of material essence, nor the five *skandhas*, bodies (*koshas*), or coverings – you are just the original nature. In another sense you are essentially an ever-changing mass of energy, material essence, or bodies depending on how far you cultivate. The objects/phenomena of the universe, including you, have various forms, names and functions but they are not different from the primordial essence. They are all characterized by its emptiness. This means that essentially you are bodiless, birthless and imperishable. What is there therefore to fear? Celebrate your life with joy and make of it what you want.

At the heart of all things is the original essence, the substance of everything. It is thus said, "There are many bodies but their governor is one." All beings/bodies are equally your True Self, and all bodies and phenomena are equally aspects of It. Therefore, all things and beings are an aspect of *you*. You are part of Shakti therefore you *are* Shakti since Shakti is one body. But you have the miracle of consciousness that allows you to guide phenomena within the All to produce everything desired, and experience joy, happiness and bliss. Insentient phenomena, which Christianity calls "darkness," are incapable of comprehension but we have illumination.

That being the case, do you not have an obligation to make all situations better, such as by relieving other beings – your brothers and sisters – of their sufferings? Do you not see your obligation to improve situations within your greater body of Shakti when you encounter them and have the

---

[36] See the *Heart Sutra* of Buddhism and *Avadhuta Gita of Dattreya Avadhuta* (translated by Swami Chetananda), which says approximately the same thing.

skills? The Buddhas, Bodhisattvas, Protector Deities and Guardian Spirits find great happiness in this way.

All things come from the original nature, so that is what you ultimately are. This is your substance, your inner being, your unchanging true existence. Being the original nature, you were never born and will never die. You are pure existence itself and are free to chart any course you want in the universe because of your abilities of consciousness. You can accomplish any vows or missions or purposes you choose. Why not take the chance to be worthy of life?

From the standpoint of the original nature there is nothing else in existence other than Itself just as the ornaments of gold are nothing but gold. Thus, there is no such thing as cause and effect, dependent arising, manifoldness (manifestations of phenomena), production or destruction, laws of physics, living beings, consciousness, holy teachings, stages of life, a path to enlightenment, wisdom, karma, suffering, attainments, codes of conduct and so forth. Ultimately there is no master nor student, no teachings nor realization. There is no state of virtue and no state of vice, no state of bondage, no state of bondage or liberation, no coming and no going. There are absolutely no modifications in It.

You can therefore say that the foundational substratum has no cause or effect, is free from cause and effect, transcends cause and effect, or is beyond the relationship of cause and effect, absent of cause and effect, cause and effect do not truly exist, cause and effect are ultimately empty and so on. Imagine if the entire universe was just empty space alone with nothing inside it. In that case, where would there be cause and effect? There would just be an endless void of nothingness.

However, in the conventional realm of manifestation there is indeed cause and effect. Conventionally, there are better apparent states of being that you can bring into existence for yourself and others, so why not do so by using your mind? Why not create states of joy and bliss absent of suffering for all?

For us, appearances (forms and phenomena, including life) do exist. You cannot say they ultimately exist as spiritual truth, but only conventionally exist as an empirical truth that is only true for now. Why are you then attached to inferior states of being rather than choosing to move ahead in the conventional realm and make things better for yourself and others?

Phenomena do not exist in an entirely pure essence for within That there is only Itself. However, they appear in the unreal, effervescent, transitory realm of causality, and only because you have a mind. Without a mind, nothing exists, does it? Even with a mind, they don't really appear in all their dimensions because you are limited by what you can see, feel, hear and so on – and thus you always experience the world incorrectly, incompletely, conditionally. Who senses their complete nature correctly? Even so, we can work to improve matters.

Phenomena appear as limited wavering illusions that appear in space, constantly changing and ultimately ungraspable. Not being changeless, they are fundamentally unreal, inherently unreal. However, they do exist non-transcendentally (conventionally) for as long as they do exist, which is always fleetingly momentary since they are ultimately transitory. Why not learn to become a master of them and guide the possible changes to more auspicious states of being? Why not choose this purpose to improve situations, and guide people on how to better live and succeed on earth?

You cannot say phenomena don't exist, but you cannot say that they exist as "realities" (non-changing ultimate entities with an independent self-so nature) either. Although you perceive a universe of objects, what you perceive is the original essence alone. The name "universe" is superimposed on It, but what we call the "universe" or "Shakti" or "The Word" is really nothing but the original essence. Thus you can say that the original nature is neither with attributes nor without attributes. You cannot say It is pure without phenomena, nor impure because of phenomena (that don't truly exist except in the nature of a dream). You cannot say It is All nor nothing (since things apparently exist). This is summarized in the *Heart Sutra* of Buddhism, but few people understand that this is its meaning.

The original nature is the one true reality and existence – single, beginningless, eternal, infinite, immaculate, pure, unchanging, and without phenomenal stain. Yet appearances somehow arise within It, but from the standpoint of the original nature there is nothing else at all except Itself. Should you not try to be like your fundamental self-nature that is blissful and free? Can your mind be like the original nature that lets appearances arise without clinging to them? That freedom and bliss is why we meditate.

If you can give up all craving like the original nature you can be blissful, happy and free. The True Reality is blissful, peaceful, tranquil, and devoid of sufferings caused by any agency. It is untouched by the grief and misery of the world, free from passion, jealousy, hatred and the rest. Can you practice so that your mind is like this? The primordial essence is by nature blissful and free. So should be your mind.

You can say that phenomena are one and the same as the original nature, or that they are the original nature, or that they are essentially the original nature, or they are inherently the original nature, or permeated by the original nature, are ultimately empty, don't truly exist and so on. Men are free to arrange phenomena as they deem fit although the results of those actions will always be bound to the rules of causality, which is the net of causation that orders phenomena in the Shakti cosmos, thus ruling them. Causality structures the infinite network of conventional existence, and is also called dependent origination or simultaneous arising. The realm of causality binds the field of emanations, but not the original nature, so the Great Learning for a sentient being is learning how to master the field of manifestations to gain any results desired.

Since phenomena appear *for us* we must learn how to master them in every realm if we wish to live better lives without suffering. The transitory nature of conventional reality, rather than the ultimate reality that is unchangeable, means that there is always the hope and chance for change to occur, and our job as beings with consciousness is to learn how to make it so to produce more fortuitous states for the future. Because phenomena are transitory and change this gives us the opportunity for altering phenomena for the better. If phenomena were not transitory, then no conditions could ever change. As a Buddha, Bodhisattva or guardian spirit you will have a lot of power to change things to help other sentient beings. Start studying and participating in the relevant charitable activities to begin doing so now.

Without doing anything, the original essence sustains the whole universe. As the universal support, It is essentially the ultimate Doer of all things that acts without acting. Armed with true knowledge, recognize that now is the time for you to also become an active doer yourself.

In summary, the original nature is neither impure nor pure; It is empty of everything and yet contains emanations, manifestations or appearances. It is neither all/everything nor none/nothing. It has neither increase nor decrease, did not come into being and is not going anywhere. It was never born and will never die, and is devoid of above and below, interior and exterior. It is eternal and everlasting, immutable, dependable and true. Somehow Shakti, or samsara, appears within it. If you say that "Maya/samsara does not exist," its appearance and *your life* is there in front of you, so this isn't true. If you say that "Maya/samsara really exists" then how can that be so? It is like a dream or illusion, lacking a permanent inherent nature. The only thing ever really present is the permanent original nature.

That is your True Self, your self-nature, your primordial self-essence. In Buddhism It is often called Emptiness. We can create whatever we want starting from emptiness, so be confident and courageous to celebrate life and improve things for everyone, your brothers and sisters. Make great art! Do great things! Be bold and creative and take great risks! Choose what you want to accomplish in the universe and then start working towards achieving that. Start from now. Since you are essentially *This One*, what then is a high, overarching mission worthy of being pursued by you? What is worthy of your life? Be a better you, be the light you want to see in the world, be the Buddha you want to be. Remember, live life like you're gonna die because you're gonna, so get going and make your life count.

From the aspect of emanations there are uncountable phenomena, including other living beings with minds who, because of the existence of consciousness can generate thoughts, perceptions, feelings and memories. They can know aspiration, joy, peace, bliss, achievement and fulfillment. Without a mind you are insentient, but because of a mind that can think, reason and know you can cultivate higher bodies, aspirations, vows and abilities to accomplish whatever you want in the universe. What goals are worthy of you as you can essentially live forever? You are essentially the undying original nature and can cultivate in any direction you choose. What joy would you want to bring to humanity everywhere?

Our fundamental nature is without fear. In boldness and freedom It has given birth to all things that will also continue transforming in endless ways throughout eternity. Can you not imitate the courageous, blissful outpouring of your fundamental essence? Of course you can! You determine what Dream has value that exteriorizes your sense of life purpose, happiness, fulfillment, aliveness, joy and direction. You determine what you will make of yourself. You determine how you will develop and what you will develop. Life runs on the principle of causality and can go in any direction you want when you start putting in the effort. Your choices and actions will determine the purpose, direction and outcome of your life.

So be bold! Be joyous and celebrate your life among the insentient phenomena. Your thoughts and actions interact with all other living beings, so start learning how to bring the best to all situations and start doing so. Grab hold of the process of causality and do something wondrous while evolving towards transcendence. Be at your best, be the light you want others to see, the Dream within yourself that reconnects you to your larger divine Self the joy you want to see in the world. Make a vow to become a Guardian Spirit, Buddha or Bodhisattva and start upon the requisite pathway of learning, practice and cultivation Yoga.

11
RAISING MONEY FOR MASTERS AND SPIRITUAL TRAINING CENTERS

Many temples and spiritual centers which train people to attain enlightenment have a constant problem of raising money to fund their operations, and need help. This includes Christian monasteries and convents/nunneries, Buddhist temples, Hindu temples, Taoist centers, and other types of centers.

As stated, I suggest giving (making offerings) twice a year - once in the Spring and once in the Fall - to effective spiritual institutions (training centers) and great masters (male or female) who train individuals. Most people only think that Indian or Tibetan masters are enlightened, but there are hundreds of individuals across the world who have achieved the subtle body attainment and higher, including within the western traditions of Christianity, Islam and Judaism. They achieve the same high states as the gurus, swamis, sadgurus, and masters of the East.

For instance, many of the high ranking Archbishops, Popes and Patriarchs of the Eastern Orthodox Christian churches are enlightened. The high ranking muftis, Sheiks and Sufis in Islam usually have several bodies too as do the Chief Rabbis of many large cities and traditions. There are hundreds of people across the world with the spiritual body attainments, but they don't tell anyone for obvious reasons.

People simply don't know this, but normally think that spiritual attainments are concentrated in masters from the East, or the "highest" only fall in their corners, but please don't fall for the misconception that they are only centered in the big names of the eastern traditions. Many individuals who shun the spotlight, and don't assume high positions such as an abbot, attain the Tao (gain the extra spiritual bodies) and arise in every tradition of spiritual practice – Shinto, Druze, Amish, Western Alchemy, etcetera. Therefore, when you are considering donations, especially do not neglect these other traditions, and in particular Christian monasteries and nunneries that are carrying on the monastic, mendicant tradition as they are also producing spiritual masters (called "saints" in Christianity), but people simply don't know about the process going on. The incorruptible bodies of Christian adepts, found within Joan Carroll Cruz's *The Incorruptibles*, list individuals whose physical body was transformed by the kundalini process as the adept went through the Twelve Year kundalini Yoga process to attain the subtle body and higher. This is why Christian, Sufi, and Jewish notables can exhibit superpowers.

Of course, the Maha Nayaka high ranking Buddhist monks in Theravada countries (Burma, Cambodia, Thailand, Laos, Vietnam, Sri Lanka), such as their Chief Patriarchs (Sangharaja), are also usually enlightened, as well as many teaching Sikhs, Jains, Bahai, Taoist, Bon, Druze, Shinto priests and others. Those who have the subtle body, or subtle plus Causal body, or subtle plus Causal and Supra-Causal body, and so on are found in countless traditions and countries, and are not restricted to just the leaders and well-known of those traditions.

Many humble mendicants and spiritual adherents attained the subtle body or higher but don't let others know it. This is why they seem to have great wisdom, know things that are impossible to know, and can often demonstrate superpowers. When a religious professional seems to have psychic abilities it might just be because that they have attained the subtle body achievement through their tradition. It can and is attained through western monastic and religious systems just as frequently as attained in the East, but everyone keeps the whole matter secret.

The point is that it is not just Tibetan, Buddhist, Taoist, Jain, Sikh and Hindu individuals who attain the subtle, Causal, Supra-Causal and Immanence bodies. There are hundreds of people around the world who have attained the higher spiritual bodies through spiritual practice. People overly focus on the Hindu, Taoist and Buddhist traditions and tend to neglect the successful adepts in all the others. Once "out" of the physical body, however, they learn how to do everything that everybody else is capable of doing. No school or tradition has a monopoly on spiritual powers or abilities.

Anyone who performs the requisite Yoga through their own religious/spiritual practices can attain the subtle body at minimum. Most mendicant traditions are designed to bring about this result, especially when they are centuries old, but they don't tell the uninitiated that this is what the spiritual path is all about. Masters don't want you to know that they have these attainments either, or what skills they are capable of doing since their major intervention is using their spiritual bodies to give you energy, thoughts and emotions at appropriate times to help you or quiet your mind.

If everyone knew your level of spiritual attainment in terms of body vehicles, imagine the constant requests you would get from individuals, as well as individuals attributing their bad fortune to your interference or lack of help. When people die they learn how things really work such as all this, and then they wonder why no one told them the truth, but that is the nature of religion. It is meant to lead the masses in a skillful way, but not to necessarily give the truth or the whole picture of reality.

Largess to help fund spiritual masters and their institutions is unlikely to be drummed up by my words alone, so here is some advice for masters and institutions struggling to raise money including the worthies in the Cisterian, Benedictine, Dominican, Augustinian, Franciscan, Carmelite, Maronite and other Christian mendicant traditions who continue to struggle to raise money as they produce enlightened adepts, thus matching the production in the East. Christianity may seem to be dying off, but that doesn't mean that its monastic systems are no longer producing enlightened individuals.

If they have a farm, once again I advise monastics or spiritual centers who need more income to study the Singing Frogs Farm (Paul and Elizabeth Kaiser), Four Seasons Farm (Eliot Coleman), Market Gardener (Jean-Martin Fortier) and Joel Salatin's Polyface Farm. While most farms make only $3-5K per acre, some farms following the organic farming principles of these leaders can make $120-150K per acre. These are among the top earners.

I am particularly impressed by the Trappist (Cisterian) monks and nuns, who both work for a living and cultivate spiritual practice. Some Trappist monks and nuns have attained the subtle body, Causal body, Supra-Causal body and higher through this monastic training system, just as do masters in the East following their own traditional cultivation streams. The Eastern Orthodox Mount Athos in Greece is commonly known to have produced many successes too. Many greats in the Eastern Orthodox Christian tradition have certainly attained the spiritual bodies of enlightenment, and many of the current leaders have these attainments.

In Christianity, the idea of "divinizing the body" is the act of attaining the spiritual body attainments, and many Christian leaders still achieve these bodies today. As said, this is why I always encourage people to also contribute to the various humble Christian sects that continue the monastic and mendicant traditions, *including convents/nunneries* rather than just male monastic centers. Many are in danger of dying off through lack of financial support even though they produce the same spiritual product as in the East - enlightened masters - but they don't parade around as spiritual teachers because this is against the rules of the tradition.

Most people also don't realize that many Christian monastic traditions are not self-centered but have the mission of "serving God, the community and fellow man." This is what enlightened Christian monks and nuns do when they attain their deva body and higher, which is work around them in their local community and elsewhere by helping to answer the prayers of the faithful in those traditions. This is also why many become recognized as "saints" in various Christian traditions. Once they attain higher spiritual bodies they are the equivalent to the "prophets" in the Bible and the "masters" or "gurus" of the East. The only major difference is that they follow a different theology and training regimen to get the exact same result, and are inferior to the easterners in no way at all.

You would be surprised to know that the humble lodgings of a Christian monk or nun – perhaps some unimpressive building with only a few adherents inside – might be occupied by someone who is actually enlightened and silently serving their community with their wisdom and spiritual bodies to perform countless untold activities. They, like the masters of eastern temples, also need financial support but this is becoming more difficult since the Christian tradition seems to be in decline. Nuns, in particular, often need your help most since people usually neglect nunneries and don't normally think of nuns as enlightened masters. However, many have attained the higher bodies that constitutes enlightenment. Once you attain the subtle body, it is just a matter of time before you attain the Causal and then Supra-Causal and then Immanence body attainments.

To raise money for their monasteries, some Trappists brew beer or engage in other manual labor occupations (often food related) and use the proceeds to produce a self-supporting community, giving any excess they make to charity. It is interesting that Bira beer, founded by a man who had no previous experience in the liquor business, became one of the best selling beers in India in less than two years after being introduced. It is all because the founder did good research and marketing when he started, which is a lesson for monasteries that aspire to become brewers. Such success can be achieved. When someone does craft beer brewing right they can definitely produce a superior product and help fund a monastery or spiritual center. In previous times, many European monasteries even supported themselves by acting as pawn shops for gold, and often created rudimentary banking systems.

See *Business Secrets of the Trappist Monks* by August Turak for some ideas on how mendicants can raise money through other self-produced products. Studying the offerings and business model of Newman's Own, founded in 1982 by the actor Paul Neuman and A.E. Hotchner, would help as well.

With custom whiskeys now quickly available from the Doug Hall team at Brain Brew (see brainbrewwhiskey.com) due to their time compression technology, which makes it possible to create unique whiskey flavors that win taste contests worldwide, this is also a liquor product that a monastery might consider producing other than just beer, especially as whiskey is one of the best selling liquors in the world. Perhaps the new whiskeys can be stored in barrels made of *bois bande* wood, instead of oak, for if *bois bande* truly had aphrodisiac powers this might contribute to a desired product and superior marketing/branding.

In addition to farming, breweries, and other manual labor activities, I should mention several other important topics related to fundraising: selling products, investing contributed funds and endowments for higher returns, and fundraising letters.

The following appendices are a collection of what I believe to be very helpful information along these lines. They concern methods for raising money or managing money, such as an endowment, for superior returns (see *Super Investing*), to hopefully produce higher income for spiritual centers and religious institutions:

Fruit Guy Interview – Michael Senoff
Warren Buffett's Real Investing Methodology – Alice Schroeder
Seasonal Stock Market Trading Via Twice a Year Switching – Bill Bodri
Building a Dividend Compounding Investment Machine - Bill Spetrino
The Most Successful Sales Letter of All Time – Martin Conwoy
100% Response College Fundraising Letter – Bruce Barton.

FRUIT GUY INTERVIEW

This is an exclusive interview provided by permission of Michael Senoff and found on his website, HardToFindSeminars.com. It teaches two things: (1) how to raise thousands in cash for a temple, monastery, convent or nunnery, spiritual center, etc. (since these institutions are always cash strapped in need of funds) during just three months of every year and, (2) the principle that every aspect of selling and marketing should be optimized.

Fruit Guy: Let's start the story. Can we start it at the beginning?

Michael: Yeah, tell me from the very beginning how it all started.

Fruit Guy: Well you know you've stopped at those roadside fruit stands ...

Michael: Absolutely, it's kind of like a nostalgic thing. You know, as a kid you can remember like if you go on vacations with your family and you stopped at the stand. It's always kind of exciting.

Fruit Guy: Whenever somebody walks up to the stands they're never unhappy.

Michael: Yeah.

Fruit Guy: They only say one or two things when they come up - *"Are they really sweet?"* or *"How much are your cherries?"* Those are the only two things they ever say, and it's beautiful. They have a big smile on their face when they say it and I always hand them a cherry and say, "The first one is always free" and they smile and we're talking. Let's start at the beginning so I can share with you how I've crafted and what I say and why I say it.

Michael: Alright, let's do it. Start from the beginning.

Fruit Guy: So as a kid, you know, I worked on that fruit stand on the side of the road. Great grandpa built it and it was grandpa's …

Michael: Where were you? What state?

Fruit Guy: A small town in Central California, farm town. You know, that whole Valley from Bakersfield to Sacramento is all just farms and fields, so there's little pastures like that I know like that all over the country but there's a lot of fruit grown in the California Valley.

Michael: Were your parents farmers?

Fruit Guy: Well, their parents were farmers and they took over. We passed it down from grandpa to son and it keeps going.

Michael: So how many generations back has your family been farming?

Fruit Guy: Every picture that we have, even those old 1800 pictures, they're all black and white, but they're all farming.

Michael: Were you all farming fruit and vegetables and all kinds of stuff?

Fruit Guy: All kinds of stuff. It was nuts, it was fruits, it was vegetables and that's how it is when you're a farmer. You start with a few trees of what you want and then over the years you build. Then your son takes over and he starts something that he likes to grow and so that's how it is. Every farm's got a bunch of stuff …

Michael: So as a kid, what do you remember about the farm?

Fruit Guy: I remember taking and knocking. That's where you took a mallet - we didn't have fancy machinery in those days - knocking things off the tree with mallets like nuts and picking our peaches or our cherries. It was the greatest life as an eight, ten, twelve year old to get paid to go run through the fields and fill up buckets with fruit and then come back. And we didn't get paid much but it was a great way to live your life as a kid, but I got to finally be on a

	stand of my own, you know, and that was when it was really fun.
Michael:	So the main money, like in farming for you guys or for your family, was your farming and then you'd take your bounty and you're selling it in bulk to the packers.
Fruit Guy:	To the packers or taking it and packaging it and sorting it and shipping it out to different areas. And most of the time no matter what city in America you live in you can get our fruit. All you got to do is call the broker - every city's got one. If there's a restaurant in the city there's likely a fruit and vegetable broker. Look in the Yellow Pages.
Michael:	That's farm fresh stuff.
Fruit Guy:	Well, that stuff that's gone to the packing house the same day it was picked and two days later it's in that broker's cooler. And so when you pick it up you're not going to really know any difference then if you got it off the farm. That's just the same thing you buy at Albertson's and Safeway.
Michael:	Okay, evolution of the fruit stand. So there's only so much money selling to the broker, so was the fruit stand an additional way for the farmer to make some money for himself?
Fruit Guy:	*Real* money because he's not now selling them for 50, 75 cents a pound. These are current numbers for his product to the packer. He's able to now put it out there on the street and get 2 bucks for that pound of cherries instead of 70 cents.
Michael:	And that means a lot.
Fruit Guy:	Well it only means a $100 a day. I mean that's all the little wooden stands on the side of the road ever bring in are $100, or if it's right in the middle of the season you got a lot of stuff you're maybe bringing in 200 bucks a day, but all the same.
Michael:	Okay. So as a kid you remember knocking the fruit down,

	growing up on the farm, working in the field and just living that farm life right.
Fruit Guy:	Yeah, that was my whole life. Well when I turned 19 grandpa threw me the keys to the truck and he said "There's a tent and cherries in the back of the truck, it's time for you to go out on your own and do it." And it was the end of the season and I didn't do very good. I only went five miles to the corner grocery store. We had a little gas station there.
Michael:	Did grandpa give you any training or tell you how to do it?
Fruit Guy:	No. I'd been on the fruit stand there for several years …
Michael:	What kind of money did gramps make on the fruit stand?
Fruit Guy:	He made about $100 a day.
Michael:	With selling cherries?
Fruit Guy:	With everything that he had it would be cherries and peaches and tomatoes and whatever we could grab off of the farm.
Michael:	Alright, you're not going to tell me how but knowing what you know now if you could go back in time knowing what you know now after all your experience could you have shown grandpa how to make more money?
Fruit Guy:	I could have, yes.
Michael:	Now what could that have meant for him?
Fruit Guy:	Maybe 200% to 300%.
Michael:	Okay, so tell me about that first day you went out. Tell me what equipment did you have that first day you remember "I'm sure selling."
Fruit Guy:	I had a piece of cardboard that I wrote "Cherries" on for my sign. I had a 4 x 8 piece of plywood that I flipped over upside on top of the cases to make a table out of.

Michael: Okay, but grandpa that's what he used right?

Fruit Guy: No, he had an actual shed that great-grandpa built on the edge of the property.

Michael: So he would go out with the truck and the produce and set up where the shed was.

Fruit Guy: He would go out, load up his truck with what wasn't taken by the packing plant that morning, bring it over to the shed, stop at grandma, my mom, my sister, everybody would work there at the shed selling the fruit. Actually we'd spend the morning just kind of sorting it, "This is bad, throw it out, this is good put it in."

Michael: So do you remember what you sold on that first day?

Fruit Guy: Like 60 dollars.

Michael: And so did you have to give it all to him or did you get to keep it?

Fruit Guy: No, it was mine.

Michael: That was yours.

Fruit Guy: Yeah.

Michael: If you didn't bring it out to the fruit stand what would have happened to it?

Fruit Guy: It would have probably have gotten sold over the next couple of days.

Michael: Did you learn anything that first day selling fruit?

Fruit Guy: To get the hell out of town. You're not going to make any money in this farm town. Every two miles there's a stand and everybody's selling them for the same price. If they want cherries why are they going to stop here at the gas station and get them?

Michael: So you had too much competition.

Fruit Guy: Competition, so my first lesson in the big business world was to find my marketplace.

Michael: So it didn't take you long to figure out to get a new market, right?

Fruit Guy: Well it took me a while, yeah, it took me a couple of years. I didn't understand what the right marketplace was.

Michael: So what are some other frustrations over the couple of years that you experienced selling fruit from the side of the road?

Fruit Guy: Well, I stayed in the Valley was my big problem. I went to Modesto and then I went over to Tracey and I went out to Stockton and I tried these cities that were too much part of the Valley. I had to figure it out that I needed to get out of the Valley. Find the long highway stretch where's there's not a store or a farm for 10 or 20 miles and people get hungry and want to stretch their legs and pull over to a fruit stand on a drive like that. I found that if I drove at 45 or 50 miles over this big barrier called the Altamont Pass and just crossed into that Bay area, even if it's the East Bay area, I'm getting 4 dollars for my 2 dollar one pound basket of cherries.

Michael: Okay, so it's kind of like with real estate - location, location, location.

Fruit Guy: I'm figuring it out as I go along. Yeah, its location.

Michael: So when you found the right location why were people stopping?

Fruit Guy: Many reasons. I mean some people just pulled over to say, "I haven't seen you here before. What made you decide to setup a tent here on the side of the road?" And then most people would come up and say, "You know, can I try one of these cherries?" And once they bit one they were mine.

Michael: I got you. Okay, let's continue. So those first years on the farm working grandpa's fruit stand and then you decided to get out of town. Tell me when you really started making things work for yourself.

Fruit Guy: I got over into the Bay area and my volume increased. Instead of pulling over 20 and 25 people, sometimes 30 or 35 people, I was now pulling over 60 or 65 and sometimes 70 people a day just because of location.

Michael: Okay, so you found a couple of secret locations that were really working.

Fruit Guy: And it wasn't just that. I have had literally hundreds of fruit stands in dozens of cities and I've worked everywhere from San Diego all the way to Seattle. I've worked hundreds of fruit stands and I've worked dozens of cities so I have a pretty good idea over time what's going to work and what isn't. At that time I was still experimenting. I would just keep trying new things - the highway, the neighborhoods, the rich neighborhoods, the poor neighborhoods, the high traffic, the business area, right in the middle of Santa Clara. I tried everywhere including the places where you couldn't believe someone would have the gall to just set their tent up there.

Michael: Tell me some areas that were just flat out losers. If you were going to show me how to make a couple of hundred bucks a day, where should I not setup?

Fruit Guy: You should not setup anywhere where there's farms, nowhere around the farms. Where all the farms are you need to get away from there. All those people know all those farms and they're not going to stop for you, I promise. You need to get where there aren't a bunch of cherry stands available, which means into town. You need to get into the big city. If you live in the farmland you need to get into the city. If you lived in the city you're right where you need to be.

Michael: Someone's going to say, "Well if I'm in the city why is someone going to stop at a fruit stand when they can just go into Vaughn's or any grocery store and pick up fruit there?" What is it that gets people to stop at a roadside fruit stand that's kind of cool? What do you think it is? Is it just that nostalgic thing or people are stopping because they know that a fruit stand is going to be a better quality fruit and it's going to taste like its fresh picked right from the farm compared to the mushy stuff in Vaughn's?

Fruit Guy: I'll say 40% to your second example and 10% to your first, but I hate to just tell you that this is the reason why because there's so many variances of people.

Michael: My wife brings fruit home from the store all the time and the peaches and the plums are just awful.

Fruit Guy: They're junk and here's the secret. I mean there's all kinds of secrets, but one of my favorite secrets is to bring one thing every day, one thing that I didn't get from the broker. I don't care if I got to go to my neighbors. I'm going to go knock on farmers doors that look like they have fresh peaches or fresh tomatoes or fresh something. Why? I want that one sign out there, that one sign that works like gold. What is it? *"Picked Today."* Better yet *"Today's Pick."* It only has to be a 2' x 1' sign it doesn't have to have anything else on it. You can have a sign over here that says *"Sweet Cherries"* and sign over here that says *"Peaches"* and a sign over here that says *"Tomatoes"* or *Nectarines"* but that one little sign over there on the edge of your stand should say *"Today's Pick"* or *"Picked Today."*

Michael: Well, that is it. That instantly telegraphs freshness. You can see the hand picking it off the tree and putting it in the basket. It's like you've picked it yourself.

Fruit Guy: It's gold. Even if you only have one thing out of everything on your table that's picked today they'll remember that. And even if you only did that for two weeks for the other 90 days of the season they're going to remember that's the fresh guy right there, that's the guy that has the *"Today's Pick"* stuff. And every time somebody comes up it's part of the spiel. The person at the stand is going to say, "This is this and this is this" and it's part of the spiel.

Michael: So working on the farm and seeing all the signs in the farm did you ever see those signs …

Fruit Guy: No.

Michael: … that said – you didn't?

Fruit Guy: No. All you ever saw and the same thing you see today … drive through the farmland and all you see is *"Cherries."* Drive a little while, next farm *"Peaches"* - that's it. And I did all those signs but I learned through time signs are key. That's the difference between pulling over 60, 70 and how I got it over 100 and in some spots pulled over a 130, 140 cars a day. For every car you pull over that was like my business thing. That was the first thing I worked on, Michael, I wanted to concentrate on. You know, I don't know much about nothing but I do know that 30 to 40 stops is not going to make me any money. I got to aim for a 100. And once I hit a 100 I wasn't satisfied. I said, "I'm looking for more. What can I do better?", so it was all about the signs. My first analogy was "How am I going to get people into my business?" and that's the signs.

Michael: How did you figure that out?

Fruit Guy: I stripped it down. I tried the hand job like a cardboard box cherries sign. And I did the stenciled letters …

Michael: That said what?

Fruit Guy: That said *"Cherries."*

Michael: Cherries.

Fruit Guy: I realized that out of every sign I tried maybe 150 signs with combinations of words, multiple fruits on the same sign, all kinds of sign combinations and the one sign that worked was *"Sweet Cherries."*

Michael: Oh, so *"Sweet Cherries"* was another sign.

Fruit Guy: That was the sign that turned it over 100. A 100 pullovers a day was no longer my goal. Now it was 125 a day. That *"Sweet Cherries"* sign just totally exploded my business.

Michael: Was that being used in combination with *"Picked Today"*?

Fruit Guy: No, I hadn't figured that out yet.

Michael: So *"Sweet Cherries"* was first.

Fruit Guy: That was first. That's when they would come up and that was the first thing they'd say, either "How much are your cherries?" or "How sweet are they?" And I learned that cherries was the key because I got 20 to 30 pullovers whenever I put any other wording out there.

Michael: Cherries is what pulls them over.

Fruit Guy: That was the key, Michael. I could tell somebody that more than anything. If you're going to run a fruit stand I don't care what else you sell just make sure you sell one thing.

Michael: In your fruit stand are you only selling cherries?

Fruit Guy: No.

Michael: Okay, but you're selling the appointment. You're selling them to pullover and stop.

Fruit Guy: Fifteen years ago I'm still trying to figure out what's going on. Fifteen years ago I figured it out, it's cherries. Ten years ago I figured it out its sweet cherries. A couple of years later I figured out I need to increase my average sale from 7 dollars to 15 dollars. How am I going to do that and that's by offering more inventory.

Michael: But would you always get them in with the cherries?

Fruit Guy: Always, it's golden. I mean there's no other fruit word out there that's going to pull them over like that one.

Michael: Sweet cherries.

Fruit Guy: And that's the golden little add to the word "cherries" as I found somewhere along that little adventure of my

	business growing. "Sweet" is that word, that word on top of cherries.
Michael:	So was your sign with the words side-by-side?
Fruit Guy:	Simple ten inch letters.
Michael:	Ten inch letters. What color?
Fruit Guy:	I like the dark red just like a cherry - real, real dark on a white or kind of a yellowish white background.
Michael:	Okay now tell me about *"Picked Today."* How did that sign come into play and how would you use it with the sweet cherries?
Fruit Guy:	Well, I've advanced since then, but back in that day I just made one little sign that said *"Today's Pick"* and it was small. It was only maybe 12" x 6" and I leaned it up against that big 2' x 4' *Sweet Cherries* sign so they understood that the cherries are today's pick. Oh, today's pick. And I'm telling you I might only have today's pick for a week or two but once that sign goes down it doesn't matter. Everybody remembers that cherries sign. *"Sweet Cherries"* is still there but the *"Today's Pick"* just didn't get put up today.
Michael:	Okay, so sometimes you'd run your stand but it may not be today's pick.
Fruit Guy:	Of course. You're going to the broker so you're no longer getting local fruit. See the fruit ripens in Bakersfield in April, and then in Stockton area in May, and then in Sacramento area in June, and then up around Redding or that area up in July, or in Oregon or in Washington in August, and then Canada's cherries come in September. The cherry is the last fruit that blossoms but it's the first fruit that's ready. And it works in a hemispheric rotation. I mean as the summer moves the fields across the states ripen in a northern direction. I like to go right to the farmer. You can go right to the farmer. I can buy my cherries for 70 cents, 65 cents a pound.

Michael: And when you go to the farmer are they already ready to be put on the truck?

Fruit Guy: They are field run which means everything on the tree has been picked, and although 60% of those cherries are perfect, 10% are way too pink and 5% are way too dark and the rest of them are somewhere in between. No cherry tree has every cherry perfect on it and ready to go at the same time.

Michael: So that's going to be your job over in the fruit stand, which is to separate them.

Fruit Guy: It is the person who's standing under the tent taking the cherries out of the farmer's cases and putting them into the baskets. That's their job is to sort that basket as the tree gave it to them. In other words, you don't give them every cherry in that basket perfect and throw away everything else. No, no, no, no, you give them 50% perfect cherries or 60% perfect cherries just like the tree gives, 10% is going to be a little too dark, 5% is going to be a little too green and the rest are going to be somewhere in-between.

Michael: So you give it to them like the tree gives it to you.

Fruit Guy: Exactly, but when you market it if you're going to give somebody a handful of cherries do you want them to see the pretty side or the not so pretty side? The girl puts them in the baskets with her gloves on. I've still to this day never seen a fruit stand, besides one of mine, where the girls wear gloves. She reaches in, she sorts that basket so it looks attractive, sets it up in a nice teepee fashion and sticks it out on the table. So let's stop there for a second.

My next lesson was packaging. I said, "Well, you know every farm has a damn scale and every farm wants to sell them by the pound and I don't want to carry a scale and I sure don't want to get stuck in a spot where people are making their own baskets and it's a mess. You know what, I'm just going to make baskets. It's about a pound. I don't know but depending on how much is in it those little green baskets are 4 bucks, 5 bucks if you're in the peninsula or

BUDDHA YOGA

San Francisco.

Michael: You'll sell one of those baskets for 4 or 5 bucks.

Fruit Guy: And it'll probably cost me 50 cents.

Michael: That's pretty good.

Fruit Guy: I've just begun. So now we're on our way. So we got ourselves 120 or 130 pullovers a day. We're moving somewhere between 400 and 500 pounds of cherries. It's a major profit and you're filling in the little stuff.

Michael: Alright, so hold on. Let's say if you've got 100 pullovers and if you sell each one of them a basket that's 4 bucks that you make about $3.30.

Fruit Guy: Well, if it was a pound, but unfortunately 30 years doing what I do and I still have never weighed this.

Michael: I mean do you think it's a pound?

Fruit Guy: No.

Michael: Not even quite.

Fruit Guy: I think it's somewhere between .75 and .85.

Michael: Alright, so on a 4 dollar basket you're going to keep around $3.50 profit.

Fruit Guy: Correct.

Michael: That's $350 bucks. When someone pulls over and they're buying cherries, what do you see the average unit of sale about?

Fruit Guy: Well, next lesson. I really needed a spiel. I thought like just standing there I wasn't getting the production.

Michael: You need to increase sales.

Fruit Guy: To increase sales. So what I did I said, "Let's put some more fruit out here. How about if I put some peaches right here? I'm only going to double my money on these peaches and I'm only going to double my money on these tomatoes and I'm only going to double my money on these other items but I'm going to fill in some of these holes and bring my average up. I don't like the 7 dollars or 7.50 dollars average on those 100 customers. I need to bring that up to a 14 dollar or 15 dollar average on these 100 customers so I can make the money I want to make. So when they come out the first thing they do is they get a cherry. Before they have a chance to get any information about why I'm here and anything else I won't even talk to you. You got to try a piece of fruit.

Michael: Alright, I want to break it down. They're driving on the side of the road. If it's a fresh pick they're going to see *Sweet Cherries Today's Pick*. They're going to pull over, they're going to get out of their car. You're standing there working or just standing there and there's no one there at the stand. They're walking to you. Do you say anything to them or do you wait for them to approach you?

Fruit Guy: I totally ignore them because part of the program is ... you know the Latino guy sitting on the corner on three cases of cherries all day and only sold a half a case. It's because he's sitting on his cases of cherries. He's bored and he looks bored. I'm busy and I look busy. I decorate my table a certain way. I have empty baskets on my table on purpose. I have full baskets all over the table but I got to have some empty ones because it looks like you just left and they cleared out half my table. And I'm not looking up at you because you're going to walk up to me and the first thing you're going to say if you don't have a warm feeling is, "How much are your cherries?" And if you do have a warm feeling you're going to say, "How sweet are they?"

Michael: You don't have your prices displayed on the table?

Fruit Guy: Never.

Michael: Do other roadside stands put their prices there?

Fruit Guy: Sometimes.

Michael: Is it a mistake?

Fruit Guy: If you let me give you the spiel, I want you to walk up to me and let me sell you.

Michael: Okay, so I'm going to come up and I'm going to say, "How much are they?"

Fruit Guy: "Our cherries? The first one's always free and grab it from me please, take it, bite, great. And I have three sizes. I have a small, medium and large. Over here the cherries are 4, 8 and 12. Here peaches are 3, 6 and 9. Here tomatoes are 2, 4 and 6. And here the nuts are 1, 2 and 3." What just happened to you?

Michael: I got confused.

Fruit Guy: You're lost. What do you care about the price? All you want is one of those. You're going to point because I'm going to tell you, "Just point to the basket you like."

Michael: You want to confuse them on purpose?

Fruit Guy: Yes.

Michael: Okay, why?

Fruit Guy: Because I don't want them calculating, "That's 4 dollars for that little one pound basket of cherries. I could go down right now for $2.99 and get them at Albertson's. They're on sale usually $5.99. They're on sale this week for $2.99 at Albertson's."

Michael: Okay, so I want you to repeat that again. So I'm going to say, "How much are they?"

Fruit Guy: "The first one's always free, try that."

Michael: Do you grab one then right there and they …

Fruit Guy: I've already got one between my fingers as I'm packing this basket, I'm preparing my next basket and I've already got a sample between my fingers or here in the corner where I know it is and I can see out of the corner of my eye, although I'm facing down towards my table. You're walking right up towards me and it's a beautiful sunny day. You're excited to see this fruit stand that suddenly popped up. You come up and you say, "Hey, how much are your cherries?" I'm going to say, "The first one is always free." You're going to feel warmth, you're going to bite that and you're going to say, "This is one delicious cherry."

Michael: What kind of gloves do you have on?

Fruit Guy: I have those food ones. What do they call them? I think they're latex.

Michael: And so you extend your arm.

Fruit Guy: I extend the hand with the cherry in it.

Michael: Do you look them in the eye?

Fruit Guy: Rarely. I'm too busy. I'm explain this as we go along because there's nothing funnier than having you walk up while one's walking away with three bags, two more are standing here trying to pay me on my right, and one over here on the left that you're trying to squeeze in-between one who's just asked the same question and finishing off their second sample. Because while you're biting that cherry and I'm doing, "Well we have small, medium and large. The cherries are 4, 8 and 12, 3, 6 and 9 over here on the peaches, 2, 4 and 6 over here on the nectarines, 1, 2 and 3 on the tomatoes, whatever it is. All I'm doing is making it so I can have them say, "Well give me a small of that, a medium of that, and a large of that." That's what I want.

Michael: Yet you've totally confused them. There's no way they can remember and because they don't remember the price you got them.

Fruit Guy: All they want is a medium cherry, or if they love their sample they want a large, or if they hated it they want a small. But I'm not done. Before they can tell me – and they probably already told me "I'll take a large," they'll say, "How many pounds are in that one?" "Honestly I don't know, probably about four for 12 which is about 3 dollars a pound. That's your better deal. If you go with the medium it's about two and a half pounds and that's 8. So you're paying maybe like $3.00, $3.25. And then if you want to get a small that one's 4 dollars. Those are around a pound."

So while you're deciphering that, if you really wanted to know more of that - rarely does it happen because about 80% go right along with the program - but you're digesting this 3, 6, 9, 2, 4, 6, 1, 2, 3, for the sale thing I threw at you and I sliced you off a very thin slice of a delicious peach and I handed that to you and you're biting into that. Before you even say "okay" I'm going to take one of those too. I've already got my hand on another sample. I don't know what it is yet, maybe a nectarine or an apricot, whatever I got my hands on that morning from the broker, whatever he had cheap that I could get that looked good and tasted good and would show good I grabbed a couple of cases of those and I got a slice of that in your hand really thin, not the big chunks. I learned a long time ago, "Oh, I got satisfied on that." No, no, no, nice and thin …

Michael:	Tell me the lesson. How did you learn that?
Fruit Guy:	Just too many sales slipping by. "Wow, this is a delicious peach."
Michael:	Because the other stands would cut it up. And I've seen it where you go to the stand – you can go and have all your fruit for lunch there, right?
Fruit Guy:	Right.
Michael:	They put it out.
Fruit Guy:	Right.
Michael:	And that's a mistake.
Fruit Guy:	Big mistake.

Michael: You've got to control it.

Fruit Guy: And then they're dying for more. When I say thin, as thin as I can slice a peach I'm going to hand it to them. When it lies on their tongue and they taste that sweetness - "Give me a small peach too, okay."

Michael: Ah, that's genius.

Fruit Guy: I don't know. It's just practice and error and I know nothing about big business but it just seems logical. So as we go along 2, 4, 6, 1, 2, 3, slice, sample, slice sample. Now the next thing that's going to happen is you're going to tell me what you want. You're going to point, you're going to point, and you're going to point. "Just point to what you like," that's what I like to say. "Well, I'll take that one, that one and that one." The next thing I'm going to do before I give them their fruit or let them touch their fruit is I want their money in the basket.

Michael: Okay, in the basket.

Fruit Guy: Well, I don't take their money by hand because I'm touching food and this impressed them so much. When I figured this out people just loved it. You know the baskets I'm talking about. They're cardboard, they're three, four times the size of the little green plastic ones and they hold fruits. They're cardboard. Every fruit stand has got them. They'll hold like three pounds or four pounds and some sizes are …

Michael: Yeah, I think I know what you're talking about. They come up about four inches.

Fruit Guy: About three inches, you're right, maybe four but that's the basket that is the large and the medium. The small ones are the little plastic ones so I've got different sizes to baskets. Well, those two large cardboard baskets are my bank. I put one on top of the other with a blank on top of that. In that blank there's a few cherries just so I can recognize that little stack of three baskets right there as my bank.

So I'm going to grab my bank with my right hand, lean it over to them, lift off the top three sample cherries that are in that top empty one and under that is going to be a bunch of $1s and $5s. And if I lift that one up it's going to be all $20s. So he's going to probably, or she's going to probably because probably 60% of the pullovers are middle-aged women. There are probably more women than men at almost any spot I've ever had except maybe the big highways where the truck drivers are.

So she's going to probably pull that $20 out of her pocket and she's going to drop it in there. She's going to look confused – "Aren't you afraid someone's going to grab all that money?" It never has happened. I've been working the basket bank for 15 years and never had anyone try to make a move. And I'll purposely turn my head, still watching out of the corner of my eye, but they never do. No one tries to steal. So she drops in her $20 and is looking confused because she's thinking she has some change coming. I draw basket two on top of the bottom basket, and now she sees a bunch of $1s and $5s, and I say, "Well, you got a medium peach that was 6, you got a large cherry that was 12, 6 and 12 … that's $18. Take two singles out of there."

Great, drop the empty basket with the three cherries on top and now they're all one little compartment again. Set them off to my side and I'm now grabbing her bags because I don't want her to take my cardboard baskets. I want her to have a plastic food bag that I've gone and bought a case of before the day started or once a week. There's a plastic bag that the cherries have been set into that's been lining that cardboard basket. I can grab the two handles to that plastic bag, lift up and all of her cherries are ready to go.

Michael:	So she thinks she's going to get the basket?
Fruit Guy:	Her first time there she might suspect but she doesn't see the basket. It's covered up by the plastic bag.
Michael:	I got you.

Fruit Guy: That's the one thing I always have a problem with whenever I'm training somebody new on the stand I tell them, "You know, nobody gets these baskets. They cost one dollar a piece."

So okay let's continue. So she's going to take her two singles change and I'm going to set my bank to the side. I'm now going to reach up onto the table, grab her two bags, the large cherry, and the medium peach and hand them to her. I don't want to rush her off. It's kind of a funny thing and I still don't understand it after 30 years. But for some reason, and it could be safety, it could be "Hey, somebody knows there's good fruit there." I don't know why exactly because everybody's a little different, but when there's somebody pulled over at my stand I guarantee you one or two people are pulling over before they leave.

It's just funny how it works. When somebody's pulled over and another car is coming along and they see them pulled over, "Hey, they're open. Hey, they must be good. Hey, it must be a safe place." I don't know but when you can slow them down a little, at least until the next car pulls up and that's my timing. It's all about your timing and how you can slow them down. I like to tell a little story, a little joke, talk fruit, I don't know … explain something. And generally when you're talking to these people they love to talk about their garden, how when they were a kid and they went to the "Pick Your Own" you-pick farm. I could write a book of all the great fruit stories that people told me.

Michael: So you want to keep them there because when there's a car there it's going to increase your chances to get another pull-over.

Fruit Guy: And, you know, the girls aren't really good at that. Not everybody needs to do that. I just found that that makes a difference. You don't need to do that to make $1000 a day, but if you can don't be surprised if your average goes up to $1250.

Michael: We should talk about the money and you've been doing this 30 years. If someone's properly trained, if they have

	the right location and if they do everything you trained them to do then what kind of money can they make?
Fruit Guy:	One thousand dollars every day where they start with $300 dollars in the morning.
Michael:	So they start with $300 in the morning and they make $1000 so they'll gross $700 a day.
Fruit Guy:	No. They'll gross $1300 and they'll net $1000.
Michael:	Oh, they'll net $1000. So the $300 in the morning … is that for their fruit?
Fruit Guy:	You need fruit.
Michael:	And this is one stand, right?
Fruit Guy:	One stand.
Michael:	One stand for a day. Look, I'm your brother, I've got a three day notice on my door, I have a truck and I'm healthy and I've got a strong back and I need to get my rent paid by Friday. What are you going to tell me to do? I'm right here in San Diego.
Fruit Guy:	If you're my brother you're going to be a millionaire in 100 days.
Michael:	A millionaire.
Fruit Guy:	You're going to make one million dollars cash in 100 days.
Michael:	I'm going to be a millionaire in 100 days?
Fruit Guy:	Correct.
Michael:	Man, I like that. How are you going to get me started?
Fruit Guy:	I'm going to start you on Day 1 with $200 dollars.
Michael:	What time do I have to wake up in the morning?

Fruit Guy: That's the thing. If you want to be a millionaire and you're my brother you need three things. One, an entrepreneurial spirit. If you want to make a few hundred dollars a day you can get up at whatever time you want and you can have whatever kind of spirit you want, but if you want to make one million dollars in 100 days you're going to have a real entrepreneurial spirit too.

Two, lazy time is over. You can't get up at 10:00 and you can't shut the stand down at 4:00. If you want to work for 100 days I'll make you a millionaire. If you're my brother and you're willing to do that we're going that route.

Three, the last thing is that you need is supplies. What are my supplies? The first thing is you need $200 dollars to go to the fruit broker and you need a tent and you need a fan or a truck to transport your things.

Michael: Like a 10' x 10' tent.

Fruit Guy: Exactly. Here's my advice because you're my brother. Don't start with a $69 dollar tent that grandpa gave you. Don't start with that thing that has four pieces for each leg and takes you a half an hour to set up and blows over. Spend the $199 bucks and get the best tent you can and make it last you five years.

Michael: Okay, I need the tent and where am I going to put everything?

Fruit Guy: You're going to slip your two tables in the side of your truck standing up sideways, your tent next to them, and you're going to stack your fruit next to those. You're going to have one 30 gallon tub with a lid that you use to keep all your supplies, your gloves, your stakes and ropes for your tent, your bags, your baskets, your hammer. All your little supplies are going to be in that one tub. That's all you need, you're done.

Michael: And my signs.

Fruit Guy: Oh yeah, and your signs, of course.

Michael: How many signs am I going to need?

Fruit Guy: Well, that's one of the things. I've done crazy stuff with signs. Michael, you're going to love it. I've done 10 signs in each direction within a mile of my stand. I've done crazy stuff that made people sick, I think because they just wouldn't stop.

Michael: That's cool. Tell me about the 10 signs one in each direction. What were they made out of?

Fruit Guy: They're all made out of the same thing. They're all made out of plywood that I cut up into little sections and I'll spend the whole month of April working on signs. Even though they're the same signs I had last year I'm not happy. When you pull up to my stand everything is clean, there's no crap on the ground, no girl's backpack is there. It's in the tub. There's nothing laying around. I don't do the hay bells anymore. I don't do any weird stuff where I tried everything in the world. Two tables, a little tub that's got supplies in it, and stacks of fruit.

Michael: You're like the farmer who just came off the field and set up his little tent and here's the fruit.

Fruit Guy: Here it is.

Michael: Okay, tell me about your 10 signs, your 10 ones going in each direction. Did they all say the same thing or did you change the words?

Fruit Guy: I use to change signs once a week. I spent so much time …

Michael: So you'd have to put the signs out daily, right?

Fruit Guy: Daily and then take them down at the end of the day. Rarely do I have spots where I can just leave them up for the whole summer.

Michael: How do you put up 10 signs? Do you have a stake on it like a real estate sign?

Fruit Guy: Well, you just get a rock and you roll it over there and lean it against the tree and then you set it up at the bottom of the sign so it doesn't fly over if the wind blows or if a car goes too close to it. And you walk another 30 feet, you put another sign down and you find some way to pry it up so it stays up. If it's a fence or the field or another tree or some rocks that have some weeds then some way it's going to stand up. Walk another 30 feet, this one says "nectarines." Walk another 30 feet, this once says "tomatoes." I've done them all but none of them worked.

Michael: None of them worked.

Fruit Guy: None of them worked. The one that worked is "Cherries." The one that really worked was "Sweet Cherries." The golden ticket: *"Sweet Cherries, Today's Pick."*

Michael: I'm your brother so that's what you're going to tell me to start with.

Fruit Guy: Yes.

Michael: "Sweet Cherries. Today's Pick."

Fruit Guy: Yes.

Michael: And how many would you say I need to start with?

Fruit Guy: You need one for each direction.

Michael: How many feet from the stand?

Fruit Guy: People can see your stand. People know you're there. You're not giving them any information by throwing all these signs out there. These dudes have one sign a quarter mile before your stand that says *"Sweet Cherries."*

Michael: And then they're looking for them.

Fruit Guy: And then walk the other direction a quarter mile and put the other one.

Michael: So I've got a good tent, I've got all my supplies that you

	told me about on the list. Okay, I'm in San Diego. How do I find my fruit? Where should I go?
Fruit Guy:	You're going to pick up the phone book and you're going to look under three sections. The first one is produce, second one is fruit brokers and you're going to make phone calls. You have your phonebook there you're going to see a whole list of them, even if you live in small town America. If there's a restaurant somebody's bringing vegetables and fruit into town. Find that company and you're going to ask them, "Hey, do you have cherries? How much are they? Will you give me cherries if you don't have them? Great, can we do that on a daily basis? Great." And then he knows he's now making a couple of bucks, whatever. I don't know, every town's going to be different, but I don't pay over one dollar a pound. I don't care if they are golden cherries I don't pay over one dollar a pound.
Michael:	Are the brokers all over the place with price?
Fruit Guy:	Yeah.
Michael:	Does price go up and down?
Fruit Guy:	It's pretty consistent. You can't control him. It's how much he wants to make. I can't tell you what that broker wants to make versus this broker.
Michael:	Well, when I'm starting, like from your experience, you'll find a couple of good relationships with some fruit brokers and you'll stick with them.
Fruit Guy:	Yes.
Michael:	I'm looking for a good relationship with a fruit broker who's got cherries under $1 a pound.
Fruit Guy:	And if you have to pay $1.50 a pound and you get 4 bucks a pound is that really going to matter to you the first season?
Michael:	No.

Fruit Guy: No. So if for twenty pound case of cherries, that's what they come in generally, the guy tells you on the phone is at 32 bucks, are you going to hang up on him?

Michael: No.

Fruit Guy: You probably you might want to think about it, at least go sample them, but you're going to make money.

Michael: You're teaching me to start with cherries, okay. It's my first day. I'm going to start with just cherries so I'm going to go out to the fruit broker. Do I walk in and buy them or do the brokers deliver? I mean what's the best way?

Fruit Guy: You're going to his place where many other people are probably doing the same thing. You're going to his place at 5:00, 6:00 in the morning. No, you're not running ten fruit stands. You're going to his place at 8:00 in the morning and you're going to be loaded and on the road at 8:20, 8:30.

Michael: They're waiting for me.

Fruit Guy: Yeah.

Michael: And I get to go grab what I want.

Fruit Guy: You get to go in and say, "Hey, what do you got in cherries?" And he's going to say, "Come on back to the back cooler." He's going to walk you back there or he's going to send somebody back there with you or he's going to just send you back there because he's too busy. Go back there and you're going to see stacks of cherries. Hopefully he's got more than one variety. He's got four or five types and prices so you can pop the lids on these cases and take one out and sample it and go to the next stack.

Michael: So what type should I get?

Fruit Guy: The ones that taste the best. Forget about the varieties or these ones come before that one. It doesn't matter. You're going to sample one from each of his cases that came from this type of a grower, and this came from this type of a packer and this came from this type of a packer and you're going to sample each one because you could care less about anything else, but when they bite into that cherry and you're looking at them as you're slicing a slice of your next sample you want their eyes to light up, you want it to explode on their chin, you want their cheeks to shoot up really high and the color to come to their face and you want them to go, "Wow, that's a great cherry." I don't care if they're 12 bucks a case. I don't want them if they don't taste great.

Michael: Okay, so when you're sampling them, I mean do I need to sample maybe a couple of them just to make sure?

Fruit Guy: I guess one's enough.

Michael: So you're good to go. You trust the rest of the batches.

Fruit Guy: So it probably took me a few times because I didn't learn that right away. You want to pop the lid on every one of those cases and make sure one of them isn't full of mold, hasn't been sitting somewhere for two weeks and he just flipped it into your stack. Because he doesn't really know what's going on. He probably has somebody loading them onto a cart and bringing them out to your truck for you - one of the many warehouse type of workers. Just check out your stuff before you leave.

Michael: Do that every time.

Fruit Guy: Every time. Take every case lid off. It's going to take you 30 seconds a box. Every box is going to bring you 72 dollars. That 20 pound case of cherries is going to bring you $72 whether you pay 12 bucks, 15 bucks or 20 bucks it's going to make you 72 bucks.

Michael: Now what time of the year could I expect that things have been "Picked Today"?

Fruit Guy: Well, if you're in California you're looking to start in mid-April. If you're in Central America you're looking to start on the 1st of May.

Michael:	This is seasonal.
Fruit Guy:	Correct. I work 100 days and then I take 265 off.
Michael:	Okay so you're going to show me how in 100 days you can make one million dollars. So this is only working 100 days out of the year.
Fruit Guy:	That's what I said.
Michael:	Wow!
Fruit Guy:	One hundred days, one million dollars.
Michael:	Okay, so the 100 days is the season.
Fruit Guy:	Correct.
Michael:	Okay, so about when in April were we starting?
Fruit Guy:	Mid-April. You can never say this is the date because of too many factors. It's all about the weather and the heat. You can't say this is always the date. Never the same day year-after-year but it's always within a week or two of each other. I've started many seasons on the 15th of April. I started many seasons on the 1st of May.
Michael:	But nothing's happening in March.
Fruit Guy:	Nothing's happening except you're running around getting permits.
Michael:	How many months are they fresh picked where I can use that "Fresh Picked" sign?
Fruit Guy:	You're going to use *Today's Pick* only the days that you can get anything on that table that was picked today.
Michael:	Well, what do you think my chances are of doing that?
Fruit Guy:	Every day. Cherries are the last fruit to blossom, the first fruit that's ready. Well, when they're not ready anymore

and the broker's now bringing them in not locally from California but he's bringing them in from Oregon because it's July, or Washington because it's August, that means your peaches are ready in California and they're picking those today. And your nectarines were ready a week before and next week will be the tomatoes and the week after will be melons. Just try to always get something if you can that was picked today.

Michael: So I can use my *Today's Pick*.

Fruit Guy: And it doesn't matter where you put it. I wouldn't put it and lean it against the sign that says *"Cherries."* I'd lean it right against my table.

Michael: So you've told me how to buy my fruit from the broker but since I'm starting off easy with cherries, if I'm just doing cherries for the day how many pounds of cherries do I need do you think?

Fruit Guy: Well, you're not going to step on yourself too bad so you want to start with a small amount until you found your spot. Once you've sold out that small amount and it's 3:00 you know the next day you're going to put an extra two cases on. And when you sold that out and its 4:00 you're going to keep adding on each day.

Michael: Do I know my spot before I buy my cherries?

Fruit Guy: You better.

Michael: Okay, so let's talk about this spot. I'm here in San Diego. What are you going to tell me as being your brother I'm going to say, "Where the hell am I going to sell these?" Where's the best place?

Fruit Guy: Actually this is the most important and the biggest challenge you're going to have, my brother, which is going to be finding your spot that's going to make you money and not going to bring you any heat. And why do I not want heat? Because I rarely get permits anymore. You want to ask me why?

Michael: Why?

Fruit Guy: Let me share you a story and then maybe you'll understand. In Northern California in the Bay area there's a kid's amusement park. It's in Vallejo and I had a great spot there. Every year I could close down at 5:00 because I already knew I had $1000 made and it was great, it was money, it was show up late, leave early, but I could just clobber that spot year-after-year. I could abuse that spot. It didn't matter, it was awesome.

Michael: And it was right by an amusement ...

Fruit Guy: Right at the exit to Marine World.

Michael: Oh, Marine World like a Sea World.

Fruit Guy: Yeah.

Michael: Okay.

Fruit Guy: As they rolled out my stand was right there and I had to go and ask the guy who ran the park there and he said, "No problem." And I said "Cool" and I set it up there. And that was good. It was great. They were happy, I was happy, customers were happy, it was easy. I would grease them, you know, once every couple of weeks I would take a case in and drop them on that guy's desk and what did that cost me? 12 bucks, 14 bucks and that's generally the best spot. So drop the spot where the guy says, "Give me 100 bucks a week." The best spots are the spots where the guys go, "Yeah, I don't care. Go ahead. Just bring me some fruit once in a while."

Michael: When you approach them what do you say, "Hey, can I set my truck up ...?"

Fruit Guy: Oh, it's April and it's beautiful and there's a technique that works like money, but let's go there when we finish this one.

Michael: Okay.

BUDDHA YOGA

Fruit Guy: Alright, where are we?

Michael: You're telling me the story about this spot that you had.

Fruit Guy: So I'm in Vallejo, greatest spot. I just love it because it's stress free. While I have, not my brother but he's like my brother, and I have this friend who's in big trouble and he needs help and so I give him a job. I know it's a mistake but I'm going to give him a job. Man, is it a mistake. Don't ever hire your friends, tip number two.

Next, he won't sell there without a permit. He doesn't want to get in trouble with the police and I try to explain to them I've done this for so many years and that I never have ever, ever gotten one ticket. And even when the police do pull over because for some reason they're usually there to buy cherries or I'm still going to be there two days later.

So, you know, you don't need a permit but every day I would get grief and I told them finally, "Here's an extra 100 bucks. Go get your permit." And it was either a Thursday or Friday and I had just shut that stand down that whole weekend and let him get his permit thing worked out. He had to go down to the police station. The city permit was like 40 bucks and then he had to go back on Monday.

He had to go get something called a Lifeline I think. To get the city permit he had to go down to the police station. Some cities have more strict standards than others. Some I'm in and out of there in 20 minutes with the permit for less than 50 bucks. Some make you run around for a month. That's why I always start early if I'm going to get any permit.

So he goes in, gets his Lifeline at the police station, a couple of days later he's got his permit, and we're good to go. Load up the truck, we're heading back to the spot in Vallejo and when we get there ...

Michael: Someone's there.

Fruit Guy: No, it's worst. The city has posted No Parking signs along the entire street that they were totally unaware of the week before I got that permit.

Michael: Wow, so you think that tipped them off.

Fruit Guy: I know it did, and that was it. So if I can tell you something if you have to get a permit great, get it, but if you don't have to get a permit my lesson that I've learned is I only get a permit when I have to.

Michael: And out of all the times you never had a permit.

Fruit Guy: Not one. A dozen cops pull over because I'm an idiot and I had to learn the hard way. What do you mean? Well you know the white line on the side of the road? If your tent is at least six feet away from that a cop is going to pull over.

Michael: Okay, so you need to be six feet back from the white line.

Fruit Guy: If you set your tent up on Skyline Ridge that's way steep and there's a big turnout but when people turn out they have to slow down and they make the whole road below them slow down to a dead stop …

Michael: Yeah.

Fruit Guy: … and they have to start in first gear again. Do you know what happens?

Michael: Yeah it's dangerous.

Fruit Guy: And do you know what happens? It's so dangerous and people get so upset do you know who they call?

Michael: They call the cops.

Fruit Guy: They call 911 and tell the Highway Patrol there's somebody out here with this tent out on the turnout stopping traffic. And when he comes he doesn't even get out of his car. He's so angry at me he just gives me this "You're out of here" thumb and he just drives off and spits a big dust ball at me. So what can I tell you? Hey, make sure your spot is safe. Make sure you're not going to cause yourself some heat. Don't get yourself in some spot where you're going to cause traffic trouble because as soon as you cause traffic trouble I promise you your spot is going away.

Michael: Okay, that's some good advice. So this is hard to find a spot. What are you going to tell me, as being your brother, where should I go? Where should I start to find my spot?

Fruit Guy: Finding the spot is really not hard. I mean how many gas stations, grocery stores, supermarkets or places that you regularly do business with are there where you can walk up and say, "Hey, you know, my family grows fruit and I've told my family that maybe I could move some of it for them this summer. Do you mind if I throw a tent out here maybe during May for a few weeks?" You're not going to ask them for a 100 day commitment. You're not going to ask them if you can take over, "You know the little corner of the parking lot back over there? I was just wondering can I throw a tent up there and sell some cherries with my daughter next weekend?" You just want to open up the door so they can see what they got.

Michael: Okay, so where am I going to go? Like in front of a grocery store?

Fruit Guy: No, that's the last place.

Michael: I'm looking for a good amount of traffic.

Fruit Guy: Traffic is the key. You're looking for a spot where cars are going by, not every one minute but every 30 seconds, some place where you can get some pullovers. It's rare that festivals work. Concerts never work and boat shows. It's been a circle and they see you once and they're not going to see you again. You're invisible to them.

Michael: So you don't want to use a concert or a festival.

Fruit Guy: No, forget all that. You want pullovers. If you want to make 1000 dollars cash in one day you've got to pull them over. You got to have the cars going by you. And you don't want to set it up at the grocery store or even a mile from the grocery store. My best spots are out on those open highways, the best spots are in those really nice neighborhoods, the best spots are those gas stations where people are standing there for four to six minutes with their hand on the pump looking over their shoulder at you thinking, "Hmm, they've got a lot of customers coming and going over there." You're on the corner of that parking lot. They're just going to put it on automatic and step over to get a free sample.

Michael: So that could be in a good residential area, right, in a gas station parking lot?

Fruit Guy: Those are money.

Michael: Because you got people coming in there all the time.

Fruit Guy: If you've got it out there towards the edge and if they're getting gas they're looking at you every second that they're getting gas.

Michael: Okay, give me some more tips for some spots like gas stations and open roads where there's cars going by every 30 seconds. Don't go to spots where there's going to be one-time events like concerts or tradeshows. You want the ones that are going to see you over and over again, right?

Fruit Guy: I want the cars that are going by me and not the people that are walking around in a circle. I don't want to see the same eyes twice in one day. I want them going by my tent.

Michael: When you get a spot, let's say you're in the corner of a gas station, but a lot of these people come get gas at the place over and over again. Does it help for them to see you over and over again, or when you get a spot can business be pretty good at first and then kind of slow down because of familiarity?

Fruit Guy: So one of my newer lessons might pertain to this. One of my newer lessons over the last five years has been how do I keep them coming back? The people come by for you early in the season, but later the grocery store is so full of all those fruits and they're already there, and that's part of their regular program. How do I take their regular program and eliminate their produce shopping and just bring it to me?

So somewhere I just said to myself, "I'm going to try stuff." I said stuff, I said stuff, I said stuff, nothing seemed to work until I starting trying, "Well, can I ask you what you like? Is there anything on this table you don't see that you would really enjoy the next time you come?" And then they say, "Well, you know, I just love apricots. Do you have any?" I'll say, "I will have them soon. You make sure you come back to this stand in a few days because I'm going to have you some apricots."

Michael: Did you ever ask and get their names or emails?

Fruit Guy: Never, but you're going to have such control and such a connection with these people that not only could you get their name and number but you could sell them your water system. All the guys that come up to me all the time and want to leave their brochures and "Do I want to be involved?" with whatever they're selling as some kind of a manager or whatever, you know. No, no, no, no, no, get that stuff off my table.

Michael: So you would recommend that if I can capture their name, number, email address, if possible?

Fruit Guy: Never done it. I have no idea how that would help me as just a Portuguese that sells fruit on the side of the road. You're probably better with knowing how that would help than I would.

Michael: Okay, so I've got a location, I've got my supplies, I've got my broker, what time should I be set up?

Fruit Guy: I'm saying at 9:00. Why? Because your traffic is going to start up at 10:00. But even when I get to a spot there'll be people waiting. I've had sometimes four or five people waiting when I get to a spot at 9:00 and I tell them, "I'm sorry folks. I cannot help you until I get everything up and it's going to take me 20 minutes." "Well, I thought you opened at 9:00?" "No, I really open at 9:20." Whatever time I get there, if its 9:15 and they're waiting and I know it's going to take me 20 minutes then I open at 9:40 today. It's my job, I'm boss, that's the greatest feeling in the world.

Michael: You just make them wait.

Fruit Guy: And here's the thing, why do I have to do that? When a person buys that bag of fruit and they're handing over their money it's not more often than not but it's so often that 30% of the people say, "Why don't you give us one of those small cherries too?" or "You know, we're going to go see our grandparents this afternoon. Why don't you give us another one of those larges?" So that's why I tell the people it's so important to keep your table full of fruit.

You're going to have three larges of everything. You're going to have three mediums of everything before you say go in the morning. Why? Because you don't want that guy to come up, buy his medium cherry and leave. You want him to buy a medium cherry, you want to hit him with some samples and maybe he'll pick up one or two more items, and you want that opportunity for him to say, "Well, these are sure good, you're going to have to give me another one for later" or "You know, my neighbor just loves cherries. I'm going to take her a bag." You have to have your table full. That's a big, big, mistake hat fruit stands only have one little basket out at a time.

Michael: So I've got cherries on my first day, I've got my location - the gas station sounds good, I'm starting in the middle of April, so I've got my sweet cherries and I've got my sign *"Today's Pick."* We're rocking and rolling. I'm selling, I've got your pricing pitch down memorized, I've got the wood crates where I have my change in there, I've got my gloves on. So if I'm starting with just cherries and then let's say I'm getting more comfortable, I've got some confidence in my own stand, now how are you going to take me to one million dollars in 100 days?

Fruit Guy: Alright, so you've done Day 1 and you're going to start Day 2. On Day 2 you're going to call home and have your girlfriend put an ad on Craigslist: *"Work on fruit stand get paid $10 cash per hour."* You're going to get about 500 phone calls before you close your stand up that day. During one of those phone calls you're going to hear somebody that sounds like it's the right person and you're going to tell them where your stand is and that you'd like to meet them right now.

Tomorrow morning when you open you're already going to have this person trained and you're going to be out looking for another spot and you're going to be bringing in twice as much fruit with your profits that you made from that day and you're going to have two tents going. Here's my goal at the end of the first week. I want four stands. You don't have to do it on your second day.

Michael: End of the first week, four stands.

Fruit Guy: Correct.

Michael: Now realistically you got some guy some from Craigslist. The training can that be frustrating or can you get them trained pretty easily?

Fruit Guy: It's pretty easy because all they're going to do for the first half of day is stand behind you and you put cherries in baskets. And you're just going to constantly be telling them "more" or "less," "cleaner" or "less clean." I don't want to sell any junk in my basket. You're going to constantly be critiquing them until they know how to make a perfect basket. The whole three, six, ten hours that he's standing there with you he's hearing you say the same thing 100 times. The next day he's good.

Michael: He is.

Fruit Guy: Yes.

Michael: Do you worry about them stealing from you?

Fruit Guy: Yes. That's the greatest thing that I've ever come up with is having those baskets and the salesperson never touches the cash. I can park three blocks away and watch with binoculars for four hours. They never steal. If they never touch the money, never touch it with their own fingers and you can keep an eye on it then you're good.

Michael: So you show him how to do that. I show him that's the program. Why? Because almost every customer the first time they come to the stand that is so great that you don't touch the money. They love that because you're touching their food. And you know what's the funniest thing? It's when you've got this person walking up to your stand while you're just finishing up with these two people as they're leaving who are just finishing talking to you because they're telling their story. And on your left you have two people coming up behind the person coming up, "Hey, how much are your cherries?" the person coming up says. You hand them a cherry and you say, "The first one's always free, and let me tell you I've got some other fruit here" and you're slicing a slice for them while these other two customers come up and are already programmed to point. They don't ever talk to you, they just point, they point to that basket. They point to that basket and you're pulling up their bags for them, you're opening up your change jar. Meanwhile you're still saying goodbye to these people while explaining to this guy what's going on. With the samples you're hitting them with the two, four, six, eight, ten blah, blah, blah, blah, and he's just engulfed. I can't explain the feeling that I'm gaining. It is really exciting.

Michael: So you get the ad on Craigslist, you get them to meet you, and it's going to be my first day. And I've used Craigslist and I'm sure I can get that phone ringing. When you put that ad on Craigslist is your girlfriend handling that or do you have the calls come into you on the cell phone or what?

Fruit Guy: I have them come to me. I make every person who works the stand shut off their phones.

Michael: So if I'm calling you about the job and you got a good feeling about me what are the expectations? I mean what do you say to them to do your best to keep them honest and service the stand properly?

Fruit Guy: Here's the first thing you say: "Are you prepared to make $100 cash a day everyday for the rest of the summer and not take the 4th of July off, Labor Day off, any day off?" That's the thing about the commitment to not being lazy, entrepreneurial spirit, having what it takes. There are no days off. If you want to make it happen you have to give all 100 days from the minute you get up until it gets dark.

Michael: Okay, because I know I've run a lot of Craigslist ads and there's a lot of lazy ass people there.

Fruit Guy: So they call up and I tell them, "You know, this is the deal. I'm looking for somebody to commit 100 days and I will give them 100 dollars cash everyday that they work for me but it has to be every day until the end of the summer." And they go, "Oh, but I want to take off and go to the – I have plans." "Sorry this is probably not for you. Thanks for calling though." And I'll go through 100 calls and I'll have five to eight people standing there by the end of the day and I'll look them over. What am I looking for? I'm looking for someone who's not going to scare grandma when she sees the fruit stand. More important than anything I want honesty. The second most important thing is that I need someone to pull people over and not scare them off. And they don't have to be a hot little 20-year-old in shorts. A middle-aged woman is great.

Michael: Do you like women better than men?

Fruit Guy: Much better. The pull over percentage is probably 20%, 25% better. People feel safer. I don't understand it, but for some reason they pull over more.

Michael: What are concerns from some of your workers?

Fruit Guy: I'll give you an example. Last year I had a new person, and actually it was a guy. I don't hire as many guys as I do girls, but I had a guy and he came down and interviewed and watched the fruit stand for half a day. He was just all over and he loved it but he said he wouldn't do it without a permit. And I said, "Hey, that's up to you, if you want to get a permit some people feel like that the first year they work for me and they go and get a permit. That's up to you and I'll pay you for it. I'll give you every dime that you pay for that permit back in your pocket. But I'll tell you something else. A lot of times the permit's just a big runaround and you don't ever get anywhere and some cities charges a mess and I just don't even get permits most of the time anymore unless I'm forced to."

Two days later he was back and ready to work. I said, "Well, you sure look pumped up. You got your permit?" And he said, "No, I just talked to some cops." And I said "What?" And he said "I just talked to cops. I've been talking to cops since I saw you and it seems like they don't want to mess with us, they don't want to touch the fruit stand, they don't even want to look at you. You're not breaking any laws, you're not selling crack, you're not doing anything bad. Unless you cause yourself some trouble, sell some crap, don't put your tent in a safe spot and cause a traffic jam."

Michael: What the hell are they going to bother with you for?

Fruit Guy: You're out selling fruit, man. You're like any person they've seen on this street that isn't trying to screw somebody. You're out there trying to make a living doing something honest. What can be better than selling fruit, Michael?

Michael: I know. It's so wholesome and natural and innocent. That's why this topic is just so cool.

Fruit Guy: It's the greatest life. It's kind of hard to believe but I would do it for free.

Michael: It just sounds like you have the confidence that you've done it so much it's just like as long as you're physically able and mentally able you'll always be able to make a wonderful living in doing something you love anywhere as long as there's a fruit broker, right?

Fruit Guy: Correct.

Michael: How old are you now?

Fruit Guy: Forty-five.

Michael: You're 45. So how long have you been doing this?

Fruit Guy: Since I was eight. But how long have I been out on my own where grandpa said, "Get your stand out there"?

Michael: Yeah since you were 19.

Fruit Guy: Thirty years.

Michael: Tell me what the lifestyle is for you.

Fruit Guy: When you run one fruit stand you wake up at 8:00. You're at the broker at 8:15. At 8:30 you're loaded up and you're on your way. You set up your stand and you want to be going by 10:00 and want to close it at 6:00. The best program is 9:00 am to 7:00 pm. You just need that extra hour in the morning to set your table up so you can get the production you want. And although you'll only pick up 50 bucks between 9:00 and 10:00 it's going to be the difference of whether you net $1000 or not. And the other thing is you're going to get a lot of traffic between 5:00 and 7:00. So you want to be 9:00 to 7:00 is how long you're going to want to work your stand. But I got to go extra early because I got more than one thing going, you know.

Michael: Okay, so yeah, I don't want to get too far off track. Okay, I asked you how I'm going to make $1 million in 100 days. So through Craigslist I'm going to get my employees, I've qualified them, I've trained them because they've watched me for four hours. I mean they're going to make a couple of mistakes at first, right?

Fruit Guy: Sure, and it's not going to hurt anything. They're going to overdo their baskets and your average is going to decrease but every day at the end of the day when they unload their cash in your living room and you do your sorting with them with the money thing and you calculate, you know, what their average and everything is before they leave it only takes a few minutes.

Michael: Well, let me ask you this. If you want four stands and you've got one truck how are you handling the move?

Fruit Guy: You need to have a trailer if you're going to make one million dollars.

Michael: So you're the guy handling all the table signage and everything, or what's their responsibility after when 7:00 rolls along? Are your employees handling your stands?

Fruit Guy: It's different with different employees. With the girls I have to almost, with every single one of them set them up and tear them down. While I'll always have at least one or two guys that I can use in several different ways, not just to run a stand but sometimes I'll need somebody to do my job for me. I'll need somebody to run cash pickups, I'll need somebody to bring lunches out to the girls, you know, I'll need to do some managerial things where I'm not able to because I'm breaking in two new spots today. I want to train these two new people but I need somebody to give Spot 7 and Spot 3 a half an hour pee break.

Michael: So you're running a crew.

Fruit Guy: That's my idea.

Michael: Can I ask you what's the most stands you've run somewhat comfortably at one time where you're just not totally freaking out?

Fruit Guy: Freaking out is when I get past 15. You're freaking out but what you want to do is you want to keep yourself in the seven to ten range and that's comfortable.

Michael: Can I do $1 million in 100 days with seven to ten?

Fruit Guy: I have one spot that brings in over $2000 grand cash a day net. I have another spot that's right there and many spots that are in the $1500 range. I have a few in the $800, $900 range but when I say you're going to make $1000 cash in your pocket every day I'm not exaggerating.

Michael:	And that's after you've paid your employee?
Fruit Guy:	Right.
Michael:	That's sweet. That's sweet cherries right there.
Fruit Guy:	Everyday has a dozen stories when you're at the fruit stand. They're interesting stories, they're fun stories, they're stories you can't wait to go home and tell your girlfriend about.
Michael:	Tell me some you just remember over the years, something that sticks out over your mind.
Fruit Guy:	Alright. This is one of my favorites, not because it's all that interesting or funny, but this one touches me. I give away fruit for about a week per year. Where the ocean meets San Francisco there's a beach there called Ocean Beach with several large parking lots. The first parking lot is clear up by the sea cliff and that's where all the surfers park. That's kind of like where we like to hangout just because we're not there to make money during that week, although we sell a lot of cherries, but if you bring me a bag off of the beach full of garbage you can come up here and trade it for any one of my baskets of fruit. And that's how we get the beach clean. We spend about a week a year giving away fruit at a beach because up here in San Francisco there's no big raking crews and machinery and all that. There's garbage on the beach and it gets really bad in the summertime.
	So every year we set up a tent there and people come up and buy cherries. But a lot of our cool-like hipsters, surfer dudes and stuff, they'll just come out and grab a plastic bag from me, take it out on the beach, fill it up with garbage, come back and take a bag of fruit. And it's great for me, it's great for them. It doesn't cost me much I know it's a couple of hundred bucks a day or whatever, but I'm making 10 times that already out there and I'm just going to run my little fun program. This Cleanup Beach Week is always for me and I'm making money. I got stands going but I got people handling that because I'm only right here for that week. I just love that week.

Anyway, let's talk about the story. Up pulled these two big yellow buses and out pour like seventy or something kids like with their red camp shirts on and they're all like waist high little kids. And I see the big burley manager guy of them all and I wave them over and we start talking and he brings them up. It's just so cool to see a line of seventy kids up to your tent and they all take a plastic bag and they all go onto the beach and they all come back. It's really great because Chandra's got a clean bag for them while she takes their dirty garbage bag, ties it and tosses it. And she gives them an empty bag and they take a couple of steps forward. I reach into the case with my glove on, pull out about a pound and drop it in their bag. I say "Thank you very much for helping us clean the beach. We really appreciate it. If you want to if you can save that bag and bring it back with more garbage and I'll give you some more."

So the seventy kids clean the beach. It was so beautiful they made like a line. It's a real wide, wide beach and they just swooped it and filled up all their bags and came up. It was great. Well guess what happened about an hour later? About half of those kids came back with another bag of garbage.

Michael: You were out of fruit.

Fruit Guy: No, no, I got lots of fruit. I'm making money at the same time we're giving it away. I'm not losing money. I shouldn't say that I'm actually ever going to lose money.

Michael: Yeah, you're selling too.

Fruit Guy: I'm selling too. And even if give away twice as much as I sell, guess what, I've made money. So the kids come back on a second round. About half of them come back on a second round of garbage drop and I tell them, "I'm sorry I cannot give you anymore cherries. Oh no, no, I would love to give everybody more cherries but you don't understand you're little kids. Two pounds of cherries equals big tummy aches past that point. I can't give you any more cherries, but next time you guys come here and you see us here I will be happy to do it again and thank you so much."

This is so cool, you know, it's all so neat to have all these little kids passing underneath you getting their input. Anyway I don't know maybe an hour and a half, two hours later I forgot all about the kids. I don't know about a dozen of them come up with bags of garbage and they set them next to the truck and I said "Guys, I don't want to give you" … "No, no, no, we don't want any more cherries." And I just felt like the kids saw something from that and I always take that with me.

Michael: But they wanted to just clean the beach.

Fruit Guy: Because they saw the value of their environment. It's something I carry with me every year. Its little things like that. You wanted a story …

Michael: That's a great story.

Fruit Guy: It just touches me when I think of them.[37]

---

[37] Michael Senoff, "Fruit Guy Interview," accessed August 29, 2018 http://www.hardtofindseminars.com/Fruit_Guy_Interview.htm.

WARREN BUFFETT'S TRUE
INVESTING METHODOLOGY

On November 20, 2008, Alice Schroeder, author of *The Snowball: Warren Buffett and the Business of Life*, spoke during the Value Investing Conference at the Darden School of Business. She provided some fascinating insights into how Warren Buffett invests that are not in the book, and which reveal his *real* methodology for evaluating investment opportunities. This should be useful to any parties managing the funds of a religious institution.

1. Much of Buffett's success has come from training himself to practice good habits. His first and most important habit is to work hard. He dug up SEC documents long before they were online. He went to the state insurance commission to dig up facts. He was visiting companies long before he was known and persisting in the face of rejection.
2. He was always thinking what more he could do to get an edge on the other guy.
3. Schroeder rejects those who argue that working harder will not give you an edge today because so much is available online.
4. Buffett is a "learning machine". This learning has been cumulative over his entire life covering thousands of businesses and many different industries. This storehouse of knowledge allows Buffett to make decisions quickly.
5. Schroeder uses a case study on Mid-Continent Tab Card Company in which Buffett invested privately to illustrate how Buffett invests.
6. In the 1950's, IBM was forced to divest itself of the computer tab card business as part of an anti-trust settlement with the Justice Department. The computer tab card business was IBM's most profitable business with profit margins of 50%.
7. Buffett was approached by some friends to invest in Mid-Continent Tab Card Company which was a start-up setup to compete in the tab card business. Buffett declined because of the real risk that the start-up could fail.
8. This illustrates a fundamental principle of how Buffett invests: first focus on what you can loose and then, and only then, think about return. Once Buffett concluded he could lose money, he quit thinking and said "no". This is his first filter.

9. Schroder argues that most investors do just the opposite: they first focus on the upside and then give passing thought to risk.
10. Later, after the start-up was successfully established and competing, Buffett was again approached to invest capital to grow the business. The company needed money to purchase additional machines to make the tab cards. The business now had 40% profit margins and was making enough that a new machine could pay for itself in a year.
11. Schroeder points out that already in 1959, long before Buffett had established himself as an expert stock picker, people were coming to him with special deals, just like they do now with Goldman Sachs and GE. The reason is that having started so young in business he already had both capital and business knowledge/acumen.
12. Unlike most investors, Buffett did not create a model of the business. In fact, based on going through pretty much all of Buffett's files, Schroder never saw that Buffett had created a model of a business.
13. Instead, Buffett thought like a horse handicapper. He isolated the one or two factors upon which the success of Mid American hinged. In this case, sales growth and cost advantage.
14. He then laid out the quarterly data for these factors for all of Mid Continent's factories and those of its competitors, as best he could determine it, on sheets of a legal pad and intently studied the data.
15. He established his hurdle of a 15% return and asked himself if he could get it based on the company's 36% profit margins and 70% growth. It was a simple yes or no decision and he determined that he could get the 15% return so he invested.
16. According to Schroder, 15% is what Buffett wants from day 1 on an investment and then for it to compound from there.
17. This is how Buffett does a discounted cash flow. There are no discounted cash flow models. Buffett simply looks at detailed long-term historical data and determines, based on the price he has to pay, if he can get at least a 15% return. (This is why Charlie Munger has said he has never seen Buffett do a discounted cash flow model.)
18. There was a big margin of safety in the numbers of Mid Continent.
19. Buffett invested $60,000 of personal money or about 20% of his net worth. It was an easy decision for him. No projections - only historical data.
20. He held the investment for 18 years and put another $1 million into the business over time. The investment earned 33% over the 18 years.

21. It was a vivid example of a Phil Fisher investment at a Ben Graham price.
22. Buffett is very risk averse and follows Firestone's Law of forecasting: "Chicken Little only has to be right once." This is why Berkshire Hathaway is not dealing with a lot of the problems other companies are dealing with because he avoids the risk of catastrophe.
23. He is very realistic and never tries to talk himself out of a decision if he sees that it has cat risk.
24. Buffett said he thought the market was attractive in the fall of 2008 because it was at 70%-80% of GDP. This gave him a margin of safety based on historical data. He is handicapping. He doesn't care if it goes up or down in the short term. Buying at these levels stacks the odds in his favor over time.
25. Buffett has never advocated the concept of dollar cost averaging because it involves buying the market at regular intervals - regardless of how overvalued the market may be. This is something Buffett would never support.[38]

---

[38] Gregory Speicher, "How Buffett Values a Business and Invests," accessed 12/01/2018, https://www.gurufocus.com/news/85318/alice-schroeder-on-how-buffett-values-a-business-and-invests.

SEASONAL STOCK MARKET TRADING
VIA TWICE A YEAR SWITCHING

This "best six months of the year strategy" comes from my book *Super Investing*, and has historically tended to outperform stock market buy-and-hold strategies while keeping investors out of many market declines. It is the simplest do-it-yourself investment strategy I have ever found that captures far more return with less risk than buy and hold stock market strategies. You basically get into the market during the best six months of every year, and get out of the market during the six months when the market tends to do its worst. One can use this for endowments or for managing monastery funds, etcetera.

A frequent argument against this automatic strategy is that an investor who misses even a small number of the best market days during the "off" investment period would underperform the market over time. The counter-argument is that an investor who misses even a small number of the worst periods would significantly outperform a buy and hold strategy over time.

Which camp is right? Historically speaking, *skipping the worst months has increased returns over buy and hold many times over*. Sometimes that means giving up some summer-autumn profits, but in terms of the total track record, this simple timing strategy has produced a better rate of return with less drawdown than staying totally invested all year long. Those results don't even take into account the interest you would have earned during the "out" periods, which would make it shine all the brighter. So here are the rules to this super investing system that uses the seasonality of the stock market ...

THE RULES:

The basic strategy has you investing in the stock market between November 1st and April 30 each year, and then getting out of the market and investing in bonds, money markets or other interest rate vehicles between May and November.

This is the idea behind the famous saying to "Sell in May and go away, but come back to be seen near favorable Halloween," which in turn is based on the original British saying to "Sell in May and go away, stay away till Saint Leger's Day." Thus, now we know approximately when we want to be in or out of the market. However, this basic strategy has a dynamic aspect to the timing that alters the exact date you would use each year to enter or exit stocks.

The strategy uses the MACD indicator (moving average convergence divergence indicator invented by Gerald Appel), favored by stock market technical analysts and found on nearly all charting software, as a trigger to determine the exact day to enter or exit the market around these two calendar poles. I tend to use the ThinkorSwim.com software to monitor the MACD as it has many other indicators, too, but you can use other services as well.

Starting in April and running through May, one waits to leave the market only after the MACD indicator finally gives a cross-over signal to "sell." Starting in October and running through November, one monitors the MACD indicator again on a daily basis and waits to re-enter the market when the indicator finally gives a "buy" cross-over signal. This little bit of dynamic behavior improves the returns of the simple six month strategy many times over! It gets you in earlier and keeps you in longer during market uptrends, and gets you out earlier and keeps you out longer when the market is in a downtrend. By making the basic calendar rule dynamic, you increase your returns and decrease drawdowns, too.

The Stock Traders Almanac, by Yale Hirsch, reports that this simple strategy, which it developed based on the initial work of seasonal analyst Sy Harding, has produced extremely reliable investment returns with reduced risk since 1950! That's a positive track record over six decades long, and having such a long term track record is one of our requirements before recommending a super investing method. Before you decide if you want to start using it, let's look at the actual performance of this method.

Starting with an investment of $10,000 (starting in 1950 for the Dow and S&P and 1971 for the NASDAQ), the following table derived from the StockTradersAlmanac.com website shows how this initial $10K would have grown for the Dow Jones Industrials, S&P and NASDAQ to the end of 2011. It also shows the compound average rate of return, or CAGR, that you would have achieved using a buy and hold strategy or the best six month seasonal period switching technique. The best six months of the year trading strategy clearly shows a far better return per year and represents far less risk and much less drawdown. Its CAGR beats buy and hold by 1-3% per annum, and that difference adds up to a lot over time.

The Compound Annual Rates of Return for Two Investing Methods

	Buy and Hold Returns		Seasonal Switching	
Dow Jones	$600,206	6.8%	$2,074,294	9.0%
S&P500	$740,484	7.2%	$1,398,585	8.3%
NASDAQ	$280,936	8.5%	$ 818,196	11.3%

These growth numbers do not even include interest earned during the six month summer period when funds are sitting idle, which would boost the compound growth rates even higher! Given that the average yearly T-bill and T-bond rates were roughly 4-5% and 6-7% over these long time frames, and assuming that we would get half of that return when we parked the idle summer funds in T-bills or bonds, we can conservatively add yet another 2-3% of yearly outperformance to the rates of return earned by the simple MACD seasonal switching system.

S&P sector analyst Sam Stovall has even suggested in *The Seven Rules of Wall Street* that investors might consider switching into either the S&P Consumer Staples (XLP) or Health Care sectors (XLV) from May to October as a rotational strategy instead of T-bonds or bills. This is yet another alternative although I have not seen computations showing how much additional return this adds to the system. People usually don't like simple investing systems because they then think they must not work due to the simplicity, but this one outperforms in spades.

If you are going to follow only one simple market timing rule rather than buy and hold, this is the one I would use.

Starting October 1, you are looking for signs of a market uptrend using a standard 12-26-9 MACD indicator, and you get into the market when it gives a "long" or "buy" cross-over signal.

Beginning April 1, you are looking to exit your position as soon as the market starts declining, once again the trade being triggered by a "short" or "sell" MACD cross-over signal.

You can trade the system using index funds to avoid management fees, and the trading rules are just that simple. People can even subscribe to the StockTradersAlmanac.com newsletter if they want to receive real time trading signals twice a year when they don't want to compute them on their own.

There are plenty of free charting programs on the web which chart the MACD indicator, so there is absolutely nothing to buy if you want to implement this system yourself. When you're not in the market, you simply park your money in a money market fund and earn interest. For a *simple strategy* that produces far better returns than a simple buy and hold strategy and which eliminates lots of risk and severe drawdown periods, I've never found anything better.

There are lots of investing strategies that are better than buy and hold, but they are not usually this simple or have such a long track record of outperformance. As stated, we're starting at the bottom of the ladder of both complexity and possible returns based on how much time you can afford to put into managing your money, and how much complexity you can handle in trying to become wealthier through investing.

While no one can say for sure why the six month summer period is so poor for trading, many logical reasons have been suggested. The clear fact is that it works in more than just the American market so something universal is going on. Thus it satisfies the criteria for a methodology that holds up over a long period of time and which captures something fundamental for its underpinnings.

It would be interesting if research were done overlaying some fundamental timing model, market climate or valuation model on these two "risk on" and "risk off" investing periods to determine if even a small amount of conditioning information could improve results. There is always the possibility that the summer-autumn returns were reasonable when the market was undervalued or interest rates were falling, or that the November to April returns were exceptional in similar circumstances. If one could determine the right conditional factors that might have identified over or underperformance conditions for this simple strategy, you could improve further upon this basic timing mechanism.

BUILDING A DIVIDEND COMPOUNDING INVESTMENT MACHINE

Bill Spetrino, editor of "The Dividend Machine" newsletter at Newsmax.com, was once kind enough to provide me the opportunity to interview him about his dividend stock picking methodology. Primarily a long-term dividend investor, Bill has achieved a very successful 20+% CAGR track record as recorded by *The Hulbert Financial Digest*. Through his investing he has achieved the investor's dream of retiring early.

Starting with just $8,000, Bill struggled to learn the principles of Warren Buffett's style of investing and ended up creating a perennial compounding machine comprised of strong dividend stocks that throws off so much cash that he could walk away from his 9-5 job and retire at the age of forty-two. He now lives comfortably just on the income from his investments alone.

For spiritual and religious institutions interested in investing, his interview, which comes from *Breakthrough Strategies of Wall Street Traders*, is instructive and is as follows. Within that book, you will also find the interviews with Fred Carach, Charles Mizrahi and Wesley Gray to be extremely helpful, especially the Fred Carach interview which changed my thinking processes an dlife. I believe that many of Carach's methods, such as buying resource stocks at multi-year lows, and the two-year holding period or 50% move upwards methodology of Benjamin Graham (see *Super Investing*) are two of the most powerful investing techniques you can learn if you want to get rich.

Bill, let's start with how you got started in stock market trading and how that moved into dividend stock investing.

I graduated from John Carroll University with a degree in accounting. I was an accountant and then I started buying and selling sports memorabilia. Then I started buying and selling tickets. All my life I wanted to build something where I didn't work and I got paid. I thought to myself, "There has to be a better way." From the start I was always focused on how to become financially independent so that I could retire.

I wanted to get into real estate but the problem with real estate was that you needed a lot of money to start. Interest rates were 10-12% at the time and I didn't understand it so I didn't get into it.

With my accounting background I bought a stock, Phillip Morris, and I started to receive dividends from it. I remember my first dividend check was for $44 back then. My dad said, "What are you going to do, buy a Happy Meal with this?" But things have now progressed to where my last dividend check is now three to four times what I made as my annual salary at my first job.

Getting into dividend investing was a gradual progression. Most people look at investing as they are buying something so that they can flip it real fast. I thought of it as, "I'm going to be buying a business that is spitting me out money and I just want the money coming. I want that check coming every quarter."

I looked at the cigarette business - at the time Philip Morris owned Miller Beer and Kraft - and I thought, "Geez, this is a great business." My investing mentor told me before he died, "If people can't eat it, drink it, smoke it, fuck it, watch it, wear it or bet on it then forget it."

So I was in a position with Kraft. They had brands like Kool-Aid, Oreos, Philadelphia Cream Cheese. They had the brands. They had Miller Beer, Marlboro and all the big brands that controlled 50% of the tobacco market in the United States and 10-12% in the world. I just thought, "This was a good safe place to put my money," and I just kept buying more shares and kept reinvesting.

Every dollar that I saved I just kept putting into that stock. It was funny because in 1996-1998 everybody was buying a stock for $20 and it would go to $50 by the end of the day. My stock kept going down but I wasn't focused on that. I was focused on a goal. I knew that my goal was to be able to get $26,000 or $27,000 a year and then my house would be paid off. I thought, "Okay, when I get to that point I can retire."

You ended up only investing in one stock?

At the time I was invested in that one stock and later I was buying other ones, but in 1998-1999 there weren't a lot of good bargains. When I started there was a whole bunch of good bargains and then there were none. I stayed in a couple of big stocks like Abbott Labs, Budweiser, McDonald's – things I could understand. Those are easy stocks to understand. When anybody is starting out in investing they should start out with stocks they understand.

You're saying that you started out as a buy and hold investor? You weren't a trader?

Absolutely, absolutely. Buy and hold was the way I went. I started trading as I got older and learned more. Investing is kind of like learning how to ride a bike and trading is like learning how to do wheelies or stunts on your bike.

I'll tell you that most people who trade lose. They are just like gamblers.

You are going to lose. I started investing with three people and they all faded out. I'll tell you why.

I was gambling since I was three years old. When you are out of money then you cannot play anymore. When you are wrong they take your money. When you bet for the short term you can have many losers. I know some of the best poker players in the world, including some of the famous ones like Doyle Brunson. They have all gone broke at one time or another in their career because they got a bad run of cards whereas if you are investing in buy and hold the story can be different.

I had a tobacco stock that dropped 50%, but I sat there and just kept buying more of it at a lower price. People were worried that tobacco was going to become illegal but the government got too much money from taxes. If you go to a state like Kentucky, Tennessee or even Virginia, you will see that there are people who grow tobacco. Tobacco cannot be illegal. The government needs the revenue from it. It was Napoleon who once said, "If I could figure out a better way to raise tax revenue then I would make smoking and drinking illegal," but he wasn't $17 trillion in debt like we are now.

Okay, so you started out in investing rather than in trading. You made that decision from the very start, which is smart. However, was this dividend investing strategy from the very start or were you originally using some other form of investing model to guide your decisions?

Yeah, it was dividend investing from the beginning. There weren't a lot of books that explained things back in pre-internet days. Today, there are tons of investing and trading articles. You couldn't really trade until the internet came.

I bought my first stock when I was in college. I made a $2,000 investment and was charged a $75 commission to buy it and $75 to sell it. That's an 8% commission. It was too expensive. You couldn't trade with those costs. Today, you can buy a million dollars worth of stock with a market order costing $5. You couldn't do that back in those days. When trading did pick up in the late '90s a lot of people got into it, but I was building my dividend machine.

I switched to doing some trading because I can do it now. Once you learn the basics of investing then it's much easier to trade. Warren Buffett can trade and Carl Icahn can trade. The reason they don't is because they have billions of dollars. They can't quickly get in and out of large stock positions but if you want to just trade with a hundred thousand dollars you can do that.

I have an account at StockTwits and I put two trades on yesterday that each made 1½% within a couple of hours. Now I didn't actually do the trades myself because I'm in a higher tax bracket now. I have what I want right now. I don't need to do it, but I know how to do it.

When you started out it was too expensive to actually do in-and-out trading so you ended up investing instead. Did you focus on a special investment style like Warren Buffett's or John Templeton's?

I was a Buffett clone. I followed Buffett. I bought some Coke a little bit after he did. I followed him into silver. I followed him into quite a few investments because at the time he knew more than I did and I wanted to know why. I needed to understand how he was thinking. There wasn't all the information there is now.

Investing is like anything else. It's a learning process. I remember Templeton saying to buy at maximum pain and being a gambler all my life I knew that you couldn't do anything obvious. If you bet football, if the outcome was obvious then everybody would make money. However, with a computer that finds things if you factor in enough data then you can make money.

I often combine long-term investing with trading. I'll put on a trade but if I have to keep it on a long time then I will because no one can predict what is going to happen in the short term. They can predict what is going to happen in the long term. It's easier.

Each person has their own skill set. My job as a dividend investor is to find imaginary fear. Like yesterday, for instance, I went long USO and long an energy stock named RIG, which is Trans-ocean. The reason I went long is because Prince Alwaleed came out and said, "Oil will never be a hundred dollars."

Well, first of all, Prince Alwaleed is one of the worst investors in the world. He was born rich. He bought Citigroup when it was way overpriced and then he bought it again right before the crisis telling everybody, "Yeah, I'm getting a bargain." He's not Warren Buffett. He didn't earn his money. He was born on third base and thinks he hit a triple. He was a pinch runner in the game. I put the trade on knowing that and then Boone Pickens came on the air and basically said, "I've made a billion dollars investing. Oil is my business and oil will be higher by the end of the year," and then the price of oil went back up.

I anticipated that would happen. I didn't anticipate Boone Pickens would come on TV. I just knew that because of Prince Alwaleed dummies were sitting at their TVs going, "Oh, I got to short this," while smart people are sitting there going, "I have to go long."

It's like when you are playing cards - if you're at the table for half an hour and you don't know who the sucker is then that means it's you. I try to combine street smarts and book smarts. I have an instinct I've developed. I've been gambling since I was five or six years old buying and selling things and if you're wrong then like I said they will take your money. That's what happened to my friends.

People ask me all the time, "My kid wants to be an investor, where do I send him?" I say, "Teach them how to gamble" because if you don't know how to get the odds in your favor then you aren't going to make money.

How do you teach them to gamble?

Well, what you would do is this. Let's say the kid likes baseball. You can get the odds off the computer and tell him, "Okay, I'm going to give you $3,000. I want you to pick what baseball team is going to win today." For instance, let's say the Yankees are playing the Red Socks and the odds are that the Yankees are 7-5 favorites, meaning if you like the Yankees you lay 7 to win 5. If you like the Red Socks you lay 5 to win 6. The difference in there is for the bookie.

When you do this for the kid he will start learning how to figure the odds. He'll start thinking, "Well gosh, if this guy pitches then ..." or he'll figure out various scenarios that affect the odds. For instance, when a team loses three in a row and they come back from a long road trip to play at home the kid will come up with scenarios like this to start figuring the odds. He will start thinking.

The trick is that you are now thinking and that you are developing a system that works for you. If I had a system, which I don't (though I have parameters that I use), but if I had a system I would never publish it because then everybody would be using it. I would destroy my advantage.

For instance, there was a theory in the old days in the NFL that if you bet against a team that played on Monday Night Football then you would win so many percent of your bets because (1) they had a shorter week and (2) they were on TV so people would overestimate them because they saw them on TV. That theory worked for a while until the bookies figured it out and then they started changing the line around. Something will work until it doesn't work.

John Templeton will tell you and Warren Buffett will also say to be greedy when others are fearful. Templeton will say to buy when there is maximum pain. You have to be able to spot imaginary fear and real fear to do that.

When the J.P. Morgan Whale incident happened I bought J.P. Morgan immediately because the fact that a trader lost money isn't a surprise. When you make big bets you are going to make mistakes the same way Michael Jordan is going to have a game where he doesn't make all his baskets. Those are the odds.

Were Warren Buffett and John Templeton your two gurus?

They were my two key gurus. I followed Buffett and I followed Templeton.

I'll tell you a funny story about Buffett's Berkshire Hathaway. I phoned them back in the old days because I wanted to buy Berkshire Hathaway stock. I called because you could get the annual report by phoning. Well, they didn't send it to me so I called them and I said, "Hey, I called previously. Please send me the report." A man answered the phone, which I now realize is Warren Buffett because he only had eight or nine people in his office. I had never heard his voice back in the old days but I've heard it now so I recognize it. He said, "I'll take care of that" real fast and before I could say thank you he hung up the phone.

I would read his annual report and my gambling background helped me because of what he said, "Be greedy when others are fearful and fearful when others are greedy," which was very helpful. He told everybody to read *The Intelligent Investor* by Benjamin Graham. To be honest, I hated that book. I'm an accountant and I couldn't follow it. It was very dry. But there were two chapters - chapters 8 and 20 - that were great.

In the book Graham talks about "Mr. Market." Mr. Market is here to serve you, not guide you, meaning that if you know what the price of something should be and everyone else doesn't know then you have a big advantage.

Just like right now to be long on oil stocks. If you believe oil is going to remain at this price for two or three years then you shouldn't be long oil. But I think that it's just not realistic that the price of gas is not going to stay this low. I just don't believe it. A gallon of gas should not sell for three times less than a gallon of milk. Something is not right about that. My instinct is contrary to the people going out onto the air saying there will be $13 oil. I don't listen to that stuff. If they really knew they wouldn't be telling anybody or they'd have billions of dollars like Carl Icahn or Warren Buffett.

Right now Buffett's down big on IBM. If you buy IBM at $150 you are going to be fine. You're getting it cheap. You are being his partner but you're getting in cheaper than him.

What I'm trying to get at is the origin of your investment philosophy. How exactly did you get into dividend stocks as your primary investment pursuit? You said you were following Warren Buffett. Are you talking about in the '80s or the '90s?

Oh, no. When I started investing in the late '80s and early '90s I started following Warren Buffett by reading his annual reports because back then the famous investors would write a book only occasionally. I couldn't get information any other way than by reading his annual report. Peter Lynch wrote *One Up on Wall Street*, but Buffett never wrote any book. As a matter of fact, the first book that I read about him - and it is the best book - was called *The Making of an American Capitalist*, by Roger Lowenstein. It exposed his relationship with Kate Graham and talks more about his personal life.

What I got from him were the principles of what you need to do. As time went on it was trial and error that produced my investing style. For example, some people talk about book value. Book value in a bank is very important. However, for a regular company or consumer goods company, it isn't important. Each company is different, just like women. There is no set way to deal with women. You could say one thing to a particular woman and it would make her upset while saying the same thing to another woman would make her happy. It's the same thing with stock investing so what you have to do is stick to what you know best.

What I know is imaginary fear and real fear. I also know what the price of something should be and I can feel when it's wrong. I'll think, "It's just a wrong number," and I can feel it. I'm not always right, nobody is always right but in investing you have to consider the odds.

When you trade you are considering something in the short term and then the probabilities are "maybe it will and maybe it won't." However, long term is different. Over time a stock like Apple will do more business five years from now than it will now because the company has money in it already that they are going to invest. If your cash coming in is a billion dollars more than your cash going out every week and you already have two hundred billion dollars of cash sitting in your company then you probably will be worth more in the future. If I ask you personally, "Are you worth more now than you were five years ago?" you probably are worth more now. If you go back another five years, you are still probably worth more now than at that time because you've had the power of compounding working for you.

I'm still not getting what I want. Let's pick up it up again on how exactly you got started in trading. You said that as a kid you got into gambling and then you bought some Philip Morris stock that somehow led to this particular niche.

I did sports memorabilia and then entered into the stock market. I started in stocks when I had $8,000, but once I had more money I couldn't put the money into tickets and sports memorabilia anymore so I went into stocks. It made sense to me. What I like about stocks is that once you put your money in then it doesn't cost you anything else.

But why did you get into dividend stocks specifically rather than growth stocks or any other philosophy of investing?

Because I wanted to retire. The object of work is so that you can retire. When you have enough money then you can retire. The reason you are working right now is probably because you need more money. I can't say that for sure because I don't know you, but 98% of the people are still working because they need more money and until you have enough money coming in from your investments you cannot retire.

Let's say you have a stock portfolio with a million dollars in it. You don't know what it is going to be worth tomorrow. Even if you have that money, a million dollars is not going to last you the rest of your life. Not if you're going to live thirty or forty more years it isn't, so you have to know what you've got to do with that money or you are going to tap it all out.

I started investing in dividend stocks for the reason that I wanted to retire. Most people invest for the wrong reason. They want to become rich. I'm all about cash flow. I want the cash to be coming in from my investments.

Now I will trade and I will buy stocks that don't pay dividends. I will do that now because I've got the dividend machine already in full gear, but for 99% of the people they should be investing and not trading. They don't know that.

I want people to understand that you started out investing with only $8,000, but you retired at age forty-two because you were able to build up a dividend machine.

Yes. Once you start seeing the dividend checks come in you get motivated. When I saw the first check of $44 I was like, "Wow! Imagine if I can start putting more money into these stocks." What I would do is get an idea like cutting my lunch budget from $5 to $3 so that I could put the extra money aside and invest it. Then I'd say, "Okay, I'm going to get free samples at the mall" or "I'm going to shop for my car insurance." I was so much more aware of saving money to invest because I was very focused on building my income. And when my stock dropped, I didn't get mad like other people. I was happy because I could buy more of it.

You never worry about the dividend being cut?

Well no, because in a stock like Altria or a consumer goods company … let me state right here that that's the type of stock everybody should be starting with because they are simple. That's why consumer good companies are so expensive now. People are finally realizing that they are the right place to be. That's why utilities are doing good now. It's because people are realizing that, for instance, if you're a New York resident then you have got to go with Con Ed. You cannot go without it. If you're in a

Coca-Cola or Pepsi Cola then it doesn't matter what the economy does.

There are some stocks that are risky, like if you buy energy or you buy banks or you buy things that are cyclical then that's a different story. You have to be able to buy some stocks at the right part of the cycle. You might have to wait years for your trade to work out whereas with the consumer goods stocks, as long as you are buying them right you are good and you should just keep adding to it.

I just kept seeing the quarterly dividend checks come out and they were bigger and bigger and bigger and bigger. I became addicted almost. And then I started using margin because I could borrow money at a certain percent. The first time I used margin was in 2000. I borrowed money at 7% and I was getting a 10½% dividend. I had an interest only loan. I didn't get it with a broker. I got it on my house. I got the 7% in the beginning when I started using margin and then I pledged my stocks off.

In other words, you looked at the whole thing as like a business where you were buying assets that were throwing off cash. You didn't really care that those asset values bobbed up and down in the marketplace as long as you knew you would be holding them for the long term and deemed that they would keep throwing off that cash flow into the future while retaining a good deal of their value. If that was your conclusion, you'd even borrow money to buy the stocks if the difference between the dividend yields and margin interest rate led to what you considered was a safe net rate of return.

Bingo. You nailed it.

Then you said, "What businesses are going to consistently do that?" That's why you focused on consumer goods stocks.

Right, because that was the easiest thing. Figuring out McDonald's or figuring out Coke or figuring out Pepsi … they are not complicated businesses so I could understand them.

Now I invest in things like Herbalife and different things. For instance, I took a position in Herbalife because I was in network marketing. I know a bunch of attorneys and I don't think that network marketing is going to be deemed illegal by the FTC especially when the guy who was the Deputy Assistant to Obama, Alan Hoffman, appointed these people. He left Pepsi to go to Herbalife. A former FTC commissioner, Patricia Harvard Jones, left her lucrative law firm to go work for Herbalife. Obviously, these people know how the political winds blow. Plus, Eric Schneiderman and Kamala Harris are the attorney generals of New York and California and have been silent about the company as has been Elizabeth Warren.

To me, Bill Ackman is trying to scare a whole bunch of people into thinking that Herbalife is doomed. When people that look at charts just say,

"Oh. The chart's broken," they aren't thinking. The minute the FTC rules then that stock is going to go up if they don't get closed down, and it will go down if they get closed down. No chart will tell you that. No financial report will tell you that. I have just done my own analysis. After doing this for thirty years I figured out the odds and I'm betting with Carl Icahn, William Stiritz, Soros, and Daniel Lowe who was in on it.

I listen to other people, too, but invariably I have to make the decision myself. But yes, to answer your question this is a business that I do. It's no different than owning a property except the beautiful thing is that it is easier. With a rental property you have to know how to fix things, you have taxes and you must do upkeep and maintenance. You also have to worry if somebody doesn't pay you. Not with stocks.

What's the chance that Apple is not going to pay their dividend or Altria? People will object and bring up to me, "Well what about Eastman Kodak, Bill?" Bill Gates pronounced Eastman Kodak dead in the '90s. The stock still ran up. It was a slow death for them. If I can see that Altria is losing share to Reynolds then I'll worry but until they start losing market share I've got a money machine that is just printing me money.

Let's consider somebody who also wants to start with investing rather than trading. Do you believe that dividend investing is the best initial road for general investors rather than growth stock investing, pure value investing that ignores dividends, momentum investing and so on?

Absolutely. It's the only way for them. There are different ways of investing. You can momentum trade, you can try to buy high and sell higher, ... all these different things. The problem with them is that you are just starting.

My philosophy is that when you are starting out you don't know what you are doing so you should go with something basic. The most basic thing in investing is to buy a company and hold it, watch it and study it.

Do you have a pet? Let's say you have a dog. That dog knows you well. You know why? Because you feed it and it's dependent on you. If you watch one company in the beginning you should watch it and learn as much as you can about it. Then you can move to another one. After that you move to another one. It's just like weight lifting or like anything else. You should have a gradual progression of making progress.

The problem is everyone gets in it to get rich quick and there are a whole bunch of charlatans telling you that they are going to make you 2% or 1% a week. If they could do all that then why are they writing a book? What do they need to do a service for? They should be rich.

I think you should start out with that and work your way up. You have to start small and build yourself up. See, that's the thing with investing. My way is boring and you are not going to get rich fast but this is the way to get started. If you want to be a trader then you need to learn how to be an investor first so you can understand what the hell are you doing.

That's fantastic advice. Now let's move to your actual stock selection process. What criteria or methodology are you using to pick your stocks?

Dividend investing. For dividend investing, I have an eighteen point system. I cannot share all the details because some criteria are actual numbers and each sector is different.

Let's just take Altria, for instance, which is in the tobacco industry. Market share is my main thing with them. I don't care what the profits are because that moves back and forth. However, I want to make sure that they are the number one brand because when you are the number one brand you then control the price increases or the price drops in the marketplace.

Now, these companies don't consciously price fix. In the tobacco industry they keep the prices high. Some companies like Barnes and Noble and Amazon keep trying to underprice each other where nobody is going to make any money in the long run. That's a bad business. I try to see if the business is good. Like Buffett says, "Give me a hundred billion dollars and let me see if I can take the business share away from it."

In other words, the first question you ask about a potential stock is whether the business is good, but you have a different set of criteria for each market sector to determine if the business is good?

Correct. Each company, each thing has different parameters.

The first step is that you want to see if the business is good. For instance, Starbucks has a great business. The problem is that it's never cheap. You're always buying it at thirty and forty times earnings. I just don't know, I'm not savvy enough to know when Starbucks is going to stop being cool. It's out of my circle of expertise but I can ask other people to help tell me that.

The first question then is about the business. What's the second question?

The second question is your valuation. You have to see if you are getting a good deal. Let's say a company earns 12% a year and it can compound that. You are only going to earn about 12% a year if you buy the stock at a fair price. If you buy the stock at the wrong price it's trouble.

I'll give you a good example, which is Coca-Cola. Buffett told everyone to buy it in 1991 when it was at a certain price. In 1991, the price was just about 10x earnings. That stock was selling for 80x earnings in 1998. I told a client to sell it when it was 55 times earnings. I said, "This is crazy. Get rid of it." He kept it and it ran up to 80x earnings because that's what momentum things do. But then in a fifteen-year span, Coca-Cola now with the splits and everything is not much higher than it was back then because that would be the return if you bought it at the wrong time.

I don't like to pay more than fifteen times earnings for something. I just don't like to do it unless it's a special situation stock like Gilead. Gilead was a biotech stock that I bought. I gave it to my subscribers when it was $14 while they were working on a hepatitis C drug and if it was going to hit then it was going to be a *big hit*. Well, it did hit. I was willing to pay a little more for that potential because I understood things.

For the formula you basically have to find a good business that you understand and you have to find a fair valuation, which takes you time.

Some companies, like Ford, are in a very capital-intensive business. A P/E of 12 isn't good for Ford. It's too high because it costs too much money. Now take a consumer goods company like Altria. What do they have? They put tobacco into a machine with a conveyor belt and a product comes out. Technology helps their businesses every year. They cut costs all the time because machines don't cost what they used to cost to fix them.

You have to determine if you think that oil is going to fall, and if so then you buy the airlines, FedEx and you buy UPS. The trouble is that UPS dropped 10% yesterday not because the company stinks but because people just bid it up too high. Smart people then took their profits. So there is no set valuation system. The thing with investing is there is not a set valuation system. There are parameters that you use to eliminate things, but in the end it comes down to experience.

Those are the basic things and then after that it just depends on the particular sector. There are different things to look at and they are not the same for every stock. For every stock I look at different things. That's why I have to give an example because for one stock I think one way and for another stock I will look at other things. In the end, I have to see whether I know something that everyone else doesn't know.

You just have to have an edge. For instance, I understand network marketing. I understand certain businesses and it varies. Everybody wants a certain valuation system they can plug into. It doesn't work like that. It just totally doesn't. Investing is not like that. Like Buffett said, "The person with a high IQ doesn't beat the person with the low IQ." It doesn't work like that. A lot of it is just trial and error. It really is.

Why do you need to know something that the market doesn't know?

Well, because then you can distinguish between imaginary fear and real fear. Let me give you two examples. With Blackberry the stock dropped because Apple was eating its lunch. The iPhone was eating its lunch. If you talked to people then you could find that out. Same thing with J. C. Penney. You could find out that no one was shopping there anymore. You could find that fact out by asking people and get information that the market doesn't know.

What I do is this: before I pick a stock every month I have a play-off. I'll play stocks against each other. I'll pick the five stocks that I think are the best ideas and then I'll number them. I'll play number five against number four just like how the old bowlers tours used to be where you would bowl and whoever wins would get to play number three, then get to play number two and so on. And then what I do is I have a panel of people that I hire. I run the questions by saying, "Okay, you are going to be the bear. Tell me why J. C. Penney stinks."

I liked J. C. Penney at one point. It looked cheap. When I kept asking women about it they kept telling me, "I don't shop there anymore. I don't like it. They took away the coupon." I couldn't find anybody that liked it and I knew it was going to go down whereas like with Herbalife, I understand network marketing. I talked to a group of attorneys and when thirty-out-of-thirty attorneys tell you there is no way they are going to shut down with or without the people that got hired from the government then I feel I've got information that the average person doesn't have. I'm not afraid of what is going on. A lot of the stuff that appears in the media is BS or like what I told you about Prince Alwaleed. He doesn't know what he's doing. He is a contra-indicator.

Because you are not a customer of a particular company you then use other people to help evaluate how it is doing, and you are always looking for fear situations in the marketplace that will depress a stock's price, and then you ...

Right. I'll give you a good example. I started buying Bank of America when it was like $10 or $11. Everyone said the bank would go broke. People kept saying that all the banks were going to go broke. The stock went from $10 to $5; I bought it all the way down and had a basis price of $7. When the stock got back to $10 I was up 30% from where I originally bought it. I was able to do this because I have the philosophy that the market is here to serve me, not guide me.

Our country doesn't work, in my opinion, without Bank of America. I thought all of the negative news was nonsense and it *was* nonsense. I was buying the stock under tangible book value, which means that if you liquidated the whole company they had more cash than the stock was selling for. To me, as long as you didn't believe that the banks were going to all go broke then the government had already proved it would step in and help the banks. That's just the way it is.

This sounds like the following story. A stock's price is depressed. Everybody is saying, "Oh, it's going to go bankrupt" or something similar so the bad news attracts your attention. You look at it and you value it. For this stock you said, "Well, let me look at the price versus book value." You then bought it after concluding it was safe and then you got a rebound in price for instant profits. But what about dividends in this story? Where did they factor into the picture? Were you buying it because of dividends?

Not Bank of America. Bank of America wasn't a dividend stock. For a dividend stock as long as I think that the dividend is good I keep buying the company and I'll even buy it down, like in 2008.

Here is a great example of a dividend stock. In 2008, Altria was selling for $21. The stock dropped in three weeks to $14. It dropped 30%. Now, the tobacco business didn't change. It's not like the company reported bad earnings and it dropped, which is real fear. It wasn't like a stock such as Radio Shack where nobody goes there anymore.

In Altria's case, it dropped because the liquidity dropped. People had to sell their flowers, not their weeds. They had to sell their good stocks in their portfolios. We had the Bernie Madoff crisis and all these people had to liquidate positions to raise cash so people just sold anything they could get their hands on. They dropped Altria from $21 to $15. In three weeks, it dropped and I knew that this was irrational so I bought it at $16. I bought it at $15. I bought it forty-seven times between $14.50 and $16.50 from October to March of 2009 and I borrowed the money to do it.

Because you knew the business wouldn't go bankrupt and you would still get dividend cash and ...

I was getting an 8½% dividend and my margin rate was 2½%. I thought, "Well geez, if I borrow $500,000 then I'm paying $12,500 to borrow the money and I'm collecting $42,000." I thought that was a good risk/reward proposition.

You never worried about your principal? You didn't worry that the stock price would go down?

No, because I'm not selling the stock so it didn't matter to me. I knew that the dividend and the earnings were not going to be messed up. People actually were going to smoke more during the crisis and that was exactly what ended up happening. People smoked and drank more because they were nervous, but the market does irrational things because nobody values it this way. They are only looking at their price charts. You know a chart person or trader is going to say, "It's dropping! It's dropping!" They don't want to know why. I want to know why. I'm looking for a bargain due to imaginary fear.

Are you then a dividend stock investor who's normally looking for "fear stocks" that you can buy?

Absolutely, because that is how you get a good price. This is where the horse racing analogy comes in. Let's say you were going to run a race against a person who is crippled. The odds are that you are going to win. Everybody knows that so they are going to make the odds accordingly. Nobody is going to bet on the cripple.

It's the same thing with investing. There are a lot of great companies. They are just overpriced and you can't afford them or you can buy them but you are not going to make any money with them going forward. The reason that Buffett, Icahn, Loeb and all the other investment stars are who they are is because they buy depressed assets and they make their money that way.

You have to be able to have the conviction to buy when prices drop. If you are worried about your principal then you're going to get scared to death. You can't worry about that. You have to focus on the dividend and the earnings because invariably the earnings are going to drive the companies forward.

You are basically saying, "Bill, here's what I do. I want a stock that I know is a good business. Warren Buffett has the same rule. I want it to keep making money and paying cash for as many years as possible into the future, which I can't fully predict, and I want to buy it at a depressed price if I can, so I look to buy it during fear situations."

Imaginary fear against real fear. Yes. That's it. You paraphrased it perfect. I buy imaginary fear.

Wonderful. You buy "imaginary fear." Do you have a list of stocks you are waiting to buy like this? Or do you just wait until a new stock, like Herbalife, is suddenly in the news so that it grabs your attention and then you analyze it to spot the imaginary fear and then pounce?

That's a great question. I have a list of stocks I want to buy. I have a shopping list. Obviously when they get into the news I start looking closer. I didn't like Herbalife at $65. At $35 I loved it.

Because that would double your yield, whatever it would be …

Exactly, exactly, exactly. See, Herbalife ended up cutting their dividend, which normally would make me nervous, but they did that to buy the stock back because Bill Ackman is short the stock big time and he has got to cover it at some point. The minute the FTC releases Herbalife from their investigation - if they release them and I'm betting they will - then the stock will shoot up. Right now, people won't put their money in it because they are afraid it's going to close. I believe that's nonsense.

You've got this Watch List and if something happens with the stock then you'll take a good look at it. Did you say that you actually hire a panel of people to help evaluate it?

Yes. I hire regular people, not investors. I know the numbers of the company. What I don't know, for instance, is whether housewives are going to J. C. Penney. Are people using Blackberrys? I don't know these things so I use a panel to tell me.

The biggest mistake that most investors make is they look at what *they like* or focus on what *they are thinking* and not what the consumer is thinking or what the world is thinking. Bill Ackman and George Soros, both famous investors, lost their shirts on J. C. Penney because they looked at the numbers. The numbers look great. The problem is nobody was going there anymore.

This idea of a panel is pretty unique and people would want to hear more on this because they might want to try this, especially when a large trade is at stake. This is one of the gems you have given me in this interview. Please explain the process of actually hiring people to help you evaluate stocks. What do you actually do?

I will tell a person that I will give him a $50 gift card for doing this. I don't pay them a lot of money and a lot of them will do it for free for me. Here is how it works. Let's say you are in the publishing business. Then I say, "Bill, I want to talk about Barnes and Noble. I want you to tell me about their future. What do you think about them?"

Okay, but how many people are you going to get for your panel to do this?

I get a panel of usually three or four. I get a person who is favorable and I get a person who is unfavorable. Sometimes I'll be the bull and they will be the bear and they will have to sell me or I sell them on the company.

Here's how I do it. I'll ask people, "Who shops at J. C. Penney?" First of all, I couldn't find anyone for this company. It took me thirty or forty people to find people who shop there. Most people never even shop there anymore. When I did find somebody they were lame like, "Well, I go there because it's traditional. My mom used to take me there" and I'll be like, "Well, do you like it?" "Well, yeah, kind of."

That told me everything I needed to know. I was trying to get them to tell me good things about J. C. Penney and while they didn't tell me bad things they just didn't tell me good things. I want to be with a company where they tell me something good. I try to find three people for each stock that will give me a bullish case, but I couldn't do it for J. C. Penney. I just couldn't. Women tell me that the company stunk and they used to shop there but they didn't anymore and that told me all I needed to know.

So for any stock you try to get several people to give you a bullish case and then what do you do?

And then I try to shoot holes in it, or I'll give a bullish case and they'll be bearish and they'll try to shoot holes into me, into my argument.

How did you find a bearish person if they are already a person who's shopping?

Well, I had people who already shopped at J. C. Penney and they didn't like it anymore. Well, they were telling me why they didn't like it and how Kohl's was beating their ass and this and that. Well, a Wall Street analyst hasn't shopped at J. C. Penney. This woman has.

This is interesting. Let's try to do this for McDonald's. What are you going to do?

I'll ask you, "Hey, you go to McDonald's, don't you?" You'll say, "Yeah, I do. I like it." I'll then say, "Good. Do you want to be part of a panel with me?" "Yeah, I'll be a part of it."

Then I'll say to someone else, "Hey, you go to McDonald's?" They'll say, "I used to, but I don't like it anymore." "What do you mean?" "I don't like it. They're not appealing to me anymore. They're concentrating on other things. I don't like it."

Then I'll put the two of them together. I'll listen to both sides of the story and I'll be in the middle. I don't need to ask them financial questions. I want to know why they like the company or why they don't like the company.

Do you get them on the phone? How does it work?

Yeah, I get them on the phone. Mostly, I get them on the phone. It'll be a three-way call or a conference call. I just try to get the information from them in order to try to find out things.

In other words, if you want to buy a stock then you find two or three people that use that company or its products or dropped them or use somebody else, you get them on the phone in a conference call and you start listening to a pro and con argument.

And then I decide it from there. Some people are adamant about the company. It doesn't mean that they are right or wrong. It just means that I need to hear their opinion. For instance, if you don't shop something then you don't know. It would be like a man trying to understand what it feels like to give childbirth. As men we don't know because we have never done it so we don't know. We need to ask a woman.

I find that this strategy works for me. It helps me find out things. It keeps me out of a lot of bad stocks that other people get involved in. Now it has kept me from some good ones, too, but in investing it's not about what you do right. It's about what you do wrong.

Do you do this for every stock, every big play?

Yes, yes. Every stock.

Wow! This costs you money every time you do this to just consider whether you want to buy a stock.

It's all relative to what I'm doing. A lot of people do this with me for free. I'll trade favors for others, like I'll say, "Hey, do you want to do me a favor?" Then in return they can call me and I'll do tax consulting for them or I will show them how to save money on their insurance. I don't always lay out money if I don't have to, but maybe I'll give them a copy of my book or my newsletter. I give them something of value, but some people don't want it. They just want to tell me if they are really bullish or bearish.

I don't want people that are lukewarm. When too many people are lukewarm about a company, that's a bad sign. They're not passionate about it.

I can evaluate the company's numbers. I don't need them for that. I need them for talking about the actual company and its products.

How long does that conversation last? You said you usually have two other people at the same time?

Well, it varies. If I can get two people arguing with each other that's what I'm trying to do. It just doesn't always happen that way. Sometimes somebody will sell somebody else and the other person will say, "Well, I kind of like the product, but I could see what you mean by, 'They are overpriced' and, 'They are this.'" Sometimes someone breaks down, generally speaking, like when you put two people in a ring and have them swinging at each other. At some point, someone is going to quit first or they are going to get knocked onto the canvass first.

This is a pretty ingenious thing that you do. Smart investors will love this because most just buy stocks after doing their own internet research or after just looking at charts. Who taught you to do this? Did you just discover this yourself?

I'll tell you where I learned this. When I was in college I had a group of guys where we would get together to watch and bet football. One morning we went to breakfast and we were arguing about a game. I really liked a certain team and I was going to bet on them and we had a discussion. This other guy said, "Look, they got three guys hurt, and every time they go from the East coast to the West, or the West coast to the East coast, they are messed up." I said, "What do you mean?" because I had never been to the West coast in my life. He said, "When you travel, like when they play a game, players get to the stadiums at seven o'clock in the morning. Well, that's four o'clock Pacific Time. Eastern people's body clocks are messed up."

He was explaining this to me because this guy had played college football, and so he explained the whole thing to me. Well, that made sense so I didn't bet on my team and of course they lost. Then I realized, "Let's get together next weekend." When we started doing this and we all agreed on a game, it hit! We didn't win all the time, but I realized that so many times I was going to bet a game and I was wrong. I learned that information, and learning and hearing things helps you make your decisions. Let's face it, if you're going to bet NFL football then everybody has the same information. They know who the quarterbacks are and they can run all the numbers in the computers all they want.

The question is, do you know something that someone else doesn't know? Or did someone bring up a point that you never considered for that stock? For instance, the other day on TV somebody brought up that last week was the first time that more hedge funds bought 30,000 long contracts for oil. It's the first time they have done this since oil was low like four or five years ago. When six smart people all see the same thing that tells me something. That helps me make decisions.

Most people move towards things. I move away from them meaning I want to avoid risks. I want to know where I'm going to die so that I don't go there. That's how you should be in investing. You want to avoid losers. That's the Buffett style. He doesn't try to hit home runs that triple in a week. He's looking for something that he knows is going to be good going forward that everyone else doesn't know is going to be good and that's how you get your edge. That's how I got the idea for doing this.

You have been doing this now for years?

Oh, yeah. I did it because I bet football until about twenty years ago. I bet football religiously. I could actually make a good amount of money betting. I even had a sports service for a while but it was pre-Internet days. It was too hard to get the money from people and stuff, but because I had an edge I was successful. In any case, from this experience I learned about getting information.

All right, you have this eighteen point system for evaluating stocks that pay dividends. You evaluate them by first asking if the business is good. If so, then you ask whether the stock is a good deal at this price. If so then you can buy it. If not because it's too expensive then you will look to buy it in any situation where the price drops as long as the future prospects are still good. You'll watch it and wait until the price drops because of some imaginary fear so that you can scoop it up at a bargain.

Right. You have to buy it on fear. That's how you get your bargain.

What are the other steps after that? You look at it as a good business ...

I mean, you are looking for valuations. Again, you are just really looking for the right price. I've been watching the stock market for twenty-five years now. I know what the price of the stock should be. Just like if you go somewhere and you have been buying watches or you've been doing something else then you know what it should be. I just have a thing in my head that tells me what the price should be.

Most people who invest do not understand numbers. That's why they get turned on by charts. It's because they don't want to use numbers, but numbers are important. I look at this company's earnings, I look at certain figures, I value the company.

Buffett talks about intrinsic value all the time. Intrinsic value is how much a company is worth. Part of it is brand so you look at its brand. You look at its balance sheet. You look at its cash flow. Those three things will tell you intrinsic value.

Then you see if you have an advantage. Does this company have an advantage over the other companies? A company like Amazon is a great company as far as making a lot of sales. It makes a lot of sales, but I don't see how it makes any money and it doesn't so I don't want to own it. I can't because owning it is for a gambler and that's not for me. I'm not going to reveal all my systems, but I'm just saying that's enough for people to work with.

Buying the imaginary fear is the key. Without the fear you don't get the bargain.

Okay, so that's the catalyst. Your catalyst for buying an overpriced but solid company is when an imaginary fear situation pops up. That's when you can buy it at a great price.

Precisely.

This is for a good stock that has a good brand, balance sheet, cash flow, and/or other advantages.

Yeah. You also want it where people don't appreciate it, like Apple two years ago. If you read the news, back then people were talking about Apple like it was going to be Eastman Kodak. Some guy compared it to Eastman Kodak.

Herbalife made investment news headlines when Bill Ackman was shorting it, so everyone was alerted to the situation. How do you know when a stock that isn't in the headlines has popped up on the radars of enough people where we can then say that the public has truly succumbed to imaginary fear?

There are fifty stocks I watch. I use my Top 50 and then I put them on a screen and then I'll get a notification from my broker if any one of them has dropped 5% or 10%. I'll get a notification that will tell me the stock dropped 10%. That tells me to keep a watch on it.

See, a lot of it is news-driven. For instance, let's take oil. In the beginning of last year, if you look there was a whole bunch of people talking about $150 oil. Now you don't hear those people anymore. Everybody is now talking about how it's going to be worth $10. I just know from the past that oil has not traded at $10 since 1998. I don't think it's going to trade at that price. If you're selling $10 bills for $10 you are not going to get many takers. At $5 you are going to get a ton of takers.

Now in investing you just don't know what the price should be. The prices are sometimes nonsensical. That's why guys like Buffett and Icahn don't have to have jobs like other people. They can invest because they know when everything is wrong. They know. That's what they do.

It's hard to explain that to somebody, but I mean as regards buying bad news if you just bought bad news all the time you would outperform. Of course sometimes the bad news is warranted. You just have to know when that sometimes is and the numbers help you.

Remember people were comparing Apple to Eastman Kodak. I look at the numbers and I'm thinking that the business is not going to go broke. This company has got $160 billion of cash and their cash flow is one billion dollars a week. How is this company bad? Is it because they are not growing as fast as people think they are going to grow? That's nonsensical to me, but that stock drops 45% and the chart guys were all against it but I was buying it.

Do you ever use charts at all?

I look at them, but I look at the numbers more importantly. I really don't look at them. No.

I know you've got eighteen points for analyzing a situation. It starts out asking whether the business is good. Is it a strong business? Next, is the price giving you a good deal on the valuation? Does the brand have cash flow? As to the balance sheet, are there any numbers there that you are looking for that are particular investment criteria?

When you see a company with no debt then you know that the company hasn't needed to borrow money. Well, if you have any children and they have never borrowed any money from you and they are doing fine then chances are they know how to handle money.

So in a super recession those guys would be good.

Well, yeah. I'll give you an example. There is a company called Insperity. They are a help for small businesses or whatever. The point is that the company has a ton of cash and no debt.

Michael Kors is a retailer. I hate retailers because they have a ton of debt and you can't predict them. I mean, everybody lost their ass in Aeropostale and all these companies. However, with Michael Kors he's a designer but he went broke fifteen years ago so now he doesn't use any debt. Same way like Steve Jobs went broke, almost, and he got bailed out by Bill Gates. He didn't use any debt. A guy like that, he's not going to go broke because he doesn't have debt. Like Buffett says, if you are smart then you don't need debt and if you're dumb it will kill you.

A lot of times I bet on the jockeys and not the horse. I won't buy GE because I hate the CEO. I hate him. I think he is not smart. I won't buy his stock because I just don't think he knows what he's doing.

How about cash flow? What are you looking for?

Well, I just want to make sure that the cash flow is consistent. It depends on the business. For instance with cornflakes things don't really change affecting whether or not people buy them. But in a cyclical business, such as the auto industry, things are determined by the economy. If the economy is bad then people aren't going to buy cars. But like Intel, I bought that stock because everybody said the PC was dead. Well, the PC is not dead. If you have a company you don't want to write a letter on a laptop. You'll want to write it on a computer.

All right. First, let me ask you about dividends. When you are looking at stocks for creating a dividend-compounding machine you are going to make sure they have dividends. Are you looking for growing dividends or are you ignoring the dividend growth rate? How important is that to you?

Yeah, I want them to grow but if you are already seven feet tall you don't have to grow taller. Ideally, I want a stock that grows their dividends. Sure, I do. It doesn't always work like that but yes, I want dividend growth and the good companies will continue to grow their dividend because they are continuing to make money.

And the dividend itself is more important to you than the share price as long as you conclude that the business is going to hold up?

Well, yeah. I mean, think of it this way. If a business is spitting out a $2 dividend would you pay $10 for it? Sure you would. It's a 20% return. Would you pay $25 for it? Yeah, it's an 8% return. Would you pay $30 for it? Yeah, that's a 6½% return.

I mean if you are going to marry a woman then you are going to want a woman who's smart, funny, rich. There are different traits you want with an investment, too. There are main things and the other stuff is … well for instance sales and growth is bullshit. Amazon keeps growing but they don't make any money. In the end, if you sold $5 bills for $4 you can make a ton of sales. However, you just won't make any money. You'll get market share but you'll almost go broke. But see, Amazon makes their money because the stock has risen from $70 to $300 because everybody kisses Jeff Bezos' ass and they are all speculators and gamblers, but at some point that stock is going to be worth $50 again.

You're saying it's like the Japanese stocks in the '80s. The companies were going after market share but they weren't profitable.

Yeah, you got it. You just have to be able to see something. For some reason, people turn on other people the same way they turn on businesses. For me, I don't hear all that. All I focus on is the numbers. When the company is not paying the dividend that's like a person who is telling you something.

If you ask someone, "I want to see your police record" they might say, "Well, I'm not showing you." If they say, "I want to see your tax return" and they respond, "I'm not showing you," then they are not showing you for a reason.

Carl Icahn and Buffett have been doing it for forty-five or fifty years. They haven't scammed anybody. Nobody is calling them liars. People don't like Icahn because he's not like everybody else, but he's good at what he does. He's better than Buffett. He just doesn't kiss everybody's ass. He doesn't care if people don't like him.

Let me ask you a hypothetical question. There's a lot of talk in the marketplace now about the potential for a depression, deflation, or hyperinflation. Let's say that one of these scenarios develops in the future where everything crashes. What type of companies would you buy in each of those situations?

I would buy the same ones - mostly consumer goods companies.

Take a stock like Coca-Cola, which is a very easy stock to figure out. In deflationary times Coca-Cola is good because what do they do? They buy sugar, they buy syrup, they have trucks to drive the stuff everywhere. With lower gas prices the deflation helps them. Now conversely it hurts Coca-Cola when we have a strong dollar because they do a lot of sales outside of the United States so they have currency headwinds that they have to worry about. But invariably Coca-Cola is a company that is going to keep making money in good and bad times.

Now I don't own Coca-Cola anymore because I happen to believe it's overpriced, but I owned it previously. It was the first stock in my dividend machine. Actually, it was the second one. I loved it but I got out of it because there were other stocks that were growing faster. Also, I don't like the CEO of the company now and I don't like the direction they are going in. I just didn't feel comfortable as time went on so I got rid of it and replaced it with something better. Everyone has limited cash. It doesn't matter who you are when cash is limited and something is better than something else so then I switched from Coca-Cola to something better.

See, you are paying for the brand. Here, I'll give you a great analogy. If you are trying to run in a race and you are racing a world-class sprinter on a track then of course they are going to beat you. If I make it muddy they are still going beat you. Do you see what I'm saying? In a bad economic situation the best companies will still do well.

Many people want to use gold as a hedge for inflation. It's nonsensical. Gold is a fear trade. It's fear. It's the antithesis of what I talk about with dividends. If you bought gold in 2000 when it was $200 an ounce it's $1,300 an ounce now. But if you had bought Altria in 2000 then with the power of the reinvested dividends you earned about 15% more a year annually than with gold. That's because of the compounding, the power of the compounding.

Gold appreciated in that timeframe like 16% a year. If you took the price of it and you put 1.16 into a calculator for the last fourteen years you get like $1,300 for the price of gold. I believe Altria grew at 30+%.

Altria grew at a compounding rate that was double gold's growth rate?

Yes, yes, because of the compounding of the dividends. Part of the reason I got richer faster than I thought was when the stock ... like in 2000 I got a 10½% dividend yield on Altria. I was like, "10½%? Wow this is crazy." But why did I get such a high dividend rate? It was because in 2000 nobody wanted dividend stocks. They wanted high flyers. They wanted to put $50 into a stock and turn it into $500 and like Buffett says, what wise people do in the beginning the fool does in the end. Just like with real estate or anything else. That's why bubbles are created.

Actually right now there is a bubble in dividend stocks. They are higher than they should be, but you'll still do better in the dividends stocks than you will in a treasury bond. That's why people continue to buy them. If you buy Altria at $54 it's higher than it was last year at $35 when you should have bought it, but it's still paying a 3½% to 4% dividend so the market price isn't as important. If you just want a return on your investment then if the dividend gets bigger the price of the stock will get bigger.

And over the long run the business isn't going to explode. It will just keep paying.

Well, unless you think somehow that somebody can knock them out of the box.

In a massive deflationary scenario, which many economists and central banks are worried about, you're saying that you would still buy consumer goods stocks?

Yes. You see, it's the same rules. At some price a stock or an investment is cheap. If I offered to work for you for free then what risk do you have? If you are not giving me your checkbook then you have no risk. I say to you, "I'm going to bring you new customers if you pay me a percentage of what I bring you." Well, there is no risk for you. The risk/reward is perfect. Well, that's the same thing with your investing. You are trying to find a company that everybody hates for some reason.

I couldn't understand why everybody hated Apple. Right now, everybody hates IBM. They hate them. IBM has been around a hundred years. This year they are going to earn $15 billion. Give me companies that are earning $15 billion of profit. There is not a hundred of them. There's probably not fifty of them but people are saying it's bad, it stinks, it's terrible. You know why? Because its stock price hasn't done anything. The company is doing okay, but see it's all perception for these people and if you are a speculator then you hate IBM because it dropped from $210 to $150. But if you are an investor like me you'll love it.

I think people now have a good bead on what you do. Like you said, you are partially a perception trader who waits. You're looking for good, solid businesses that will pay you dividends and then you just wait until the perception is bad so you can buy the company for cheap. You want that asset at a cheap price.

The reason I tell you all these stories is the light needs to go off in your head so you can see what I'm talking about.

Your strategy sounds familiar to what Buffett or some other famous investors have done, such as buying when there is "blood in the streets." That's when you get the greatest bargains of solid firms. We know that applying this principle consistently over the years has enabled you to compound your returns at about 20% annually and retire at age forty-two. Over time you have no doubt invested in a large number of companies. Do you look at dividend yield tables to find stocks paying the highest dividends and say, "These are the ones I'm going to buy when the price is right?"

No, no, no, because a lot of times a high dividend is evidence that there is a problem. I own a stock called Transocean. The dividend is going to get cut because the price of oil went to $48. I didn't see that coming. Now, at what price will the dividend get cut I don't know but the point is that I think the company may cut the dividend to buy the debt at 70¢ on the dollar, which is actually a better use of the money. When they announce that then the stock price will probably go up and not go down. I'm anticipating that this is going to happen, but I don't know.

Are you ever looking at a table of high dividend yielding stocks to spot possible purchase candidates?

No, no, no, no, no. I look at the companies.

So you have a list of roughly fifty good companies that you thought about over the years, which you know are good companies and which you want to own when the price is right. Those are the ones you want to buy.

Yes. I'd like to own them. I'd love to own Panera Bread, but it's just never the right price for me.

You take a company like VISA, okay? It's a great, or MasterCard. They are both great businesses. People are spending money all around the world. They are not going to stop.

A company like eBay - they own PayPal and they are going to spin it off. I think Paypal is worth more than eBay and PayPal combined. I own eBay, that's one I own.

There are really good companies like Starbucks. It's a great company but everybody knows it. It's just never cheap. It's never been cheap for me.

I like companies where there is a lot of fear about it. Like IBM is the redheaded stepchild now. Everybody hates it and that gets me interested. When everybody hates something that is when I start liking it.

My Top 50 list is all the big companies like Apple, Google, Starbucks,

Visa, MasterCard, Qualcomm. They are all good businesses. You can't try to replace them. Johnson & Johnson is another.

All the banks are good at certain prices so I watch them. You just have to buy them at the right time. The biggest banks - Citi, Wells Fargo, J.P. Morgan and Bank of America - control like 45% of the deposits in the United States. They are big.

I watch Kimberly Clark. They are in consumer goods. I look at Pepsi. I look at companies where I think you can't knock them out of the box.

This is a list of just good businesses. They will still be here in ten years but they might be too expensive to buy at any one particular moment in time. Therefore, you just buy these things when they are cheap and then compound your cash by reinvesting in any great opportunities when you get them.

You just let it roll. Just let it roll.

Is that pretty much it?

You summed it up. When you marry someone you are picking somebody that you hope over time is going to be somebody who can grow with you and learn with you. It's the same analogy as for picking a stock. You pick your stock like you pick your best friend. I pick a stock that I want to own for the next twenty or thirty years. I don't pick a stock that I want to jump in and jump out of.

If you ask half the people who buy stocks what the company's price earnings ratio is they don't know. You ask them, "Does it have any debt? Who is the CEO?" They don't know the answer to those questions either. When I pick stocks I try to know what I'm getting into.

Amazon is not on the list because ...

No, it's a bad business to me.

What are some other good businesses people should keep watching besides the ones you mentioned?

Well, I told you about eight. I'll tell you some more. Exxon is a good business, not a great business. I shouldn't put Exxon in there because it's not a consumer goods company, but Kraft is a good business. I previously said Visa and MasterCard. Abbott Labs. AIG the insurance company ... believe it or not is a good business. They just made a couple of mistakes a while back but it's a good business. IBM is a good business. Oracle is a good business. Microsoft is a good business. Intel. Cisco.

They are all powerful businesses. Think of the people you do business with. You readily do business with them. McDonald's is a good business. It's run poorly right now but it's a good business. GE is a good business that is run poorly now, but they are a good business. They have been around for a hundred years.

There is a stock called National Oilwell Varco. It's been around since 1862. It's been around a long time. It's been through all sorts of economic times.

You pick a stock like Johnson & Johnson or Altria. They have been around through depressions, they have seen 18% interest rates, they have seen 30% unemployment rates and they have survived through both good and bad. The dinosaur was the most powerful animal on earth at one time but it is gone now. The ant is still around. Survivors tend to be strong.

People think that I'm a gambler. The fact is that I'm betting with the house. I feel like I own a casino, I really do. I feel like I own the casino. I may have a bad day or week but I know that check is coming every three months.

Now we know exactly what you are doing and how you made your money. How would you compare yourself to Warren Buffett?

Buffett does the same things I do. When Buffett started out it was different for Buffett because when he started in the '50s and '60s nobody knew the game he was playing. It was like playing against blind people. It's like playing poker. How good you are at poker often depends on whom you are playing against. You could be a champion if you played against a bunch of bad people.

Investing is the same way. It's a game where you are competing against the smartest people on earth. You have to see something that they don't see. Buffett was like that. Buffett was an investor. He didn't try to jump in and jump out of stocks. He bought stocks and then he held them.

Once you get to a certain point you have to become a buy and hold investor because the tax ramifications of doing otherwise just don't make any sense. Buffett never sold a share of his Berkshire. Now Berkshire as a company paid tax but he never paid a dime of tax and then he gave everything away to Gates. Holding without selling is like having an interest-free loan from the government.

I have three stocks that I have enormous capital gains on. Obama is talking about raising the tax on capital gains. My friends asked, "What do you think of that?" I said, "I don't care. I'm not selling these stocks. He can make the capital gains tax 80% for all I care. I'm not selling them." All he is going to do is hurt the people he is trying to help.

You won't sell because you calculate that the business is going to last and the stock is still paying dividends. Even if the price of the stock went back to where you bought it you are still making good money.

I'd have to pay enormous capital gains so my wealth would go down. The alternative to that is when people say to me, "Okay, what happens if you need money?" If I need money I can go on margin. I can borrow money against my stocks.

I've been on margin straight for fourteen years because I'm borrowing money. You can borrow money at Interactive Brokers for 1.5% or 1.6%. If I can't make 1.6% on my money then I need to go somewhere else. I can just borrow from them and buy a stock that yields 5% or 6% and make the difference.

Now I do have to worry that the stock is going to crash, but a stock like Altria won't crash because their sales are going to be consistent. People are not just going to wake up and stop smoking. They're just not. They are not going to do that.

What websites are doing any hard work for you for your dividend investing?

I look at Yahoo Business. It's very good. You can see the cash and you can see the shares. Before I make an investment I spend fifty to one hundred hours studying a stock. Before I put a dime up I'm going to spend fifty to one hundred hours in study.

Someone says, "Fifty to one hundred hours? What do you do?" I look at the annual reports from the last twenty years. I talk to people about the company. I'll make a list of people who are friends of mine. I'll say, "Do you do business with this company or do you buy Johnson & Johnson bandages?" or "Do you do this?" I try to delve into things and try to get a feel on where the company is.

This is my life so I'm real serious about this. I say this to people all the time. If you were going to go up in a plane then you wouldn't want to find out in midair that the person who is flying the plane doesn't know what they are doing.

It is the same thing with investing. Most people are gamblers. I'm an investor.

When you get married you bet on your wife. When you buy a stock or you pick a friend then you are also betting. Before I know something, information is king. I can't study a universe of 60,000 stocks. I'm never going to know about Eaton Corporation even though it's based in Cleveland. I don't know about that. But if you tell me something about Altria, I know the CEOs. Nothing has happened in the last twenty-three years that I don't know about for that company.

A lot of people don't like the stock because it's not a Dividend

Aristocrat since they didn't raise their dividend every year. Well, the one year they didn't raise their dividend was because they were being investigated by the government, which was trying to close them down, so what they did is they didn't raise their dividend. They didn't eliminate it. They just didn't raise it. They are not part of the Dividend Aristocrats because of that. Well, that's a stupid rule.

You have got some really wonderful gems here other than just the simple story of investing in good stocks that pay dividends when the price is right. The interesting thing is that you were a gambler, which is a similar history to that of many highly successful traders, and you then used those skills for investing. Many people would want to know about you and your techniques just because of this alone.

I did it because I'm the casino owner. The odds are in my favor in the sense that if you own a stock for a long time then go look at a chart, which is what I tell to chartists. Go look at a chart of any big company like Apple, Johnson & Johnson or whatever. You know where the chart is going? Higher. They are all going higher.

Now the trick is that if you knew Walmart thirty years ago then you had an advantage over someone else. I'm trying to get people to understand that if you just stick with what you know, not just in investing but in life, then you will be fine versus doing something you don't know. People just think they can jump in and jump out of things.

I have a friend of mine who is a trader. He showed me a system that he has. He's doing very good with it and obviously I can't share it. It works fine but he's not going to share it with anybody because if he shared it then it wouldn't work anymore.

Yes, he would lose his advantage. Everyone would copy it and then arbitrage its success away so that it wouldn't work anymore. That's what happens when something becomes too popular.

There is a book called *The Smart Money*. It's about this guy who bet with a professional gambler and they had this computer that picked the games. They were geniuses that put it together. The key to winning was that they had information that the average person just doesn't have.

If you have that information you have an edge like the people who knew oil prices were going to drop and bet accordingly. I didn't know that. I was short oil but then I got long some companies. I thought it would start to rebound in the $70s and it didn't. But long term, I know at some point the price of oil will be over $70 again. That will happen. I don't know when but I can just sit back and collect my dividend. If you own Exxon or Chevron … well, Chevron pays a 4% dividend. You can just sit back and collect your money and you'll be good. Oil companies aren't going to go out of business. They can't. You need oil to live. That's the difference between oil and gold.

You mentioned a couple of books. Are there any other books that have really impressed you that you think people should read to help them understand dividend investing?

Stocks for the Long Run, by Jeremy Siegel. It's the truth. It shows you how dividend investing can give better returns than growth stocks or index funds. That's a good book. That's a very good book so I recommend it to people. He shows you statistically why dividend stocks are better. He doesn't know how to pick them himself, mind you, but his numbers are correct and he shows you how to beat valuations.

I don't agree with some of the other things he says, for instance he thinks that you are going to have a hard time selling stocks in the future because of the baby boomers. I don't get into all the macroeconomic stuff. It's just about buying value. If you buy value you are going to be fine and if you don't you are going to have trouble. Otherwise, you are gambling.

I think that my own book, *The Great American Dividend Machine,* doesn't have all the numbers in it but my book will pay for itself because I have a chapter in it that has a ton of ways to save money that will more than pay for the book. I say my book is informational and inspirational as well. There is information like the basics that I gave you about investing but it's inspirational, too, because of the stories.

I'm not one that's big on books. Most books are full of hype. Someone is not going to tell you their secrets. Now, if you are a trader there is a book, there is a guy named Mark Fisher. For a trader, Mark Fisher wrote *The Logical Trader* and it's a very good book. If you are going to trade then you should read this book. It's good. He makes total, total sense. He trades in and out of a position in ten or twenty minutes. I'm more of a swing trader. While I'll take a position I may take it off in a day or two days or I may hold it for six months. It depends. If I'm wrong with the trade I sit and hold it unlike most people who just cut and run. I don't do that.

I believe that people can now understand your basic method for dividend investing. In terms of the 80/20 rule applied to dividend investing, what are the fewest but also the very most important investment lessons you have learned over the years that people absolutely have to know, have to institute and have to master for success?

The first two things I talked about. You have to pick good businesses. That's the first thing you have to do right. Buying a good business at a bad price is not the mistake that people make, rather it's buying a bad business at a good price or they buy a bad business at a bad price.

You want to pick good businesses. Pick a company that you think thirty to forty years from now is going to be good. A company that you like and that you understand. You should try to understand the company. My biggest money is made on the easiest stocks. When I start trying to get complicated, it's hard.

Warren Buffett made his money on American Express, Coke, and Wells Fargo. He made his money backing up the truck and loading up with these issues. He wasn't trying to invent anything. Bill Gates made his money because he owned Microsoft that invented software. He's a terrible investor. Terrible. He's an intelligent guy but bad investor. Same thing with Jeremy Siegel.

As an investor, you have to be able to buy something. I would tell everyone what Buffett said, "Be greedy when others are fearful." That doesn't really tell you anything though. It's too general. Like I said, I think it's very important to find good businesses and then be able to spot bargains. You have to look at the numbers. You can't overpay for something. You have to buy it at the right price. The right business and the right price are crucial. Once you have that then you're good. You're good.

If you just bought a stock that had a P/E of under 15 and they raised their dividend every year and had a good predictable income then you'd do fine. The problem is that's like telling a person who golfs, "Make your eight foot puts and you're fine." It doesn't always work like that. And sometimes some stocks are on their way down. For a stock like Amazon, someone thinks it's a good business but they haven't looked at the numbers otherwise they would realize that the company doesn't make any money.

For your 80/20 rule of doing the fewest things with the biggest impact on success it would primarily come down to these two rules?

Yes, that's what I would say. I would say that those two rules are it because that's where you make your money.

When you see something you like then you have to be able to bet big and buy. Diversification is a bunch of baloney. For somebody who is brand new diversification is okay but if you are somebody who knows what they are doing then when you get an opportunity of a lifetime you have to be able to know that. You can't be scared of taking advantage of those situations. If you like a company you need to buy it.

But you have to check the numbers. If the numbers are good and it's a good business, chances are you'll do good. Obviously, you want something with some bad news. You want to buy some imaginary fear. That's going to give you the good price. Really, that is number two, which is getting the right price.

Is there any economic situation that you are hoping might happen to produce a fear situation for some of these stocks that you really want to buy on your Watch List?

I don't sweat things, I really don't. The people who are in charge of the country, contrary to what conspiracy people and other people will say, are watching matters. For instance, everybody worried that the banks would shut down. If the banks were going to shut down then the Chinese were going to come in and take them over. They wouldn't let it happen.

I'm not macroeconomic. There are two things that I can say that are kind of controversial but I'll say them. I don't ever believe interest rates are going to get high again. I also don't believe we are ever going to have hyperinflation. I just don't believe it's going to happen. Not because I'm pie in the sky but because inflation is caused by people chasing too few goods. There are plenty of goods today and there are plenty of people. I just don't see it. The real enemy is not inflation. It's deflation.

With deflation nobody wants to buy a house because they're saying, "Why should I buy something since it's going to be worth less?" That's why people are driving cars longer. I have a jeep that is twelve years old. Why should I buy a new one? It only has 40,000 miles on it so I don't need a new one. I can buy a Bentley if I lived in Florida, but I don't live in Florida. Why should I buy a nice car here in Cleveland? It doesn't make any sense. Do you follow me? I just don't think it will happen.

Try not to worry about the math. For me, how I look at macroeconomic things is that I'll look at the price of oil from a numbers point of view. Oil hasn't been this low since the world was in recession. Now why is the oil market this low? Well, there are a bunch of reasons. The Saudis are trying to hurt our fracking. They are trying to hurt Iran. They are trying to hurt Venezuela. They are trying to hurt Russia. But at some point the people that hold the debt on these people don't want things to crash. If the oil market crashes you are going to have a problem. The central banks around the world don't want that.

Right now countries are so much in debt. Everybody is borrowing money cheap. People say, "Well, how much lower can interest rates get?" Trust me, they can get lower. People can't afford to do things.

This has all been a big boon for me because I've been able to borrow money on margin. When I started using margin I was paying 7½%. I'm now paying less than 2%. That's crazy. That is why the rich get richer and the poor get poorer, but that's like saying that people who eat right and workout are getting in better shape than those who don't work out and don't eat right. That's common sense.

How could a regular person who doesn't invest any money in the stock market try to buy dividend stocks? How are they going to get ahead? You see what I'm saying? They are going take $10,000 and try to trade with it, or

$50,000. That's like going to a casino with $50,000. The casino has more money than you do. You're going to lose that $50K before they lose their $40 million, trust me. Or billion. And that's the way things are today.

But with dividends it doesn't matter. You're in your own world. If you have a stock called Con Ed or Southern Company then you are just going to be waiting for your check to come in. You want to make those checks as big as possible so you could quit working. The object of work is so that you can make enough money so that you don't have to work, right? You like what you do, obviously, but you wouldn't do it for free.

That's the part you have to be thinking about. For macroeconomic stuff the real pros don't think like that. They don't. The real investor does. I can trade because I know the odds of things. I know when something is cheap. If I buy something that's cheap then at some point it is going to go up. Whether I use margin or options or whatever I'm going to make money. That's what I know.

Are there any other important things you want to tell people as advice that might correct some of the common mistakes you are always encountering?

First of all, the most important thing is that you save 10% of every dollar that comes in. At least 10% at the minimum. If you don't do that then anything else doesn't matter because you're not going to have any chips to play with. You have to save at least 10% of your money. That's the best financial advice you could ever give another human being.

Take that money and invest it in good paying dividend stocks. Just keep doing it. You can pass it on your children. I have a machine that I'm going to pass on to my daughter. My dividends at some point will be over a million dollars a year.

Your BillSpetrino.com website says, "A 25 year old who's portfolio is only $30,000 can buy a stock like with a dividend of about 8%. The $2,700 of annual dividends should double about every nine years at least. With no further investment this particular Dividend Machine should return over $86,000 annually at age seventy. Sound impressive? By reinvesting dividends the first fifteen years this amount should be well over $200,000 annually at age seventy. How many of your friends do you think will have done that? Not bad for a one time investment. See the importance of a dividend machine now?" Bill, do you have a rate of return on your portfolio I can report so they know how powerful this type of investing can be over the long run? I always want people to see many different styles of trading and investing, understand how they work and how to do them and understand the potential returns.

My newsletter has documented returns. The documented returns since I've started I believe are like 24% compounded. Now I'm not going to keep doing that because when I started the market was cheap. Going forward it wouldn't be that way. My goal is 12% a year.

That is for six years of *The Dividend Machine* newsletter.

If someone is going to buy an investment newsletter, they should check with *The Hulbert Financial Digest* to make sure the person is ranked because if they are not ranked by Mark Hulbert then you have to ask why not? Why wouldn't they want that accreditation?

How's your personal account?

For my personal investing returns, I can't document that number but on my personal account I've averaged 22% since I started.

That's as good as the best of the best value investors like Warren Buffett and Walter Schloss.

Well, it's easier for me because I'm managing less money. I'm not saying that I'm better than them. It gets harder when you are managing more money. The last three years I've done real well. I did 55%, 74%, and 44%, but that's not going to happen going forward. It can't. My personal goal this year is 20%. I use options, I use leverage, I use dividends. There are a bunch of things that I use to spike it but the trees don't grow to the sky. This low margin rate really helps me, though. I couldn't do that without margin.

Are you buying any high-yielding MLPs or Oil and Gas Trusts?

My next trade that comes out in my newsletter is going to be gas. I'm looking in that industry now. Anything that you buy in the energy industry that has a good balance sheet will do fine going forward. Those stocks are priced for $48 oil. I just don't believe that is going to be sustained. Things can happen for a short term but think of what it cost to produce a gallon of gasoline.

When you go to your pump and pay $1.75 there is a state and federal tax on that. The company only sees $1.20 or $1.30. Think about that. It doesn't make any sense. It just doesn't. It's out of whack right now. I just know that because I know how business works. At some point someone is going to bid the price of oil up. They are going to be buying it at $48. They are going to push it higher. It's just a matter of time.

If people want to really learn more about your investing style and stock picks, how can they find you?

I have three different things going on.

I have my book, *The Great American Dividend Machine*, which I recommend that everybody get. I have a chapter in there with a bunch of different tips for direct savings that will help the book pay for itself.

Then I have my Newsmax newsletter, *The Dividend Machine*. It's a $99 newsletter. You get a three-month trial. If you don't like it you get your money back. I've got around 65,000 subscribers to that and with people on trial it's probably around 80,000 subscribers.

And then if you want to trade or you want to learn how to be an investor I have an interactive school, BillSpetrino.com. The price on that is usually around a $600 deal. For your readers, however, I'll make it just $299 as a favor. If you just identify that you are one of Bill's readers you'll get it for $299. Again, if they don't like it I'll give them their money back. I don't need to take other people's money. That's not my thing.

I think with those three things they can understand how I do things. For $99 you can hire me through *The Dividend Machine*, or for $299 you can get on my interactive thing and ask me questions. I have an all-star team of people and this is another place where I get my group of people. I have BillSpetrino.com. I call it the "BIO" forum. It's By Invitation Only because I don't want just any clown coming in there. I've got sixty people in it. It's like an all-star game.

I've got people from all over the world in it telling me things. That's like when people say Philip Morris stock isn't selling in Malaysia or the iPhone then I have people in Malaysia to give me the real deal. People will tell me, "It was selling great when I was standing in line." One guy told a story about how there was like a monsoon coming and the people wouldn't get out of the line. That's a pretty powerful product if people are willing to do that. "Get us tents." That's what they were telling the people from Apple. "Get us tents so we can stay out here."

That's a really valuable source of information when you are trying to figure out how strong the sales are for a company. That's pretty unique. It reminds me of Peter Lynch's fundamental analysis advice to get a feel for the actual product of a company and its marketplace sales before buying that stock.

My track record is good. With all my conservative stocks I have never had a loser. None. I had one loser on the aggressive side, but I tell everybody that 90% of your money should go into conservative stocks. Until you are rich you shouldn't be gambling.

If you have children you don't teach them the wrong things first. You teach them the right things first. They can learn how to drink and smoke and do other things once they get down the important lessons first.

The trick to investing is compounding. I do have good math skills and that helps me. There are a lot of guys with PhDs in statistics but they can't think. They have never gambled before. They don't understand. They just see a number, but they don't see what led to the number. They don't want to know. Because of their egos they don't want to ask some regular person. I don't mind asking a housewife for example. I think you should do this.

My greatest stock pick came from a nine-year-old when I took her shopping and she told me, "Daddy it's obvious. Everybody has the same case for Apple." That's how you learn. I'm constantly trying to learn. I read a lot and I study the companies. I still read for about three hours every day. I am on a constant quest to learn from the wisdom of others. From the very beginning that I entered this field I read every book I could find from some of the greatest investors of the world like Graham and Buffett.

People say it to me all the time, "Do you want to do this?" and I'll say, "No." They say, "Why not?" "Well, it has a 20% or 30% chance of losing." I'll also say, "Would you go up on a plane if you thought you had a 30% chance of it crashing?" They don't know the answer to that.

That's just it. If people save the money ... you have got to save money or you won't have any chips to play with. That's the greatest thing you can teach your children. When $100 comes in then you take $10 and you don't ever spend it.

Beautiful. Bill, I want to thank you for this interview and revealing the principles involved with your investment technique. I sincerely hope that many people take your wisdom to heart to investigate this particular investment path because of the income, safety, and growth factors it has all bundled up into one.

THE MOST SUCCESSFUL COPYWRITTEN
SALES LETTER OF ALL TIME

Most religious institutions need to raise money, and do so through fundraising letters. If they do this on their own, they are advised to consider AWAI's home study course on fundraising letters: "Copywriting for Nonprofits: How to write inspiring copy for the fundraising market."

Amazon.com also has a number of books on fundraising for non-profit organizations such as *Breakthrough Fundraising Letters* (Alan Sharpe), *How to Write Successful Fundraising Letters* (Mal Warwick), *How to Write Fundraising Materials that Raise More Money* (Tom Ahem), *The Fundraiser's Guide to Irresistible Communications* (Jeff Brooks), etcetera. There are gems you can learn from studying, such as the fact that the words "Donating = Loving" added to collections can increase voluntary contributions by nearly 100% without asking.

While not specifically for fundraising, I want to introduce to you perhaps the most successful direct marketing sales letter ever of some 800 words, which might spark some ideas. *The Wall Street Journal*, in order to sell subscriptions, for years would mail out this two page solicitation letter that has been called "the greatest direct mail sales letter of all time." This letter ran continuously with minor changes from 1975 to 2003. It was sent to millions of people and brought in over $1 billion dollars in subscription revenues. It has worked longer and better than any other direct mail piece in history.

This sales letter, written by Martin Conwoy, was the workhorse circulation builder for *The Wall Street Journal*. The beauty of the letter was its simplicity. Written in plain language, it told the story of two young men who were very much alike at the start of their careers, but whose fortunes diverged because over time one consistently read *The Wall Street Journal* while the other did not. That, of course, is what the letter was designed to make you believe since it was selling *The Wall Street Journal* subscriptions.

First the letter sold you on the premise that knowledge equals success and then the idea that *The Wall Street Journal* possessed this "success knowledge." Finally, it sold you on a subscription. Here is the letter in its entirety:

> On a beautiful late spring afternoon, twenty-five years ago, two young men graduated from the same college. They were very much alike, these two young men. Both had been better than average students, both were personable and both – as young college graduates are – were filled with ambitious dreams for the

future.

Recently, these men returned to their college for their 25th reunion.

They were very much alike. Both were happily married. Both had three children. And both, it turned out, had gone to work for the same Midwestern manufacturing company, and were still there.

But there was a difference. One of the men was manager of a small department of that company. The other was its president.

What Made The Difference

Have you ever wondered, as I have, what makes this kind of difference in people's lives? It isn't always a native intelligence or talent or dedication. It isn't that one person wants success and the other doesn't. The difference lies in what each person knows and how he or she makes use of that knowledge.

And that is why I am writing to you and to people like you about The Wall Street Journal. For that is the whole purpose of the Journal: To give its readers knowledge – knowledge that they can use in business.

A Publication Unlike Any Other

You see, The Wall Street Journal is a unique publication. It's the country's only national business daily. Each business day, it is put together by the world's largest staff of business-news experts.

Each business day, The Journal's pages include a broad range of information of interest and significance to business-minded people, no matter where it comes from. *Not just stocks and finance*, but anything and everything in the whole, fast-moving world of business ... The Wall Street Journal gives you all the business you need - when you need it.

Knowledge is Power

Right now, I am reading page one of The Journal, the best-read front page in America. It combines all the important news of the day with in-depth feature reporting. Every phase of business news is covered. I see articles on new inflation, wholesale prices, car prices, tax incentives for industries to major developments in Washington, and elsewhere.

And there is page after page inside The Journal filled with

fascinating and significant information that's useful to you. The Marketplace section gives you insights into how consumers are thinking and spending. How companies compete for market share. There is daily coverage of law, technology, media and marketing. Plus daily features on the challenges of managing smaller companies.

The Journal is also the single best source for news and statistics about your money. In the Money & Investing section there are helpful charts, easy-o-scan market quotations, plus "Abreast of the Market," "Heard on the Street" and "Your Money Matters," three of America's most influential and carefully read investment columns.

If you have never read The Wall Street Journal, you cannot imagine how useful it can be to you.

A Money-Saving Subscription

Put our statements to the proof by subscribing for the next 13 weeks just for just $44. This is among the shortest subscription terms we offer – and a perfect way to get acquired with The Journal.

Or you may prefer to take advantage of our *better buy* – one year for $149. You save over $40 off the cover price of The Journal.

Simply fill out the enclosed order card and mail it in the postage-paid envelope provided. And here's The Journal's guarantee: Should the Journal not measure up to your expectations, you may cancel this arrangement at any point and receive a refund for the undelivered portion of your subscription.

If you feel as we do that this is a fair and reasonable proposition, then you will want to find out without delay if The Wall Street Journal can do for you what it is doing for millions of readers. So please mail the enclosed order card now, and we will start serving you immediately.

About those two college graduates I mentioned in the beginning of this letter: They were graduated from the same college together and together got started in the business world. So what made their lives in business different?

Knowledge. Useful knowledge. And its application.

An Investment in Success

I cannot promise you that success will be instantly yours if you start reading The Wall Street Journal. But I can guarantee that you will find The Journal always interesting, always reliable, and always useful.

Sincerely,

Peter R. Kann Publisher

P.S. It's important to note that The Journal's subscription price may be tax deductible. Ask your tax advisor.

100% RESPONSE COLLEGE FUNDRAISING LETTER

Bruce Barton, the founder of the global ad agency BBDO, is often referred to as the one of the first men to do supporter-driven fundraising. Among his many famous campaigns, Barton created the character of "Betty Crocker" and is credited with naming General Motors and General Electric. Politically conservative, over the years he offered his public relations expertise to many Republican candidates and even served two terms in the United States House of Representatives (1937-1941).

In 1925, Barton visited Berea College in Kentucky, which served the purpose of educating the local towns. The students at the college were poor so they raised their own food, milked their own cows, and were a model of self-reliance, self-improvement and responsibility. Berea College was running a deficit when Barton visited. It had two bad options to keep going. It could turn down students, thus depriving them of an education, or start charging tuition that few could afford.

After seeing this, Barton wrote a fundraising letter to ask for donations. He sent this letter to 24 of his friends and asked for $1000 each to help kids in the South. He described the students at Berea College and how they lived in order to humanize them to his readers and illustrate the college's urgent need for funding.

The result? All 25 friends donated – a 100% response rate. In today's money, they gave $300,000 to provide 250 students with an education. Today, Berea College still provides tuition-free education to low-income students. It was the first college in the south to be integrated too. Here is Barton's letter that produced a 100% response rate:

Dear Mr. Blank,

For the past three or four years things have been going pretty well at our house. We pay our bills, afford such luxuries as having the children's tonsils out, and still have something in the bank at the end of the year.

So far as business is concerned, therefore, I have felt fairly well content.

But there is another side to a man, which every now and then gets restless. It says: "What good are you anyway? What influences have you set up, aside from your business, that would go on working if you were to shuffle off tomorrow?"

Of course, we chip in to the Church and the Salvation Army, and dribble out a little money right along in response to all sorts of appeals. But there isn't much satisfaction in it. For one thing, it's too diffused and, for another, I'm never very sure in my own mind that the thing I'm giving to is worth a hurrah and I don't have time to find out.

A couple of years ago I said: "I'd like to discover the one place in the United States where a dollar does more net good than anywhere else." It was a rather thrilling idea, and I went at it in the same spirit in which our advertising agency conducts a market investigation for a manufacturer. Without bothering you with a long story, I believe I have found the place.

This letter is being mailed to 23 men besides yourself, twenty-five of us altogether. I honestly believe that it offers an opportunity to get a maximum amount of satisfaction for a minimum sum.

Let me give you the background.

Among the first comers to this country were some pure blooded English folks who settled in Virginia but, being more hardy and venturesome than the average, pushed on west and settled in the mountains of Kentucky, Tennessee, North and South Carolina. They were stalwart lads and lassies. They fought the first battle against the British and shed the first blood. In the Revolution they won the battle of King's Mountain. Later, under Andy Jackson, they fought and won the only land victory that we managed to pull off in the War of 1812. Although they lived in southern states they refused to secede in 1860. They broke off from Virginia and formed the state of West.

Virginia; they kept Kentucky in the Union; and they sent a million men into the northern armies. It is not too much to say that they were the deciding factor in winning the struggle to keep these United States united.

They have had a rotten deal from Fate. There are no roads into the mountains, no trains, no ways of making money. So our prosperity has circled all around them and left them pretty much untouched. They are great folks. The girls are as good-looking as any in the world. Take one of them out of her two-roomed log cabin home, give her a stylish dress and a permanent wave, and she'd be a hit on Fifth Avenue. Take one of the boys, who maybe never saw a railroad train until he was 21: give him a few years of education and he goes back into the mountains as a teacher or doctor or lawyer or carpenter, and changes the life of a town or county.

This gives you an idea of the raw material. Clean, sound timber – no knots, no wormholes; a great contrast to the imported stuff with which our social settlements have to work in New York and other cities.

Now, away back in the Civil War days, a little college was started in the Kentucky mountains. It started with faith, hope, and sacrifice, and those three virtues are the only endowment it has ever had. Yet today it has accumulated, by little gifts picked up by passing the hat, a plant that takes care of 3000 students a year. It's the most wonderful manufacturing proposition you ever heard of. They raise their own food, can it in their own cannery; milk their own cows; make brooms and weave rugs that are sold all over the country; do their own carpentry, painting, printing, horseshoeing, and everything, teaching every boy and girl a trade while he and she is studying. And so efficiently is the job done that —

- o a room rents for 60 cents a week (including heat and light)
- o meals are 11 cents apiece (yet all the students gain weight on the faire; every student gets a quart of milk a day)
- o the whole cost to a boy or girl for a year's study — room, board, books, etc., - is $146. More than half of this the student earns by work; many students earn all.

One boy walked in a hundred miles, leading a cow. He stabled the cow in the village, milked her night and morning, peddled the milk, and put himself through college. He is now a major in the United States Army. His brother, who owned half of the cow, is a missionary in Africa. Seventy-five percent of the graduates go back to the mountains, and their touch is on the mountain counties of five states; better homes, better food, better child health, better churches, better schools; no more feuds; lower death rates.

Now we come to the hook. It costs this college, which is named Berea, $100 a year per student to carry on. She could, of course, turn away 1500 students each year and break even on the other 1500. Or she could charge $100 tuition. But then she would be just one more college for the well-to-do. Either plan would be a moral crime. The boys and girls in those one-room and two-room cabins deserve a chance. They are of the same stuff as Lincoln and Daniel Boone and Henry Clay; they are the very best raw material that can be found in the United States.

I have agreed to take ten boys and pay the deficit on their education each year, $1,000. I have agreed to do this if I can get twenty-four other men who will each take ten. The president, Dr. William J. Hutchins (Yale 1892), who ought to be giving every minute of his time to running the college, is out passing the hat and riding the rails from town to town. He can manage to get $50,000 or $70,000 a year. I want to lift part of his load by turning in $25,000.

This is my proposition to you. Let me pick out ten boys, who are as sure blooded Americans as your own sons, and just as deserving of a chance. Let me send you their names and tell you in confidence, for we don't want to hurt their pride, where they come from and what they hope to do with their lives. Let me report to you on their progress three times a year. You write me, using the enclosed envelope, that, if and when I get my other twenty-three men, you will send President Hutchins your check for $1,000. If you will do this I'll promise you the best time you have ever bought for a thousand dollars.

Most of the activities to which we give in our lives stop when we stop.

But our families go on; and young life goes on and matures and gives birth to other lives. For a thousand dollars a year you can put ten boys or girls back into the mountains who will be a leavening influence in ten towns or counties, and their children will bear the imprint of your influence. Honestly, can you think of any other investment that would keep your life working in the world so long a time after you are gone?

This is a long letter, and I could be writing a piece for the magazines and collecting for it in the time it has taken me to turn it out. So, remember that this is different from any other appeal that ever came to you. Most appeals are made by people who profit from a favorable response, but this appeal is hurting me a lot more than it can possibly hurt you. What will you have, ten boys or ten girls?

Cordially yours,

Bruce Barton

APPENDIX
SAMPLE TYPES OF EMPTINESS MEDITATION

Individuals who want to practice meditation can try many different types of emptiness meditation. Here is a short list you can try, excerpted from *Meditation Case Studies*:

- Set your mind on the highest ether of consciousness that is above all thought-constructs. Let go of thoughts and remain there.

- You should concentrate intensely on the idea that this universe is totally an ephemeral, effervescent illusion populated by transparent images, ungraspable like mirages that lack inherent existence. Let your mind become like that empty (void) substrate in which they appear.

- Go to an empty plane and stare into space. Take no notice of the clouds in the sky but become the space itself, infinitely everywhere. Rest in that state ignoring any thoughts that arise without suppressing them. Let them appear with clear knowing but don't attach to them since you are bodiless and limitless like space.

- Imagine that, like a fish, you are swimming in an infinite ocean of pure consciousness without any obstruction whatsoever. Now, maintaining that imagination, imagine that you lose your fish body and you are a bodiless observer.

- Imagine you are a pot of water immersed in water, and what it is then like if the pot breaks and there is water both inside and outside. Now imagine as if you are a pot of air resting in space, and similarly the pot disintegrates. What are you like?

- Imagine that you are a point of light within an ocean of infinite light. Next, try to feel that you are that ocean of light, which has no form. Make that point of light merge in the infinite ocean of light.

In some of these approaches you are the center of your consciousness and try to feel that you are infinite, and in others you try to make the infinite the center of your consciousness and think of yourself as a manifestation of that infinite. You must try each way to see what works best for you. When you find that your internal energy stirs because of using some technique, that is a good sign of progress.

The *Vijnana Bhairava*, which is a how-to meditation book from the tradition of Kashmir Shaivism, contains instructions for practicing over one hundred different types of meditations. *Meditation Techniques of the Buddhist and Taoist Masters* (Daniel Odier) has quite a few methods too. Several of these meditation practices embody different roads to cultivating mental emptiness. In order to avoid getting into a rut, I suggest you devote yourself to a new one each week and cycle through them on a yearly basis. This is one of the quickest ways to develop meditation progress! Some of the relevant emptiness meditation practice instructions are:

- Visualize the Qi of your body arising from your root chakra (your pelvis) as getting subtler and subtler until at last it dissolves into emptiness and remains there. Let your mind become empty like the final dissolution state of that Qi.

- Fill the center of your brain with Qi (visualize it coming into the brain from the spine, or draw it into the top of the head from the cosmos, or imagine it being a projection into your head from a spiritual great or your guru master, etc.) and keep letting go of any thought-constructs. Let your mind become un-minded. Let your thoughts go to the state of being unmanifest. Your consciousness will eventually become empty if you continue letting go of whatever arises within your mind after bringing Qi into your head.

- Meditate by locating your consciousness in your heart, holding your thoughts and energy there so that discursive thought disappears. Upon its disappearance stay absorbed in that emptiness. Alternatively, restrain your mental activities in the heart chakra (or on a flame that appears therein) and try to cultivate an empty mental state therein that eventually envelops your body.

- Recite the sound "Aum" and observe the void of emptiness at the end of the protracted syllable. Doing this each time, you will eventually attain an experience of mental emptiness. For some people "Om" works better than "Aum," so see which works best for you.

- Imagine that you are empty space in all directions simultaneously without any thought-constructs, experiencing emptiness all around you. Imagine being the spatial vacuity in all directions around you and rest your mind in that state. If anything arises, let it arise within you because you are just infinite emptiness, bodiless, boundless and limitless like space. Being space you cannot grasp anything so just let go of whatever arises.

- Imagine there is endless space above your head, below your feet and within your heart. Rest your mind in that visage of empty space without holding onto any thoughts that arise. Simultaneously imagine that the upper part of your body (where consciousness resides) is void and the lower side of your body is void. In your consciousness there is nothing, in the lower half of your body is nothing, and in everything everywhere there is nothing.

- Contemplate that the constituents of your body (such as the bones, flesh, etc.) are pervaded with mere vacuity (emptiness). Imagine that they are empty inside. Imagine that there is nothing inside your body's components. In time, the contemplation of having empty body parts will become steady and you can then extend the idea of emptiness to resting your mind in empty space as well.

- Contemplate that the skin of your body is like an outer wall and that there is nothing inside it but empty space. After you imagine that the body becomes like an empty sack, imagine that your mind becomes limitless, infinite in all spatial directions. All things you experience appear within this infinite spaciousness, but you know them without attaching to them because nothing is you, you are just the empty space that cannot attach to anything. Rest your mind in empty space like that.

- Bring your mind and your senses into the interior space of your heart – the ether or voidness of the heart - and exclude everything else from consciousness.

- Penetrate all parts of your body by consciousness, feeling all the parts of your body as a unified wholeness of soft energy, and then bring your mind into the brain and dissolve it into emptiness.

- Imagine that the whole universe is successively dissolved from a gross state into a subtle state, from a subtle state into emptiness, and then from emptiness into an even more transcendental formless supreme state that lacks any attributes or distinctions. Allow your mind to be dissolved away the same way into pure empty consciousness and then the emptiness of non-existence. This is called the technique of *sadadhva* where you trace the entire universe back to its source.

- You should concentrate intensely on the idea that this universe is totally void, without substance, completely empty. Imagine that it is a nothing. In that emptiness (void) let your mind be absorbed.

- You should cast your eyes in the empty space inside a jar or any other empty object leaving aside the enclosing partitions. Let your mind get absorbed in that empty space, and then imagine that your mind then becomes absorbed in a total void of infinite emptiness. Let yourself become identified with that infinite voidness.

- Cast your gaze on a region in which there are no trees, such as going to a mountain plateau or high wall and looking into the empty sky. Let your mental state become like the empty sky you observe. Let thought-fullness become thought-lessness. Let your thoughts dissolve as you become the empty space. Cast aside the body and ignore the fluctuations of your mind as you become the empty space you see.

- Contemplate with an unwavering mind that your whole body and the entire universe simultaneously are the nature of consciousness. Since your consciousness is what sees everything as pictures, then what you are seeing is only consciousness (only images within your consciousness). Therefore the body you normally take yourself to be and the universe you see are just mental images of consciousness-only. Stay in that realization that the "you" ("I") that you take yourself to be is therefore ultimately pure consciousness that is pure without perturbations like space.

- Contemplate that your whole body and the universe simultaneously are in their totality filled with bliss. After being fully saturated, fully permeated with this bliss, let go of all consciousness and let the mind rest in this blissfulness feeling without thinking.

- Concentrate on your self in the form of a vast firmament, unlimited in any direction whatsoever.

- One should contemplate thus: "Within me the inner apparatus consisting of the mind does not ultimately exist for it is just brought about by the combination of energy forces in a particular structure that make consciousness happen. In the absence of thought-constructs, I will be rid of all thought-constructs and will abide as pure consciousness." Try to become that ultimate state free of thoughts but without suppression.

- Observe your mind and any desires or afflictions that spring up. When you observe a desire or affliction that springs up, put an end to it immediately. Don't let it function at all. Let your mind become absorbed in that very place from which it arose. In time the mind will become pure and clear like space.

- Consider, "When knowledge has not arisen in me, then what am I when in that condition?" Become absorbed in the reality of that emptiness lacking thoughts.

- After rejecting attachment to your body, you should with firm mind that has no consideration for anything else contemplate thus, "I am everywhere."

- Cast your gaze on an object, withdraw it and slowly eliminate the knowledge of that object along with the thought and impression of it so as to abide in non-knowing (without suppression).

- When a person perceives a particular object, absence is established regarding all other objects (including what you perceived just prior to this object). If one contemplates on this vacuity with a mind freed of all thought, then even though the present particular object is still known or perceived your mind will settle into a tranquil state.

- Fix your mind on the vast, limitless external space that is empty and without support. By prolonged concentration practice on becoming boundless external space, you will gradually acquire the capacity of mentally becoming like supportless, objectless, vacant space. Let your mind become absorbed in this experience.

- Towards whatever object the mind goes, one should remove it from there immediately by that very mind, and thus make it supportless by not allowing it to settle down anywhere. Just push the mind away from any point upon which it settles. Wherever the mind moves to, withdraw it to clinglessness/emptiness. Do not attach to thoughts that arise within the mind.

OTHER RELATED BOOKS BY THE AUTHOR

Twenty-five Doors to Meditation
The Little Book of Meditation
Easy Meditation Lessons
What is Enlightenment?
Socrates and the Enlightenment Path
Meditation Case Studies
The Little Book of Hercules
Nyasa Yoga
Internal Martial Arts Nei-gong
Visualization Power
Sport Visualization for the Elite Athlete
Detox Your Body Quickly and Completely
Look Younger, Live Longer
Husbands and Wives Were Connected in the Past
Color Me Confucius
Culture, Country, City, Company, Person, Purpose, Passion, World
Move Forward
Quick, Fast, Done